Triathlon Science

Joe Friel
Jim Vance

Editors

Human Kinetics

Library of Congress Cataloging-in-Publication Data

Triathlon science / Joe Friel, Jim Vance, editors.
p. cm.
Includes bibliographical references and index.
1. Triathlon. 2. Sports sciences. I. Friel, Joe. II. Vance, Jim.
GV1060.73.T77 2013
796.42'57--dc23

2012036423

ISBN-10: 1-4504-2380-9 (print)
ISBN-13: 978-1-4504-2380-9 (print)

This publication is written and published to provide accurate and authoritative information relevant to the subject matter presented. It is published and sold with the understanding that the author and publisher are not engaged in rendering legal, medical, or other professional services by reason of their authorship or publication of this work. If medical or other expert assistance is required, the services of a competent professional person should be sought.

The web addresses cited in this text were current as of December 2012, unless otherwise noted.

Developmental Editor: Cynthia McEntire; **Assistant Editor:** Elizabeth Evans; **Copyeditor:** Bob Replinger; **Indexer:** Nan Badgett; **Permissions Manager:** Martha Gullo; **Graphic Designer:** Joe Buck; **Graphic Artist:** Kim McFarland; **Cover Designer:** Keith Blomberg; **Photograph (cover):** Daniel Swee/Action Plus/Icon SMI; **Photographs (interior):** Neil Bernstein, except where otherwise noted; **Photo Asset Manager:** Laura Fitch; **Visual Production Assistant:** Joyce Brumfield; **Photo Production Manager:** Jason Allen; **Art Manager:** Kelly Hendren; **Associate Art Manager:** Alan L. Wilborn; **Illustrations:** © Human Kinetics, except where otherwise noted; **Printer:** Sheridan Books

Human Kinetics books are available at special discounts for bulk purchase. Special editions or book excerpts can also be created to specification. For details, contact the Special Sales Manager at Human Kinetics.

Printed in the United States of America   10 9 8 7 6 5 4 3 2 1

The paper in this book is certified under a sustainable forestry program. The paper in this book was manufactured using responsible forestry methods.

Human Kinetics
Website: www.HumanKinetics.com

United States: Human Kinetics
P.O. Box 5076
Champaign, IL 61825-5076
800-747-4457
e-mail: humank@hkusa.com

Canada: Human Kinetics
475 Devonshire Road Unit 100
Windsor, ON N8Y 2L5
800-465-7301 (in Canada only)
e-mail: info@hkcanada.com

Europe: Human Kinetics
107 Bradford Road
Stanningley
Leeds LS28 6AT, United Kingdom
+44 (0) 113 255 5665
e-mail: hk@hkeurope.com

Australia: Human Kinetics
57A Price Avenue
Lower Mitcham, South Australia 5062
08 8372 0999
e-mail: info@hkaustralia.com

New Zealand: Human Kinetics
P.O. Box 80
Torrens Park, South Australia 5062
0800 222 062
e-mail: info@hknewzealand.com

E5643

Contents

| **Part XI** | Psychology of Multisport | 553 |

Introduction

The Tri-Knowledge Advantage

—Joe Friel, MSc

Whether you are a triathlete, coach, sport scientist, or student of the sport, if you are passionate about the science of triathlon, you are in for a treat. Human Kinetics, Jim Vance, and I have brought together some of the most knowledgeable people in the many fields related to sport science to contribute to this book. Here you will find the scientific underpinnings of a wide range of triathlon topics from physiology, gender, and genetics to biomechanics, training methods, and psychology—and more. The book is a treasure trove of information that will help you understand what it takes to succeed in this complex sport.

No project like this has ever been done for triathlon. I promise that you will learn a lot. I know I did, having read each of the chapters before publication. And I've been around the sport for a long time.

I came to triathlon in 1983 when I did my first race in Longmont, Colorado, a race just short of what we now call the Olympic distance. It was a pool swim. After many years of only running before trying this new sport, my stroke mechanics were pathetic. In those days we didn't believe that technique was important. It was all about building fitness in the pool with endless intervals. The bike I rode was decent for the early 1980s—a Fuji road bike that probably weighed 25 pounds (11 kg). In those days there was no such thing as a triathlon bike. It would be 6 more years until the first of those appeared in bike shops. I came from a running background, but my ego was deflated on that race day by how slowly I ran after an hour of pushing my limits on the bike. Of course, power meters, GPS devices, and accelerometers were unheard of. I would get my first heart rate monitor later that summer. Racing back then was only about going as hard as you could for as long as you could.

In those early days we had no reason to think that triathlon would be anything other than a fun way for swimmers, cyclists, and runners to compete with each other. We never dreamed that it would one day become the fastest growing sport in the world or that in less than 20 years it would be an event in the Olympic Games. Triathlon was just something we all did as a break from our "real" sports.

In the 1970s I had gone back to school to work on a master's degree in exercise science, in part so I could become a better runner. I had high aspirations as an athlete and had always been curious about how to train to run faster. I figured the answers to all my training questions could be found within those ivy-covered walls. After 3 years of study I came away with few answers, but with much better questions. And along the way I learned of the role of research in seeking answers to such questions. Ever since then I have been a student of the science of training for sport. To this day I read research studies the way most people read novels—just for fun. So when I was asked to be a part of this book project, I jumped at the opportunity.

I knew I would need help with such a huge project, so I asked Jim Vance to come onboard to assist. Jim has been a coaching associate with me for 4 years. He also comes from a running background, having competed in track and field at the University of Nebraska. After graduation, he took up mountain bike racing, which eventually led him to triathlon. He soon turned pro and moved up to the Ironman distance. Jim was a public school teacher before becoming a coach, so he understands how to help athletes become more fit and faster by learning as well as doing. I was Jim's coach before he retired from professional racing to become a full-time coach. So I knew that we could work well together on this book.

We started on the project in the spring of 2011 by deciding what should be included, and we then made a list of people we would like to have onboard as contributors. The list was impressive—and we got them all. They each fall into one of three categories: academics with advanced degrees, coaches with high levels of certification and unparalleled experience, and medical practitioners known for their treatment of endurance athletes. Several of the contributors fit in two of these categories. All are athletes, and many have competed or continue to compete at remarkably high levels given their busy lives. They come from five countries—Australia, France, Russia, South Africa, and the United States—on four continents. You can read brief biographies about each of them in the About the Contributors section. Their accomplishments are remarkable. In the sport of triathlon, never has such a high-powered group with so much cutting-edge information been brought together with a single mission: to help you understand better what it takes to excel as a triathlete.

Here's a brief overview to what you can expect from the contributors to *Triathlon Science*:

> In **part I** you will learn about the physiology of triathlon from Randy Wilber, PhD; about genetics from Ildus Ahmetov, PhD, and Malcolm Collins, PhD; and about the training needs of special populations from Romuald Lepers, PhD.
>
> **Part II** takes an in-depth look at the movement skills of each of the three disciplines. Chapters are written by David Pease, PhD, from the Australian Institute of Sport; Jeff Broker, PhD; and George Dallam, PhD.
>
> **Part III** examines the effect of environmental conditions and equipment, including computer software, on performance. Contributors are Bruce

Mason, PhD; Gina Sacilotto; Jeff Broker, PhD; Sean Langlais; George Dallam, PhD; and coach Hunter Allen.

Ross Tucker, PhD, of the Sports Science Institute of South Africa, contributed all of **part IV** on the physiological determinants of success in triathlon.

U.S.-based coach David Warden applies much of what preceded his **part V** with a discussion of the application of science to training for triathlon. David is well known for in-depth discussions of the science of training in his Tri-Talk podcasts.

In **part VI** Stephen McGregor, PhD, and coach and author Matt Fitzgerald provide an overview to training in three disciplines using a periodization-based model.

In **part VII** Jim Vance; Neal Henderson; and George Dallam, PhD, explain the details of building general, or base, fitness as a component of the periodization model.

Long-time coach, author, and associate Gale Bernhardt shows how to build beyond base fitness to prepare to race at the standard distances in **part VIII**.

In **part IX** two of the leaders in sports medicine for endurance athletes, John Post, MD, and Nate Koch, PT, ATC, describe their cutting-edge injury prevention and treatment techniques.

Well-known coach, author, and nutritionist Bob Seebohar explains how triathletes can fuel their bodies to perform better in **part X**.

Finally, in **part XI** noted sports psychologist JoAnn Dahlkoetter, PhD, describes mental preparation for competition. This aspect of the sport is probably the least understood among triathletes at all levels.

In all, the book contains 43 chapters, each written by a leader in the field to explain the cutting-edge concepts and methods that will help serious triathletes train and race to their potential. I'm certain that after you've read *Triathlon Science* you will have a much deeper understanding of what it takes to train and perform better in all three disciplines.

PART

I

Physical Attributes
of Triathletes

CHAPTER 1

Physiology and the Multisport Athlete

—Randall L. Wilber, PhD, FACSM

This chapter provides advanced information on exercise physiology necessary for coaching or participating in triathlon. Here we will examine the athlete's energy production systems, cardiopulmonary physiology, and skeletal muscle contraction.

The sport of triathlon presents a unique physiological challenge in endurance sport. Whether you participate recreationally in the local sprint triathlon or are dedicated to competing in the grueling Ironman triathlon, the three-in-one triathlon format requires a demanding but intelligent and well-balanced training program. Knowledge of the science of triathlon has become critical to success in the sport, particularly in the Ironman race format.

Although each of the three disciplines in triathlon offer unique training challenges, some basic physiological principles can be applied to swimming, cycling, and running. This chapter will help triathletes and their coaches understand the basic physiology of endurance sport. Three primary topics will be presented: energy production, cardiopulmonary physiology, and skeletal muscle contraction. Better scientific knowledge means better performance.

The goal of this chapter, therefore, is to build a strong physiological foundation from which triathletes and coaches of triathletes can design effective and successful training programs. Added to the basic scientific information presented here is expertise in swimming, cycling, and running provided in subsequent chapters.

Energy Production

Every triathlete has experienced the bonk, most likely in competition but perhaps on a long training ride or run. A significant amount of physical energy is required to train for and compete in triathlon. This section deals with the physiology of energy production. It will help you understand how your body produces energy. Practical knowledge of the three energy systems can help you design effective workouts and pace yourself more effectively during races.

What exactly is energy? How is energy produced and used in a triathlete's body? The answers to these questions rely heavily on the sciences of biology and biochemistry.

Energy Systems

The basic unit of energy within the human body is *adenosine triphosphate* (ATP). A simple way to think of a molecule of ATP is as an energy dollar bill. Millions of molecules of ATP in the human body are providing energy. Triathletes are constantly using and replenishing ATP, even when not exercising. ATP utilization and production is similar to the daily scenario of spending money to pay bills and maintain a lifestyle.

The molecular structure of ATP is shown in figure 1.1. ATP is made up of three unique subunits: adenine, ribose, and the phosphate groups. Notice the wavy lines that connect the three phosphate groups, each of which represents a high-energy bond.

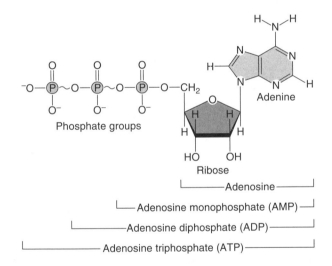

▶ **Figure 1.1** Structure of adenosine triphosphate (ATP).

The basic biochemical reaction whereby ATP produces energy is shown in figure 1.2. A single molecule of ATP is represented on the left side of the reaction. When ATP comes in contact with water and the enzyme ATPase, one of its high-energy bonds is broken, or cleaved, which releases a burst of chemical energy. This burst of chemical energy can be used for several important physiological functions including nerve transmission, blood circulation, tissue synthesis, glandular secretion, digestion, and the physiological function that we will focus on later in this chapter, skeletal muscle contraction.

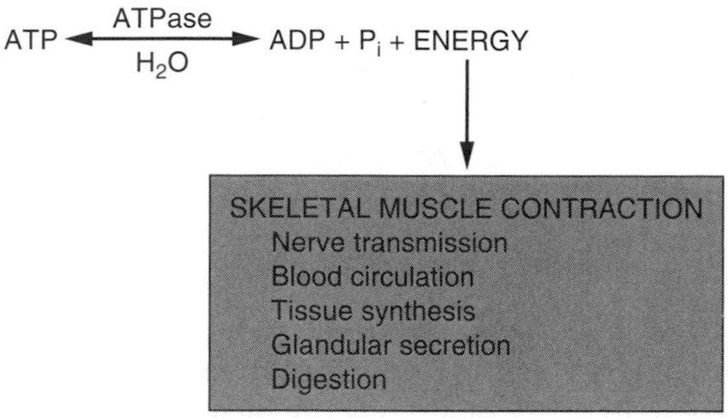

$$ATP \xleftrightarrow[\text{H}_2\text{O}]{\text{ATPase}} ADP + P_i + ENERGY$$

SKELETAL MUSCLE CONTRACTION
Nerve transmission
Blood circulation
Tissue synthesis
Glandular secretion
Digestion

▶ **Figure 1.2** Biochemical conversion of ATP to ADP + P_i + energy.

There are three energy-producing systems (see figure 1.3): the adenosine triphosphate–creatine phosphate (ATP–CP) system, which is immediate; glycolysis, which is short term; and oxidative phosphorylation, which is long term. The three energy systems are similar in that they all produce ATP, but they differ in how quickly and how much ATP they produce. Two of the three energy systems—immediate and short term—are anaerobic energy systems. In other words, these two energy systems do not require oxygen to produce ATP. In contrast, the long-term energy system is aerobically dependent, requiring oxygen to produce ATP.

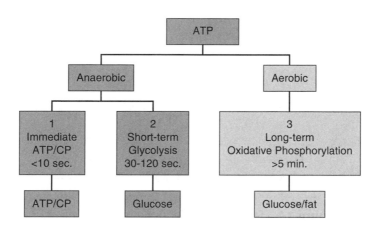

▶ **Figure 1.3** The three energy-producing systems.

Immediate Energy System

The first energy system is the *immediate energy system,* one of the two anaerobic energy systems. The technical name for this energy system is the *adenosine triphosphate (ATP)–creatine phosphate (CP)* system. The immediate energy system is for immediate use. The biochemical reactions involved in this system are shown in figure 1.4. Notice that the first reaction is the same one described earlier in the chapter that showed the conversion of ATP to chemical energy (see figure 1.2). Recall that one of the high-energy bonds was cleaved in that reaction, which resulted in adenosine triphosphate (ATP), which contains three phosphate groups, being converted to adenosine diphosphate (ADP), which contains two phosphate groups. Notice that ADP is not simply thrown away after the initial reaction (figure 1.4). Rather, it goes through a recycling process with CP, which donates its phosphate group to ADP (two phosphate groups) to produce a new molecule of ATP (three phosphate groups).

The immediate energy system has the advantage of producing ATP quickly but the disadvantage of producing only a limited supply of ATP. In terms of athletic performance, the immediate energy system is the dominant energy system during high-intensity, short-duration exercise lasting approximately 10 seconds or less. The immediate energy system is used in athletic performances like the 100-meter sprint in track, 10-meter diving events, and weightlifting events.

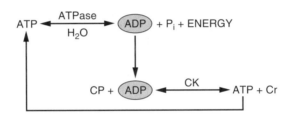

▶ **Figure 1.4** Two basic biochemical reactions of the ATP–CP energy system, the immediate energy system.

Short-Term Energy System

The second energy system is the *short-term energy system*. Like the immediate energy system, it is anaerobic because it does not require oxygen to produce ATP. The technical name for this system is *glycolysis* because the first of several biochemical reactions in this energy system involves the conversion of glycogen to free glucose. A simplified version of glycolysis is shown in figure 1.5. One molecule of glucose is converted to two molecules of pyruvic acid, and then, in the absence of oxygen, the two molecules of pyruvic acid are converted to two molecules of lactic acid. Notice that in glycolysis two molecules of ATP are produced per one molecule of glucose.

The short-term energy system has the advantage of producing more ATP than the immediate energy system but the disadvantage of taking longer to do so. Another disadvantage is that the short-term energy system produces lactic acid, which is quickly converted to lactate and positively charged hydrogen ions (H^+) (see figure 1.5). High concentrations of H^+ create the acidic burning sensation in exercising skeletal muscle that, along with other biochemical, neural, and biomechanical factors, contributes to premature fatigue.

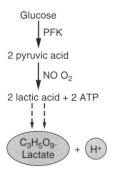

▶ **Figure 1.5** Biochemical reactions involved in glycolysis, the short-term energy system. PFK = phosphofructokinase.

In terms of athletic performance, the short-term energy system is the dominant energy system during high-intensity, moderate-duration exercise lasting approximately 30 to 120 seconds. Examples of the short-term energy system being used in athletic performance include the 400-meter sprint in track, 100-meter sprint in swimming, and 1,000-meter track cycling event.

Long-Term Energy System

The third energy system is the *long-term energy system*, which is aerobic in nature and requires oxygen to produce ATP. The technical name for this energy system is *oxidative phosphorylation*. A simplified version of this relatively complex energy system is shown in figure 1.6. Notice that the long-term energy system starts out the same way as the short-term energy system does as a single molecule of glucose converted to two molecules of pyruvic acid. Because oxygen is available, however, pyruvic acid is not converted to lactic acid as in the short-term energy system. Rather, pyruvic acid is converted to acetyl coenzyme A (acetyl CoA), which then enters one of several mitochondria in

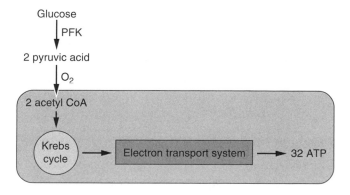

▶ **Figure 1.6** Biochemical reactions involved in oxidative phosphorylation, the long-term energy system. PFK = phosphofructokinase.

the cell and goes through a series of biochemical reactions (Krebs cycle and electron transport system [ETS]) that ultimately produce 32 molecules of ATP.

The long-term energy system has the advantage of producing very large amounts of ATP compared with the other energy systems, but it has the disadvantage of taking more time to produce that relatively large amount of ATP. The long-term energy system takes longer because it uses oxygen to produce ATP. The only place in the cell where oxygen can be used to produce ATP is in the mitochondrion, which is essentially a large ATP factory that requires several steps for processing, increasing the time needed for the final production of ATP.

In terms of athletic performance, the long-term energy system is the dominant energy system in low- to moderate-intensity, long-duration exercise lasting longer than 5 minutes. The long-term energy system is used in athletic performances like the marathon, 800-meter swim, and road cycling events. The long-term energy system is the dominant energy system used during triathlon training and racing, but it is not the only energy system used in triathlon.

Energy Dynamics During Exercise

The previous section examined each of the three energy systems separately. But note that more than one energy system can function at once. Consider a symphony orchestra, in which several different instrument groups play soft or moderate or loud depending on the musical score. At the beginning of the symphony, the string group may be loud, the woodwind group may be moderate, and the percussion group may be soft. These musical emphases may be reversed by the end of the symphony to reflect soft music by the string group and loud music by the percussion group. The same is true for energy production during exercise. Each of the three energy systems is in a state of dynamic flux. Like the various instrument groups, each of the energy systems is operating constantly during exercise but at a different level of ATP production depending on the intensity and duration of the exercise.

An example of the symphony orchestra effect is shown in figure 1.7, which shows energy dynamics during a cycling road race. During pack riding, the exercise intensity is moderate and the duration is relatively long. As described in the previous section, the dominant energy system during moderate-intensity, long-duration exercise is the oxidative phosphorylation (long-term) energy system. Notice that it is dominant but not the only energy system used during pack riding. The other two energy systems are active but playing softly.

During a hill climb, the intensity picks up but the duration is shorter compared with pack riding. This type of high-intensity, moderate-duration exercise requires the glycolytic (short-term) energy system to play loudest, the ATP–CP system to play louder, and the oxidative phosphorylation system to play softer versus pack riding. Finally, notice how the energy dynamics are reversed during the high-intensity, short-duration final sprint to the finish.

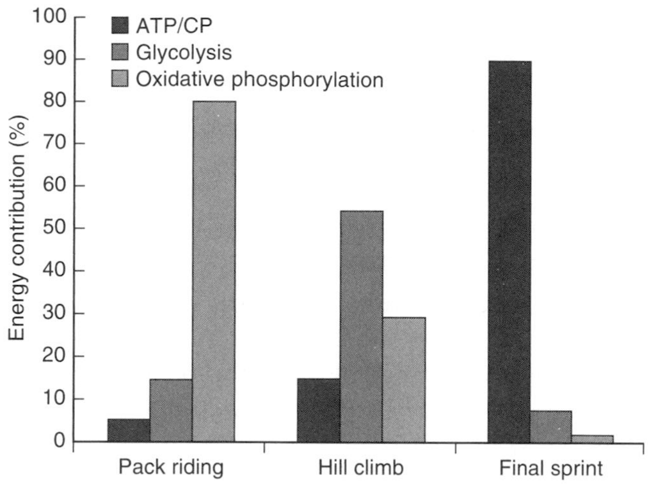

▶ **Figure 1.7**   Energy dynamics during a cycling road race.

Here the ATP–CP system is clearly the loudest, whereas the glycolytic (short-term) and oxidative phosphorylation (long-term) energy systems are relatively quiet.

In triathlon the dominant energy system is the oxidative phosphorylation system. But remember the role of the ATP–CP and glycolytic energy systems to triathlon performance. Knowing when to train and how much time to devote to training each of the three energy systems is an important ingredient of success in triathlon and is reflective of a well-designed and scientifically based training plan.

Cardiopulmonary Physiology

Because triathlon relies heavily on the oxidative phosphorylation energy system, understanding the basic concepts of cardiopulmonary physiology is important. The term *cardiopulmonary* refers to the heart and lungs and to the way in which those vital organs work in synchrony to ensure that the blood is carrying oxygen and nutrients optimally to the working skeletal muscles during exercise.

Cardiopulmonary Anatomy

The primary anatomical structures of the cardiopulmonary system are illustrated in figure 1.8, which shows the lungs (top), heart (center), and skeletal muscles (bottom). An anatomical tour of the cardiopulmonary system begins in the lungs. Blood passes through the capillary beds of the lungs where it unloads carbon dioxide (CO_2) and picks up oxygen (O_2). This *oxygen-enriched* blood travels from the lungs to the heart through the pulmonary vein.

Oxygen-enriched blood initially enters the heart in the left atrium and then flows into the left ventricle. When the heart contracts, oxygen-enriched blood is ejected from the left ventricle and exits the heart through the aorta. The aorta ultimately branches into several smaller arteries that carry oxygen-enriched blood to the entire body. After the oxygen-enriched blood reaches, for example, the leg muscles during cycling or running, it unloads O_2 and picks up CO_2. Blood exiting the exercising muscles is *oxygen reduced* and returns to the heart through the venous system.

Oxygen-reduced blood is ultimately delivered to the heart by two large veins, the superior and inferior vena cava. The vena cavae deliver oxygen-reduced blood to the right atrium of the heart, where it then flows into the right ventricle. When the heart contracts, oxygen-reduced blood is ejected by the right ventricle and travels through the pulmonary artery to the lungs, which brings it back to the starting point of the tour.

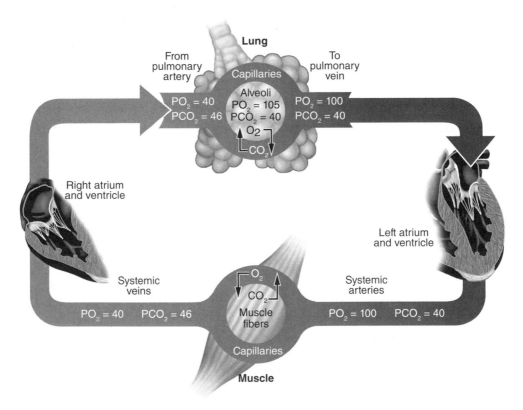

▶ **Figure 1.8** Cardiopulmonary anatomy and partial pressure gradients that promote O_2 and CO_2 movement in the body. $PO_2 = O_2$ partial pressure, $PCO_2 = CO_2$ partial pressure.

Oxygen Transport

Triathlon is heavily dependent on the oxidative phosphorylation energy system for ATP. In the previous section, O_2 transport was referred to in general terms: oxygen enriched and oxygen reduced. In this section, O_2 transport is described in more detail, focusing on the gas physics and physiology of O_2 transport.

What exactly carries oxygen around in the body? A small percentage of O_2 travels through the body dissolved in the fluid portion of the blood. But the primary way by which O_2 is transported through the body is by the *red blood cells* (RBCs), also called *erythrocytes*.

Human blood contains trillions of red blood cells. The RBC portion of the blood is referred to as the *hematocrit* (Hct), which is expressed as a percentage of the total number of RBCs relative to total blood volume. Hematocrits for healthy people residing at low elevation range from 35 to 45 percent for women and 40 to 50 percent for men. A single RBC contains about 250 million molecules of *hemoglobin* (Hb). The hemoglobin molecule transports oxygen throughout the body. A single molecule of Hb can transport four molecules of O_2. Thus, a single RBC has the capacity to transport 1 billion molecules of O_2.

Next, it is important to understand how oxygen-*reduced* blood becomes oxygen-*enriched* blood in the lungs (see figure 1.8). The entire process of O_2 transport is regulated by changes in the *partial pressure of oxygen* (PO_2) that take place from the moment ambient air is inhaled through the nose and mouth until it reaches the body's tissues and organs. PO_2 decreases as the inspired air moves from the nose and mouth to the lungs.

Specifically, the PO_2 of inspired air at sea level is approximately 149 millimeters of mercury (mm Hg), which drops to 105 mm Hg in the lungs. As previously described, blood entering the lungs through the pulmonary arteries contains RBCs that are relatively low in O_2, or oxygen reduced. The PO_2 of this oxygen-reduced blood is approximately 40 mm Hg. This pressure difference (105 mm Hg in the lungs versus 40 mm Hg in the oxygen-reduced blood), or *pressure gradient*, favors the diffusion of O_2 from the lungs to the oxygen-reduced blood where it binds to hemoglobin molecules. The diffusion of O_2 from the lungs to the blood takes only about 0.75 seconds and occurs across a sheer membrane in the pulmonary capillaries that is approximately 1/10,000 the width of a facial tissue. Because of this pressure gradient and diffusion of O_2 in the lungs, oxygen-enriched blood exits the lungs with a PO_2 of 100 mm Hg. The oxygen-enriched blood is transported by the pulmonary vein to the left ventricle of the heart, from which it is then circulated throughout the body.

When oxygen-enriched blood arrives at the capillary bed of a skeletal muscle, the pressure gradient favors the release of O_2 from hemoglobin (PO_2 of approximately 100 mm Hg) to the skeletal muscle (PO_2 of about 30 mm Hg) (figure 1.8). The oxygen unloaded in the skeletal muscle can now be used by the mitochondria to produce ATP by the oxidative phosphorylation energy system. Finally, the blood exits the skeletal muscle capillary bed in an oxygen-reduced state (PO_2 of about 40 mm Hg) and returns to the right ventricle of the heart to repeat the process of oxygenation in the lungs and O_2 transport throughout the body.

Training Effects

The ability to transport oxygen efficiently is clearly an important factor contributing to optimal performance in triathlon, which is heavily dependent on oxidative energy production. Of course, one question that immediately comes to mind among triathletes and coaches is, Can the cardiopulmonary system and oxygen transport capabilities be improved through training? The answer is yes.

One way to improve O_2 transport is to undertake altitude training, which has the effect of increasing the number of RBCs and Hb molecules, resulting in an increased capacity to get oxygen to the exercising muscles. (Unfortunately, some unethical athletes have chosen to induce the same physiological effect by using illegal pharmacological ergogenic aids such as recombinant human erythropoietin [rhEPO].) Many athletes, however, do not have the time or resources to undergo altitude training for a duration that will bring about an increase in RBC and Hb.

Note that several positive cardiopulmonary training effects can be acquired at sea level by a well-designed and scientifically sound training program that involves regular endurance training. Regular endurance training is defined here as a minimum of 30 to 45 minutes per training session and a minimum of three to five training sessions per week for at least 8 weeks. Several beneficial cardiopulmonary adaptations occur:

- Decrease in resting and exercise heart rate
- Increase in total blood volume
- Increase in cardiac output
- Increase in exercise respiratory capacity
- Increase in maximal oxygen uptake ($\dot{V}O_2$max)
- Improvement in lactate threshold (LT)
- Improvement in maximal exercise performance
- Improvement in exercise economy
- Improvement in endurance performance
- Improvement in heat tolerance
- Decrease in total body weight
- Decrease in body fat
- Decrease in blood pressure (if moderate or high blood pressure exists)

Lower Resting and Exercise Heart Rates

Through regular endurance training, the heart becomes stronger because of progressive overload. Because the heart is stronger, heart rate at rest and during exercise is lower than it was before the endurance training program began. During exercise, athletes can expect heart rate to be lower at a specific workload. For example, if heart rate taken immediately after running 800 meters on the first day of training was 175 beats per minute (bpm), after 8 weeks of endurance training heart rate should be significantly lower after running 800 meters at the same pace. The magnitude of the reduction in exercise heart rate will be difficult to determine because it will vary from person to person.

Recovery heart rate will also improve because of endurance training. Using the previous example, if it took 3 minutes for the heart rate to drop from 175 bpm to 125 bpm after running 800 meters on the first day of training, after 8 weeks of endurance training heart rate should drop to the same rate in much less than 3 minutes. Again, the improvement in recovery heart rate will vary from person to person. Despite this individual variability, after a minimum of 8 weeks of endurance training, improvements should occur in heart rate at rest (lower), during exercise at the same workload (lower), and during recovery following a hard effort (less time to recover).

Increased Blood Volume and Cardiac Output

Endurance training increases the level of specific hormones that regulate the body's volume of blood. These hormones act to increase the fluid portion of the blood, called plasma. The overall effect of this hormonal response is an increase in *total blood volume*. An increase in total blood volume, along with the fact that the heart is stronger and more powerful, means that the heart can pump more blood through the body in a single minute, an amount referred to as *cardiac output*.

An increase in cardiac output is important because more blood is delivered to the brain, liver, kidneys, and other important organs. During endurance exercise, increased cardiac output is important because more blood is delivered to the working skeletal muscles. As a result, more oxygen is delivered to the exercising muscles for energy, and carbon dioxide and other metabolic byproducts are removed from the muscles more rapidly.

Higher Maximal Oxygen Uptake

Endurance training improves the capacity of the lungs during exercise. Both respiratory rate (breaths per minute) and tidal volume (liters of air per breath) improve. These improvements in lung capacity contribute to an increase in maximal oxygen uptake ($\dot{V}O_2max$).

Maximal oxygen uptake is defined as the highest volume of oxygen that an athlete's body is capable of taking in and using for aerobic energy production. $\dot{V}O_2max$ can be expressed in absolute units (liters of oxygen per minute [$L \cdot min^{-1}$]) or relative units (milliliters of oxygen per kilogram of body mass per minute [$ml \cdot kg^{-1} \cdot min^{-1}$]). $\dot{V}O_2max$ is usually expressed in milliliters of oxygen per kilogram body weight per minute ($ml \cdot kg^{-1} \cdot min^{-1}$) to allow comparisons between individuals. $\dot{V}O_2max$ can rise to levels of 65 to 75 $ml \cdot kg^{-1} \cdot min^{-1}$ and 75 to 85 $ml \cdot kg^{-1} \cdot min^{-1}$ in well-trained female and male endurance athletes, respectively. By comparison, typical values for untrained females and males may range from 35 to 40 ml · kg^{-1} · min^{-1} and 45 to 50 ml · kg^{-1} · min^{-1}, respectively.

An improvement in $\dot{V}O_2$max is important because it means that more oxygen is available to the exercising muscles for energy production. Research has shown that a high $\dot{V}O_2$max is one of several physiological factors that contribute to success in triathlon.

Higher Lactate Threshold and Maximal Exercise Performance

A couple of additional physiological factors recently identified by scientific research to be important contributors to endurance performance are lactate threshold (LT) and maximal exercise performance. These physiological parameters are typically measured under laboratory conditions. The lactate threshold represents the point during an increasingly demanding endurance training session or race that requires a greater contribution from the glycolytic energy system and a lesser contribution from the oxidative phosphorylation energy system. As a result, lactate production exceeds lactate removal, and blood lactate levels increase exponentially.

In evaluating LT capabilities in triathletes, swimming velocity in meters per second (m · sec^{-1}), cycling power output (watts [W], watts per kilogram of body weight [W · kg^{-1}]) and running velocity (m · min^{-1}) are the measurements of interest. The higher the LT is, the better endurance performance is. A triathlete can expect to see significant improvement in these LT parameters by executing a well-designed endurance training program, both over the course of a single season and from season to season, depending on how many years he has been in training.

Maximal exercise performance is simply the objective quantification of an endurance athlete's athletic capability at the point of volitional exhaustion that occurs at the conclusion of a laboratory-based maximal exercise test, such as a treadmill test. In evaluating maximal exercise performance in triathletes, the same physiological measurements are of interest, although now under maximal-effort (versus LT-effort) conditions: maximal swimming velocity (m · sec^{-1}), maximal cycling power output (W · kg^{-1}), and maximal running velocity (m · min^{-1}).

As with the LT, the higher the maximal exercise performance is, the better endurance performance is. An athlete can expect to see the same type of improvement in maximal exercise performance as seen in the LT within a single season and from season to season by executing a well-designed endurance training program.

Improved Economy

Another physiological factor contributing to endurance performance is economy. The concept of physiological economy is the same as fuel efficiency or economy in an automobile. A more economical or efficient car uses less fuel at a specific speed and achieves greater miles per gallon than a less economical car.

The same is true for endurance athletes. For example, athlete AA and athlete BB have a similar $\dot{V}O_2$max value of 65 ml · kg^{-1} · min^{-1}. Athlete AA, however, uses 50 ml · kg^{-1} · min^{-1} while running at a 5:00 per mile (3:06 per km) pace in the first half of a 10K race, whereas athlete BB uses 53 ml · kg^{-1} · min^{-1} while running at the same 5:00 per mile pace in the first half of a 10K race. Thus, athlete AA is more efficient and economical in terms of energy expenditure than athlete BB because he uses less oxygen at the same pace. Logically, then, athlete AA will have a competitive advantage over athlete BB over the second half of the race because of better physiological economy.

Physiological economy can be affected by several factors including use of a well-designed endurance training program, as well as running biomechanics, uphill running, training in heat and humidity, bungee running, and plyometric training.

Additional Training Effects

The combined effect of the training-induced improvements in cardiac output, maximal oxygen uptake, lactate threshold, economy, and maximal exercise performance clearly have a positive effect on endurance performance.

In addition, the ability to work and exercise in heat and humidity improves significantly through endurance training. As mentioned earlier in this section, the body produces more plasma volume and total blood volume because of endurance training. Total blood volume acts like a radiator coolant found in a car or truck. By having more plasma and greater blood volume, an athlete is able to produce more sweat and dissipate heat more effectively from the body, particularly when exercising in a hot and humid environment. This benefit is particularly helpful for triathletes who compete in tropical environments.

Endurance training can lower total body weight and reduce body fat. This result is probably not a major concern to well-trained triathletes, who are typically lean, but it may become more important as athletes get older and have less time to train than they did earlier in their careers.

For people with moderate to high blood pressure, regular endurance training can have a significant lowering effect, thereby decreasing the risk of cardiovascular disease and premature death. Similar to total body weight and body fat, high blood pressure is probably not a major concern to most well-trained triathletes, whose blood pressure is typically normal. But elevated blood pressure may become an issue as an athlete gets older and potentially less active.

Skeletal Muscle Contraction

The physiological process of skeletal muscle contraction is operating during daily activities, even when not exercising. Walking up stairs, lifting a book, even reading this sentence involves skeletal muscle contraction. Of course, the process of skeletal muscle contraction is extremely active during exercise, and it is an important training consideration for people who compete in triathlon. This section describes the process of skeletal muscle contraction, focusing on the unique anatomical structure of skeletal muscle fiber and the fascinating step-by-step process of muscular contraction.

Skeletal Muscle Anatomy

The anatomical structure of skeletal muscle is similar to a suspension-bridge cable. A bridge cable has several internal smaller-diameter cables wrapped in an overlapping configuration that significantly enhances the strength and stability of the mother cable. The anatomical structure of skeletal muscle is similar in that deeper into the muscle, the tightly bundled muscle fibers are progressively smaller in diameter. They are reinforced by various connective and overlapping anatomical structures that provide additional support.

Figure 1.9 shows this suspension-bridge cable characteristic of a skeletal muscle. In viewing the figure, notice how the muscle fibers become progressively smaller in diameter. Also, notice the connective and supportive tubelike structures that surround each sequential layer of skeletal muscle. The main structure in skeletal muscle fiber is the *sarcomere*. The sarcomere is important because it is the basic unit of all skeletal muscle contraction. Figure 1.10 shows a detailed version of the sarcomere and surrounding structures. Note the structures that surround the sarcomere, described in the next section: T-tubule, tubules of the sarcoplasmic reticulum, and terminal cisternae of the sacroplasmic reticulum. Notice also the mitochondria, where ATP is produced by oxidative phosphorylation.

Finally, notice the two most important structures in skeletal muscle contraction, actin and myosin, as illustrated in figure 1.11. The anatomical structure of myosin is shown in the inset. Notice that myosin is made up of a tail segment and several large heads. An important feature of myosin is that the heads have the ability to move, for coupling and contraction, as detailed in the next section. The anatomical structure of actin is shown in the inset. Actin is the double strand of egg-shaped structures lined up in an end-to-end configuration. Notice also the thinner protein strand tropomyosin, which overlaps the outer surface of actin, and the troponin complex, which is attached to and positioned at regular intervals on tropomyosin.

Contraction of Skeletal Muscle

A sequence of neural, biochemical, and physiological events allows skeletal muscle contraction to take place. The process of skeletal muscle contraction occurs in three phases: excitation, coupling, and contraction. Each of these phases involves several steps.

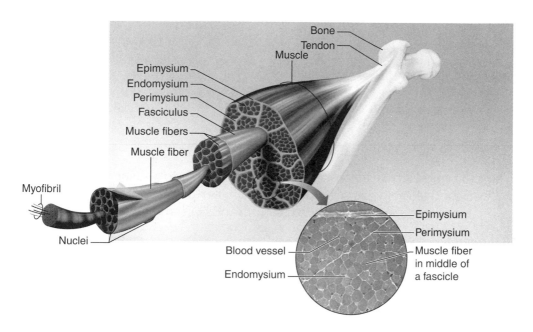

▶ **Figure 1.9** Structure of skeletal muscle.

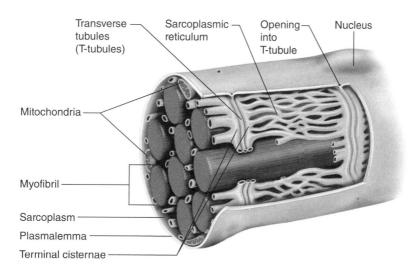

▶ **Figure 1.10** Skeletal muscle sarcomere and surrounding structures including the T-tubules, tubules of the sarcoplasmic reticulum, and the terminal cisternae of the sarcoplasmic reticulum.

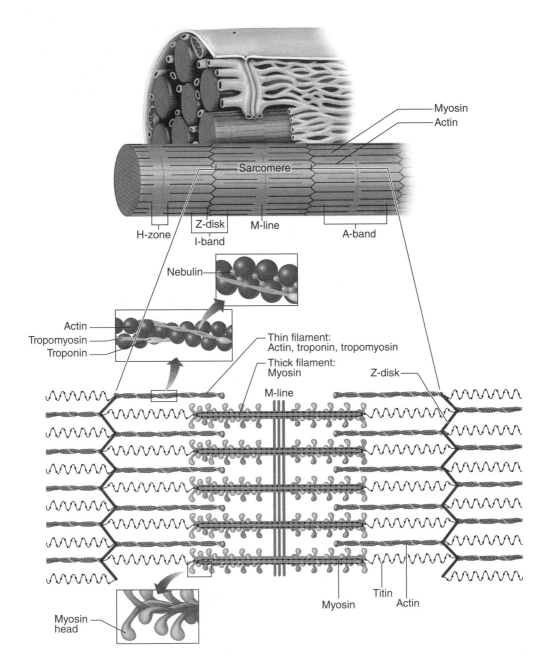

▶ **Figure 1.11** Contractile filaments, actin and myosin, shown individually and in relation to one another.

The *excitation phase* of skeletal muscle contraction is shown in figure 1.12. Excitation refers to the neural impulse that serves to spark the sequence of biochemical and physiological steps that result in skeletal muscle contraction. The excitation phase includes three key steps:

1. Motor nerves imbedded in the muscle fire off electrical impulses called *action potentials*. These action potentials move through the muscle fiber like electricity traveling through a power line (figure 1.12*a*).
2. The action potential moves along the sarcolemma and down the T-tubules of the sarcoplasmic reticulum (figure 1.12*b*).
3. The action potential triggers the release of calcium (Ca^{2+}) from the terminal cisternae of the sarcoplasmic reticulum (figure 1.12*b*).

The *coupling phase* of skeletal muscle contraction is shown in figure 1.12*c*. Coupling refers to the interconnection of the contractile filaments, actin and myosin. The key steps in the coupling phase of skeletal muscle contraction are as follows:

1. Ca^{2+} binds to the troponin complex.
2. The troponin complex changes its shape and configuration, thereby allowing *tropomyosin* to recede into the space between the actin strands.
3. As tropomyosin recedes from the outer surface of actin, it no longer blocks the outer surface of actin from interfacing with myosin.
4. The binding sites on actin are now fully exposed. The myosin heads quickly attach, or couple, to actin at the binding sites.

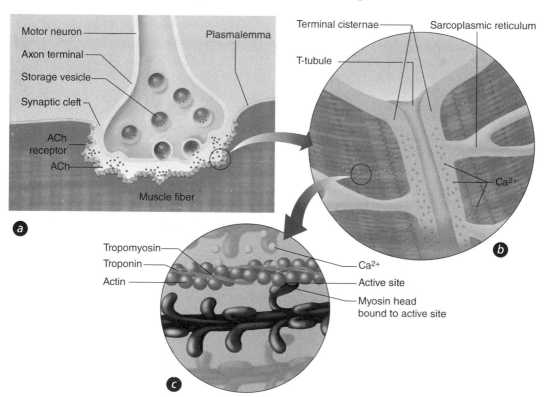

▶ **Figure 1.12** Excitation phase and coupling phase of skeletal muscle contraction.

The *contraction phase* of skeletal muscle contraction is shown in figure 1.13. Contraction refers to the sequence of events whereby myosin essentially pulls on actin, thereby drawing the two contractile filaments closer together, resulting in muscular contraction. This phase is typically referred to as the *sliding filament theory*. Note that the contraction phase of skeletal muscle contraction cannot occur unless ATP is present. The key steps in the contraction phase of skeletal muscle contraction are as follows:

1. Myosin and actin are attached. This process is called myosin–actin *cross bridging*.

2. ADP and P_i are released from the myosin head. When ADP and P_i are released, the myosin head pivots and pulls the actin filament toward the middle of the sarcomere. This step is called the *power stroke*.

3. A new ATP molecule attaches to the myosin head. When this occurs, the myosin head briefly releases from its attachment to actin.

4. The new ATP molecule is quickly converted to ADP and P_i and energy. When this occurs, the myosin head quickly reattaches to actin.

5. Steps 1 through 4 are repeated continuously, provided that ATP is supplied at the appropriate rate. (If ATP is not present and myosin–actin cross bridging occurs, then the muscle is in a state of *rigor mortis*.)

A good analogy for the contraction phase is a tug-of-war contest. In tug-of-war, the hands of several people are constantly grabbing, pulling, quickly releasing, and regrabbing a rope. Similarly, in the contraction phase several myosin heads are constantly grabbing (step 1 above), pulling (step 2), quickly releasing (step 3), and regrabbing (step 4) on an actin "rope." The contraction phase cannot continue indefinitely. Skeletal muscle will return to the relaxed, noncontractile state when the motor nerve action potential ceases, which in turn shuts off the release of Ca^{2+} from the terminal cisternae of the sarcoplasmic reticulum. Without Ca^{2+} present, tropomyosin and the troponin complex resume their noncontractile positions, where they serve to block myosin from attaching to actin.

Skeletal Muscle Fiber Types

Traditional exercise physiology textbooks typically identify three basic types of human skeletal muscle fiber. Recent animal and human research, however, has provided compelling evidence of several additional pure and hybrid skeletal muscle fiber types.[1, 2, 3] Nevertheless, for the purpose of this chapter we focus on the three main skeletal muscle fiber types:

Type I: slow oxidative (SO); for example, the soleus muscle

Type IIa: fast oxidative glycolytic (FOG); for example, the diaphragm

Type IIx: fast glycolytic (FG); for example, the gastrocnemius muscle

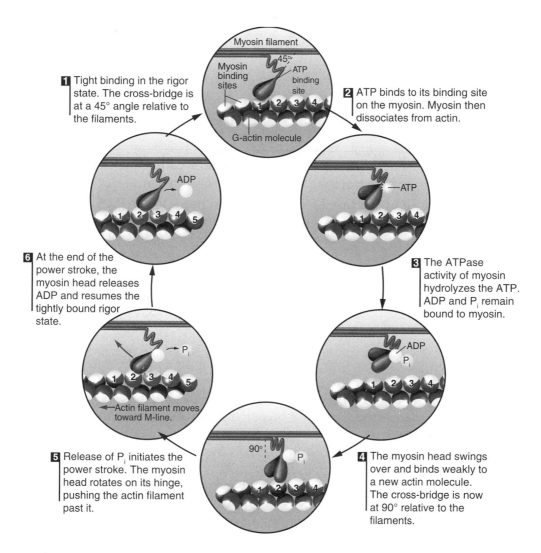

1 Tight binding in the rigor state. The cross-bridge is at a 45° angle relative to the filaments.

2 ATP binds to its binding site on the myosin. Myosin then dissociates from actin.

3 The ATPase activity of myosin hydrolyzes the ATP. ADP and P_i remain bound to myosin.

4 The myosin head swings over and binds weakly to a new actin molecule. The cross-bridge is now at 90° relative to the filaments.

5 Release of P_i initiates the power stroke. The myosin head rotates on its hinge, pushing the actin filament past it.

6 At the end of the power stroke, the myosin head releases ADP and resumes the tightly bound rigor state.

▶ **Figure 1.13** Contraction phase of skeletal muscle contraction.

SILVERTHORN, DEE UNGLAUB, HUMAN PHYSIOLOGY: AN INTEGRATED APPROACH, 4th, © 2007. Printed and electronically reproduced by permission of Pearson Education, Inc., Upper Saddle River, New Jersey.

Note that most muscles have a certain percentage of type I, type IIa, and type IIx fibers. In other words, the soleus muscle is not made up exclusively of type I fibers. Rather, it is composed predominantly of type I fibers but includes lower percentages of type IIa and type IIx fibers. Similarly, the diaphragm muscle is predominantly composed of type IIa fibers, whereas the gastrocnemius muscle is primarily made up of type IIx fibers.

Type I and type IIx fibers have distinct metabolic features. Type I fibers are designed to facilitate oxidative phosphorylation energy production and are found in relative abundance in endurance athletes. In contrast, type IIx fibers are designed to facilitate glycolytic energy production and are found in relative abundance in sprint and power athletes. Type IIa fibers are essentially a hybrid of type I and type IIx fibers and therefore have the capability of producing ATP by oxidative phosphorylation or glycolytic metabolism.

Training Effects

In describing the effect of training on skeletal muscle, a useful first step is to categorize the specific types of training that alter the physiological and biochemical characteristics of skeletal muscle. Skeletal muscle can be affected by aerobic endurance training, anaerobic training, and resistance training.

Aerobic Endurance Training

Endurance training stresses and challenges type I (slow oxidative) muscle fibers more than it does type IIx (fast glycolytic) muscle fibers. As a result, type I fibers tend to enlarge with endurance training. Although the percentage of type I and type IIx fibers does not appear to change, endurance training may cause type IIx fibers to take on more type IIa (fast oxidative glycolytic) fiber characteristics.

The number of capillaries supplying each muscle fiber increases with endurance training. The capillary bed is a microscopic, meshlike structure that is embedded deep in the muscle. The capillaries serve as a transfer point whereby oxygen and nutrients (glucose) are delivered to the exercising muscles by arterial blood, whereas carbon dioxide and metabolic by-products (lactate + H^+) are removed by venous blood. This delivery-and-pickup process is enhanced if the number of capillaries is increased, thereby allowing the exercising muscles to perform more efficiently.

Endurance training increases both the number and size of the mitochondria in skeletal muscle, particularly for type I muscle fibers. The mitochondria are microscopic, capsule-shaped units located in the muscle cell that are essential for the production of ATP by the oxidative phosphorylation energy system (figure 1.6). By increasing both the size and number of mitochondria through endurance training, oxidative energy production is enhanced.

The activity of many oxidative enzymes is increased with endurance training. Figure 1.6 is a simplified representation of the oxidative energy system. It shows how two molecules of acetyl CoA enter a mitochondrion, move into the Krebs cycle, and then move on to the electron transport system (ETS) to produce 32 molecules of ATP. The Krebs cycle is a series of biochemical reactions that are essential to the production of the 32 molecules of ATP, which are ultimately synthesized in the ETS. Most of the oxidative enzymes that are enhanced by endurance training are located in the Krebs cycle phase of the oxidative phosphorylation energy system. Similar to the increase in mitochondria, an increase in the activity of oxidative enzymes serves to enhance oxidative energy production.

Finally, endurance training increases muscle myoglobin (Mb) content by 75 to 80 percent. Myoglobin is the "smaller brother" of hemoglobin and has many similar structural characteristics. Like hemoglobin, myoglobin has as its primary physiological function the transport of oxygen. Whereas hemoglobin carries oxygen from the lungs to the exercising muscles by the bloodstream, myoglobin picks up oxygen after it has been dropped off in the capillary bed by hemoglobin. Next, myoglobin transports oxygen to the mitochondria where it is used to produce ATP by the oxidative phosphorylation energy system. By increasing myoglobin content through endurance training, oxygen delivery within the exercising muscle is enhanced.

Anaerobic Training

Anaerobic training increases ATP–CP and glycolytic enzymes in skeletal muscle. Some of these enzymes are shown in figure 1.4 (ATP–CP) and figure 1.5 (glycolytic). Similar to the increase in the oxidative enzymes, increases in the ATP–CP and glycolytic enzymes serve to enhance the production of ATP by those two energy systems.

Skeletal muscle buffering capacity is enhanced by anaerobic training. As described earlier, lactate and H^+ are metabolites that are produced in the glycolytic energy system. High concentrations of H^+ can slow the release of Ca^{2+} in the excitation phase of skeletal muscle contraction, thereby contributing to premature fatigue of the muscle. Because of anaerobic training, the amount of bicarbonate (HCO_3^-) in skeletal muscle is increased.

As shown in figure 1.14, bicarbonate acts as an effective buffer for reducing acidosis in the exercising muscle. Bicarbonate essentially picks up the potentially detrimental H^+ and subsequently removes it safely from the body in the form of H_2O and CO_2.

$$C_3H_5O_8^- + \boxed{H^+} + \boxed{HCO_3^-} \longrightarrow H_2CO_3 \longrightarrow H_2O + CO_2$$

Lactate   Bicarbonate

▶ **Figure 1.14** Bicarbonate reduces acidosis in exercising muscle.

Resistance Training

Although triathletes use various types of resistance training programs (heavy weight and low repetitions versus moderate weight and high repetitions), the following physiological adaptations occur because of regular resistance training. Regular resistance training means a minimum of three to five training sessions per week for at least 8 weeks.

An increase in the size of the skeletal muscle fiber is known as hypertrophy. Most research studies have shown that regular resistance training in combination with an adequate diet will produce skeletal muscle hypertrophy. The degree of skeletal muscle hypertrophy will vary depending on the specific resistance training program used, as defined by weight, repetitions, and number of training sessions per week.

Regular resistance training also increases the number of active muscle motor units. A single muscle motor unit is made up of several muscle fibers along with the nerve that innervates them and stimulates the muscles fibers to contract in unison. After several weeks of resistance training, the skeletal muscle produces additional active motor units.

Muscular strength increases because of resistance training. Muscular strength is defined as the maximum force that is generated by a muscle or muscle group. Muscular strength is usually measured using a one-repetition maximum lift (1RM), or the maximum amount of weight that a person can lift just once. An athlete who can bench press 300 pounds (136 kg) in a 1RM has twice the muscular strength of an athlete who can bench press 150 pounds (68 kg).

Resistance training also increases muscular power, which is not the same as muscular strength. Muscular power is the explosive aspect of strength and is the product of muscular strength and the speed of a specific movement. For example, athlete AA and athlete BB can both bench press 150 pounds (68 kg) in a 1RM. Athlete AA, however, completes the lift in 1.0 second, whereas athlete BB can complete the lift in 0.5 second. Although athlete BB has the same muscular strength as athlete AA, he has twice the muscular power because he can lift the same weight in half the time.

An important performance characteristic for triathletes is muscular endurance, which is also enhanced by regular resistance training.[4, 5, 6] Muscular endurance refers to the capacity to sustain repeated muscular actions, such as when running for an extended period. It also refers to the ability to sustain fixed or static muscular actions for an extended period, such as when attempting to pin an opponent in wrestling. Muscular endurance is usually measured by counting the number of repetitions that an athlete can perform at a fixed percentage of her 1RM. For example, if an athlete bench presses 140 pounds (64 kg) in a 1RM, her muscular endurance can be measured by counting how many repetitions she can complete at 75 percent of 1RM, or 105 pounds (48 kg).

Conclusion

After reading this chapter, triathletes and their coaches should feel confident in their understanding of the physiology of triathlon. Triathletes should apply the scientific principles of the three energy systems (ATP–CP, glycolysis, oxidative phosphorylation) to the design of daily workouts to meet the specific goals of their training programs. The principles of the three energy systems should be applied to race-day strategy for all triathlon formats—sprint, Olympic, and Ironman.

An understanding of cardiopulmonary anatomy and physiology will help triathletes and coaches apply these principles to create training programs that are designed to enhance the four most important contributors to endurance performance: $\dot{V}O_2$max, economy, lactate threshold, and maximal exercise performance (swimming and running velocity, cycling power output).

Knowledge of skeletal muscle anatomy and physiology will optimize the triathlete's training capacity while simultaneously reducing the chance of injury or overtraining. Applying this knowledge will maximize positive training effects on skeletal muscle that are derived from aerobic training (e.g., enhancement of oxidative enzymes) and anaerobic training (e.g., enhanced muscle buffering capacity), which ultimately serve to improve race performance.

CHAPTER 2

Genetics and Inheritance in Triathlon Performance

—Ildus I. Ahmetov, PhD, and Malcolm Collins, PhD

Athletic performance and the occurrence of sports-related injuries are both multifactorial conditions, which are determined by the complex and poorly understood interactions of both environmental and genetic factors. Although much work has been done to identify the nongenetic components associated with performance and susceptibility to injuries, an ever-growing body of research is investigating the genetic contribution to these observable characteristics or traits, known in the field of genetics as *phenotypes*.

It has long been recognized that the interindividual variability of physical performance traits and the ability to become an elite athlete have a strong genetic basis. The genetic factors that influence these performance and sports-related injury phenotypes are now being sought. Several family, twin, case-control, and cross-sectional studies suggest an important role of genetics along with epigenetic (i.e., stable and heritable changes in gene expression) and environmental factors in the determination of individual differences in athletic performance and training responses.

Research has shown that a genetic component of the variance in any phenotype (i.e., height, muscle mass, athlete status, and so on) is determined by small changes in the structure of DNA (composed of about 3 billion genetic letters or nucleotides and about 25,000 genes), which are called *polymorphisms*. In other words, any position in the genome where more than one nucleotide base is found among a population of individuals is known as a polymorphism, and each variant letter found at a polymorphism is known as an *allele*. In most cases, two different alleles are found at any polymorphism in the genome (e.g., the nucleotides G and C are both possible at position −634 of gene *VEGFA*; see figure 2.1). Across a population, the frequency of each allele can be measured. Because most genes come in pairs (inherited from father and mother), each person has a pair of alleles within his or her genome for any polymorphism. This combination of alleles at any variant site is known as a *genotype* (for example GG, GC, and CC genotypes).

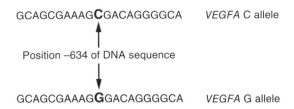

GCAGCGAAAG**C**GACAGGGGCA   *VEGFA* C allele

↑

Position −634 of DNA sequence

↓

GCAGCGAAAG**G**GACAGGGGCA   *VEGFA* G allele

▶ **Figure 2.1** Scheme of possible genetic variations (alleles) at position −634 of gene VEGFA. This example shows that people may possess two different types of alleles (G or C) of a given DNA sequence.

The human genome has no less than 50 million polymorphic variants, which make all individuals different. The most common type of DNA sequence variant is the single-nucleotide polymorphism, or SNP. Other types of DNA polymorphisms exist as well. Insertion/deletion (I/D) polymorphisms are the presence or absence of a stretch of specific DNA nucleotides at a certain position in the genome (e.g., I/D polymorphism of the *ACE* gene). Another type of genetic variation is known as a repeat polymorphism. These polymorphisms are repetitive stretches of DNA sequences (e.g., CAG repeats in the *AR* gene).

Genetic variations can affect the amount and structure of mRNA/protein and therefore may account for the main share of genetic factors in human phenotypic variability, but most of these polymorphisms remain to be discovered. If any allele is associated with a certain phenotype, it is called a *DNA (or genetic) marker*. Based on final effect, DNA variations generally can be classified as genetic markers associated with endurance athlete status, height, increased proportion of slow-twitch muscle fibers, risk of injury, and so on. These and other genetic markers are considered in the sections that follow.

DNA Effect on Height, Body Composition, and Muscle Fiber Composition

Physical characteristics and body composition are heritable traits and are known to be fundamental to excellence in athletic performance. Specific athletic events require different body type, height, weight, and muscle fiber composition for maximal performance. Mean height, body mass index, and percentage of slow-twitch muscle fibers of elite triathletes reflect the preferred anthropometric and morphologic measures for this type of sport.

Height

The mean body height of elite male and female triathletes typically is around 71 inches (180 cm) and 67 inches (170 cm), respectively (e.g., 2012 Olympic champions Alistair Brownlee and Nicola Spirig are 176 cm and 166 cm tall, respectively.) The consensus within the scientific literature is that height is highly heritable; 80 percent of its variance is determined by small contributions of multiple genes.[1] Of note, heritability refers to the proportion of the phenotypic variance attributable to all genetic effects. Initially, 47 common genetic variants, which explain 5 percent of the variance in height within Caucasians, were identified during a meta-analysis of genomewide association studies (GWAS).[1]

Recently Yang and colleagues[2] estimated that approximately 295,000 common SNPs explained 45 percent of the variance and that the remaining 35 percent of the genetic variance could be explained by genetic linkage between the causal variants and the genotyped SNPs. In summary, besides the effects of nutrition, which determines most of the 20 percent of the environmental variance,[1] height is determined by small contributions of sequence variants within thousands of genes.

Body Composition

Body composition is most often viewed in the context of the two-compartment model: Body mass is a combination of fat-free mass (FFM; includes muscle mass, bone mass, and other lean components) and fat mass. Total body fat is defined as the absolute amount of energy stored in the form of triacylglycerol in the body. Total body fat content is generally estimated using the body mass index (BMI = kg/m^2). The mean BMI of elite male and female triathletes is around 23.0 and 20.5 kg/m^2, respectively.

Any estimate of genetic effects on BMI is influenced in unknown proportions by the contribution of the genotype to fat mass, muscle mass, skeletal mass, and other components. Heritability estimates range from 44 to 90 percent for BMI. An excessive amount of fat is associated with greater risk of a variety of morbid conditions. Low body fat content is associated with better performance in most endurance activities. Researchers have found that the athletes with lower body fat percentage had higher maximum oxygen uptake ($\dot{V}O_2max$). In other words, the athletes with lower body fat percentage seemed to use oxygen most efficiently, and the excess of body fat was reported to be a deterrent to physical performance. Furthermore, percent body fat is negatively correlated with total race time in male Ironman triathletes.[3]

On the other hand, muscle mass (with heritability from 52 to 90 percent) is considered a favorable factor for endurance performance. Skeletal muscle is the largest tissue in the body and the main energy-consuming and work-producing tissue, providing the propulsive force to perform physical activities.

Support for a role of genes in variation in body fat and muscle content has been obtained by several approaches including association studies. To date, more than 50 gene polymorphisms associated with BMI have been reported. These polymorphisms are located in genes mainly involved in appetite control, fat absorption, lipid storage, and fatty acid oxidation.[4]

The genetics of fat-free mass or muscle mass is less studied. The genetic markers associated with increased FFM or muscle mass are located within genes involved in regulation of vascular tone, muscle contraction, hormone metabolism, and cell signaling.[5]

Muscle Fiber Composition

The ability to perform aerobic or anaerobic exercise varies widely among people, partially depending on muscle fiber composition. In untrained people, the proportion of slow-twitch (type I) fibers in the vastus lateralis muscle is typically around 50 percent (range 5 to 90 percent), and it is unusual for them to undergo conversion to fast-twitch fibers. Endurance-oriented athletes are reported to have a remarkably high proportion of type I fibers in their trained muscle groups, whereas sprinters and weightlifters have muscles that consist predominantly of type IIa and IIx fibers.

Indeed, triathletes have a high percentage of type I fibers in their gastrocnemius, vastus lateralis, and posterior deltoid muscles.[6] It has been suggested that the genetic component for the observed variability in the proportion of type I fibers in human muscles is of the order of 40 to 50 percent, indicating that muscle fiber type composition is determined by both genotype and environment.[7] The genetic variance is that portion of the individual differences associated with differences in DNA sequence at relevant genes and other DNA regions. It incorporates the effects of single genes, gene–environment interactions, and a variety of gene–gene interactions.

Environmental variance depends on factors such as nutritional habits, level of habitual physical activity, nonheritable intrauterine influences, and a variety of other lifestyle components and factors from the social and physical environment. Such environmental factors modulate muscle phenotype through epigenetic mechanisms, activation of transcription factors, and activation of transcriptional coactivators.

Environmental and genetic factors associated with muscle fiber composition are shown in table 2.1. To date, reports have shown that five gene polymorphisms are associated with muscle fiber composition. These polymorphisms are located in genes involved in biochemical processes in mitochondria, glucose and lipid metabolism, cytoskeletal function, hypoxia-related growth of

Table 2.1 Factors Associated With Muscle Fiber Composition

Factors	Factors that induce increased proportion of ST fibers	Factors that induce increased proportion of FT fibers
Environmental (intrinsic or extrinsic)	Tonic activity; reduced thyroid hormone level (hypothyroidism); high-intensity endurance training	Phasic pattern of activity; increased thyroid hormone level (hyperthyroidism); resistance training; spaceflight and unloading; spinal cord injuries
Genetic	Gene variants associated with high percentage of ST fibers (e.g., *ACE* I, *ACTN3* 577X, *HIF1A* Pro582, *PPARA* rs4253778 G, *VEGFR*2472Gln)	Gene variants associated with high percentage of FT fibers (e.g., *ACE* D, *ACTN3* R577, *HIF1A* 582Ser, *PPARA* rs4253778 C, *VEGFR*2 His472)

new blood vessels, and circulatory homeostasis. Interestingly, most of these gene variants are associated with physical performance, athlete status, and various metabolic and cardiovascular diseases.[8, 9]

DNA Effect on Endurance Training

The effects from aerobic exercise differ greatly among people, depending on lifestyle factors and genetic backgrounds. An understanding of genetic backgrounds will help to clarify criteria of daily physical activities and appropriate exercise for individuals including athletes, making it possible to apply individualized preventive medicine and medical care. Note that at the molecular and cellular levels, people with the same genotype respond more similarly to training than do those with different genotypes, indicating that genes play an important role in determining individual differences in response to training.[5]

Research on aerobic endurance clearly shows that some people respond more to training than others.[10] In the same study the maximal heritability estimate of the $\dot{V}O_2$max response to training adjusted for age and sex was reported to be 47 percent. This result means that genetically gifted athletes have a much greater response to training.

For example, evidence that many of the world's best endurance runners originate from distinct regions of Ethiopia and Kenya, rather than being evenly distributed throughout their respective countries, appears to sustain the idea that the success of East African runners is genetically determined. Studies have shown that African distance runners have reduced lactic acid accumulation in muscles, increased resistance to fatigue, and increased oxidative enzyme activity, which equates with high levels of aerobic energy production.

At least 65 genetic markers have been shown to be associated with endurance phenotypes in response to training.[5, 8, 11, 12] These genes are primarily involved in ATP, glucose and lipid metabolism, hypoxia, mitochondrial processes, regulation of muscle fiber type composition, oxygen transport, vascular tone, and the development of new blood vessels.

Most recently, Bouchard and colleagues[12] have identified a panel of 21 gene polymorphisms that account for 49 percent of the variance in $\dot{V}O_2$max trainability. The study included 473 sedentary adults who followed a standardized 20-week exercise program. Subjects who carried 9 or fewer favorable alleles at these 21 gene polymorphisms improved their $\dot{V}O_2$max by 221 milliliters per minute (ml/min), whereas those who carried 19 or more of these alleles gained, on average, 604 ml/min.

Genes and Triathlete Status

Athlete status is a heritable trait: Around 66 percent of the variance in athlete status is explained by additive genetic factors. The remaining variance is because of nonshared environmental factors. Fifteen genetic markers have been reported to be associated with triathlete status (table 2.2). For instance, one elite Russian triathlete possesses the following combination of seven favorable genotypes: *PPARA* GG, *PPARD* CC, *PPARGC1A*Gly/Gly, *PPARGC1B*Ala/Pro, *UCP2*Ala/Val, *ACTN3* RX, and *ACE* ID (carrier of 10 favorable alleles).

All three triathlon disciplines are endurance events. Therefore, it is not surprising that investigators have shown that genetic variants associated with endurance performance are associated with performance during the Ironman triathlon.[13, 14, 15, 16] Some common sequence variants are associated with the performance of Ironman triathletes.[13, 14] Many of these sequence variants are associated with improvements in biochemical pathways within skeletal muscle that improve endurance performance.[17]

A certain genotype is associated with reduced sprint and power performance in several studies.[18] It was not associated with ultraendurance performance in the South African Ironman triathlons study,[19] but the frequency of this genotype was significantly lower in Russian Olympic triathletes in comparison with controls.[20] In the same group of Russian triathletes the frequencies of specific variants located in genes involved in lipid and glucose metabolism, fatty acid oxidation, muscle fiber regulation, mitochondrial processes, muscle fiber regulation, and thermoregulation were significantly higher than in nonathletes.[8, 21, 22]

Different sets of sequence variants have generally been associated with endurance performance and sprint or power events in a sport-independent manner. Discipline-specific associations, however, have recently been reported

Table 2.2 Gene Variants Associated With Triathlete Status

Gene	Polymorphism	Favorable marker	Cohort
ACE	Alu I/D	I	Caucasian Ironman triathletes
ACTN3	R577X	R	Russian Olympic-distance triathletes
BDKRB2	+9/−9	−9	Caucasian Ironman triathletes
COL5A1	rs12722 C/T	rs12722 T	Caucasian Ironman triathletes
COL6A1	rs35796750 C/T	rs35796750 T	Caucasian Ironman triathletes
EPAS1	rs1867785A/G rs11689011C/T	rs1867785G rs11689011T	Australian Ironman and Olympic-distance triathletes
NOS3	Glu298Asp	Glu298	Caucasian Ironman triathletes
PPARA	rs4253778G/C	rs4253778 G	Russian Olympic-distance triathletes
PPARD	rs2016520 T/C	rs2016520C	Russian Olympic-distance triathletes
PPARGC1A	Gly482Ser	Gly482	Russian and Polish Olympic-distance triathletes
PPARGC1B	Ala203Pro	203Pro	Russian Olympic-distance triathletes
TFAM	Ser12Thr	12Thr	Russian Olympic-distance triathletes
UCP2	Ala55Val	55Val	Russian Olympic-distance triathletes
UCP3	rs1800849 C/T	rs1800849 T	Russian Olympic-distance triathletes

with the cycling and running legs of the Ironman triathlon.[15, 16] Variants within the genes that produce the collagens that form a fibrous protein that connects and supports body tissues are associated with the cycling and running times in an Ironman triathlon, respectively.[15, 16] Types V and VI collagen are important structural proteins within the connective tissue components of the musculoskeletal system. These results, however, need to be confirmed in other similar subjects.

Adding to the complexity, multiple genes that remain to be investigated, each encoding for proteins involved in different biological systems and having a small influence on the systems, are likely involved in determining the innate performance ability of a triathlete.[23] Therefore, the limited number of studies (South Africa Ironman, Russian Olympic distance, Australian Ironman and Olympic distance) investigating the genetic contribution to triathlon performance and the extremely small number of sequence variants analyzed to date should not be overinterpreted by athletes and coaches. More study is needed before affective assessment of genes for performance can be done.

Genetic Contribution to Injuries

Triathletes are at increased risk for muscle, tendon, ligament, and other injuries as a result of training and competition.[24] Thirty-nine percent of the 433 triathletes who completed a general medical history questionnaire during the 2006 and 2007 South African Ironman Triathlons reported suffering from a painful, swollen, or stiff tendons or ligaments during their triathlon careers (unpublished data). Acute and chronic or overuse musculoskeletal tissue injuries can negatively affect an athlete's ability to train and perform during competition. In extreme cases these injuries could end an athlete's competitive career or prevent him or her from reaching full potential. Certain athletes seem to be predisposed to specific injuries, whereas others, in spite of training harder and longer, appear to be protected.[25, 23]

No single factor causes musculoskeletal tissue injuries; instead, typical injury risk models include multiple intrinsic and extrinsic factors that are associated with these injuries.[23] A typical injury risk model for Achilles tendon injuries is illustrated in figure 2.2.[26] The individually associated factors do not cause these injuries. Instead, they are believed to increase the risk for musculoskeletal injuries to a lesser or greater extent.

The current level of scientific evidence used to include risk factors in the risk models varies significantly. The inclusion of increased age and weight, for example, as an intrinsic risk factor for Achilles tendon injuries is based on weak scientific evidence, whereas strong evidence indicates that a previous injury increases the risk for Achilles tendon injuries.[26] The current injury risk models are therefore unable to identify athletes who are at risk for Achilles tendon injuries. The biological processes that result in these injuries are poorly understood, and the traditional injury risk models have not been developed on the underlying biological and biomechanical processes that cause these injuries.

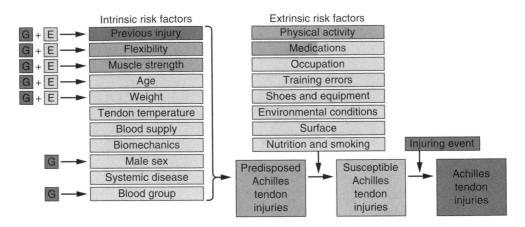

▶ Figure 2.2 Relationship between intrinsic and extrinsic risk factors as the role of the injuring event in the etiology of Achilles tendon injuries.[23, 26] Many of the individual intrinsic risk factors are also in their own right multifactorial phenotypes determined by, to a lesser or greater extent, both genetic (nature, G) and environmental (nurture, E) factors. A high level of scientific evidence suggests that a previous Achilles tendon injury (listed in black boxes) is an intrinsic risk factor for a subsequent injury. A moderate to low level of evidence suggests the intrinsic (gray boxes) and extrinsic (white boxes) are risk factors. Intrinsic risk factors merely predispose athletes to the injury. The predisposed athlete becomes more susceptible to injury when exposed to the appropriate extrinsic factors. A specific event results in a complete or partial rupture or the volume of tissue damage becomes symptomatic. Blood supply refers to the blood supply in the tendon.

Most of the intrinsic factors included in the typical risk models are in their own right multifactorial traits determined to varying degrees by both genetic (nature) and environmental (nurture) factors (figure 2.2).[23] Many are polygenic traits, and each individual gene has a small effect on the phenotype. Added together, they have a significant contribution.[23] In spite of this, specific genetic sequence variants within genes that contribute to the structural components of tendons and ligaments have recently been identified as intrinsic risk factors for some tendon and ligament injuries. Genetic variants previously associated with musculoskeletal soft tissue injuries have been extensively reviewed and are summarized in table 2.3.[23, 25]

Whether these genes are directly or indirectly associated with these injuries remains to be determined. For example, one particular genotype has been reported to protect athletes from developing chronic Achilles tendinopathy.[27] It was recently reported that this genotype also protected healthy, physically active people against an age-related decline in range of motion measurements. Because this gene is associated with both range of motion measurements and chronic Achilles tendinopathy, it is not surprising that flexibility has been reported to be an intrinsic risk factor for Achilles tendon injuries.[27] The involved gene, which produces type V collagen, plays a critical role in the regulation of type I collagen fibril assembly and lateral growth in tendons, ligaments, and other connective tissues (fibrillogenesis).

Table 2.3 Summary of the Genes Previously Associated With Musculoskeletal Soft-Tissue Injuries

The genes encode for structural components of the matrix (collagens and glycoproteins), signaling molecules (cytokines and growth factors), and extracellular matrix (ECM) proteinases (MMPs) have been identified as intrinsic risk factors for some tendon and ligament injuries.

MATRIX		SIGNALING MOLECULES		ECM PROTEINASES	
Gene	**Injury**	**Gene**	**Injury**	**Gene**	**Injury**
COL1A1	ACL ruptures	GDF5	Achilles tendinopathy	MMP3	Achilles tendinopathy
COL5A1	Achilles tendinopathy Female ACL ruptures	IL-1β[a] IL-1RN[a] IL-6[a]	Achilles tendinopathy	MMP10[b] MMP1[b] MMP3[b] MMP12[b]	ACL ruptures
COL12A1	Female ACL ruptures				
TNC	Achilles tendinopathy				

The data within this table is more extensively described in Tucker and Collins.[23]

COL1A1, α1 chain of type I collagen; COL5A1, α1 chain of type V collagen; COL12A1, α1 chain of type XII collagen; TNC, tenascin C; GDF5, growth and differentiation factor 5; IL-1β, interleukin-1β; IL-1RN, interleukin-1 receptor antagonist; IL-6, interleukin-6; MMP3, matrix metalloproteinase 3; MMP10, matrix metalloproteinase 10; MMP1, matrix metalloproteinase 1; MMP12, matrix metalloproteinase 12; ACL, anterior cruciate ligament.

[a]A pathway-based approach was used to investigate the association of genes within the inflammatory pathway and Achilles tendinopathy.

[b]These four MMP genes have been mapped to chromosome 11q22 and a haplotype within this region associated with ACL rupture.

Collins and Posthumus[27] have recently suggested that the type V collagen connect in the Achilles tendon and other tissues may alter their mechanical properties and susceptibility to injuries.

Note that none of the genetic risk factors or any of the other intrinsic risk factors causes musculoskeletal injuries. They merely modulate or contribute to the risk for these injuries. Predisposed athletes need to be exposed to appropriate extrinsic factors, and an event that causes the rupture, tear, or the volume of accumulated damage within the tissue becomes symptomatic.

Physiological Responses During Participation in Triathlons

Besides being subject to individual variations in performance and susceptibility to injury, not all triathletes respond identically to the stresses of training and participating in a triathlon. These physiological responses are also complex phenotypes determined by both genes and environment. This notion is best illustrated by the large individual variation in body weight changes during participation in the Ironman triathlon and the practical recommendations on how much and how often triathletes should drink while competing.

Weight losses, mainly because of dehydration, of up to 12 percent have been reported.[28] Inappropriate replacement of this fluid loss during exercise can lead to disregulation of sodium homeostasis, resulting in either hypernatremia, hyponatremia, or in rare cases potentially fatal encephalopathy (EAHE).[28] EAHE is caused by abnormal fluid retention in athletes who drink to excess during prolonged exercise, usually lasting more than 4 hours, and is preventable when athletes drink only to thirst during exercise. It has been proposed that drinking behavior, water losses, and electrolyte homeostasis during exercise are determined partially by genetics. An association of certain genes with weight loss during the South African Ironman triathlons has previously been reported.[29, 30] The products of these genes regulate water and electrolyte homeostasis by controlling thirst and water reabsorption.[29, 30]

Practical Recommendations Regarding Genetic Profiling

Large variations occur within the responses to training and participation in a triathlon, performance, and susceptibility to sports-related injuries. This variation is caused by complex interactions of environmental and other factors with an athlete's genetic makeup. Although these traits have an inheritable component, athletes and coaches need to understand that no single genetic test or panel of genetic tests can be used to determine performance, response to training, or susceptibility to injuries.

Recognize as well that because all these phenotypes are multifactorial, genetic testing can never be used to predict or diagnose any of these phenotypes. Predictive and diagnostic genetic testing is limited to the rare, classical genetic disorders caused by a single genetic mutation. But genetic testing may one day be incorporated into multifactorial models, consisting of both genetic and nongenetic components, to determine risk for injuries and response to training. These models would enable clinicians and coaches to optimize training programs to reduce the likelihood of injury and maximize training responses. The ethical issues associated with the development and implementation of any model including genetic testing, however, need to be considered.

Conclusion

Physical performance is a complex phenotype influenced by multiple environmental and genetic factors, and variation in human physical performance and athletic ability has long been recognized as having a strong heritable component. The question is no longer whether there is a genetic component to athletic potential and endurance and strength trainability, but exactly which genes are involved and by which mechanisms and pathways they exert their effect. Our current progress toward answering these questions represents only the first steps toward understanding the genetic factors that influence human physical performance.

The current review provides evidence that hundreds of genetic markers are linked to morphological phenotypes, elite athlete status, training responses, and risk of injuries. Of those, 15 gene polymorphisms are linked with triathlete performance. Although more replication studies are needed, the preliminary data suggest an opportunity to use some of these genetic markers in an individually tailored prescription of lifestyle and exercise for health and sport performance.

CHAPTER 3

Gender and Age Considerations in Triathlon

—Romuald Lepers, PhD

Both gender and age can affect performance in triathlon. During these last decades, female triathletes have reduced the gap in triathlon with their male counterparts, especially in long-distance triathlons such as Ironman distance. Female triathletes such as Chrissie Wellington have led triathlon performance to a higher level. In addition to the improvement in female triathlete performance, an increase in participation of masters triathletes (more than 40 years old) has been observed recently. Masters triathletes can still achieve extremely high levels of performance: Dave Scott finished second overall at the Hawaii Ironman Triathlon at 42 years old in 1996; more recently, in 2012, Natascha Badmann finished 6th at Hawaii at 46 years old. Moreover, some unique older triathletes (up to 80 years of age) have begun to push the limits of the interaction between aging and human endurance. In this context, we could wonder how training and outcome expectations for the standard triathlon distances should be modified to the unique needs required by gender and age.

Gender Differences in Triathlon Performance

The gender difference in endurance performance has received considerable attention in these last decades, but most studies have focused on running. Previous studies that have investigated the participation and performance trends of female endurance athletes in running reported an increase in female participation and an improvement in performance during the last three decades.[1]

Although some authors have suggested that the gap in gender difference in endurance performance could be closed, more recent studies could not confirm this assumption, showing that the gender difference in endurance performance is no longer diminishing.[2] For elite runners the gender difference in marathon running performance has remained about the same since the 1980s at a difference of approximately 10 percent.[3] Gender difference in triathlon regarding participation and performances has been less investigated.

Physiological Considerations

Physiological and morphological characteristics may be responsible for gender difference in triathlon performance. Little information was available on the physiological determinants of endurance performance in women until the 1970s. The current available data, while limited in comparison to those available on men, suggest that maximal oxygen uptake ($\dot{V}O_2$max), lactate threshold, and running economy interact in women as determinants of endurance performance in a manner similar to that in men.

The current explanation of gender differences in $\dot{V}O_2$max among elite athletes when expressed relative to body mass is twofold:

- First, elite females have more body fat than males (about 13 percent versus about 5 percent). Much of the difference in $\dot{V}O_2$max disappears when it is expressed relative to lean body mass.
- Second, the hemoglobin concentration of elite athletes is 5 to 10 percent lower in women than in men.

Concerning lactate threshold, there is no reason to believe that values will be lower in women than in men because mitochondrial adaptations in the skeletal muscles of highly trained male and female athletes appear similar. Finally, the average oxygen cost to run a given speed (i.e., running economy) by groups of elite male and female athletes appears to be similar and probably plays the same role in determining success in endurance performance. Therefore, the major physiological reason to explain the slower record performances by women than men is probably the lower $\dot{V}O_2$max values observed in women. Although a number of elite male and female athletes have similar $\dot{V}O_2$max values, these values are at the low end of the elite range for men versus the upper end of the elite range for women.

Male triathletes possess a larger muscle mass, correlating with greater muscular strength and lower relative body fat compared with females. Low body fat is an important predictor variable for total time performance in triathlon. For example, Knechtle, Knechtle, and Rosemann[4] showed that low body fat was associated with faster race times in male Ironman triathletes but not in females. Males retain on average 7 to 9 percent less percent body fat than females, which is likely an advantage for males. Therefore, gender differences in percentage body fat, oxygen carrying capacity, and muscle mass appear to be responsible for gender difference in triathlon performance. Note also that pregnancy and the menstruation cycle may affect training and racing.

Gender Difference in Participation and Performance Density

The number of females competing in triathlon has increased progressively since the 1980s. For example, the number of females finishing the Hawaii Ironman Triathlon increased from 20 in 1981 (6 percent of the participants), to more than 470 in 2010 (27 percent of the participants). By comparison, women represented 32 percent of the participants at the New York Marathon during the last 10 years. In Europe, a progressive rise in the number of female Ironman finishers also occurred, but the rate was lower. For example in 2010 females accounted for 8, 11, and 13 percent of the field at the France, Austria, and Switzerland Ironman triathlons, respectively. The lower rate of female participation in Europe is presumably explained by the fact that Ironman triathlon in Europe is younger compared with Hawaii Ironman Triathlon (first event held in 1978). Female participation in European Ironman triathlons will probably increase in the future.

For short-distance triathlon, the rate of female participation appears greater than for Ironman triathlon. For example, in 2010 at the Zurich (Switzerland) short-distance triathlon, females accounted for 26 percent of the field, but females made up only 13 percent for the Ironman distance held in the same city. Interestingly, the increase in female participation this last decade at the Zurich short-distance triathlon only appears for females between 40 and 54 years old and not for younger female triathletes. In contrast, the participation of male triathletes at this event did not change during the last decade.

Nowadays, female triathletes have the same opportunities to train and compete as males do. Females may be gaining more competitive opportunities as they age, or they may be seeking out competition later in life, after childbirth, or later in their careers. Another aspect linked to the increase in participation of female triathletes is motivation. If winning prize money can be an additional motivation for elite triathletes, having fun and staying in good health may be the main motivations for recreational female triathletes.

The performance density in triathlon, quantified by the time difference between the winner and 10th place, is greater in males than in females, whatever the event (see table 3.1). For example, at the Hawaii Ironman Triathlon between 1981 and 2010, the average time difference between the winner and 10th place was 5.8 percent for the males and 7.5 percent for the females. During the last 5 years, the time difference between the winner and 10th place decreased for both males (about 3.1 percent) and females (about 5.7 percent), suggesting that elite female performance density will probably become similar to what is seen among males in the future.

Table 3.1 Time Difference Between the Winner and 10th Place, Expressed as a Percentage of the Winner's Performance for Males and Females at Various Events in 2009

Difference 10th to 1st in 2009	Male	Female
Olympic Triathlon World Championship Grand final (with drafting) Gold Coast, Australia	0.7%	1.1%
Xterra Triathlon World Championship Maui, Hawaii, USA	4.5%	11.7%
Half-Ironman World Championship Clearwater, Florida, USA	3.5%	6.8%
ITU Long-Distance World Championship Perth, Australia	3.8%	9.8%
Ironman World Championship Kona, Hawaii, USA	2.3%	8.8%

Long-Distance Triathlon: The Example of the Hawaii Ironman Triathlon

The analysis of male and female performances during the Hawaii Ironman Triathlon World Championship, considered as the premier race in the field of long-distance triathlon, provides accurate insights into gender difference in long-distance triathlon. A study conducted by Lepers[5] in 2008 showed that overall performance time of elite male and female triathletes at the event decreased rapidly between 1981 and the late 1980s and then plateaued thereafter for both males and females (figure 3.1). During the last two decades, while swimming times for males and females and running times in males tended to stagnate, running times in females marginally improved. In contrast, cycling performance over time was more stochastic, presumably caused by the substantial effect of wind conditions. Between 1988 and 2010, the gender difference remained stable and practically identical for swimming (+0.8 percent per decade), increased a little for cycling (+1.3 percent per decade) and decreased somewhat more for running (–1.8 percent per decade).

Gender Difference in Swimming is Smaller Than in Cycling or Running

The average gender difference in swimming performance at the Hawaii Ironman over the last 25 years was 10.3 percent (figure 3.2). The gender difference in Ironman 3.8-kilometer swimming is consistent with values found for various swimming events from 50- to 400-meter freestyle but is lower than the gender difference found for 100-meter freestyle. It has been suggested that swimming gender difference became progressively less with increasing distance between 50 and 1,500 meters.[6]

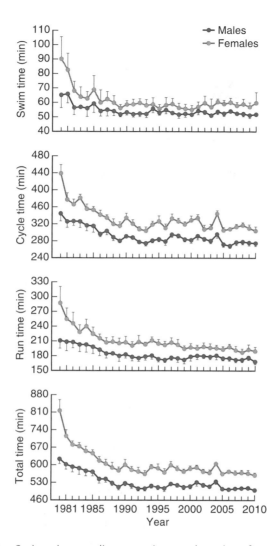

▶ **Figure 3.1** Swimming, cycling, running, and total performance times at the Hawaii Ironman Triathlon for the top 10 males and females from 1981 to 2010. Values are mean ± SD. Two races took place in 1982, in February and October.

Two factors could explain the reduced gender difference for longer distances, especially for ocean swimming compared with sprint events in the pool. First, the denser salt water compared with fresh water would likely raise more of a female's body out of the water because females have more body fat than males do. This positioning would reduce surface area in the water and total drag compared with swimming in fresh water and give some specific advantage to females. Second, according to swimming studies, at lower velocity a woman's drag coefficient drops somewhat compared with a man's in any similar water condition.

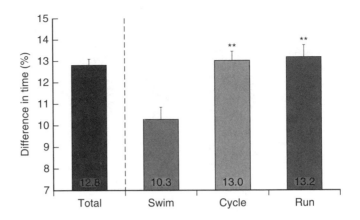

▶ **Figure 3.2** Average gender difference in time performance for total event, swimming, cycling, and running at the Hawaii Ironman Triathlon for the top 10 males and females from 1986 to 2010. Values are means ± SE. **Significantly different from swim, P < 0.01.

The swimming gender difference in time (10.3 percent) appears on average smaller compared with cycling (13.0 percent) and running (13.2 percent) (figure 3.2). The difference between swimming and the two other disciplines could be explained in part by the biological gender difference in relative body fat (body mass in females is 7 to 9 percent higher). Indeed, greater body fat may represent a limit in weight-bearing activities such as running, but in contrast it increases buoyancy in water.

Moreover, it has been shown that the underwater torque, a measure of the tendency of the feet to sink, is lower for females than for males. In addition, the mechanical efficiency of swimming corrected to body surface area is greater for females than for males. Upper-body strength differences between males and females are larger compared with differences in the lower body, so presumably buoyancy issues outweigh this difference. These factors could explain the reduced difference between males and females in swimming compared with running and cycling.

Cycling Gender Difference Comparisons Are Difficult

The average gender difference in cycling at the Hawaii Ironman is 13.0 percent in performance time. Cycling performance comparison between genders in single cycling events is difficult because cycling does not have an official time-trial championship with a distance close to 180 kilometers at the same distance for males and females. For example, at the 2007 world cycling time-trial championships, the difference between the male champion's pace and the female champion's pace was 11.5 percent, but males rode 44.9 kilometers and females rode 25.1 kilometers. Schumacher, Mueller, and Keul[7] reported that in track cycling the gender gap difference between males and females appeared constant (about 11 percent) for distances between 200 and 1,000 meters.

The available data suggest that the difference in cycling between males and females is of similar magnitude for much longer time-trial cycling. Greater muscle mass and aerobic capacity in males, even expressed relative to lean body mass, may represent an advantage during long-distance cycling, especially on a relatively flat course such as Ironman cycling, where cycling approximates a non-weight-bearing sport. Indeed, it has been shown that absolute power output, which among elites is greater for males than females, is associated with successful performance. In addition, a significant correlation has been reported between 40-kilometer time-trial performance and body mass.[8]

Running Gender Difference is Slightly Decreasing

Over the last 25 years, the top 10 males have run the Hawaii Ironman marathon on average 13.2 percent faster than the top 10 females. The physiological differences between males and females in running performance that are well identified in the literature persist in the marathon of an Ironman. Morphological (body fatness) and physiological gender differences, such as oxygen carrying capacity (hemoglobin concentration) may partly account for the gender difference in distance running performance.

Interestingly, during the last 25 years elite female triathletes improved their running time by 0.8 minutes per year while running time remained stable for males. The reasons for such an improvement in female running performance at Ironman distance is not clear because both males and females had the opportunity to use new training methods (e.g., altitude training) and advances in nutrition. If females continue to improve their running performance at Ironman in the future, they could reduce the gender difference in the marathon and therefore in overall performance. The best example is Chrissie Wellington, who astonishingly reduced the gap in running with her male counterpart in Roth Ironman (Germany) to the world's fastest Ironman distance performance for both males and females (see table 3.2).

Table 3.2 World Best Total Event Performance Times (h:min:s) for Males and Females With Corresponding Split Times Without Transition Times for Swimming, Cycling, and Running at the Hawaii Ironman Triathlon and Roth Ironman (Germany) Gender difference is expressed as a percentage of the male's time.

Ironman course records	Total	Swim 3.8 km	Cycle 180 km	Run 42 km
HAWAII IRONMAN TRIATHLON				
Male, Craig Alexander (2011)	8:03:56	51:56	4:24:05	2:44:02
Female, Chrissie Wellington (2009)	8:54:02	54:31	4:52:06	3:03:05
Gender difference	10.3%	5.0%	10.6%	11.6%
ROTH IRONMAN (GERMANY)				
Male, Andreas Raelert (2011)	7:41:33	46:18	4:11:43	2:40:52
Female, Chrissie Wellington (2011)	8:18:05	49:49	4:40:39	2:44:35
Gender difference	7.9%	7.6%	11.5%	2.6%

Observations on ultratriathlons such as double- or triple-Ironman-distance triathlon show greater gender difference in performance compared with Ironman distance.[9, 10] For example, the gender difference in total time performance for both double- and triple-Ironman distance triathlons is close to 19 percent, which is greater than that found for an Ironman (about 13 percent). But nonphysiological factors may have contributed to these observations. For example, the widening of gender difference with increased distance could be caused in part by the fewer number of female finishers in ultratriathlons.

Comparison Between Short and Long Distances

Surprisingly, gender differences in short-distance triathlon (consisting of a 1.5-kilometer swim, 40-kilometer bike, and 10-kilometer run) performances for elite athletes have been less investigated. One reason may be that the top international Olympic-distance triathlons (i.e., World Championship Series events) have all been draft legal for several years and therefore finding a reference of high-level Olympic-distance triathlon without drafting for comparison is difficult. The addition of several nondrafting international-distance triathlons that offer a competitive platform for professional triathletes should help in analyzing gender difference in short-distance triathlon performance in the future.

Gender differences in times for swimming, cycling, running, and total event have been compared for triathlons with distances from Olympic to Ironman distance for the top 10 elite males and females (figure 3.3). Gender difference in time for swimming was lower for Olympic distance triathlon (5.4

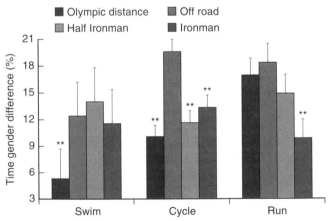

▶ **Figure 3.3** Mean percentage difference in time for swimming, cycling, and running at four triathlon events of different types (2007, 2008, and 2009; data pooled) between the top 10 females and males: Olympic distance, World Cup Triathlon (Des Moines, Iowa, USA); off-road, Xterra Triathlon World Championship (Makena, Hawaii, USA); half-ironman, Half-Ironman Triathlon World Championship (Clearwater, Florida, USA); Ironman, Ironman Triathlon World Championship (Kona, Hawaii, USA). Values are means ± SE. **P < 0.01, significantly different from off-road triathlon.

percent) than for other triathlons (about 10 to 13 percent). For cycling, gender difference did not differ between the three conventional distances (about 10 to 13 percent). Gender difference in time for running was lower for Ironman triathlon (9.7 percent) than for other triathlons (about 14 to 18 percent).

Gender and Age Interaction in Triathlon Performance

Knowing that the physiological (e.g., muscle strength, oxygen carrying capacity) and morphological (e.g., percentage of body fat, muscle mass) functional characteristics change with advancing age, gender difference in triathlon performance may also change with advancing age. After age 55, the decline in athletic performance increases exponentially in both sexes, but this decline is typically more pronounced in women than in men.[11] This change in gender difference with advancing age has been examined at the Hawaii Ironman Triathlon[12] (see figure 3.4).

Figure 3.4 shows that gender difference in total event performance time increased significantly with advancing age from 55 years. Male triathletes at the age of 60 years were on average 27 percent slower than the 30- to 40-year-old triathletes, and the difference reached 38 percent for women.

Age- and gender-related differences in swimming, cycling, and running performances likely result from physiological, sociological, and psychological changes that occur. The exact reasons for these sex-related differences

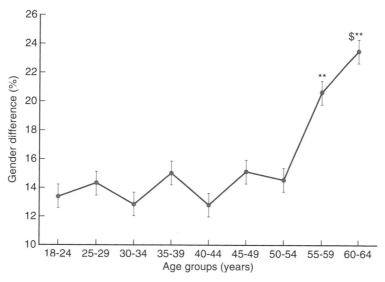

▶ **Figure 3.4** Average gender difference in time for total event at the Hawaii Ironman Triathlon (2006, 2007, 2008 pool data). Values are means ± 95 percent CI. **Significantly different from all age groups from 20 to 24 to 50 to 55 years, $P < 0.01$. $ Significantly different from age group 55 to 59 years, $P < 0.05$.

Reprinted, by permission, from R. Lepers and N.A. Maffiuletti, 2011, "Age and gender interactions in ultraendurance performance: Insight from the triathlon," *Medicine & Science in Sports & Exercise* 43(1), 134-139.

are not clear. A greater decline of one or more physiological determinants of endurance performance for women compared with men (e.g., maximal oxygen uptake, lactate threshold, and exercise economy) has not been evidenced.

Age-related changes in body composition (i.e., increase in percentage body fat and loss of muscular mass), hormonal changes, and fluid balance changes (e.g., decline in the thirst mechanism) could also differ between males and females and affect triathlon performance. Finally, the reduction in training volume and intensity could contribute to the larger declines in endurance performance of elderly athletes. Differences in terms of years of training, training volume, and intensity between elderly men and women triathletes performing Ironman triathlon may exist, but further work is required to clarify this.

Interpretation of cross-sectional comparisons of triathlon performance times across ages and sexes must be made carefully. Compared with men, fewer women are competing in triathlon events, especially in the older age categories. For example, the percentage of women participating at the Hawaii Ironman Triathlon during 2007 to 2009 corresponded on average to 27 percent, but women finishers in the age group 60 to 64 years represented only 3 percent of the women's field. This participation difference will no doubt diminish over the next couple of decades. As a result, triathlon performances of the oldest women will probably improve more rapidly than those of the oldest men as the new generation of well-trained young female athletes moves into older age group competition.

Age-Related Decline in Triathlon Performance

Even if it is possible for an 80-year-old male athlete to finish an Ironman triathlon in less than 17 hours (e.g., Lew Hollander finished the Hawaii Ironman Triathlon in 15:48 in 2010; see table 3.3), the gradient in declining performances increased notably after the age of 55 years for both sexes, and female performances tended to decline faster than those of males. According to Reaburn and Dascombe,[13] the physiological factors affecting endurance performance with increasing age are maximum oxygen consumption ($\dot{V}O_2max$), maximal heart rate, stroke volume, lactate threshold, economy of movement, muscle-fiber type, activity of aerobic enzymes, blood volume, and skeletal muscle mass.

The decline in endurance performance appears primarily because of an age-related decrease in $\dot{V}O_2max$. The decrease of muscle mass with advancing age plays a role in the age-related decrease in $\dot{V}O_2max$ in master endurance athletes. On average, the muscle area decreases by about 40 percent between 20 and 80 years old. Both slow- and fast-twitch fibers decline with increasing age, although the loss of fast-twitch fibers is greater.

Table 3.3 Best Total Performance Times for Male and Female Age Groups With Corresponding Split Times at the Hawaii Ironman Triathlon

	MALE									
Year	2011[a]	1996[b]	2009	2006	2005	2010	2011	2011	2005	2012
Age group (years)	18–39	40–44	45–49	50–54	55–59	60–64	65–69	70–74	75–79	>80
3.8 km swim (h:min:s)	51:56	53:16	56:55	1:03:32	1:07:09	1:16:20	1:14:11	1:47:46	1:37:47	1:49:34
180 km cycle (h:min:s)	4:24:05	4:49:55	5:04:47	4:51:44	5:00:17	5:19:17	5:42:08	5:47:33	6:39:35	7:42:08
42 km run (h:min:s)	2:44:02	2:45:20	3:04:21	3:24:51	3:34:03	3:25:28	4:14:52	3:52:47	4:55:43	5:41:51
Total (h:min:s)	8:03:56	8:28:31	9:11:24	9:26:23	9:47:29	10:08:15	11:19:07	11:45:05	13:27:50	15:38:25
	FEMALE									
Year	2009[c]	2010	2012[d]	2005	2010	2010	2010	2000	2005	NA
Age group (years)	18–39	40–44	45–49	50–54	55–59	60–64	65–69	70–74	75–79	NA
3.8 km swim (h:min:s)	54:31	1:13:52	1:06:21	1:08:08	1:06:18	1:32:16	1:21:02	1:37:54	1:45:05	NA
180 km cycle (h:min:s)	4:52:06	5:25:00	5:06:07	5:31:56	5:35:36	6:27:46	6:47:28	7:24:33	7:25:17	NA
42 km run (h:min:s)	3:03:05	3:17:48	3:09:18	3:47:23	4:00:08	4:05:22	4:59:01	6:07:02	6:19:43	NA
Total (h:min:s)	8:54:02	10:02:35	9:26:25	10:35:59	10:51:43	12:17:24	13:16:32	15:19:19	15:54:16	NA

[a]Craig Alexander, 38 years old; [b]Dave Scott, 42 years old; [c]Chrissie Wellington, 32 years old; [d]Natascha Badmann, 45 years old.

Effect of Locomotion Mode

The age-related decline in triathlon performance is specific to the discipline. For both short- and long-distance triathlons, the age-related decline in cycling performance is less compared with running and swimming performances[14, 15, 16] (see figure 3.5). The question of whether there is better maintenance of cycling performance or a greater decline in running and swimming performances with advancing age can be raised.

One explanation for the different age-related declines in cycling and running may involve the mechanical power required by those disciplines. Mechanical power output (P) in running depends on the velocity (V) because $P = k \times V$ (k is a constant), whereas it depends on the third power of velocity in cycling ($P = k \times V^3$). If we assume that the changes in aerobic capacity (e.g., $\dot{V}O_2max$) with age are directly related to the decline in mechanical power, a similar reduction in power output for running and cycling with advancing age would induce a lower reduction in cycling velocity compared with running velocity. This relationship may explain, in part, why the magnitude of the decrease in cycling performance with age was less than that for running.

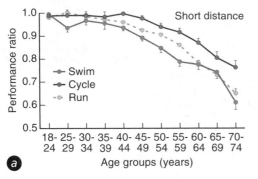
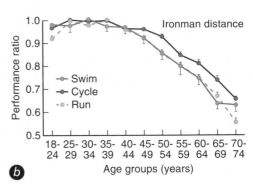

▶ **Figure 3.5** Age-related decline in swimming, cycling, and running performance for (a) short-distance triathlon and for (b) Ironman-distance triathlon (mean ± SE). For short-distance triathlon the cycling performance ratio remained significantly ($P < 0.01$) greater than swimming from age group 40 onward, and from age group 45 the cycling performance ratio remained significantly ($P < 0.01$) greater than running. For Ironman-distance triathlon, the cycling performance ratio remained significantly ($P < 0.01$) greater than swimming from age group 45 onward, except for age group 70, and from age group 50 the cycling performance ratio remained significantly ($P < 0.01$) greater than running.

Adapted, by permission, from R. Lepers, F. Sultana, T. Bernard, et al., 2010, "Age-related changes in triathlon performance," *International Journal of Sports Medicine* 31(4): 251-256.

Running involves stretch-shortening cycles (SSC) with eccentric muscle contractions, whereas cycling is a non-weight-bearing activity that involves dominant concentric muscle contractions. Fast-twitch fibers, however, atrophy more than slow-twitch fibers do with age. Because fast-twitch fibers seem more susceptible to damage than slow-twitch fibers during SSC, the greater reduction in running performance compared with cycling could be related to muscle typology changes with age.

But the changes in muscle fiber type distribution (i.e., the percentage of type I muscle fibers) with advancing age seem less pronounced in well-trained masters athletes compared with untrained older adults. Moreover, in terms of muscle damage, although some animal studies have shown that recovery from eccentric exercise-induced muscle damage is lessened in older subjects compared with the young, the results from human studies are not as clear. Results might differ among muscle groups, but there is no evidence that the muscles of older triathletes are more susceptible to muscle damage than muscles of young triathletes.

Findings for competitive long-distance runners indicate that the decline in running times parallels the age-related reductions in maximal oxygen uptake and lactate threshold. The contributions of these respective physiological factors to age-related declines in cycling performance, however, are unknown at present.

Indeed, few studies are available on the effect of age on cycling performance. For example, Balmer, Bird, and Davison[17] characterized the decline in maximal oxygen consumption and maximal aerobic power with age in cycling. These authors found that the relative intensity expressed as a percentage of maximal heart rate or maximal oxygen uptake as well as economy was not affected by age during a 20-minute time trial. Thus, the possible lesser decline in cycling performance with advancing age, because of a lesser reduction in lactate threshold or economy compared with running, needs to be confirmed by additional studies.

An alternative explanation for the smaller age-related performance decline in cycling compared with running is the maintenance of a relatively greater exercise training stimulus in cycling. An overall reduction in the exercise training stimulus generally occurs with advancing age. In running, the decline in exercise performance with age has been partly attributed to an increased incidence of orthopedic injuries, which would limit running training volume of many older athletes. This factor may influence cycling performance to a much lesser extent.

Moreover, it has been shown that the protein synthesis rate decreases in older subjects compared with young subjects, which could limit running training volume in older triathletes in which muscle damage occurs. With advancing age, triathletes would likely spend more training time cycling than running because of changes in physical factors (e.g., increased prevalence of injuries). Further prospective studies are necessary to quantify the changes in training volume in triathletes with age because training history is an important aspect of performance status at older age.

Comparison Between Short and Long Distances

The triathlon duration exerts an important influence on the age-associated changes in triathlon performance.[15] It has been shown that age-related changes in swimming performance were not influenced by triathlon duration; the magnitudes of decreases in swimming performance were similar for Olympic versus Ironman triathlon (see figure 3.6). Swimming is the first discipline during a triathlon, so triathletes perform it without suffering from accumulated fatigue, in contrast to the cycling and running disciplines. On average, swimming performance declines by about 15 percent at 50 years old and reaches about 38 percent by 70 years of age.

Previous studies showed no effect of task duration for shorter-distance swimming events. For example, Tanaka and Seals[6] found no significant differences in the magnitude of performance decline with age (about 32 percent at 70 years) among distance events ranging from 100 to 1500 meters in a pool. The lower performance decline observed by these authors for the same age (70 years old) compared with triathlon data might be related to differences between water conditions: calm in swimming pools versus stochastic in open water for triathlon.

In contrast to swimming, cycling and running with advancing age had a less pronounced decline at Olympic triathlon than at Ironman triathlon. It is not clear why task duration in triathlon exerts an influence on age-related declines in cycling and running performance.

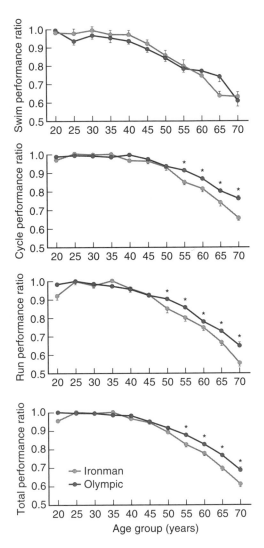

▶ **Figure 3.6** Age-related decline in swimming, cycling, running, and total performance for short-distance and Ironman distance triathlons (mean ± SE). There was no distance effect for swimming performance, but age-related declines in cycling, running, and total performance were less pronounced for short-distance triathlon. *P < 0.01, significantly different from Ironman distance triathlon for the same age group.

Adapted, by permission, from R. Lepers, F. Sultana, T. Bernard, et al., 2010, "Age-related changes in triathlon performance," *International Journal of Sports Medicine* 31(4): 251-256.

For the 70 to 74 year age group, the finish time is about 3 hours for the Olympic triathlon versus about 15 hours for Ironman triathlon. Certainly, the Ironman triathlon induces greater neuromuscular fatigue in cycling and running compared with Olympic triathlon. Furthermore, muscle damage during a 10K run of Olympic distance is limited compared with that occurring during the Ironman marathon. Endurance exercise increases the use of endogenous fuels to provide energy for working muscles.

It has been suggested that older subjects oxidize more glucose and less fat during moderate-intensity exercise.[18] Compared with young adults, older adults seem to oxidize less fat during endurance exercise performed at either the same absolute or relative intensity.[19] This shift in substrate use is presumably caused by age-related changes in skeletal muscle, including decreased skeletal muscle respiratory capacity. Therefore, changes in substrate availability and utilization with advancing age may explain in part the task duration effect on triathlon performances, at least in cycling and running.

Additional studies examining the changes in training volume and physiological characteristics of older triathletes are required to understand the age-associated changes in triathlon performance. Such studies will provide valuable information for understanding how to maintain physical capacity and performance with advancing age.

Conclusion

Physiological factors (e.g., percent body fat and oxygen carrying capacity) and nonphysiological factors (e.g., rate of participation) may be responsible for gender difference in triathlon performances. The difference in triathlon total performance between elite males and females (about 10 percent) is similar to differences seen in other endurance sports such as marathon running. Swimming gender difference in time is generally smaller compared with cycling and running and can be explained in part by the biological difference in relative body fat. Female triathletes now have the same opportunities as males do to train and compete, and an increase in female participation in the future will probably improve the female performance density that remains, to date, smaller than that in male races.

Age-related decline in triathlon performance depends on locomotion mode (swimming versus cycling versus running) and distance (short versus long distance). Although younger triathletes still have the advantage with regard to overall performance, masters triathletes have shown in these last decades a relative improvement of their performances in the three disciplines.[20]

The question as to whether older triathletes have reached their limits in triathlon performance should therefore be raised. Most health care providers agree that racing an Ironman triathlon after 50 years of age is not good for the body. But most older triathletes say that training for triathlon is one of the healthiest things that they can do. Where should the limits be set? If masters triathletes perform at a high level for a long time, it is reasonable to expect that those destined to maintain that intensity could do so because they remained largely injury free. A framework for preparticipation evaluation, training programs, and injury prevention is required to help older triathletes reach their participation and performance goals injury free, to maximize the benefits and minimize the risks.

PART

II

Technical Execution
and Efficiency
in Each Event

CHAPTER 4

Swimming Biomechanics for Triathlon

—David Pease, PhD

For humans, one of the most inefficient ways to move through space is to swim. In fact, most swimmers are only about 5 percent efficient, whereas at other activities such as running athletes can be almost 90 percent efficient.[1,2,3] That finding means that the amount of power that a swimmer is able to create by pushing and pulling on the water to propel herself is equal to only about 5 percent of the total amount of power that her body is using to generate those movements.

Because of that inefficiency, swimming is the most challenging of the three disciplines for most triathletes. But this low efficiency also allows triathletes to achieve substantial improvements in performance with relatively small improvements in stroke efficiency.

Triathletes can achieve these improvements in efficiency in many ways. Common technique faults may lead to inefficient swimming, but these faults can be addressed. The primary forces that act during swimming—propulsion and drag—can be manipulated to increase swimming efficiency and thereby improve overall performance.

Technique

One of the most important aspects in improving efficiency in swimming is to maintain a smooth stroke while holding a relatively streamlined body position. Just how a person does that comes down to the techniques used. This section describes key aspects of optimizing technique and limiting some of the errors that triathletes often exhibit.

Center of Mass

Mass can be thought of as the weight of a given object, whether it is a person or a ball or a mass of water. In conjunction with mass is center of mass. Because center of mass represents all the parts of the body at once, it moves according to the movement of various parts of the body (see figure 4.1).

In terms of swimming, the position of the center of mass will influence how a person sits in the water. When streamlining off a wall after pushing off, the hands should be outstretched above the head. In this position the center of mass will move closer to the lungs where most of the buoyancy is found and put the triathlete in a more balanced position (floating more level).

If the swimmer lowers the arms to the sides, the legs sink more because the center of mass is moving farther from the lungs and torque is created around the center of mass. Just to clarify, torque is essentially a force, but instead of trying to create motion in a straight line, torque is trying to cause motion about an axis of rotation. Think of the axis of rotation as the axle of a wheel. Using a hand to spin a wheel generates torque. Although a force acts through the center of mass of an object, torque is created any time the line of action of a force doesn't pass through the center of mass of an object.

▶ **Figure 4.1** Center of mass position with arms (*a*) lowered and (*b*) raised.

In the example of the streamlined swimmer, the buoyant force, mostly from the lungs, acts to lift the upper body relative to the center of mass. Similarly, the less buoyant mass of the legs creates torque that causes the legs to sink relative to the center of mass.

Momentum

Essentially momentum is the amount of motion an object has. Momentum is determined by multiplying the mass of the object by its velocity. Therefore, a 100-kilogram athlete moving at 2 meters per second and a 50-kilogram athlete moving at 4 meters per second will have the same amount of motion or momentum. Momentum is also described in Newton's first law: When an object has momentum in a given direction, it will continue moving in that direction until a force acts on it to change its momentum.

For optimal performance and greatest efficiency in swimming, the swimmer wants the amount of forward momentum to be as constant as possible. The athlete achieves this goal by keeping velocity as consistent as possible. If velocity is going up and down as the triathlete goes through a stroke cycle, then he is using more energy. The best way to maintain velocity is to maintain a consistent level of propulsion and minimize any drag acting on the body.

Propulsion

Propulsion is a force that moves the swimmer in the desired direction, forward through the water. A force generates movement of an object in a given direction. In the case of swimming propulsion, this direction is the forward swimming direction. Drag is the opposite. Drag is any force that tries to move the swimmer backward or at least slow her down.

One of the most confusing aspects of dealing with forces is the concept of a reaction force. Many have likely heard the saying "For every action there is an equal and opposite reaction." This fundamental principle in physics is derived from Isaac Newton's third law of motion. In its most basic form this principle means that when a person pushes on something with a given force, the object pushes back with the same amount of force. In swimming the water pushes back on a swimmer's body with the same amount of force that the swimmer pushes on the water. This force pushing back on the swimmer is actually moving him through the water or slowing him down. This water force is termed the reaction force because it is a reaction to the force generated by the swimmer.

The counterintuitive notion of reaction forces leads to some confusion when describing the propulsive forces generated by a swimmer. We can find instances in which propulsion is termed either lift generated or drag generated. In that context the drag is referring to the force generated by the swimmer, which is directed back toward the feet in the drag direction. The propulsion is then a reaction to that force. This just means that the force is acting in the same direction as the swimmer's hand is moving and is generated by a paddlewheel type of motion.

Propulsion described as being generated by lift indicates a force generated during a sculling or lateral motion of the hand. This movement creates a propulsive force similar to the way that a propeller creates propulsive force for a boat. Although the propeller doesn't move in the same direction as the boat, it is able to elicit a reaction force from the water that creates propulsion.

Again, this force is the reaction force to the forces generated by the hand. Substantial discussion has occurred over the last 40 years about how swimmers generate propulsion.[4-12] The current thinking is that propulsion is a mixture of the two types, and a majority of the force is likely generated by the drag type of propulsion.[4, 13] This thinking largely dictates how athletes are coached to perform the techniques used in swimming, in particular the hand paths that are taught.

Pull

Because it takes advantage of both the lift and drag forces, the S pattern is generally accepted as the best arm pull pattern (see figure 4.2). The hand enters the water between the shoulder and the center of the head and then moves laterally as the arm extends such that the hand ends up just wide

▶ **Figure 4.2** S pull pattern.

of the shoulder. This wide point is often described as the end of the catch phase of the swimming stroke. From this wide point the insweep begins, in which the hand moves on a slight angle and gets to the midline of the body at a point about level with the shoulders. The hand then changes direction slightly again and sweeps outward until it exits the water next to the body at about the level of the hip.

To maximize propulsive forces, the fingers should be pointing toward the bottom of the pool throughout the entire pull. During the insweep phase this positioning is achieved by bending at the elbow, not at the wrist. If the wrist is flexed, the elbow tends to drop and point toward the bottom of the pool. This dropping limits the ability of the forearm to create propulsive force. This technical flaw, and the way to correct it, is discussed in detail later in the chapter. Additionally, flexing the wrist during this phase of the stroke tends to overuse the smaller muscles of the forearm, which are more prone to fatigue, and therefore reduces the amount of propulsion generated during a pull.

Two additional concepts often used when talking about technique are impulse and power.

Impulse is the rate at which a force is applied. It is determined by multiplying the force (or torque) by the amount of time over which it is acting. In swimming, impulse is used when describing the pull. A swimmer who applies a relatively low force over a long period can achieve the same impulse as a swimmer who applies a large force over a short period.

Some athletes use a long stroke length and low stroke rate, whereas others use a very high stroke rate but shorter stroke length. They can elicit the same impulse using different techniques, although the athlete with the longer, slower stroke is generally more efficient and can maintain the stroke for a longer time.[14, 15]

Related to impulse is *power*. Instead of looking at the time over which a force is applied, power is the product of the force or torque and the velocity at which it is applied. Again, in swimming terms, if a hand moving at a higher velocity can apply the same force as a hand that is moving more slowly, then the faster hand creates more power.

Kick

To this point we have focused on the propulsive forces generated by the hands. Obviously, most people can generate propulsion with both the hands and the feet. Particularly for triathletes, the kick acts in two other ways that are highly beneficial to performance. Fortunately, neither of these functions requires high kicking rates, thereby helping to save the legs for the later stages of the race. The first and probably most important function in terms of triathlon swimming is the generation of vertical forces that help keep the legs higher in the water and maintain a more streamlined position. This action provides the same function as a wetsuit, which increases the amount of buoyancy, thereby keeping the legs elevated. In nonwetsuit swims, the triathlete needs to be able to use the legs to fulfill this function.

The final role of the kick is to help maintain balance in the stroke by providing a counteraction to the movement of the arms. This situation is also present in running when the contralateral arm swings forward with each forward stride. In swimming, however, the balance needs to occur around the entry and extension phases of the stroke. At that point in the stroke the contralateral leg should be kicking downward. As seen in figure 4.3 this motion promotes a coordinated roll between the shoulders and hips and keeps the muscles of the trunk in better alignment, thereby enhancing the stability of the body in the water and allowing enhanced force delivery to the water.

▶ **Figure 4.3** Proper balance between pull and kick. Note the right leg kicking down at point of catch for the left hand.

Drag

While discussing ways of increasing propulsion in swimming, to maximize performance, the triathlete also needs to look at ways of reducing the resistance, or drag, experienced while moving through the water. Triathletes experience three primary types of drag in the water.

Form Drag

The first main type of drag is known as form drag, or pressure drag. This type of drag is caused by the frontal area of the swimmer being exposed to the oncoming water flow.

The easiest way to picture this is to imagine that a coach is taking a picture of an athlete swimming from directly in front, just below the surface of the water. The more of the body that appears in the picture, the greater the drag acting on the body will be. Form drag increases with the square of velocity, so someone trying to swim twice as fast will experience four times the amount of drag. Minimizing form drag is obviously highly beneficial.

The primary technique aspect used to minimize form drag is streamlining (see figure 4.4). This point is related to the lifting role of the kick. If the legs are allowed to drag low in the water, then the area of the body increases substantially, causing an increase in drag.

Form drag is reduced when buoyancy is increased. Obviously, an athlete who is more buoyant rides higher in the water, exposing less frontal area to the flow of the water. By increasing buoyancy and reducing drag forces, triathletes are able to use less energy to travel at a given speed through the water. For that reason, triathletes generally find swimming in a wetsuit easier than without. The wetsuit provides the extra lift force that is normally provided by the kick.[16]

▶ **Figure 4.4** (a) Good and (b) poor streamline positions.

Frictional Drag

The second main type of drag is frictional, or skin, drag. This type of drag results from the slipperiness of the surface of the swimmer's body. Generally, skin is not slippery. Wetsuits and normal swimsuits made of materials more slippery than skin have been developed in recent years.

Although form drag has a squared relationship to swimming speed, frictional drag has only a linear relationship. The magnitude of frictional drag is therefore relatively small compared with other types of drag, so the benefits of reducing it are not as great as those found by reducing other types. Other than wearing suits designed for drag reduction, swimmers can do little to reduce frictional drag.

Wave Drag

The final primary type of drag experienced during swimming, and the most difficult to reduce, is wave drag (see figure 4.5). Wave drag is created when the swimmer moving through the water creates waves by pushing water up. To push the water, the swimmer needs to use energy that would otherwise be used to create propulsion. The bigger the waves are, the greater the amount of energy is lost.

The biggest problem with wave drag is that it increases with velocity to the sixth power, which means that if the swimmer doubles her speed, wave drag increases 64 times! The easiest way to limit wave drag is to develop a

▶ **Figure 4.5** A wave generated during swimming, leading to the creation of wave drag.

smooth swimming technique that consists of a good streamline position in the water and long, smooth movements that maximize the amount of motion in the horizontal direction and minimize motion in the vertical.

Common Mistakes and Corrections

So far discussion has focused on the main factors underlying swimming performance. At this point it may be useful to discuss some further biomechanical issues common among triathletes.

Kicking

The problem: The triathlete generates only a slight amount of force through kicking. Some even say that they move backward when kicking.

The cause: Generally, the cause is lack of ankle plantar flexibility (toe pointing), as shown in figure 4.6.

The result: Because the primary source of propulsion from the kick results from drag-type forces, the foot needs to be in a position in which it can push back on the water to get the propulsive reaction force from the water. The lack of ankle plantar flexibility often leads to another common problem with triathlete swimming technique—initiating the kick by flexing the knee excessively.

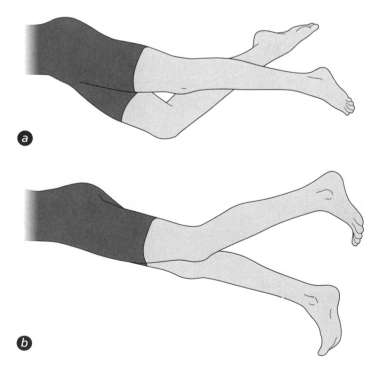

▶ **Figure 4.6** Examples of (a) good and (b) poor ankle plantar flexibility on the kick.

Although flexing the knee does indeed get the foot into the proper position, it also exposes the back of the leg to the oncoming water flow. The flexed knee can also lead to driving the knee down as the hip flexes, which exposes the front of the thigh to the oncoming water. The motion looks similar to someone riding a bike. Both of these positions increase resistance and counteract any benefits of getting the foot into a propulsive position. Additionally, a substantial amount of additional effort is required to perform this larger kicking motion, which wastes energy that will be required during the bike and run legs of the race.

The solution: The best way to improve kicking is to enhance ankle plantar flexibility and focus on kicking from the hip with only slight flexion at the knee.

Side-to-Side Imbalance

The problem: One of the most common faults demonstrated by triathletes during their swimming is a side-to-side imbalance in their movement patterns (see figure 4.7).

The cause: The imbalance is seen most often as a difference in pull widths of the hands; one hand often pulls much wider away from the midline of the body than the other. This situation is similar to trying to row a boat with oars of two different lengths. The result is that the boat continually veers off to one side.

The result: The same thing happens in swimming. If the arms are pulling at different distances away from the midline of the body, then the torque around the center of mass will not be balanced and the swimmer will continually turn to one side (see figure 4.7). This flaw can be especially costly

▶**Figure 4.7** Example of (a) a proper-width pull and (b) a too-wide pull. The combination of these two creates an imbalance and poor course control.

in open-water swims where the swimmer cannot follow a black line on the bottom and make corrections to keep moving in a straight line. In open water the constant veering off course and resulting course corrections lead to extra distance swum and a significant amount of wasted energy.

The solution: A simple way to test a triathlete's stroke for imbalance is to have the person swim in the middle of a lane in a pool with his eyes closed. The key is that the swimmer must not peek; the stroke must be allowed to guide his movement. If the triathlete ends up running into a lane line, an imbalance is present somewhere in the stroke. If an imbalance is present in the stroke, the fix is to adjust the path that the hands are travelling. The best hand path follows an S shape. Observed from the point of view of the swimmer, however, the path is much straighter because of body rotation. A good drill to help monitor hand path is to swim down the middle of the lane and watch the position of the hand relative to the line on the bottom of the pool. The hand should track pretty much right down the line. A key to success in this drill is that the swimmer must be using a significant amount of body rotation (or roll) around the long axis (head to toe) of the body.

Reduced Body Roll

The problem: A reduced amount of body roll is a common issue with triathletes.

The cause: Insufficient rotation causes several consequences that can limit performance.

The result: Being flatter in the water increases drag forces compared with rotating. Underrotating also increases the difficulty of moving the arms through the recovery phase of the stroke. The arms move closer to the surface of the water, necessitating greater rotation at the shoulder. The increased rotation at the shoulder can lead to shoulder pain in those who have inadequate shoulder flexibility.

The solution: Ideally, the body roll should be about 30 to 45 degrees to both sides (see figure 4.8). This technique not only remedies the problems with flat body position but also enhances the extension at the front of the stroke after the hand enters the water, thereby adding to the propulsive impulse when a high elbow catch is used. To achieve this amount of body roll, a bit of exaggeration is useful. Therefore, the best drill is the shark fin drill. For this drill, as the swimmer finishes the pull and the hand comes out of the water, she places the hand on the hip and pretends to be a shark while rolling all the way onto her side. While doing this she keeps the other arm extended out in front and the head aligned with the body, looking down toward the bottom of the pool. She stays in that position for about six kicks and then repeats on the other side. As the swimmer gets better at the drill, she should reduce the number of kicks but maintain the same amount of body roll. When triathletes start swimming normally, they should begin to feel more natural with the greater amount of body rotation.

▶ **Figure 4.8** Good shoulder rotation. Rotation should be around 30 to 45 degrees.

Dropped Elbow

The problem: The final and most common flaw, not only in triathlon swimming but also in competitive swimming, is the dropped elbow (see figure 4.9).

The cause: Although a high elbow, sometimes seen as early vertical forearm (EVF), has definite advantages in terms of propulsion, it requires specific strength as well as flexibility at the shoulder joint. Although poor shoulder flexibility is not usually much of a problem in competitive swimmers, it is common in triathletes. This weakness limits the ability of many triathletes to use a high elbow catch effectively.

The result: The dropped elbow position redirects the reaction forces from the water, making them vertical rather than horizontal, and therefore limits the amount of propulsion gained.

The solution: Most triathletes should try to get as much of a high elbow as they can given their limitations. If a line were to be drawn from the shoulder to the wrist of the pulling arm, the minimum should be that the elbow should lie on that line at the time of the catch (see figure 4.10). As the pull progresses

▶ **Figure 4.9** Dropped elbow position common to many triathletes.

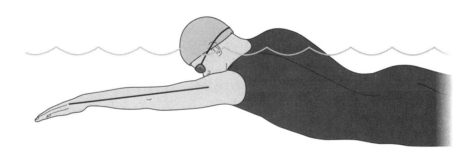

▶ **Figure 4.10** Arm position that should be deemed the minimum high elbow catch position with the elbow lying on the line drawn between the shoulder and wrist.

through the remainder of the insweep, maintaining a high elbow becomes easier because of the more natural position of the shoulder joint as compared with that needed during the initial catch. As flexibility and strength increase, the aim should be for the elbow to be a greater distance above the line between the shoulder and the wrist. The easiest way to work on fixing this problem is to forget about the hands for a while. Triathletes should imagine that they are trying to catch the water with the forearm only. By doing so they will naturally adopt a higher elbow position (see figure 4.11). Swimming with closed fists is another way to help achieve this in combination with the forearm catch.

▶ **Figure 4.11**   Example of a high elbow catch. Although uncommon shoulder flexibility is required to achieve an even higher elbow catch position, most triathletes should be able to achieve close to this position with coaching.

Conclusion

This chapter describes the basic biomechanics of triathlon swimming and offers some useful ideas for correcting common flaws in triathlon swimming. As with all sport movements, swimming is controlled by some relatively simple concepts of physics. By studying these factors, triathletes should gain at least a rudimentary grasp on these issues, which should allow them to think about how they can change their movements to improve performance.

As we've seen in this chapter, many of the common flaws in the swimming style of triathletes can be easily corrected by thinking about how swimmers generate propulsion and what positions can optimize those forces. Remember that the biggest factors in improving swimming performance are to keep the stroke smooth and consistent to maintain momentum, to keep the stroke balanced so that the forces from the right and left sides are equal, and to use techniques that produce the maximum amount of propulsion and the minimum amount of drag. If the triathlete can achieve these few things, he will be well on his way to improving his swimming performance and therefore his overall triathlon performance.

CHAPTER 5

Cycling Biomechanics for Triathlon

—Jeff Broker, PhD, and Sean Langlais, MSc

Among the three events in a triathlon competition, the bicycle leg stands alone as the event upon which performance is directly related to the effective integration of human and machine. This integration attracted the attention of biomechanists decades ago, partly because of the fascination with optimal coupling of human to machine but also because of the relative ease with which cycling can be used to study musculoskeletal performance. In recent years triathletes have benefited from the sciences targeting the optimal integration of athlete and machine, specifically when triathlon equipment options, body positions, and training methods are visited.

This chapter presents relevant scientific findings concerning the biomechanics of cycling for the triathlete. First, the nature of *cycling power* and its importance to triathletes is introduced. As cycling power is explored, the critical elements defining resistance to motion are exposed. The chapter then shifts to the pedals, where energy derived from muscular effort is delivered to the bicycle. Pedaling is explored in detail, focusing on pedaling mechanics, its sensitivity to body position, myths surrounding effective pedaling, and drills to improve pedaling. Next, the aerodynamics of cycling, with a general focus on the triathlete, is described. Last, perhaps as an ironic transition into the next chapter on running, we briefly focus our attention on the fascinating T2 transition, in which triathletes must run effectively and safely immediately after cycling.

Cycling Power

Cycling power is the rate of performing work, usually expressed in watts (W). Work represents force applied over a distance. Thus, cycling power represents the propulsive force moving the bicycle and cyclist forward, through a given distance, over a specific period.

Two variants of a simple power equation can be developed:

$$\text{power} = (\text{force} \times \text{distance}) / \text{time} \quad \text{(equation 5.1)}$$

or, by rearranging parentheses,

$$\text{power} = \text{force} \times (\text{distance} / \text{time}) \quad \text{(equation 5.2)}$$

The term within the parentheses in equation 5.2, distance per unit time, is simply cycling velocity. Thus,

$$\text{cycling power} = \text{force} \times \text{cycling velocity} \quad \text{(equation 5.3)}$$

In equation 5.3 cycling power (W) equals the product of the force applied by the rear wheel against the ground to produce forward motion (in newtons, N), and cycling velocity (in meters per second, m/sec). A cyclist overcoming total resistive forces of 7.8 pounds (3.5 kg) (35 N) at a velocity of 19.2 miles per hour (8.58 m/sec) requires an average power delivery to the rear wheel of roughly 300 W. To put these numbers into perspective, 1 horsepower (HP) is equivalent to 746 W; thus, our triathlete would produce roughly 0.4 HP to ride at 19.2 miles per hour under these conditions.

An alternative form of mechanical work is represented by a torque applied through an arc of rotation. This represents the rotational variant of work. Because power equals work performed per unit time, another formula representing mechanical power is developed as follows:

$$\text{power} = (\text{torque} \times \text{angular rotation}) / \text{time} \quad \text{(equation 5.4)}$$

or, by rearranging parentheses,

$$\text{power} = \text{torque} \times (\text{angular rotation} / \text{time}) \quad \text{(equation 5.5)}$$

The rotational variant of power (equation 5.5) applies when cycling power is measured. By measuring crank torque within the chainring and angular velocity of the cranks, power at the cranks can be calculated. Alternatively, torque at the bicycle rear hub, multiplied by rear wheel angular velocity, provides a measure of cycling power. Notably, the difference between power measured at the cranks and at the rear hub represents drivetrain energy losses.

Resistance

Cyclists deliver energy to the pedals to overcome resistive elements associated with bicycle movement.

Resistance to bicycle motion can be expressed in relation to five specific elements:

- Resistance to bicycle acceleration
- Resistance to climbing (change in height along a grade)

- Static rolling resistance
- Dynamic rolling resistance
- Aerodynamic drag

Rider-plus-bicycle mass figures linearly into the first three elements listed, so a 5 percent increase in rider-plus-bicycle mass (and thus weight) results in a 5 percent increase in cycling power connected with bicycle acceleration, climbing hills, and rotating the tires. Herein lies the advantage of lighter bicycles and, for that matter, lighter riders. The effect of hill climbing on cycling power is addressed further in chapter 8.

Next, power to overcome dynamic rolling resistance, associated with deformation of the tire as it contacts the ground, is not dependent on rider and bicycle mass but increases as the square of cycling velocity. Doubling cycling velocity quadruples the power needed to overcome dynamic rolling resistance. Fortunately, the magnitude of this energy loss is relatively small.

Finally, and most important, the power to overcome aerodynamic forces increases as the third power of cycling velocity. Thus, doubling cycling speed increases the power needed to overcome aerodynamic forces by a factor of eight.

When considering these resistive elements, triathletes may want to think through which of these elements they can control and which they cannot. Weight reduction clearly plays a role, most notably when the bicycle is being accelerated and when climbing hills. High-pressure tires reduce resistive loads at the tire–pavement interface. Body position, bicycle frame and component selection, and clothing and helmet features play an important role in managing aerodynamic resistance.

What cannot be controlled is the magnitude of any grade, the presence of headwinds (particularly in nondrafting races), and air density (a factor in aerodynamics and a function of the local temperature, humidity, and altitude).

Pedaling Mechanics

Perhaps second only to bicycle–rider geometry and fit, the term *pedaling mechanics* seems synonymous with cycling biomechanics. An interest in what happens at this critical interface between the cyclist and the machine dates back more than 100 years, when Sharp (1896) developed the first instrumented bicycle pedal.[1] Since then, instrumented pedals of varying designs have emerged.[2] Our understanding of how a cyclist delivers energy to the bicycle has benefitted tremendously from these developments.

Pedal forces are typically described in their component terms. A *normal force* acts perpendicular to the surface of the pedal, and a *tangential force* acts parallel to the pedal surface (in the fore–aft direction). If we know the orientation of the pedal relative to the bicycle crank, these components can be mathematically resolved into *effective* and *ineffective* components. The effective component drives the crank around the pedal circle, always acting perpendicular to the bicycle crank. The ineffective component performs no useful work, because it acts parallel to the crank at all times. Some researchers use these terms to describe pedaling quality.[3, 4]

Typical normal and tangential force profiles measured during pedaling are illustrated in figure 5.1. The effective component associated with these forces is shown in figure 5.2. Note here that crank torque is simply the product of effective force and crank arm length; thus, the effective force profile shown in figure 5.2 mirrors the crank torque profile, derived from each pedal.

As indicated, effective force (and thus crank torque) peaks roughly when the crank is level and forward in the pedal stroke, about 100 degrees past top dead center.

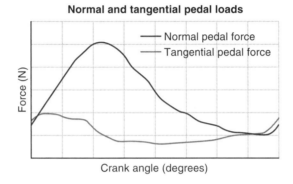

▶ **Figure 5.1** Average normal and tangential components of pedal loading for cyclists riding at 350 watts and 90 revolutions per minute (rpm) (n = 17). Crank angles of 0 and 360 degrees represent pedal top dead center positions. The left half of the graph represents the downstroke (0 to 180 degrees), and the right half of the graph represents the upstroke (180 to 360 degrees).

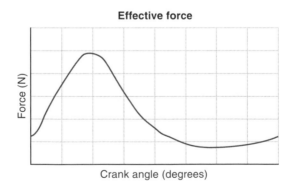

▶ **Figure 5.2** The effective component of pedal loading derived from the normal and tangential components shown in figure 5.1, again for the 350 W, 90 rpm condition. This effective component always acts perpendicular to the crank, providing the force needed to propel the bicycle forward.

Effective force is negative during the upstroke, because the force on the pedal acts downward as the pedal rises. Note as well the low effective force magnitudes at the top and bottom of the pedal cycle.

A more effective way to visualize how pedal forces vary during the pedal cycle is to present the data in clock diagram format (figure 5.3). Pedal forces are represented as force vectors (arrows). Their lengths are proportional to their magnitudes, and their directions are consistent with the manner in which they are applied. Clock diagrams dramatically illustrate why effective forces peak midway through the downstroke; force magnitudes are high and the forces are directed nearly perpendicular to the crank.

The clock diagram also exposes regions of the pedal stroke where effective force is low. For example, effective forces and crank torque are low through the top of the pedal stroke, predominantly because of the low magnitude of forces during this phase of the cycle.

By contrast, low effective forces, and thus low crank torque, are present through the bottom of the pedal stroke, not because of low force magnitudes but because of the orientation of the force vectors, which are largely parallel to the crank. Lastly, the negative effective force during the upstroke is clearly explained in the clock diagram, because forces are applied to the pedal in the opposite direction of crank rotation.

The effective force profile shown in figure 5.2 tells only half the story. Because the two pedals on a bicycle are connected to each other through the bottom bracket, *net crank torque* develops from the combined effect of the forces applied to each pedal.

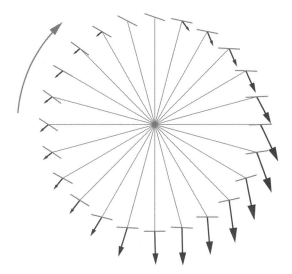

▶ **Figure 5.3** Clock diagram for cycling showing the magnitude and direction of forces applied to the pedal, as well as pedal orientation. The major torque applied to the crank during the downstroke is evident, and forces through the bottom of the pedal cycle are large but contribute little to crank rotation.

Net crank torque is shown in figure 5.4, highlighting substantial variation in instantaneous torque throughout the pedal cycle. Two distinct peaks in crank torque are evident, generated during the right- and left-pedal downstrokes. The left-pedal downstroke peak is larger than the other for this particular cyclist. Peak net torque is usually less than single-leg peak torque, because as the downstroke pedal receives its greatest positive torque, the upstroke pedal simultaneously experiences negative torque. (In essence, loading of the downstroke pedal acts partially to lift the upstroke leg.)

Also evident in figure 5.4 are distinct minima, occurring just after the pedals pass through their respective vertical positions. These minima are explained by low effective forces on both pedals when the cranks are vertical.

The difference in peak torque for the right- and left-pedal downstrokes shown in figure 5.4 deserves comment. Recall that the net torque pattern shown represents the combined effects of both pedals. When one of the net crank torque peaks is higher than the other, the explanation could be that the effective force on the downstroke pedal (for the left pedal shown in figure 5.4) is larger.

That would be the traditional interpretation. Alternatively, the peak torque difference may be explained by different force magnitudes during the upstroke. Thus, the asymmetry could be an upstroke imbalance rather than a downstroke imbalance. This analysis of asymmetry, although seeming trivial, exposes a common pitfall regarding commercially available devices that claim the ability to assess pedaling asymmetry. The rider represented in figure 5.4, in fact, generates nearly identical downstroke effective force magnitudes yet is heavier during the upstroke on his right side.

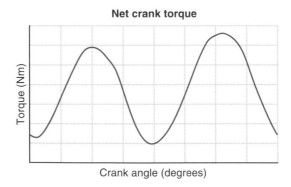

Net crank torque

Torque (Nm)

Crank angle (degrees)

▶ **Figure 5.4** Total crank torque developed from the combined effects of right- and left-pedal loading for a cyclist demonstrating pedaling asymmetry. The first peak in crank torque occurs during the right-pedal downstroke; the second occurs during the left-pedal downstroke. A first glance suggests a downstroke asymmetry; the left leg appears to drive the crank more powerfully than the right. But the real asymmetry is an upstroke effect; the right leg is more active during its upstroke.

The source of a net crank torque asymmetry cannot be isolated by measuring only net crank torques or externally measuring bicycle power output.

Crank Torque and Crank Power

As discussed earlier, pedaling power is mathematically equal to the product of the net crank torque and instantaneous crank angular velocity. When instrumented pedals are used to assess cycling biomechanics, the nature of energy delivered to the pedals can be quantified. Average instantaneous total power at the pedals for 17 road cyclists riding at 350 W and 90 rpm is depicted in figure 5.5. Notably, power fluctuates between roughly 110 W and 600 W within a single pedal revolution. These fluctuations characterize the nature of energy delivery to the pedals.

Interestingly, the magnitude of the oscillations in the instantaneous power (figure 5.5) qualitatively describes how smooth a given rider pedals. A rider who develops most of her crank torque during the downstroke of the pedal cycle will exhibit greater oscillations in instantaneous power than a rider who distributes crank torque more evenly throughout the pedal circle, particularly the top and bottom regions of the pedal cycle.

Effective and Ineffective Forces: Relations With Natural Pedaling Dynamics

In the 1980s the terms *effective forces* and *ineffective forces* were introduced by researchers to describe pedaling quality quantitatively.[3, 4] The implication was that ineffective forces, those parallel to the crank, do not contribute to the pedaling motion and therefore represent wasted energy. Recent research, however, suggests that the use of these terms to describe pedaling effectiveness may not be appropriate.

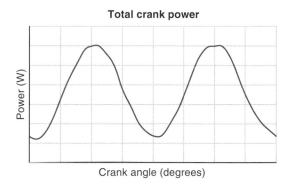

Total crank power

Power (W)

Crank angle (degrees)

▶ **Figure 5.5** Average instantaneous crank power associated with riding at 350 W, 90 rpm (n = 17). Notice how crank power oscillates substantially around the average power level of 350 W. The two minima in total power occur when the cranks are nearly vertical.

Consider a cyclist sitting on a bicycle with his feet in the pedals but the cranks are not rotating. Both right and left pedals experience forces from the weight of the legs acting downward. If the pedals are placed at the top and bottom of the pedal cycle, these forces would act parallel to the cranks and would not contribute to crank torque development. The question arises: Are these forces wasted? Because these forces require no muscular work, being developed solely by gravitational effects, the answer must be no. In this case, the pedals and crank serve to maintain the position of the limbs.

Now let's consider the normal pedaling condition, involving rotation of the crank as depicted in the clock diagram of figure 5.3. As indicated, large downward forces are seen through the bottom of the pedal stroke. These downward forces, often labeled ineffective in that they act to lengthen the crank and do not assist in rotating the crank, are dominantly generated by the interaction between the pedal and the leg. The pedal supports the leg under the influence of gravity and assists in changing the movement direction of the leg from downward to upward.

Critically, if a cyclist were asked to pedal in such a way that these forces were minimized or eliminated, significant muscular work would be required, yet no additional pedaling power would result. These forces acting downward along the axis of the cranks are highly functional and free of metabolic energy expenditure.

Kautz and Hull reported a method to separate the naturally occurring components of pedal loading from the total pedal loads.[5] The natural component of pedal loading is derived from gravitational and inertial effects acting on the leg and is thus nonmuscular. When pedal forces are separated into elements derived from muscular contractions versus those developed from gravitational and inertial effects, fascinating observations emerge. First, a significant portion of the measured downward loading at the bottom of the pedal cycle (figure 5.5) is indeed caused by gravitational and inertial effects, not muscular actions. During the upstroke, the measured forces seen acting downward on the pedal are also gravity and inertia based. Thus, the cyclist is not actively pushing down as the pedal rises.

By contrast, the muscular component of total loading represents more of what cyclists perceive. Muscular actions drive the pedal downward during the first half of the pedal cycle, rearward through the bottom of the pedal stroke, and upward during the upstroke. Despite these muscle actions, however, the gravitational and inertial-based pedal forces produce the seemingly ineffective pedal forces. These findings should alter our interpretation of pedaling technique and pedaling skills training.

In summary, effective pedaling mechanics requires the appropriate recruitment of muscles to generate forces on the pedal acting dominantly perpendicular to the crank. These muscular-based forces will act in concert with forces arising from gravitational and inertial effects, such that power delivery to the pedals oscillates dramatically, predictably, and naturally but ultimately feels and looks smooth.

Pedaling Mechanics: Triathletes Compared With Cyclists of Other Disciplines

Since 1992 more than 150 pedaling mechanics evaluations were performed at the U.S. Olympic Training Center in Colorado Springs, Colorado.[2] These evaluations included more than 125 cyclists from road, track sprint, track endurance (pursuit), mountain, and triathlon. Many of the riders were national team riders at the peak of their cycling careers. The following important observations were made:[2]

- Cyclists move their feet in circles during pedaling, but applied forces in no way appear circular. The clock diagram discussed earlier (figure 5.3) clearly demonstrates how forces vary during the pedal cycle.

- Cyclists of all abilities generate counterproductive forces on the pedal during the upstroke during steady-state cycling. Experienced cyclists generate smaller counterproductive forces during the upstroke because of active lifting of the leg during this phase. An effective way to visualize the upstroke during cycling is to recognize that the proficient cyclist lifts her leg actively during the upstroke, but not as fast as the pedal is rising. The pedal helps lift the leg during the upstroke.

- Counterproductive forces during the upstroke are larger in magnitude at high cadences and are less negative at high power outputs for a given cadence. They may even be positive (productive) during sprinting and climbing.

To compare cyclists across disciplines, every rider tested at the Olympic Training Center during a 10-year period was evaluated under the same cycling condition, 90 rpm and 250 W. Many riders were also evaluated at 90 rpm and 350 W.[2]

Comparison of the disciplines revealed sprinters to be the mashers of the cycling community, generating large downstroke peak effective forces with the largest peak-to-peak power oscillations. Road and mountain bike riders performed greater work in the top quadrant than other riders did, notably at higher power conditions. Peak-to-peak power oscillations were lowest with the mountain and road specialists.

Finally, triathletes pedaled similar to the road specialists, but they were often less proficient at generating work through the top quadrant of the pedal stroke. Further, triathletes, when faced with an increase in cycling power (from 250 W to 350 W), generally demonstrated increased downstroke effective forces, compared with road riders who used more of the pedal cycle to generate power. The triathletes, although internationally competitive, were relatively new to competitive cycling, often coming from swimming or running backgrounds.[2] Their limited exposure to competitive cycling and perhaps an interaction with their running and swimming muscular development may explain the differences.

Aerodynamics, Rider Position, and Pedaling Mechanics

Bicycles and cycling accessories are responsible for roughly 20 to 35 percent of the total aerodynamic drag on a cyclist; the remaining 65 to 80 percent is attributed to the cyclist's body. Wind tunnel tests and controlled experiments using on-board power measuring devices have invariably shown that a cyclist can dramatically reduce aerodynamic drag by assuming a flat-back, tucked-head posture with the hands and arms atop aero bars held nearly parallel to the bicycle top tube (figure 5.6).

© AP Photo/Daniel Roland

▶ **Figure 5.6** A triathlete in an aerodynamic, flat-back position. Note the horizontal position of the arms atop aero bars.

A simple real-world example highlights the importance of aerodynamic positioning. Wind tunnel experiments performed in the mid-1990s quantified aerodynamic drag across rider positions centered on the time-trial and pursuit cycling postures.[6] One U.S. national team cyclist achieved a 0.28-pound (1.25 N) decrease in aerodynamic drag at 22.5 mph (10 m/sec), by tucking his head, narrowing his shoulders and arms atop the aero bars, and dropping his handlebars less than 1 inch (2.5 cm). This 0.28-pound (127 g) reduction in drag translates into a 1.26 mph (0.56 m/sec) increase in cycling velocity for the same power output, providing an advantage of 3 minutes and 30 seconds over a 40-kilometer race![6]

As many triathletes recognize, the flat-back, streamlined posture can wreak havoc on the ability to pedal effectively. A triathlete's pedaling mechanics are shown in figure 5.7, representing his on-the-hoods position as well as his time-trial position (on aero bars). As the triathlete rotated his torso into an aerodynamic orientation, the effective force generated on the pedal through the top of the pedal stroke decreased. Further, effective force magnitudes during the upstroke (between 180 and 360 degrees in figure 5.7) were more negative. To offset the losses in torque at the top of the pedal stroke and through the upstroke, greater effective force (greater torque) was needed during the downstroke (surrounding 90 degrees in figure 5.7). In essence, the flat-back position turned this triathlete into a masher.

The musculoskeletal explanation for this phenomenon is that the hip flexors, responsible for torque generation through the top of the pedal cycle and during the upstroke, are shortened when the pelvis is rotated forward to support the flat-back position. Muscles lose some of their force generating capacity at shortened lengths. Further, in some cyclists, physical interactions between the thighs and the torso through the top of the pedal stroke can interfere with power generation.

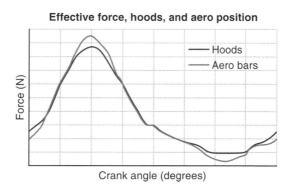

Effective force, hoods, and aero position

Force (N)

Crank angle (degrees)

— Hoods
— Aero bars

▶ **Figure 5.7** Effective force profile for a triathlete exhibiting sensitivity to aerodynamic positioning. When the rider rotated forward onto aero bars his effective force (and thus crank torque) through the top of the pedal cycle decreased (0 and 360 degrees), his effective force during the upstroke became more negative (225 to 315 degrees), and he needed to apply greater force during the downstroke to make up for the pedaling weakness.

For triathletes demonstrating sensitivity to aerodynamic positioning an effective method to recapture pedaling effectiveness involves changing the geometry of the bicycle. Simply, bicycle geometry with a steeper seat tube facilitates recapture of the normal hip angle range of motion during pedaling. This steeper geometry, so intimately linked with present triathlon cycling, is fundamentally a result of musculoskeletal-based needs, balancing aerodynamic concerns and muscular capabilities. For more information concerning triathlon-specific bicycle geometry, bike fit, and related aerodynamic enhancements, see chapter 8.

Drills to Improve Pedaling

Serious cyclists, coaches, and trainers recognize the importance of working on pedaling technique. But what elements of pedaling technique should be emphasized, in light of our knowledge concerning the biomechanics of pedaling? And what methods work best for refining pedaling technique?

The clock diagram in figure 5.3 shows that the top and bottom of the pedal cycle represent relative dead spots where little torque is developed. A masher produces almost all of her power during the downstroke, accomplishing little if anything through the top and bottom. By contrast, the smooth-pedaling cyclist applies forces at the top and bottom of the pedal cycle partially in the direction of pedal motion. The resulting total power curve has no dead spots, or regions where power delivery falls to near zero.

Early-season training should incorporate methods to promote the development of these torque patterns. These methods include spinning at a relatively high cadence on rollers, focusing on the elimination of the fluctuating power characteristics. One mental image would be to drive the foot into the front of the shoe through the top of the pedal cycle and to scrape the shoe rearward through the bottom.

Emphasis on single-limb cycling during indoor and outdoor riding encourages the distribution of pedaling work over a greater part of the pedal cycle. Single-leg riding on a fixed indoor trainer is one of the more uncomfortable methods to improve pedaling technique but may be the most effective. Placing one leg on a box or in a fixed pedal mount allows cyclists to work on right and left legs separately. Productive torque generation through the top and bottom of the pedal cycle should be emphasized.

Pedaling technique can also be practiced on the road. Emphasizing crank torque through the top and bottom of the pedal cycle is recommended. When cyclists first attempt to pedal in this manner, they immediately notice bicycle acceleration because they are delivering power to the cranks and regions of the pedal cycle that were previously power passive. An important lesson gained from this acceleration is that cyclists do not have to push harder to go faster. By developing the ability to apply power to the cranks over more of the pedal cycle, pedaling is smoother, muscular resources are developed to deliver more power when needed, and cycling performance can improve.

Finally, triathletes may suffer from their multidiscipline sport training when attempting to refine pedaling technique. In a comparison between highly trained cyclists and highly trained triathletes, Chapman and colleagues reported clear differences in muscle recruitment between cyclists and triathletes during cycling.[7] These researchers reported recruitment pattern differences between trained cyclists and triathletes, pedaling at common work rates, in all five of the tested lower-extremity muscles (tibialis anterior, tibialis posterior, peroneus longus, gastrocnemius lateralis, and soleus). Differences included greater variation between athletes, greater variation between pedal cycles, more extensive and variable muscle coactivation, and greater electromyographic amplitudes in triathletes. The results indicate that control of muscle recruitment is less developed in triathletes than in experienced cyclists, suggesting that multidiscipline training might interfere with adaptation of the neuromuscular system to cycling. More research is needed to determine whether multidiscipline interference represents an unavoidable and permanent aspect of triathlon training and racing, or whether countermeasures can be developed to reverse or minimize the deleterious effects.

Bike-to-Run Transition

A unique challenge for the triathlete is the need to run, and run effectively, immediately after finishing the bike leg. The feeling of heavy legs reported by many triathletes has drawn the attention of physiologists, neuromuscular control specialists, and biomechanists. Scientific studies focusing on this transition have grown in number in recent years, designed to explore and understand the phenomenon, and possibly direct mitigating measures. The heavy-leg phenomenon is thought not only to affect performance (reduced running velocity) but also to place triathletes at risk of lower-extremity injuries. Although a section of chapter 6 in this book is devoted to the bike-to-run transition, we briefly address this transition here from a cycling perspective.

From a neuromuscular standpoint, cycling and running differ in a couple of important respects. First, and most obvious, running involves short-duration impacts that place loads exceeding two times body weight on the skeletal system.[8] Cycling, by contrast, involves nonimpact, smoothly fluctuating forces that rarely exceed body weight. Cycling is clearly nonimpact, particularly when compared with running.

Cycling is also generally represented muscularly as a *concentric* activity, in which the major muscles dominantly shorten in performing the mechanical work of pedaling. *Eccentric* muscle actions, in which muscles are active yet lengthened, occur only in small isolated regions of the pedal cycle.[9]

By contrast, running involves substantial eccentric–concentric cycles, in which muscles are significantly stretched, while active, and subsequently shortened. These stretch–shorten cycles have been shown to enhance muscle force production as well as contraction efficiency (reduced metabolic cost).

Researchers wonder whether a sudden switch between a smooth and largely concentric activity to an impact-heavy, eccentric–concentric activity might cause problems.

Chapman and colleagues at the University of Queensland and the Australian Institute of Sport examined joint kinematics (movement patterns), muscular activity, and metabolic expenditure in experienced and elite triathletes performing a run following a strenuous bout of cycling, compared with running without a preceding cycling effort.[10, 11, 12] These researchers generally report transient yet significant alterations in neuromuscular control and energy expenditure, absent significant changes in running mechanics (kinematics). Notably, clear intersubject differences in response to prerunning cycling emerged. Some triathletes (including elite) demonstrate minimal or no effect of cycling on subsequent running muscular activity patterns, whereas other triathletes exhibit noticeable alterations.[10]

Sutter and colleagues evaluated the effect of cycling intensity on running economy and vertical running center of mass excursion (VCOM) in well-trained triathletes.[13] If altering cycling intensity late in the cycling leg of a triathlon influences running performance, intensity management might be useful in pacing during races. Unfortunately, in nine triathletes (six males and three females, $\dot{V}O_2$max 63.5 +/− 7.2) running economy and VCOM were unaffected by prerun cycling intensity. The only measures affected by cycling intensity were ventilation rates and blood lactate levels.

A recent study with important practical implications introduced plyometric training into the normal triathlon training regimen, attempting to elicit neuromuscular adaptations that might mitigate the cycle–run transition effects.[14] Eight elite triathletes who demonstrated altered joint mechanics and muscle recruitment patterns during running following moderate to intense cycling were identified. In these eight triathletes, four were subjected to controlled plyometric training targeting lower-extremity explosiveness, in addition to their normal triathlon training. The remaining four triathletes trained normally, without plyometric elements.

Follow-up testing after 8 weeks of training found that running mechanics and muscular recruitment patterns were not altered by prerun cycling in the triathletes who incorporated plyometrics into their training regimes. In the four control triathletes, two maintained altered running mechanics and muscle recruitment in response to cycling. Although the small sample limits the extrapolation of these findings to triathletes as a whole, the findings, in elite-level triathletes, suggest that plyometric training may be advised to mitigate the transition-mediated running performance. As is the case in many areas of triathlon performance science, future research will continue to unravel this interesting aspect of triathlon racing.

Conclusion

In this chapter the focus has been cycling biomechanics. We first focused on the energy (power) demands on the rider and bicycle system. Triathletes should be attentive to the sources of drag while riding: rolling resistance, grade (or hill climbing), bicycle acceleration, and aerodynamic forces. Of these, managing aerodynamic drag is the most important. A flat-back, time-trial position on the bicycle should be developed if possible. This positioning traditionally requires a bicycle with steeper seat tube geometry to prevent the pedaling stroke from becoming choppy and less efficient. Concerning grade, riding uphill dramatically increases cycling power, although less so when bicycles (and triathletes) are lightweight. Power meters are useful in providing feedback to the rider during climbing and helpful in modulating physiological effort. This topic will be addressed further in chapter 8.

We then turned our attention to how pedal forces, generated to manage energy demands, fluctuate in response to both muscular and nonmuscular influences. Research indicates that triathletes, like their traditional cycling partners, should abandon the pursuit of true circular pedaling because the legs and cranks naturally capitalize on the noncircular dynamics of the coupled legs and bicycle cranks. Instead, triathletes should work to develop the ability to power the cranks through the top and bottom of the pedal cycle, specifically when higher cycling power is desired. Indoor one-legged pedaling drills, high-cadence riding on rollers, and a focus on delivering energy to the cranks through the top and bottom of the pedal cycle are effective methods of improving pedaling technique.

Finally, as a logical step into the next chapter, recent findings were presented concerning the cycle-to-run transition. The triathlete, like the road-racing time-trial specialist, seeks a unique solution to the optimal human–machine integration challenge. Aerodynamic positioning without compromised pedaling technique is an achievable goal, but for the triathlete, running performance off the bicycle must be considered. Recent research suggests that plyometric training may be useful in mitigating both the perceived and measured difficulties in running following cycling. Future research will further define and refine our understanding of the triathlete as a cyclist and even characterize the triathlete who runs fast, right off the bike.

CHAPTER 6

Running Biomechanics for Triathlon

—George M. Dallam, PhD

Running form is potentially an important part of successful performance in triathlon.[1, 2, 3, 4, 5, 6] The pattern of movement used when running is referred to scientifically as running biomechanics. This pattern represents interplay between the biological lever systems (bones, joints, muscles, and nervous system) and the physical principles that guide effective movement.

Importance of Running Economy

In the scientific study of running, a long-held notion is that the movement pattern that people adopt naturally is the most efficient way to run and consequently should not be changed. This view evolved from early studies examining the effect of making changes in the stride length and stride frequency on running economy.[1] The early studies often found the same thing: Changing the stride rate and length away from those used freely (used naturally) increases the oxygen cost of running over the short term, whereas typical training without changing technique has no effect on oxygen cost over the short term.[7]

This oxygen cost is referred to as running economy. Because other studies have implicated running economy as one of the major factors responsible for running performance,[1, 5, 8] the assumption is often made that increasing oxygen cost will make running harder and hinder performance. Consequently, many scientists who study running economy recommend that runners not attempt to change how they run naturally.

But some running and triathlon coaches attempt to create new and improved running technique, or running biomechanics, particularly when runners appear to overstride, to take steps that appear longer than optimal. Additional coaching concerns include taking steps that are too short, allowing body posture to slump during each foot support, creating excessive vertical movements with each step, twisting the upper body and crossing over the arms excessively with each step, leaning forward too much or too little, allowing the pelvis to dip with each step, forcing the low back to arch excessively, and moving the head about unnecessarily. Of course, coaches commonly measure the outcome of a change in the running movement more directly than scientists do. Rather than measuring energy cost, coaches simply measure performance—how fast the athlete can run any given distance. Unfortunately, few of the typical form changes recommended by coaches have been directly studied scientifically, so they remain theoretical at best.

Consequently, the notion of trying to improve how someone runs is contentious and widely debated. Numerous viewpoints and approaches exist. But some useful scientific evidence does exist concerning various theories about the development of running technique. Among those the pose method of running has been studied scientifically and appears to hold some promise.[2, 9, 10, 11] This approach to running technique focuses on maximizing the use of gravity for forward propulsion by creating running movements that more closely resemble the movements of a wheel. More recently, new studies have examined the concept of running without shoes as a mechanism by which running technique may change naturally.[12, 13] Such an approach is widely thought to allow the hardwired running motor pattern that we are born with to reemerge in those who have altered their running movements by wearing heavily cushioned shoes that inhibit the normal reflexive responses associated with natural running biomechanics. There are generally three widely accepted reasons to change how someone moves in an athletic activity. These include

- improving efficiency (making it easier to move),
- improving performance capability (allowing a person to move faster, farther, or higher), and
- reducing risk of injury caused by repeating the movement.

The traditional scientific studies of changing running technique primarily address the first reason, and indirectly at that because they measure running economy as the outcome variable. More recently, science has begun to address the other two reasons by examining the influence of changing running technique on both performance and potential injury risk factors as well.[9, 11]

Mechanical Efficiency and Performance

The mechanical efficiency of movement refers to the energy cost required to perform a given level of mechanical work output. For instance, a more efficient runner creates the same work using less energy than a runner who is less efficient. Measuring this concept in running is complicated by the fact that measuring the mechanical work of running (to calculate power output, for instance) is problematic.[14]

The simple work formula (force times distance) is hard to apply because the muscle forces created in running are used to store energy and return it, rather than simply to generate movement of the limbs directly. Running stores and returns substantial amounts of the energy used elastically, like a rubber band, with each step. How much energy is conserved in this way is not now directly measureable, not known, and probably varies from runner to runner.[14]

Consequently, although measuring how fast someone runs from point A to point B is easy, consistently measuring the amount of work required to do so is not possible, although numerous approaches and formulas exist.[14, 15] Consequently, sport scientists typically measure running energy consumption only by the oxygen cost of running, making the assumption that work will be constant when two individuals are running at a given speed. They next make inferences about mechanical efficiency (work kilocalories divided by total energy consumption kilocalories) from there.

A common assumption is that when two runners run at the same speed and one uses less oxygen to do so, that runner is more mechanically efficient. But another possibility is that the runner using less oxygen is doing less mechanical work and is not more efficient when comparing work to oxygen cost. For instance, this difference in oxygen cost may result from factors such an anthropometrics, improved neuromuscular activation patterns, or training status[5] and not be related to running mechanics at all.

Improving Running Economy

The most definitive statement that can be made when evaluating someone's running economy is that it will improve over long periods through simple repetition if technique remains constant. This result happens through the natural process of decreasing coactivation of agonist and antagonist muscle groups against each other in a process called reciprocal inhibition. When learning a new motor pattern the early conscious regulation that we create through the cerebral cortex is gradually replaced by autonomic regulation in the cerebellum and through spinal reflexes as overlearning occurs. This process takes considerable time, especially when a runner is replacing an already well-developed motor pattern with a different but similar one.

The result of reduced coactivation is that the same movement becomes easier to perform because the opposing muscles around each joint work against each other less to produce the same outcome in force. Gradual inhibition of cocontraction is the natural outcome of many millions of consistent repetitions. Although this concept has not been studied directly in running, the existence of increased oxygen cost during walking because of excessive cocontraction has been demonstrated in children with cerebral palsy.[16]

Of course, this concept helps to explain the large body of research that illustrates that a significant change in running technique results in increased oxygen costs over the typical period of a research study, 6 to 12 weeks. We likely increase coactivation of opposing muscles (lose coordination) when learning a new version of a motor skill, even if the new skill may be more effective mechanically in producing the performance outcome that we want.

An example might be found in learning to pedal at higher cadence. Doing so initially requires our attention and is usually more energy intensive, yet it results nearly immediately in a reduced fatigue level in our working muscles. As a result, the only effective measure of the utility of changing running technique over short time frames is found by measuring running performance itself rather than by measuring the energy cost of running. Economy is then improved primarily through accumulated training repetition with constant biomechanics at the particular velocities targeted, as well as through adaptation to training interventions such as movement-specific strength training, higher-speed interval training, and increased altitude training.[5]

Factors That Affect Economy

Considering the aforementioned limitations in studying running economy, the aspects of technique that are most commonly associated with a reduced running energy cost at a given speed include reduced braking forces upon foot strike, reduced vertical oscillations (up and down movements), and lower peak vertical and horizontal ground reaction forces with each step taken.[1, 4, 5, 17] These differences are generally associated with shorter steps, a higher stride rate, reduced contact or support time, and a resulting reduction in ground reaction forces with each step at a given speed in comparison with less economical runners.

A range of 90 to 100 strides per minute and a vertical oscillation with each step of 8 to 10 centimeters have been associated with higher-performing runners as well. It is further theorized that an increased ability to use energy elastically to capture the force of gravity and translate it into a horizontal stimulus should also be associated with lower energy cost,[11] although this hasn't yet been demonstrated experimentally. Basically, the kinetic energy associated with the falling body during each step is captured by stretching muscles and tendons during landing and translated into an optimal projection angle as the tissues return to their original length and the body's momentum continues to carry the center of mass forward, much like the way that a spring works. Therefore, an optimal body position and the appropriate level of reflexive muscle contraction during support are critical to creating efficient forward propulsion. Runners who have poor body position at landing (foot too far forward and dorsiflexed, knee too straight, upper body slumped) give away some of the free energy that they could absorb from gravity. Runners who project themselves at too high or too low an angle sacrifice distance covered while airborne from the same projecting force.

Figure 6.1 shows the theoretical relationships between the angle of projection of the body's center of mass from the ground and the resultant vertical oscillations and step distances. Imagine a dot on the side of the head moving up and down with each step. The darkest line represents the optimal (45-degree) projection angle, which results in the greatest distance covered because the vertical forces and horizontal forces at push-off perfectly offset the downward force of gravity to maximize distance traveled in the air. The optimal projection angle is associated with a vertical oscillation of about 8 to 10 centimeters for typical step lengths. The higher angle of projection reduces step length because forces are applied in too vertical a manner—a runner appears to bounce up with each step. The gray line represents forces applied too horizontally without an adequate vertical component to offset gravity. Gravity then forces the body down prematurely, resulting in short, rapid steps. Imagine a baseball thrown at too low or too high an angle. Either trajectory reduces the distance of the throw for a given force applied. Keep in mind that these are not on a time scale, just distance. The oscillations represented by the gray line represent the slowest step rate because of the time spent to reach peak height. This might represent a stride rate of 60 to 80 strides per minute. The dotted line associates with a more optimal stride rate of 90 to 100 strides per minute, and the darkest line associates with an excessive stride rate of more than 100 strides per minute.

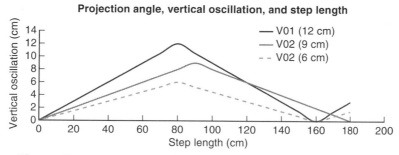

▶ **Figure 6.1** Projection angle, vertical oscillation, and step length.

The Pose Method

It has been demonstrated that a global alteration in running technique, using pose method instruction, could create the more efficient running mechanics just described (reduced vertical oscillation and increased stride rate) but also resulted in increased oxygen cost when running on a treadmill over 12 weeks.[10] The pose method uses a series of drills designed to develop the ability to land on the ball of the foot just forward of the center of mass in a springlike body posture, to remove the foot vertically from the ground while simultaneously shifting the body weight to the opposite and falling foot, and to lean forward so as to fall into each step, in turn maximizing the use of gravity to project the body. As the lead researcher in this study, I was intrigued by the fact that this increased energy cost occurred in spite of repeated anecdotal reports of improved running performance among the vast majority of participants in the pose method treatment group. Unfortunately, performance measures were not directly used in the study.

Following completion of the study I formally questioned the treatment group using a Likert scale survey that included questions about performance improvements, chronic injury effects, and desire to continue using the altered technique. Six of seven treatment group subjects reported improvements in performance, positive or no effects on existing chronic injuries, and a desire to continue using the new technique despite knowledge of the results of the study concerning running economy.

A later pose method experimental study that examined both running economy while running overland and running performance at 1.5 miles (2.4 km) found no loss in running economy and a 24-second improvement in 1.5-mile running time in the pose method treatment group in comparison with no meaningful change in the control group.

This result occurred after just 1 week of instruction in the pose method and concurrently with measureable changes to running kinematics in line with those discussed previously.[2] Considering that the loss of economy in the first study may have been at least partially a result of testing on the treadmill, which has been shown to alter running mechanics in comparison with testing overland,[18] and which created a novel environment for the subjects to attempt to regulate a newly learned technique, the overall potential for effective change in running technique and the resulting improvement in running performance through pose method instruction can be viewed optimistically.

Barefoot Running and Minimalist Shoes

Along these same lines of thinking the science studying barefoot, or unshod, running clearly demonstrates the immediate potential to change running biomechanics[13, 19] and reduce oxygen cost by simply running without shoes.[20] When running without shoes, people immediately adopt[19, 20] and eventually adapt[13, 21] running mechanics that parallel those described previously for running with lower energy cost. They also experience an immediate reduction in oxygen cost.

Barefoot running results in a shorter step and higher stride rate, a ball-of-the-foot landing (see figure 6.2), shorter support time, and reduced ground reaction forces in comparison with shod running at a given speed.[13, 19] In addition, the use of glovelike footwear induces similar immediate changes in running biomechanics.[19] Unfortunately, no published experimental trials studied the immediate effect of barefoot running changes on performance. This approach may offer the theoretical advantage, in comparison to more conventional instruction, of allowing the athlete to adopt an already existing, and some would argue innate, motor pattern, thereby avoiding the coactivation issues and increase in oxygen cost described earlier.

Extreme caution, however, must be observed to avoid injury, as often occurs when a previously habitually shod athlete attempts to adapt too quickly to the conditions of running without shoes. This caution may be particularly applicable to those who use glovelike shoes rather than simply run without shoes, because the shoes remove significant cushioning yet prevent the normal limitation to excessive barefoot running, which is the accumulation

▶ **Figure 6.2** Barefoot runner landing on the ball of the foot.

of external skin abrasion and soreness. Wearing glovelike shoes may tempt athletes to progress distance in a new running style too quickly and has been associated with case study reports of metatarsal injury.[22]

In practical terms, barefoot or minimalist shoe running offers potential as a means of practicing and reinforcing running technique when risk is minimized.[23] To do so, a person can attempt such running in conditions such as the artificial turf now used on many athletic fields, slowly progress the running volume while barefoot or in minimalist shoes, and gradually transition to lighter footwear in normal running conditions. This approach should naturally reinforce improved technique while minimizing risk for overuse injuries caused by the adjustment process.

Following is a suggested progression in shoe type, under the assumption that each shoe will be worn to its normal wear duration during normal running conditions. Such a progression should occur over a period of years rather than weeks or months. Barefoot running, technique instruction, and minimalist shoe running can then be used to learn and reinforce the techniques applied during regular shoe running. This selection of shoes assumes a change in running technique to the ball-of-the-foot striking pattern associated with barefoot running and anthropometrics that are suitable to the new technique. At the first sign of problems the runner should retreat to a previously successful shoe and then consider providing more time for adaptation.

1. Start with the current supportive or heavyweight training shoe, ideally using a version with a minimum heel-to-forefoot height differential.
2. Move to a more neutral training shoe with no overt features designed to control foot motion.
3. Move to a lighter weight neutral shoe designed for performance training.
4. Move to a racing flat or a well-cushioned minimalist-style shoe such as the Nike Free.
5. Move to minimalist-style shoe with less cushion.
6. Move to bare feet if desired. If planning to do so, gradually increase walking time in bare feet.

Triathlete Versus Runner Efficiency

Although triathletes are less skilled in both swimming and cycling than their comparably trained counterparts in those individual sports,[40, 41] the same is apparently not true for running.[42] The first observations mentioned raise the concern that cross-training, meaning simultaneous training for more than one sport in a common timeframe, may negatively influence neuromuscular development and skill level in a single sport. But the greater likelihood is simply that multisport athletes possess less ability than their elite single-sport counterparts in the first place.

This result likely occurs as less-than-elite-level swimmers, cyclists, and runners take up multisport at a later stage in their athletic development while their more skilled counterparts remain committed to the individual sports of swimming, cycling, and running. Any comparison between elite single-sport athletes and multisport athletes will then naturally include a wider variation in skill level among the multisport athletes.

Because most triathletes come to the sport from a competitive running background, neuromuscular coordination (or skill) levels is likely more comparable between triathletes and runners completing similar volumes of run training.[42] Finally, running is the most natural of the three disciplines that typically make up triathlon; consequently, the role of learning in differentiating running skill development is greatly reduced between runners and triathletes. Despite these explanations for the differences in skill between single-sport and multisport athletes, multisport athletes can still improve tremendously by improving their running skill.

Injury Prevention

The rate of musculoskeletal injury that results in lost training time in competitive triathletes at some point in the training and competition process has been reported to be as high as 75 percent.[24] Unfortunately, studies of running and triathlon injury risk factors invariably fail to examine general movement technique factors that may relate to injury such as foot strike pattern, vertical oscillation, or ground reaction force patterns.

Some studies do address what can be more accurately viewed as anatomical movement limitations that seem to influence injury potential.[25] Among these are limited dorsiflexion capability of the ankle (see figure 6.3), hip immobility in rotation, leg length differences, excessive joint laxity, excessively high or low arches,[25] and more recently pelvic positioning during support (see figure 6.4).[26] Such factors, although certainly elements of the overall biomechanical profile, do not represent conscious choices in technique. Rather, they are inherent limitations of an individual's anatomy and should be addressed through physical therapy–based methodologies such as functional training.

▶ **Figure 6.3** Limited ankle dorsiflexion.   ▶ **Figure 6.4** Pelvic drop during support.

Most studies of running injury risk factors examine training factors such as total training hours and years of actively competing. A review of such studies concludes that total training volume and previous injury are the most important risk factors for injury.[27]

One scientific review paper has addressed the effects of impact forces in running.[28] The finding is that relatively higher impact forces generally provide the strongest predictive value for increased injury rate.[28] Trials examining the effects of both pose method instruction[2, 10] and a change to barefoot running[13, 20] suggest that these approaches to modifying running technique offer the promise of reducing injury potential by reducing impact forces. Each approach has been shown to reduce total ground reaction forces absorbed with each step taken at a given speed in comparison to heel–toe running[9] and running with shoes,[12] respectively.

The pose method has also been shown to reduce torque at the knee and increase torque at the ankle,[9] thereby rebalancing total-body force absorption across the knee and ankle. Although the short-term incidental effect of the second change is often increased muscle soreness in the calf muscles as the runner adapts to the new loading pattern, the long-term effect appears to be a more balanced force distribution pattern that allows a higher total impact load to be placed on the body while running.

Barefoot running appears to improve muscular response at foot strike, resulting in more effective ankle and foot pronation and an improvement in shock absorption.[13, 21] This likely results from improved sensory input upon landing on the ball of the foot without the insulating effect of running shoes.[21] Further, the use of modern running shoes has been shown to increase joint torque at both the knee and hip.[29]

Note, however, that the recent rush to minimalist footwear and barefoot running has also produced case study reports of metatarsal stress fracture in experienced runners.[22] This result is not surprising because a lifetime of walking and running in padded shoes is not likely to prepare someone for a rapid transition to unshod walking and running. Of course, the pragmatic solution for a runner who hopes to improve performance and resistance to injury is likely to be found in a combination of both instruction and footwear individually applied in relation to both current training level and physical characteristics. In the same vein, it is reasonable to suggest that runners who are satisfied with their current performance level and relatively injury free need not attempt such changes.

Effect of Prior Cycling on Running Performance

Triathlon competition requires the peculiar need to run following swimming and cycling in the most typical multisport racing order.[18, 30] Therefore, the athlete runs in a relatively fatigued state.[8, 30, 31] Several studies have illustrated that this running condition results in minor changes in running technique, as well as losses in economy or performance.[8, 30, 31, 32, 33, 34]

But an additional study suggests that elite triathletes in World Cup competition suffer little or no loss in efficiency.[35] Three variables are the most likely to influence this outcome. The first is the legality of drafting other cyclists during International Triathlon Union competitions such as the World Cup and World Championship Series events. Many athletes in these events are able to reduce average power output significantly in comparison with traditional nondrafting or arbitrary positioning–style cycle segments. Lesser decrements likely occur in both running efficiency and running performance in the following run segment for those athletes who use their energy wisely during the cycle segment, and in some cases the cycle segment may even exert a warm-up effect.[18, 30, 35]

A second factor is the greater likelihood that elite athletes use specific combination or brick training to prepare for competition. In this training approach athletes move back and forth rapidly between training disciplines, simulating the conditions that they experience in racing. This approach to training has been shown to improve both transition speed and early running speed during triathlons.[36]

A third factor is that high-level cyclists in drafting-legal forms of cycle racing prefer a higher cadence than that commonly used in nondrafting cycling triathlons.[37] Higher cadences are likely used in elite draft-legal triathlon competition as well. Higher-cadence cycling has been shown to increase stride rate and run speed during early subsequent running,[32, 38] and it appears to result in more economical running than a low-cadence (60 rpm) cycling approach.[38] This last point further illustrates the value of a higher stride frequency approach to running in the specific context of multisport racing.

Further, one study supports the value of using a triathlon-specific bicycle with a high seat tube angle. The use of a seat tube with an angle greater than 76 degrees (see figure 6.5) results in substantial improvements in early

▶ **Figure 6.5** Seat tube greater than 76 degrees.

running speed following cycling as well as both greater overall run speed and faster combined cycle and run time.[39] In theory, using a higher seat tube angle allows the triathlete to sit more forward on the bike, resulting in a more relaxed acute hip angle and higher cadence potential while pedaling. Such changes appear to minimize the negative effects of the cycling position on subsequent running.

Conclusion

Improved running biomechanics and efficiency appear to offer a significant avenue by which triathletes can improve overall performance, and those who desire to improve speed should actively develop them. Current running technique development approaches such as the pose method and the use of minimalist shoes or barefoot running show promise as either parallel or intertwined methods to improve running mechanics and performance, primarily for those whose performance outcomes are less than satisfactory or are compromised by injury. These methods should be applied cautiously, allowing time for successful adaptation. After effective running mechanics are learned, running economy and efficiency will improve primarily because of sustained successful running training without injury or further variation in running mechanics. The specific issue of improved running following cycling will benefit from high-cadence cycling, the consistent use of combination cycle–run training, and the use of a triathlon-specific bicycle with a steep seat tube angle.

Environmental Factors and Equipment Options

CHAPTER 7

In the Water

—Bruce R. Mason, PhD, and Gina Sacilotto

Many factors affect the swim performance of competitors participating in triathlon events specifically because of the unpredictable nature of an open body of water. According to the International Triathlon Union (ITU), swim distances range from 300 to 4,000 meters. Because of the variety of uncertainties encountered in an open-water setting, these distances can become difficult for triathletes to complete. Coaches and triathletes need to understand several points:

- Differences between swimming in a pool compared with swimming in an open body of water
- Potential water conditions that triathletes may face during competition
- The use of swimsuits in triathlon events
- The use of wetsuits in triathlon events
- The use of other swim gear in preparation and training for triathlon competition

This chapter covers these topics and presents ideas for coaches and triathletes to use to make the most of the swim leg of the triathlon.

Pool Versus Open Body of Water

Anyone who has swum in a standard swimming pool and an open body of water will attest to being exposed to a greater variety of conditions in the open water. The main difference between swimming pools and open bodies of water is the lack of control over the environmental factors that triathletes endure while competing. For example, in pool swimming competitions most international events are held indoors, therefore almost eliminating weather elements. In triathlons, however, almost all international events are held outdoors, therefore exposing competitors to environmental factors such as extreme air and water temperatures, tide changes, turbulent water flow, aquatic life, and chemical or bacterial contamination in the water.

Specifically, within competitive pool swimming, guidelines for the setup of a competition pool are outlined by the governing body, Federation Internationale De Natation (FINA). Within a competitive pool event, mandated FINA guidelines include the level of lighting, the length and depth of the pool, the lane widths, lane ropes, starting platforms, lane markings, specifications for the bulkheads, and the element that affects triathlons the most, water temperature. In pool swimming competitions, FINA requires the water temperature to be maintained between 25 and 28 degrees Celsius (77 to 82 degrees Fahrenheit).

In triathlon events, the ideal temperature that the International Triathlon Union (ITU) outlines for competition is also between 25 and 28 degrees Celsius, but this temperature range is impossible to maintain because of environmental factors, discussed later in the chapter. Realistically, water temperatures have been known to range between 13 and 32 degrees Celsius (55 to 90 degrees Fahrenheit).[1] Open-water swimming events take place in an open body of water and more closely resemble a swim leg in a triathlon than other FINA events. FINA guidelines state that the minimum water temperature for open-water swimming competitions is 16 degrees Celsius (60 degrees Fahrenheit). Allowable temperature ranges for competition are greater in triathlons than in open-water swimming events because triathletes may possibly use wetsuits in colder water. This issue is discussed later in the chapter. Similar to open-water events, triathlons have a swim course marked out with accurately measured and highly visible buoys that are secured to minimize movement even in severe wave conditions.

Another difference between pools and open bodies of water is how the race starts. In pool events the start involves a dive from individual blocks into the athlete's individual lane. Open-water swimming and the start of a triathlon involve starting in a small area with all competitors in the same space of water. The start can be chaotic. Three main start types are involved in triathlons: in-water starts from a treading-water position, a beach run into the water, and diving from a pontoon.

In-Water Starts

For in-water starts, the triathletes are positioned in rows, usually bookended by two buoys. After the starter declares the beginning of the event, the triathletes change from a vertical treading-water position to a horizontal position, requiring greater surface area per competitor. This change in position causes chaos as each athlete tries to make a break and swim in her own space.

Because all the triathletes are packed closely together while treading water, the water can become turbulent, possibly causing athletes who are weak swimmers to be sucked under the water. Novice triathletes should therefore start from the back and to the side of the starting pack so that they can learn how to start in the water without the risk of harm. After the triathlete becomes more confident and wants to avoid hindering his performance time by starting from the back, he should stay to the side of the pack but move closer to the front. Advanced triathletes tend to start in the front row toward the middle to create the straightest line possible to the first course marker.

Beach Starts

When the swim leg of a triathlon is contested in the ocean, competitors often do a beach run to enter the water. As with an in-water start, all participants are positioned in rows between two markers, although here the markers are on the sand. When the starter declares the start of the race, triathletes run down the beach and into the water. The best time to dive and commence swimming is when the water is level with naval.[2]

Because ocean swims involve swimming through the wave breaks, triathletes must learn how to swim out beyond the break. Suggested techniques include diving over the waves, dolphining underneath the waves if the water is deep enough, or standing side on to the wave so that the water moves around the body rather than crashes against it, which could cause the triathlete to be pushed over. In confronting the wave breaks, knowing when to dive underneath the waves is imperative.

Before the event, triathletes should practice a run in and out to determine the shore gradient in relation to the water, which can involve gradual changes in depth as well as an uneven floor. These factors may change how the triathlete approaches the entry.[2] All these start procedures, particularly with beach starts, may create anxiety, so the triathlete may want to start on the outer edge or back of the pack and wait a few seconds after the starting signal to allow more room to swim.[3]

Diving Starts

The final option for a start in triathlons is a dive from a pontoon into the water. This type of start procedure is described in the ITU competition guidelines and therefore can be assumed to be the main form of commencing a triathlon at the elite level.[4] Amateur triathletes seldom have the opportunity to start from a pontoon in competition.

This starting procedure has two phases. The first is the starting position selection. Triathletes are usually ordered according to their competition number, which is usually relative to their ranking in the field. The second is the starting procedure. One starting official calls, "On your marks," and the triathletes move forward to the start line. Then a second starting official signals the start of the event. To minimize the risk of harm during the actual event, triathletes should investigate all aspects of the swim leg before the competition.

Water Conditions

In triathlon events, the swim leg is conducted in a variety of settings such as saltwater oceans and bays and freshwater inland lakes and rivers. Ocean swims tend to be colder and may have significant turbulent flow and offshore currents. Ingestion of saltwater may cause participants to become nauseated or seasick in ocean swims.[1] Ocean swims also involve a greater possibility of interaction with troublesome aquatic life,[1] such as jellyfish, stingrays, or even sharks.

With inland swim venues, the water generally remains calm and has weaker currents. But if a strong wind is present, the water may become choppy and swimming may be as difficult as it is in the ocean. These elements will govern not only participation, swim distance, and the use of a wetsuit but also the type of stroke technique to be used in the race.[2] For example, when water conditions are rough, the triathlete will have to raise her head more often to locate the course markers.

As a consequence of swimming with the head up more often, the body position of the swimmer changes because the hips drop lower in the water. This alteration in swim position increases the amount of surface area exposed to the oncoming water, which amplifies the amount of resistance that the triathlete has to encounter. When the water is calm, the swim phase will generally be faster because the triathletes can minimize the time that their heads are above the water looking for the course markers and thus maintain a more streamlined technique.

Water Temperature

According to the ITU, the water temperature for a triathlon event is taken 24 hours beforehand and approximately 1 hour before the start of competition on race day. The water temperature is taken from the middle of the course and two other locations around the course at a depth of 60 centimeters. The lowest temperature is used as the official water temperature.

The water temperature governs whether the competitors are permitted to wear wetsuits and whether the swim distance will be modified or cancelled. The water temperatures outlined for the use of a wetsuit are discussed later in this chapter. Table 7.1 outlines when swim distances will be modified or cancelled because of the water temperature.

If the measured air temperature is lower than the water temperature, the water temperatures used can be decreased accordingly (see table 7.2).

These temperature-related modifications are intended to minimize the potential harm to competitors, because extreme water temperatures mixed with long durations of exposure are known to influence hyperthermia and hypothermia. According to the British Triathlon Federation guidelines, a sufficient number of blankets should be on hand to supply a minimum of 20 percent of the entrants in an event.[5] This provision ensures that treatment can be offered to a number of people if they experience hypothermia.

Table 7.1 ITU Water Temperature for Modification or Cancellation of the Swim Component

Original swim distance (m)	Water temperature				
°C	16.9–16.0	15.9–15.0	14.9–14.0	13.9–13.0	Below 13.0
°F	62.4–60.6	60.6–59.0	58.8–57.2	57.0–55.4	Below 55.4
750	750	750	750	750	Cancel
1,500	1,500	1,500	1,500	750	Cancel
3,000	3,000	3,000	1,500	Cancel	Cancel
4,000	4,000	3,000	1,500	Cancel	Cancel

Table 7.2 ITU Water Temperature Modified by Air Temperature

		AIR TEMPERATURE (°C)							
		15	14	13	12	11	10	9	8
WATER TEMPERATURE (°C)	20	17.5	17.0	16.5	16.0	15.5	15.0	14.5	14.0
	19	17.0	16.5	16.0	15.5	15.0	14.5	14.0	13.5
	18	16.5	16.0	15.5	15.0	14.5	14.0	13.5	13.0
	17	16.0	15.5	15.0	14.5	14.0	13.5	13.0	Cancel
	16	15.5	15.0	14.5	14.0	13.5	13.0	Cancel	Cancel
	15	15.0	14.5	14.0	13.5	13.0	Cancel	Cancel	Cancel
	14	14.0	14.0	13.5	13.0	Cancel	Cancel	Cancel	Cancel

Tables 7.1 and 7.2 adapted, by permission, from International Triathlon Union, 2012, *ITU competition rules*, 21/02/2012 edition pp. 15, 16. [Online]. Available: http://www.triathlon.org/images/uploads/itusport_competition_rules_20120215.pdf [December 3, 2012].

Furthermore, all first aid personnel should be trained in handling the symptoms of anxiety conditions and cold temperatures.

Other race factors that may be affected are the triathlete's ability to reduce the resistive forces encountered while swimming. According to Clarys,[6] in water temperatures of 18 to 24 degrees Celsius (64 to 75 degrees Fahrenheit), the amount of resistive forces (commonly termed *active drag*, which is an accumulation of pressure, wave, and frictional drag) that the swimmer encounters significantly decreases as the temperature increases.[6] Therefore, triathletes participating in events in which water temperatures are on the upper limit of the range of 18 to 24 degrees Celsius would be able to generate greater propulsion and reduce the loss of wasted kinetic energy into the water. Note, however, that several other factors influence the level of resistive forces, such as anthropometry, swim technique, and swim speed.

Adverse Conditions

Along with reducing swim distance because of adverse water conditions, senior race officials can incorporate race cutoff times or change the venue of the swim if they deem conditions unsafe. These conditions could include strong water currents, large waves, breakers, or strong undertows (water movement under the surface waves). If cutoff times are evoked, they must be advised to all the entrants at least 7 days before the event.[5]

According to USA Triathlon, the operation of an event must be in accordance with the established guidelines of the government agency that controls the body of water where the competition is to occur. After water quality is established as suitable for human swimming, the certificate or notification must be kept for a period of 7 years after the event.[7] Similarly, the Canadian triathlon medical manual mentions that organizers should consult the guidelines for Canadian recreational water quality in determining an adequate venue for an event.[8]

The ITU dictates that the technical and medical delegates may enforce limits on the swim length as well as provisions about wetsuit use in the case of adverse weather conditions. The final decision should be made 1 hour before the start of the event.[4] The Triathlon Canada medical manual advises that a swim leg could be cancelled if competitors or potential rescuers are not able to see the buoys marking the course when sighting from water level.[8] When competing in an international triathlon, competitors must have access to course specifications, which should be distributed to all competitors before race day. Each triathlete should investigate factors including temperature, water conditions, and aquatic life in preparation for the event.

Swimsuits

Swimsuits are to be worn at all times throughout all legs of a triathlon. Where wetsuits are not permitted, the international competitor must wear an ITU-approved uniform for the swim portion as well as the bike and run legs of the event. If the competitor chooses to wear a second suit, it must be worn underneath the approved uniform.[4]

The uniform can be either a one piece or a two piece. The ITU prefers the suit to be a one piece. If a two piece is worn, the two garments must overlap so that the torso is not exposed during any part of the race.[9, 10]

Elite U23 and junior competitors must complete the entire triathlon in an unaltered race competition uniform.[11] Where wetsuits are permitted, the wetsuit must be worn over the top of the swimwear and must display only the manufacturer's logo, which must not exceed a size of 80 square centimeters.[10] An example of an approved age-group male and female uniforms can be seen in figures 7.1 and 7.2.

In competitive pool swimming in recent years, much controversy has arisen about the use of swimsuits (or "super suits") because of the performance-enhancement capabilities of such suits. The competitive swimming govern-

▶ **Figure 7.1**   ITU example of approved age group male uniforms.[12]

▶ **Figure 7.2**   ITU example of approved age group female uniforms.[13, 14]

ing body, FINA, now has strict criteria for swimsuit manufacturers, and swimmers must compete in FINA-approved suits, which are listed on the FINA website.[15] Triathlon federations are also amending competition rules to mirror FINA in the move to allow only textile swimsuits (or speed suits).[16]

Similar to the swimsuits used in competitive pool swimming, triathlon swimsuits reduce the water resistance encountered by the triathlete, but the suits differ in offering an increased amount of movement and durability that is needed in a triathlon event. These features enable the triathlete to complete the three legs of the event as well as address the thermoregulatory aspects of the suits to maintain a near normal core body temperature through the event. The USA Triathlon website has a list of approved swimsuits that can be worn in any water temperature.[17] When unsure of the legality of a swimsuit, the triathlete should contact the pertinent governing bodies before purchasing or competing in the suit.

Wetsuits

Whether wetsuits can be used depends on the water temperature taken 24 hours before and on race day. As mentioned earlier in this chapter, the water temperature must fall within a certain range for the officials to allow the use of wetsuits. The sole purpose of the suits is to maintain a stable body temperature in colder water temperatures. Tables 7.3 and 7.4 outline those temperature ranges.

Note that national federations or unions have specific guidelines for wetsuit use and that some events may even use different guidelines altogether. Therefore, before competing, a triathlete should check the event guidelines to determine whether a wetsuit may be worn.

Back in the mid-1980s it was shown that swim speed was enhanced by up to 7 percent by a wet suit.[18] Toussaint et al.[19] also established that speed increased by 5 percent because of a 14 percent decrease in the triathlete's active drag while wearing a wetsuit. A study completed in the mid-1990s found that wetsuits aided the swim performance of triathletes by 6 percent.[20]

Table 7.3 ITU Guidelines for Wetsuit Use in Elite U23 and Junior Competitors

| Swim length (m) | FORBIDDEN ABOVE | | MANDATORY BELOW | | Maximum stay in water |
	(°C)	(°F)	(°C)	(°F)	
300	20	68	14	57	10 min
750	20	68	14	57	20 min
1,500	20	68	14	57	30 min
3,000	22	72	16	61	1 h 15 min
4,000	22	72	16	61	1 h 45 min

Table 7.4 ITU Guidelines for Wetsuit Use in Age-Group Competitors

| Swim length (m) | FORBIDDEN ABOVE | | MANDATORY BELOW | | Maximum stay in water |
	(°C)	(°F)	(°C)	(°F)	
750	22	72	14	57	30 min
1,500	22	72	14	57	1 h 10 min
3,000	23	73	16	61	1 h 40 min
4,000	24	75	16	61	2 h 15 min

Tables 7.3 and 7.4 adapted, by permission, from International Triathlon Union, 2012, *ITU competition rules,* 21/02/2012 edition, p. 15. [Online]. Available: http://www.triathlon.org/images/uploads/itusport_competition_rules_20120215.pdf [December 3, 2012].

These enhancements in swim speed while wearing a wetsuit were revealed only with triathletes and not with competitive swimmers. The explanation was that competitive swimmers have a more streamlined technique and therefore do not gain as much from wearing a wetsuit as triathletes do. Wearing a wetsuit allows triathletes to expend less energy in maintaining a horizontal position, thereby conserving more energy for propulsion.[21] This energy conversation is important, particularly in the longer triathlon events, in storing energy for the bike and run legs. According to Chatard and Millet[20] wearing a wetsuit decreases the energy cost of a triathlete by 7 to 22 percent. Recent research has reached similar conclusions.[22]

For those reasons, wetsuit guidelines were introduced to create a level playing field among competitors who may not be able to afford the more advanced suits.[18] As was the case with competitive pool swimming swimwear, because of the performance enhancement capabilities of previously designed wetsuits, the ITU now restricts wetsuit thickness. For example, no suit may be more than 5 millimeters thick because any greater thickness will further increase the buoyancy of the competitor, providing a potentially unfair advantage.

Wetsuits also vary in thickness around the body; for example, in some brands the thickness under the arms is only 1 millimeter. This change in suit thickness allows the body to continue to thermoregulate during the longer-distance swims. Because of their typically lean body compositions,[1] elite triathletes have been assumed to have relatively poor tolerance to colder temperatures; therefore, first and foremost, wetsuits are permitted as a health and safety aid when the water temperature is low.

Other Swim Gear

During the swim leg of the triathlon the competitor is not allowed to use any floatation or swim-enhancing aids, such as kickboards, fins, snorkel, or paddles. Swim gear allowed during an event includes swimming caps, goggles, and nose clips. The ITU outlines that triathletes must wear the swimming cap given to them at the commencement of the event. If the triathlete chooses to wear another swimming cap, the event cap must be worn over it. The caps given to the competitors are bright and enable event officials to monitor the triathletes throughout the swim leg.

Goggles, which are designed, of course, to keep water out of the triathletes' eyes and allow them to see clearly, are permitted. In training before an event, triathletes should practice the technique of looking for buoys because stroke mechanics used in training in a pool differ from those used when competing in an open body of water.

Nose clips are used by competitors who find it uncomfortable to have water up their noses or wish to limit airflow to only their mouths. Some triathletes have not sufficiently practiced the mechanism of breathing properly in water (out through the nose by blowing bubbles in the water and in through the mouth). A nose clip limits the possibility that water will enter the nose and become unpleasant for the triathlete, which may cause anxiety during the swim.

Although equipment is restricted during competition, triathletes can use several aids during training to assist in technique and power enhancement. A list of equipment and their application to training can be found in table 7.5.

Table 7.5 Description of Swim Training Equipment

Equipment	Description	Advantages
Short fins	Fins with short blades	Promote concentration on muscle strength in overspeed drills
Long fins	Fins with long blades	Used in overspeed drills to increase stroke rate
Pull buoy	Floatation device placed between the legs	Focuses on improving the stroke without concern for the legs
Drag suit	Mesh pants with mesh pockets	Resists the athlete, which encourages an increase in power per stroke
Kickboard	Floatation board shaped device	Focuses on improving kicking without concern for the arms
Snorkel	Breathing tube	Allows the athlete to practice technique without concern for the breathing movement
Hand paddles	Large paddles that fit on the hand and can be attached over the wrist and at least one finger	Enhance propulsion through the water if used correctly or suddenly change direction or come off if used incorrectly
Finger paddles	Small, half-moon-shaped paddles usually attached only to the athlete's middle finger	Same as hand paddles but less extreme if wrong technique is used; also can be used to "feel the water"

Conclusion

Because of the unpredictable nature of open-water swimming during the first leg of a triathlon, several factors need to be considered when preparing for an event.

First, the triathlete should learn the course—how the course will be set out, what type of course markers will be used, what type of water the event will be contested in, whether wetsuits will be allowed, and what type of start will be used. Answers to these questions will aid in the preparation for an event because each aspect can be practiced before race day.

Second, the triathlete should learn how to swim in various water conditions, specifically in both oceans and inland bodies of water. An easy way to prepare for these conditions is to enter open-water events. These events also allow the triathlete to practice various race starts, adjust stroke technique to the water conditions, and become more confident swimming in an open body of water. Another benefit of entering these open-water swims is that they are structured events, so the participants will be monitored and medical care is close by if the triathlete gets into trouble.

Third, if a wetsuit is permitted, the triathlete should wear one. Wearing a wetsuit will enable a quicker swim. Before race day the triathlete should practice removing the wetsuit quickly to enable a fast first transition.

Finally, the triathlete should learn to use training equipment. Joining a competitive swimming squad will enable the triathlete to learn not only correct swim technique but also the proper use of training equipment. The structure and consistency of squad training also will maintain interest in training for the swim leg of the triathlon. Because the swim leg is the shortest part of the triathlon, athletes often minimize their training for this section.

Foremost in any competition to be undertaken, the triathlete must consider safety in the water on the day of the event.

On the Bike

—Jeff Broker, PhD, and Sean Langlais, MSc

Optimum performance during the cycling portion of a triathlon is heavily influenced by equipment selection and triathlete–bicycle integration. A triathlete with a top-of-the-line bicycle will not have success if he is poorly integrated to (fit to) his bicycle. Likewise, at the highest competitive level, state-of-the-art equipment can separate medalists from nonmedalists. Ultimately, optimal integration of the rider with the bicycle and proper selection of equipment will provide a competitive advantage, saving precious seconds.

In this chapter we build on the concepts presented in chapter 5 concerning cycling biomechanics. After briefly visiting the rules concerning the cycling leg of triathlons, we turn our discussion to bicycle selection and configuration. We begin by discussing concepts of the steeper seat tube of the tri-bike, highlighting its role in reducing aerodynamic drag without compromising the triathlete's physical performance. The discussion then turns to frame element design, handlebar selection, and wheel considerations. We then shift our focus to bike fit, outlining guidelines for saddle placement and handlebar configuration. The chapter concludes by exploring the demands of hill climbing, bicycle acceleration, the quantitative rationale for drafting (when legal), and ways to solve the aerodynamic challenge.

Governing Body Rules

All participants of a triathlon must follow the rules set forth by the organizing body, typically USA Triathlon (USAT) in the Unites States or the International Triathlon Union (ITU). Small local or recreational races may not operate under a governing body and therefore may have their own rules. Generally, ITU cycling equipment and racing rules follow the guidelines set forth by the Union Cycliste Internationale (UCI). Much of the following discussions concerning equipment and drafting are provided with the USAT and ITU regulations in mind. For further information, consult the ITU and UCI websites.

Bicycle Choice and Geometry Options

The triathlete's bicycle should provide an appropriate balance among comfort, handling, pedaling effectiveness, and aerodynamic quality. Unfortunately, many of these characteristics are conflicted; that is, an overemphasis on one characteristic may be detrimental to another. Maximal pedaling power, for example, cannot be achieved in the most aerodynamic cycling position. Further, the aerodynamic position can be fatiguing to the neck extensor musculature and places more load on the front wheel, which can negatively affect handling.

Elite triathletes ride bicycles specifically built for triathlon racing (tri-bikes) that attempt to balance the characteristics listed previously. These bicycles, which are themselves aerodynamic, place the rider in a streamlined position compatible with reasonable power delivery.

Based on pedaling mechanics research (see chapter 5) as well as real-world observations of elite triathletes, it can safely be concluded that the preferred operating condition for triathletes involves a flat-back, streamlined riding position incorporating a more traditional hip angle range of motion. Here *traditional* refers to the range of motion specific to non-time-trial riding in which the hands are on the hoods or dropbars of a standard bicycle. Seat tube angles associated with this traditional position center around 72 degrees. In a flat-back aerodynamic cycling posture, the equivalent seat tube angle rises to 78 degrees or more (figure 8.1). Specifically, to achieve a traditional hip angle operating range in the more aerodynamic position of a tri-bike, the seat tube must be steepened from 72 to 78 degrees.

Triathlon-specific research concerning seat tube angles has provided a scientific basis for triathletes to use steeper seat tube angles. Ricard and colleagues[1] looked at muscle activation patterns across various seat tube angles while performing Wingate tests. Wingate tests evaluate a cyclist's peak anaerobic power, anaerobic capacity, and fatigue profile over a 30-second maximal cycling effort. They discovered that riders were able to maintain similar cycling power outputs at steeper seat tube angles (e.g., 82 degrees) while significantly reducing the muscular activity of the biceps femoris muscle. They hypothesized that reduced recruitment of the biceps femoris (a hamstring) may facilitate the triathlete's transition to running. These results are consistent with the data of Browning,[2] which showed a slight shift of pedaling demand from the hamstrings to the quadriceps with forward saddle movement in elite triathletes.

On the topic of seat tube angles and the effects on the T2 transition, Garside and Doran[3] compared triathlete's self-selected 10-kilometer running performances after riding 40 kilometers at two seat tube angles, 73 degrees and 81 degrees. The subjects were nearly 2.3 minutes (on average) faster during the first 5 kilometers of the run after riding with the steeper seat tube geometry. The detected physiological differences included increased heart rate, increased stride length, and increased stride frequency in the steeper seat tube condi-

© Nigel Farrow

▶ **Figure 8.1** A triathlete riding a tri-bike with an aggressive steep seat tube in an aerodynamic position. Note how the hip is not excessively flexed as the left pedal moves through the top of the pedal cycle. Also notice a slightly humped thoracic spine, possibly associated with pelvic inflexibility.

tion. During the second half of the run, the effects were less noticeable. This research coincides with the perception of many triathletes that a steeper seat tube is more beneficial to running performance. For more discussion of the T2 transition, see chapters 5 and 6.

The draft-illegal competitive triathlete should select a tri-bike. Entry-level or recreational triathletes, however, may start with a road bike, especially if cost is an issue. Modifications to traditional road bikes can address the hip angle range of motion issue to some extent. Seat posts that allow forward positioning of the saddle can make the effective seat tube angle steeper, circumventing the need to replace the frame of the bicycle. Simply moving the saddle forward, however, reduces the distance between the saddle and bottom bracket, shortening the effective saddle height. Thus, to maintain appropriate saddle height, the saddle should be moved upward as well as forward. A general guideline used with Olympic pursuit riders was to raise the saddle 1 centimeter for every 2 centimeters of forward adjustment.

Another consideration when modifying a traditional bicycle for triathlon use involves handling. Simply moving the saddle forward and slightly upward moves the rider's center of mass closer to the front wheel, thus altering handling characteristics. If bicycle handling is seriously compromised with a simple saddle position change, forcing a triathlon position atop a standard bicycle may not be advised. Further, if forward positioning of the saddle causes interference between the knees and the handlebars during pedaling, this modification is not appropriate. Assessment of proper aerodynamic positioning, coupled with an evaluation of pedaling effectiveness and bicycle handling capability, is best done with a specialist trained in bicycle design and fitting for triathletes.

ITU rules govern aspects of bicycle frame design.[4] The ITU has adopted many of the UCI rules governing bicycle racing and includes modifications depending on whether the triathlon is draft legal or draft illegal. ITU rules state that a vertical line dropped from the nose of the saddle cannot be more than 5 centimeters forward of the bottom bracket axle.[4] This geometrical relationship limits the forward positioning of the athlete to the preferred ranges discussed previously. Additional ITU regulations control the overall length of the bicycle, the front-to-center distance (front axle to bottom bracket spindle), and the width of the bicycle.[4]

Frame Materials

Today, most competition bicycle frames are made of carbon fiber, a lightweight and highly responsive material. Manufacturers can design a carbon fiber frame to suit the elite or recreational triathlete, seeking to optimize performance through superior handling, aerodynamics, vibration attenuation, and other key elements. The negative features of carbon fiber are price, impact resistance, and deterioration over time.

Bicycle frames are also made of aluminum, steel, titanium, and other metals. The most common frame material is aluminum, a cheaper, heavier substitute for carbon fiber. An aluminum frame bicycle will likely weigh 3 pounds (1.4 kg) more than a carbon fiber frame with similar components. As with all equipment choices, the decision should be based on the level of competition, performance, comfort, and price.

Frame Elements

As with saddle position, the ITU regulates the design of a triathlon bike differently for draft-legal and draft-illegal racing. In general, the ITU adopts the UCI time-trial rules for draft-illegal triathlons and uses the UCI road race rules for draft-legal triathlons. For draft-legal races, the bicycle frame must be formed around a main triangle of three tubular elements that may be round, oval, flattened, teardrop shaped, or otherwise in cross-section.[4] Bicycle elements specifically designed to enhance aerodynamics are prohibited; for example, fairings are not allowed.

Aerodynamic tubular elements are allowed. Notably, a tapered tube section with a long dimension (length, parallel to the airstream) that is two to three times longer than the short dimension (width, perpendicular to the airstream) will exhibit one-quarter to one-half of the drag of a round tube of the same width. Prototype "superbikes" developed by the U.S. Olympic team in 1996 were fashioned from helicopter blades for this reason. (The Olympic race versions employed carbon fiber aerodynamic frame elements.) Many commercially available triathlon bikes incorporate such aerodynamic tubing.

Handlebars

The sport of triathlon contributed substantially to the advent of the aerodynamic handlebar and clip-on handlebar system. In 2003 Kyle attributed the invention of the modern aero handlebar to a California engineer, Pete Penseyers, who developed custom handlebars to support a record performance in the Race Across America.[5] Manufacturers Scott and Profile introduced commercially available aerodynamic handlebars shortly thereafter, and by 1988 triathletes were using them in Ironman competitions.[5] Simply stated, aerodynamic handlebars allow a cyclist to ride comfortably in an aerodynamic position while still being able to control the bicycle. Wind tunnel tests and on-road assessments with power meters confirm the performance advantage of aerodynamic handlebars. Triathletes should capitalize on the performance advantage of aerodynamic handlebars when they are allowed by race organizers.

As is the case with frames, the ITU regulates the form and configuration of aerodynamic handlebars.[4] Traditional drop handlebars must be used in draft-legal racing, and clip-on handlebars are permitted provided that they do not project beyond the brake levers. Gear shifters are not allowed on the ends of the clip-on handlebars. For draft-illegal races, handlebar systems including traditional drop bars with clip-on aero bars must not extend beyond the leading edge of the front wheel. [5]

Wheels

Several types of bicycle wheels are available to the triathlete, including simple rounded-spoked wheels with flat rims, bladed-spoked wheels with aero rims, disk wheels fashioned from material composites, membrane aero wheels, and composite molded three- and four-spoked wheels allowed in unlimited competitions. These wheels differ in stiffness, weight, strength, durability, and aerodynamic performance. As pointed out by Kyle, almost any wheel can be designed to support the strength, durability, stiffness, and braking surface needs, but not all wheel types have low weight and low aerodynamic drag.[5]

The ITU dictates wheel selection as follows: For draft-legal competitions, wheel diameters must be between 55 and 70 centimeters, including the tire, and both wheels must be of equal size and have at least 12 spokes. For draft-illegal competitions, covers are allowed on the rear wheel only, subject to race-specific governance (for example, to address high-wind conditions).[4] National or local rules may differ; for example, USAT allows the front wheel to be of different diameter than the rear, but the front wheel must be of spoke construction, whereas the rear wheel may be spoke or solid.[6]

Wheel size matters little as far as aerodynamics are concerned because the aerodynamic advantage of a smaller frontal area for a smaller front wheel is largely offset by the increase in rotational speed.[5] Smaller wheels, however, are lighter and stronger, so they offer an advantage during climbing and accelerating. Smaller wheels may also be superior to larger wheels in crosswinds. The only apparent scientific disadvantage to small wheels, within reason, is their higher rolling resistance.[5] Wheel size is best determined based on cost (including the frame changes involved), wheel and tire availability, and personal handling preference.

The aerodynamic performance of different wheel types is a hotly debated topic among wheel manufacturers. In general, composite aerodynamic wheels have lower drag than the best bladed-, oval-, or rounded-spoked wheels.[5] When legal in competition, three- and four-spoked wheels are similar in performance to flat disk wheels, and the three- and four-spoked aero wheels perform better than flat disks in crosswinds.[5]

Rolling resistance is the loss of energy at the contact patch where the tire meets the road. Energy losses occur here because of deformation of the tire–tube combination. Rolling resistance is affected by the tread design, tread construction, sidewall construction, and tube configuration. Rolling resistance is also affected by the road conditions, load (weight) on the wheel, tire pressure, tire size (i.e., 23 versus 27), wheel diameter, steering, and temperature. Generally, high-pressure tires with thinner and more flexible casings have lower rolling resistance.

Bike Fit

For triathletes racing in draft-illegal events, the time-trial position has emerged as the position of performance. Although pedaling mechanics may be slightly compromised in this position, the advantages gained from superior aerodynamics are unquestioned. Fitting a bicycle to a triathlete should seek to strike a balance among comfort, injury prevention, and, of course, cycling performance.

A rider has only three points of contact with a bicycle: the pedals, the saddle, and the handlebars. Optimal positioning involves the manipulation of these three contact points in relation to one another. Fitting a triathlete to a bicycle is part science and part art. Although many guidelines can be used to direct appropriate bike fit, no two triathletes are exactly alike; each triathlete has unique needs for comfort and performance. Following are brief guidelines developed over the years that are useful in fitting triathletes to bicycles. These guidelines are similar in many respects to those used with road cyclists, but they are specifically modified to the forward, flat-back time-trial position ubiquitously used by triathletes.

Saddle Height

Optimal saddle height in cycling has been studied for decades. Variables used to study saddle height include power output, caloric expenditure, muscle activation patterns, joint forces and torques, and even pedal force effectiveness. In general, oxygen consumption is minimized at a saddle height (measured in a straight line from the bottom bracket to the middle top of the saddle) of roughly 100 percent of greater trochanteric height, or 106 to 110 percent of pubic symphysis height. Both of these measurements are made while the cyclist is standing barefoot. These measurements require detailed knowledge of anatomy and are not practical for triathletes. Practical alternatives developed over the years for setting a cyclist's saddle height, based on optimization studies and observations of elite cyclists, are briefly summarized as follows:

Leg extension method: Perhaps the simplest method for quickly setting saddle height involves the rider sitting atop the bicycle, mounted in a stationary trainer. The rider sits comfortably and centered in the saddle, unclips her shoes from the pedals, and puts the heels of her shoes on top of the pedals. The cyclist then slowly pedals backward. Saddle height is set such that the heels stay in contact with the pedals throughout the pedaling motion, just reaching the pedals at the bottom of the pedal stroke without rocking of the hips. Clipping into the pedals will provide the additional leg length and associated knee flexion during pedaling. This saddle height will be slightly lower than those developed from the methods to follow.

Crotch height method: Here, the cyclist stands in cycling shoes with his back to a wall and feet roughly 2 inches (5 cm) apart. A thin book or broomstick is gently pulled up between the legs in a horizontal orientation until slight resistance in the crotch is encountered. The distance measured from the floor to the top of the book or broomstick is noted and multiplied by 1.09. This computation provides the distance from the pedal spindle axis to the top middle of the saddle when the crank arm is down and parallel with the seat tube. This method, first developed by Hamley and Thomas in 1967,[7] provides an upper limit to saddle height.

LeMond method: Greg LeMond developed a method similar to the crotch height method in which crotch height is multiplied by 0.883 to estimate the distance from the center of the bottom bracket to the top middle of the saddle.[8] LeMond further recommended a 3-millimeter reduction from this final number when using clipless pedals. Pruitt and Matheny noted that the LeMond method slightly overestimates saddle height because riders now wear thinner cycling shoes than those used when the method was developed.[9] Also, riders with long feet or considerable soft tissue over their ischial tuberosities (sit bones) may think that this saddle height is too low.[9] This method is also specific to 172.5-millimeter crank arms; a cyclist using 175-millimeter crank arms would subtract 2.5 millimeters from the estimate computed.

Dynamic knee angle method: This last method requires the cyclist to ride the bicycle on a fixed fork trainer. While riding, the knee should flex 25 to 30 degrees from its fully extended position when the pedal is at the bottom of the pedal cycle. Ideally, the knee angle is measured from video images captured while the cyclist pedals (a dynamic measure). Fortunately, many bicycle shops now have video equipment for obtaining these important dynamic measures. Lacking video equipment, the cyclist can position her legs at the bottom of the pedal strokes, and this angle can be measured using a goniometer. Recognize, however, that dynamic pedaling may differ from the static method described here, so this method is generally not preferred.

These methods represent estimates to be modified based on individual preference, comfort, and performance. No one method is the best because every triathlete will make modifications. Small, incremental modifications to saddle height may be necessary to identify the optimal height. Also, recent research at the University of Colorado in Colorado Springs suggests that cycling kinematics in the laboratory (fixed fork) differ from the kinematics of on-the-road cycling for the same rider and bicycle.[10] Cyclists may alter their position on the road in response to changes in work rate, fatigue, and comfort, an important observation when the concept of optimal positioning is considered.

Fore-Aft Saddle Position

The fore–aft position of the saddle is critical for the triathlete's performance and comfort. The rule of thumb used for fore–aft placement of the saddle for road cycling places the anterior (most forward) aspect of the knee directly above the pedal spindle axis when the crank is halfway through its downstroke (see figure 8.2a). This approach is referred to as the knee-over-pedal-spindle (KOPS) method. This position has been developed over the years to facilitate power delivery to the cranks without overstressing the knee joint.

For triathletes the KOPS position cannot be achieved with a flat-back, time-trial posture. As described earlier, the steeper seat tubes used on tri-bikes induce forward and upward positioning of the saddle relative to the conventional road-cycling position, increasing the hip angle to facilitate effective pedaling. This movement of the saddle places the front of the knee up to 3 centimeters forward of the pedal spindle (see figure 8.2b). This forward position increases the torque requirements for the knee extensors (quadriceps), placing higher stresses on the knee joint.[2] Triathletes should use higher cadences (lower gears) for the first few weeks after changing to the more forward position (after switching to the more aerodynamic position of a tri-bike, for example), to reduce the likelihood of knee problems.

▶ **Figure 8.2** (*a*) Road cyclist with the knee directly above the pedal spindle axis when the crank is halfway through its downstroke; (*b*) the more forward position for triathletes.

Upper-Body Position With Aero Bars

Reach and reach length are the traditional terms used to describe handlebar placement relative to the saddle. Bicycle top tube length and stem geometry are manipulated to achieve proper reach. For road cyclists, whose positioning is somewhat applicable to triathletes who compete in draft-legal events, the cyclist's nose should be above or slightly behind the stem clamp when the hands are in the drops position and the elbows are slightly flexed (15 to 20 degrees). The top surface of the handlebars should be 2 to 4 inches (5 to 10 cm) below the top of the saddle, less for shorter riders and more for taller riders.

For draft-illegal racing, aero bars and clip-on bars are used, which narrow the triathlete's arms and shoulders, thus reducing the rider's frontal area. The elbows are brought somewhat together atop armrest pads, ideally without compromising bicycle handling (see figure 8.3). This position requires practice and accommodation.

The height of the aero bars is adjusted to achieve a flat-back position. The entire back will not be flat, only the upper portion of the back behind the head and neck. This posture requires forward rotation of the pelvis, necessitating the forward and upward positioning of the saddle as previously discussed. In practice, triathletes with limited low-back flexibility and tight hamstrings have difficulty getting the middle of their backs into a flat position.

Considerable debate surrounds the best position of the arms in relation to aero bar usage. Many coaches recommend that the aero bars be configured to have the forearms horizontal and the elbows flexed roughly 90 to 110 degrees (see figure 8.3). This positioning places the upper arms nearly vertical, a position in which the arms and shoulders can relax. Others recommend tilting the aero bars up so that the hands are above the elbows, more in front of the face. In this configuration the upper arms should still be nearly vertical.

The debate probably arises because wind tunnel tests have demonstrated considerable variability among athletes and bicycles. Positions that represent the lowest drag for one triathlete may not be optimal for another. Further, comfort, power generation, and handling capabilities may differ among triathletes for the same aerodynamic position.

Testing of U.S. national team cyclists by the U.S. Olympic Committee in 1995 revealed considerable subject-specific aerodynamic features surrounding aero bar placement. Many athletes achieved lower drag forces with their forearms horizontal. One athlete positioned his forearms below horizontal, with his hands lower than his elbows, yet suffered no aerodynamic consequences. He felt particularly powerful with his hands in this position.

One concept to keep in mind is the degree to which the arms are used to direct the wind about the triathlete's body. With the hands together and the aero bars tipped upward, the triathlete directs the airflow more around

▶ **Figure 8.3** Triathlete with the elbows together atop armrest pads.

the shoulders and along the outside of the body. With the forearms level and the hands slightly separated, the midline airflow is directed between the arms, down between the legs, and across the frame and rear wheel. The optimal condition for a given triathlete likely varies, and wind tunnel testing or cycling power meter testing may be required to establish which position is preferred. The author's experience is the former position may be preferred for cyclists with larger legs or less aerodynamic bicycles (nonaero seat tube, nonaero rear wheel). Here, directing the airflow around the body may be best. For the rider with smaller thighs or an aero bicycle frame and rear wheel, the flat forearm position may be preferred.

Terrain, Drafting, and Solving the Aero Challenge

Bicycle selection and optimal rider–bike integration are important steps that triathletes should take before they even roll out of the garage. On the road, triathletes must manage environmental conditions including hills, wind, and other cyclists.

Power of Climbing and Descending

Many cyclists and triathletes attempt to decrease bicycle weight to manage the implications of gravitational forces. Obviously, the influence of gravity is realized during hill climbing, when the power to climb must be added to the power required just to ride. Unfortunately, the energy saved during a descent does not offset the energy required to climb because of differences in aerodynamic drag. Therefore, flat courses are faster than hilly courses of the same length.

Briefly, the power necessary to climb is directly related to mass of the rider and bicycle system and the magnitude of the grade. Figure 8.4 illustrates the power necessary to climb in relation to grade and velocity (ignoring aerodynamics and rolling resistance). Power is expressed in watts per pound for ease of application. For example, the power required for a 150-pound (68 kg) rider to climb a 10 percent grade at 10 miles per hour (4.4 m/sec) is roughly 300 watts (2 watts per lb × 150 lb).

Figure 8.4 also demonstrates the penalty paid by heavier riders and by riders atop heavier bicycles. For our example (10 percent grade at 10 mph), every 5 pounds (2.3 kg) of extra weight increases the power needed to climb by 10 watts. This relationship has a dramatic effect across a given race population because differences in rider weight can exceed 50 pounds (23 kg). Not surprisingly, the best climbers in the world (of road cyclists) are generally slight of build.

Acceleration

Bicycle acceleration occurs when the energy delivered to the rear wheel exceeds the total resistive forces acting on the rider and bicycle. Acceleration for a given force application is inversely proportional to the total mass of the bicycle and rider combination. Therefore, lighter riders with lighter bicycles will accelerate faster under the same propulsive force. Consider a rider accelerating uniformly from rest over a distance of 200 feet (61 m) in 10 seconds. At the 200-foot mark this rider will reach a velocity of 27.3 miles per hour (12.2 m/sec). The same propulsive force developed by a rider on a bike weighing an additional 5 pounds (2.3 kg) will result in the cyclist's being 5.25 feet (1.6 m) behind at the 200-foot mark. Clearly, a rider on a lightweight bike has an advantage, particularly in a race with many acceleration opportunities.

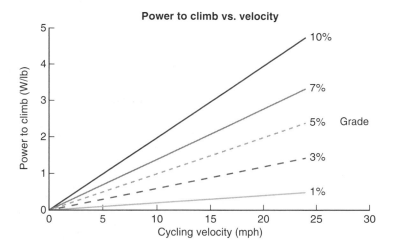

Figure 8.4 Power to climb as a function of hill grade (percent) and cycling velocity. Power is expressed in watts per pound of rider weight. Aerodynamic and rolling resistive forces are not included in the power measure here.

When bicycles accelerate, their wheels increase their rotational velocity (accelerate) as well. Wheels have rotational inertia, representing their resistance to rotational acceleration. Rotational inertia increases with mass and increases more so when the mass is distributed farther from the rotation axis (axle). Light wheels with their mass concentrated closer to the hub are easiest to accelerate.

Aerodynamics Revisited

Cycling aerodynamics was briefly addressed in chapter 5, and the aerodynamic performance features of frames, wheels, and rider body positioning were discussed earlier in this chapter. In many elite ITU triathlons, drafting is legal. Drafting is simply riding within the wake of another rider ahead (figure 8.5). The effect of drafting on cycling power and thus energy expenditure is dramatic.

Several methods have been used to study the effects of drafting. A fascinating study by Hagberg and Nicole quantified the benefits of drafting using oxygen consumption measurements.[11] Riders cycled on the road in various drafting configurations (pacelines and small pelotons) while boom-mounted breathing systems measured oxygen consumption. Using this method, Hagberg and Nicole reported metabolic energy savings of 26 percent plus or minus 7 percent connected with paceline drafting in the second, third, and fourth positions behind a lead rider. Centered at the back of an eight-rider peloton, a rider enjoys a reduction in energy expenditure of 39 percent plus or minus 6 percent.

▶ **Figure 8.5**   One triathlete drafting another. The drafting triathlete can reduce power output by up to 35 percent by drafting effectively.

A modern and simpler method for studying the effects of drafting requires a crank-based, pedal-based, or hub-based power meter. These systems are now widely available, providing many cyclists the opportunity to explore and appreciate the effects of drafting.

Finally, wind tunnel tests provide a unique look at the drafting phenomenon. U.S. national team cyclists preparing for the 1996 Olympics were rotated through a four-rider paceline in a wind tunnel.[12] In these optimal conditions, where bicycle spacing and alignment could be completely controlled, energy savings in the second, third, and fourth positions behind a lead rider were 37 percent, 45 percent, and 46 percent, respectively. Actual racing advantages, quantified using power meters with the same athletes and bicycles on velodromes, were 5 to 10 percent less (still providing an advantage of 30 to 40 percent across the three drafting positions).

Given the substantial advantage offered by drafting in cycling, the ITU and national triathlon federations have set strict guidelines concerning drafting in draft-illegal races. The ITU has established a draft zone measuring 10 meters in length and 3 meters in width. The long dimension of this zone begins at the most forward position of the front wheel of the lead bicycle and projects rearward. A rider cycling within this draft zone at a constant speed is in violation of the drafting rule. USAT has a similar rule, except the draft zone is only 7 meters long and 2 meters wide. ITU and national federation rules permit riders to be in draft zones when preparing to overtake other riders (completed within 20 seconds for the ITU and within 15 seconds for the USAT); for safety reasons when entering aid stations, transition areas, or sharp curves; and in race-specific situations in which exclusions are necessary because of narrow lanes, construction, and detours.

Finally, using on-board power meters in controlled and systematic test situations, the effects of various aerodynamic modifications can be explored for any level of triathlete. Figure 8.6 illustrates a sample power meter–based assessment of cycling aerodynamics. Ideally, a cyclist rides on an indoor velodrome or in calm conditions on a flat road, and power measurements are made across a range of cycling velocities. The data are plotted, adjustments in rider geometry on the bike or componentry are incrementally made, and the test is repeated. The goal is to shift the power versus velocity curve to the right, documenting an ability to cycle at higher speed for a given energy expenditure or at lower energy expenditure for a given cycling speed.

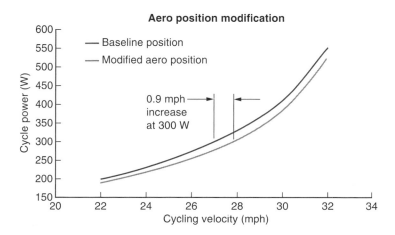

▶ **Figure 8.6** A power versus cycling speed characteristic derived from power meter data collected at a velodrome. When modifications are made to improve aerodynamics, the effects of cycling performance are highlighted. (Shown: an increase of 0.9 miles per hour [0.4 m/s] with no change in cycling power.)

In 1993 Lance Armstrong was tested at the 7-Eleven Velodrome in Colorado Springs shortly after his Cycling World Championship victory. The goal was to improve his time-trial position. Through careful and incremental modifications to handlebar and saddle positions, coupled with a helmet change, Lance was able to ride at a sustainable power output over 1 mile per hour (1.6 km/h) faster in his newly modified, more aero position. Ironically, in response to the findings Lance said that he could ride comfortably in that position because he had used it years earlier when he was a triathlete.

Conclusion

Triathletes are no different from serious cyclists when it comes to the selection of cycling equipment. Competitive triathletes recognize the tangible, scientific advantages offered by superior bicycles and componentry and the importance of optimal rider and bicycle integration

Triathletes should invest in tri-bikes or modify their existing bicycles to achieve a more rotated and streamlined time-trial position. Aero handlebars should be part of the racing package, when allowed by race organizers. The aerodynamic advantages of the streamlined position are tangible, and a more forward position of the rider facilitates pedaling while in this flat-back posture. Modifying road bicycles to place the rider forward must be done carefully, however, because handling can be compromised when weight is shifted forward on a standard road frame.

Bike fit is part science and part art. The various methods of setting saddle position are useful steps to achieving a saddle position within a centimeter or two of the probable rider-specific ideal. Trial and error involving on-the-road testing, preferably with a power meter, will dictate further refinements to saddle position. A comfortable yet powerful position is the goal.

The effects of hill climbing and drafting on cycling power output must be appreciated. Weight-saving measures benefit cyclists on hills, and drafting, when legal, can lead to power savings of up to 40 percent. The smart triathlete can use this information to improve race strategy, race course and type selection, and even training program design.

The author's experience is that triathletes, as athletes, actively seek out scientific information concerning their sport and freely explore techniques to improve performance. As scientists we are heartened to recognize that research findings concerning the cycling leg of triathlons are actively consumed and considered by triathletes and triathlon coaches. As Dr. Chester Kyle, renowned cycling scientist and aerodynamicist said regarding cycling science directions, "Improvements in cycling technology and performance advancements are the result of evolutionary processes, not revolutionary processes." Triathletes as cyclists will continue to evolve, closely tracking emerging scientific findings, and will undoubtedly figure out how to go faster than ever before.

CHAPTER 9

For the Run

—George M. Dallam, PhD

Numerous factors influence running performance and injury resistance beyond training and running technique. These items include the surfaces chosen for training and racing, the types of shoes worn (or not), the use or disuse of orthotics in shoes, and the conditions of the environment including temperature, humidity, presence of pollutants, and altitude. Awareness and an appropriate decision-making process regarding these variables can enhance both the training process and the performance outcome.

Running Surfaces

Although the choice of running surfaces used for training may seem either mundane or irrelevant, the surface is in fact important to a successful training and racing outcome. In particular, this choice can influence training performance, race specificity and the transfer of training, and the potential for overuse and acute injury occurring because of the training process.

Softer Surfaces

A widely held notion is that natural surfaces such as dirt and grass are easier on the body than harder surfaces such as asphalt (on roadways and recreation trails) and concrete (on sidewalks and some roadways and trails; see figure 9.1). But during running we tune our muscle activity (create a level of tension or stiffness) to minimize muscle vibration at impact and presumably to reduce damage to the muscle fibers.[1] In other words, we adapt how we use the body as a spring by varying muscle tension to absorb force effectively for a variety of surface characteristics. This modulation of the impact forces means that there are not large differences in impact between different surfaces.

As a result, it has been hypothesized that any variation in impact forces across varying surfaces is not significant to injury potential.[2] Rather, we simply change our running mechanics by varying muscle tension and the resulting flexion of our joints under load to accommodate variations in surface and midsole hardness. Impact forces on surfaces of varying hardness are thus comparable.[3]

▶ **Figure 9.1**   Different running surfaces do not vary significantly in their effects on the body.

Therefore, in practical terms, a triathlete can generally adapt effectively to running on a variety of surfaces.

Harder Surfaces

Harder surfaces are less resilient (return less energy), meaning that our springlike muscle and joint structure must work harder to maintain acceptable impact forces. In such conditions (running on concrete or a hard track, for instance) muscle contraction levels and stiffness must be higher to create the appropriate damping effect.[4] An efficient runner loses little energy, and runners can run faster than they can on softer surfaces such as dirt or natural grass (see figure 9.2). Faster running, however, causes higher impact forces, higher peak muscle activations, and greater fatigue.[5]

▶ **Figure 9.2** Faster running produces higher impact forces, higher peak muscle activation, and greater fatigue.

Resilient Surfaces

Highly resilient surfaces allow a runner to regain energy with each step, allowing for a reduction in muscle activity at a given speed.[6, 7] Think of bouncing on a trampoline in comparison with jumping up and down on the ground. Of course, this action requires that our movements match the movements of the surface to maximize energy return with each step. Too much resilience can hinder running speed by forcing our exchange of supports to occur too slowly. For example, have you ever tried to run on a trampoline?

Examples of optimally resilient surfaces that match typical running stride rates include wooden tracks and the newest versions of synthetic turf, which are infused with rubber particles. Treadmills often offer a spring-loaded deck, which can be viewed as a highly resilient surface as well. Such conditions produce running that is easy on the body and can be the fastest if running stride rate matches surface resiliency.

Finally, soft energy-absorbing (with minimal return) surfaces such as sand do not promote the springlike behavior of efficient running. Such surfaces minimize ground reaction impact forces but also dramatically slow running speed and increase metabolic effort substantially by reducing elastic energy return.[8]

Practical Applications

Several practical applications come to mind. First is the need for training specificity. A triathlete who races on hard surfaces should train adequately on such surfaces at race speeds to minimize fatigue in racing conditions. From an injury-prevention perspective, large volumes of slower paced training can then be carried out on optimally resilient or softer surfaces such as dirt trails, grass, and artificial turf to minimize accumulated fatigue. Those adjusting to barefoot running may find the rubberized artificial turf optimal for early adaptation. Finally, running speed may be optimized by using appropriately tuned resilient surfaces for speed work.

Additional concern in selecting running surfaces include the regularity and incline of the surface and the effect of impact forces on foot strike hemolysis, the loss of red blood cells that results from each impact. Increased hemolysis further increases the need to replace red blood cells thereby adding additional risk of anemia. Although extended aerobic running appears to induce hemolysis, the irregularity of natural grass surfaces increases this to a greater degree than more evenly developed artificial surfaces such as asphalt.[9] In addition, the greater impact forces associated with downhill running increase the rate of hemolysis in comparison with flat and uphill running.[10]

Combining downhill and uphill speed work has been demonstrated to create a greater positive influence on speed improvement than simply running fast on flat surfaces (see figure 9.3).[11] Performing fast race-pace training

▶ **Figure 9.3** Hill running during training has been shown to improve running speed.

increases the rate of hemolysis and muscle inflammation in comparison with slower running, although surface types (grass versus asphalt) no longer appear to matter.[12] Finally, running on surfaces that are canted sideways has been shown to induce distinct muscle activation changes,[13] likely resulting in mediolateral (side-to-side) changes in both posture and running biomechanics if pursued habitually or without balanced compensation (running equally on cants in the opposing direction).

The main applications of this information are found in the need to assess iron status in those who pursue a complex approach to run training including a variety of levels of running speed and the use of uphill and downhill training, as well as either to avoid or to counterbalance canted-surface running.

Running Shoes

The paradigm that exists around the use of specialized running shoes reflects the belief system that doing so will prevent chronic running injuries and improve performance. But the scientific evidence can be viewed as suggesting the opposite.[14, 15, 16, 17]

A 2009 review of the available scientific literature addressing the prescription of running shoes to prevent overuse injuries concludes that this practice is not evidence based.[15] Further, the available scientific evidence on running without shoes illustrates a lower level of running injury among populations who are unshod in comparison with those who wear shoes habitually, suggesting that successful adaptations to barefoot running may be more effective in the prevention of injury than the wearing of specialty running shoes.[16]

Studies on Running Barefoot

In a review of the literature on running barefoot published in 2001,[17] the author concludes that the use of specialized running shoes can be a negative factor in the development of some injuries including ankle sprain and plantar fasciitis. He states that ankle sprains may be increased either by decreasing awareness of foot position or by increasing the twisting torque on the ankle during a stumble, and that plantar fasciitis and other chronic injuries of the lower limb may be increased by modifying the transfer of shock to muscles and supporting structures. Further, he adds that running without shoes offers concern for puncture wounds, bruising, thermal injury, and overuse injury during the adaptation period. Finally, he observes that running shoes play an important protective role on some courses, in extreme weather, and with certain pathologies of the lower limb.[17] Consequently, the decision to wear or not wear specialty running shoes is neither clear cut nor simple. Triathletes interested in gaining the potential benefits of running barefoot or in minimalist shoes should consider multiple factors including their own running history, biomechanics, and typical running surfaces used. In addition, any change away from conventional running shoes should be made gradually.

In regard to the performance-enhancing potential of running without shoes, clear experimental data illustrate that running economy is improved in the range of 2 to 4 percent as a result of both reduced weight on the foot and altered running biomechanics that are likely to increase elastic energy return[18] (see figure 9.4). Running shoes, by contrast, absorb energy that is not returned to the musculoskeletal system for forward propulsion and are therefore less economical than running without shoes.[18]

▶ **Figure 9.4** Running barefoot may improve running economy.

Advantages of Training With Shoes

In the real world of racing and training, the potential for improved performance from running with shoes in comparison with running without shoes might come from several avenues including

- enhanced energy return versus absorption,
- improved stance stability because of the external friction characteristics of the shoe,
- reductions in impact forces and stiffness during stance to reduce muscular fatigue over time, and
- reduced anxiety in relation to landing impacts in terrain with uneven surfaces or rocks.

Reviews of the available literature on the energetics of running with shoes suggest that effective mechanisms to enhance energy return to meaningful levels are not yet in existence in running shoe technology.[19] Rather, running shoes have been designed primarily to absorb energy.[19] Consequently, the best approach for performance improvement by this mechanism that is currently available is most likely to be found by using shoes with minimal cushioning and the lowest weight possible to minimize energy absorption.

Further, relatively stiff midsoles in the ball of the foot appear to minimize energy loss through flexion of the metatarsal phalangeal joints (the toes).[20] Cross country spikes, for example, accomplish this by virtue of the relatively stiff plate necessary under the ball of the foot to provide a base for the installation of the spikes.

The enhancement of external friction characteristics is effectively accomplished by the selection of shoe outsoles appropriate for the nature of the surface run on, including minimal or no lugging for road shoes in optimal conditions, increased lugging for loose dirt and slippery road conditions, and spikes for conditions such as grass and ice.

The effective reduction of impact forces is accomplished primarily by alterations in running biomechanics and muscle forces and is less affected by running shoe cushioning.[21, 22] Consequently, the use of highly cushioned shoes is more likely to create a performance disadvantage when running on harder surfaces. A preferred strategy is to adapt to running on such surfaces in the shoes intended for racing.

All runners have a level of protection to which they have both adapted and habituated that likely provides them with the confidence to run at the speeds to which they are adapted. Protection may range from a barefoot condition to the wearing of heavily cushioned shoes, and the conditions of running may vary from the most compliant rubberized turf to rocky or hard terrain covered with small obstacles. Although the concept has not been scientifically studied, exceeding our current habituated behavior is likely to induce anxiety and alter running mechanics in a way that reduces speed. To embrace this concept, imagine the effect of running over broken glass.

Recommendations

Overall, the shoes most likely to provide the best performance will be as lightweight as possible, relatively stiffer in the area of the ball of the foot, equipped with the appropriate outsole to suit conditions, and designed not to inhibit the normal actions of barefoot running. In multisport competition such shoes should also be relatively easy to pull on bare feet while standing. Of course, such a shoe must be progressively adapted to in training and adequately cushioned to provide the psychological confidence at foot strike necessary for the full expression of individual running technique at racing speed. For some relatively small number of people in a modern population, this guideline does not rule out the concept of running without shoes in certain conditions.

A conservative application of this knowledge, in consideration of the lack of scientific data that directly reflect modern conditions in developed societies, being that the vast majority of triathletes have grown up wearing shoes and running in specialty running shoes, is that any transition to lighter weight, less cushioned, less supportive footwear should be done with extreme caution and a slow patient progression.

Orthotics

Orthotics are custom-made insole appliances often prescribed by physicians to assist in overcoming running- and walking-related chronic injuries. Such appliances range from minimalistic, soft support systems to full-foot semi-rigid systems. The intent of such devices is to support the foot through its longitudinal and transverse arches in either their current condition or an idealized condition.

The original intent of orthotic devices was to limit the process of pronation, which occurs in the ankle and foot as a means of absorbing shock upon foot strike, to align the rest of the body properly during locomotion. Excessive pronation was thought to predispose a runner to a variety of lower-body injuries. The occurrence of such injuries rose nearly exponentially during the increased participation of people in recreational running during the running boom of the 1970s and 1980s.[23]

But we have since learned that pronation is a necessary function and that attempts to control it through shoe construction and orthotic devices may unproductive over time for many runners.[24] The more conservative approach advocated recently is to prescribe orthotics to those for whom there are clear rationales for treating specific injuries such as plantar fasciitis.[25] A review of the variety of potential applications of orthotics found them to be generally favorable, particularly for pain management.[26] Further, the use of orthotics in a prophylactic manner in a military population undergoing basic training, a situation known to produce extremely high injury rates, reduced injury occurrence in the treatment group to a third of that in the control group among recruits considered at increased risk for injury.[27]

Another rationale for the use of orthotics in sport and physical activity is the reduction of energy use. In other words, if the orthotic device aligns skeletal movements in a productive way, muscle activations and oxygen consumption should be reduced.[28] This theory, however, has not been supported in the scientific literature. A mid-1980s study of running economy comparing conditions when unshod, when shod, and when shod with orthotics found no improvement with orthotics and higher oxygen cost in general when wearing shoes. The same study found less angular displacement of the knee in the barefoot condition as well.[29]

In summary, orthotics should not be considered as performance-enhancing devices for running. Rather, their use should proceed from individual diagnosis and custom fitting after changes in training, running biomechanics, and footwear have proved inadequate to resolve specific overuse injury issues known to be treatable with orthotics. Finally, the use of orthotics may also be warranted in short-term training situations in which the normal rates of progression are likely to be violated.

Environmental Conditions and Running

Triathletes race across a variety of environmental conditions in temperature, humidity, altitude, and pollution level. Extremes of temperature and humidity negatively influence endurance-performance capability and exercise safety, but triathletes can reduce concerns and improve performance in such conditions by using acclimatization or acclimation methods in training. Increased altitude exposure also reduces performance capability, an effect that can be negated to some degree by using training acclimatization and acclimations. Further, such training strategies may offer performance benefits even when competing in optimal conditions. Pollutants, on the other hand, serve only to inhibit performance capability and exacerbate breathing difficulties, so avoidance strategies become important.

Temperature and Humidity

Increasing ambient temperature beyond some optimal range inhibits running performance. Two recent studies examining historical race data show that marathon racing performance begins to degenerate at 5 degrees Celsius (41 degrees Fahrenheit) and continues to degenerate further through the available data at 25 degrees Celsius (77 degrees Fahrenheit). This loss in performance occurs to a progressively greater degree with lower-performing runners.[30, 31]

Even greater performance decrements at higher temperatures are certain to occur with the additional concern for heat-induced illness including heat stroke and heat exhaustion. In triathlon, in which the running portion may occur at temperatures above 35 degrees Celsius (95 degree Fahrenheit),[32] heat injuries are a predominant reason that athletes end up in the medical tent. In multisport this phenomenon is further exaggerated by prior dehydration that occurs during the swimming and cycling legs of the event.[33]

A study that examined the occurrence of heat-related injuries in both an early season and a later season triathlon event illustrates the large reduction in heat-related injuries that occur after changing general environmental conditions later in the racing season have allowed heat acclimatization to occur.[32] Although most heat illness prevention strategies focus on taking in fluids during the race, wearing optimal clothing, and slowing the pace appropriately for the conditions,[33] prior heat acclimatization or acclimation may be even more critical to successful performance in the heat.

Acclimatization refers to the process of adapting to environmental conditions by living in them naturally. This strategy is problematic for most athletes because they must move to a new training location for a period of days to weeks and suffer a loss in performance capability while completing the adaptive process. In addition, they may not even experience positive adaptations beyond that which occurs through training alone.[34] Further, the process is difficult to control in terms of progressively increasing exposures.

Acclimation refers to the process of increasing tolerance using manmade conditions. This approach allows the minimum necessary progressive exposures so as to minimize the detrimental effect of the process on current training. In addition, acclimation can be carried out in the triathlete's home location. A recent review of such practices concludes that heat acclimation can be effective in 5 or fewer days, may be manipulated to produce a more significant response than natural acclimatization, and is more likely to be beneficial even in already well-trained athletes.[35]

Practical strategies for implementing heat and humidity acclimation in running include using treadmill running with controlled heat and humidity levels indoors, using heavier clothing in normal ambient conditions, and using passive exposures through devices such as hot tubs or saunas. The advantage of the third approach is that normal training intensities can be maintained by training in more optimal conditions while heat acclimation proceeds passively. Concern for adequate fluid replacement and the minimization of increases in body core temperature should always be exercised.

Altitude

Increased altitude and the resulting reduction in barometric pressure and oxygen availability produce decrements in maximal oxygen uptake at as little as 300 meters (984 feet) above sea level in well-trained athletes. This reduction in oxygen uptake increases linearly with increasing altitude through the available measurements at 2,800 meters (9,200 feet).[36] With the increasing amount of competition in multisport events, such as off-road triathlons, occurring at altitudes well above sea level, strategies for minimizing the deleterious effect of increased altitude become important for many athletes. Prior acclimatization to altitude clearly improves altitude performance by reducing this deficit.[37] Further, it appears that even as few as seven intermittent exposures to increased altitude can significantly reduce the performance decrement.[38]

The effects of altitude acclimatization on performance at sea level are less clear cut.[39] Acclimatization to moderate altitudes of 2,000 to 2,500 meters is likely to increase maximal oxygen carrying capacity. But running power output or training velocities may be hampered by reduced oxygenation levels, particularly when efforts extend beyond 1 to 2 minutes. Over an extended period this effect is likely to offset any gains made in oxygen carrying capacity when competing at sea level. This outcome appears to result from a loss in peripheral muscle adaptations that facilitate faster running at sea level if high-quality training at altitude is not addressed.

With the advent of what is called the high–low training model, whereby athletes live at moderate altitudes and incorporate training in conditions that allow for sea-level work output, this problem has been largely rectified. A general review of the literature addressing the high–low altitude training model suggests that an average performance improvement of 1 to 2 percent, maintainable for up to 3 weeks upon return to sea level, is possible beyond that which can be accomplished with an optimal training program alone.[40] Success using such a model has been demonstrated at both 3,000 meters and 5,000 meters of running.[41]

Criteria suggested necessary to make this model effective in marathoners are as follows: 20 or more hours a day of natural environmental exposure at altitudes ranging from 2,100 to 2,500 meters per day for 4 weeks combined with appropriate higher-velocity low-altitude or hyperoxic training. Further, athletes attempting to adapt successfully to such training should ensure that their iron stores are adequate.[42] Producing adequate training velocities for the low-altitude training has been accomplished by using supplemental oxygen, travel to lower altitudes, and shortened training intervals whereby sea-level speeds can be maintained.[37, 39, 40, 42] Also proposed is a more complex scheme that combines low-altitude training with high supra-threshold training completed in short interval fashion.[43]

For all practical purposes several methods of implementing this model exist. These include habitual residence at moderate altitude combined with supplemental oxygen training on treadmills, habitual or part-year residence at moderate altitudes with interspersed travel to lower altitudes for high-quality training, constant shifting of training locations between moderate altitudes and sea-level locations in 3- to 4-week periods, and periodic moderate-altitude camps typically preceding periods of intensive training at sea level before major competitions.

In summary, increased altitude compromises endurance performance, although the compromise can be minimized by prior acclimatization. Longer-term acclimatization to altitude can also be used to improve sea-level performance as long as exposures are adequate and a high–low training model is used.

Pollution

Before the Beijing Olympic Games, the United States Olympic Committee conducted a scientific symposium that had the primary purpose of helping coaches and athletes prepare for competition in one of the most polluted cities in the world in recognition of the importance of this topic. The pernicious effect of both acute and chronic forms of air pollution results in both performance decrements[44] and the potential for destructive changes to respiratory health.[45, 46]

Considering that exercise can increase the rate of ventilation 10-fold or more in comparison with resting ventilation, while simultaneously encouraging an oral breathing route that delivers largely unfiltered air to the lungs, it is not surprising that air pollutants have a powerful effect on human physiology. Recently, an increase in exercise-induced bronchospasm among nonasthmatic athletes has been identified, further illustrating the chronic effects of high levels of ventilation and the inhalation of airborne irritants and chemicals.[47] Current treatments emphasize a pharmacological approach,[47] but additional preventative strategies should be considered as well.

The primary polluting gas of concern is carbon monoxide, a by-product of the incineration of gasoline and tobacco products as well as many industrial processes. Carbon monoxide directly binds to hemoglobin, competing successfully with oxygen to reduce oxygenation. Consequently, one important strategy is to avoid training where people smoke and drive cars, as well as in industrial areas. A Canadian study conducted in Toronto concluded that carbon monoxide levels were lowest before 7:00 a.m. and after 8:00 p.m. and highest during morning rush hour. The study further suggested the prevention strategy of exercising indoors during periods of high pollution or when conducting the most intense training to minimize carbon monoxide exposure[48] (see figure 9.5).

Of further concern is the airborne fine-particulate matter associated with incineration or dust in the air. Exercise has been shown to increase the deposition of this material in the lung by 4.5 fold.[49] Avoiding this problem requires the same strategies mentioned previously as well as wearing a mouth filter or adapting to nasal breathing during exercise training.

Addressing the problems created by air pollution for triathletes requires a multidimensional avoidance strategy:

1. Avoid training in areas of high vehicular traffic.
2. Avoid training outdoors during periods of high vehicular traffic.

3. Conduct high-ventilation training in the areas available where pollution is lowest, often indoors.

4. Use filter masks, perform nasal breathing, or reduce ventilation as able if exposed to high concentrations of particulate matter in the air, as in a dust storm or smoke.

▶ **Figure 9.5** Consider running indoors on a treadmill to avoid pollution exposure.

Conclusion

A variety of environmental factors and equipment options influence both performance and injury resistance in running, including temperature, humidity, altitude, and pollution levels along with the selection of running surfaces and shoes.

Although most triathletes can successfully adapt to a variety of running surfaces without increasing injury risk, to develop speed, they should seek optimal running surfaces that are resilient but do not absorb too much force. Applying conventional wisdom regarding the utility of dirt trail running to limit fatigue comes at the cost of the slower running that this approach will necessitate. The incorporation of uphill and downhill running along with running at higher speeds requires attention to maintaining serum iron levels. Running on banked surfaces requires altered muscle-activation patterns that likely will change running biomechanics over time. These surfaces should be avoided or counterbalanced as able.

Ideal running shoes can increase performance and improve injury resistance. Such shoes will be lightweight, minimally cushioned, and lacking the gait control features present in many modern running shoes. The use of such shoes, however, requires a slow and patient progression from current running footwear. Orthotic use should be limited to diagnostic prescription for specific running-related injuries when training and biomechanical modifications have proved unsuccessful.

Heat acclimation strategies should be used to improve performance and deter heat injury when competing in hot and humid conditions. Altitude acclimatization should be used before competitions at altitudes higher than the triathlete's altitude of residence. A high–low altitude training model can maximize performance at sea level.

Airborne gaseous pollutants and particulate-matter intake should be minimized through avoidance strategies to ensure maximum performance potential and minimize the potential to develop respiratory problems associated with exercise.

CHAPTER 10

Triathlon Training Technologies

—Hunter Allen

Technological advancements in recent years have made lives easier and simpler and have even advanced knowledge about training. For technology to be useful to triathletes and coaches, it needs to help them become faster and stronger and increase their stamina. If technology is truly a breakthrough tool, it will help triathletes achieve their goals in a shorter time and with less effort. Many technological tools can do this, and triathletes and coaches should learn to use and integrate these tools into their triathlon training and racing. This chapter introduces the most current and useful training tools in the marketplace today.

Improving Training Through Technology

One of the most important advances in technology with all electronic training devices (GPS, power meters, heart rate monitors, and so on) is that each now records a complete history of every workout second by second. These recordings have fundamentally changed how triathletes train, giving them the ability to review every training run, ride, and race and to analyze the data for signs of improvement. Triathletes can learn many things through the scientific method, which incorporates observation, hypothesis testing, data collection, and conclusions about what is effective and what is ineffective. Training with these devices can help triathletes learn their strengths and weaknesses, their relative fitness as related to themselves and to others, the effectiveness of their training regimens, the quickness of their response to training, the way in which they should pace energy expenditure, and ways to plan and predict peak performance. Of course, triathletes can learn many other things along the way—these are only the highlights.

All coaches and triathletes are looking for improvement. In doing so, they constantly consider what they can change to improve their training—whether they should increase their volume, adjust the training frequency for one of the disciplines, train the $\dot{V}O_2$max energy system more or less, and more.

The primary question is always, "Should the triathlete change something?" If a technology tool isn't answering that fundamental question, then it's not an effective tool.

Keep this fundamental question in mind when examining each of the tools used in triathlon. Of course, a triathlete may already possess an effective tool but not have enough knowledge to use it effectively. The coach and triathlete must learn how to do this by doing research using a book like this or possibly by hiring a coach to shorten the learning process.

Heart Rate Monitors

Heart rate monitors (HRM) are ubiquitous in the endurance sports world. They are relatively inexpensive, give the user some basic feedback on exertion level, and allow the user to understand his response to a training dose and establish training zones, which can be used to help direct training.

Understanding the Limits of Heart Rate Monitors

Heart rate is only a response to a training dose. A heart rate monitor does not quantify training load or work, and understanding that distinction is important. Heart rate is the dependent variable in the equation, and many factors affect it, such as heat, humidity, fatigue level, number of hours slept the night before, hydration status, and even level of excitement. If heart rate reaches 160 beats per minute (bpm), it could mean that a dog chased the runner down the road or that the runner was doing a 20-minute threshold interval. It could also mean that the triathlete is just standing at the start line and anxious about beginning the race.

The other key understanding about heart rate is that it lags behind effort. Heart rate can lag up to 30 seconds behind the current effort, and this presents a couple of problems:

- First, it means that triathletes are constantly chasing the perfect heart rate number—overshooting it, easing off, going hard again to get it back where it should be, and repeating this process over and over, which creates an inconsistent rhythm and suboptimal effort.

- Second, for shorter efforts, heart rate is largely irrelevant because in many cases effort is already over before heart rate even begins rising. A peak heart rate could be achieved after the effort is finished.

Although heart rate is not the perfect training tool because it tells only half the story, even knowing half the story is better than not knowing any of it.

Establishing a Training Zone

A testing protocol to establish training zones is an important first step. The testing protocol must be a maximal sustained effort long enough for heart rate to stabilize and for the noise, or small fluctuations, to be eliminated during the test itself. This test also needs to be done on a relatively flat course or steady climb to avoid downhills that help triathletes rest and lower their heart rate. The test must be done at the maximal, sustained effort for at least 20 minutes; 30 minutes would be even better because a longer time will better account for the initial effort.

The average heart rate of the last 10 or 20 minutes of the test will be a good number to represent threshold heart rate and establish training zones. Each of the many training zone systems has its positives and negatives. One of the best is Joe Friel's zones, first introduced in *The Triathlete's Training Bible*.[1] Friel's cycling heart rate zones are listed in table 10.1.

Thousands of cyclists and triathletes have used these zones because Friel recognized how big the difference is between the perceived exertions of the athlete and heart rate as the athlete approaches threshold. The difference between riding or running just below threshold, just at threshold, and then pushing to just above it is a large one from the perceived exertion standpoint, but not from the pure heart rate number standpoint. The difference might be only five or six beats, but there is a world of difference in how it feels. Physiological changes occur in that narrow window as well.

Clearly separating these areas is an important and necessary component in learning to train in the proper zone. Note also that a triathlete will likely have to deal with two sets of zones, one for cycling and one for running. Generally, in running the heart rate will be higher because more of the upper body is engaged in the activity than in cycling. In most circumstances a triathlete's running threshold heart rate is about four or five beats above her cycling threshold heart rate, but triathletes need to do a running test along with a cycling test to quantify the difference between how the heart responds to both sports. Joe Friel's running heart rate zones are in table 10.2.[2]

Using a Monitor for Pacing

Pacing is an important part of triathlon, and using a HRM for this purpose is a practical and simple way to help accomplish goals. Many triathlon coaches use heart rate as a governor in Ironman distance races to prevent overexertion during the bike leg and to compensate for heat and hydration issues. This approach may or may not be a good idea, depending on the individual triathlete. Based on the fitness level of the triathlete, the percentage of threshold heart rate should be adjusted for the distance of the race.

For example, a strong age-group triathlete will be able to hold 87 to 90 percent of threshold heart rate (*not* max HR) for a half-Ironman quite easily

Table 10.1   Cycling Heart Rate Zones

Zone 1	Zone 2	Zone 3	Zone 4	Zone 5a	Zone 5b	Zone 5c
<109	109–122	123–128	129–136	137–140	141–145	146+
<110	110–123	124–129	130–137	138–141	142–146	147+
<110	110–124	125–130	131–138	139–142	143–147	148+
<111	111–125	126–130	131–139	140–143	144–147	148+
<112	112–125	126–131	132–140	141–144	145–148	149+
<113	113–126	127–132	133–141	142–145	146–149	150+
<113	113–127	128–133	134–142	143–145	146–150	151+
<114	114–128	129–134	135–143	144–147	148–151	152+
<115	115–129	130–135	136–144	145–148	149–152	153+
<116	116–130	131–136	137–145	146–149	150–154	155+
<117	117–131	132–137	138–146	147–150	151–155	156+
<118	118–132	133–138	139–147	148–151	152–156	157+
<119	119–133	134–139	140–148	149–152	153–157	158+
<120	120–134	135–140	141–149	150–153	154–158	159+
<121	121–134	135–141	142–150	151–154	155–159	160+
<122	122–135	136–142	143–151	152–155	156–160	161+
<123	123–136	137–142	143–152	153–156	157–161	162+
<124	124–137	138–143	144–153	154–157	158–162	163+
<125	125–138	139–144	145–154	155–158	159–163	164+
<126	126–138	139–145	146–155	156–159	160–164	165+
<127	127–140	141–146	147–156	157–160	161–165	166+
<128	128–141	142–147	148–157	158–161	162–167	168+
<129	129–142	143–148	149–158	159–162	163–168	169+
<130	130–143	144–148	149–159	160–163	164–169	170+
<130	130–143	144–150	151–160	161–164	165–170	171+
<131	131–144	145–151	152–161	162–165	166–171	172+
<132	132–145	146–152	153–162	163–166	167–172	173+
<133	133–146	147–153	154–163	164–167	168–173	174+
<134	134–147	148–154	155–164	165–168	169–174	175+
<135	135–148	149–154	155–165	166–169	170–175	176+
<136	136–149	150–155	156–166	167–170	171–176	177+
<137	137–150	151–156	157–167	168–171	172–177	178+
<138	138–151	152–157	158–168	169–172	173–178	179+
<139	139–151	152–158	159–169	170–173	174–179	180+
<140	140–152	153–160	161–170	171–174	175–180	181+
<141	141–153	154–160	161–171	172–175	176–181	182+
<142	142–154	155–161	162–172	173–176	177–182	183+
<143	143–155	156–162	163–173	174–177	178–183	184+
<144	144–156	157–163	164–174	175–178	179–184	185+
<145	145–157	158–164	165–175	176–179	180–185	186+
<146	146–158	159–165	166–176	177–180	181–186	187+

Zone 1	Zone 2	Zone 3	Zone 4	Zone 5a	Zone 5b	Zone 5c
<147	147–159	160–166	167–177	178–181	182–187	188+
<148	148–160	161–166	167–178	179–182	183–188	189+
<149	149–160	161–167	168–179	180–183	184–190	191+
<150	150–161	162–168	169–180	181–184	185–191	192+
<151	151–162	163–170	171–181	182–185	186–192	193+
<152	152–163	164–171	172–182	183–186	187–193	194+
<153	153–164	165–172	173–183	184–187	188–194	195+
<154	154–165	166–172	173–184	185–188	189–195	196+
<155	155–166	167–173	174–185	186–189	190–196	197+
<156	156–167	168–174	175–186	187–190	191–197	198+
<157	157–168	169–175	176–187	188–191	192–198	199+
<158	158–169	170–176	177–188	189–192	193–199	200+
<159	159–170	171–177	178–189	190–193	194–200	201+
<160	160–170	171–178	179–190	191–194	195–201	202+
<161	161–171	172–178	179–191	192–195	196–202	203+
<162	162–172	173–179	180–192	193–196	197–203	204+
<163	163–173	174–180	181–193	194–197	198–204	205+
<164	164–174	175–181	182–194	195–198	199–205	206+

Table 10.2 Running Heart Rate Zones

Zone 1	Zone 2	Zone 3	Zone 4	Zone 5a	Zone 5b	Zone 5c
<120	120–126	127–133	134–139	140–143	144–149	150+
<120	120–127	128–134	135–140	141–144	145–150	151+
<121	121–129	130–135	136–141	142–145	146–151	152+
<122	122–130	131–136	137–142	143–146	147–152	153+
<123	123–131	132–137	138–143	144–147	148–153	154+
<124	124–132	133–138	139–144	145–148	149–154	155+
<125	125–133	134–139	140–145	146–149	150–155	156+
<125	125–134	135–140	141–146	147–150	151–156	157+
<126	126–135	136–141	142–147	148–151	152–157	158+
<127	127–135	136–142	143–148	149–152	153–158	159+
<128	128–136	137–143	144–149	150–153	154–158	159+
<129	129–137	138–144	145–150	151–154	155–159	160+
<130	130–138	139–145	146–151	152–155	156–160	161+
<131	131–139	140–146	147–152	153–156	157–161	162+
<132	132–140	141–147	148–153	154–157	158–162	163+
<132	132–141	142–148	149–154	155–158	159–164	165+
<133	133–142	143–149	150–155	156–159	160–165	166+
<134	134–143	144–150	151–156	157–160	161–166	167+
<135	135–143	144–151	152–157	158–161	162–167	168+

(continued)

Table 10.2, *continued*

Zone 1	Zone 2	Zone 3	Zone 4	Zone 5a	Zone 5b	Zone 5c
<136	136–144	145–152	153–158	159–162	163–168	169+
<137	137–145	146–153	154–159	160–163	164–169	170+
<137	137–146	147–154	155–160	161–164	165–170	171+
<138	138–147	148–155	156–161	162–165	166–171	172+
<139	139–148	149–155	156–162	163–166	167–172	173+
<140	140–149	150–156	157–163	164–167	168–174	175+
<141	141–150	151–157	158–164	165–168	169–175	176+
<142	142–151	152–158	159–165	166–169	170–176	177+
<142	142–152	153–159	160–166	167–170	171–177	178+
<143	143–153	154–160	161–167	168–171	172–178	179+
<144	144–154	155–161	162–168	169–172	173–179	180+
<145	145–155	156–162	163–169	170–173	174–179	180+
<146	146–156	157–163	164–170	171–174	175–180	181+
<146	146–156	157–164	165–171	172–175	176–182	183+
<147	147–157	158–165	166–172	173–176	177–183	184+
<148	148–157	158–166	167–173	174–177	178–184	185+
<149	149–158	159–167	168–174	175–178	179–185	186+
<150	150–159	160–168	169–175	176–179	180–186	187+
<151	151–160	161–169	170–176	177–180	181–187	188+
<152	152–161	162–170	171–177	178–181	182–188	189+
<153	153–162	163–171	172–178	179–182	183–189	190+
<154	154–163	164–172	173–179	180–183	184–190	191+
<155	155–164	165–173	174–180	181–184	185–192	193+
<155	155–165	166–174	175–181	182–185	186–193	194+
<156	156–166	167–175	176–182	183–186	187–194	195+
<157	157–167	168–176	177–183	184–187	188–195	196+
<158	158–168	169–177	178–184	185–188	189–196	197+
<159	159–169	170–178	179–185	186–189	190–197	198+
<160	160–170	171–179	180–186	187–190	191–198	199+
<160	160–170	171–179	180–187	188–191	192–199	200+
<161	161–171	172–180	181–188	189–192	193–200	201+
<162	162–172	173–181	182–189	190–193	194–201	202+
<163	163–173	174–182	183–190	191–194	195–201	202+
<164	164–174	175–183	184–191	192–195	196–202	203+
<165	165–175	176–184	185–192	193–196	197–203	204+
<166	166–176	177–185	186–193	194–197	198–204	205+
<166	166–177	178–186	187–194	195–198	199–205	206+
<167	167–178	179–187	188–195	196–199	200–206	207+
<168	168–178	179–188	189–196	197–198	199–207	208+
<169	169–179	180–189	190–197	198–201	202–208	209+
<170	170–180	181–190	191–198	199–202	203–209	210+
<171	171–181	182–191	192–199	200–203	204–210	211+

Tables 10.1 and 10.2 adapted, by permission, from J. Friel, 2009, *The triathlete's training bible,* 3rd ed. (Boulder, Co: VeloPress), 54, 55.

and still have plenty of energy for the run. An elite professional might hold 91 to 95 percent of threshold heart rate, whereas a beginner will need to be more conservative and keep heart rate lower at around 80 to 85 percent. Of course, many other factors could affect heart rate, so the triathlete should do plenty of training with a HRM to understand this critical relationship. Triathletes and coaches looking for a more reliable tool with less variability should consider a power meter.

Power Meters

A power meter is fast becoming as ubiquitous a training device as the heart rate monitor in the triathlon world, and it has certainly proven its worth over the past 10 years. Power meters measure the amount of cycling work done by the triathlete in watts. Wattage is force (how hard the triathlete pushes on the pedals) multiplied by angular velocity (how fast the triathlete pedals, or cadence). Therefore, the triathlete can create 1,000 watts by pushing very hard in a big gear at a low cadence or by pedaling very quickly but not very forcefully. Wattage is the dose in the training dose-response system, and heart rate is the response. Wattage measures the actual work completed by the rider.

A power meter a near perfect training tool because wattage is not dependent on the weather, amount of sleep, or fatigue. Three hundred watts is 300 watts, whether in the rain, snow, or at the end of a 100-mile (160 km) ride. Three hundred watts as a work rate is the same for everyone regardless of size, weight, and fitness. One of the greatest benefits of measuring wattage is that it tells triathletes exactly their ability to complete work and is easily comparable with others.

Among the reasons to use a power meter are the following:

• **Tracking fitness changes**. A power meter allows triathletes to know with certainty whether fitness is improving and when they have reached a peak. Measuring improvement by tracking speed or heart rate on a bike leaves too many variables to influence it, such as wind, temperature, road surface, elevation profile, packs of riders, and more. With power data, the triathlete knows for certain whether he is improving.

• **Race analysis**. A power meter can help analyze race performance. A coach can easily see when the triathlete burned a match or used too much energy in parts of the race that weren't decisive. Did she make a tactical error in a race but not realize it? Did she pace herself properly?

• **Pinpointing strengths and weaknesses**. With a power meter, a triathlete can analyze performance and training to find out what his natural talents are and whether he should stick with hilly events or flatter ones. By learning his strengths and weaknesses, the triathlete can determine which event is best suited to him and identify any holes in his training so that he can excel in many types of events.

• **Improved interaction between triathlete and coach**. A coach can instantly see what the triathlete is doing in races and training rides and make suggestions to achieve further improvements. A power meter doesn't lie!

• **Optimize training time**. Triathletes who train with a power meter can concentrate on the workload and find extra motivation to improve their efforts. For example, the triathlete who watches average watts drop near the end of a 5-minute effort will likely find additional motivation to achieve a 5-minute wattage goal.

• **Pacing of efforts**. Power meters allow triathletes to pace their effort better in interval workouts, hill climbs, and time trials. By knowing threshold power, triathletes can hold to it like glue in a time trial or hill climb, so they will know that they went as hard as they possibly could.

• **Mobile testing lab**. A power meter allows coaches and triathletes to test on a regular basis, to see quantitatively what areas have improved and what still need work. By testing regularly, the triathlete can better understand potential for improvement while avoiding overtraining. Training is testing, and testing is training. Every training session can be a peak performance.

• **Coordinate sport nutrition for best performance**. Knowing how much work (in kilojoules) triathletes do in training allows postexercise meals to be planned so that energy intake meets energy expenditure. As a result, they can recover faster and be able to train harder sooner.

One of the downfalls of training with a power meter is becoming obsessed with the numbers and forgetting that a personal best is not possible on every ride. The power meter does not lie, so workouts can be mentally challenging when fitness is not as high as desired. Triathletes tend to be critical of themselves, so having a "truth meter" on the bike might not be the best idea for hyper-self-critical triathletes.

Beginning to Use a Power Meter

What should a coach or triathlete do first after purchasing a power meter? Collect data. The first mission is just to ride with the meter on the bike and download every ride. Every ride is important, and every download is key to understanding. The triathlete should not change training for the first week or two and just follow a normal routine while collecting the data.

These downloads will soon begin to give some valuable information on current training: how much time is spent in the new power training zones, at what wattage level the triathlete consistently pedals, what her preferred cadence is, how many kilojoules it takes before she becomes significantly fatigued, and more. In this first step, the goal is to learn some basic things about the triathlete as a cyclist that will apply later in training and help her improve.

Learning the Functional Threshold Power

After becoming accustomed to the device, testing begins. The second step in this process is to learn the triathlete's functional threshold power (FTP). FTP is defined as the highest power that a rider can maintain in a quasi-steady state without fatiguing for approximately 1 hour. When power exceeds FTP, fatigue will occur much sooner, whereas power just below FTP can be maintained considerably longer. Therefore, FTP is the best average watts for a 1-hour time trial.

There are many ways to find a triathlete's FTP, but the best way is just to go out and hammer all out for an hour and see what can be done. This effort is a painful but necessary part of the process. Triathletes will need to test for FTP many times in the future, because this is one of the best ways to see how much they have improved over time.

An alternative field test is to do 20 minutes as hard as possible and then subtract 5 percent. This will give a close approximation of FTP.

Establishing Power Training Levels

The third step is to establish power training levels. After FTP is known, the triathlete can determine power training levels. The power training levels are anchored on the triathlete's FTP; level 4 (in the middle of the 7 levels) is defined at 91 to 105 percent of FTP.[3] With FTP as 100 percent, the rest of the training levels can be determined (see table 10.3). Understanding at what level triathletes are training is critical to creating the training response that they and coaches are looking for. If triathletes want to improve their anaerobic capacity, then intervals should be between 120 and 150 percent of FTP. At this level they will know that they are training at the correct level to induce training adaptation.

Table 10.3 Power Training Levels

Level	Name/purpose	% of threshold power	% of threshold HR	RPE
1	Active recovery	≤55%	≤68%	<2
2	Endurance	56.75%	69.83%	2–3
3	Tempo	76.90%	84.94%	3–4
4	Lactate threshold	91–105%	95–105%	4–5
5	$\dot{V}O_2$max	106–120%	>106%	6–7
6	Anaerobic capacity	121–150%	N/A	>7
7	Neuromuscular power	N/A	N/A	(maximal)

Adapted, by permission, from H. Allen and A. Coggan, 2010, *Training and racing with a power meter*, 2nd ed., (Boulder, Co: VeloPress), 48.

Creating a Power Profile

After establishing training zones, the triathlete can create a power profile. Figuring out the triathlete's relative strengths and weaknesses is the fourth step. In a project with Dr. Andrew Coggan the power profiling chart (table 10.3) was created, initially to help riders compare themselves to the best in the world and with their racing peers. Once created, however, it became an important tool in figuring out the riding style of triathletes and the areas where they need help. Are they better sprinters or time trialists? By comparing wattages with their power profiles, coaches and triathletes can tell exactly what their strengths and weaknesses are.

Unfortunately, figuring out power profiles involves more testing. To establish a power profile, triathletes need to test their best 5-second, 1-minute, and 5-minute wattages. These represent neuromuscular power (level 7), anaerobic capacity (level 6), and $\dot{V}O_2$max (level 5) wattages respectively. To produce the best numbers, the testing should be done on a day when the triathlete is fresh and not tired from a long block of training. The importance of learning a triathlete's power profile cannot be understated. Relative strengths and weaknesses will determine the training plan going forward to attack and improve weaknesses and to monitor the improvement in strengths. For example, a triathlete with a strong $\dot{V}O_2$max (level 5) but poor FTP (level 4) has the potential to improve FTP but has just not trained it sufficiently yet. Understanding a triathlete's power profile will direct the training that best suits upcoming events and addressees the triathlete's specific needs.

Using a Power Meter as a Pacing Tool

One of the most useful things that a triathlete can do with a power meter is to use it as a pacing device. Pacing is incredibly important in triathlons of any distance, and most successful triathletes use a power meter to optimize pacing. Pacing in the swim, on the bike, and in the run is critical, and the longer the races are, the more critical pacing becomes to success.

Pacing is a skill learned through trial-and-error experiences on the training grounds every day and at races. Pacing on the bike can also be learned using a power meter to give an objective, real-time view. The reason that pacing for triathlon is difficult is that for races at the Olympic distance and longer, the perceived exertion at the correct pace is much lower than triathletes know they can do if they were racing in only one event instead of three.

The rating of perceived exertion (RPE) is an important feeling that every triathlete needs to associate with power output. One of the best ways found for triathletes to learn this is by doing progressively longer intervals at different intensities, becoming keenly aware of the feelings associated with each level of intensity.

The key to pacing for triathlons is learning the proper wattage output to maintain for the bike leg and still be able to have a good run leg and then calibrating that with the correct perceived exertion. The problem with this calibration is that RPE changes daily and is affected by sleep, stress, hydration level, and more, just as heart rate is affected by those factors. On race day, RPE will likely be lower than the actual effort. Here a power meter can play a significant role in a triathlete's race.

Table 10.4 helps illustrate the appropriate intensities and pace guidelines for various distances of triathlon races when using a power meter or analyzing pacing skills in postrace analysis.

Table 10.4 Pacing Guidelines for Triathlon Events

Type of triathlon	Distance	Intensity factor (fraction of NP)	Percentage of FTP as a percentage of average power	Corresponding Coggan training level
Sprint	10 km (6.2 mi)	1.03–1.07	100–103%	4
Olympic	40 km (24.8 mi)	0.95–1.00	95–100%	4
Half-Ironman	90 km (56 mi)	0.83–0.87	80–85%	3
Ironman	180 km (112 mi)	0.70–0.76	68–78%	3
Double Ironman	361 km (224 mi)	0.55–0.67	56–70%	2

Pacing at the Proper Percentage of FTP

Triathletes relatively new to triathlon or competing in their first Ironman-distance event are advised to be conservative and maintain a pace between 68 and 71 percent of their FTP. This pace will solidly be in their endurance zone and allow them to ride comfortably and conserve plenty of energy for the run. Triathletes who are more experienced and who have been training consistently for 3 years or more could consider riding between 70 and 74 percent of FTP; this pace should be just intense enough. They will ride quickly and still have energy for the run. The most experienced triathletes and those going for a personal best or for a top placing can safely ride between 75 and 80 percent of FTP and still be able to run hard. Elite triathletes need to be solidly between 80 and 84 percent of their threshold power to be in contention for the win.

Speed Distance Devices

Speed distance devices are another relatively new technology training tool. The latest of these are global positioning system (GPS) watches and swimming accelerometers. GPS watches are excellent tools for triathletes because they display pace on the screen while the triathlete is running so that she can know immediately whether she is running at too fast or slow a pace and then adjust quickly. Along with providing instantaneous pace data, a GPS device records workouts and races in a second-by-second fashion, allowing triathletes to understand whether they are improving by analyzing the data in a training analysis software package such as TrainingPeaks.[4]

Running Devices

Just as with the heart rate monitor and the power meter, triathletes needs to learn their threshold pace for running (FTP, or functional threshold pace) and then use pace zones to train optimally. For runners, the threshold test is a 15-kilometer run, or about 45 minutes of all-out running, to find FTP. Running is much harder on the musculosketal system than cycling is and hence requires only a solid 45-minute test rather than the full hour that a cycling threshold test requires. After the threshold pace is known, athletes can use that number to create running pace zones. A couple of common zone methodologies are available. One of the easiest to understand is Joe Friel's pace zones,[2] which are shown in table 10.5.

Table 10.5 Running Pace Zones in Minutes and Seconds Per Mile Based on Recent 5K or 10K Race Times

5K time	10K time	Zone 1	Zone 2	Zone 3	Zone 4–5a	Zone 5b	Zone 5c
14:15–14:44	30:00–30:59	6:38+	5:52–6:37	5:27–5:51	5:09–5:26	4:37–4:58	4:36–max
14:45–15:14	31:00–31:59	6:50+	6:02–6:49	5:37–6:01	5:18–5:36	4:45–5:06	4:44–max
15:15–15:44	32:00–32:59	7:02+	6:13–7:01	5:47–6:12	5:27–5:46	4:53–5:15	4:52–max
15:45–16:09	33:00–33:59	7:13+	6:23–7:12	5:56–6:22	5:36–5:55	5:01–5:24	5:00–max
16:10–16:44	34:00–34:59	7:25+	6:33–7:24	6:06–6:32	5:45–6:05	5:10–5:33	5:09–max
16:45–17:06	35:00–35:59	7:36+	6:43–7:35	6:15–6:42	5:54–6:14	5:18–5:41	5:17–max
17:07–17:34	36:00–36:59	7:48+	6:54–7:47	6:25–6:53	6:03–6:24	5:26–5:50	5:25–max
17:35–18:04	37:00–37:59	8:00+	7:04–7:59	6:34–7:03	6:12–6:33	5:34–5:59	5:33–max
18:05–18:29	38:00–38:59	8:11+	7:14–8:10	6:44–7:13	6:21–6:43	5:42–6:08	5:41–max
18:30–18:59	39:00–39:59	8:23+	7:24–8:22	6:53–7:23	6:30–6:52	5:50–6:16	5:49–max
19:00–19:29	40:00–40:59	8:34+	7:35–8:33	7:03–7:34	6:39–7:02	5:58–6:25	5:57–max
19:30–19:54	41:00–41:59	8:46+	7:45–8:45	7:12–7:44	6:48–7:11	6:06–6:34	6:05–max
19:55–20:24	42:00–42:59	8:58+	7:55–8:57	7:22–7:54	6:57–7:21	6:14–6:43	6:13–max
20:25–20:49	43:00–43:59	9:09+	8:05–9:08	7:31–8:04	7:06–7:30	6:22–6:51	6:21–max
20:50–21:19	44:00–44:59	9:21+	8:16–9:20	7:41–8:15	7:15–7:40	6:31–7:00	6:30–max
21:20–21:49	45:00–45:59	9:32+	8:26–9:31	7:51–8:25	7:24–7:50	6:39–7:09	6:38–max
21:50–22:14	46:00–46:59	9:44+	8:36–9:43	8:00–8:35	7:33–7:59	6:47–7:17	6:46–max
22:15–22:41	47:00–47:59	9:56+	8:47–9:55	8:10–8:46	7:42–8:09	6:55–7:26	6:54–max
22:42–23:09	48:00–48:59	10:07+	8:57–10:06	8:19–8:56	7:51–8:18	7:03–7:35	7:02–max
23:10–23:37	49:00–49:59	10:19+	9:07–10:18	8:29–9:06	8:00–8:28	7:11–7:44	7:10–max
23:38–24:04	50:00–50:59	10:31+	9:17–10:30	8:38–9:16	8:09–8:37	7:19–7:52	7:18–max
24:05–24:34	51:00–51:59	10:42+	9:28–10:41	8:48–9:27	8:18–8:47	7:27–8:01	7:26–max
24:35–24:59	52:00–52:59	10:54+	9:38–10:53	8:57–9:37	8:27–8:56	7:35–8:10	7:34–max
25:00–25:24	53:00–53:59	11:05+	9:48–11:04	9:07–9:47	8:36–9:06	7:43–8:19	7:42–max
25:25–25:54	54:00–54:59	11:17+	9:58–11:16	9:16–9:57	8:45–9:15	7:52–8:27	7:51–max
25:55–26:29	55:00–55:59	11:29+	10:09–11:28	9:26–10:08	8:54–9:25	8:00–8:36	7:59–max
26:30–26:49	56:00–56:59	11:40+	10:19–11:39	9:36–10:18	9:03–9:35	8:08–8:45	8:07–max
26:50–17:19	57:00–57:59	11:52+	10:29–11:51	9:45–10:28	9:12–9:44	8:16–8:53	8:15–max
27:20–27:44	58:00–58:59	12:03+	10:39–12:02	9:55–10:38	9:21–9:54	8:24–9:02	8:23–max
27:45–28:14	59:00–59:59	12:15+	10:50–12:14	10:04–10:49	9:30–10:03	8:32–9:11	8:31–max
28:15–28:44	60:00–60:59	12:27+	11:00–12:26	10:14–10:59	9:39–10:13	8:40–9:20	8:39–max

Reprinted, by permission, from J. Friel, 2009, *The triathlete's training bible*, 3rd ed. (Boulder, Co: VeloPress), 49.

Training with a GPS device is similar to training with a power meter because the athlete needs to test, assess strengths and weaknesses, understand training zones, develop a training plan around those zones, and finally analyze the data to confirm workout adherence and improvement.

Swimming Accelerometers

Swimming accelerometers are a new entry into the training with technology market and have merit. An accelerometer is a watch that uses motion sensors to record data accurately for every lap that the triathlete swims. The device makes these data easily available for analysis both on the watch screen and by downloading to a computer.

The accelerometer records total training distance, training load, and calories burned in every session. It also captures the structure of every session exactly as the athlete swims it so that coaches get a complete record of every workout performed in the pool. Accelerometers can monitor stroke rate (strokes per minute) and facilitate study of how it varies with distance, training pace, and fatigue. The ability to monitor stroke count on every lap is probably one of the most helpful features of the watch for postworkout analysis. Split times taken on every lap can be used to assess pacing skills.

Some accelerometers have easy-to-use data-transfer and analysis software including a full online training log or diary to record training sessions and data along with full integration with other training analysis software programs, such as TrainingPeaks WKO+. For triathletes who use a power meter on the bike and a GPS or foot pod when running, an accelerometer completes the picture, allowing them to measure complete training load in all three disciplines.

Training Analysis Software

The software takes a training gizmo and turns it into a training tool. Without downloading and analyzing the data, a triathlete has nothing more than an expensive watch or bicycle speedometer. Training analysis allows the triathlete to review individual workouts, look at data over the past season, and develop a clear understanding of the optimal training load.

Each of the training devices mentioned in this chapter comes with its own basic training software that generally downloads and displays one day's worth of data in graphic form. Each workout is important to understand, and the analysis should assure that the proper training zones were addressed, that intervals were completed, and that the correct muscular stress was created to facilitate the greatest training adaptation. By parsing out the individual intervals within the analysis software, a triathlete can begin to understand the training pattern and response to that pattern.

In figure 10.1 a triathlete has completed a set of intervals on the bike that addressed the level 4 power training zone (lactate threshold) and the level 5 zone ($\dot{V}O_2max$), both of which are excellent zones to train for triathletes.

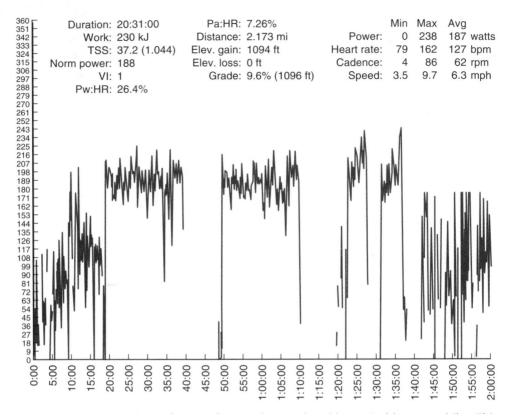

▶ **Figure 10.1** Analysis of a set of intervals completed by a triathlete on a bike. This triathlete completed two 20-minute intervals at threshold and then did two 5-minute $\dot{V}O_2$max intervals to prepare for an upcoming Ironman-distance event.

By using analysis software such as TrainingPeaks WKO+, the triathlete is able to review data over a longer period. WKO+ software houses charts detailing performance improvements, which can be more informative than individual workout results.

One of the most critical charts for a triathlete is the performance management chart. This chart explains the relationship between chronic training load (CTL), or fitness; acute training load (ATL), or fatigue; and training stress balance (TSB), or performance. Critical to peaking or creating a peak of fitness is the balance of fitness and fatigue. On the day that a triathlete wants to peak, fitness should be the highest possible and fatigue should be low enough to create a personal best performance. (See chapter 23 for more on this tapering and peaking concept.)

In figure 10.2 the triathlete has properly peaked for two Ironman-distance events by timing the taper correctly, performing a rational and progressive recovery after the first event, and executing a sane buildup to the next peak.

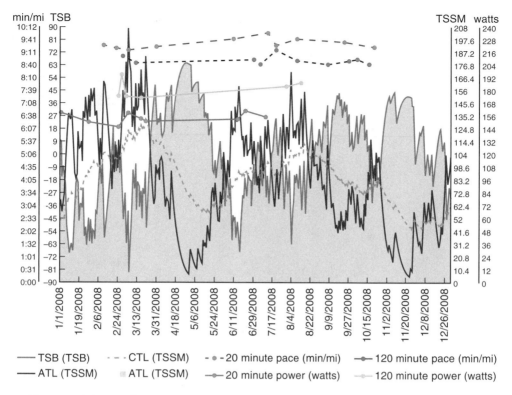

▶ **Figure 10.2** Performance management chart showing proper peaking for two Ironman-distance events. The darker line shows the fitness (CTL), the lighter line shows fatigue (ATL), and the shadow demonstrates the ability to perform (TSB). The solid line is the triathlete's best 10 runs for the year. The dashed line represents the best 10 rides for the year.

Mobile Training Applications

Mobile applications currently provide limited analysis features for triathletes and coaches compared with more robust analysis programs, but they do show merit for improving communication between triathletes and coaches, which is a key component of making appropriate training decisions. Improvements in these apps will likely address these limitations.

Conclusion

Training with technology has become an essential part of triathlon success, and triathletes who monitor their training dose and response have an edge on those who do not. Although technology adds complexity to training, capturing workouts daily and downloading them into training analysis software is highly beneficial to performance. Optimizing training time is one of the greatest benefits of training with technology. Because most triathletes have tight time constraints, technology has to be considered to create the greatest opportunity for personal bests on the bike, in the run, and during the swim.

PART

IV

Physiological Function in Triathlon Training

CHAPTER 11

Aerobic Capacity

—Ross Tucker, PhD

Aerobic capacity is recognized as one of the crucial physiological attributes for success in endurance sport, to the point that it has perhaps been overvalued as a predictor of performance and a marker for training status. Maximal aerobic capacity, expressed as $\dot{V}O_2max$, is measured relatively easily in laboratories and is deemed a good indication of overall cardiovascular fitness. When applied to a large population, $\dot{V}O_2max$ is also a strong predictor of performance, but this predictive power diminishes significantly to the point of being dissociated from performance in a homogenous group of triathletes, because other factors related to the metabolic, neurological, and muscular systems contribute to performance.

The result of this preoccupation with measurement, and the ever-increasing understanding of exercise physiology, means that the concept of $\dot{V}O_2max$ is often misunderstood and overapplied. In this chapter we describe the key concepts of aerobic capacity, including measurement, interpretation, and implications for training and performance.

Historical Perspectives and Measurement of $\dot{V}O_2max$

Maximal oxygen consumption is measured using progressive or incremental exercise trials to exhaustion. Triathletes typically run or cycle at increasing workloads until volitional fatigue occurs, while inspired and expired air are measured. The progressive increase in exercise intensity demands increasing levels of muscle activation and metabolic work. The result is that oxygen consumption increases as a function of intensity. The highest achieved workload as well as the highest oxygen consumption measured are recorded and used to obtain information on the maximal performance and physiological level of the athlete.

Nobel laureate A.V. Hill introduced exercise physiology, and thus coaches and athletes, to the concept of $\dot{V}O_2max$ in 1925.[1] He was able to measure oxygen consumption during running using a method known as the Douglas bag method. Briefly, he ran at a range of progressively increasing speeds while breathing into a large apparatus resembling a backpack connected to his face by a tube and mask. He found that as running speed increased, so too did oxygen use, until he could no longer increase his running speed. He noted that "the oxygen requirement increases continuously as the speed increases, attaining enormous values at the highest speeds: The actual oxygen intake, however, reaches a maximum beyond which no effort can drive it." Hill surmised that the reason for this maximum was "limitations of the circulatory and respiratory system."[1]

Later, Taylor et al. described the presence of a plateau when they observed an increase in $\dot{V}O_2$max of less than 150 milliliters between two successive workloads, and the concept of a $\dot{V}O_2$max plateau was created.[2] Beyond this point, at higher exercise intensities, any further energy requirement would have to be met from oxygen-independent sources, and the theorized anaerobic limit to exercise would be exceeded.

The question over whether exercise performance is limited by the attainment of this plateau in oxygen consumption, or whether the peak in oxygen consumption is in fact limited by other factors, is the subject of much debate in the scientific literature[3] and is not our primary focus here. But two important practical points should be considered, both with implications for the understanding of measurement and application of $\dot{V}O_2$max.

First, the presence of a plateau is actually relatively rare during laboratory tests of $\dot{V}O_2$max (see figure 11.1) and may be the exception rather than the norm. For example, Lucia et al. found that less than half of elite cyclists displayed a plateau[4] and concluded, "In a good number of highly trained humans, the main factor limiting maximal endurance might not necessarily be oxygen-dependent."[4] The prevalence of the plateau has been found to be even lower in Olympic-level runners, and was found in only 12 out of 71 subjects in another study.[5]

Second, tests for $\dot{V}O_2$max terminate despite submaximal levels of muscle activation. That is, muscle fibers remain inactive at the point of volitional exhaustion, which is significant because these inactive fibers could be recruited to continue exercise, with a resultant increase in oxygen consumption. That this does not occur has led to the theory that exercise is terminated by the brain at submaximal levels of muscle activation and that the measured $\dot{V}O_2$ at this point is a consequence, rather than a determinant, of the underlying physiology and performance.[6] For the same reason, the highest oxygen consumption measured in a test to fatigue is sometimes called the $\dot{V}O_2$peak, to distinguish it from a max where the plateau would supposedly be reached.[3]

Regardless of the model or theoretical explanation, the measurement of $\dot{V}O_2$max can provide important information on training status and, potentially, performance levels in triathletes because the peak speed or power output achieved as well as the oxygen measurement are both performance outcomes. Thus, as part of a controlled training program, repeated measurements can be conducted to identify training responses and predict performance.

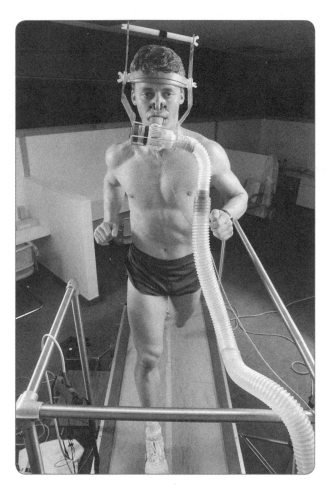

▶ **Figure 11.1** Testing for $\dot{V}O_2$max.

Protocols for Measurement of $\dot{V}O_2$max

A number of protocols exist for the measurement of $\dot{V}O_2$max. The selection of protocol has important implications for the measured aerobic capacity and, perhaps more important, the maximal power output or running speed that is associated with $\dot{V}O_2$max. For example, Lucia et al. used a protocol for elite cyclists that began at a power output of only 25 watts and increased by 25 watts every minute until exhaustion,[4] whereas Hawley and Noakes used a protocol that began at 3.3 watts per kilogram, increased by 50 watts after 2.5 minutes, and increased again by 25 watts every 2.5 minutes.[7] For cyclists who reach 400 watts, both protocols would be expected to last approximately 20 minutes, but the former begins at a significantly lower power output and may be more suitable for sedentary people, whereas the latter entails spending far longer at a given power output, which may facilitate measurement of steady-state physiology during the trial. Hawley and Noakes, using this protocol, established an accurate equation for the prediction of $\dot{V}O_2$max using peak power output:

$$\text{Estimated } \dot{V}O_2\text{max (L/min)} = 0.01141 \times \text{PPO} + 0.435.^{[7]}$$

Padilla et al.[8] have used an intermittent protocol on world-class cyclists, using a starting power output of 110 watts, increasing by 35 watts every 4 minutes, and allowing a 1-minute recovery interval after each stage. This protocol is designed to last approximately 1 hour for elite cyclists. Clearly, this has implications for the measurement of work rates at $\dot{V}O_2$max, as well as the metabolic demand of exercise, and should be borne in mind by coaches and scientists wishing to assess aerobic capacity and performance.

An additional factor to consider for triathlon is the exercise modality used for testing. In the same way that heart rate is affected by exercise modality,[9] $\dot{V}O_2$max measured during running is greater than that measured during cycling and swimming, because of the involvement of a larger muscle mass and the weight-bearing nature of running. (Cross-country skiing is generally considered to produce the highest $\dot{V}O_2$max.) But this result is highly dependent on the state of training, because this influences the ability to achieve the high workloads necessary to produce a higher $\dot{V}O_2$max. For example, a cyclist performing a running protocol would be expected to underperform relative to his performance using a cycling protocol, and vice-versa for runners.

Triathletes may thus have context-dependent aerobic capacity, depending on the method of assessment and state of training within each of the three disciplines at the time of testing. This has important implications for the prescription of training zones based on aerobic capacity.

$\dot{V}O_2$max Benchmarks

Table 11.1 depicts the measured $\dot{V}O_2$max levels in elite triathletes, as well as moderately trained and sedentary people in various sports. Large differences clearly exist between high-performing triathletes and sedentary people. As noted later in this chapter, these differences are partly a result of differences in starting $\dot{V}O_2$max levels (genetically influenced) and partly because of the response to training, which has a genetic component.

Differences in training status make direct comparisons between studies and modalities difficult. In triathletes, $\dot{V}O_2$max values have been found to range between 39 to 49 milliliters per kilogram per minute during tethered swimming, 57 to 61 milliliters per kilogram per minute during cycling, and 61 to 85 milliliters per kilogram per minute during running.[10] These values are marginally lower than values measured in single-event endurance specialists.[11] Males tend to have higher $\dot{V}O_2$max values than females, even when expressed relative to body weight. $\dot{V}O_2$max increases into adulthood, and adolescents have significantly lower aerobic capacity than adults do.

Table 11.1 Varying Levels of $\dot{V}O_2$max

Athlete and level	$\dot{V}O_2$max (ml · kg⁻¹ · min⁻¹)	Reference
Elite male triathletes measured during running	78.5 ± 3.6	12
Elite male triathletes measured during cycling	75.9 ± 5.2	12
Elite junior (<18 yr) triathletes tested during running	67.9 ± 5.9 (males) 56.1 ± 2.4 (females)	13
Junior regional level triathletes	62.7 ± 2.5	14
Elite Tour de France cyclists	72 ± 1.8 with a range from 62.5 to 82.5	15
Elite Tour de France champion	71.5, measured 3 months post Tour	16
Olympic-level runners (middle and long distance)	79.1 ± 0.7 (males) 66.1 ± 1.2 (females)	5
Elite junior swimmers (<18 yr)	61.6 ± 3.6 (males) 52.1 ± 3.6 (females)	13
Sedentary people during running	30.6 ± 7.9	17, 18, 19, 20

Of significance is the observation that a relatively large range of measured $\dot{V}O_2$max values can occur within the elite population, as shown by Lucia et al.[15] in which the $\dot{V}O_2$max of elite cyclists differed by 20 milliliters per kilogram per minute (over 30 percent). As mentioned previously, other factors contribute to performance, such as running economy (see chapter 12) and the ability to sustain a high relative intensity during competition. The result is that $\dot{V}O_2$max is a poor predictor of performance within a relatively homogenous or narrow performance range of individuals.

Aerobic Capacity, Aerobic Metabolism, and Training Responses

Apart from providing an indicator of cardiorespiratory and performance capacities, the measurement of aerobic metabolism during progressive exercise has numerous other important applications. One is the determination of running economy or cycling efficiency (described in chapter 12), and another is to allow the determination of the metabolic cost and fuel utilization during exercise.

As exercise intensity increases, oxygen consumption rises because of the increasing metabolic demand. The oxidation of carbohydrate and fat meets this energy demand and can be estimated based on the measurement of the respiratory exchange ratio, or RER. (Note that this is different from respiratory quotient, or RQ, in that RER is measured at the mouth using expired gases, whereas RQ refers to the measurement taken at the tissue level.) RER is calculated as the ratio of oxygen consumed to carbon dioxide produced and, because of the metabolic reactions involved in the oxidation of carbohydrate and fat, provides an accurate estimate of the relative contribution of each to energy. The exclusive oxidation of carbohydrates results in an RER of 1, whereas the exclusive oxidation of long-chain fatty acids results in an RER of 0.7.

Therefore, when exercise is performed below the anaerobic threshold, RER will range between 0.7 and 1.0. At some point RER rises above 1, reflecting the liberation of carbon dioxide from the body's bicarbonate pool because of acidosis, and is interpreted as an indication of anaerobic metabolism, the point at which the anaerobic threshold has been crossed (see chapter 13). Beyond this point, the estimation of energy use is fraught with difficulty, requiring assumptions or more invasive measurement. As a result, economy and fuel utilization are typically measured at submaximal levels.

Returning to RER, the contribution of fat and carbohydrate to energy metabolism can be estimated using table 11.2. Here, each RER value corresponds to a percentage of energy contributed by both carbohydrate and protein. (Note that these do not factor in protein contributions to energy, which may be a factor for ultraendurance activity.)

For example, at an RER of 0.76, 18.4 percent and 81.6 percent of the energy consumed are from carbohydrate and fat sources, respectively. This can be converted into a caloric equivalent, in which the energy consumption in kilocalories per liter of oxygen is estimated. (At an RER of 0.76, for example, each liter of oxygen contributes 4.751 kilocalories of energy.)

As exercise intensity rises, a larger proportion of energy demand is met by carbohydrate until, at an RER of 1.0, energy is entirely provided by carbohydrate sources. One of the benefits of endurance exercise training is to

Table 11.2 Respiratory Exchange Ratios Showing Fat and Carbohydrate Contributions to Energy Metabolism

RER	Cho %	Fat %	kCal/L O_2
0.7	0	100.0	4.686
0.72	4.8	95.2	4.702
0.74	11.6	88.4	4.727
0.76	18.4	81.6	4.751
0.8	25.2	74.8	4.776
0.82	38.8	61.2	4.801
0.84	45.6	54.4	4.825
0.86	52.4	47.6	4.850
0.88	59.2	40.8	4.899
0.90	66.0	34.0	4.924
0.92	72.8	27.2	4.948
0.94	79.6	20.4	4.973
0.96	86.4	13.6	4.998
0.98	93.2	6.8	5.022
1.0	100.0	0	5.047

improve the body's capacity to oxidize fat as a fuel, which allows higher exercise workloads to be achieved before this point is reached. The metabolic adaptations allowing increased fat oxidation are explained in more detail in chapter 14, but the result is that highly trained triathletes use glycogen at lower rates, which has implications for fatigue and performance (chapter 15). Indeed, the capacity to use fat is one of the crucial attributes that enables ultradistance triathlon performance.

Effects of Training on Aerobic Capacity

Some dispute has arisen about the capacity to increase $\dot{V}O_2$max with training because some studies have shown a large range of responses among individuals. These results may have occurred because of differences in the training status of athletes before the controlled training program, as well as genetic differences among people.[17]

Three large-scale studies have looked at how an aerobic training program can improve $\dot{V}O_2$max in previously sedentary people.[17,19,20] Collectively, the Heritage studies, the DREW study, and SSTRIDE studies have found that a 5-month training program increases $\dot{V}O_2$max by 15.2 percent plus or minus 9.7 percent,[17,19,20] and that further improvements are likely with a longer training period and possibly the introduction of higher intensity training.

But the trainability of aerobic capacity varies significantly among individuals. For example, approximately one in seven people (14 percent) improved $\dot{V}O_2$max by less than 8 percent compared with baseline, whereas 8 percent of the population improved by almost 30 percent.[17]

Genetic Factor

These disparate responses are strongly associated with genes. Using a genomewide association approach, it was found that 21 single-nucleotide polymorphisms, or SNPs (gene variants), account for 49 percent of the trainability of $\dot{V}O_2$max.[17] Those who carried 9 or fewer of the 21 SNPs were found to improve by less than 10 percent, whereas those who carried 19 or more of these alleles improved their $\dot{V}O_2$max by 30 percent.[17] Clearly, the presence of certain SNPs has a strong influence on the response to training and points to the importance of genetic factors, and thus talent identification. It seems reasonable to suggest that those who show a greater improvement in $\dot{V}O_2$max may also show the largest improvements in performance with training.

Effect of Training on $\dot{V}O_2$max

For this reason it is important to recognize that the measurement of $\dot{V}O_2$max involves a performance test. Because oxygen consumption is a function of the exercise work rate (running speed or cycling power output) achieved, then it makes sense that an effective training program that improves endurance performance will also result in an increase in $\dot{V}O_2max$ as a result of reaching higher exercise intensities after training.

The 16 percent improvement in $\dot{V}O_2max$ in three large cross-sectional studies is largely because of an increase in performance capacity, which is a function of cardiorespiratory factors as well as muscle, metabolic, and neurological adaptations to training. The measurement of aerobic capacity with training is therefore not simply a function of changing cardiorespiratory function; other systems also contribute to performance.

Because of this complex interaction between performance and aerobic capacity, changes in performance can often be dissociated from changes in $\dot{V}O_2max$. One reason may be that training improves economy or efficiency, as we shall discuss in chapter 12. The result is that at the same workload, oxygen consumption will be reduced. Further, any increases in performance because of training may not necessarily be reflected as an increase in $\dot{V}O_2max$. For coaches and triathletes, the value of the test should be extended beyond the measurement of aerobic capacity to the exercise intensity at which $\dot{V}O_2max$ is measured, because this is a performance measure.

Training to Improve $\dot{V}O_2max$

In terms of the most effective training method for improving $\dot{V}O_2max$, recent research has found that aerobic, high-intensity interval training is more effective than low- and moderate-intensity training in trained athletes.[21] In this study, four methods of training were compared:

1. Long, slow distance running—continuous running at 70 percent of HR^{max} for 45 minutes
2. Lactate threshold running—approximately 25 minutes of running at 85 percent of HR^{max}
3. Short interval running—47 repetitions of 15 seconds of running at 90 to 95 percent of HR^{max} with 15 seconds of slow running recovery
4. Long interval running—4 repetitions of 4 minutes at 90 to 95 percent of HR^{max} with 3 minutes of recovery

All training sessions were performed 3 days a week for 8 weeks. The largest increases in aerobic capacity were achieved with the higher intensity training (the short and long interval sessions), which increased $\dot{V}O_2max$ by 5.5 percent and 7.2 percent respectively, probably because of increases in stroke volume (see figure 11.2). $\dot{V}O_2max$ was unchanged by the long, slow distance and lactate threshold running.

A similar finding has been made for cycling exercise, performance, and metabolic changes associated with training,[22] in which higher intensity interval training produces similar effects to traditional endurance training with less than a third of the training time (see chapter 14). This suggests that the addition of higher intensity work, or possibly even the replacement of lower

▶ **Figure 11.2**   Running high-intensity intervals.

volume training, may have a timesaving effect, as well as being physiologically more effective.

But this result does not negate the need for longer duration endurance training, because other benefits may accrue during lower intensity training (running economy was shown to improve similarly in all four groups, for example), and practical reasons may come into play as well. The risk of injury is higher during sprints, which may make them unfeasible for triathletes wishing to improve performance and become more competitive.

Conclusion

The measurement of oxygen use as an indication of performance is relatively simple and has some important implications for the identification of inherent ability and for tracking the physiological changes that occur with training. The most commonly used index is aerobic capacity, or $\dot{V}O_2max$, which can provide valuable information for coaches and scientists. But $\dot{V}O_2max$ should be interpreted in the context of performance, rather than being viewed as the limiting determinant of exercise ability. Other indices include the measurement of fuel substrate utilization and energy use during exercise. Aerobic function during triathlon is an important component of performance, but it should not be viewed in isolation from other key attributes, such as economy and anaerobic threshold, which are discussed subsequently.

CHAPTER 12

Economy

—Ross Tucker, PhD

Economy refers to how efficiently oxygen is used at submaximal intensities, and it provides an indirect measure of the energetic cost of swimming, cycling, or running. In running and swimming, economy is measured as the volume of oxygen used to cover a given distance at submaximal intensities, whereas for cycling economy can be expressed as mechanical efficiency because it is possible to make accurate measurements of useful work (power output) as well as total energy use by means of respiratory gas analysis. Therefore, in the same way that a car is economical if it uses less fuel at a given speed, humans are classified as economical when oxygen consumption (and therefore energy consumption at submaximal speeds) at a given workload is lower than it is for other athletes.

Measuring Economy

Running economy is normally measured as the volume of oxygen used per kilogram per kilometer. For example, if an athlete with a mass of 70 kilograms uses 4 liters of oxygen per minute when running at a speed of 18 kilometers per hour (33:20 10K pace), economy is calculated by first converting the volume of oxygen used to a value relative to body mass (64 milliliters per kilogram per minute) and then expressing it as the total oxygen used to cover 1 kilometer. In this case, the athlete would have an economy of 190 milliliters per kilogram per kilometer, which is a typical value for an elite athlete whose running economy ranges between 180 and 210 milliliters per kilogram per kilometer.[1] A slower athlete would use much more oxygen to accomplish the same pace.

Swimming economy is similarly measured as the oxygen consumption required to cover a given distance, usually a meter. This value for oxygen consumption can easily be converted to an energy cost in kilojoules, and the energetic cost can be expressed per meter swum. For example, studies of elite swimmers have found that at a speed of 1.5 meters per second, the energy cost of swimming is 1.23, 1.47, 1.55, and 1.87 kilojoules per meter for freestyle, backstroke, butterfly, and breaststroke, respectively.[2] Freestyle is thus the most economical stroke, approximately 50 percent more economical than breaststroke, the least economical stroke.

For cycling, it is possible to calculate gross or delta efficiency because, unlike for running, power output can be accurately measured. Cycling efficiency is then calculated as the ratio of the useful work done (the power output) to the total energy expended. For example, consider a cyclist whose oxygen consumption is measured as 4 liters per minute while cycling at 300 watts on a cycle ergometer. The total energy cost of producing this power output can be calculated. To do this, we need to measure the respiratory exchange ratio, or RER, which provides an indication of the relative contribution of carbohydrate and fat to energy supply (see chapter 11). In our example, assume that RER is measured as 0.85, which implies that approximately 50 percent of the energy comes from fat and 50 percent from carbohydrate sources.

At that RER, the caloric equivalent, defined as the energy consumed per liter of oxygen, is 4.862 kilocalories. Knowing that the cyclist is consuming 4 liters of oxygen per minute, we can calculate that energy consumption is equal to 19.45 kilocalories per minute. This measure is easily converted into joules per second, or watts, and we can then calculate that the total energy consumption of our cyclist is 1,335 joules per second, or 1,335 watts. Therefore, because the cyclist is producing 300 watts of useful work, the gross efficiency of the cyclist is calculated as 22.1 percent.

Significance of Economy

Economy is increasingly recognized as a crucial determinant of swimming, running, and cycling performance. Despite its recognized importance, however, economy remains a relatively poorly understood physiological attribute. In a 2007 review of running economy published in *Sports Medicine*, exercise physiologists Carl Foster and Alejandro Lucia described running economy as "the forgotten factor in elite performance."[1]

In an endurance activity such as triathlon it is clearly beneficial to use less oxygen and energy at a given intensity because performance is regulated in part by the ability of the body to supply and use oxygen and provide energy for work over the long duration of endurance exercise. Studies of elite cyclists in the Tour de France reveal that the best performing cyclists often have typical or even lower levels for $\dot{V}O_2$max (see figure 12.1) but are distinguished instead by their exceptionally high cycling efficiency.[3] That is, they use less oxygen at a given workload than their peers do and are able to convert a greater proportion of total energy into useful work or power output.

Logically, of course, those who are most economical would also have lower $\dot{V}O_2$max values. By definition, the most economical athletes will use the least oxygen at a given workload, so even at peak intensities oxygen consumption will be significantly lower. For that reason in elite athletes economy and $\dot{V}O_2$max typically show an inverse relationship.[3, 4]

© Pierre Teyssot/Action Plus/Icon SMI

▶ **Figure 12.1** The best cyclists at the Tour de France typically have lower levels for $\dot{V}O_2$max and use oxygen more efficiently.

Differences in running economy are also used to explain differences in running performances and to account for the observation that within a performance-matched group of runners, $\dot{V}O_2$max is a poor predictor of performance. But because $\dot{V}O_2$max can be easily measured and perhaps more important because it can be improved with training, it has received disproportionate attention from exercise physiologists, coaches, and athletes, when devoting more attention to running economy may unlock better results, particularly for triathletes

Training Influences on Economy

Despite the recognized importance of economy on performance, data are scarce on how and why training alters economy in each of the three triathlon disciplines. In isolation, both running and cycling economy, which have been extensively studied, appear to have the potential to be improved with training, although the magnitude of the possible improvement is debated in the scientific literature.

But because of the multidisciplinary nature of triathlon, it may be that there is more scope to train to overcome the normal impairments in economy associated with training the different disciplines, in particular the transition between cycling and running. That is, it has been found that running economy is impaired during running after cycling compared with running in isolation.[5, 6] This impairment, however, appears to be related to the ability level and experience of the triathletes; elite triathletes display little to no change in running economy after cycling.[7]

Training may thus attenuate the normal impairment in running economy after cycling, and this topic is discussed subsequently. But first we briefly consider the three disciplines independently.

Swimming Economy

Research has shown that both physiological and biomechanical factors influence swimming economy. These factors include body length, body mass, body surface area, buoyancy (a function of body composition), passive torque, and differences in swimming technique and stroke length. (See reference 8 for discussion.) Clearly, some of these factors cannot be altered by training and are a function of body size and dimensions, emphasizing the importance of talent identification and selection.

Swimming technique is clearly a crucial component of swimming economy. The metabolic power needed to swim at a certain velocity depends on propelling efficiency, gross efficiency, and drag, all of which can be influenced through equipment and correct swimming technique, particularly a focus on body position or angle in the water[8] (figure 12.2). Coaches inherently recognize that efficient technique is crucial for triathlon success. The ability to swim with lower oxygen use, longer strokes, and reduced drag points to the

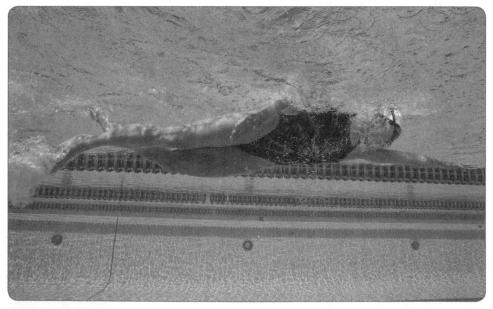

▶ **Figure 12.2** Correct swimming technique, especially body angle, is critical to improved economy.

value of focusing on correct technique for triathlon. For more on effective and optimal swimming technique, refer to chapter 4.

Cycling Efficiency

There has been much debate about the potential to improve cycling efficiency with training. A recent review by Hopker[9] concluded that in well-controlled and rigorously designed studies, training has a positive influence on gross efficiency, defined as the ratio of power output to energy expenditure. (Note that this measure differs from delta efficiency, which is the ratio of the change in power output to the change in energy expenditure, and thus includes metabolic rate at rest, whereas gross efficiency does not.)

The specific mechanisms by which training may improve cycling efficiency have yet to be determined but may include muscle fiber type alterations, changes to muscle fiber shortening velocities, changes within the mitochondria, and neural characteristics.[9, 10, 11, 12, 13, 14] Recent research has also found a correlation between maximal muscle strength and efficiency, particularly in older cyclists, so it appears that training interventions can improve cycling efficiency.[11]

In terms of cycling-specific training, changes in gross efficiency are significantly correlated with both the volume and the intensity of training, but it appears that high-intensity training is most strongly related to improvements in gross efficiency. For example, as little as 6 weeks of high-intensity training (above OBLA) increases gross efficiency in endurance-trained cyclists by approximately 1.5 percent.[14] This margin is similar to that found when comparing the gross efficiency of professional and elite cyclists,[15] the efficiency of trained and untrained cyclists,[12] and the change in efficiency that has been found to occur during a competitive cycling season.[13]

Strength is another factor identified as predictive for cycling efficiency. Younger cyclists have been found to be more efficient compared with older cyclists,[10, 11] but this difference disappears if the older cyclists perform strength training,[11] which suggests that one of the key predictors of cycling efficiency, at least in older athletes, is maximal muscle strength.

In this study,[11] the cycling efficiency in master cyclists (over the age of 50) improved within 3 weeks of beginning a strength training program consisting of three weekly sessions of leg extension exercises performed at 70 percent of a predetermined one-repetition maximum. Ten sets of 10 extensions were performed, with a 3-minute recovery between sets, and this was sufficient to improve cycling efficiency from 19.66 percent to 22.86 percent. In young cyclists (26 years old), the same strength training program produced a small but nonsignificant improvement in cycling efficiency.

In terms of the effect on performance, mathematical methods have been used to estimate that a 1 percent improvement in efficiency would result in a 63-second improvement during a 40-kilometer time trial,[16] although this potential performance advantage has yet to be assessed in controlled studies.

Running Economy

Training is thought to improve running economy primarily because of neuromuscular adaptations including improved muscle power and more efficient use of elastic energy stored during the stretch-shortening cycle.[17] Running-specific training improves running economy because of learned patterns of motor control and improved coordination, and runners are most economical at the speeds that they are more familiar with as a result of training.

Recent studies have shown that resistance and plyometric training produce significant improvements in running economy within relatively short durations, ranging from 6 weeks to 14 weeks (as reviewed by reference 17). Plyometric training, including explosive exercise such as hopping, jumping, and bounding, is thought to be effective because it improves the function of the neuromuscular system during running[18, 19] (see figure 12.3). Improvements include increased levels of preactivation (muscle activity before ground contact), increased stiffness of the leg, and enhanced function of the stretch-shortening cycle, in which an eccentric contraction is followed immediately by a concentric contraction.[18, 19] These changes combine to produce measurably lower ground contact times and changes in EMG activity, and are thought to be the primary mechanism for improved running economy because of training.

Another intervention that has received much attention is flexibility training. Theories differ about how stretching and improving flexibility may influence running economy. One theory holds that stretching will reduce the visco-elastic properties of muscles and tendons, making it easier to move the limbs. On the other hand, improved flexibility may reduce the ability of the muscle–tendon to store and harness elastic energy, which may reduce running economy.[17] Running economy has been negatively correlated with flexibility—economical runners tend to have reduced flexibility.[20, 21] But these studies are correlative only, and intervention studies are required to determine whether changes in flexibility affect running economy in the same predicted manner.

Only three controlled studies have examined this question. Two found that flexibility training had no influence on economy,[22, 23] whereas a third showed that running economy was in fact improved by a stretching program.[24] But in this last study, the volunteers all had tight hip extensor and flexor muscles to begin with, and economy was measured immediately after stretching. Subsequent reviews have suggested that stretching may acutely improve running economy but that a stretching program has no long-term effect on it. Further research studies are required to examine this theory. Evidence is presently insufficient to warrant the incorporation of stretching as a means to improve economy, although there are other reasons, of course, to advise regular stretching.

For comprehensive reviews on running economy and the factors influencing it, readers are referred to review articles by Foster and Lucia[1] and Bonacci et al.[17]

▶ **Figure 12.3** Plyometric training improves the function of the neuromuscular system and economy.

Neuromuscular Function in Triathletes— the Effect of Multidiscipline Training

One of the challenges in triathlon training is the requirement to alternate between disciplines. This switching has implications for economy, in particular the neuromuscular function that may underpin it. For example, trained triathletes display muscle activation patterns that are more similar to novice cyclists than trained cyclists.[25]

This result occurs even when the cycling training loads are matched, so it is not simply a case that triathletes perform relatively less cycling training. Specifically, triathletes show more variation between pedal strokes and more muscle coactivation (quadriceps and hamstrings being active simultaneously, for example) than trained cyclists, even though cycling loads are similar.

This finding suggests that multidisciplinary training interferes with learning the patterns of muscle activation during cycling. This conclusion is supported by studies of motor learning, which have found that when two activities are practiced within a short time of one another, learning the second task is biased by the previous task and that training adaptations can be partly overwritten by interference. The same patterns are not observed for running, which may be a function of great variability of running kinematics and muscle activation patterns to begin with but may also reflect the difficulty of conclusively finding these differences in research studies.

Note that the studies investigating differences between triathletes and cyclists or runners are typically underpowered (small sample number), short in duration, and unable to control for training volume and intensity precisely. Therefore, stronger evidence for these theories remains absent.

Practically, one implication of this observation of interference is that improvements in economy may be slowed by a multidisciplinary approach. Therefore, a triathlete who is seeking improved performance in one discipline through improved economy or technique may need to consider prolonged periods of single-discipline focus, when she can attempt to address this discipline without interference from the other two. This approach is speculative and has the obvious downside of reducing focus and training time on two disciplines, although it may be considered in specific cases.

Effect of Prior Cycling on Running Economy

In support of the concept that multidiscipline training exerts a negative effect on economy, it has been found that triathletes show reduced running economy when running after cycling compared with running only.[5,6] This result seems to be associated partly with changes in muscle activation patterns and the resultant changes in running kinematics, but it may also be influenced by metabolic and whole body physiological responses that occur during cycling, such as glycogen depletion, ventilatory muscle fatigue, dehydration, and leg muscle fatigue during the cycling leg.[5,6]

Recent work has shown that this impairment in economy is not present in elite triathletes. They use the same volume of oxygen during a run after a short low-intensity cycle, a longer high-intensity cycle, and during an isolated run and have the same patterns of muscle activation in all the conditions. Therefore, cycling did not influence running economy or neuromuscular control.[26]

This study is significant for triathlon performance and training because the ability to run with maximum efficiency after the cycle leg is crucial for performance. The extent of the change appears related to experience and ability level because the best performing triathletes show the smallest impairments in running economy off the bike.[26, 27]

No doubt this result occurs in part because of the training level of the athletes, which suggests that training to improve the ability to run economically immediately after cycling is crucial for triathlon success. But some athletes may have some innate characteristics, and it has been suggested that triathletes who are able to preserve their neuromuscular control and running economy after cycling may be those who could be most successful at the sport.

Conclusion

Economy is a crucial component for success, particularly in triathlon, in which multidiscipline training may compromise this variable in any given discipline. Although in part genetically influenced, economy can clearly be improved by a combination of specific training, strength training, plyometrics, and high-intensity training, and this should be a focus for those wishing to achieve a higher level of performance. When combined with high aerobic capacity, economy is a powerful predictor of endurance performance. Therefore, technical aspects of training for each discipline should be prioritized for optimal performance.

CHAPTER 13

Anaerobic Threshold

—Ross Tucker, PhD

The concept of the anaerobic threshold dates back over 50 years, to research published by Wasserman and McIlroy.[1] Because of differences in terminology, confusion regarding the identification and definition of thresholds, and the recognition that there may be more than one threshold, uncertainty surrounds the precise meaning of the anaerobic threshold, and more important, its physiological significance. As was the case for aerobic capacity and the measurement of $\dot{V}O_2$max, a tendency to rely on measurable physiological changes often leads coaches and athletes to overvalue these concepts. Aerobic capacity, economy, and anaerobic threshold are three sides of a triangle. The elite triathlete possesses all three.

The ability to sustain a high relative workload, as a percentage of either $\dot{V}O_2$max or peak exercise work rate, for long periods is crucial to success in triathlon. We have seen that within a group of similarly performing endurance athletes, aerobic capacity is often a poor predictor of success. One of the reasons for this is the crucial importance of being able to sustain high relative exercise intensities in competition. Regardless of the definition, the threshold concept is a key success factor for triathlon. In this chapter, we describe the concept, measurement, and significance of the anaerobic threshold.

Defining Anaerobic Threshold

The anaerobic threshold (AT) is defined as either the oxygen consumption or, more practically, the exercise intensity beyond which any further contributions to total energy supply come from oxygen-independent sources.[1, 2] That is, the AT is the maximum exercise intensity that the triathlete can maintain without producing a significant increase in lactate above resting levels.

Recall from chapter 11 that energy demand is a function of exercise intensity and is met by the oxidation of fat and carbohydrate. As exercise intensity increases, the demand for energy requires that oxygen-independent, or so-called anaerobic, metabolic pathways contribute to the total energy supply. As a result, measurable physiological changes occur, some of which are used as markers to identify the AT intensity.

Marker 1: Lactate

One of these markers is an exponential increase in the concentration of lactate in the blood, used most widely to identify the AT. Lactate is a molecule formed as the end-product of glycogenolysis and glycolysis, and it is often implicated as a limiting factor for exercise, despite evidence suggesting that it has beneficial effects and is in fact a crucial substrate for energy production and a signaling molecule (as discussed later).

Lactate has also been wrongly blamed for the acidosis that occurs when exercise intensity increases beyond the so-called anaerobic threshold. In reality, lactate is only indirectly involved in the decrease in pH that occurs during high-intensity exercise, and the acidosis actually occurs because the formation of lactate involves the transfer of hydrogen ions to coenzymes. But lactate remains implicated as the key marker of the anaerobic threshold, and for this reason AT is also called the lactate threshold.

Marker 2: Increase in the Respiratory Exchange Ratio

Another physiological variable used to detect the anaerobic threshold is an increase in the respiratory exchange ratio (RER) above 1.0.[2, 3] This is the point at which the volume of carbon dioxide produced exceeds oxygen used as a result of liberation of carbon dioxide from the body's bicarbonate buffer pool. (See chapter 11 for a more detailed explanation of RER.) The excess CO_2 is breathed out, and the result is the increase in RER above 1.

In the absence of direct lactate testing using blood samples, many laboratory studies infer the anaerobic threshold using this method, which has been shown to give comparable results to blood measurement and has the benefit of being noninvasive.[2, 3]

Marker 3: Onset of Blood Lactate Accumulation

Onset of blood lactate accumulation (OBLA) is the point at which the lactate concentration begins to increase exponentially, using mathematical definitions to identify this point.[3] This definition is much the same as that for anaerobic or lactate threshold, as described earlier. But in the original research this point happened when blood lactate concentrations were approximately 4 millimoles per liter, so the concept of OBLA being the point at which blood lactate levels reaches 4 millimoles per liter has persisted, although this was not originally intended as the definition. As a result, OBLA differs from anaerobic threshold in some studies, although it was and still is intended to convey the same concept.

Marker 4: Ventilatory Threshold

In addition to the anaerobic threshold, the ventilatory threshold (VT) has also been identified. (There are in fact two VTs.) VT has numerous mathematical and physiological definitions,[3, 4] but it is generally identified as the point at which the ventilation increases at a more rapid rate as a function of workload. That is, it is the ventilatory equivalent of lactate in the LT definition, and the workloads eliciting the AT and VT are generally similar, but differences in the method used to identify them,[5] as well as a significant subjective component, mean that the workloads at which they occur are slightly different.

This difference has implications for the prescription of training zones based on LT or VT because they are a function of the method used to measure them. Coaches and triathletes implementing one or more of these markers to prescribe training volume and monitor performance and adaptations to training thus need to understand that they are defined somewhat arbitrarily. Comparisons within an athlete for tracking changes over time should be made using the same threshold or marker, as well as the same method of determining the threshold.

Other Markers

Other functional applications of the threshold concept include that of functional threshold power, or FTP, which has been defined as the highest average power output or pace that an athlete can sustain for 1 hour. FTP is thus similar in concept to AT, which is defined as the highest intensity that does not cause a rise in lactate concentration, because the requirement to sustain power output for 1 hour means that FTP is at or near the level where this physiological change would occur.

In our laboratory, we have found that the average power output achieved for a maximal 40-kilometer cycling time-trial is also a good approximation of the AT because for well-trained cyclists a 40-kilometer cycling time trial lasts approximately an hour. These methods are attractive, because they allow the workrate or intensity to be measured without the requirement for time-consuming, expensive, and invasive specialized testing.

Finally, for all the preceding intensities, the workrate eliciting the threshold can be identified as either speed or power output, as well as the heart rate. Heart rate is, of course, susceptible to numerous factors such as diet, temperature, diurnal variations, stress, and hydration status, but it may, under controlled conditions, provide an alternative means of prescribing and monitoring training intensities.

Aerobic Versus Anaerobic Metabolism and Lactate

The metabolic processes responsible for anaerobic metabolism are complex but worth considering briefly. The metabolic pathway responsible for the production of lactate is glycogenolysis, an 11-step pathway involving the sequential breakdown of glycogen to pyruvate.

Pyruvate is then converted to acetyl CoA through a reaction catalyzed by the enzyme pyruvate dehydrogenase (PDH). When this occurs, acetyl CoA is next converted to citrate before undergoing a series of reactions in a pathway known as the TCA, or Krebs, cycle, followed by oxidative phosphorylation of the resultant electron carriers, the final one of which is oxygen. As a result of this series of reactions, adenosine triphosphate (ATP), the energy currency of the cell, is generated in what are known as the oxidative pathways (refer to chapter 1 for more about ATP).

But pyruvate can also be converted to lactate by the enzyme lactate dehydrogenase (LDH), and this reaction is the final step in the glycolytic pathway. This occurs because the flux, or rate of metabolic reactions, through glycolysis exceeds the capacity of the PDH to catalyze the conversion of pyruvate to acetyl-CoA. The result is that pyruvate concentrations rise and LDH converts it to lactate.

This process has an important metabolic function, because the formation of lactate allows NADH, the coenzyme, to be converted back to NAD+, which then facilitates the production of ATP molecules earlier in the glycolytic pathway. Because of lactate formation, glycolysis can continue at sufficient rates to provide ATP to muscle, albeit for a limited time only.

Rate of Glycolysis

The driving factor for the formation of lactate, rather than acetyl CoA, is the flux or rate of reactions occurring in glycolysis. The formation of pyruvate is driven in part by the energy charge of the cell (a depletion in ATP or NADH or an increase in ADP or NAD+ stimulates glycolytic enzymes, producing more pyruvate), and by sympathetic nervous system hormones such as adrenaline, which increase the breakdown of glycogen, ultimately leading to more pyruvate formation. Because the sympathetic response and a decrease in the energy charge of the cell occur as intensity increases, the rate of glycolysis and thus pyruvate formation is a function of exercise intensity.

PDH, however, represents a rate-limiting enzyme in the pathway, and excess pyruvate is converted instead to lactate. Indeed, one of the key metabolic effects of endurance training is that PDH levels increase significantly, which means that the capacity to convert pyruvate to acetyl CoA increases, with the result that lactate levels at the same exercise intensity are reduced. Put differently, people with greater oxidative capacity, either because of training adaptations or genetic factors, will achieve a higher steady-state exercise intensity before lactate levels begin to rise—that is, their exercise workrate at AT will increase. For that reason AT is often a good predictor of triathlon or endurance performance.

With respect to training effects on lactate production, it is known that endurance training shifts the AT to higher exercise intensities. This result occurs primarily because the oxidative capacity is improved, and we describe the mechanisms for this in chapter 14. The outcome is that endurance-trained triathletes are able to swim, cycle, and run at a higher relative speed or power output, which has performance implications (described subsequently).

Lactate Shuttle

A final consideration when monitoring lactate is that the level measured in the blood is a function of both the production of lactate in the cell and the reuptake for oxidation in other tissues. This reuptake and oxidation form part of the lactate shuttle, which was described by Brooks.[6,7] The lactate shuttle concept is that lactate is formed continuously under aerobic conditions and then oxidized in other tissues as a source of energy. Brooks describes how lactate is shuttled between glycolytic and oxidative muscle fibers within a working muscle bed, between working skeletal muscle and the heart, brain, liver, and kidneys.

Effectively, this model proposes that rather than being viewed as alternative pathways, glycolytic and oxidative pathways should be viewed as linked because lactate is the product of one (glycolysis) and the substrate of another (oxidative pathways), albeit in different cells as a result of shuttling between compartments.[6,7]

Lactate transfer occurs through monocarboxylate transporters, which shuttle lactate into and out of cells. Endurance training enhances the function of these transporters, the result being that lactate can be removed from the blood more rapidly.[7] This is another reason why highly trained athletes often have lower lactate levels than less trained athletes at a given exercise intensity, not solely because of reduced production but also because training enhances the reuptake and oxidation of lactate.

Lactate levels at steady-state intensity and AT intensities are thus a predictor of exercise performance because they are markers of the cellular ability to use oxidative pathways rather than glycolytic pathways for the formation of ATP. This is in turn influenced by the hormonal and metabolic responses to exercise, including the sympathetic responses to exercise and the capacity of oxidative enzymes, which enable higher exercise intensities to be reached before higher lactate, and thus hydrogen ion concentrations, occur.

Influence of Exercise Intensity on Energy Supply

The predominant pathway responsible for providing energy is strongly influenced by exercise intensity, which is inversely related to the exercise duration. That is, shorter sprint activities are performed at a high intensity, whereas ultraendurance events including Ironman triathlons are performed at lower intensities, so they use different energy pathways.

Energy Pathway for Sprints: Phosphocreatine System

For exercise lasting less than 20 seconds, the predominant energy pathway responsible for ATP formation is the phosphocreatine system, which is able to form ATP at rapid rates from another high-energy compound, phosphocreatine. This system has limited capacity, however, and for exercise lasting longer than a few seconds, other sources of ATP must be used. One such source is glycolysis, described previously, which produces ATP and pyruvate. This pathway is responsible for energy supply for exercise lasting minutes.

Beyond this, oxidative pathways assume most of the ATP production in the form of carbohydrate oxidation and fat oxidation. Note that there are not distinct intensities at which one pathway is switched on while another is switched off—all contribute to energy but in vastly different amounts depending on the demand, which is a function of intensity.

Energy Pathway for Triathlon: Oxidative Metabolism

For triathlon events, the predominant source of energy, even for sprint triathlons, is oxidative metabolism. But the ability to exercise above the AT level is crucially important, not only because the stochastic nature of competition demands it but also because evidence from training studies indicates that training at higher intensities improves performance and economy (see chapter 12).

In terms of competition, research on the cycling leg of Olympic-distance triathlon events in the World Cup has shown that most of the time (51 percent plus or minus 9 percent) is spent below VT1 (which is an approximation for AT), whereas 17 percent plus or minus 6 percent of the 40-kilometer leg was spent at workloads higher than maximal aerobic power (MAP).[8] These periods of higher intensity are crucial to racing success, because they influence the triathlete's ability to respond to surges, to bridge gaps following the swim leg, and to negotiate variable terrain and climbs.

Over longer distances, as expected, the relative intensity is further reduced. Laursen et al. found that highly trained Ironman triathletes completed the cycle leg of an Ironman at a power output that was considerably below the power output measured at the ventilatory threshold.[9]

Need for High-Intensity Training

In terms of training, despite the observation that the most time is spent below AT, evidence suggests a crucial role for training at higher intensities. As described in chapter 12, high-intensity training has been found to improve cycling efficiency.[10]

Further, short-duration, high-intensity sprint training produces physiological adaptations similar to those produced by low-intensity, higher volume training.[11] In a study, four to six repeats of 30 seconds at 250 percent of $\dot{V}O_2$max, corresponding to the training intensity usually associated with predominantly glycolytic pathways, induced increases in muscle oxidative capacity, muscle buffering capacity, and glycogen content that were similar to those achieved by a group of cyclists who performed 90 to 120 minutes of continuous cycling at 65 percent of $\dot{V}O_2$max.[11]

Triathlon Performance and Anaerobic Threshold

The ability to sustain high relative power outputs is clearly important for endurance performance. The definition for AT implicitly includes performance, because it is defined as the maximal intensity that can be sustained before an exponential increase in blood lactate levels can occur. For this reason FTP is a relatively good approximation of AT intensity.

Regardless of the mechanism for the resultant fatigue when this intensity is exceeded, athletes who are able to sustain higher speeds at this exercise intensity will be successful. Research from Van Schuylenbergh has found that the best predictors of triathlon performance are running speed and swimming speed at the maximal lactate steady state, or anaerobic threshold.[12]

Schabort et al. have further shown that blood lactate measured during steady-state cycling at a workload of 4 watts per kilogram or during running at 15 kilometers per hour can be combined with peak treadmill running velocity and $\dot{V}O_2$max during cycling to predict triathlon performance.[13] Using stepwise multiple regression analysis, they produced an equation to predict performance in Olympic-distance triathlon using two of the previously mentioned variables:

$$\text{Race time (in seconds)} =$$
$$-129 \times \text{PTRS (km/h)} + 122 \times \text{lactate at 4 W/kg (mM)} + 9{,}456.$$

For example, a high-level triathlete would typically achieve a PTRS speed of 22 kilometers per hour and may have a lactate concentration of 4 millimoles at a power output of 4 watts per kilogram. This athlete's predicted race time would be 7,106 seconds, or 1 hour and 58 minutes. An increase in the PTRS (an indication of improved running ability, a function of numerous physiological adaptations) or a decrease in lactate (which indicates improved aerobic and anaerobic function) would reduce the predicted time.

Of course, the prediction will be influenced by the method used to determine the input characteristics, as described in chapter 11.

Finally, Hue et al. found that the lactate concentration at the end of a 30-minute laboratory cycling bout and the distance covered during a 20-minute performance run immediately following this cycling bout were the only factors that could be correlated with triathlon race performance in elite triathletes.[14]

Clearly, the measurement of submaximal performance variables, when combined with measurements of lactate concentrations in controlled conditions, provides an accurate prediction of triathlon performance. The explanation for this was described previously, namely that the lactate concentration is a marker for the metabolic and hormonal capacity and response to exercise. Genetic factors and the influence of training on these variables means that laboratory or field measurements of lactate can provide accurate predictions of performance.

But this is true only when laboratory conditions and other physiological variables are tightly controlled. For example, Swart et al. have described that the monitoring of lactate as a means to track training status and performance over time is unreliable and potentially misleading.[15] This inaccuracy is the result of multiple confounding factors, such as accuracy of portable lactate analyzers, carbohydrate depletion, mode of exercise (particularly important for triathlon), ambient temperature, muscle damage, and overtraining, all of which affect the normal relationship between lactate concentration and exercise intensity, and thus the AT. They concluded, "Changes in blood lactate concentration should be interpreted with caution as the changes do not track training status or exercise intensity with sufficient precision to have a practical application."[13]

Similarly, Pyne et al. have shown that in elite swimmers the swimming velocity at lactate threshold improves with training, as does lactate tolerance, but those changes were not associated with changes in swimming performance.[16] This finding challenges the notion that coaches or athletes should regularly monitor lactate to gauge the effectiveness of a training intervention.

Conclusion

The concept of thresholds is crucial for triathlon performance. Despite some confusion about variable definitions for the many possible thresholds and their measurement, the ability of the triathlete to sustain a high relative workrate is crucial to success and is thus a focus of training. The key is to recognize the concept and to ensure that the prescription of training and monitoring of intensities is consistent over time.

Endurance training produces many physiological changes, but in terms of the effect on performance, one of the most significant is the ability to exercise at a higher intensity before the AT intensity is reached. This improvement occurs primarily because of muscle adaptations to training and enables the triathlete to sustain a higher power output or pace for long periods. For this reason, AT has been identified as a predictor of performance. The specific muscle adaptations responsible are considered in the next chapter.

CHAPTER 14

Muscle Types and Triathlon Performance

—Ross Tucker, PhD

One of the most persistent and perhaps misapplied concepts in exercise physiology is the theory of muscle fiber types and function. Coaches and athletes recognize that some people possess greater speed or explosiveness than others and that training produces different responses among individuals. Muscle biopsy methods early on established that not all muscle was equal in terms of the speed and force produced or fatigue characteristics of the muscle, and athletes were quickly separated into somewhat oversimplified, polarized groups of fast-twitch athletes (sprinters), and slow-twitch athletes (endurance athletes).

The development of improved molecular methods has allowed much better understanding of muscle fiber types, function, and characteristics, making it clear that the binary approach is indeed an oversimplification and that muscle fiber type and function are more complex than was initially believed.

Despite unanswered questions, research has provided an answer to the age-old question from both athletes and coaches: Can we change the fiber-type composition of our muscles through training? Based on the available evidence, the short and somewhat disappointing answer is, Not really.[1, 2] In the words of Andersen and Aagard, "Both coaches and scientists know that it is not possible to turn a donkey into a race horse by means of exercise and training. Hard work will, at most, turn the donkey into a fast and explosive donkey."[2]

But a longer answer to the posed question is available, including various nuances that point to the significant physiological and metabolic changes that occur within muscle because of training. In this chapter we introduce the concept of muscle fiber types and discuss how training affects not only the general fiber type classification of muscle but also muscle metabolic properties, leading to improved performance.

Muscle Fiber Type Physiology and Characteristics

The ability of a muscle to contract at high speeds and forces is largely explained by the composition of the individual fibers of that muscle. Muscle fibers are distinguished by contractile and metabolic factors, and the type of myosin is the key difference between the three recognized muscle fiber types. Myosin, one of several contractile proteins, makes up the thick filament of the muscle fiber.

The heavy chain of the myosin molecule exists in three forms, and the differences between these isoforms confer to skeletal muscle its unique properties, particularly its speed of contraction.[1] The three isoforms are MyHC I, MyHC IIA, and MyHC IIx, and from these isoforms the muscle fiber types are named.[2] That is, the three recognized pure fiber types are type I fibers, type IIa fibers, and type IIx fibers. There are also hybrids of these isoforms, muscle fibers that coexpress MyHC I and MyHC IIA or MyHC IIA and MyHC IIx.[2]

In terms of the characteristics of the muscle fiber types, numerous functional differences exist among the three identified types (see table 14.1). These differences lead to the more common functional classification of muscle fibers into type I slow oxidative fibers and type II fibers, in which type II fibers comprise three subtypes: IIa, IIx, and IIb.

This method of classification more comprehensively reflects the differences among fiber types, not only according to contraction speed and MyHC type but also by metabolic properties. These properties are summarized in table 14.1 (adapted from Zierath and Hawley[3]) and discussed subsequently.

Table 14.1 Muscle Fiber Type Characteristics

ST oxidative fibers (type I)	FT oxidative fibers (type IIa)	FT glycolytic fibers (type IIx)
Myosin heavy chain I	Myosin heavy chain IIa	Myosin heavy chain IIx
High aerobic (oxidative) capacity and fatigue resistance	Moderate aerobic (oxidative) capacity and fatigue resistance	Low aerobic (oxidative) capacity and fatigue resistance
Low anaerobic (glycolytic) capacity and motor unit strength	High anaerobic (glycolytic) capacity and motor unit strength	High anaerobic (glycolytic) capacity and motor unit strength
Slow contractile speed	Fast contractile speed	Fast contractile speed
10 to 180 fibers per motor neuron	300 to 800 fibers per motor neuron	300 to 800 fibers per motor neuron
Low sarcoplasmic reticulum development	High sarcoplasmic reticulum development	High sarcoplasmic reticulum development
High mitochondrial density	Moderate mitochondrial density	Low mitochondrial density
High capillary density	Moderate capillary density	Low capillary density
55% in untrained people	30% in untrained people	15% in untrained people

These functional differences center on the speed of contraction in the three muscle fiber types. According to the literature, muscle fibers can be ranked from slowest to fastest as follows: MyHC I, MyHC I/IIa hybrid, MyHC IIa, MyHC IIa/IIx hybrid, and then MyHC IIx.[4, 5] The difference in contractile speed has been measured at approximately 1:2 for MyHC I: MyHC II-containing fibers,[6] meaning that fast-twitch fibers take half the time to reach peak tension compared with slow-twitch fibers.

But other significant differences exist, most notably those relating to the metabolic differences among fiber types.[7] Here the characteristics of the type I fibers that make them less suitable for explosive, short-duration sprint events make these fibers more suited to endurance activity. Their increased capacity for oxidative metabolism, for example, confers an endurance advantage, because it enables more efficient energy production through oxidative pathways, as described in chapter 13.

Influence of Muscle Fiber Composition on Athletic Performance

Functionally, the result of the characteristics listed in table 14.1 means that an athlete who possesses a large proportion of type II (FT) muscle fibers will be able to achieve higher muscle force and power output during fast movements. These differences in force don't appear at slow speeds because the type I fibers have sufficient time to build up force. The differences are present only at higher speeds, particularly during acceleration and sprinting-type activities. For this reason, athletes who have a large proportion of type II muscle fibers are most suited to sports in which acceleration and explosive force production is a requirement for success.

In contrast, triathlon, which is an endurance activity even during sprint triathlons (see chapter 13 for the metabolic explanation), would be more suitable for people who have a higher percentage of type I, or slow-twitch, muscle fibers because aerobic characteristics (chapter 11), economy (chapter 12), and fatigue resistance (chapter 15) are the key factors for triathlon success.

The research generally bears this out. For example, one study of elite middle- and long-distance runners revealed that they had a higher proportion of type I fibers in the vastus medialis than did wrestlers, kayakers, and powerlifters.[8] Research also generally shows that successful endurance athletes possess higher ST proportions than successful sprinters do[9, 10, 11] and that elite endurance athletes have a higher proportion of ST fibers than subelite endurance athletes do.[12]

But this principle, although true in general, does not translate into the simple dichotomy of athlete that is often thought to exist. That is, successful endurance athletes do not always have the greatest proportion of ST muscle fibers. For example, large ranges exist among people who are similarly trained within the same endurance activities. Also, successful endurance performance does not require an exceedingly high percentage of type I muscle fibers.

For example, Fink et al. showed that two performance-matched marathon runners (2 hours and 18 minutes) differed enormously with respect to the proportion of ST fibers—50 percent compared with 98 percent.[9] These large ranges are seen elsewhere,[8] and a linear relationship clearly does not exist between proportion of ST fibers and endurance performance, despite the general finding that elite endurance athletes have more ST fibers than subelite or untrained individuals do.[9]

Ultimately, although certain fiber-type compositions are considered advantageous for certain events, the relationship does not appear sufficiently close to allow the conclusion that fiber-type composition is the key factor driving performance.[13] Rather, factors such as $\dot{V}O_2max$, economy, and thresholds appear to be more crucial determinants of performance.

Effect of Training on Muscle Fiber Type

Having described that elite endurance athletes possess a higher percentage of ST fibers than subelite and untrained people, it is compelling to ask whether these high ST proportions are the result of training or whether these individuals are selected because of a genetic difference that persists despite training? Considerable debate has swirled around this question,[14, 15, 16] and the exact capacity to alter fiber type ratios by converting one type to another remains unknown.

As described earlier, there is limited plasticity in the muscle fiber type composition, but endurance training seems to lead to some changes in muscle fiber composition because of its effects on various signaling pathways. That is, fast-twitch glycolytic fibers may be converted to FT oxidative fibers and to ST fibers as a result of calcium-signaling pathways that are activated specifically by endurance training.[3] In rats the experimental activation of the PPAR-δ receptor leads to muscle fiber transformation,[17] which further suggests that fiber conversions may be possible through the exercise-stimulated activation of these and other receptors that are known to be activated by exercise and to modulate gene expression.

Other animal studies have shown that exposing a muscle with predominantly fast muscles fibers to low-frequency electrical stimulation, similar to what is received by slow muscle fibers, leads to a gradual shift toward MyHC I isoforms. Complete removal of the motor nerve, as well as paralysis caused by spinal cord injury, can shift fiber type from FT to ST.[2] These situations are hardly physiological, however, and are not relevant to a triathlete or coach. Therefore, it is more important to consider training interventions that have studied changes in muscle fiber-type composition.

In 1973, in the first study to examine the effects of training on muscle fiber type, Gollnick et al. had six untrained volunteers cycle for 1 hour per day, 4 days a week, for 5 months.[18] They found that limited conversion of fast-twitch to slow-twitch muscle fibers occurred (32 percent to 36 percent) and concluded that endurance training did not alter fiber type.

Subsequent studies have found similar percentage changes, although some of these have been statistically significant,[19] probably because of differences in individual responses to training and different sample sizes used in the studies. The magnitude of changes, however, is consistently small, suggesting that the conversion of FT to ST fibers is limited.

A more important consideration is that these early studies were able to distinguish only between FT and ST fibers, and not between the subtypes of FT fibers. Research has subsequently shown that the conversion of type IIb to type IIa fibers does occur in greater magnitudes with endurance training, and, to a lesser extent, that type IIa fibers can be converted to type I fibers. These changes are often put forward as part of the explanation for the observed, albeit slight, improvements in cycling efficiency or running economy that occur with endurance training (see chapter 12).

Ultimately, the capacity to change muscle fiber composition and to convert among fiber types may be limited, at least in magnitude. But the metabolic properties of muscle have enormous plasticity, and the result is that endurance training can induce large performance differences, not necessarily by altering fiber-type composition, but through its effects on the function and performance of existing muscle fibers, which are considered next.

Effect of Training on Muscle Physiology and Metabolism

Endurance exercise training has been shown to produce profound changes in muscle structure, function, and metabolism. These changes are reviewed comprehensively elsewhere.[14] Early research established that prolonged endurance training increased the activities of all the major enzymes of metabolism, including hexokinase, phosphofructokinase (PFK), and lactate dehydrogenase (LDH) in the glycolytic pathways, and pyruvate dehydrogenase, malate dehydrogenase, 3-hydroxyacyl-CoA dehydrogenase (HADH), NADH dehydrogenase, succinate dehydrogenase, cytochrome oxidase, and oxoglutarate dehydrogenase (OGDH) in the oxidative pathways.[14]

Role of Mitochondria

The primary factor responsible for these increases, particularly in the oxidative enzyme pathways, is an exercise-induced increase in mitochondrial mass caused by contractile activity. (The increase in mitochondrial enzyme activity is present only in the legs of runners and cyclists, for example.) The increase in mitochondrial mass is the result of an increase in both the size and number of mitochondria in the muscle.[14] The result is that more pyruvate can be oxidized, which in turn reduces the accumulation of lactate at a given exercise intensity (see chapter 13 for explanation). These changes also mean that endurance-trained muscle has increased capacity to oxidize fatty acids, with a resultant glycogen-sparing effect and its benefits for reducing fatigue (see chapter 15).

These metabolic adaptations occur rapidly after the onset of training. Within 5 days of starting training, lactate concentrations and glycogen depletion are reduced, despite the fact that oxidative capacity and mitochondrial changes occur only later (31 days).[14] Also, detraining produces a more rapid loss of oxidative potential than glycolytic potential.

Metabolic Benefits of Training

The recent discovery that higher intensity training may produce greater improvements in aerobic capacity than traditional endurance training (see chapter 11) also extends to the metabolic benefits associated with training.[21, 22] Specifically, sprint interval training consisting of four to six repeats of all-out 30-second sprinting with 4 to 5 minutes of recovery produced similar metabolic adaptations compared with higher volume, lower intensity endurance training.[21, 22]

That is, all the mitochondrial markers for oxidative metabolism were increased (including pyruvate dehydrogenase and HADH), glycogen use was decreased, and fat oxidation increased regardless of training method. The difference in time commitment between these two training methods is enormous—an average of 90 minutes per week for sprint training compared with approximately 5 hours per week for endurance training, and a 90 percent reduction in training volume (measured as energy consumption in kilojoules).

Intense Training Leads to Muscle Adaptation

This finding, along with those showing that aerobic capacity and economy are both effectively increased with high-intensity interval training[20] (chapters 11 and 12), is important because it shows that high-intensity interval training is an effective strategy to induce rapid adaptations in skeletal muscle and exercise performance that are comparable with the changes induced by endurance training.

But these findings do not dispel the need for traditional endurance training. Higher volume training unquestionably has a place, notably to produce improved function of the cardiovascular system, neuromuscular adaptations, and adaptation in joints, tendons, and muscles. Also, these studies are typically performed on untrained or moderately trained athletes, who have greater potential than competitive or highly trained athletes to improve as a result of training.

It is debatable whether high-intensity interval training alone can elevate physiological and metabolic function, and hence performance, to the level that a competitive triathlete may aspire to. But these findings do suggest that for triathlon, for which time constraints are of particular concern, the addition of high-intensity interval training, at appropriate times, has physiological benefits usually thought to be obtained solely through high-volume endurance training.

Conclusion

Muscle fiber type appears to play a role in the ability of people to excel in a particular type of sport. Those with a high proportion of FT fibers are likely to succeed in explosive events, whereas endurance success requires a higher proportion of ST fibers. But this relationship is by no means rigid, and other physiological variables appear to exert more influence over performance than muscle fiber type does. The ability to convert one fiber type to another appears to be limited, although conversions from FT glycolytic to FT oxidative and, to a lesser extent, to ST fibers, have been shown to occur.

The more crucial recognition is that endurance training results in significant adaptations that increase the metabolic efficiency and oxidative capacity of the muscle. The result is that fuel substrate utilization is altered, the metabolic implications of a given workrate are favorably changed, and fatigue may be delayed. The type of training that produces these responses has recently been questioned, because higher intensity intervals are now known to be as effective as traditional endurance training. For practical reasons, however, the coach must balance the various training stressors to maximize performance.

CHAPTER 15

Fatigue Resistance and Recovery

—Ross Tucker, PhD

An overriding purpose of training is fatigue resistance. All training is designed with the ultimate purpose of improving triathlon performance, which is to say, avoiding or tolerating the onset of fatigue. Of course, some sessions are designed to assist with technical aspects of the swim, bike, and run, and these are directly concerned with improving technique, but they too indirectly contribute to increasing the intensity achievable before the debilitating effects of fatigue are felt.

Fatigue is an ill-defined phenomenon, having physiological, psychological, and emotional qualities, and numerous factors contribute. As a result, fatigue is hotly debated and somewhat polarizing in the scientific literature. Coaches and most athletes are well aware of when fatigue happens, why (in the broader picture) it happens, and how to train to improve performance, which is essentially either delaying fatigue or achieving a higher speed before fatigue kicks in.

In this chapter we address some of the theoretical explanations for fatigue and explain how training alters fatigue and thus performance.

Context-Specific Fatigue

To appreciate the influence of training on fatigue, we first need to appreciate the physiology of fatigue. The key concept is that fatigue is contextual. It is a multifactorial phenomenon, and the result is that the physiology of fatigue is usually dependent on the point of view.

The parable of blind men trying to describe what an elephant looks like by touching only one part of it is appropriate to how we tend to view and understand fatigue. A blind man who touches the leg describes an elephant as a pillar; the man who feels the tail describes it as a rope; to the man who feels the trunk, it is like a tree branch; the man who touches the tusk says that the elephant must be a solid pipe. All are correct, of course, in a narrow way, but all are completely wrong. The men's ability to describe the elephant is limited by their inability to see it from afar and to touch different areas of it.

But this story is not different from how fatigue has been viewed and explained in the scientific literature. As a result, an integrated model for fatigue, accounting for a wide range of observations and exercise situations, remains somewhat elusive.

To illustrate the contextual nature of fatigue, recall that in chapter 13 we described the predominant energy pathways used for exercise of different durations and intensities. Clearly, an athlete in the final 2 miles of a 26.2-mile (42 km) run after 12 hours in an Ironman triathlon experiences an entirely different metabolic, thermoregulatory, cardiovascular, and hormonal challenge compared with an Olympic-distance triathlete sprinting the final 500 meters of an event lasting less than 2 hours. As a result, the physiological underpinning of fatigue will differ significantly.

In the Ironman event, a hot day produces a different physiological explanation of fatigue compared with a cool day. Attributing fatigue to the same physiological changes in these athletes would be entirely incorrect. The key point is that training to manage fatigue requires that all the physiological factors be recognized and managed in training. In so doing, the first paradigm that must be challenged is the theory that fatigue is a failure of physiology.

Failure Concept of Fatigue

Fatigue, in a real-world, practical sense, cannot be viewed as a failure of physiology, although science has often explained it that way. For example, the theory exists that fatigue occurs because a critical level of hyperthermia is reached.[1, 2, 3] Another theory holds that fatigue occurs because of a limitation in oxygen supply, often as a result of failing to pump sufficient blood to the working muscles.[4] "Hitting the wall" in marathon running or longer-distance triathlons is the conceptualization of one of many failure models for fatigue—in this case, the failure to maintain normal blood sugar levels (euglycemia) because of the depletion of liver glycogen.

In all these explanations, fatigue occurs because of the loss of "homeostasis in one or more homeostatic systems."[5, 6] But that model is incomplete, the result of laboratory studies that have traditionally approached fatigue using a model in which exercise is performed to exhaustion at a fixed work rate. Here, the exercising volunteer is made to exercise literally to the point of exhaustion, and the cause of exercise failure is then inferred through measurement of the physiological milieu at that point of exhaustion.

For example, cycling trials to exhaustion at lower workloads have led researchers to deduce that fatigue occurs because of insufficient energy supply or glycogen depletion in either muscle or liver. Cycling trials to exhaustion in hot conditions resulted in a rise in body temperature to 104 degrees Fahrenheit (40 degrees Celsius)—normal is 99 degrees Fahrenheit

(37 degrees Celsius)—and the conclusion was that fatigue occurred because of the high body temperature.[1, 2] And, of course, like the man who describes the elephant as a pillar while touching the leg, the researchers are not incorrect; their interpretation is just incomplete.

Fatigue: From Failure to Regulation

A newer paradigm has recognized the concept of self-paced exercise and regulation, which introduces the concept of pacing strategy to how we understand fatigue. Here, fatigue is a sensation, not a distinct event that happens only at the point of homeostatic failure.[5, 6] That is, rather than being the result of failure to maintain homeostasis, fatigue is relative and regulated specifically to prevent this failure.[7] And training, in terms of its effect on fatigue, acts by improving homeostatic regulation, so that both the physiology and the sensation of fatigue are altered from the first moment of exercise.

To understand this concept fully and to understand how training alters the physiology of fatigue, we consider three common examples: heat, energy supply, and oxygen availability.

Effects of Heat

Heat imposes an enormous physiological challenge on athletes. Heat is a common challenge in triathlons, particularly in the Ironman distances, during which the run leg takes place during the hottest part of the day, so it is a relevant and practical illustration of the physiology of fatigue.

People had previously believed that exercise in hot conditions was negatively affected because our bodies could not deliver enough blood to the skin for cooling while still matching the demand for muscle blood flow.[8] The theory was that the requirement from the muscles to supply oxygen and energy and remove carbon dioxide and other by-products would be in conflict with the demand from the skin during exercise in the heat, creating internal competition for blood supply.

But in 1979 Nadel et al. showed that this theoretical problem was not a factor because the body was more than capable of meeting both demands simultaneously by diverting blood from the renal and splanchnic circulations to match the demand.[9] This conclusion was subsequently confirmed by Savard et al.[10], and it became clear that other factors were responsible for impaired performance in the heat.

Effect of Heat on the Brain and Muscle Function

Researchers noticed that exercising volunteers in the laboratory in hot conditions often lost coordination and had impaired motor and cognitive function at the point of complete exhaustion.[10, 11] That finding implicated the brain, and when it was observed that exhaustion almost always happened at the same temperature of approximately 40 degrees Celsius (104 degrees Fahrenheit), researchers proposed that there was an upper limit to body temperature beyond which exercise would not continue.[1, 2]

As technology improved, so did our ability to study how the brain and muscle function were affected by high temperatures. One of the key studies came in 2001 from Denmark, where Nybo and Nielsen were able to use electromyography to measure muscle activation levels after exercise in hot and cold environments. They found that when cyclists had fatigued at a body temperature of 104 degrees Fahrenheit (40 degrees Celsius), they were able to activate less muscle than when their body temperature was only 100 degrees Fahrenheit (37 degrees Celsius). The hot brain therefore failed to maintain the required level of muscle recruitment, so the conclusion was that the high body temperature caused fatigue because it prevented the central drive for the recruitment of muscle fibers.[1]

Again, this conclusion is not necessarily incorrect. The study, in fact, provides crucial information about what happens at the very end of exercise. It is incomplete, however, and perhaps inappropriate, for an obvious practical reason. We rarely exercise at the same speed until we literally have to stop exercise altogether. In training and in races, we slow down well in advance of complete termination of exercise, so studies of self-paced exercise were needed to complete the picture. Those came in 2002, in the form of numerous research studies that began to accumulate evidence for physiological regulation in advance of hyperthermia.[12, 13, 14]

Adjusting for Heat

Marino et al. found that athletes doing an 8-kilometer time trial in hot conditions started slower than they did in cool conditions even though their body temperatures were no different between conditions and were not close to the theoretical ceiling that had been proposed by previous research on the "critical hyperthermia hypothesis."[14] The key was that the bigger athletes slowed down more, right from the start of the time trial, which says that it is not a direct effect of body temperature but rather an anticipatory reduction in speed that affects performance. The fact that bigger runners are more affected by this anticipatory reduction is probably because they have higher rates of heat storage, suggesting that the brain monitors not the actual temperature but how the rate of heat gain is changing, and then slows us down.

That was followed by a study by Tucker et al., in which cyclists slowed down in hot conditions during a 20-kilometer cycling time trial from the first 5 kilometers onward, although they too had submaximal core temperatures that were no different from those measured in a cool environment.[15] This reduction in power output was associated with a reduction in EMG activity in the quadriceps muscles, and it was concluded that the centrally regulated activation of muscle fibers was decreased in advance of an excessive rise in body temperature so that the required 20-kilometer time trial could be completed in the fastest possible time without either premature fatigue or potentially harmful changes in homeostasis.[15]

Nybo and Nielsen had shown that if the body does overheat, fatigue occurs as a distinct event and that a dramatic reduction in muscle activation is the cause.[1] But the physiology of fatigue happens well in advance of this point during self-paced exercise, such as a race or training session.[14, 15] Here, muscle activation is reduced in anticipation of that critically high body temperature.

Equally significant is the increase in muscle activation levels and thus power output at the end of exercise. This result is typical. Every athlete who approaches the finish line of a race has experienced finding the necessary energy to increase pace for the final spurt. This spurt is a significant observation, because it shows that during exercise, the body maintains a muscle activation reserve and can recruit those muscles to enable the sprint at the end of exercise.

For example, Tucker et al. showed a significant increase in skeletal muscle activation and power output at the end of 20-kilometer cycling time trials in the heat. The increase in EMG activity and power output happened despite body temperatures that were significantly elevated compared with those measured earlier in the trial, showing that a direct effect of high body temperature was not responsible for a reduction in EMG activity as Nybo and Nielsen had previously suggested. The maintenance of a reserve is a crucial component of anticipatory regulation.

How is this anticipatory reduction achieved? This discussion is complex and not directly relevant here, but it is described in detail elsewhere.[5, 7] But it has been proposed that the brain is constantly making calculations based on changes that happen throughout exercise. If the pace is too high on a hot day, then the brain activates less muscle; the pace drops, and the rate of heat storage and body temperature are returned to acceptable levels. Central to this occurrence is the rating of perceived exertion, or RPE, a subjective but crucial component, because it explains why fatigue is now viewed as a sensation, not an event. In this RPE-regulated model, athletes compare how they feel to how they expect themselves to feel at any moment during exercise and adjust their intensity accordingly. This modulation is likely a result of both conscious processes (the conscious awareness of RPE) and subconscious processes, including the underlying physiology responsible for, in this case, thermal homeostasis, as well as the generation of RPE and the expectation of RPE during exercise.

Energy Stores

The same is true during longer duration endurance exercise during which the depletion of energy stores is a potential limiting factor. Glycogen depletion in either the muscle or liver is known to result in fatigue. The levels of these fuel stores, however, appear to be regulated during self-paced exercise, and this would prevent the premature fatigue associated with depletion and the even more dire physiological consequences of total glycogen depletion.[16, 17]

According to this theory, the RPE would be elevated for a given workload,[7, 18] and the pace would be adjusted so that the RPE, and therefore the rate of fuel use, would be reduced specifically to ensure that this limit is not reached. Of course, in ultradistance events, this failure does occur. Athletes do hit the wall, and glycogen depletion does occur, as does the attainment of critically high body temperatures. Athletes who are sufficiently motivated or who are unable to reduce the workload sufficiently (even reducing to walking speed on a run may be insufficient on a hot day or during an ultradistance event) remain in danger of reaching these physiological limits.

Oxygen Supply

In the case of an Olympic- or sprint-distance triathlete, who may be running at an intensity approaching 90 percent of $\dot{V}O_2$max during the final stages of a race, the physiological systems contributing to fatigue involve oxygen content of the arterial blood, oxygen delivery to muscle, or the removal or accumulation of metabolic by-products such as hydrogen ions, ADP, and the depletion of ATP.

In these situations, where exercise intensity is greater, it is less clear what system or systems are responsible for the sensation of fatigue. Recently, however, Amman proposed that adjustments in the recruitment of muscle and thus exercise intensity were made based on afferent feedback from the muscle, specifically to ensure that excessive peripheral fatigue (loss of muscle function) does not occur.[19, 20, 21] That is, muscle function was protected during higher intensity exercise because of inputs that include chemical changes in muscle and oxygen content of the arterial blood.

In all these exercise situations, workload is reduced through a reduction in muscle activation before the known or theorized point of failure is reached, and the rating of perceived exertion is central to this regulation. When the pace is fixed, fatigue is detected as an increase in the RPE—holding that pace becomes more difficult. If the pace is free to vary, then fatigue is seen as a slowing down at the same overall effort.

Crucially, we are aware only of our subjective judgment of effort. We do not have a warning light like a car to alert us to the fact that we are running low on fuel or oxygen or that our body temperature is increasing. But we do have a subjective perception of discomfort or exertion, which may be viewed as a subconscious warning light, and this subjective perception of effort is what allows us to adjust our pace and in turn our physiological cost of exercise.

Training and Fatigue: A Three-Pronged Approach

The key to understanding the influence of these theories on training is to appreciate several points:

1. **Fatigue should be viewed not as a distinct event at which the athlete fails but rather as a drop in output pace or power for the same effort.** Alternatively, fatigue occurs when the perception of effort is elevated for a given workrate. This notion has clear implications for the management of training quantity and quality, as described subsequently.

2. **Training will alter the physiology that determines perceived exertion.** That is, the signals that are responsible for this regulation of perceived exertion, the sensation of fatigue, will change with training, so that the stimulus to increase the RPE occurs later and the anticipatory regulation is attenuated.

3. **Our interpretation of the brain's signal of fatigue is crucial to performance**, and although we cannot completely override the brain's regulation, we can recognize that a reserve exists and begin to approach our limits more closely.

Effect of Training on Exercising in the Heat

In the case of exercise in the heat, both heat loss and heat production at the same exercise workload change favorably as a result of endurance training. That is, heat loss capacity improves while heat production decreases.

Athletes increase sweat capacity as more sweat glands are recruited and because heat loss ability is greatly enhanced by the plasma volume expansion that occurs because of training. (This mechanism largely explains acclimatization to heat.[22]) In addition, heat production declines because any given workload corresponds to a reduced relative intensity (as a percentage of maximum), which has been shown to be a key predictor of body temperature.[22]

The result is that the rate of heat storage is reduced at a given workload and core body temperature rises at a lower rate because of training or acclimatization to heat. This outcome is reflected in the subjective rating of perceived exertion, which has been found to increase at a lower rate because of repeated exposures to heat. Six consecutive exercise bouts to volitional exhaustion in hot environments can produce full acclimatization. In practice, the time required is likely longer because the physiological demand of exercising to exhaustion on 6 consecutive days is both unrealistic and disruptive to normal training. Full acclimatization may therefore require up to 2 weeks of planned training. Ultimately, the exercising athlete is able to sustain a higher pace, experience less fatigue, and delay the point at which a critical level of hyperthermia may occur.

Effect of Training on Energy Use

Similarly, for energy use, training has numerous benefits. As described previously, one of the key adaptations to training is an increase in mitochondria, which results in an increase in the capacity to oxidize fat as a source of fuel and a resultant glycogen-sparing effect. As for heat, the fact that a trained athlete competes or trains at a lower relative exercise intensity (as a percentage of maximum) means that the sympathetic response to exercise is reduced, and this further favors the preferential use of fat and sparing of muscle glycogen.

As a result, a trained athlete oxidizes significantly more fat at a given intensity than an untrained athlete does. In addition, glycogen storage capacity increases with training, resulting in a larger fuel store with which to begin exercise. The brain is therefore monitoring an entirely different set of physiological signals, so the point of glycogen depletion is delayed because of metabolic adaptations to training.

Again, it has been shown that the RPE increases at a rate that is influenced by the level of glycogen in the muscle; low levels are associated with a rapid rise in RPE.[18] Therefore, altering the rate of glycogen utilization, or optimizing fuel use, is reflected as a change in the rate at which the RPE, or sensation of fatigue, rises during exercise. In both instances, it is easy to appreciate that the changes with training will completely alter the signals that the brain monitors during training and racing.

Importance of RPE

As for the significance of fatigue being a sensation,[23] this point is crucial. It means that athletes can monitor physiology by monitoring the subjective ratings of perceived exertion during training sessions. Scientists may balk at the idea that a subjective rating of perceived exertion can outperform sophisticated technology such as heart rate variability and chemical tests, but the global trend towards fatigue monitoring does indeed reflect the realization of the importance of the RPE. The astute triathlete or coach who recognizes the physiological value of the RPE is able to control exercise intensity and volume to manage and avoid fatigue that occurs with overtraining.

Conclusion

Our understanding of fatigue has evolved in recent years to explain more broadly what is known to occur during self-paced exercise. A complex regulatory process integrates input such as body temperature, oxygen availability, energy supply, and metabolic status from various physiological systems and then enables the adjustment of exercise intensity by means of alterations in muscle activation levels to ensure that performance is optimized and that homeostasis is maintained.

The effect of training is to alter the input to the brain because training enables higher workloads to be achieved before potentially limiting perturbations can occur in these systems. For example, fat oxidation increases, glycogen depletion is delayed, and body temperature rises less rapidly, thus delaying the critical level of hyperthermia at which the athlete would be forced to stop exercise.

Although this theory does not fundamentally change the practice of coaching or making training decisions (the triathlete must still perform the same training to induce the same adaptations; there are no shortcuts here), it does inform a novel approach to the management of performance, pacing strategy, and fatigue, particularly in physiologically stressful conditions such as hot and humid environments, high altitude, and limited energy supply. In these situations, the pacing strategy and the coach and triathlete's ability to understand how pacing strategy is regulated is crucial to success.

Training Modes and Methods for Triathletes

CHAPTER 16

Warm-Up and Cool-Down

—David Warden

In the complexities of training, triathletes and coaches often forget that the mass of the human body is subject to the same physical laws as all other matter. Specifically, the effect of temperature on any solid or liquid is to change its physical state. When a solid is heated, energy is added to the system, increasing the vibration of the particles. When cooled, the particles slow down. The blood, muscles, and other tissues of triathletes respond to this phenomenon as any physical matter does, and the effect on performance can be significant. Although triathletes of all abilities practice warm-ups and cool-downs, implementation varies. Triathletes who implement specific warm-up and cool-down protocols based on certain variables are likely to see an improvement in performance and recovery.

Warm-Up for Performance

At the most basic level, the benefits of warm-up could be summed up as reducing resistance in the triathlete's body. Reduced resistance is a natural consequence of the heated state of any material. In early examinations,[1, 2] a 20 percent reduction of resistance was reported in some joints following a light warm-up, as was a decrease in muscle fiber stiffness. But the physical, physiological, and metabolic consequences of warming up are much broader, and some of the benefits are unrelated to temperature change.

The two forms of warming up are passive and active. Passive warm-up is the act of heating the body using an external source, such as a shower, hot tub, or heating pad. Active warm-up, during which the triathlete duplicates the movement of an activity, such as by jogging, is more common. Although the passive method contributes to an elevated temperature and the associated benefit of energy conservation in the triathlete, it does not introduce the physiological and metabolic benefits of an active warm-up and will not be discussed in this chapter.

The focus of this section is warm-up before an event, but the applications are similar for a warm-up before the main set of a workout. The principles laid out can be applied to any workout that includes intervals of moderate intensity or simulated racing. Additionally, like all effective training, any warm-up incorporated into a competitive event should be frequently practiced in training.

Benefits of Warm-Up

The benefits of warm-up are diverse. They include increased blood flow, an increase in oxygen uptake, an elevated baseline $\dot{V}O_2$, reduced muscle stiffness and soreness, injury prevention, and even reported psychological benefits.

Increased Blood Flow and Oxygen Uptake

The immediate results of the heated state of blood, muscles, and tissues include higher core and muscle temperatures, which in turn improve and increase blood flow. This increased blood flow and its associated oxygen content promote a potential increase in oxygen uptake,[3] a significant predictor for endurance performance. In addition, as early as 1909 researchers demonstrated that hemoglobin gives off twice as much oxygen when its temperature is raised by 5 degrees Celsius.[4] With muscle temperature increased by as much as 6 degrees Celsius from warming up,[15] the temperature of hemoglobin will likely rise by a similar amount. Although oxygen delivery to the muscles is only one component in determining $\dot{V}O_2$max, an increase in the supply of oxygen to the muscles is key.

Elevated Baseline $\dot{V}O_2$

The warm-up has additional performance benefits possibly related to temperature change and the resulting metabolic consequences of a warm-up (figure 16.1). A primary advantage is that the triathlete enters the main workout or competition with an elevated baseline $\dot{V}O_2$.[5, 6] This "excited" state of oxygen consumption may allow the triathlete to maintain aerobic workload early in the activity, lowering the risk of early anaerobic work, using less glycogen for fuel, and increasing time to exhaustion.

Decreased Muscle Stiffness

Additionally, general muscle movement reduces muscle stiffness by breaking the bond between actin and myosin filaments.[7] These filamentous protein molecules continue to bond at rest, which can lead to muscle stiffness. Taking a muscle group through a range of motion tends to break these bonds, decrease stiffness, and maximize range of motion.

Psychological Consequences

The warm-up may even offer psychological benefits. Athletes who visualize a warm-up report improved performance.[8] In interviews, 75 Canadian

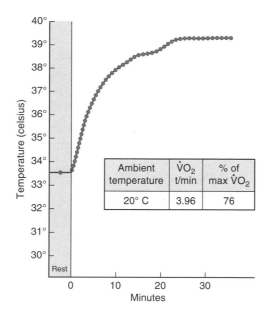

▶**Figure 16.1** Muscle temperature before and after warm-up.

Adapted, by permission, from B. Saltin, A.P. Gagge, and J.A. Stolwijk, 1968, "Muscle temperature during submaximal exercise in man," Journal of Applied Physiology 25(6): 679-688.

Olympians identified a preperformance routine as a distinguishing characteristic of an Olympic-level athlete. They also found that athletes who maintain a regular prerace checklist, including a warm-up, appear to be more likely to duplicate the success of previous performances.

Muscle Soreness and Injury Prevention

Although most of this chapter focuses on warm-up in relation to performance, evidence also shows that warm-up has postexercise advantages. These benefits include reduced muscle soreness in the days following exercise and a reduction in overall potential soft-tissue injury. Even 10 minutes of slow walking before eccentric exercise reduces muscle soreness 48 hours later.[9]

Additionally, although there is conflicting evidence that warm-up prevents injury, research suggests that active warming of the muscles increases elasticity and range of motion,[10, 11] thus reducing the chance that the muscle will stretch beyond capacity during intense exercise.

Risks of Warm-Up

Despite the documented performance advantages of warm-up, some risks are involved. These possibilities include an increase in core temperature, a decrease in glycogen stores, and a general increase in fatigue before the event.

In endurance sports, the triathlete's capacity to store heat becomes a limiting factor in performance,[12] particularly for longer exercise sessions during which the ambient temperature may continue to rise throughout the event. A warm-up that increases the triathlete's initial core temperature carries the risk that the athlete may start the event at an elevated core temperature,[13] thus reducing the overall capacity to store heat later in the exercise and reducing performance. In cool environments, a warm-up is unlikely to contribute to overheating.

Although exercise of less than 3 hours' duration carries little risk of glycogen depletion for a moderately trained triathlete, the conservation of glycogen stores must be carefully considered for longer events. A 30-minute warm-up for a moderately trained male could reasonably consume hundreds of calories of glycogen. Although this risk can be easily mitigated through ingesting additional calories during the warm-up and controlling intensity, a triathlete who enters long-term endurance exercise with reduced glycogen stores risks a decrease in overall performance.

Perhaps the most ironic risk of warm-up is the potential to introduce fatigue to the triathlete before the onset of desired peak performance. A warm-up of unnecessary duration or intensity crosses the line between warm-up and intense exercise, thus prematurely placing the triathlete in a fatigued state.[14] This potential for fatigue is relative to the triathlete's fitness. Risk is significantly reduced in trained triathletes, and warm-ups should be practiced and experimented with in training.

Warm-Up Duration

Because the primary benefits of warm-up are the elevation of blood and muscle temperature, increased baseline $\dot{V}O_2$, and increased range of motion, the warm-up time should be of sufficient length to introduce these three benefits but short enough to avoid the risks of diminished heat storage capacity, glycogen depletion, and general fatigue.

Although muscle temperature does not continue to rise significantly after 20 minutes of exercise,[15] core temperature, which is the primary factor in the heat-related decrease in performance, does continue to rise with increased exercise duration, giving incentive to the triathlete to keep the warm-up short. In fact, healthy males reached a steady $\dot{V}O_2$ after just a 10-minute warm-up.[16] Finally, trained cyclists achieved a higher power output with a 16-minute warm-up when compared with a 50-minute warm-up.[17]

Therefore, for endurance exercise, a warm-up of up to 20 minutes appears to promote the physical and metabolic benefits that increase performance without the negative fatiguing effects that accumulate with an increase in warm-up duration.

Despite the documented performance advantages of warm-up, under some circumstances it should be adjusted or eliminated from the workout or event. Based on an understanding of the benefits and risks of warm-up, the warm-up duration should be varied based on three factors:

- Duration of the exercise or event
- Fitness of the individual
- Ambient temperature of the exercise environment

Adjusting Warm-Up Duration Based on Event Length

As the length of an endurance event increases, the need for warm-up declines, not only because of the warm-up risks previously discussed, which increase with a longer event, but also because of the low intensity associated with increased exercise or race duration. For the purposes of this discussion, *long* refers to an endurance event during which complete glycogen depletion would be possible if additional carbohydrate is not ingested throughout the event, perhaps 3 hours for a moderately trained male or an event that lasts longer than an Olympic-distance triathlon. The triathlete can take advantage of the lower intensity associated with long events by treating the first 20 minutes as the warm-up, which would provide similar benefits without introducing the risks.

For short events, the requirement for early intensity is great, as is the need to call on close-to-peak power at the onset of the event, particularly for elite or draft-legal triathletes who must stay with the lead swimming pack. This early intensity further increases the risk of prematurely achieving an anaerobic state. The need for increased muscle temperature, elevated baseline $\dot{V}O_2$, and range of motion are immediate. Additionally, the risk of glycogen depletion for a short endurance event of less than 3 hours is low, as is heat storage capacity for early- to mid-morning performance. Therefore, a warm-up is recommended for shorter endurance events.

For triathletes, a specific recommendation is to warm up for sprint- and Olympic-distance events and to avoid additional activity for half- and full-Ironman events.

Adjusting Warm-Up Duration Based on the Triathlete's Fitness

The triathlete's fitness must also be considered in warm-up. The more fit the individual is, the longer the warm-up that she can tolerate without an effect on performance. When the risk of undue fatigue is considered in association with warm-up, the onset and degree of fatigue from activity varies from one triathlete to another based on fitness. A 20-minute warm-up for a 90-minute event is a significant share of the activity for many triathletes. Anecdotal observation of elite triathletes often reveals a warm-up of 60 minutes or longer for a 60-minute event (half marathon) without an apparent decrease in performance.

Although no evidence shows that this longer warm-up promotes increased physical or metabolic benefit, the high fitness level of the individuals allows them to perform that extended activity without the risks that would apply to untrained people. The decision about duration of warm-up should be made and applied in training to verify tolerance and the consequences to race-day performance.

Adjusting Warm-Up Duration Based on Temperature

Although less a consideration than fitness and event duration, the ambient temperature should also be considered when structuring a warm-up. The warmer the temperature is, the greater the risk that the warm-up will contribute to higher core body temperature. Although the objective of the warm-up should still be to increase muscle temperature, rarely does increasing core body temperature offer an advantage.

Conversely, on cool or cold days, more than 20 minutes may be needed to warm the muscles sufficiently, so a longer warm-up would be necessary to reach the desired muscle temperature. Additionally, a cool environment does not carry the same risk of elevated core body temperature during either the warm-up or the subsequent event.

Although little specific literature addresses the effect of exercise on muscle temperature in varying ambient environments, a warm-up of longer than 20 minutes may be justified for events in cool conditions, perhaps 30 to 40 minutes for short endurance events, to ensure that blood and muscle temperature have been properly elevated. For warm days, when the temperature could affect performance later in the event, the warm-up should be reduced to less than 20 minutes.

Warm-up Intensity and Specificity

Researchers reported a stable elevated baseline $\dot{V}O_2$ after 10 minutes at 90 percent of $\dot{V}O_2$max.[16] But this intensity is fairly high, and the duration may not be adequate to raise blood and muscle temperature. Other research supports an intensity of between 60 and 70 percent of $\dot{V}O_2$max output,[11, 14] which can be tolerated well for 20 minutes and is intense enough to promote the physical and metabolic benefits of warm-up without risk of undue fatigue. Although the consequences of warm-up on fatigue vary by fitness level, because this intensity (60 to 70 percent of individual $\dot{V}O_2$max) is relative to the athlete's fitness level, a 20-minute warm-up at this intensity presents low risk of premature fatigue before events of less than 3 hours in length.

The intensity should include brief bursts of higher-than-race-intensity speed, or at least the maximum intensity estimated for the event. These 10- to 30-second intervals should be intense enough to prep the body for the upcoming race-intensity stress, activate the neuromuscular systems, and put the muscles through a greater range of motion. The number of intervals should be three to five, each 10 to 30 seconds in duration, should include long recoveries of several minutes, and should be performed at somewhere between 100 percent and 150 percent of $\dot{V}O_2$max output, depending on the triathlete's fitness level, race length, and ambient temperature. A higher fitness level, shorter event, and cooler day justify a longer and more intense interval. See table 16.1 for a specific example of a race-day warm-up.

Ideally, the warm-up should include activities specific to the event. Although doing so is relatively simple for an individual running, cycling, or swimming event, it becomes complicated for a triathlete. A preferred triathlon warm-up would include 5 to 10 minutes of activity in all three disciplines, in reverse order (run, bike, swim).

Although performing a run and swim warm-up before the event is often easy, a bike warm-up can be impractical and even impossible in the final 30 minutes before a triathlon. Research is limited on the warm-up effects of one activity on performance in another, but it is the author's opinion that the bike warm-up can be eliminated from the triathlete's routine on race day and replaced with run and swim warm-up activity. Although this approach contradicts the activity-specific principle of warm-up, many of the physical and metabolic benefits of warm-up would theoretically transfer from one activity to another.

Table 16.1 Suggested Warm-Up for Sprint- and Olympic-Distance Triathlon*

Activity	Time (min)
Run at velocities between 60 and 70% of $\dot{V}O_2$max velocity**	10
Run three to five intervals of 10 to 30 seconds at 100 to 150% of $\dot{V}O_2$max velocity** with long easy recoveries	10
Return to transition area, check equipment, put on wetsuit	10
Continue warm-up in water at 60 to 70% of $\dot{V}O_2$max velocity** or perform 10- to 30-second intervals at anticipated swim start intensity	5

*Cool-day warm-up for events at which maximum anticipated competitive temperature is less than 80 degrees Fahrenheit (27 degrees Celsius). For warmer days, reduce warm-up time by 50%.

**See chapter 20 for determining $\dot{V}O_2$max swim and run velocity.

Warm-Up Timing

Unfortunately, the benefits of warm-up dissipate with inactivity, but they can be maintained for some time after warm-up. Baseline $\dot{V}O_2$ returns to its normal profile after 20 to 45 minutes of inactivity.[18] But the greatest increase in baseline $\dot{V}O_2$ after warm-up occurs when the activity begins within 10 minutes of the end of the warm-up (figure 16.2).

Muscle temperature appears to be more tolerant of inactivity. Temperature drops by less than 1 degree Celsius 15 minutes after exercise and remains elevated by over 2 degrees relative to preexercise for over an hour after exercise at an ambient temperature of 22 degrees Celsius.[19] Muscle stiffness and range of motion can change quickly during prolonged inactivity.

In any competitive athletic event, timing the warm-up to end within 10 minutes of the start to gain the benefit of elevated $\dot{V}O_2$ is challenging. For a triathlete, precise timing can be exceptionally difficult, depending on the logistics and layout of the race. For this reason, a triathlete should consider a "broken" warm-up consisting of 15 to 20 minutes of running with associated intervals, followed by a final check and setup of the transition area, and then possibly putting on a wetsuit and reporting to the swim venue to continue the warm-up.

The time from the end of the run warm-up to the start of the swim warm-up will likely be more than the recommended 10 minutes. Therefore, the triathlete must continue the warm-up in the water at the swim venue to mitigate any muscle temperature loss and to reinstate a high baseline $\dot{V}O_2$ before the start. The swim warm-up should be consistent at a relatively high percentage of $\dot{V}O_2$ velocity (60 to 70 percent), both to regain the metabolic benefits potentially lost from inactivity and to maintain or increase blood and muscle temperature.

Even this broken warm-up will not be possible or feasible at some events, such as a dry-land start or in extremely cold water in which muscle temperature could decrease even with activity. In such cases, the triathlete should consider a warm-up of only running to realize the remaining psychological

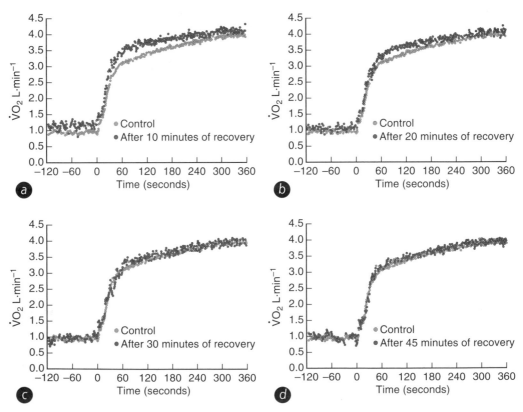

▶ **Figure 16.2** Baseline and activity-driven $\dot{V}O_2$max after 10, 20, 30, and 45 minutes between warm-up and activity.

Reprinted, by permission, from M. Burnley, J.H. Doust, and A.M. Jones, 2006. "Time required for the restoration of normal heavy exercise $\dot{V}O_2$ kinetics following prior heavy exercise," Journal of Applied Physiology 101(5): 1320-1327.

and postexercise benefits, as well as the physical benefits of increasing blood and muscle temperature, breaking the bond between actin and myosin filaments, and increasing range of motion. These warm-up effects appear to be somewhat tolerant of brief inactivity and can still provide an increase in performance.

Cool-Down for Recovery

The term *cool-down* has been incorporated into exercise science with multiple definitions. For the purpose of this chapter, cool-down will be defined as two distinct postexercise protocols: active cool-down and passive cool-down.

Active Cool-Down

Active cool-down is the gradual reduction in exercise intensity at the end of a training session. The triathlete remains active, although at a fraction of the previous exercise intensity. The most common form of cool-down is the equivalent intensity of a jog or even a walk for approximately 10 minutes at the end of an exercise session.

Despite the lack of evidence-based benefits of active cool-down, no research indicates that it is harmful or detrimental to performance. Triathletes who perform more than one workout a day may benefit from a 20-minute active cool-down at very low intensity. Active cool-down is traditionally believed to have multiple benefits, including the dissipation of lactic acid, reduced muscle soreness, and reduced likelihood of dizziness or fainting.

Clearing of Lactic Acid

Research does show that an active cool-down of 5 minutes at 32 percent of $\dot{V}O_2$max (a brisk walk or light jog) is more effective than 5 minutes of compete rest in reducing lactate in the blood after anaerobic activity.[20] The same research also indicates an increase in peak short-term power in repetitive exercise bouts following an active cool-down, which was associated with reduced lactate in the blood from cool-down.

But the lactate buildup in this study resulted from peak power of only 6 seconds, not the much smaller buildup of lactate that would be expected from endurance exercise. In addition, lactate, once viewed as the enemy and a primary cause of fatigue, is not a contributing factor in fatigue for aerobic activity.[21] Lactic acid accumulates only in brief high-intensity efforts of less than 1 minute. Although the dissipation of large accumulations of lactate after anaerobic exercise may provide some benefit when calling upon additional anaerobic power, lactate dissipation is a concern neither during nor after exercise for aerobic activity. For the triathlete, who rarely incorporates maximum-effort anaerobic training of less than 1 minute, large accumulation of lactate is rare, as is the need to call on repetitive bouts of peak power.

Cool-Down and Muscle Soreness

Lactic acid is also anecdotally blamed for muscle soreness felt a day or two after intense exercise (delayed-onset muscle soreness, or DOMS). The theory is that the lingering lactic acid adds to muscle soreness. Not only is this accumulation unlikely for aerobic activity, as related previously, but the soreness theory has been widely dismissed, in part because of a study that showed that runners who reported less muscle soreness actually had higher concentrations of lactate during a 45-minute run in a controlled environment.[22] A previously cited study concluded, "There was no evidence of an effect of cool-down on either measure of soreness or tenderness."[9] DOMS appears to have much more to do with eccentric muscle contraction leading to structural damage, not lingering lactic acid.

An active cool-down study more applicable to triathletes, who often train twice a day, was based on a 30-minute time trial followed by 20 minutes of one of five different recovery methods (variations on passive, compression, and active cool-down). The subjects then rested and repeated the time trial. The only recovery method to improve performance in the second time trial was an active cool-down at 80 watts, suggesting that a 20-minute cool-down at a light spin may be beneficial for triathletes who train twice a day.[23]

Prevention of Fainting

Perhaps the most likely benefit of active cool-down is to prevent postexercise dizziness by allowing the "muscle pump" to stay active and prevent the pooling of blood in the extremities.[24] The alternating contraction and relaxation of skeletal muscle creates a pumping action in the veins to aid with venous return, which reduces the risk of light-headedness or fainting after exercise.

Passive Cool-Down

Passive cool-down is the process of cooling the body using external, inactive methods, such as ice baths, hydrotherapy, cryotherapy, or contrast baths. Intense or sustained exercise causes microtrauma, or tiny tears in muscle fibers. Although fitness is ultimately increased by introducing measured stress and even minor damage (followed by rest) to muscles and tissue, the ability to speed the recovery process allows the triathlete to return quickly to additional intense or sustained exercise.

Passive-cool down is thought to minimize exercise-induced damage and speed recovery by reducing swelling and inflammation, decreasing metabolic activity, slowing down physiological processes, and constricting blood vessels to flush, or squeeze, waste products out of the affected tissues. With contrast baths, repetitive cooling and rewarming the body is thought to increase blood flow and circulation by pumping the blood in and out of the tissues because of the constriction and expansion of blood vessels from the variations in temperature.

Scientific research supporting passive recovery is rich. In one study, cyclists performed 5 consecutive days of 105 minutes of moderately intense exercise, including a 9-minute time trial.[25] The exercise was followed by 14 minutes of either cold-water immersion, hot-water immersion, contrast bath, or inactivity. Both the cold-water bath and contrast bath recovery showed a slight improvement in time-trial performance over the 5-day period compared with hot water or inactivity. Another study looked at performance 24 and 48 hours after 3 days of intense exercise and found that cold-water recovery resulted in a faster return to baseline performance compared with contrast baths.[26] With the literature leaning toward cold-water recovery over contrast baths and the consideration of the complexity of contrast baths compared with cold water only, an effective and practical approach for the triathlete is to use cold-water recovery.

Although the studies supporting passive cool-down vary in terms of water temperature and duration, a common protocol would be water temperature between 10 and 15 degrees Celsius (50 to 60 degrees Fahrenheit) with submersion for 10 to 20 minutes. For triathletes, this would rarely include the need for whole-body submersion and could be limited to the lower body, for example, by returning to the water start and standing waist deep in water after a race.

Finally, stretching after exercise could be considered part of a cool-down protocol. The benefits of stretching and flexibility and ways to incorporate stretching into a triathlon training program are covered in chapter 17.

Conclusion

These protocols require a relatively small investment of time from the triathlete while returning potentially significant physiological and even psychological benefits. For example, an increase in baseline VO_2 and oxygen uptake would normally take months or years of regular training to develop. Yet a brief warm-up can provide an immediate, although temporary, increase in these critical components of endurance performance. Likewise, investment in passive cool-down allows a quicker path to recovery, effectively extending the triathlete's training week by reducing recovery time.

Like all training techniques, warm-up and cool-down should be practiced during training and low-priority races before implementing them on race day. When implemented properly, active warm-up can play a significant role in improving a triathlete's performance on race day, and passive cool-down can speed the ability to return to intense training sessions so that new fitness can be gained.

CHAPTER 17

Flexibility and Core Strength

—David Warden

Theoretically, flexibility, or range of motion, should have a direct positive correlation with improved athletic performance and injury prevention. Intuitively, a triathlete's ability to maximize movement should result in increased power, particularly for cyclic disciplines such as swimming, cycling, and running. Additionally, because soft-tissue injury is caused almost exclusively by pushing a muscle or joint beyond its strength or range of motion, increased flexibility would theoretically reduce the risk of injury. Empirical data on flexibility, however, present a complex and sometimes contradictory picture.

Often developed concurrently with flexibility is core strength, or postural stability. A popular concept among triathletes, its role in injury prevention appears positive. Although flexibility may lengthen the lever, core strength appears to play a crucial role in stabilizing the lever.

Research suggests that a triathlete's performance can be improved when specific (but not all) joint and muscle groups increase in flexibility. Although stretching appears to offer little in terms in terms of injury prevention, it does offer other limited benefits. Additionally, a core strength program appears to provide significant benefit in terms of injury prevention.

Flexibility and Performance

To illustrate the inconsistent relationship between flexibility and athletic performance, the flexibility of over 200 elite athletes, including 90 Olympians, was compared with the total-body flexibility of nonathletes.[1] Elite male athletes in sports such as basketball, soccer, judo, rowing, and fencing were found to be less flexible than, or equal in flexibility to, the general public, whereas swimmers, cyclists, and tennis players were found to be more flexible. Elite female athletes in swimming, but not in cycling, showed increased flexibility.

The researchers concluded that only swimming appears to benefit from an increase in flexibility across genders.

Although increased flexibility appears to lead to increased performance in some sports, the trend is not universal. Variations also occur by gender. Because the focus of this book is triathlon, let's review how flexibility affects performance in swimming, cycling, and running.

Swimming

Whether evidence is considered anecdotally or empirically, swimming performance and flexibility appear to be directly related. Unlike cycling or running, during which the legs are rarely required to extend to their fullest reach, outstanding swimming requires maximum length and reach of the arms to lengthen the lever.

In freestyle swimming, limited shoulder flexibility results in a low elbow during the recovery phase of the stroke. (Figure 17.1 shows good shoulder flexibility.) The effect of drag in swimming is so great that ankle flexibility is required to produce a streamlined lower leg and pointed foot. Additionally, the ability to whip the foot across a wide arc during a flutter kick adds propulsion to the swim. A 2009 study found a direct correlation between ankle flexibility, flutter kick speed, and 50-meter swim times,[2] and knee flexibility, or the ability to hyperextend the knee slightly, is directly associated with swim volume.[3]

Although swimmers would theoretically benefit from flexibility in multiple joints and muscles in the upper body, the primary areas of focus should be

▶ **Figure 17.1** Good shoulder flexibility.

ankles (tibialis), lats (latissimus dorsi), shoulders, pectorals (pectoralis), and knees. See the section Sample Flexibility Exercises for good stretches to try.

Cycling

Unlike swimming and running, empirical literature on the relationship between cycling and flexibility is scarce. Among coaches and elite athletes, there is a common anecdotal belief that flexibility of the legs will allow an increase in power. For example, tight hamstrings could theoretically restrict the downstroke of the pedal cycle. Or, even more likely, they could reduce the speed with which the leg can reach the bottom of the stroke. This same logic applies to the soleus and gastrocnemius muscles of the lower leg. As referenced earlier, a correlation exists between flexibility and elite male cyclists, which provides a compelling case for flexibility in cycling.

Most research on flexibility and athletic performance focuses on the relationship between flexibility and propulsive force. In cycling, however, triathletes have another unique benefit from flexibility unrelated to propulsion. The ability to maintain an aggressive aerodynamic position for 30 minutes in a sprint-distance triathlon to over 6 hours for a long-course event has a direct effect on cycling speed. Flexibility in the back, shoulders, and neck allows an aerodynamic and comfortable ride. In addition, inflexibility in the aerodynamic position, which leads to discomfort or pain, could reduce overall power output when cycling.

The primary areas on which to focus to improve flexibility in triathlon cycling would be the shoulders, hamstrings, and lower back. See the section Sample Flexibility Exercises for good stretches to try.

Running

Perhaps no discipline has more conflicting data on performance and flexibility than running. As with swimming and cycling, at first glance it appears logical that increasing the range through which force can be applied should increase propulsion. But multiple studies support the theory that the unique biomechanics of running may require a decrease in range of motion for maximum economy and performance.

Less Flexible, More Economical

For example, a review of 34 international runners[4] measured age, height, body mass, and trunk flexibility (sit-and-reach test) and correlated those measurements with running economy. Although no correlation was found within that group between aerobic running economy and age, height, or body weight, an inverse relationship was found between economy and flexibility. The least flexible runners were also the most economical.

The researchers theorized that "stiffer musculotendinous structures reduce the aerobic demand of submaximal running by facilitating a greater elastic energy return during the shortening phase of the stretch-shortening cycle."[5] This study was repeated in 2009 using subjects' 10K running times, and again an inverse relationship was found between the sit-and-reach test and running economy.[6]

This inverse relationship between running economy and flexibility extends to more than just the trunk. For example, runners with decreased range of motion in standing hip rotation and dorsiflexion of the foot (toes pointed upward) also have an increase in running economy.[7] The theory is that the stiff joints led to "increasing storage and return of elastic energy and minimizing the need for muscle-stabilizing activity."[8]

Other research on the effect of flexibility on running performance is more ambivalent. Male and female runners adding 2 hours a week of stretching to their regimens for 10 weeks were compared with male and female runners who did not add the stretching routine.[9] Although the stretching group was able to increase their sit-and-reach test by approximately 3 centimeters over their nonstretching counterparts, the stretching group exhibited neither a decrease nor an increase in running economy.

Static Stretching Before Running

The previous studies focused on the effect of general, long-term flexibility on running economy, but we also want to know about the effect on performance of static stretching just before running. Multiple studies[10, 11, 12] have looked at prerun static stretching and come to the conclusion that although prerun stretching does temporarily increase range of motion, it has no effect on subsequent running economy.

The argument that flexibility can improve running performance is mostly speculative, but that speculation is logical. As previously mentioned, if flexibility increases the range of force (produces a longer lever), then the action is more energy efficient. Other theories also support the link between flexibility and performance. For instance, because run speed is a result of both stride rate and stride length, flexibility could allow the triathlete to increase the length of the stride. Tight hip flexors could cause a reduction in stride length, but an increase in stride length could theoretically compensate for any elastic muscular energy efficiency lost in those more flexible muscles.

Good running form also requires a sustained forward drive on the part of the end of the foot. The longer the forefoot can drive forward before leaving the ground, the longer the overall stride length will be. If the toes leave the ground too early, forward thrust and distance are reduced or may even be channeled upward instead of forward. For the foot to maintain a longer plantar flex (toes pointed down) in the foot strike cycle, it must have adequate range of motion. Conversely, inflexible ankles could result in premature separation from the ground and reduced stride length, as illustrated in figure 17.2.

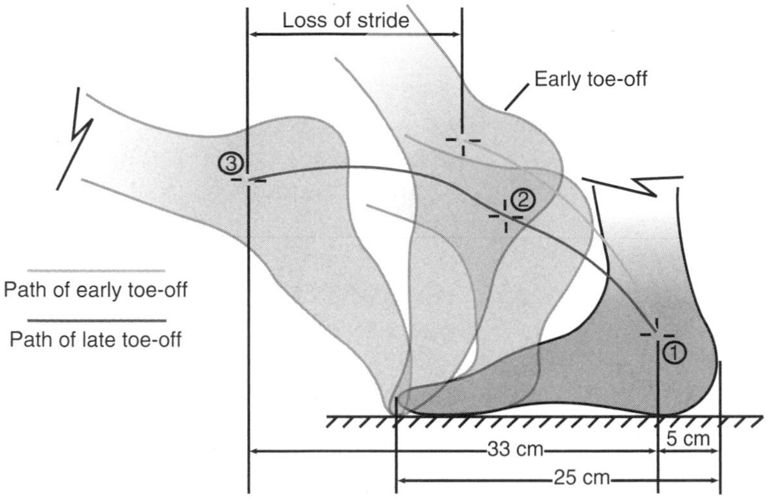

▶ **Figure 17.2** Foot strike cycle illustrating inflexible ankles resulting in premature separation from the ground and reduced stride length.

Reprinted, by permission, from D.E. Martin and P.N. Coe, 1997, Better training for distance runners, 2nd ed. (Champaign, IL: Human Kinetics), 27.

Upper-Body Range of Motion

Can upper-body range of motion affect stride length in running? A compelling theory by Pritchard is that if a runner's foot crosses over the midline, the total distance run is longer.[13] Any path taken by the foot or leg that deviates from a straight line in the direction of desired travel could add several centimeters per stride, and those centimeters would add up. Over the course of a 10K run, for example, 2 extra centimeters per stride at 620 strides per kilometer would add 124 meters of running.

Pritchard postulates that although there could be multiple causes for crossover, one cause is upper-body torque (UBT). UBT occurs when an inflexible shoulder or pectoral pulls the upper body back along with the swing of the arm, causing the opposing leg to cross over in a compensating movement.

A triathlete who implements a performance-motivated flexibility program should therefore focus on the plantar flexion of the ankles, shoulders, pectoralis, and hip flexors. See the section Sample Flexibility Exercises for good stretches to try.

Considerations for the Triathlete

The conflicting information on flexibility and performance is particularly challenging for a triathlete, because the three disciplines compete with one another in terms of ideal flexibility. How does the triathlete decide between increased dorsiflexion, which improves the kick in swimming but causes a reduction in running economy? Will the decreased hip rotation correlated with better running harm swim performance? Would it be better to keep trunk flexibility limited to maximize running and accept the potential trade-off of reduced cycling power or aerodynamics?

Although significant research supports decreased range of motion in the lower body for increased run performance, equally compelling evidence supports increased range of motion to improve performance in all three triathlon disciplines. When all is carefully considered, the best choice for triathletes is to incorporate a flexibility program into their training, targeting the joints and muscle groups linked to performance in swimming, cycling, and running.

Finally, if all other risks and rewards are relatively equal, the decision for a triathlete on flexibility could reasonably be based on just one consideration: potential injury prevention.

Sample Flexibility Exercises

The following exercises may help the triathlete improve flexibility in the ankles, upper back, shoulders, chest, knees, hamstrings, lower back, and hip flexors. Follow the guidelines in table 17.1 for static stretching.

Table 17.1   Static Stretching Guidelines

Frequency	Stretching 2 or 3 days per week is effective in improving joint range of motion. The greatest gains occur with daily flexibility exercise.
Intensity	Stretch to the point of feeling tightness or slight discomfort.
Time	Hold a static stretch for 10 to 30 seconds (recommended for most adults).
Volume	A reasonable target is to perform 60 seconds of total stretching time for each flexibility exercise, perhaps 3 × 20 seconds per muscle.
Pattern	Two to four repetitions of each flexibility exercise is recommended. Flexibility exercise is most effective when the muscle is warmed through activity.

Adapted from American College of Sports Medicine, 2011, "Position stand. Quantity and quality of exercise for developing and maintaining cardiorespiratory, musculoskeletal, and neuromotor fitness in apparently healthy adults: Guidance for prescribing exercise," *Medicine & Science in Sports & Exercise* 43(7): 1334-1359.

Kneeling Ankle Stretch   Kneel on both knees with the feet close together, toes pointed, and the tops of the feet resting on the floor. Keeping the knees together as much as possible, lean back over the feet, using your hands to support your weight (figure 17.3).

▶ **Figure 17.3**   Kneeling ankle stretch.

Ankle Motion   Sit with the legs straight and feet together. Alternate pointing the toes (figure 17.4a), flexing the feet (figure 17.4b), and rotating the feet in a circle (figure 17.4c).

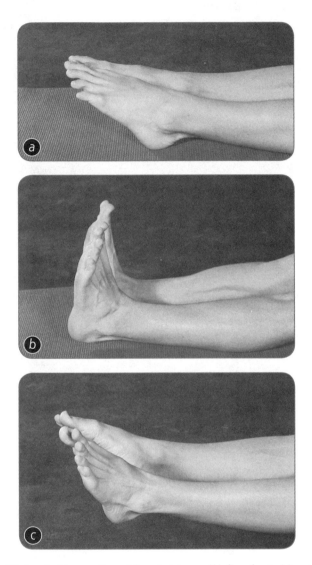

▶ **Figure 17.4**   Ankle motion: (a) point toes; (b) flex feet; (c) rotate feet.

Standing Lat Stretch   Stand with the feet shoulder-width apart and keep the knees soft. Lift the arms overhead. Bend the left arm and lower the left hand behind your head. With your right hand, grasp the left elbow and gently lean to the right, feeling the stretch up the left side (figure 17.5). Switch sides and repeat.

▶ **Figure 17.5**   Standing lat stretch.

Kneeling Physioball Lat Stretch   Kneel in front of a large physioball. Place your forearms on the ball and press your torso toward the ground (figure 17.6), keeping the back straight and abdominals engaged.

▶ **Figure 17.6**   Kneeling physioball lat stretch.

Doorway Shoulder Stretch   Stand in a doorway or other sturdy frame and place the left leg forward in lunge position. Place both forearms on the frame and lean into it. Depending on your flexibility, the arms can be lower (elbows aligned with waist), medium (elbows aligned with shoulders; figure 17.7), or high (elbows aligned with ears).

▶ **Figure 17.7**   Doorway shoulder stretch.

Up-and-Over Shoulder Stretch   Stand with the feet shoulder-width apart and keep the knees soft. Reach the right arm overhead, bend the right elbow, and lower the right hand behind the back. If flexibility allows, grasp the right hand with the left hand (figure 17.8). Switch sides and repeat.

▶ **Figure 17.8**   Up-and-over shoulder stretch.

Lying Full-Body Stretch   Lie on your back with your legs straight and arms reaching overhead. Point your toes and stretch your arms overhead as much as possible (figure 17.9).

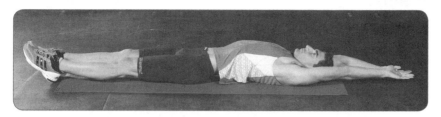

▶ **Figure 17.9**   Lying full-body stretch.

Pec Stretch   Stand with the feet close together, keep the knees soft, and position your left side beside a wall, doorway, or other sturdy frame. Place your left hand on the wall at shoulder height and slightly behind your shoulder to feel a stretch in the left side of the chest. Turn your head to the right and gently press right to deepen the stretch (figure 17.10). Switch sides and repeat.

▶ **Figure 17.10**   Pec stretch.

Corner Pec Stretch Stand in a corner, facing the corner, and have your feet together and legs straight. With the elbows at shoulder height, place your forearms on opposite walls. Lean into the corner to feel the stretch in the chest (figure 17.11).

▶ **Figure 17.11** Corner pec stretch.

Knee Stretch Sit with your back against a wall, the left leg bent, and the right leg straight with the ankle propped on a small box or foam block. Gently press the right knee toward the floor (figure 17.12), being careful not to hyperextend the knee. Switch sides and repeat.

▶ **Figure 17.12** Knee stretch.

Sitting Hamstring Stretch   Sit with the right leg straight, the foot flexed, and the left leg bent, resting the left foot against the inside of the right thigh. Reach with both hands toward the right foot, keeping the back straight (figure 17.13). Grasp your ankle, if flexibility permits. Switch sides and repeat.

▶ **Figure 17.13**   Sitting hamstring stretch.

Standing Hamstring Stretch   Stand with the feet about hip-width apart and keep the knees soft. Bend at the hips, keep the back flat, and reach with both hands toward the feet (figure 17.14).

▶ **Figure 17.14**   Standing hamstring stretch.

Chair Lower-Back Stretch   Sit in a chair with the feet flat on floor about shoulder-width apart. Lean forward and reach with both hands toward the floor between the feet (figure 17.15).

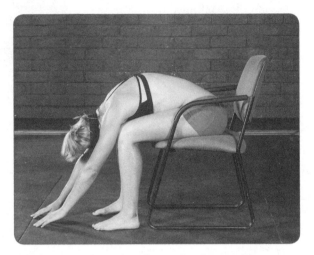

▶ **Figure 17.15**   Chair lower-back stretch.

Child's Pose   Kneel on the floor on both knees, keeping the knees and feet as close together as possible, depending on your flexibility. Reach the arms overhead and lean forward, pressing the buttocks back toward the ankles and the hands on the floor in front of the head (figure 17.16).

▶ **Figure 17.16**   Child's pose.

Standing Lower-Back Stretch Stand with the feet wide apart and keep the knees soft. Link your fingers behind your head. As you inhale, turn at the waist to the left. Exhale as you lower your torso toward your left knee. Inhale, reaching with the hands to the left of your left foot (figure 17.17). Return to the starting position and repeat to the other side.

▶ **Figure 17.17** Standing lower-back stretch.

Runner's Lunge Hip Flexor Stretch Stand with the feet together. With the left foot, take a big step forward into a lunge position, keeping the left knee over the left ankle and the right leg straight. If flexibility allows, place both hands on the floor on either side of the left foot (figure 17.18). Press the hips down slightly to stretch the hip flexors. Return to the starting position and repeat with the right leg.

▶ **Figure 17.18** Runner's lunge hip flexor stretch.

Kneeling Hip Flexor Stretch   Kneel on the ground on both knees. With the left foot, step forward into a lunge position, keeping the right knee and shin on the floor. Place the hands on the hips and gently press the hips forward to stretch the hip flexor (figure 17.19). Switch legs and repeat.

▶ **Figure 17.19**   Kneeling hip flexor stretch.

Roles in Injury Prevention

In 2003 the University of Heidelberg surveyed 656 active Ironman triathletes.[14] Seventy-five percent reported experiencing at least one injury during their times as triathletes. Because this number included all injuries, including bruises and abrasions, the rate does not seem unexpectedly high. But when limiting the scope to include only injuries to muscles, tendons, or ligaments, the rate was an alarming 62 percent. Considering that regular runners have a muscular tendon injury rate of 65 percent,[15] triathletes, despite lower run volume, are at about the same risk of injury as pure runners.

Although the Heidelberg study covered injury rate over the entire career of the triathlete, a British study found a 37 percent injury rate over just 8 weeks of triathlon training.[16] Because of this extraordinarily high rate of injury among triathletes, the prevention of injury and the resulting increase in the ability to train could play a major role in the improvement of a triathlete's performance. The triathlete should consider potential injury a real threat, and look for methods to reduce its likelihood, which may include flexibility.

Flexibility Linked to Injury Prevention

Although many factors influence rates of injury in triathlons, including age, training volume, and intensity, evidence shows that under certain conditions flexibility could play a role in injury prevention. For example, over 200 college athletes in various sports were tested for flexibility in the iliopsoas, iliotibial band, hamstring, rectus femoris, and gastrocsoleus muscles.[17]

At the end of the season, a direct correlation was found between injuries sustained during the season and preseason tightness in males, but not in females. But because this study included athletes from disciplines other than swimming, cycling, and running, it may not be sufficient evidence for preseason flexibility in the triathlete in and of itself.

Further research about flexibility and injury prevention also indicated a correlation between stretching and injury.[18] Although stretching before exercise reduced injury, the link was limited to female cyclists only and the benefit was isolated to groin and buttocks conditions.

Plausible reasoning stands behind the theory that an increase in flexibility should reduce injury. If the fibers of the muscles are compared with the fibers of a rope, it is easy to accept the analogy that a more flexible and pliable rope would have fewer fiber tears when stretched. If soft-tissue injury were caused exclusively by a combination of lack of strength and lack of flexibility, it would make sense that an increase in flexibility would decrease injury.

Flexibility Not Linked to Injury Prevention

Ample research, however, indicates that stretching offers no benefit in reducing injury. Although the assumption that flexibility was linked to injury prevention had been ubiquitous among athletic professionals for decades, it came into question as early as 1998 with this statement from the American College of Sports Medicine: "There is a lack of randomized, controlled clinical trials defining the benefit of flexibility exercises in the prevention of musculoskeletal injuries."[19] As a result, a flurry of studies on stretching and flexibility took place over the next decade.

Perhaps one of the best studies was presented at the American Academy of Orthopaedic Surgeons' 2011 Annual Meeting.[20] Half of 1,400 runners were introduced to three stretches for the quadriceps, hamstrings, and calf muscle groups. The stretch time was 3 to 5 minutes immediately preceding running. The other half performed no stretching before running. The researchers concluded that there was no difference in injury risk for the two groups.

Reinforcing this theory is a review of 361 studies (a meta-study) related to stretching and injury prevention.[21] This panel of researchers also concluded, based on the combined data from these hundreds of studies, that there was no link between stretching and an increase or decrease in injury. Unlike the study of 1,400 runners, which focused on stretching before exercise, this meta-analysis reviewed stretching both before and after exercise.

Additional Flexibility Considerations

These studies would seem to be a devastating blow to the flexibility camp, but some additional points need to be considered. First, note that no evidence in these studies indicated an *increase* in injury linked to stretching. Although stretching does not seem to offer much benefit regarding injury prevention, it seems to present little risk. Additionally, because some previously cited research does support preseason flexibility as a way to mitigate injury, the scale would seem to be tipped in favor of at least preseason flexibility to combat injury.

Although the focus of this chapter has been the relatively narrow effect of flexibility on performance and injury, flexibility can provide other benefits as well. In his book *The Science of Flexibility*, author Michael J. Alter argues that the benefits of a flexibility program include a wide range of research-based outcomes, including relaxation, relief of low-back pain, and enhanced sleep, all of which significantly benefit triathletes.[22]

Additionally, the studies that refute flexibility for injury prevention also tend to be limited in scope in terms of muscle groups, focusing largely on the hamstrings, quadriceps, and gastrocsoleus muscles. In some circumstances flexibility in other muscle groups plays a critical role in the prevention of injury.

For example, an established treatment of iliotibial band syndrome (ITBS), a common injury among runners and cyclists, is an increase in flexibility of the iliotibial band.[23] Ober's test, which tests shortening of the iliotibial band, is a reliable method to confirm the cause of knee pain linked to ITBS. Stretching is also a key consideration in both prevention and treatment of Achilles tendinopathy.[24]

Although increased risk of injury does not appear to result from either stretching or not stretching, there does appear to be a risk in rapidly changing an existing stretching program. Runners who usually stretched and were then assigned to a no-stretch group had a 40 percent increased risk of injury, and nonstretchers who were assigned to stretching had a 30 percent increased risk of injury.[20] In other words, no difference in injury risk occurred in either the stretch or no-stretch group, but risk significantly increased if the runner abruptly adopted or abandoned an established stretching routine.

Similar to flexibility relative to performance, flexibility relative to injury prevention is equivocal in the data establishing benefits and risks. It is the author's opinion, based on available research, that the benefits (not limited to injury prevention) of a general flexibility program outweigh any risks. The most promising and logical strategy to reduce injury through flexibility is to increase slowly and then maintain general flexibility through stretching frequency and duration. The stretching should take place after, not before, exercise.

Core Strength

Core strength, or postural stability, is a mature concept. In the 1920s Joseph and Clara Pilates opened a studio in New York City. Their method, which they originally called *contrology*, focused on core postural muscles that help keep the human body balanced and provide support for the spine. A triathlete's core has since been commonly defined as the transversus abdominis, multifidus, internal oblique, paraspinal, and pelvic floor muscles (figure 17.20). A broader interpretation of the core is any muscle in the region between the buttocks and chest, which would include some muscles below the pelvic floor, such as the gluteus medius.

Although the link between postural stability and performance was assumed for decades, it was only recently revealed that the cocontraction of the transversus abdominis and multifidus muscles occurred before any movement of the limbs.[25] In other words, all movement starts at the core.

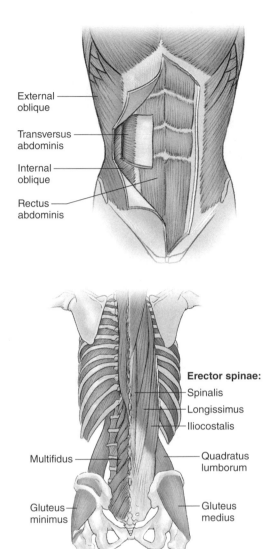

▶ **Figure 17.20**   Core muscles: (*a*) front; (*b*) back.

Core Strength and Injury Prevention

Most research on injury prevention associated with core stability or strength is linked to the reduction of chronic low-back pain unrelated to exercise. But some research indicates that core strength prevents athletic injury as well. Subjects with patellofemoral (knee) pain demonstrated 26 percent less hip-abduction strength and 36 percent less hip external-rotation strength than similar age-matched controls who did not report knee pain.[26] The collapse of the hip when running, because of poor lower-core strength, is thought to place the knee in a misaligned position, adding stress and increasing the risk of injury.

A similar study was done among college track athletes. Researchers found that athletes who did not sustain an injury over a season were significantly stronger in hip abduction and external rotation, and the researchers further concluded that hip external-rotation strength was the only useful predictor of injury status among this group of athletes.[27]

Another common running and cycling condition, ITBS, was found to be directly related to weakness in the gluteus medius.[28] In this study, females with ITBS were able to lift only 7.82 percent of their body weight through hip adduction compared with 10.19 percent for noninjured female runners. Injured males scored even worse, lifting only 6.86 percent of their body weight compared with 9.73 percent for noninjured males. The injured runners were then enrolled in a 6-week, standardized rehabilitation protocol that directed special attention to strengthening the gluteus medius.

After rehabilitation, the females demonstrated an average increase in hip abductor torque of 34.9 percent in the injured limb, and the males had an average increase of 51.4 percent. After 6 weeks of rehabilitation, 22 of 24 athletes were pain free with all exercises and able to return to running. At a 6-month follow-up there were no reports of recurrence.

Further research reviewed the recurrence of hamstring injury in relation to a complete core strengthening routine.[29] Twenty-four athletes who were suffering from an acute hamstring strain, including 10 triathletes and runners, were placed into either a core strengthening program or a hamstring strengthening and stretching program. The core strengthening routine consisted of a full regimen of core exercises, including side steps, crossover steps, multiple bridges, and push-up stabilization with trunk rotation, allowing the complete range of core muscles to be exercised.

In the first 2 weeks after returning to their sport, the reinjury rate was significantly greater in the strengthening and stretching group, in which 6 of 11 athletes had reinjured the hamstring. None of the 13 athletes in the core strengthening group had reinjured the hamstring after 2 weeks. After 1 year, the reinjury rate was again significantly greater in the strengthening and stretching group, in which 70 percent of the athletes had restrained the hamstring, but only 1 athlete in the core strengthening group had reinjured the hamstring.

Even further evidence indicates that core strength is associated with other athletic maladies that would, on the surface, appear completely unrelated. One example is exercise-related transient abdominal pain (ETAP). These painful side stitches, characterized by a sharp, localized abdominal pain, plague runners of all abilities. People with poor posture (weak core) were more likely to experience ETAP, and the level of pain is directly correlated to posture.[30] The worse the posture is, the more severe the ETAP pain is.

Although the link between core strength and hamstring, knee, IT band, and ETAP may seem unrelated at first, it is consistent with the theory that all movement starts at the core. Thus, the core exercises are strongly recommended for triathletes of all abilities to mitigate a wide variety of potential injuries.

Core Strength and Performance

The research on core strength is almost exclusively linked to injury prevention. Few significant findings correlate core strength to performance other than finding that all movement starts at the core,[25] which does not necessarily imply a link between core strength and performance. One study did find an impressive 30-second improvement in 5K run performance.[31] The overwhelming evidence suggests no link between core strength and performance, including research on swimming and running, which found no performance improvement after incorporating a core stability program,[32, 33] and additional research that found no link between core strength and run performance or general functional movement.[34]

Certainly, a reduction in injuries would have a positive effect on endurance performance by allowing the athlete to perform a greater volume of high-quality training. But a reasonable expectation is that core strength would positively affect the biomechanics of a triathlete's swim, bike, and run disciplines and thus improve performance. The techniques described in part II of this book could not be executed properly without core strength.

For example, the proper running posture described in chapter 6 could not be maintained indefinitely without core strength to support the position. Without core strength, an ultimate breakdown in form is likely during this last and arguably most difficult portion of a triathlon. Because of the unique nature of swimming, in which the triathlete has relatively little resistance for the limbs to utilize, the core theoretically becomes a primary mover. Even without a strong empirical link between core strength and performance, the argument for core strength to improve performance through biomechanical efficiency is reasonable.

Sample Core Strength Program

These six exercises will help a triathlete strengthen the core muscles. Follow the guidelines in table 17.2. Perform the exercises three times a week.

Table 17.2   Recommended Core Exercises

Perform three times per week.

Exercise	Duration	Repetitions
Plank (bridge)	20 to 60 seconds	4
Side plank (bridge)	20 to 60 seconds	4 per side
Side step	60 seconds	3 per direction
Grapevine step	60 seconds	3 per direction
Hip abductor	60 seconds	3 per side
Push-up stabilization with trunk rotation	n/a	2 × 15 each side

Plank or Bridge   Use the abdominal and hip muscles to hold the body in a facedown, straight plank position, having the elbows and feet as the only points of contact (figure 17.21).

▶ **Figure 17.21**   Plank or bridge.

Side Plank or Side Bridge   Use the abdominal and hip muscles to hold the body in a straight plank position with the right side toward the floor (figure 17.22). One elbow and one foot are the only points of contact. Perform on both sides.

▶ **Figure 17.22**   Side plank or side bridge.

Side Step Wrap a resistance band around the ankles or shins. Step to the side, keeping the feet low to the ground (figure 17.23). Step in both directions.

▶ **Figure 17.23** Side step.

Grapevine Step Step laterally with the trail leg going over the lead leg (figure 17.24) and then behind the lead leg. Step in both directions.

▶ **Figure 17.24** Grapevine step.

Hip Abductor Lie on one side with the lower leg bent and the upper leg straight. Lift the upper leg up and down (figure 17.25). Perform on both sides.

▶ **Figure 17.25** Hip abductor.

Push-Up Stabilization With Trunk Rotation Start in push-up position. Lift the left hand and rotate the chest to the left, lifting the left hand to point to the ceiling (figure 17.26). Pause and return to the starting position. Repeat on the other side.

▶ **Figure 17.26** Push-up stabilization with trunk rotation.

Conclusion

Although limited empirical evidence supports the notion that stretching and flexibility prevent injury, the evidence shows that a consistent stretching program does not offer any risk and may provide at least some benefit. Triathletes motivated by injury prevention would be better served by adopting a core strengthening program, which has a well-established link to injury prevention. In terms of endurance performance, swimming speed is closely correlated to flexibility, but running performance appears to be inversely related to lower-body flexibility. The relationship between cycling performance and flexibility is ambiguous, as is the link between core strength and performance.

CHAPTER 18

Strength Training

—David Warden

Dr. Tudor O. Bompa, considered the father of modern periodization, was once asked about the biggest training mistakes that triathletes make.[1] He responded that the two biggest mistakes were not using evidence-based training methods and not implementing a year-round strength training program. With this endorsement, justifying the exclusion of strength training for the serious triathlete would be difficult.

In his breakthrough book *Periodization: Theory and Methodology of Training*, which introduced the method of periodization, Dr. Bompa lays out three critical biomotor abilities: strength (force), endurance, and speed.[2] Although each discipline requires a different balance of these abilities, some element of all three is necessary to maximize performance in any sport. Furthermore, Dr. Bompa states that the development of strength "should be the prime concern of anyone who attempts to improve an athlete's performance."[3]

For the triathlete especially, strength is paramount. For example, running performance is often simplified as a calculation of only two factors—stride frequency and stride length. True run performance, however, is the result of three factors—stride frequency, stride length, and force,[4] force being the ability to accelerate a mass in a desired direction.

Weyland et al. found that when comparing slower runners with faster runners, the faster runners indeed had a stride length 1.69 times greater than the slower runners did, a stride frequency 1.16 times greater, and a force applied to the running surface 1.26 times greater. Force was more closely associated with run speed than stride frequency was. The researchers concluded that force played the primary role in reducing contact time with the ground. The more force that a runner applied to the ground, the shorter the time was between the end of the contact period of one foot and the beginning of the contact period of the opposite foot.

Additionally, strength is one of two abilities required to develop the advanced ability of muscular endurance, which is the combination of strength and endurance. Although some strength is developed as a residual of endurance training, true force can be developed only through a specific and dedicated strength training program.

Strength Training and Performance

Unlike endurance and speed training, strength training can be seen by triathletes as contrary to the training principle of specificity. The nature and scope of strength training, particularly gym-based training, mimics the movement of the triathlon disciplines only superficially. Triathlon is a steady-state sport and, with the exception of draft-legal ITU-style racing, exhibits little need for bursts of brief power and explosive force. Rather, the triathlete will perform best with a constant and measured intensity consistent with the distance of the event.

For that reason, strength training has a poor reputation among triathletes. Performing it is sometimes seen as stealing time from precious sport-specific training, or even worse, as the cause of weight gain that leads to reduced economy and performance.

Strength Training Benefits

Despite the lack of sport-specific movement and the theoretically unnecessary development of power and mass, a considerable body of research indicates that strength training can improve a triathlete's endurance performance in cycling and running in particular. The two primary benefits from strength training appear to be increases in both endurance and economy.

In a frequently-cited study,[5] researchers added three strength training sessions for 10 weeks to the regimens of athletes trained in both cycling and running. As expected, leg strength increased significantly, but thigh girth remained unchanged.

More important, cycling time to exhaustion at 80 percent of $\dot{V}O_2$max increased from 71 to 81 minutes, an exercise duration and intensity highly applicable to triathletes. Short-term endurance performance (from 4 to 8 minutes), which would add power to the final push in a triathlon event, also improved 11 to 13 percent in both cycling and running. Additionally, 12 weeks of strength training resulted in a 33 percent increase in cycling to exhaustion at 75 percent of $\dot{V}O_2$max, also an intensity particularly relevant to triathletes.[6]

Another study found that concurrent strength and endurance training resulted in a significant improvement in 5K run time unrelated to an increase in $\dot{V}O_2$max.[7] This improvement would be quite useful in the final minutes of triathlon, specifically in sprint-distance triathlon events.

Specific to endurance running, researchers found that adding strength training concurrently with run training significantly improved endurance running.[8] The strength regimen was 8 weeks long, but this research divided the group into three types of strength training: heavy (high load), explosive (high power), and muscular endurance (high duration). All three types of strength training resulted in improved run endurance, and the muscular endurance training resulted in the highest gains. This finding suggests that although any type of strength training can improve endurance, the best results will come from the most sport-specific strength training.

Much of this research supports the positive relationship between strength and endurance performance for durations of 4 to 80 minutes. But what will the effect of strength training be on exercise of 2 hours' duration or longer? Although the research on endurance of this duration is limited, significant science supports a positive correlation between strength training and both cycling and running economy. Any improvement in economy (usually measured as the relative oxygen cost in milligrams of oxygen per kilogram per minute to run at a given velocity) is almost certain to improve endurance, particularly at longer distances.

For example, eight well-trained runners completed an 8-week strength training program on 3 days per week, in addition to their regular training.[9] They were compared with nine control runners who did not include strength training in their regimens. The strength training group improved running economy by an impressive 5.0 percent, which likely contributed to a 21.3 percent improvement in time to exhaustion at maximum aerobic threshold.

Similar results were seen with a group of 15 triathletes assigned to either an endurance-only group or a group that did endurance training and two sessions of strength training per week for 14 weeks.[10] The endurance-plus-strength group had a significant improvement in running economy.

Perhaps even more compelling evidence than these individual studies comes from two systematic reviews of multiple studies on strength training and endurance performance. After reviewing several studies and using a scale to determine the quality and consistency of the research, the researchers concluded that "resistance training likely has a positive effect on endurance running performance or running economy,"[11] and "replacing a portion of a cyclist's endurance training with resistance training will result in improved time trial performance and maximal power."[12]

How Strength Training Improves Endurance and Economy

How could strength training contribute to this increase in endurance and economy? Strength training appears to promote a combination of biomechanical and metabolic changes that directly affect endurance and economy.

Because run speed is a result of stride length, stride frequency, and force, a triathlete who can maintain stride length late in the run has an increased likelihood of maintaining run speed. This notion is borne out in a study in which 18 very quick endurance runners were placed into periodized strength and nonstrength groups for a period of 8 weeks.[13] At the end of that period, the runners performed a workout of three intervals, and the researchers measured the stride length of the first and third intervals. The periodized strength group had no significant loss of stride length during the third interval, whereas the nonstrength group lost almost 3 percent of stride length in the final interval.

Additionally, researchers from Ohio University used an MRI to measure the contrast shift (activation) of muscles before and after a 9-week strength training program.[14] After the strength training, the MRI revealed less contrast shift for a given amount of work. These results suggest that resistance training results in the use of less muscle to lift a given load. This finding has significant potential application for triathletes. Less use of muscle for a given amount of work would not only delay muscular fatigue and reduce muscle glycogen use but also reduce oxygen consumption for that given load and thus help explain the increase in economy seen after performing a strength training program.

At a metabolic level, strength training has been shown to introduce remarkable changes. Healthy males were tested for levels of phosphocreatine (an essential molecule in the formation of ATP), lactate, and glycogen after approximately 1 hour of exercise at 72 percent of $\dot{V}O_2$max.[15] They were tested again for those levels postexercise after 4 to 12 weeks of strength training three times a week. The results were a 39 percent increase in phosphocreatine, a 37 percent decrease in lactate, and a 37 percent increase in glycogen levels after exercise, when compared with the period before strength training. In a previously cited study,[6] the 33 percent increase in time to exhaustion at 75 percent of $\dot{V}O_2$max after 12 weeks of strength training was attributed to a 12 percent increase in lactate threshold.

Controversy Regarding Elite Male Triathletes' Need to Strength Train

Despite this notable body of evidence supporting strength training in endurance triathletes, many triathletes and coaches believe that strength training may not benefit performance in elite male triathletes. Additionally, they often express concern regarding weight gain and the limited time available for task-specific endurance and speed training.

Strong research supports strength training for endurance performance specifically for female athletes,[16] junior athletes,[17] and masters athletes.[18] Because female, junior, and masters athletes maintain less muscle mass than young men do, elite male triathletes could theoretically benefit less (or not at all) from strength training.

Additional arguments against strength training for elite male endurance triathletes include the difficulty of fitting additional work into a schedule that often already exceeds 20 hours a week. This considerable volume of specificity may eclipse any benefit from strength training. Finally, some studies refute the performance benefit of strength training in both cycling[19] and running.[20] These studies concluded that female cyclists had no improvement in a 1-hour cycle test after 12 weeks of twice weekly strength training and that middle-aged runners had no improvement in $\dot{V}O_2$max, stride length, or stride frequency.

Most Evidence Shows Strength Training to Be Helpful to Cycling and Running

The evidence supporting strength training for endurance performance is therefore far from unequivocal. The majority of evidence, however, suggests a positive relationship. Even the limited studies refuting strength training for endurance performance do not find a decrease in performance. Rather, they simply find no performance increase, which means that there is little risk to the triathlete in a trial of strength training. These negative studies represent a small portion of the literature, whereas significantly more research indicates that strength training improves endurance performance.

More specifically, the concerns regarding elite triathletes—weight gain and sacrificing training time—are themselves refuted in multiple studies. For example, previously cited studies supporting the benefits of strength training[11, 12] included advanced cyclists who rode more than 90 miles (145 km) a week and advanced runners who ran more than 30 miles (48 km) per week. Further research concluded that strength training can lead to enhanced long-term (greater than 30 minutes) endurance capacity, in both well-trained and highly trained top-level endurance athletes.[21]

Concerns regarding strength training and weight gain are certainly justified. A triathlete's mass is a critical factor in performance, both physiologically and even aerodynamically. But weight gain by itself becomes irrelevant when measuring economy or power-to-weight ratio. Because running economy is the measure of oxygen cost for a given velocity, when economy improves any concurrent increase in the mass of the triathlete is immaterial.

In elite cycling, a gain of 1 kilogram of body weight can be alarming but becomes insignificant if the triathlete's power has increased by 2 percent because the total power-to-weight ratio has increased. Rather than focusing on simple weight gain, a triathlete or coach should avoid uneconomical weight gain. Note also that although many studies reported an increase in limb girth and weight with strength training, other studies reported no weight gain from the regimen.[7]

Finally, objections to redirecting precious training time to strength training, particularly for time-constrained age-group triathletes, seem to be addressed in the scientific literature. Most of the studies cited in this chapter had the subjects add strength training to an existing endurance program. But other studies showed the benefits of strength training when athletes replaced as much as 32 percent of their endurance training with strength training.[5, 9] In fact, strength training was most effective when replacing existing endurance training rather than being used as an additional approach.[12]

Effect of Strength Training on Swimming

The research discussed in this chapter has hereto focused on the benefits of strength training on cycling and running performance. Not surprisingly, the three disciplines of triathlon may have different responses to strength training. In swimming, swim coaches at all levels have used dry-land strength training extensively. Despite this consistent use by swim professionals, the empirical data supporting dry-land strength training are weak.

Greater Strength, Yes; Better Swimming, No

In one study collegiate swimmers added strength training on 3 days per week to their existing 6 days per week of in-water training.[22] Despite an increase of 25 to 35 percent in dry-land strength, no change in distance per stroke was observed compared with the control group, and no significant differences were found in any of the swim power and swimming performance tests.

Similar results were found with another group of collegiate swimmers. Again, although dry-land power improved, no difference was seen in stroke length or performance time in a 400-yard (366 m) swim time trial between the swimmers who did and did not perform dry-land strength training.[23]

Furthermore, despite claiming six gold and two bronze medals at the 2004 Olympics in Athens, Michael Phelps reported in a 2004 interview, "I've never lifted a single weight in my life. It's all from training in the water, period."[24] Although Phelps did begin dry-land training in 2005 before an even more impressive 2008 Olympic performance, the benefit was reported as limited to his push-off from the wall,[25] a benefit not relevant to open-water triathletes.

A study from the University of Colorado may have described it best: "In contrast to running and cycling, traditional dry-land resistance training or combined-swim-and-resistance training does not appear to enhance swimming performance in untrained individuals or competitive swimmers, despite substantially increasing upper-body strength."[26]

The anecdotal evidence supporting dry-land strength training, stemming from its extensive use by swim professionals, is difficult to ignore, but the empirical evidence is equally convincing. Note that no evidence suggests that dry-land strength training impedes performance. The studies cited earlier did not find any detrimental effects of strength training on swim performance.

When discussing swimming and strength training, it is essential to distinguish the research regarding dry-land strength training from that regarding in-water strength training. The latter has positive results on swim performance. In-water strength training is discussed later in this chapter.

Dry-Land Strength Training Not Needed

It is the author's opinion that the relative importance of flexibility and strength are related to the technique required to perform the task. For example, cycling certainly requires a certain amount of skill, but it is relatively easy compared with the technique required in swimming. An inverse relationship may exist between the complexity of a sport and the role of strength, and a direct relationship may be present between complexity and the role of flexibility.

Because of the complexity of swimming, dry-land training for swimming appears to be unhelpful. In previously cited research, the authors suggested that "the lack of a positive transfer between dry-land strength gains and swimming propulsive force may be due to the specificity of (swim) training."[22] Other research postulated that "resistance training may be a valuable adjunct to the exercise programmes followed by endurance runners or cyclists, but not swimmers; these latter athletes need more specific forms of resistance training to realise performance improvement."[27]

The hypothesis of the relationship between strength and flexibility and the three triathlon disciplines is supported in the literature cited in this chapter and in chapter 17, but further research is required to confirm this supposition.

Gym-Based Strength Training

With the benefits of strength training well established, how do triathletes incorporate it into their endurance training? The most successful approach is a program that is both sport specific and periodized. Sport-specific means that the strength training focuses on the prime movers, or multijoint exercises that mimic the movements of the discipline. Periodized means the strength training follows a preparatory-to-specific path. For example, strength training was found to benefit stride length in runners only when the strength training was periodized.[13] In this particular study, the runners spent 4 weeks in a prep phase of easy lifting to adapt the muscles to the additional upcoming stress, 8 weeks in a specific period in which the strength training mimicked the increased intensity of running, and finally 4 weeks in a period of strength maintenance.

Sport-specific strength training is, of course, unique to every sport. For triathlon, table 18.1 lists the recommended exercises and the associated discipline that receives the greatest benefit.

In his book *The Triathlete's Training Bible,*[28] author Joe Friel proposes four distinct periodized strength training phases: anatomical adaptation (AA), maximum transition (MT), maximum strength (MS), and strength maintenance (SM). This chapter also proposes an additional strength training phase, the competition maintenance (CM) phase.

Table 18.1 Multijoint Exercises and Applicable Discipline

Multijoint exercise	Applicable disciplines
Squat or leg press	Cycling, running
Bent-arm lat pull-down	Swimming
Chest press or push-up	Swimming
Seated row	Cycling (particularly climbing)

Anatomical Adaptation

Consistent with the theory of endurance periodization, anatomical adaptation is a preparatory phase introduced at the beginning of an overall triathlon training program or season, usually in the early season preparation phase lasting into the early weeks of base training. Long, slow repetitions both promote slow-twitch muscles and prepare the body for the increased demand in load as the strength program progresses. Use caution when introducing this training, particularly for the first time, and increase the load slowly over the AA period. Failure to introduce this new type of training can result in severe soreness that can disrupt days of training or even cause injury, requiring an even longer recovery time. Table 18.2 lists the suggested implementation of the AA phase.

Table 18.2 Anatomical Adaptation (AA) Phase

Total AA sessions	8 to 12
Sessions per week	2 or 3
Load (% of 1RM)	40 to 60
Sets per session	3 to 5
Reps per set	20 to 30
Recovery time	60 to 90 seconds
Speed of lift	Slow

Triathlon exercises (in order of completion)	
1. Squat or leg press	
2. Bent-arm lat pull-down	
3. Squat or leg press	
4. Chest press or push-up	
5. Personal weakness (hamstring curl, knee extension, heel raise)	
6. Seated row	
7. Core (see chapter 17)	

Adapted, by permission, from J. Friel, 2009, *The triathlete's training bible*, 3rd ed. (Boulder, CO: VeloPress), 243.

Maximum Transition

The MT phase is designed to prepare the body for the heavier loads of the critical MS phase. Use caution when introducing this phase and the increase in load. Note that only certain exercises (in bold in table 18.3) move to the MT phase; all others remain in the AA phase. This approach promotes long, lean, fat-burning muscles that will not be required to generate as much force as the key prime movers. See table 18.3 for the MT phase.

Table 18.3 Maximum Transition (MT) Phase

Total MT sessions	3 to 5
Sessions per week	2 or 3
Sets per session	3
Reps per set	10 to 15
Recovery time	90 to 180 seconds
Speed of lift	Slow

Triathlon exercises (in order of completion)	Load goal
Squat or leg press*	Squat: 1.3 to 1.7 × body weight Leg press: 2.5 to 2.9 × body weight
Seated row*	0.5 to 0.8 × body weight
Personal weakness (hamstring curl, knee extension, heel raise)	40 to 60% 1RM
Bent-arm lat pull-down*	0.3 to 0.8 × body weight
Core (see chapter 17)	

*Carried over from the AA phase.

Adapted, by permission, from J. Friel, 2009, *The triathlete's training bible*, 3rd ed. (Boulder, CO: VeloPress), 244.

Maximum Strength

The MS phase is the primary purpose of gym-based strength training. This phase is when power is primarily developed for the triathlete. Although power is rarely called on in a steady-state event, it is crucial in draft-legal events, when climbing, or when finishing a race. The work done in the AA and MT phases prepares the triathletes for these heavy MS loads to solidify the ability to generate force and power. Like the MT phase, only specific exercises move to the MS phase; all others remain in the AA phase.

Be aware that endurance and speed training may suffer during this phase because the MT phase introduces a significant level of fatigue. To minimize this effect, strength training should be periodized and coordinated with endurance training so that the MT phase ends by the first part of the base training phase. This approach allows the later stages of base training and further phases to focus on sport-specific improvement without the heavy legs introduced in the MT phase.

Additionally, scientists found that the fatigue introduced from strength training can be mitigated by ordering the strength sessions to take place after an endurance set, which allows a high-quality endurance set and improves results from the strength session.[29] See table 18.4 for details about the recommended MS phase.

Table 18.4 Maximum Strength (MS) Phase

Total MS sessions	8 to 12
Sessions per week	2
Sets per session	3 to 6
Reps per set	3 to 6
Recovery time	120 to 240 seconds
Speed of lift	Slow

Triathlon exercises (in order of completion)	Load goal
1. Squat or leg press	Squat: 1.3 to 1.7 × body weight Leg press: 2.5 to 2.9 × body weight
2. Seated row	0.5 to 0.8 × body weight
3. Personal weakness (hamstring curl, knee extension, heel raise)	40 to 60% 1RM
4. Bent-arm lat pull-down	0.3 to 0.8 × body weight
5. Core (see chapter 17)	

Adapted, by permission, from J. Friel, 2009, *The triathlete's training bible,* 3rd ed. (Boulder, CO: VeloPress), 246.

Strength Maintenance

Like any other fitness or skill developed, strength must be maintained. The SM phase is designed to sustain the new abilities to generate force while not interfering with critical sport-specific endurance and speed training beyond the base phase. Note in table 18.5 that the standing, bent-arm lat pull-down

Table 18.5 Strength Maintenance (SM) Phase

Total SM sessions	Until race or competition phase
Sessions per week	1
Load (% of 1RM)	60, 80 (last set)
Sets per session	2 or 3
Reps per set	6 to 12
Recovery time	60 to 120 seconds
Speed of lift	Moderate

Triathlon exercises (in order of completion)	
1. Squat or leg press	
2. Seated row	
3. Personal weakness (hamstring curl, knee extension, heel raise)	
4. Bent-arm lat pull-down	
5. Core (see chapter 17)	

Adapted, by permission, from J. Friel, 2009, *The triathlete's training bible,* 3rd ed. (Boulder, CO: VeloPress), 247.

reverts to AA phase repetition frequency in the SM phase, whereas the hip extension and seated row alone, in bold, continue with the lower reps of the SM phase.

Competition Maintenance

Many coaches recommend the termination of strength training at the onset of the race phase to avoid the buildup of additional fatigue. Continuing limited strength training into the race phase, however, will result in better performance than abruptly ending strength training.[30] This plan is particularly relevant for female and masters triathletes, who may lose muscle mass faster than younger men do.

The CM phase is designed to provide limited strength training benefit without introducing resistance-induced weakness in competition. Because of this, a CM session should be completed at least 72 hours before competition. Table 18.6 outlines the recommended CM phase. Note that all exercises follow the same load and repetition goals in the CM phase.

Table 18.6 Competition Maintenance (CM) Phase

Total CM sessions	Through race or competition phase
Sessions per week	1
Load (% of 1RM)	80 to 85%
Sets per session	2
Reps per set	5
Recovery time	60 to 120 seconds
Speed of lift	Moderate

Triathlon exercises (in order of completion)	
1. Squat or leg press	
2. Seated row	
3. Personal weakness (hamstring curl, knee extension, heel raise)	
4. Bent-arm lat pull-down	
5. Core (see chapter 17)	

Load Goals

Naturally, the repetitions recommended here would be easy to achieve with little resistance. Appropriate load must be administered to stress the body sufficiently to gain new fitness. Load goals are generally determined either as a percentage of body weight or as a percentage of 1 repetition maximum (1RM).

Several formulas and protocols can be used to determine 1RM. One author proposed the following protocol for 1RM testing:[31] Begin with a warm-up of 5 to 10 repetitions at 40 percent to 60 percent of the triathlete's estimated maximum. After a brief rest period, the load is increased to 60 percent to 80 percent of the triathlete's estimated maximum, and the triathlete attempts to complete 3 to 5 repetitions. At this point small increases in weight are added to the load, and a 1RM lift is attempted. The goal is to determine the triathlete's 1RM in three to five trials. The triathlete rests for 3 to 5 minutes before each 1RM attempt.

A more practical approach, or at least an approach to estimate the 1RM that initiates the preceding method, is a formula that states that a 1RM can be calculated based on the resistance and number of repetitions to exhaustion, as follows:[32]

$$1RM = 100 \times weight / (102.78 - 2.78 \times reps)$$

For example, an athlete is able to squat 200 pounds (91 kg) 15 times. Using the preceding formula, his 1RM would be estimated as follows:

$$1RM = 100 \times 200 \text{ lb} / (102.78 - 2.78 \times 15 \text{ reps}), \text{ or a 1RM estimate of 327 pounds (148 kg)}$$

Strength Training Exercises

Here we describe the exercises listed in tables 18.1 through 18.6. Follow the specific guidelines for each phase regarding number of sets, repetitions, and load.

Squat   Stand with your feet shoulder-width apart and toes out slightly. If using a barbell, hold it across your upper back in a closed grip. If using dumbbells, hold them to your sides, palms turned in. Maintaining a natural curve in the lower back, slowly squat, moving the buttocks back as though sitting on a chair, making sure that the knees do not move over the toes (figure 18.1). When the thighs are parallel to the floor, straighten the legs to return to the starting position.

▶ **Figure 18.1**   Squat.

Leg Press Sit in an incline leg press machine or sled with your back flat against the seat back, your feet shoulder-width apart on the platform, and your legs straight. Slowly bend your knees to lower the weight, bringing the knees to a 90-degree angle (figure 18.2). Do not lock your knees. Straighten your legs to return to the starting position.

▶ **Figure 18.2** Leg press.

Bent-Arm Lat Pull-Down   Stand facing a cable machine with your feet shoulder-width apart or sit on the seat of the cable machine, facing it, feet flat on the floor. Using a wide grip, grasp the bar with the palms facing away from your body and your arms extended overhead. Bend the arms to pull the bar down to the upper chest (figure 18.3). Extend the arms to return to the starting position.

▶ **Figure 18.3**   Bent-arm lat pull-down.

Chest Press   Lie on a weight bench or stability ball with your feet flat on the floor. Using a closed, overhand grip, grasp the barbell with your hands about shoulder-width apart. Slowly lower the barbell toward your chest (figure 18.4). Push the barbell up to return to starting position. If using dumbbells, hold a dumbbell in each hand with the palms turned toward the feet and lower the dumbbells until they touch your chest.

▶ **Figure 18.4**   Chest press.

Push-Up   Lie face down on the floor with your hands under your shoulders and toes pointed. Push up with your hands until your body is in a straight line from the ankles to the top of your head. Bend the elbows to lower your torso toward the floor (figure 18.5). Then push up again.

▶ **Figure 18.5**   Push-up.

Seated Row   Sit on the bench facing a pulley machine. With palms facing each other, grab the handles of the machine and have your arms straight. Keeping your back still, pull the handles toward your torso (figure 18.6), pulling your shoulder blades together. Pause before straightening the arms to return to the starting position.

▶ **Figure 18.6**   Seated row.

Hamstring Curl   Lie face down on a hamstring curl machine with your ankles under the pads. Slowly bend your knees to pull the pads toward your buttocks (figure 18.7). Return to the starting position by slowly straightening your legs.

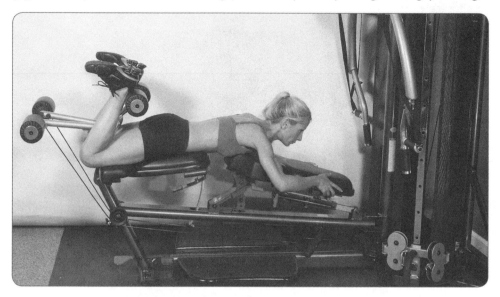

▶ **Figure 18.7**   Hamstring curl.

Knee Extension   Sit on a leg extension machine with your ankles under the pads and knees bent. Slowly straighten your knees to lift the weight (figure 18.8). Return the weight to the starting position by bending your knees.

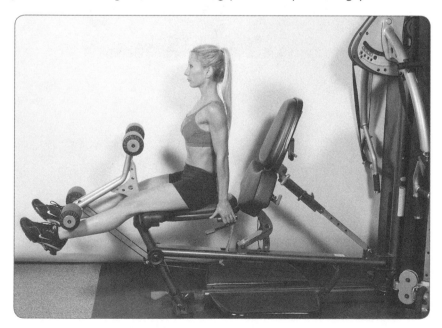

▶ **Figure 18.8**   Knee extension.

Heel Raise   Stand on a small plyometric box with your heels off the edge of the box. Hold on to a sturdy object for balance, if you wish. Press through the toes to lift your heels (figure 18.9), keeping the knees soft. Slowly return to the starting position.

▶ **Figure 18.9**   Heel raise.

Distance-Specific Strength Training

Is the approach to strength training the same for the various triathlon distances? The cycling and running improvements in force, endurance, and economy that occur with strength training are certainly desirable for triathletes participating or specializing in any distance. But incorporating the recommended strength training frequency and volume to an already busy week of training can be challenging. Recovering from strength training in an 8-hour training week is much easier than recovering from the same strength training that is part of a training week of 15 hours or more.

Therefore, the long-distance triathlete, who will often exceed 15 hours of training in the latter stages of a training season, needs to map out an annual training plan that ensures that the MS phase of strength training is complete before the heaviest volume of training begins, usually in base training. This plan is practical even for short-distance training, but it is crucial for the long-distance triathlete, who must complete the strength training periodization plan and move to a once-weekly strength maintenance program as soon as possible.

Sport-Specific Strength Training

If gym-based resistance training shows promise of improving endurance performance, then combining strength training within the specificity of a workout for a particular discipline might be even better. Here, power workouts using swim paddles, plyometrics, and hills can play a role in a triathlete's training. As with gym-based resistance training, the purpose is to apply high levels of quick force for a portion of the workout. Unlike dry-land resistance training, in-water swim resistance training has robust support from scientific studies. One report found that the measured use of swim paddles may help a swimmer develop a feel for stroke length (a predictor of swim performance), because paddles were shown to increase stroke length.[33] A swimmer who becomes accustomed to the velocity and feel of distance per stroke when using paddles may be able to translate that skill to open-hand swimming.

Other in-water resistance devices and programs have been shown to improve performance. A device similar to hand paddles improved stroke length and 200-meter race time by 2.3 seconds.[34] Additionally, an in-water bungee resistance device tethered to the swimmer improved distance per stroke and velocity more than either an assisted device (pulling the swimmer) or using no device at all.[35]

Endurance runners have long claimed that hill work (a form of plyometrics) has improved their performance, and some evidence backs that up. An increase in running economy of 2 percent occurred after just 6 weeks of plyometrics in speeds up to 12.88 kilometers per hour,[36] and three plyometric sessions of 30 minutes per week improved running economy by 4.1 percent during even faster speeds of 18.0 kilometers per hour.[37]

The addition of force to an endurance workout should include brief intervals of 30 to 60 seconds at a low cadence with high force, using short recoveries of only 15 to 30 seconds. This kind of workout is best done in hills for cycling and running. When swimming with paddles to introduce force, the reduced load-bearing fatigue of swimming would allow the triathlete to swim at a constant state for 5 to 30 minutes, depending on paddle size.

Conclusion

With the overwhelming endorsement and evidence supporting strength training for triathletes, strength training should be treated as the fourth discipline. Triathletes can expect results with predictability similar to that of core endurance training. As with flexibility, the benefits of strength training are not universal. Swim performance lacks a strong link to dry-land training. But the overall established benefits of increased ability to generate force, economy, and endurance from a periodized gym-based and sport-specific strength program would be a welcome gain for triathletes of all distances and experience.

CHAPTER 19

General and Specific Training

—David Warden

A common observation from the casual triathlon spectator is that relative to more popular athletic events, triathlon lacks an element of surprise. No one can dispute that triathlons are exciting, rich with storyline and the conquering of remarkable individual challenges. But at any given event with a prize purse, the top 1 percent is relatively consistent. In part because of the chaotic nature and interplay of team sports, in part because of the individualistic nature of triathlon, endurance performance is somewhat predictable.

But more important, whether genetically or through hard work (or both), endurance performance results almost exclusively from, and can be predicted by, the general abilities of aerobic capacity and endurance, the ability to resist fatigue (muscular endurance), economy (skills), lactate threshold, and metabolic efficiency. Although an interdependency and a cause-and-effect relationship certainly exists among these abilities, this chapter seeks to isolate and address many of these general predictors of endurance performance and distinguish them from more specific training.

Aerobic Base Building

This book addresses numerous essential training components and issues (devices, skills, intervals, nutrition, and so on) to help triathletes maximize success. Although it would be difficult to support the claim that any one training component is more important than another, if we were to make the attempt, aerobic endurance training would be an excellent candidate.

The human body uses two kinds of energy producing systems: aerobic (with oxygen) and anaerobic (without oxygen). Although the definition of energy system use is unequivocal, defining *aerobic exercise* can be difficult. If aerobic exercise were to be defined as exercise intensities that use the aerobic energy system, it would then include virtually all exercise intensities, because even at maximal intensities a combination of the two energy systems is used.

If it were to be defined as exercise that uses the aerobic energy system only slightly more than the anaerobic system, triathletes would still find themselves exercising at unsustainable intensities.

Aerobic exercise could potentially be quantified as the intensity at which sufficient oxygen is available for all carbohydrate to be converted into energy. But this technical threshold is inconvenient for a triathlete to measure without real-time access to a lab. For the purposes of this chapter, therefore, aerobic exercise will refer to deeply aerobic exercise at intensities of less than 60 percent of $\dot{V}O_2$max.

Need for a Highly Trained Aerobic System

An analysis of the energy system contribution at various run distances found that the aerobic–anaerobic usage ratio of 400-meter running was approximately 40–60 but that at 800 meters it changed to 60–40.[1] Therefore, the crossover point for the primary energy system usage from anaerobic to aerobic is probably somewhere around the intensity required for 600-meter performance, or perhaps 75 to 90 seconds. Thus, for an exercise event that lasts beyond 90 seconds, total energy output is mostly aerobic. Because all triathlon distances cover far more distance and time than that and the aerobic to anaerobic ratio can reach as much as 95–5, we can see how much an endurance triathlete needs to depend on a highly trained aerobic system.

This dependency on the aerobic system is evident in the structures of the training programs of elite endurance athletes. For example, elite Norwegian cross-country skiers record the highest levels of maximal oxygen uptake,[2] and 71 percent of those skiers' training is performed at less than 2.0 millimoles blood lactate, a deeply aerobic intensity. Furthermore, 7 percent is between 2 and 4 millimoles, still below the traditional lactate threshold intensity.[3] Note that these elite athletes essentially trained either very easy or very hard, avoiding moderate intensities.

Almost 2,000 miles (3,200 km) away, Spanish researchers in Madrid went a step further and attempted to correlate time spent in aerobic intensities to performance with elite-level runners. With fascinating consistency, these researchers found that the elite athletes spent 71 percent of their training time at low intensity, although they defined low intensity as less than 60 percent of $\dot{V}O_2$max or less than 70 percent of maximum heart rate, as opposed to specifying lactate levels.[4] Additionally, this research found a relationship between total training time at low intensities and 10K run performance, in which the total time spent at intensities less than 60 percent of $\dot{V}O_2$max resulted in better run performance.

Another impressive comparison reviewed two training groups that spent approximately 80 percent or 65 percent, respectively, of total training in a low-aerobic intensity and 12 percent or 25 percent, respectively, at a tempo pace over 21 weeks.[5] Both groups also spent a similar remaining percentage of time at high intensities above 90 percent of $\dot{V}O_2$max. The group spending

80 percent of their time at low intensity improved their 10K run performance by 157 seconds plus or minus 13 seconds, compared with an improvement in the group spending 65 percent of their time at low intensity of 121.5 seconds plus or minus 7.1 seconds.

Simply accepting and mimicking the highly aerobic training programs of elite athletes would be convenient. But the serious triathlete or coach should also ask these questions: What are the adaptations taking place with aerobic training that lead to this increase in performance? How can we confirm that an aerobic base has been achieved?

Adaptations From Aerobic Training

An impressive array of metabolic and physiologic adaptations from aerobic training can be found in table 19.1, which lists some of the differences between untrained and trained men. Although each of these adaptations is crucial, triathletes may be most interested in the increase in glycogen storage, percentage of muscle fiber type, $\dot{V}O_2$max, and fat utilization.

Table 19.1 Metabolic and Physiologic Adaptations to Endurance Training

Variable	Percentage difference of trained vs. untrained men
Glycogen	+41
Max lactate	+36
Slow-twitch muscle fibers	+20
Fast-twitch muscle fibers	−50
Max cardiac output	+75
Max stroke volume	+50
$\dot{V}O_2$max	+107
Body fat percentage	−27
Muscle glycogen utilization*	−41
Increase in fat utilization*	+63

*Data from B.F. Hurley, P.M. Nemeth, W.H. Martin, et al., 1986, "Muscle triglyceride utilization during exercise: Effect on training," *Journal of Applied Physiology* 60(2): 562-567.

Adapted from W.D. McArdle, F.I. Katch, and V.L. Katch, 2010, *Exercise physiology: Nutrition, energy, and human performance*, 7th ed. (Baltimore: Lippincott Williams & Wilkins), 457.

Fat Utilization as an Indicator of Fitness

Although the ability to use fat as a primary source of fuel is not the sole indicator of aerobic fitness, it is widely used by triathletes and coaches as a relatively inexpensive and accessible way to determine the level of aerobic fitness. Metabolic testing cannot provide the measurements of aerobic fitness variables listed in table 19.1, but it is assumed that if a metabolic profile shows a high level of fat utilization through broad levels of intensity, the other variables must also be strong.

For example, slow-twitch muscle fibers (with high fat oxidation) are unlikely to be well developed if a metabolic profile indicates low fat utilization. Figures 19.1 and 19.2 contrast the fat utilization of two similarly built cyclists at different levels of fitness. Note that the well-trained cyclist maintains a high level of fat utilization (6 or more kilocalories per minute) deeply into high intensity, whereas the untrained cyclist peaks quickly (3 kilocalories per minute) at a lower rate of fat usage and it continues to drop as intensity increases.

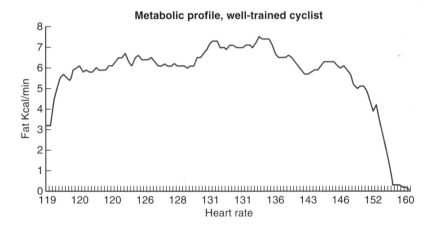

▶ **Figure 19.1**   Metabolic profile of a well-trained cyclist.

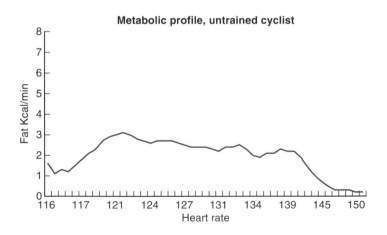

▶ **Figure 19.2**   Metabolic profile of an untrained cyclist.

The implications of substrate utilization (fat versus carbohydrate) are particularly significant in half- and full-Ironman training. Even a simple calculation shows that, assuming similar total energy expenditure, the triathlete represented in figure 19.1 will use more than twice as much fat for fuel as the triathlete represented in figure 19.2. Similar results were found at relatively high intensities of 75 percent to 85 percent of $\dot{V}O_2$max; endurance-trained men used 58 percent more fat for energy compared with untrained men.[6]

The finding of a dramatic increase in fat utilization found in table 19.1 took place over just 12 weeks of endurance training. This fits well with a triathlete's annual training plan, and perhaps suggests spending the initial mesocycles (the base periods) at approximately 90 percent of total volume in intensities below 70 percent of velocity or power at $\dot{V}O_2$max. Even during the build phases, elite athletes focus on aerobic training at 70 percent of total training time in deeply aerobic intensities. See chapter 22 for more about periodization training.

Anaerobic Base Training

No serious discussion of aerobic base building can be complete without a review of anaerobic base building. The typical triathlete, however, rarely needs to call on true anaerobic power. Not only is it rarely needed, it is rarely recommended. As previously defined, true anaerobic intensity can last only approximately 75 seconds, and the consequence to the triathlete of going anaerobic in an endurance event can be dire. What many triathletes think of as anaerobic is really highly aerobic intensity, such as climbing for several minutes or going very hard for the last mile of a race.

Still, anaerobic intensity has application in triathlon. Triathletes training for draft-legal triathlon must be able to maintain proximity to the lead swimmers and cyclists, because participation in the lead peloton is a requirement for success. They must be able to call on anaerobic intensities to avoid being dropped. Triathletes participating in sprint-distance events, in which the margin of victory is often just a few seconds, may have to depend on the anaerobic system in the final few hundred meters of the event. Finally, anaerobic interval training of approximately 30 seconds for several weeks has been shown to increase $\dot{V}O_2$max, which would improve performance across all triathlon distances as well as help maintain fitness during the low-volume competitive phase of a training plan (see chapter 20).

Other than limited interval training to increase and maintain $\dot{V}O_2$max, the decision of how much anaerobic training to include in a training program should ultimately be based on specificity. If the triathlete expects to call on anaerobic intensity when racing, it should be included in training.

General Versus Race-Specific Preparation

Triathletes training for all distances share a set of fitness goals. Despite the significant difference in event duration from the shortest to the longest triathlon, some general abilities build the foundation for peak performance for any steady-state endurance event lasting more than even a few minutes.

At the same time, after those general abilities have been developed, the skill requirements for a 60-minute event are quite different from those needed for a 14-hour event. As the competition period nears, the triathlete must alter training to simulate the stresses and intensities expected for the particular distance.

General Preparation

Although the history and theory of periodization are covered in chapter 22, the application of its method and mode in triathlon training fits well within this section. What is race specific? What is not?

A common misconception among triathletes is that general preparation in the early phases of a training plan is exclusively long, slow, distance training. Consistent with the research on aerobic training mentioned previously, 70 percent or more of all training should indeed be deeply aerobic. But what of the other 30 percent? General preparation does indeed require long, slow distance, but it does not exclude high-intensity training.

General preparation should focus on increasing the working capacity of the triathlete by increasing abilities such as aerobic capacity ($\dot{V}O_2max$), aerobic endurance, economy, metabolic efficiency, flexibility, speed, force, and muscular endurance. These abilities are essential for any triathlete competing at any distance, because they provide the foundation for the subsequent and specific phases of training.

Achieving these abilities in the general phase often requires the triathlete to train at intensities or with techniques that appear contrary to his selected triathlon distance. An Ironman triathlete might question the need to perform intense intervals at wattage three times what he expects to perform when racing. A sprint-distance specialist may question the need to perform a 2-hour bike ride, which is four times her expected cycling duration when racing. But because all endurance triathletes need these abilities they are considered an essential part of general preparation, as illustrated in table 19.2.

Additionally, modern triathletes face competition periods that include triathlons of all distances. Although not recommended for mastery of event-specific racing, because of personal restrictions and choice many triathletes find themselves racing both sprint and Ironman in the same season. In such situations, developing general abilities becomes paramount for the multidistance, multidiscipline triathlete.

See table 19.2 for a list of general abilities applicable to all triathlon distances and their associated training methods.

Table 19.2 General Triathlon Abilities and Methods

Ability	Definition	Benefit	Training methods
Aerobic capacity	Ability to use oxygen to produce energy. Often measured as $\dot{V}O_2$max, a significant predictor of performance at any triathlon distance.	High $\dot{V}O_2$max. The more oxygen that can be delivered to the muscles, the more intense the exercise that can be maintained. A higher $\dot{V}O_2$max allows higher velocity at a lower percentage of $\dot{V}O_2$max.	Interval training above, at, or near $\dot{V}O_2$max making up 15% of total training volume (see chapter 20).
Aerobic endurance	Ability to sustain prolonged exercise by maintaining oxygen delivery to working muscles.	Develops a high oxygen transport system, stroke volume, and cardiac output. Promotes quick recovery.	Long, slow endurance training at approximately 60% of $\dot{V}O_2$max making up more than 70% of total training volume.
Economy	A measure of how efficiently a person uses oxygen at a given output or velocity.	Use less oxygen and therefore less energy for a given output or velocity.	Long, slow endurance training at approximately 60% of $\dot{V}O_2$max making up more than 70% of total training volume. Drills that promote stride and stroke length, high cadence, foot strike, and general technique. Strength training.
Metabolic efficiency	Ability to oxidize a high level of fat as a percentage of overall energy use.	Preserves carbohydrate stores.	Long, slow endurance training at approximately 60% of $\dot{V}O_2$max making up more than 70% of total training volume. Nutrition.
Flexibility	Ability to move joints and soft tissues through a wide range of motion.	Increase the range through which force is applied and support injury prevention (see chapter 17).	Routine stretching after exercise (see chapter 17).
Speed	Ability to quickly perform a technique properly.	Improve cadence and reaction time.	Cadence drills. Overspeed training.
Force	Capacity for muscles to overcome resistance.	Overcome difficulty in hills, improve economy and, support injury prevention (see chapter 18).	Intervals with low cadence (hills, paddles, plyometrics). Strength training (see chapter 18).
Power	Ability to apply force quickly.	Limited use but applicable to draft-legal races or the final moments of a race.	Strength and interval training at intensities above $\dot{V}O_2$max.
Muscular endurance	Ability for muscles to overcome fatigue and apply force over prolonged exercise.	Resist fatigue and maintain race-pace velocity throughout the race. Particularly helpful for time-trial type performance and the end of a triathlon.	Intervals of 2 to 12 minutes at highly aerobic intensities (see chapter 20).

Specific Race Preparation

As the triathlete nears the competition phase, training must become more race specific. The goal of the specific training period is to mimic the conditions and stress of racing to the point that race day feels like an intense, routine workout.

As the triathlete transitions from general to race-specific preparation, the combined duration and intensity should begin to simulate the stress expected on race day. The abilities developed in general preparation are not abandoned; rather, they are gradually replaced by specific training. In many cases, the methods used to promote general abilities are identical to the methods used to promote specific abilities.

For example, Ironman triathletes may spend 70 percent of their time at a deeply aerobic intensity in the general phase and then continue with that level of intensity in the specific phase. Sprint triathletes may invest time performing muscular endurance in general preparation and maintain the same frequency and intensity into their specific training. Table 19.3 lists some examples of possible race-specific workouts.

Specific Tactical Training

Specific training is not limited to aerobic exercise. Tactics and strategy must be implemented and practiced early so that they become second nature on race day. Triathlon training requires as much planning around the characteristics of the racecourse as around the characteristics of the triathlete.

Tactical training should include sessions that use the same nutrition and equipment to be implemented on race day. The terrain and environment must also be considered. Although hill training would be considered a general ability (to develop force), if the run course for the race includes hills, hill training should be frequent in the specific phase. If high temperatures are expected for the event, the triathlete should train in a similar environment.

Humans also respond to diurnal cycles, and the triathlete who performs all run training at 6:00 a.m. may be in for an unpleasant surprise when she hits the run at noon on race day. Although more relevant for sprint and Olympic training, expediting transitions is an important task for which to train specifically. A triathlete who has not used the specific period to train for all expected nutritional, equipment, environmental, and strategic contingencies cannot expect peak performance.

Table 19.3 Specific Triathlon Training Sessions

Distance	Swim workout	Bike workout	Run workout	Training race
Sprint	10 × 100 meters leaving every 2 minutes 750-meter time trial Open-water sessions	2 × 15 minutes at 95 to 100% of threshold power, 5 minutes of recovery 30-minute time trial at 95 to 100% of threshold power	10 minutes off an intense bike session at goal race pace 5K time trial 4 × 1 mile (1.6 km) on 1 minute of rest	Sprint-distance race
Olympic	3 × 500 meters on 30 seconds of rest 1,500-meter time trial Open-water sessions	3 × 20 minutes at 90 to 95% of threshold power, 10 minutes of recovery 5 × 12 minutes at 90 to 95% of threshold power, 3 minutes of recovery	20 minutes off an intense bike session at goal race pace 2 × 20 minutes at goal race pace with 10 minutes of recovery 4 × 1 mile (1.6 km) on 1 minute of rest	Sprint-distance race
Half-Ironman	10 × 200 meters leaving every 4 minutes 2,000-meter time trial Open-water sessions	3 × 30 minutes at 80 to 85% of threshold power, 10 minutes of recovery 3-hour ride with tempo finish at 80 to 85% of threshold power	45 minutes off an intense bike session at goal race pace 3 × 20 minutes at 80% of $\dot{V}O_2max$ velocity on 5 minutes of rest 2-hour long easy run	Half-marathon race Cycling stage race
Ironman	4 × 1000 meters on 1 of minute rest 4,000-meter time trial Open-water sessions	3 × 60 minutes at 75 to 80% of threshold power, 15 minutes of recovery at 60% of threshold power 6-hour ride building from 65% to a finish at 75% of threshold power	1 hour off a long bike session at goal race pace 3 × 20 minutes at 70 to 75% of $\dot{V}O_2max$ velocity on 5 minutes of rest 2-hour long easy run	Half-Ironman race
Draft-legal	With paddles, 10 × 100 meters sprint on 1 minute of rest 50-meter sprints on a diving start 1,500-meter time trial Open-water sessions	10 × 30 seconds at 175% of peak power (see chapter 20) on 30 seconds of rest Follow Olympic-distance bike training	Follow Olympic-distance run training	Cycling criterion Olympic-distance race

General ability workouts continue into the specific phase, but the frequency and volume change to support the specificity of the upcoming competition phase.

Muscular Endurance Training

Muscular endurance plays a special role for the triathlete. Muscular endurance is the ability of a skeletal muscle or group of muscles to continue contracting and applying limited force over a long period; it is the combination of force and endurance. Although a triathlete's upper limit of aerobic capacity and endurance, lactate threshold, and metabolic efficiency will not change during a triathlon, muscular fatigue is likely the first ability to betray the triathlete and cause him to slow down, most often during the run. Therefore, muscular endurance becomes one of the more important general abilities to develop.

To develop muscular endurance, the triathlete cannot simply develop force and endurance independently. Although these two abilities must indeed be developed as a prerequisite, true muscular endurance is born from the simultaneous application of force and endurance. This training is most commonly performed at intervals of highly aerobic intensities as discussed in chapter 20.

Skill Training

Identifying skill training as a general or specific ability would be difficult. Skill work is certainly a general ability, because it is a required base from which to build new levels of muscle memory and fitness before moving on to more specific training. Skill work is also required in the specific phase of training, because desired race intensities cannot be obtained without the supporting technique. Additionally, general aerobic economy is largely a result of efficient movement permitted by the development of a skill. Therefore, skill training is an essential part of the entire training season, from aerobic base building to general preparation and through the specific phase before competition.

Swim Skill Training

For the triathlete entering the sport as an adult, the swim can be the most daunting, discouraging, and depressing part of training. Fortunately, age-group triathletes have had a long history of success in mastering the swim. Unlike cycling and running, in which a triathlete can gain substantial velocity from years of muscling through, achievement in swimming can never be realized by brute force and determination alone. Swimming success requires skill work.

A substantial swim literature reflects various philosophies. Researchers Toussaint and Beek proposed a formula[7] that swim velocity could be determined by

1. drag,
2. power input (aerobic capacity),
3. efficiency (mechanical), and
4. power output (force).

In other words, half of the components that lead to great swimming are technique based. At the risk of oversimplifying the hundreds of books and philosophies on swim technique, the common principle that they share is to reduce drag and increase propelling efficiency. Table 19.4 attempts to summarize the most common and effective drills used to support these two pillars of swimming.

Table 19.4 Swim Drills to Reduce Drag and Increase Propelling Efficiency

Drill	Reduce drag	Increase propelling efficiency
Swim with snorkel, buoy, or fins		X
Swim golf[a]	X	X
High elbow		X
Catch-up drill	X	
Kick drills[b]	X	X
V-line		X
Buoy press	X	
Fist drill		X
Kick, count, stroke drill	X	X
Finger spread[c, d]		X
Swim on side	X	

[a]Alberty, M.R., Potdevin, F.P., Dekerle, J., Pelayo, P.P., and Sidney, M.C. 2010. Effect of stroke rate reduction on swimming technique during paced exercise. *Journal of Strength and Conditioning Research*, 25(2), 392–397.

[b]Deschodt, V.J., Arsac, L.M., and Rouard, A.H. 1999. Relative contribution of arms and legs in humans to propulsion in 25-m sprint front-crawl swimming. *European Journal of Applied Physiology*, 80(3), 192–199.

[c]Marinho, D.A., Barbosa, T.M., Reis, V.M., Kjendlie, P.L., Alves, F.B., Vilas-Boas, J.P., and Rouboa, A.I. 2010. Swimming propulsion forces are enhanced by a small finger spread. *Journal of Applied Biomechanics*, 26(1), 87–92.

[d]Minetti, A.E., Machtsiras, G., and Masters, J.C. 2009. The optimum finger spacing in human swimming. *Journal of Biomechanics*, 42(13), 2188–2190.

Swim With Snorkel, Buoy, or Fins Use a snorkel, buoy, or fins while swimming. Focus on specific arm phases of each stroke to isolate and observe the phases without the distraction of breathing or kicking. Swim aids can be used in conjunction with all drills.

Swim Golf For each lap, have someone record the lap time in seconds and add the stroke count. Try to reduce stroke rate and distance per stroke to achieve a lower score.

From Alberty, M.R., Potdevin, F.P., Dekerle, J., Pelayo, P.P., and Sidney, M.C. 2010. Effect of stroke rate reduction on swimming technique during paced exercise. Journal of Strength and Conditioning Research, 25(2), 392-397.

High Elbow Swim with an exaggerated high elbow.

Catch-Up Drill   Do not begin the catch phase until the opposite hand has entered the water (figure 19.3). This drill promotes quadrant swimming.

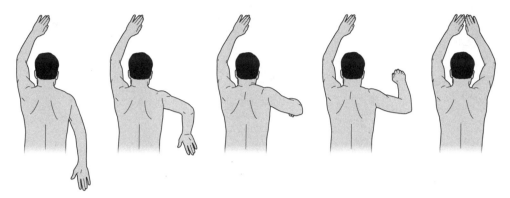

▶ **Figure 19.3**   Catch-up drill.

Kick Drills   Swim with a kickboard or swim on your back with your arms extended and hands together. This drill increases total velocity by making arm strokes more efficient and reduces drag by keeping the legs high.

From Deschodt, V.J., Arsac, L.M., and Rouard, A.H. 1999. Relative contribution of arms and legs in humans to propulsion in 25-m sprint front-crawl swimming. European Journal of Applied Physiology, 80(3), 192–199.

V-Line   Swim with the hands slightly outside the shoulders when extended (figure 19.4) to avoid crossing over the midline of the body.

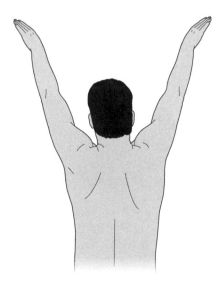

▶ **Figure 19.4**   V-line drill.

Buoy Press   Using a snorkel with this drill is best. Consciously press the chest while kicking with your face down and in the water. Hold your arms at your sides or extend one arm.

Fist Drill   Swim with your fists clenched or while holding tennis balls. This can be done with both fists clenched at the same time or one hand at a time to enhance the contrast. Focus on using a high elbow.

Kick, Count, Stroke Drill   With one arm extended, kick on your side for a count of 4, 5, 6, or 7. Take one to three full arm strokes to rotate to your other side for a new count. Focus on the rotation.

Finger Spread   Swim with your fingers slightly spread.

From Marinho, D.A., Barbosa, T.M., Reis, V.M., Kjendlie, P.L., Alves, F.B., Vilas-Boas, J.P., and Rouboa, A.I. 2010. Swimming propulsion forces are enhanced by a small finger spread. Journal of Applied Biomechanics, 26(1), 87–92; and Minetti, A.E., Machtsiras, G., and Masters, J.C. 2009. The optimum finger spacing in human swimming. Journal of Biomechanics, 42(13), 2188–2190.

Swim on Side   Swim with your navel facing the wall, with or without one arm extended (figure 19.5). Wearing fins for this drill is best.

▶ **Figure 19.5**   Swim on side drill.

Bike Skill Training

Although not as complex as swimming, cycling can be improved through specific skill training. Like swimming and running performance, cycling performance is ultimately a product of stroke rate and distance per stroke. In a relatively fixed position, the cyclist can either increase distance per stroke through force (big gear) or increase the efficiency of the stroke. Triathletes should therefore include cycling drills that promote a high cadence and pedal stroke efficiency.

Cadence

Even a cursory review of professional cyclists reveals that they use a cadence within a few revolutions of 90 rpm unless they are climbing. A formal review of professional cyclists competing at the Giro d'Italia, Tour de France, and Vuelta a España revealed a mean cadence of 89.3 plus or minus 1.0 during the group stages and 92.4 plus or minus 1.3 during time trials.[8] Although many studies prove that a high cadence reduces gross efficiency[9, 10] (comparing total work performed to total energy expenditure), this drawback appears to be compensated by advantages including better run times off the bike, more work done in the recovery phase of the stroke, increased pedaling efficiency, and more fat oxidation.

Additional benefits of a high cadence include improved subsequent run performance,[11] an increase in pedaling efficiency, and recruitment of more muscle groups in the recovery phase of the stroke.[12] Furthermore, a lower cadence requires more force and therefore more recruitment of fast-twitch muscle fibers. Long-term cycling with a low cadence theoretically changes the triathlete's metabolism to use more carbohydrate. In contrast, a high cadence promotes slow-twitch development. Although perhaps not a concern for short-course triathletes, long-course nutrition could be affected by decreased fat utilization from a low cadence.

But the preceding does not mean that a triathlete should spend all her time drilling at a 90 or more rpm. The development and maintenance of force and power developed through low cadence can translate into improved hill work, time-trial performance, and aerobic capacity.[13, 14] In summary, the triathlete's bread and butter should be a high cadence, but force should be developed and maintained year-round.

To drill for increased cadence,

- practice 30 right or left foot cycles in 20 seconds (equals 90 rpm),
- practice cadences of 100 or more rpm for several minutes at a time, and
- use a cycling computer with a cadence function year round to obtain real-time feedback.

Pedal Stroke Efficiency

Like any machine, a cyclist increases efficiency by administering power uniformly through the range of motion of a lever. The cyclist must overcome the tendency to rely on the downstroke of one leg to assist the recovery of the opposite leg during the pedal stroke. This "free ride" from the recovery leg is lost power.

To overcome this common cycling deficiency, the triathlete must practice drills that encourage the hip flexors and hamstrings to lift during the recovery phase, thus changing the recovery phase to an active phase. This ability can be accomplished through a combination of the following drills and equipment:

- Single-leg drill (indoor only). With one leg resting on a stool, the opposite leg is isolated and cycles independently. The focus should be on the upstroke and a smooth transition from downstroke to upstroke.
- Scraping drill. As the downstroke finishes, imagine scraping mud off the bottom of the shoe and pulling the foot back toward the rear of the bicycle.

- PowerCranks are an independent crank system that forces each leg to complete the stroke independently. These devices are best added to a separate bike because they replace your existing crank system.
- Various power meters including the CompuTrainer bike trainer system provides real-time feedback on pedaling efficiency through the SpinScan software interface, including the amount of power generated during each point in the pedal cycle. The Polar CS600X and LOOK Kéo Power power meters display a pedaling index, the ratio between the minimum and maximum forces of a single pedaling cycle to determine how round the distribution of power is.

Run Skill Training

The primary goal of the runner should be to increase running economy or the oxygen cost for a given velocity through a quick cadence, reduced braking and contact time from a midfoot strike, and a proud posture. Here are some drills to improve running economy.

Cadence Practice 30 right or left foot strikes in 20 seconds (equals 90 rpm).

Landers, G.J., Blanksby, B.A., and Ackland, T.R. 2011. Cadence, stride rate and stride length during triathlon competition. International Journal of Exercise Science, 4(1), article 6. Available at http://digitalcommons.wku.edu/ijes/vol4/iss1/6.

High Knees With a slight forward lean, stay tall while quickly lifting and driving down the knees. Cadence is rapid. Forward movement is not relevant. Striking at the heel is impossible if the drill is done properly.

Hands on Head Alternate between normal running and running with the hands on the head. Any lateral movement in your running gait (inefficiency) will be amplified.

Glute Kicks With the thigh pointing directly down and a slight lean, kick the legs up to the gluteal muscles. Forward movement is not relevant. The purpose is the quick action toward the gluteal muscles.

Ballerina Overemphasize the forefoot strike on the toes with high cadence. This running form is not optimal. The purpose is to discourage rear or heel strikes in favor of a midfoot strike.

From Hasegawa, H., Yamauchi, T., and Kraemer, W.J. 2007. Foot strike patterns of runners at the 15-km point during an elite-level half marathon. Journal of Strength and Conditioning Research, 21(3), 888–893; and Ardigo, L.P., Lafortuna, C., Minetti, A.E., Mognoni, P., and Saibene, F. 1995. Metabolic and mechanical aspects of foot landing type, forefoot and rearfoot strike, in human running. Acta Physiologica Scandinavica, 155(1), 17–22.

Knee Drive Lead the body with the knees, driving forward.

Strides Perform 6 × 30 left-foot strikes at $\dot{V}O_2$max velocity and then walk back for 90 seconds to rest. Focus on using a high cadence and lifting the heel directly up to the gluteal muscles.

Conclusion

Although the triathlete may be tempted to despair at the assertion that triathlon performance is largely predictable, this realization should be considered largely good news. Armed with an understanding of some of the primary predictors of endurance performance, including aerobic capacity and endurance, the ability to resist fatigue (muscular endurance), and economy (skills), the triathlete can modify training to develop these primary and other general abilities that will coalesce for race-day success.

CHAPTER **20**

Interval Training

—David Warden

The interval may be a triathlete's most effective tool. Interval training involves repeated short to long periods of high-intensity exercise, broken up with recovery periods of light exercise or rest. Intervals allow triathletes to perform more work at higher intensities than they could if they attempted those same high intensities without a rest interval.

In an early study of intervals, athletes were able to double the total amount of work done at high intensity when the rest interval was doubled.[1] When the rest interval was tripled, the total amount of work done at high intensity had no measurable limit. People performing run intervals at a duration of 50 percent of the time to exhaustion, with rest periods of the same duration, were able to spend more than twice as much time at the same velocity as they did when running one set to exhaustion.[2]

Benefits of Interval Training

Intense interval training not only allows the individual to do more total work than when doing uninterrupted intensities but also allows the body to maintain $\dot{V}O_2max$ for a longer period of the workout. Run interval training at 100 percent of $\dot{V}O_2max$ velocity, interspersed with rest periods at 50 percent of $\dot{V}O_2max$ velocity, allows runners to stay at $\dot{V}O_2max$ even during a portion of the rest interval, resulting in nearly three times the amount of time at $\dot{V}O_2max$ compared with continuous running at the same intensity.[3]

This ability to complete more work at higher intensities and to spend more time at $\dot{V}O_2max$ contributes directly to a triathlete's increase in fitness. Theoretically, by more than doubling the amount of time spent at high intensities, positive physiological changes would follow more rapidly than from less total time spent at high intensities.

Performance Improvements

Empirically, intervals have been proved to improve performance over endurance training alone. Although the interval work intensities in these studies vary from as low as 80 percent of $\dot{V}O_2$max output to as high as 160 percent of $\dot{V}O_2$max output, considerable improvement from interval training has been measured in several predictors of performance as well as actual performance results.

An interval study found significant improvement in overall $\dot{V}O_2$max, the running velocity at $\dot{V}O_2$max, the time that the runner could spend at $\dot{V}O_2$max velocity, and overall 3,000-meter run time.[4] This improvement over multiple measures of performance occurred after 10 weeks of two sessions of interval training per week. No improvement occurred in the control group, which performed only endurance training.

Fortunately for triathletes, the literature supporting positive results from high-intensity training is common across all three disciplines. Thirty-nine well-trained cyclists and triathletes found that two sessions of interval training per week, in addition to their endurance training, improved their 40-kilometer time trial performance by 4.4 to 5.8 percent, an improvement of approximately 3 minutes.[5] The cyclists and triathletes who maintained only endurance training had no improvement in their time trial.

When competitive young swimmers were split into two groups, high volume and high intensity, the high-intensity group spent 50 percent less total time swimming (30 minutes versus 60 minutes of main set) but swam at higher intensity intervals.[6] The result for these high-intensity swimmers was a 2.8 percent improvement in 2,000-meter swim performance, compared with a 1.8 percent improvement for the high-volume swimmers.

Physiological Changes

Although the ultimate goal of any elite triathlete is to reduce the total amount of time to complete a specific distance, the physiological changes associated with the improved time trial have broad implications. In a previously cited study, the cyclists' and triathletes' measures of peak oxygen consumption before interval training were already an enviable 64.5 plus or minus 5.2 (as measured in milliliters per kilogram per minute).[5] The interval training not only improved 40-kilometer time trial performance (a factor in Olympic-distance triathlon success) but also increased peak oxygen consumption between 5.4 and 8.1 percent from the already elite preinterval levels.

Similar increases of 5.5 milliliters per kilogram per minute in peak $\dot{V}O_2$ after 6 weeks of interval training[7] were found in moderately trained athletes. This increase in general $\dot{V}O_2$max from interval training in both elite and moderate athletes has implications across all triathlon distances because $\dot{V}O_2$max is a general predictor of endurance performance.

Enjoyment of Interval Training

Perhaps as important as the performance increase itself, interval training may play an important role in training adherence and overall enjoyment of training. Runners who performed either 50 minutes of moderate-intensity running, without intensity variation, or 50 minutes of high-intensity intervals (total interval work equaled 18 minutes) were asked to rate their level of enjoyment of the workout using the Physical Activities Enjoyment Scale (PACES).[8] Despite no difference between the two groups in average heart rate and total work completed within the 50-minute run, the high-intensity interval group scored 9 points higher on the enjoyment scale.

The result of this increase in pleasure is likely not because of the increased intensity but because of the intensity spread over the intervals. Multiple research[9, 10] supports the concept that an increase in the intensity of continuous exercise generally leads to a decrease in enjoyment. Intervals allow the total workout intensity to be higher with more total intense work completed, and breaking up the intensity with rest intervals allows more total pleasure in the workout. A more enjoyable training regimen results in an increased chance of exercise adherence and therefore improved performance.[11]

Interval Volume

If interval training is so effective, then why not either include it in every workout or use it for a high percentage of total training volume? Although a triathlete may be tempted to add high volumes of intensity, either as continuous or interval sessions, because of their effectiveness, doing so carries significant risks, including injury, compromised recovery, metabolic inefficiency, and overtraining.

People generally agree that the total amount of exercise is associated with increased risk of injury. Total amount of exercise, or exercise volume, is a combination of exercise frequency, duration, and intensity. An increase in any of these elements, particularly intensity, can increase the risk of injury to the athlete.

Additionally, an increase in intensity often occurs at the expense of aerobic work. The benefits of an aerobic base will not be discussed in detail in this chapter, but they include fat oxidation, development of slow-twitch muscle fibers, and an increase in the total number of red blood cells, to name just a few, and they develop only after considerable aerobic duration. A disproportionate level of interval training will likely reduce the volume of this important low-intensity training. Aerobic training volume should always make up the bulk of a triathlete's training.

In fact, an aerobic base facilitates the ability to perform intervals more effectively. Aerobic fitness translates into faster recovery from interval sets because of increased aerobic response, improved lactate removal, and enhanced phosphocreatine regeneration.[12] In other words, a triathlete desiring quality anaerobic intervals must maintain an aerobic base to support an effective recovery interval and therefore an effective overall interval session.

Perhaps the greatest consequence of high-intensity interval training is the risk of overtraining. Although overtraining is a complex condition that includes physiological, physical, and emotional elements, reduction in hematocrit, hemoglobin, and red blood cell count are all associated with overtraining.

Unfortunately, interval training can play a direct role in the reduction of these essential oxygen-carrying cells and molecules. In one study, hematocrit, hemoglobin, and red blood cell count were all significantly reduced in just 3 weeks of interval training 5 days per week.[13] Serum ferritin, an indirect measure of iron in the blood, remained low even after the interval training was completed, despite an iron supplementation throughout the training at 260 percent of the U.S. recommended daily allowance. Although this weekly interval frequency (five) is abnormally high, it illustrates just how quickly a triathlete's iron stores can be depleted from interval training. Like severe injury, overtraining because of insufficient iron stores can cause months of training interruption.

Because of these collective disadvantages of too much intensity, an optimal training program includes approximately 15 percent of total training duration at highly aerobic or anaerobic intensities, as demonstrated by multiple studies.[14, 15, 16, 17]

Interval Structure

The interval structure is composed of the work interval duration and repetitions, total interval duration, intensity, and rest period. For example, an interval set of 5 × 5 minutes on 1-minute rest would have a total interval duration of 25 minutes (5 × 5 minutes), a work interval of 5 minutes, a work interval repetition of 5, and a rest period of 1 minute.

Interval structure depends on the interval type and purpose. Intervals can be categorized into two types. General intervals are designed to increase broad fitness parameters such as $\dot{V}O_2$max and muscular endurance. These are typically high-intensity, anaerobic, or highly aerobic short-duration work intervals at outputs between 15 seconds and 6 minutes. The purpose of these intervals is to increase a triathlete's base speed, which can translate into a faster steady-state aerobic output.[18] Triathletes training for any distance would benefit from this increase in base thresholds by incorporating general intervals into the early period of an annual training plan.

Specific intervals are intervals performed at or close to the pace specific to the triathlete's race distance. For example, the sprint-distance triathlete may perform specific intervals at 100 percent of his 1-hour threshold intensity, whereas a long-distance triathlete's specific intervals may be performed at only 80 percent of 1-hour threshold intensity. These intervals are designed to prepare the triathlete for the particular stress and duration of an endurance event. They are highly aerobic work intervals lasting several minutes to hours. As the triathlete approaches her competition period, the number and volume of intervals done at specific race intensity should replace the more intense general intervals.

General Intervals

General intervals appear to increase $\dot{V}O_2$max and muscular endurance best at work interval durations anywhere from 15 seconds to 6 minutes,[5, 17, 18, 19, 20] but not necessarily all durations within that window. For example, benefit in work interval duration was specifically found at either 15 seconds or 4 minutes at 90 to 95 percent of maximum heart rate.[19] Similarly, work intervals of 30 seconds or 4 minutes are better at increasing muscular endurance compared with intervals at 1, 2, and 8 minutes because intensities increased inversely to the work interval duration.[18]

Considerable improvement in muscular endurance and $\dot{V}O_2$max was found at work interval durations of approximately 2 to 3 minutes,[5, 20] or, more specifically, interval durations at 60 percent of the time that $\dot{V}O_2$max output could be maintained, typically around 4 to 6 minutes for a well-trained triathlete.

Other interval research showed that increased performance used intensities below $\dot{V}O_2$max output of 4 to 5 minutes in duration.[17, 18, 19, 21] This finding supports an interval training program that includes either very short intense work intervals above $\dot{V}O_2$max output of 15 to 30 seconds (supramaximal), intervals at intensities associated with $\dot{V}O_2$max of 2 to 3 minutes (maximal), or intervals of 4 to 5 minutes at intense but submaximal outputs. Figure 20.1 quantifies the physiological effects of incorporating these various interval intensities into a training program.

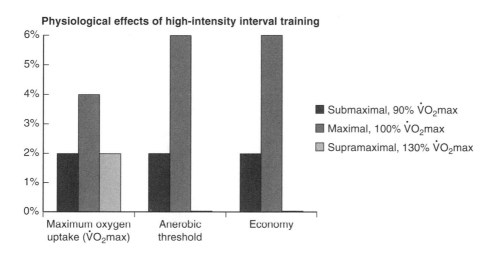

▶ **Figure 20.1** Physiological effects of high-intensity interval training.

Adapted from C.C. Paton and W.G. Hopkins, 2004, "Effects of high-intensity training on performance and physiology of endurance athletes," Sportscience 8: 25-40.

General Interval Intensity

Naturally, the intensity of the interval increases as the duration of the work interval or rest period decreases. Work intervals in the 15- to 30-second range show positive results at intensities of 90 to 95 percent of maximum heart rate for running[19] and 175 percent of peak power output (defined as peak 30-second power in a progressive exercise test) for cycling.[18]

Intensity for running or cycling working intervals of 2 to 3 minutes also appears to be best at output associated with $\dot{V}O_2$max.[5, 20] For longer intervals of 3 to 6 minutes, submaximal intensities of 80 to 85 percent of 30-second peak power for cycling all had positive results.[5, 20, 21]

A protocol for determining $\dot{V}O_2$max output and 30-second peak power can be found in the sidebar Determining Peak Power and $\dot{V}O_2$max Velocity or Output.

Intuitively, a triathlete might assume that shorter, more intense anaerobic intervals would be best for increasing $\dot{V}O_2$max and the longer highly aerobic intervals would be best for improving muscular endurance. The evidence reviewed here seems to suggest that both work interval durations can increase $\dot{V}O_2$max and muscular endurance, although the literature leans toward the longer 2- to 6-minute work intervals as the superior duration. But although both 15- to 30-second and 3- to 4-minute intervals increase $\dot{V}O_2$max, the increase is more significant with 2- to 4-minute intervals.[4, 5, 19, 22]

Additionally, a review of 22 studies on interval training revealed that the greatest benefit across a spectrum of fitness measures occurred with intensities associated with $\dot{V}O_2$max lasting several minutes.[23] When comparing

---

Determining Peak Power and $\dot{V}O_2$max Velocity or Output

Peak 30-second power protocol (bike with power meter)

1. Warm up for 5 minutes at a self-selected pace.
2. Begin at a workload of 100 watts.
3. Increase the workload by 15 watts every 30 seconds until exhaustion.
4. Peak power is the highest 30-second power output completed during the incremental test.

$\dot{V}O_2$max velocity or output (all disciplines)

1. Warm up for 20 minutes at a comfortable pace and include several 10-second bursts at estimated $\dot{V}O_2$max velocity or output.
2. Perform a 5-minute time trial at maximum maintainable pace.
3. $\dot{V}O_2$max velocity or output is the average velocity or power output during the time trial.

work interval intensity and durations of submaximal (greater than 10 minutes), maximal (2 to 10 minutes), and supramaximal (less than 2 minutes), this review found overwhelming benefit from the maximal intervals over supramaximal intervals in measures of submaximal endurance, maximal endurance, peak power, $\dot{V}O_2$max, anaerobic threshold, and economy. Therefore, a triathlete should consider a training mix of both short and longer general intervals, with the frequency skewed toward intervals of 2 to 6 minutes.

General Interval Duration

Work interval repetitions should be inversely related to the work interval duration. As the work interval decreases, the number of repetitions increases. When considering how to structure the repetitions of an interval workout, the total interval duration (work interval duration times repetitions) should be considered.

For supramaximal intervals, repetitions of 10 to 20 at 30 or 60 seconds have been shown to be effective,[23] and additional research shows improvement in 15-second intervals.[19] The consistent total interval duration of these studies was 4 to 6 minutes, although one study was a clear outlier at 20 minutes of total interval duration[24] (20 repetitions times 1-minute work interval at 100 percent of peak power).

But that study found that 1-minute intervals resulted in improvement only in peak power and ventilatory thresholds, not in $\dot{V}O_2$max. The other studies of shorter, more intense 30-second intervals (i.e., 175 percent of peak power as well as the research about 15-second intervals at up to 95 percent of maximum heart rate) all found increases in either $\dot{V}O_2$max or time-trial performance, measurements much more desirable than peak power in a steady-state endurance athlete. Therefore, the triathlete should structure the workout to include these general supramaximal work interval durations of 15 to 30 seconds and total interval duration of 4 to 6 minutes.

Research on interval intensities associated with $\dot{V}O_2$max (maximal intervals) supports a total interval duration of 15 to 45 minutes made up of individual work intervals ranging from 2.5 to 5 minutes. Although no empirical evidence is available on an upper limit to the total interval duration, the literature suggests that effective performance can result from a total interval duration of up to 45 minutes at intensities close to or at $\dot{V}O_2$max.

This total volume of intensity in a given workout appears to have an effective balance of risk and reward; the risk of overtraining or injury is relatively low, but the documented fitness reward is high. The triathlete should structure the workout to include work interval durations of 2 to 6 minutes at or close to $\dot{V}O_2$max output and total interval duration of 15 to 45 minutes. Intensities should be at $\dot{V}O_2$max output closer to the 15-minute range and just under $\dot{V}O_2$max output closer to 45 minutes.

General Interval Rest Period

The rest period between work intervals is the key to intervals and the primary reason that triathletes can perform more total high-intensity work than they can when training at uninterrupted intensities. Interval training must be implemented in a way that allows sufficient recovery to promote increased total work but does not permit excessive rest that would compromise fitness gains.

General intervals in this chapter have been divided into either very short work intervals of 15 to 30 seconds at intensities well above $\dot{V}O_2$max output (supramaximal), work intervals of 2 to 3 minutes at outputs associated with $\dot{V}O_2$max (maximal), or intervals of 3 to 6 minutes at outputs below $\dot{V}O_2$max (submaximal). Studies on rest periods for these three work interval intensities are consistent, but the structure changes based on work interval intensity and repetitions.

For example, Billat et al. found positive results in total time at $\dot{V}O_2$max from a 1:1 ratio of work interval duration to rest interval duration at $\dot{V}O_2$max velocity, but the work and rest interval durations were only 30 seconds at this maximal intensity.[3] Similar results were found with a 1:1 ratio at 15 seconds.[19] At supramaximal intensities, the rest interval must become longer. A 1:9 ratio at 30-second intensities at 175 percent of peak power resulted in a significant increase in $\dot{V}O_2$max.[5] Running velocities of 30 seconds at 130 percent of $\dot{V}O_2$max velocity also showed a 1:9 ratio.[4]

The 1:1 ratio is appropriate for maximal intervals of less than 30 seconds; work of 2 to 6 minutes requires a change in that ratio. A 1:2 work-to-recovery rest interval promoted an increase in performance at maximal intensity intervals of 2 to 3 minutes,[5, 20] whereas a rest interval of 1 minute for submaximal intervals of 4 to 6 minutes is consistently used in testing that resulted in improved performance.[17, 18, 21]

Perhaps the most interesting research on rest intervals was done with the work interval intensity, duration, and repetitions identical and the only difference being that the interval set was either an approximate 1:1 or 1:2 work-to-rest ratio.[5] Intuitively, the assumption would be that the same amount of work in a shorter period would be more likely to improve performance. Although both rest intervals promoted nearly identical improvement in $\dot{V}O_2$max, the group of athletes using the 1:2 work-to-rest interval ratio actually did more work in a subsequent time-to-exhaustion test. In the case of rest intervals, shorter is not always better. Triathletes can safely use a 1:2 work-to-rest ratio at maximal intensities of 2 to 3 minutes.

The term *rest interval* should not imply completely inactive (passive) rest. Several studies [25, 26, 27] have shown that an active rest interval (anything from brisk walking or light spinning to easy running) at intensities of 30 to 65 percent of $\dot{V}O_2$max velocities is superior in clearing lactate when compared with complete rest.

General Interval Frequency

The frequency of interval training for improved performance appears to be well established at two to three times per week. Interval training of two times per week is superior to one time per week, and the magnitude of improvement is related to frequency.[28]

But like many aspects of triathlon training, more is not always better. One study found no difference in $\dot{V}O_2$max improvement when comparing interval training at two or four sessions per week.[29] Significant improvement in multiple markers of performance was present in as little as four sessions in 6 weeks,[21] two sessions per week,[5, 17, 18, 20] or three times per week.[19, 22]

Considering the evidence that more than three interval sessions per week is no more effective than four per week and the evidence that five sessions per week can rapidly lead to potential overtraining, it appears that triathletes should aim for two or three high-intensity general interval sessions per week, or perhaps one session per discipline per week of either a supramaximal, maximal, or submaximal interval set. An example in a given week might include a swim interval session of 12 × 25 meters on 20 to 30 seconds of rest (supramaximal), a run interval session of 6 × 800 meters on 6 minutes of rest (maximal), and a cycling interval session of 6 × 6 minutes on 1 minute of rest (submaximal).

Theoretically, a triathlete could use interval training to work on sport-specific weaknesses. For example, a triathlete who is strong in run performance but weak in swim performance could modify the weekly training plan to include two run sessions and one cycling session per week.

Periodization of General Intervals

In the research cited in this chapter, positive results occurred in as little as 3 weeks,[18] although other studies lasted 4 to 8 weeks. But when comparing interval training of 7 or 13 weeks, the trend was to see greater improvement at 13 weeks.[29] In a periodized training plan, this finding would suggest that the triathlete do 2 to 3 months of general interval training (perhaps during the base phase; see table 20.1) before moving into more race-specific interval training and doing interval intensities at race pace in later phases.

This plan does not mean that general high intensity would be eliminated from the training plan as the triathlete moves into more race-specific training or actual racing. Researchers experimented with high-intensity intervals during the competitive phase in highly trained cyclists. The results were an increase in endurance performance when continuing high-intensity interval training during the competitive phase compared with a control group that did not participate in high-intensity training.[30]

As expected, the interval duration and repetitions were short at 5 × 30 seconds on 30 seconds of rest on 2 or 3 days per week, enough to promote a significant increase in performance without adding additional fatigue in the

Table 20.1 General Interval Structure, Base Training Period

Interval type	Intensity	Work interval	Total work duration	Rest period (work-to-rest ratio)	Frequency per week (total, not per discipline)
Supramaximal	175% of peak power (cycling) 130% of $\dot{V}O_2$max velocity (running, swimming) 90 to 95% of max heart rate	15 to 30 seconds	4 to 6 minutes	1:9	≤1
Maximal	100% of $\dot{V}O_2$max output	2 to 3 minutes	15 to 30 minutes	1:2	1 or 2
Submaximal	80 to 85% of peak power (cycling) 90% of $\dot{V}O_2$max velocity or output (cycling, running, swimming)	4 to 6 minutes	30 to 45 minutes	4:1 to 6:1	≤1

Supramaximal intervals of 5 × 30 seconds with 30 seconds of rest 2 or 3 days per week can be continued into the competition phase.

competition phase of training, and used the philosophy of 2 to 3 months of general intervals followed by limited interval training replaced by specific intervals.

Specific Intervals

Unlike general high-intensity intervals, race-specific intervals have had little attention directed to them in the scientific literature. Although the interval data on the individual disciplines of swimming, cycling, and running are mature and rich, the relatively immature sport of triathlon has been little studied by the scientific community.

Fortunately, we have the principle of specificity to guide the triathlete. Although general intervals will place the triathlete at an increased baseline of $\dot{V}O_2$max and muscular endurance (predictors of performance at any triathlon distance), specific intervals must be the primary method of interval training as the triathlete nears the competition phase. The goal is to introduce the specific intensities and stress that the triathlete will encounter during the race.

Coaches and triathletes widely believe that although interval training must begin to mimic the actual race intensity as the competition phase approaches, the maintenance of muscular endurance (or the ability to generate force for long periods) is critical for all triathlon distances. Intervals that promote muscular endurance should be continued from the general phases of training (as submaximal intervals) even into the more specific phase.

Although part VIII of this book will cover event-specific training, including interval training for sprint, Olympic, half-Ironman, and Ironman distances, some brief examples of specific interval training are listed in table 20.2.

Table 20.2 Specific Interval Structure Examples, Base or Build Phases

Race distance	Intensity	Work interval	Total work duration	Rest period	Frequency per week per discipline
Sprint	At goal race pace	6 to 12 minutes	30 to 60 minutes	2 to 3 minutes	1 or 2
Olympic	At goal race pace	6 to 12 minutes	30 to 60 minutes	2 to 3 minutes	1 or 2
Half-Ironman	At goal race pace	10 to 30 minutes	30 minutes to 3 hours	2 to 5 minutes	1 or 2
Ironman	At goal race pace	10 to 60 minutes	30 minutes to 6 hours	2 to 10 minutes	1 or 2
All distances (muscular endurance maintenance)	80 to 90% of $\dot{V}O_2max$ velocity or output (cycling, running, swimming)	6 to 12 minutes	30 to 60 minutes	2 to 3 minutes	1 or 2

Conclusion

The impressive increase in $\dot{V}O_2max$ from interval training is reason enough for triathletes to implement this type of training, but interval training offers additional benefits. Triathletes rarely perform only one distance during their triathlon careers. Many find themselves participating in triathlons lasting from 60 minutes to 17 hours.

To be prepared for events that have this significant spread of duration and intensities, the triathlete can maintain base fitness for an event of any length through general interval training and then switch to specific intervals before the particular event. Thus, the triathlete can maintain a dynamic annual training plan and be prepared to enjoy all triathlon events. Finally, although the performance benefits of interval training are well established, the additional benefit of increased enjoyment and associated increase in training compliance add an unexpected advantage from interval training.

PART

VI

Training Strategies in Triathlon

CHAPTER 21

Duration, Frequency, and Intensity

—Stephen J. McGregor, PhD

When contemplating the overall training program, triathletes and coaches alike are confronted with a profound question: How much, how often, and how hard should I train? For triathletes in particular, a complex set of variables complicates the answer to this question since triathletes must attain, or maintain, proficiency in three disciplines, as opposed to other endurance athletes who typically need to train for only one. Because of this, the answer to the question of how the athlete should structure his or her training is not necessarily straightforward.

This requirement to spend time training in each discipline dictates the need for a relatively high frequency of training that ultimately results in a high volume of total training time. At the same time, the intensity (or difficulty) of the training must be modulated to stimulate fitness adaptations but allow recovery and rejuvenation. Therefore, the demands of training present special challenges to triathletes that are unique among endurance sports.

Generally, three principles guide training for any kind of sport: overload, specificity, and reversibility.[1, 2]

- The principle of overload states that for a tissue or system to adapt, it must be exposed to stress that is greater than that to which it is accustomed.

- The principle of specificity asserts that for a tissue or system to adapt to a specific requirement, it needs to be stressed in a manner similar to that requirement. A simplistic example might be the intuitive notion that the legs can be trained for endurance by running or cycling, but they will adapt to each discipline in a specific fashion.

- Finally, the principle of reversibility maintains that after a stress is removed, the adaptation that was elicited will be lost; in simple terms, Use it or lose it.

Each of these principles should be considered with regard to training for triathlon, but in this chapter we focus primarily on overload. That said, specificity and reversibility are part of the subtext underpinning the overall approach to training. An approach designed to manipulate intensity will depend to some extent on the nature of the event (e.g., sprint, Olympic, Ironman) and will therefore be determined by the principle of specificity. Similarly, the principle of reversibility should be considered when devising the sequence of individual discipline training sessions, because if overload is neglected in a particular discipline (e.g., reducing swim overload to accommodate run overload), the adaptations in that discipline may suffer, relatively speaking.

Overload can be manipulated in one of three ways: frequency of stress, duration of stress, and intensity of stress. Another factor to consider is volume, which is a function of duration and frequency. Further, each of these main factors can be applied in different ways. For example, intensity could be manipulated by increasing the load in strength training, the speed in running, or the power in cycling. Similarly, frequency can be manipulated in terms of sessions per day, per week, per month, or a combination thereof. In the case of individual disciplines, we will consider intensity overload in swimming primarily in terms of pace, in cycling in terms of power and heart rate, and in running in terms of pace and heart rate.

Frequency

The frequency of training is an important parameter to consider because it contributes to total training volume. But in the context of triathlon, the challenge is maintaining sufficient frequency of training stress for three individual disciplines that collectively contribute to overall sport success.

Few studies have examined the direct effect of training frequency, particularly in highly trained athletes. The response of untrained people to various training frequencies has been well established for decades, though. Optimal results are achieved with three to five training sessions per week, and performing more than five sessions does not increase cardiovascular adaptations.[3, 4, 5, 6] Because serious triathletes will likely be training more than five times per week, these guidelines are of little value.

On the other hand, in recently trained people, training adaptations ($\dot{V}O_2$max) can be maintained with as little as 2 to 4 days per week of training.[7, 8] Because training adaptations, even within the endurance domain, are somewhat specific to the activity being practiced, the observation that optimal adaptations occur within 2 to 4 days per week, with diminishing returns above that, may be applicable to each individual discipline within triathlon. Therefore, a training regimen that incorporates 3 or 4 workouts per discipline per week would result in 9 to 12 training sessions per week, which, anecdotally, is a common weekly training frequency range for triathletes.

Duration and Volume

The duration of time for individual training sessions depends on a number of factors, such as event specificity (e.g., Olympic versus Ironman), periodization, and injury prevention. The latter factor is an important consideration because injuries are common in triathlon, particularly as a result of running.[3, 4, 5, 6] For athletes focused on Ironman-distance events, though, large volumes of training will be necessary, consisting of some training for long duration.

There is no evidence, though, regarding the individual contribution of training duration on adaptations in trained triathletes, so factors such as those mentioned previously need to be considered for this training variable.

Training volume is a function of frequency and duration, and because three disciplines need to be trained, global training frequency will likely be high for most triathletes, as mentioned previously, in the range of 9 to 12 training sessions per week or more.

Because a relatively high training frequency is a necessary component of triathlon training, changes or manipulations of training volume will come primarily from manipulations of training duration. Total training volume will be dictated by a number of factors but will depend largely on event specificity. Recently, Knechtle et al.[9] compared participants in Triple-Ironman Germany and Ironman Switzerland. The authors reported that the Triple-Ironman athletes (n = 64) trained on average approximately 19 hours per week whereas the Ironman athletes (n = 71) trained approximately 14 hours per week. In another recent study, Neal et al.[10] reported that 10 masters-level triathletes (42 years of age) trained between 8 and 11 hours per week over the course of 6 months.

In both of the aforementioned studies, the majority of the training volume (approximately 50 to 60 percent) was allocated to cycling. The second greatest volume was devoted to running, and the least to swimming. These were not elite triathletes, so it's not clear whether these training volumes are optimal, but these data can serve as benchmarks for age-group triathletes. Anecdotally, for elite or professional-level triathletes, training volumes commonly exceed 20 hours per week (unpublished observations).

Although it is important to consider the training variables frequency, duration, and volume, in many cases the answer to the question of how much to do regarding these variables is simply to do as much as possible. In other words, because training for the ultraendurance sport of triathlon requires proficiency in three individual disciplines, most triathletes, particularly age-group triathletes, will be relatively time constrained due to nonsport obligations and will be unable to realize sufficiently high training volumes to elicit optimal adaptations. Therefore, manipulating frequency and volume will likely result in suboptimal adaptations, which leaves intensity as the primary training variable that the triathlete can modulate.

Intensity

Possibly the most controversial training variable to consider is intensity. Particularly in triathlon, debate continues about the optimal intensity and even the role of intensity with regard to training for the triathlon. If the debate with regard to training intensity in endurance sport were divided into two camps, these camps would be the high-intensity training (HIT) camp[11, 12, 13, 14] and the high-volume, and hence, low-intensity camp.[15, 16]

High-Intensity Training (HIT)

Advocates of the HIT approach argue that intense training performed above the lactate threshold will elicit adaptations that result in improved performance that cannot be obtained through standard low-intensity endurance training, particularly in highly trained athletes.[13, 17, 18] Several investigations have demonstrated dramatic improvements in endurance performance from HIT in previously untrained or recreationally active individuals,[19, 20, 21, 22] but evidence indicates that such an approach can be beneficial for highly trained athletes as well.[14, 17, 23, 24, 25, 26, 27]

Several investigators have used 4- or 5-minute efforts at 80 to 85 percent of peak power for 4 to 6 weeks and demonstrated improvements in 40-kilometer time-trial cycling performance in highly trained athletes.[24, 25, 27] Other investigations have used shorter efforts (30 to 60 seconds) at higher intensities (100 to 175 percent of peak power) and demonstrated improvements in endurance performance as well.[23, 25, 27] Although relatively high intensity, these efforts are performed within the aerobic domain, or slightly above it, so it is not surprising that improvements in endurance performance would be observed with such efforts. Iaia and Bangsbo have performed extensive investigation of training that falls in more of the anaerobic domain, what has been coined *speed endurance* training.

The term *speed work* can impart different connotations, depending on the context or circumstances. Speed work should be considered in two primary ways:

- anaerobic training performed with the objective of improving the rate of anaerobic energy provision or anaerobic capacity or
- neuromuscular training performed at powers corresponding to anaerobic metabolism but more with the objective of increasing neurological or biomechanical aspects of movement patterns to improve performance.

Iaia et al.[11] have added criterion definitions for several components of speed work training. First, they define speed training as bouts that consist of short, maximal efforts (e.g., 2 to 10 seconds) interspersed with relatively long recovery periods (e.g., 50 to 100 seconds). Speed training is used to develop maximal-speed generation and neurological training.

Metabolic Responses to Anaerobic Training

Despite the fact that maximal efforts of 30 seconds in duration generally are considered anaerobic, repeated efforts of this duration or shorter become increasingly aerobic. Investigators have shown that repeated maximal efforts of 5 to 30 seconds in duration become primarily aerobic largely because of the reduced contribution from glycolytic and glycogenolytic metabolism.[30, 31, 32, 33] In fact, after only three maximal efforts of 30 seconds in duration with 4 minutes of recovery, the total anaerobic contribution during the third 30-second effort is reduced to less than half and aerobic metabolism accounts for approximately 60 percent of total energy provision, which makes them, by definition, aerobic.[34]

Aside from the obvious potential benefits to anaerobic performance, several investigators have reported aerobic adaptations to various types of training programs that are based on anaerobic efforts.[11, 20, 35, 36] So, although anaerobic training may not seem appropriate for an endurance sport such as triathlon, regardless of the distance, some foundational evidence supports the potential benefits of this type of training to aerobic performance. An argument can be made that anaerobic training may actually be a stimulus for aerobic adaptations, but it is likely not an optimal stimulus.

Although maximal efforts of short duration become mostly aerobic, short-duration efforts are not long enough to elicit $\dot{V}O_2$max or are too short to elicit large volumes of accumulated aerobic work. Therefore, anaerobic training may have a place in the overall training scheme, but it should likely be used judiciously.

Speed endurance training is defined as any other anaerobic training and is further divided into speed production and speed maintenance training.

In speed production training, the effort lasts less than 40 seconds and is followed by relatively long recovery periods, generally five times the work period.

Speed maintenance training consists of efforts lasting 5 to 90 seconds but has shorter recovery periods of less than three times the work period. The distinction between speed production and speed maintenance is the relatively higher intensities that can be maintained during speed production work because of the proportionally longer recoveries. With speed maintenance work, intensities will be lower, particularly because fatigue ensues with the shorter recovery periods.

As previously stated, the purposes of speed training can be targeted either at neuromuscular learning, with the intention of improving movement patterns that result in greater speed development, or at metabolic processes that illicit increased ability to generate energy from anaerobic sources faster (i.e., rate) or in greater amounts (i.e., capacity). This type of training has been shown to improve performance as well as some underlying physiological parameters that were not previously investigated in relation to endurance performance.[11, 12, 28, 29]

High-Volume, Low-Intensity Training

In contrast to the HIT approach to intensity application, an intensity and volume distribution that is heavily weighted to the lower-intensity spectrum is advocated by some authors. In particular, Seiler has argued for an approximate 80–20 percentage distribution, in which 80 percent of training is performed below the lactate threshold and 20 percent above.[15, 16] He cites as support for this contention that, anecdotally, this distribution seems to be the one that many high-level endurance athletes in various disciplines have come to use through the process of trial and error.

Additionally, he cites evidence from Esteve-Lanao et al.,[15] who examined two groups of subelite distance runners, one that trained with an 80–20 distribution and the other that trained with a 67–33 distribution. Over a 5-month period, the 80–20 group improved significantly more than the 67–33 group in a standardized performance test (–157 plus or minus 13 seconds versus –122 plus or minus 7 seconds).

Other data in support of the high-volume, low-intensity approach come from Fiskerstrand and Seiler,[37] who examined training data for elite rowers over the course of 30 years. Evidence showed that over this time, total training volume had increased, with a 20 percent increase in volume of training below the LT but a decrease in volume of training above the LT. At the same time, $\dot{V}O_2$max increased by approximately 10 percent and rowing ergometer performance improved by 10 percent. Note that rowers primarily compete in the 2,000-meter event, which requires approximately 6 to 7 minutes to complete, a time that corresponds closely to the $\dot{V}O_2$max,[38, 39] yet the majority of training is performed below the LT.

Training Adaptations Similar Across Event Durations

This finding demonstrates a principle that some astute practitioners have been aware of for decades—aerobic performance relies on similar training adaptations regardless of the duration of the event. In particular, Arthur Lydiard, the legendary coach of numerous Olympic medalists in running from the 800 meters to the marathon, argued that he trained all his runners regardless of discipline in much the same way. From a speech in 1990 he said,

> Even my middle distance runners like Snell and Davies also did the same mileage. Because what does the middle distance runner and distance runner require? They require the high oxygen uptake level as the governing factor in their performance level. They need speed and they need anaerobic development. So, this is why I trained them all the same, except for the last 10 weeks when we decided which event they were better suited for and changed the training to co-ordinate their efforts for that particular event."[40]

Training Volume Distribution

To illustrate this point further, in figure 21.1 data are presented from three athletes with regard to their training volume distribution. In figure 21.1*a*, the run training volume distribution for an Ironman World Championships (IMWC) age-group podium winner is presented. This data were collected for every run training session by GPS speed distance devices over the course of 4 months leading up the IMWC.

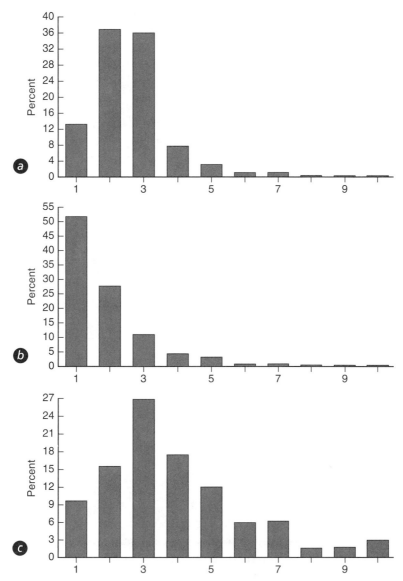

▶ **Figure 21.1**   Running pace zone distribution generated from speed and distance data obtained from global positioning system (GPS) devices in (*a*) Ironman World Championships (IMWC) age-group competitor for 4 months before IMWC; (*b*) subelite national-caliber runner for one season; and (*c*) elite amateur triathlete for one season

With regard to the runner presented in figure 21.1*a*, more than 90 percent of training volume was performed below the functional threshold pace (FTP), or maximal lactate steady-state pace (MLSS). Similarly obtained data from a subelite national-caliber distance runner are presented in figure 21.1*b*. In this case, the runner exhibits an extreme distribution in which more than 95 percent of training was below the FTP–MLSS.

Finally, in figure 21.1*c*, data from an elite amateur triathlete show a distribution pattern different from the other two. In this case, 81 percent of run volume was performed below the FTP–MLSS, but apparently this athlete performed more training closer to the FTP–MLSS than the other two athletes did. In comparison with the other two athletes, this athlete was the only one to improve run FT pace over the course of the training year.

Pace Zone Distribution

The data are divided into a pace zone distribution that this author has presented previously,[41] in which the FTP, which is analogous to the MLSS, occurs in zone 6. The pace zone determination approach used for these runners is presented in figure 21.2, in which the FTP is determined through testing or based on extrapolation from recent performances such as the 3K, 5K, or 10K, and then the other zones are centered on associated physiological responses or adaptations (e.g., Z8 = $\dot{V}O_2$max, Z10 = speed).[41]

Recent race (Min: Sec)			Target training pace (Min: Sec/Mile)						
3K	5K	10K	PZI	2: L Aero	3: M Aero	4: H Aero	6: Thresh	8: $\dot{V}O_2$max	10: Speed
18:10-17:41	33:55-32:01	66:04-66:21	50	14:41-13:21	13:20-12:15	12:14-11:37	11:01-10:41	10:08-9:55	9:38-2:40
17:40-17:13	32:00-31:05	66:20-64:37	49	14:22-13:02	13:01-11:57	11:55-11:19	10:44-10:24	9:51-9:41	9:22-2:40

10:21-10:13	18:30-18:13	33:23-37:49	23	9:10-8:00	7:59-7:11	7:10-6:43	6:26-6:15	5:50-5:44	5:26-2:40
10:12-10:03	18:12-17:57	37:48-37:14	22	9:03-7:53	7:52-7:04	7:03-6:37	6:21-6:10	5:44-5:38	5:20-2:40
10:02-9:54	17:56-17:41	37:13-36:41	21	8:56-7:46	7:45-6:58	6:57-6:31	6:15-6:04	5:40-5:34	5:16-2:40

▶ **Figure 21.2** Pace zone index (PZI) chart extract for pace zone determination in running. The PZI can be extrapolated from performances in races such as the 5K. In this case, a 5K performance of 18:00 would correspond to a PZI of 22. The corresponding pace zones to the right of that value would then be applied. The FTP would lie within zone 6: threshold.

Data from McGregor, S.J, and Fitzgerald, M. 2010. The Runner's Edge. Champaign, IL: Human Kinetics.

Cycling Power Distribution

In figure 21.3 data collected from portable power meters in cycling are presented. In figure 21.3*a*, an example comes from an elite espoir (i.e., U23) bicycle racer for an entire season in which he placed in the top five in his national professional time-trial championship and competed in the espoir world championships. Data are collected from an onboard power meter for all training sessions and most races and are presented in a power distribution scheme developed by Allen and Coggan[42] in which the functional threshold power (FTP) occurs in the zone labeled TH.

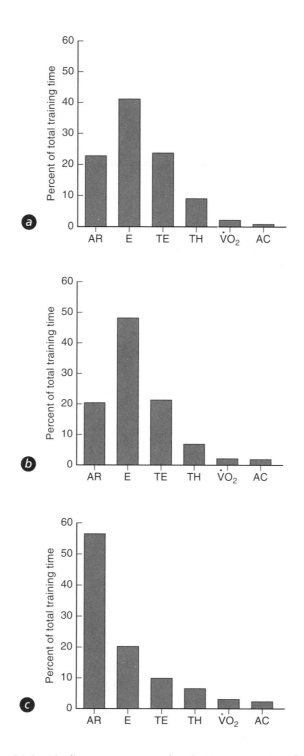

▶ **Figure 21.3** Cycling power zone distribution generated from portable onboard power meter data obtained for (*a*) an elite espoir professional cyclist for one season; (*b*) an elite amateur national-caliber cyclist for one season; and (*c*) an elite amateur age-group national champion cyclist for one season.

As with the FTP for running, the FTP in cycling corresponds approximately to the maximal lactate steady state effort (MLSS), but in this case is power based, as opposed to pace based for running. With regard to training structure, despite the inclusion of high-intensity efforts produced during elite-level road racing included in the dataset, 87 percent of total training and racing volume is performed below the FTP–MLSS.

In figure 21.3b data are presented from an elite amateur cyclist who placed fourth in his national elite time trial. In this case 88 percent of total training volume, including races and training, was performed below the FTP–MLSS. In the case of both of these athletes, performance at the FTP improved approximately 5 percent over the course of the season.

Finally, in figure 21.3c power meter data are presented from a masters-level national champion cyclist who won several elite category time trials. Data include all racing and training sessions, and although the total training volume is approximately two-thirds of the other elite-level cyclists, over the course of the season, 88 percent of all training was performed below the FTP.

Note that despite the apparent overwhelming weight of sub-FTP training distribution, these athletes either raced or performed supra-FTP efforts on a frequent, almost weekly, basis. So, HIT training was a component of the training program, but a relatively small component. These anecdotal observations coming from quantitative data collection methods in runners, triathletes, and cyclists support the notion that a large majority of training is performed below the FTP or MLSS, regardless of discipline.

Further, the difference among individuals in the distribution pattern of volume in the various training zones presented in figures 21.1 and 21.3 is somewhat striking, yet the relative proportion of training below FT in general terms is essentially the same among individuals. This begs the question, How important are differences in intensity between subthreshold exercise intensities for optimal development? The data from triathletes and runners, though, might indicate that a 90 percent distribution is the upper limit for sub-FTP training because improvements were not observed in athletes who trained with this distribution. With the proliferation of electronic training devices (e.g., portable power meters and GPS), more information in this regard will likely be accumulated in the future and shed more light on this issue.

Conclusion

The basic training variables frequency, duration, volume, and intensity, which contribute to the principle of overload, are foundational to training for triathlon, yet there is no clear evidence about the optimal application of these variables to elicit the maximal training effect and performance. Nevertheless, several general guidelines regarding these variables can be offered:

- In simple terms, because most triathletes will be time constrained, the frequency and volume of training should be as high as practical.
- A training intensity distribution consisting of approximately 80 to 90 percent of total training performed below the FTP–MLSS is advisable.
- Within the confines of this distribution, HIT training is likely required as a component of the overall training program to address the 10 to 20 percent of training that should be performed above the FTP–MLSS.
- Intensive training should probably be more aerobic in nature as opposed to anaerobic to assist with the overall aerobic development of the triathlete.

CHAPTER **22**

Periodization

—Stephen J. McGregor, PhD

Most triathletes anticipate and accept, even relish, that they need to train a great deal to be successful in their sport. But simply training a lot with no particular plan or objective is unlikely to lead to success. A key element to success in triathlon, or most endurance sports for that matter, is an organized approach to training that allows the athlete to gain fitness and ultimately optimize performance for target events of the season without becoming overstressed. So, at the start of each season, the triathlete is faced with the daunting task of organizing the yearly training plan in a way that will result in the best possible performance at the target events of the season. The approach that most triathletes typically take is called periodization.

In general terms, periodization is the systematic planning of training over a relatively long time frame (e.g., year, several years, and so on), in which the larger time scale is subdivided into smaller periods or cycles. A pictorial example of one of the earliest documented approaches to periodization can be seen in figure 22.1. In this example, the training year is divided into small periods consisting of *preparatory*, *competitions*, and *transition* phases, which are further divided into *general preparatory*, *specific preparatory*, *precompetition*, *main competition*, and *transition* phases. As we will see later in this chapter, this traditional approach to periodization is made up of one monocycle and gross manipulations of volume and intensity designed to elicit optimal performance at one target competition late in the year during the competition phase. This periodization approach has been modified extensively since its original introduction in 1965, but many coaches and triathletes still use the basic elements.

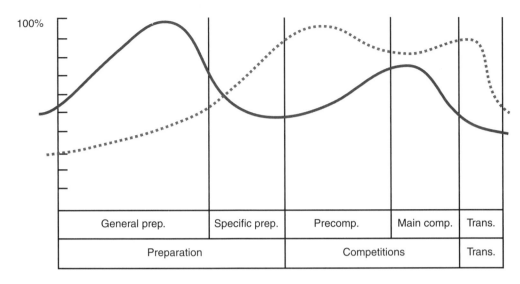

100%					
	General prep.	Specific prep.	Precomp.	Main comp.	Trans.
	Preparation		Competitions		Trans.

▶ **Figure 22.1** Original periodization model presented by Matveyev. The main competition year is subdivided into several phases of training. The solid line represents the volume of training, and the dotted line represents the intensity of training.

From L. Matveyev, 1965, *Periodization of sports training (Moscow: Fizkultura i Sport).*

Rationale for Periodization

Much of the rationale for periodization theory is based on the work of Hans Selye and his model of General Adaptation Syndrome (GAS)[1, 2, 3] (see figure 22.2). From this model, it has been proposed that any stress on the system can result in an adaptation whereby the body becomes more fit, or resistant to this

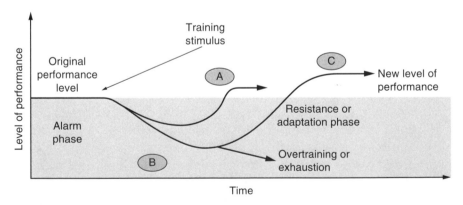

▶ **Figure 22.2** Illustration of Selye's general adaptation syndrome (GAS) theory. A = typical training that results in positive adaptation; B = overtraining that results in detrimental adaptation; C = overreaching or supercompensation that results in superior adaptation to that from typical training.

Reprinted, by permission, from T.O. Bompa and G.G. Haff, 2009, *Periodization: Theory and methodology of training,* 5th ed. (Champaign, IL: Human Kinetics), 14. Adapted, by permission, from A.C. Fry, 1998, The role of training intensity in resistance exercise overtraining and overreaching. In *Overtraining in sport,* edited by R.B. Kreider, A.C. Fry, and M.L. O'Toole (Champaign, IL: Human Kinetics), 114.

stress. In general, this fitness is simply a resistance or tolerance to stress—any stress to which the system is exposed, not just training stress.

An important point is that a recovery period is required for the adaptation to the stress and increased fitness to occur. People often say that the adaptation to training stress does not occur during the training session itself but during the subsequent rest or recovery period. In a larger context, this same principle applies in that if a training stress is imposed in a continuous fashion, the system may adapt, but if the stress is not removed, the system will become overstressed and break down.

Therefore, the periodization approach allows for the application of stress and recovery in a systematic fashion to optimize the adaptation and minimize, or avoid, the potential for overstressing the system and causing a breakdown (i.e., overtraining or underperformance).

Specifically with regard to training, the rationale for periodization is several fold. First, it is generally accepted that periods of training stress followed by recovery result in a supercompensation that produces improved performance.[1,4,5] The degree of supercompensation resulting from training depends largely on the magnitude of the overload imposed;[6] hence, periodization allows for progressive increases in training load, interspersed by recovery. Second, periodization is a systematic approach to this pattern of overload and recovery that allows for planning of training, adaptation, and competition. Further, conceptually, periodization facilitates the visualization of short-term training objectives and benchmarks within the context of the longer-term goals that are the primary objectives of the season. Therefore, the periodization plan serves as a temporal guide for the application of training loads in a sequential fashion such that optimal performance may be achieved for the primary target events.[1,3,4,7,8,9,10,11] Finally, another purpose of periodization may simply be to relieve training monotony, which in turn may result in greater physiological adaptations.[1]

Periodization Cycles

In periodization theory, cycles are the subdivisions by which the larger timeframes are broken down. An unfortunate problem in the periodization literature is the lack of standardization, and therefore some discrepancies in this nomenclature exist. For instance, in some cases, the yearly or seasonal plan would be referred to as the macrocycle, the 8-week increments would be mesocycles, and the 7-day increments would be microcycles.[4,11,12,13] Others might consider a macrocycle one of several divisions of the yearly or seasonal plan, and they would not use mesocycles.[1,14] For purposes of consistency, in this text we will use the macrocycle to describe the largest timeframe for a given training objective, typically a year or season. Mesocycles are the subdivisions of the macrocycle that typically focus on a particular attribute of overall training objective (e.g., base, specialization, competition, peak). In this context, an attribute is any skill or characteristic that can be affected by training. As such, the term can be broadly used to describe physiological characteristics (e.g., anaerobic capacity or $\dot{V}O_2$max) or technical skills and abilities (e.g., swimming technique or running economy). Microcycles are the smallest division of organized training apart from the actual training sessions themselves.

Traditional Periodization in Triathlon

Probably the most prolific application of periodization in triathlon comes from the popular text by Friel.[7] In this work, Friel presents a linear model of traditional periodization (figure 22.3). Using this approach, if each mesocycle is condensed by approximately half, the periodization scheme could be applied for a period as short as 20 to 22 weeks, but as presented it would typically be applied for a year. An in-depth analysis of the suggested components of each mesocycle and microcycle is beyond the scope of this chapter, but the reader is encouraged to seek out Friel[7] as a reference and an exemplar of linear periodization approach that is widely used in triathlon and other endurance sports.[1, 7, 15] In the text, Friel provides this template as a generalized approach that is founded on the commonly accepted traditional model of periodization for endurance sports, but he acknowledges that other approaches may be effective as well. Possible alternative approaches are presented later in this chapter.

Other examples of traditional periodization applied to triathlon found in the literature include Rowbottom et al.,[5] in which the authors examined highly trained triathletes over the course of 9 months. During this period, the triathletes doubled their training load. This approach of continually increasing the training load over the course of 9 months consisting of a 5-month preparatory mesocycle (July to November) and a 4-month competition mesocycle (December to March) would be considered a traditional linear periodization approach.[5, 16]

Macrocycle	Training year																	
	Preparation									Competition			Transition					
Mesocycles	General preparation							Specific preparation	Pre-comp	Competition			Transition					
	Prep	Base						Build	Peak	Race			Transition					
Microcycles	1	2	3	4	5	6	7	8	Weeks 9-42		43	44	45	46	47	48	49	50	51	52

▶ **Figure 22.3** A traditional periodization plan as presented by Friel that is composed of one macrocycle. The single macrocycle is divided into several mesocycles, which are further divided into microcycles. This approach could be used for a yearly monocycle approach or for a multicycle approach in which two or more of these macrocycles would be planned within a calendar year.

Reprinted, by permission, from J. Friel, 2009, The triathlete's training bible, 3rd ed. (Boulder, CO: VeloPress), 38.

Note that 6-week microcycles were used with a 1-week regeneration period before testing and beginning the next microcycle. Numerous physiological parameters were examined, but the only significant change occurred in run speed at anaerobic threshold, which increased from 15.6 to 16.6 kilometers per hour (approximately a 6 percent increase) from the start to the finish of the 9-month period.

Several arguments have been raised against the traditional periodization concept.[4, 17, 18, 19] In particular, competing frequently at a consistently high level, as elite and professional athletes do, may conflict with the periodization scheme.[20] Another problem rests in coordinating the periodization of three disciplines that may have conflicting training approaches (e.g., LSD for running versus intervals for swimming).[21, 22, 23, 24, 25] So, for triathletes who must develop proficiency in three disciplines with disparate approaches, a singular overarching traditional periodization scheme may be problematic to develop.

Alternative Periodization Approaches

In response to the aforementioned criticisms of the traditional periodization approach, alternative methodologies have been developed. An alternative termed *block periodization* is primarily advocated by Issurin.[4, 18, 26] Another is *undulating*, or *nonlinear, periodization*.

Block Periodization

Block periodization is an approach whereby the annual cycle is divided into three mesocycles that are cyclically repeated in a fashion that depends on the nature of the competitive season. The three mesocycles *(accumulation, transmutation,* and *realization)* are joined together in a sequential fashion much like in traditional periodization, but it is argued that during these mesocycles, the triathlete can focus on a more limited number of attributes, or abilities, than in the traditional mixed approach. Therefore, the triathlete can achieve intensified training and development of these attributes using the block periodization approach.

During the accumulation mesocycle, volume is typically higher and intensity is low, as is typical with the early mesocycles of a traditional periodization approach. This mesocycle is said to last only 2 to 6 weeks, though, before the triathlete moves into the more intense transmutation mesocycle. During this mesocycle, intensity is high. This period is considered the most stressful, but it lasts only 2 to 4 weeks, depending on the overall structure of the annual plan. The final realization phase consists of drills to prepare specifically for competition using a sport-specific program, which also allows for recovery from the fatigue of the preceding mesocycle.[4] One main advantage to this approach as proposed by Issurin can be seen in figure 22.4, in which periodization is structured around several competitions throughout the year, culminating with the targeted primary objective at the end of the annual plan.[4] This plan shows how the pattern of the three mesocycles is repeated sequentially, enabling relative rest, a high fitness level for competitions, and repeated intensified training in the interim.

A potential limitation to the block periodization approach, which is identified by Issurin himself, lies in the fact that during each mesocycle, particular attributes are targeted while nontargeted attributes may be ignored. For example, the triathlete who focuses on anaerobic capacity during a mesocycle may ignore aerobic endurance. So, the issue of detraining is of concern if a previously targeted attribute is ignored and fitness of that nontargeted attribute is lost in a subsequent mesocycle. Therefore, Issurin argues that the coach must be aware of the duration of the training residuals of each attribute so as not to leave attributes with short-lived training residuals untargeted too long. Training residuals are either the delayed adaptations to training or persistent adaptations, which can remain for various periods after a training overload has been removed. For example, Issurin states that both aerobic endurance and maximal strength adaptations persist for approximately 30 days, whereas anaerobic glycolytic endurance will dissipate after only 18 days and alactic speed will last approximately 5 days.[18]

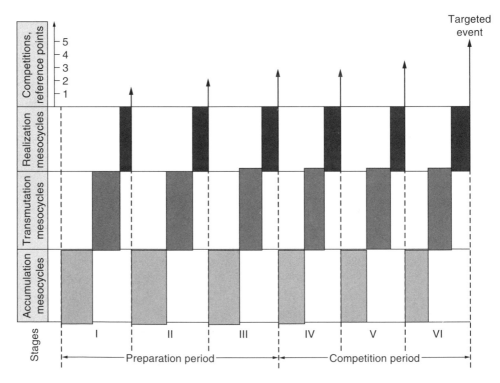

▶ **Figure 22.4** Presentation of a block periodization annual plan with competitions placed at the end of each block and with the plan culminating with the sixth primary targeted competition.

Reprinted, by permission, from V.B. Issurin, 2010, "New horizons for the methodology and physiology of training periodization," Sports Medicine 40(3): 189–206.

At the same time, Issurin argues that the training residuals are a central aspect of the block periodization approach, in that the relatively short meso-cycle approach relies on training residuals to maintain fitness of particular attributes over the course of the rapid fluctuations in training load and focus. This approach is claimed to have been responsible for the success of the former USSR canoe–kayak team (6 Olympic and 17 world championship medals from 1988 to 1990) as well as Alexander Popov, multiple Olympic and world champion swimmer.[4, 27]

Undulating, or Nonlinear, Periodization

Another periodization approach that has been developed in response to per-ceived problems with the traditional approach is termed *nonlinear periodization*. In the traditional approach, each period is designed for a specific purpose (e.g., preparation, base, build, and so on) that should be followed in a sequen-tial fashion, but the nonlinear approach does not adhere to these strictures.

Few studies address this approach as it applies to endurance sport, and fewer still are specifically related to triathlon, but in the field of strength training, numerous peer-reviewed studies have been done.[28, 29, 30, 31, 32, 33, 34, 35] Although it may seem counterintuitive to extrapolate the validity of strength training studies to an endurance sport such as triathlon, performance mod-eling studies have shown that global training adaptations can be modeled similarly in sports as disparate as the hammer throw and triathlon based on quantification of training loads.[36, 37] Therefore, until more data are available specifically regarding triathlon, the aforementioned strength training studies will have to suffice.

Anecdotally, in terms of endurance sport, the nonlinear approach contrasts traditional periodization by not adhering to a more segregated distribution of training loads whereby the early base mesocycles consist of low intensity and high volume and progress to specialized mesocycles consisting of lower volume and high intensity. Instead, nonlinear periodization consists of a more balanced application of intensities throughout the entire macrocycle. The various training modalities (e.g., LSD, aerobic intervals, anaerobic train-ing) are applied more consistently throughout the entire macrocycle and are periodized over the course of days as opposed to segregated by mesocycles.

A primary argument in favor of this approach is along the lines of the block periodization rationale—that more frequent competitions spread throughout the year require a more consistent, higher fitness level over the course of the macrocycle. Numerous practitioners have likely been applying this approach over the years not as the application of a grand theoretical design, but as a matter of necessity, because competition schedules have dictated it.

In fact, a popular training manual for cycling, written by Greg LeMond more than two decades ago,[38] recommended such an approach, as espoused by Cyrille Guimard and Paul Koechli, to accommodate the greater frequency of cycling competitions relative to other endurance sports.[18] Further, Haff has argued that the nonlinear approach is synonymous with the traditional model in that both approaches use day-to-day variations in training load to optimize adaptation and avoid overtraining.[17] So, the hallmark of nonlinear periodization that distinguishes it from a traditional approach with regard to endurance sports is simply the lack of a sequential series of mesocycles that progress from low intensity and high volume to high intensity and low volume, and a more consistent distribution of training intensities throughout the year or macrocycle.

Evaluating Periodization Through Performance Modeling

When devising the overall periodization plan, it is difficult for the triathlete to objectively see the changes and adaptations that may be occurring on multiple time scales. So, how can the triathlete or coach see the forest for the trees, if you will, when evaluating the periodization plan?

One technique that has shown some promise in simplifying the complexities of the overall periodized program is mathematical performance modeling. Modeling the effects of training on performance has been of interest in the scientific literature since Calvert et al.[39] first proposed an impulse–response (IR) modeling approach more than three decades ago. They devised their approach based on the ideas that an acute training bout (impulse) elicited two antagonistic responses: an initial negative component (i.e., fatigue) that detracted from performance and a delayed positive component (i.e., fitness) that ultimately contributed to improved performance after dissipation of the negative component.

These concepts of reduced performance because of incurring fatigue through training and increased performance with reestablishment of homeostasis and subsequent supercompensation are essentially synonymous with those of periodization. Therefore, the performance modeling approach developed by Calvert et al.[39] (see figure 22.5) could be thought of as mathematical approach to modeling the result of periodization.

Now understandably, for nonmathematicians such an equation will likely be intimidating, but in simple terms, the concept is straightforward.

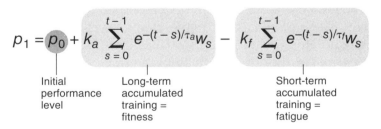

$$p_1 = p_0 + k_a \sum_{s=0}^{t-1} e^{-(t-s)/\tau_a} w_s - k_f \sum_{s=0}^{t-1} e^{-(t-s)/\tau_f} w_s$$

Initial performance level

Long-term accumulated training = fitness

Short-term accumulated training = fatigue

▶ **Figure 22.5** Performance modeling approach.

A performance at any given time in the future (p_t) is determined by the initial performance level at day 0, the positive effects of training that can be thought of as fitness, and the negative effects of training that can be thought of as fatigue. So, the effects of training can be mathematically reduced to fitness and fatigue components that essentially dictate performance at a given time. In their initial work, Calvert et al. quantified training using a heart rate metric termed TRIMPS, or training impulse.[39] Again, though, for practitioners such as coaches and triathletes, this mathematical approach may be too esoteric and complex, so a simplified approach has been developed specifically for the cycling and running subdisciplines of triathlon.

In essence, all derivations of the mathematical model can be simplified to

$$\text{Performance} = \text{fitness} - \text{fatigue}$$

Therefore, Coggan devised an approach that eliminates much of the complex math and can be performed using simple spreadsheet calculations[40, 41] (better yet, this approach has been incorporated into user-friendly consumer software packages). By removing several of the components of the original model (e.g., k_a and k_f), Coggan argued that performance on a given day depends on the training stress balance (TSB), which is determined by an interaction between the positive chronic training load (CTL) and the negative acute training load (ATL). The CTL is essentially synonymous with fitness and the ATL with fatigue. Therefore, performance on a given day is proportional to

$$\text{TSB} = \text{CTL} - \text{ATL}$$

In other words, a triathlete's TSB is equal to the chronic training that he or she has been exposed to over a long period of time minus the acute training that he or she has undergone in recent days. Conceptually, every triathlete should intuitively understand this idea; the purpose of training is to accumulate fitness by incurring a chronic training load over a long period (months or years). At the same time, training imparts some negative consequences in the near term that result in fatigue and reduced performance. The balance of these two factors dictates performance, and managing them appropriately results in optimal performance.

Quantifying Daily Training Loads

Again, the trick to periodization for the triathlete is being able to visualize and manage training loads over multiple time scales. Fitness will accumulate over months and, in terms of residuals, may persist for approximately a month or more. Fatigue, on the other hand, will accumulate immediately and typically dissipate within a matter of days to a week.

To determine the chronic and acute training loads, Coggan devised a training stress score (TSS) to quantify the daily training load using cycling power meters in terms of volume and intensity. A benchmark TSS score was determined to be 100 based on a maximal effort that was performed for 1 hour, which corresponded to the functional threshold (FT).

The CTL and ATL are determined from daily TSS based on exponentially weighted rolling averages of 42 days for CTL and 7 days for ATL. The 42- and 7-day periods reflect the time scales on which each respective training load dissipates. The practical importance of these time scales and their use will be demonstrated in reference to an elite runner later in this chapter, but the general concept of the relationship among TSB, CTL, and ATL can be seen in figure 22.6, which presents performance modeling of an age-group triathlete.

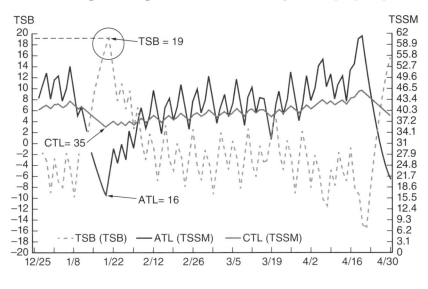

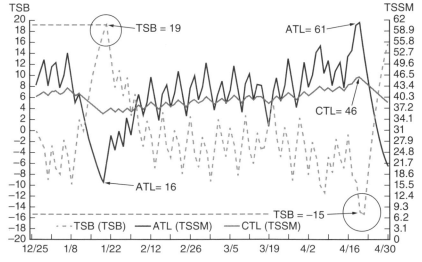

▶ **Figure 22.6** Performance modeling chart for an age-group triathlete over the first 4 months of a season for running. Top: positive TSB of 19 results from a CTL of 35 and ATL of 16. Bottom: negative TSB of −15 results from a CTL of 46 and ATL of 61.

We can see changes in TSB, CTL, and ATL over the course of the early season. In January (top), a positive TSB is shown, whereas in March (bottom), a negative TSB is shown. This relationship also demonstrates a concept that may not be otherwise readily apparent—when fitness (CTL) is relatively stable, as in this case, changes in performance (TSB) are inversely related to changes in fatigue (ATL). In simple terms, then, when fatigue is high, performance is low, and when fatigue is low, performance is high.

Determining the Optimal Level of Fitness Based on Training Load

Coggan's approach to performance modeling was devised for cycling, but as previously mentioned, McGregor et al.[20,42] (figure 22.7) used a derivative of the approach and analyzed an Olympic middle-distance runner's training and performances over a 7-year span. The authors found that this performance modeling approach provided valuable insight regarding the overall periodization structure that could be of value to the coach or athlete who used it on a regular basis. In particular, the optimal level of fitness (CTL) based on training load that elicited best performances was determined.

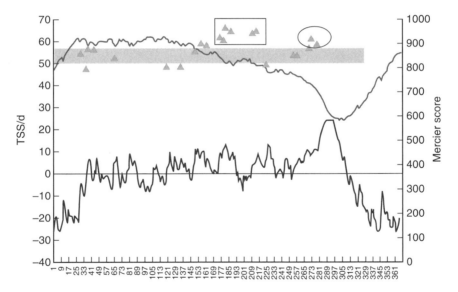

▶ **Figure 22.7** Plot of impulse response (IR) model parameters versus performance for 2000 Olympic year. Top line = chronic training load (CTL); bottom line = model response output (TSB); triangles = Mercier score (MS). The shaded area highlights the range of CTL values for which the top 10 percent of performances occurred for this athlete during the 7 years of study. The square indicates when the personal best performances for this athlete occurred in 2000, and the circle indicates performances during the Olympics.

Adapted, by permission, from S.J. McGregor, R.K. Weese, and I.K. Ratz, 2009, "Performance modeling in an Olympic 1500-m finalist: A practical approach," *Journal of Strength and Conditioning Research* 23(9): 2515-2523.

McGregor et al. converted performances in the 800-meter through 3,000-meter events to Mercier scores, which is a system for comparison of different athletic events that are all based on world record performances and given a maximum value of approximately 1,020:

> Briefly, they are the end-result of a linear fit to the weighted average of the 5th, 10th, 20th, 50th, and 100th world-ranked performances in each event over the past 4 years. The performances from more recent years are given a higher weighting, which can tend to skew the comparisons if one of the events had a weak year.[43]

This approach allowed the authors to use different performances from 800 meters through 3,000 meters for performance evaluation.[20] They reported a parabolic relationship between fitness (CTL) and performances expressed as Mercier scores whereby best performances were observed when CTL was relatively high, but as CTL increased, at a certain point (approximately 55), performance declined (figure 22.8).[20]

Taken together, these data showed that this middle-distance runner needed to have a CTL of at least 50 TSS/d for optimal performance. At the same time a CTL of more than 55 TSS/d caused performance to decline. But as the athlete tapered over the course of the season, as can be seen in figure 22.7, the CTL dropped below 50 TSS/d and performances declined relative to earlier in the season when CTL was higher.

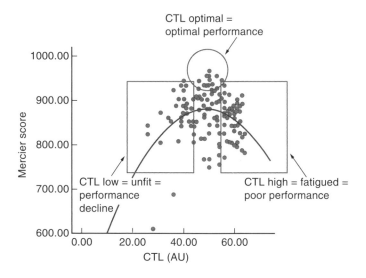

▶ **Figure 22.8** Quadratic relationship between Mercier score (MS) and chronic training load (CTL). A quadratic relationship was identified when model parameter CTL values for the day of competition performances (n = 141) were fit to MS calculated for the performance ($P = 0.001$).

Adapted, by permission, from S.J. McGregor, R.K. Weese, and I.K. Ratz, 2009, "Performance modeling in an Olympic 1500-m finalist: A practical approach," *Journal of Strength and Conditioning Research* 23(9): 2515-2523.

Even if a statistical analysis is not performed, by following the curve (figure 22.7) it should be evident that CTL (fitness) is declining rapidly at the end of the season and performances will soon decline. Therefore, graphical presentation of these modeling data can provide the triathlete with the big picture perspective of training adaptations and the effects on performance.[42]

Aside from CTL values, triathletes and coaches also need to consider the TSB, which is arguably of most importance to target events because the TSB is the output function of the modeling equation, which should be directly related to performance. Coggan has presented data indicating that personal best performances for efforts longer than 5 minutes in cycling are obtained when TSB is slightly positive. As with CTL, however, above a certain level of positive TSB, performances decline as well (figure 22.9).[40]

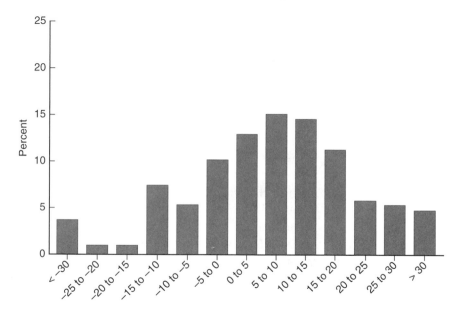

▶ **Figure 22.9** Training stress balances (TSBs) for personal best (PB) performances of cycling efforts of a duration of 5 minutes or longer. The highest frequencies of PBs for these performances occurred with a TSB between 5 and 10; above 15, performances decline substantially.

Reprinted, by permission, from H. Allen and A. Coggan, 2010, Training and racing with a power meter, 2nd ed. (Boulder, CO: VeloPress), 158.

Balancing Performance With Fitness: How Much Training Is Too Much?

Balancing a positive TSB (performance) with a high level of CTL (fitness) is a difficult task. It is self-evident that low fitness (low CTL) is not conducive to optimal performance, but triathletes and coaches often ask two questions: How much training is enough, and how much is too much?

Table 22.1 Chronic Training Load (CTL) Guidelines for Triathletes in Cycling and Running Based on Experience Level and Distance Focus

Triathlete level	Cycling TSS/d	Run TSS/d	Combined TSS/d (cycle and run)
Novice	30 to 50	10 to 15	40 to 65
Experienced ager	50 to 70	20 to 30	70 to 100
Elite short course	50 to 70	20 to 30	70 to 100
Elite long course	70 to 90	30 to 50	100 to 140

Anecdotally, some guidelines for CTL values for individual disciplines in triathlon are provided in table 22.1. Note that a novice triathlete who targets an arbitrarily high CTL may be misplacing her priorities. Particularly in running for those without a running background, seeking a high CTL will likely lead to injury. The principles presented in chapter 21 regarding progressive overload should be observed as the triathlete attempts to increase fitness. Along those lines, anecdotal observations are that a CTL increase of 5 TSS/d per week in individual disciplines is reasonable, but in triathlon the combined stress of a more rapid increase in CTL can lead to injury or underperformance.

It may be tempting to express CTL as a singular combined value for both disciplines or graphically on one chart, but CTL for individual disciplines are not additive. For example, neither a cyclist who exhibits a CTL of 120 TSS/d in cycling alone nor a runner who exhibits a CTL of 100 TSS/d in running alone will perform on par in triathlon with an elite triathlete who exhibits a CTL of 70 TSS/d in cycling and 40 TSS/d in running despite the comparable combined CTLs. Similarly, the triathlete would not compete on par with either of the individual sport specialists in their respective sports. The combined CTLs are not additive across sports.

That being said, training load likely has some upper limit that can be tolerated, and this limit may be reflected in the combined CTL value, so it warrants attention in that respect. On the other hand, tracking performance modeling for the individual disciplines separately can show the triathlete how fitness and performance in the individual discipline is affected by the overall periodization plan.

On a related note, the modeling of Fitz-Clark et al.[44] supports the most commonly used approach to periodization in endurance sport, that being a traditional linear approach for optimal performance at one target event. Therefore, some of the alternative approaches (e.g., block periodization or nonlinear periodization) may be necessary for athletes who compete in frequent competitions of equal relative importance or where a larger number of consistent results may be more desirable than one high-profile result at a given point in time (e.g., world championships). On the other hand, a more traditional linear approach may be preferable if one primary performance is of utmost importance.

Conclusion

Periodization is the most common approach to overall training plan design in endurance sports such as triathlon. The literature does not provide evidence of a clearly superior way to periodize the overall training program, but the traditional linear, monocyclical schema is likely the approach most often used. Because the traditional linear approach has been so widely used and was advocated by such successful practitioners as Lydiard[21] before formalized scientific study on the topic had been pursued, it may be close to an optimal approach.

In particular, for a sport such as long-course triathlon that depends heavily on aerobic endurance of the athlete, emphasizing this development over other factors such as anaerobic capacity, strength, or short-term maximal power production is likely important. This pattern of development lends itself to a traditional linear approach. On the other hand, short-course athletes who may need to compete more frequently and may require more speed to be competitive may benefit from using an alternative approach such as block periodization or nonlinear periodization.

Performance modeling may be used to assist the triathlete in seeing the big picture regarding the overall periodization plan. This information supports the notion that optimal performance comes from the triathlete possessing a high CTL and a slightly positive TSB, which is synonymous with high fitness and good performance at target events. These characteristics would be evident from a heavy training load and an appropriate taper before target competitions, and performance modeling could be used to envision this approach in an objective fashion. Finally, performance modeling can be used to assess the effects of the overall periodization plan on the individual disciplines.

CHAPTER 23

Tapering and Peaking for Races

—Stephen J. McGregor, PhD

The taper is an intentional reduction in the athlete's training load in the final days to weeks before an objective competition with the aim of optimizing performance at targeted competitions.[1, 2] Further, Mujika[3] has noted the distinction made previously by Houmard[4] that a taper is not simply a reduction in training load, but a progressive reduction in load over time, culminating with the objective competition.

A further clarification should be added that the taper typically follows an extended period of fitness building by the application of large training loads and that the taper will allow the dissipation of accumulated fatigue while a state of supercompensated fitness is present. This combination will promote optimal performance within a relatively narrow time window. This window of optimal performance is typically referred to as the peak. Therefore, the taper is the reduction in training load that will lead to a peak in fitness, but the two terms are often used interchangeably. From the aforementioned points we can derive several criteria that distinguish a taper from a simple reduction in training:

1. An intentional, planned reduction in training load
2. A progressive reduction as opposed to a constant reduction in training load
3. A period of reduced training load that follows an extended period of persistently heavy training to maximize fitness
4. A reduction in training load that is finite in duration and relatively short term

Each of these criteria is specifically addressed in detail in this chapter so that recommendations for taper optimization in triathlon can be presented.

For more than 25 years, numerous studies have investigated the physiological and performance effects of reduced training and the taper.[1, 3, 5, 6, 7]

From this data, it has been determined that a reasonable expected performance gain from a taper would be approximately 2 to 3 percent, with a range from 0.5 to 6 percent being possible.[3, 7] At the highest level of sport, Mujika et al. have shown that performance improvements on the order of 2 to 3 percent in swimming were greater than the difference between the gold medal and fourth place in the 2000 Sydney Olympics.[8]

For elite athletes, the taper can mean the difference between winning outright versus not medaling at international competitions. Do not expect performance improvements greater than 8 percent in any discipline because in the studies performed in endurance sports (not including time to exhaustion or incremental protocols), the greatest reported performance improvements are about 6 to 8 percent across various disciplines.[5, 9, 10, 11] Therefore, although the performance improvements elicited by the taper might appear modest, in highly trained athletes they could have significant effect at the elite level of competition.

Elements of the Prerace Taper

Because the precompetition taper is a programmed reduction in overall training load and because the physiological consequences of reduced training (i.e., detraining) are well documented,[12, 13, 14] the nature of the reduction in training load is an important consideration. Because reductions in central cardiovascular parameters as well as peripheral muscle metabolic parameters are to be expected with a period of reduced training, the question becomes, How best can the triathlete reduce the overall training load while maintaining the capacity for optimal performance? Which parameters—intensity, volume, or frequency—should be maintained or increased, and which should be reduced?

Intensity

Conventional wisdom might suggest that an optimal taper would include a reduction in intensity, but much evidence indicates the contrary. Numerous investigators have reported that physiological adaptations can be maintained and performances improved during periods of reduced overall training loads if high-intensity training is maintained or increased.[1, 7, 15, 16, 17]

In runners, time to exhaustion at 1,500-meter pace improved by 22 percent with a high-intensity, low-volume taper.[18] In recently trained subjects who reduced training intensity by 33 percent (high intensity) or 66 percent (low intensity) over an extended period, performance in a 5-minute test effort did not change in the high-intensity group, but it declined 30 percent in the low-intensity group.[19] Within a group of 24 distance runners, those who reduced volume 85 percent while maintaining interval intensity work during run training improved 5K run performance by 3 percent whereas a control group did not.[19] Thus, evidence consistently shows that intensity should be maintained and not reduced during a taper.

Volume

If intensity appears to be a critical parameter to maintain during the taper, then volume appears to be a critical parameter that should be reduced during the taper. Total training volume is a function of frequency and duration, but in most cases, training volume is manipulated primarily by duration as opposed to frequency.

Numerous studies have provided evidence in support of the argument that large reductions in training volume can be implemented during the taper and performance improved as long as intensity is maintained. Bosquet et al. performed a meta-analysis of 27 studies in the literature that met various stringent criteria required for inclusion. They found that optimal performance improvements were obtained with tapers that included a 41 to 60 percent reduction in training volume with no change in intensity and frequency.[1]

Their analysis showed that when all disciplines (swimming, running, bicycling) were included in the analysis, the positive effect of the taper dropped at training volume reductions greater than 61 percent and less than 40 percent. Therefore, in general, substantial reductions in training volume seem to be a necessary component of a properly executed taper.

An interesting aspect of the Bosquet et al. study was apparent when the data were examined by individual discipline. For example, in the case of both cycling and swimming, the greatest positive effects during the taper were still observed when training volume was reduced between 41 to 60 percent. On the other hand, in running, the strongest and only significant effects were observed when the training volume was reduced 21 to 40 percent. Although the authors did not recommend a smaller reduction in training volume for running versus the other disciplines, this approach appears to merit consideration.

One explanation for the discrepancy between disciplines may be that, in general, training volumes are typically lower for running than in other disciplines. Because total training volumes are lower, corresponding accumulated fitness will be lower, resulting in lower end-taper fitness after a reduction in training volume. Some have argued that fitness level does not affect the optimal approach to the taper,[3, 7] but a slightly different approach to training volume reduction should possibly be considered by triathletes for running because larger volume reductions are clearly of benefit for cycling and swimming.[1]

Frequency

If the critical nature of maintaining intensity and reducing volume during the taper are well established, the importance of the role of frequency during the taper is less clear. Numerous studies have demonstrated that both physiological parameters and performance can be maintained or improved in the face of reduced training frequencies over a period of 2 to 4 weeks.[10, 20, 21, 22, 23]

Houmard has suggested that swimmers maintain daily high-intensity work during the taper, that ideally they should not reduce frequency by more than 20 percent, and that reductions of 50 percent or more would be detrimental.[24] One factor that seems to be an issue with frequency reductions during the taper is that of feel for the activity. This aspect is likely of greater importance at higher levels of ability and competition.

Insight regarding this issue can be gleaned from the work of Neufer et al.,[25] in which they reduced training frequency to 1 or 3 days per week in competitive collegiate swimmers. In the group that trained 1 day per week, after 4 weeks swim stroke rate was significantly higher and stroke distance was significantly lower than before reduced training. At the same time, the group that trained 3 days per week maintained those parameters. So, aside from the physiological characteristics contributing to performance, the technical characteristics should be considered as well.

Taper Duration

Probably the best evidence in support of an optimal duration of the taper comes from the meta-analysis performed by Bosquet et al.[1] As previously mentioned, the authors examined data from 168 studies of competitive athletes that met certain criteria, which ultimately led to the inclusion of 27 studies in the analysis. Their analysis showed that when all disciplines were combined, the overall effect of tapering was greatest when the duration was 2 weeks and was reduced for shorter and longer durations.[1]

When the data were examined by individual discipline, a greater margin for error seemed to occur with a swimming taper than with a run taper. In other words, the positive effects of a taper could be observed in swimming for durations as short as 8 to 14 days up to more than 22 days. On the other hand, positive effects of the taper could be observed in running only up to 14 days, after which the positive effects dissipated.[1] For cycling, positive effects from a taper could be observed for durations less than 7 days, but they were significant and much stronger for 8 to 14 days. No data were available for durations longer than 14 days, so it is not clear whether the positive effects of the taper are more long lasting as in swimming or dissipate faster as in running. But in all three disciplines optimal positive effects are observed at 2 weeks, so this duration is recommended across disciplines.

Shape of the Taper

Another question that should be considered when planning a taper is, What should the shape of the taper be? In other words, should the training load be reduced over time in a progressive linear fashion, a stepwise, square-wave fashion, or a progressive exponential fashion?

If a taper is considered a reduction of training load over a given period, the reduction can be applied in three main ways:

- First, a *linear taper* is a reduction whereby the training load immediately preceding the taper would be considered 100 percent and the final desired training load would be a given proportion of 100 percent (e.g., 50 percent). The training load would be reduced in a linear fashion over the course of the taper to end up at the final reduced level.

- Second, a *step taper* is an approach in which the load is reduced by the given amount (e.g., 50 percent) at one time and remains at the reduced amount for the remainder of the taper.

- Finally, in an *exponential taper* the load is reduced by an exponential factor, which will lead to relatively larger initial reductions in load and smaller reductions as the taper progresses. The exponential taper is further divided into fast-decay and slow-decay varieties. Conceptually, these different taper approaches can be seen in figure 23.1. In particular, note how the fast decay tapers (fast exponential and fast variable exponential) initially decrease more rapidly than the slow decay taper.

In general, researchers believe that the progressive taper (e.g., linear or exponential) is more beneficial for performance improvements compared with the step taper.[1, 5, 26, 27] Further, Banister et al.[26] and Zardakas et al.[27] reported that the exponential approach with a fast decay is preferable to either exponential slow decay or linear approaches. Additional work is necessary in this area, but the most beneficial type of taper to use appears to be an exponential, fast-decay approach.

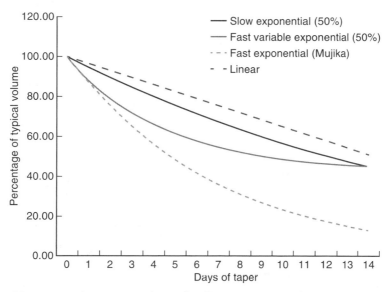

▶ **Figure 23.1** Tapering approaches. The figure presents the main types of taper approaches (linear, exponential fast decay, exponential slow decay) that result in an approximate 50 percent reduction in training volume at the end of 14 days. Also, for comparison, an exponential fast decay is presented that corresponds closely to what Mujika has proposed.[5]

Mujika[5] has presented a conceptual comparison of the various taper approaches and compares an exponential slow-decay taper that results in an approximate 70 percent reduction in training load over 14 days versus an exponential fast-decay taper that results in an approximate 90 percent reduction over the same period. Because the optimal volume reduction appears to be in the 40 to 60 percent range,[1] this author suggests an alternative approach that results in an approximate 50 percent reduction in volume over 14 days regardless of the approach.

To achieve this, a variable exponent that changes each day must be applied. This method results in a proportionally greater reduction in volume early in the taper and a lesser reduction later in the taper. Figure 23.1 shows a comparison of the three tapering approaches (linear, exponential slow decay, variable exponential fast decay) in which all result in an approximate 50 percent reduction in volume over 14 days.

Table 23.1 presents the daily volumes as a percentage of typical volume resulting from these two exponential approaches and the percentage difference between a variable fast decay versus slow decay. The fast decay results in a greater initial reduction of training load, but in the final days before the competition, the volumes are similar between the variable fast and slow approaches.

Table 23.1 Comparison of Taper Approaches to Reduce Volume by Approximately 50 Percent Over 14 Days

Days of taper	Exponential slow decay	Variable exponential fast decay	Difference between variable fast versus slow*
	100.00	100.00	
1	94.50	87.75	6.74
2	89.30	78.51	10.79
3	84.38	71.38	13.00
4	79.74	65.81	13.93
5	75.35	61.39	13.97
6	71.21	57.84	13.37
7	67.29	54.96	12.33
8	63.59	52.60	10.99
9	60.09	50.66	9.43
10	56.78	49.05	7.73
11	53.66	47.71	5.95
12	50.71	46.59	4.11
13	47.92	45.65	2.27
14	45.28	44.85	0.43

*The right-hand column presents the difference in volume percentage on each day between the two approaches.

Triathlon-Specific Studies

Numerous studies have used triathletes or a multisport design, and these may provide special insight into aspects of the taper that might be particular to triathlon. In a study of 16 highly trained triathletes, half of whom supplemented with an antioxidant compound, Margaritis et al. examined the effects of a 2-week taper in which training load was reduced between 32 and 46 percent following a 4-week period of standardized overloaded training. As a test of performance, the athletes completed a pretaper and posttaper duathlon (5K run, 20K bike, 5K run). Both supplemented and control athletes significantly improved duathlon performance after the taper by an average of 2.6 percent, and $\dot{V}O_2$max increased 3.0 percent.[28]

Vollaard et al.[29] examined the effects of a 2-week taper following a 2-week period of training overload in highly trained triathletes. As a test of performance, the athletes performed weekly standard 45-minute cycling efforts at 70 percent of maximal aerobic power followed by a 1-minute time trial. The overload training period consisted of a 40 percent increase in training load, and the taper used a 40 percent reduction in load. Because of the taper, time-trial performance improved 4.9 percent.

Eleven Ironman triathletes were examined[26, 27] over a 3-month training period that was broken up by two taper periods of 10 and 13 days. During each taper period the triathletes were divided into two groups to examine separate taper effects. Each of the progressive tapers resulted in a performance improvement in a 5K run ranging from 2 to 6 percent, whereas the step taper did not improve performance. In another study 16 experienced triathletes who performed a 2-week taper following a period of intensified training improved 3-kilometer running performance by 7 percent.[30, 31]

Collectively, these results demonstrate that in trained triathletes, a progressive taper over the course of 1 or 2 weeks will result in performance improvements in running and cycling. How these improvements would be extrapolated to real-world competition, especially in events of much longer duration (e.g., half-Ironman and Ironman distance) is difficult to ascertain with certainty. One limitation in the tapering literature with regard to triathlon is the relative lack of data for events lasting several hours, so this avenue of research offers interesting possibilities for the future.

Despite this, Pyne et al. argue that the results of existing tapering literature indicate that the duration of the event is of little consequence and that general tapering principles and results are broadly applicable across various disciplines and durations.[7] Therefore, current evidence may be valid for extrapolation to efforts of longer duration such as half-Ironman or Ironman events.

Performance Modeling

Experimental approaches and observational reports are of great value, but their utility is limited because of both the small number of high-level athletes who can be recruited into studies and the constraints placed on high-level athletes by their competitive schedules. Therefore, mathematical performance modeling studies have provided unique insights into aspects of tapering that might otherwise not be possible.

Much of the performance modeling literature[26, 32, 33, 34, 35, 36, 37, 38, 39] is based on the work of Calvert et al.'s impulse–response model.[40] This modeling approach was tested in highly trained athletes over the course of a calendar year.[37] The authors present individual data of one of the athletes, an Olympic finalist, in graphical form. As can be seen in a figure 23.2 from the Hellard et al. paper, an extended period of reduced training load occurred starting with the training block at week 33, a full 23 weeks before the primary objective of the world championships (WC). Performances approximately equivalent to those observed at the WC occurred 14 weeks earlier in the season in week 45.

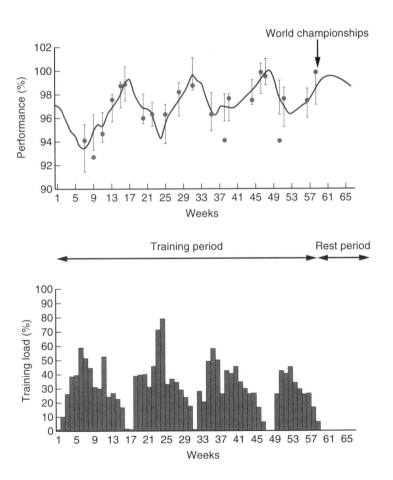

▶ **Figure 23.2** Modeling of training load based on the Banister model in an Olympic finalist swimmer.

From P. Hellard, M. Avalos, L. Lacoste, et al., 2006, "Assessing the limitations of the Banister model in monitoring training," Journal of Sports Sciences 24(5): 509-520. Reprinted by permission of Taylor & Francis Ltd.

These performances resulted from the taper at the end of the training block preceding the WC block. These performances indicate that multiple peaks of fitness can be elicited by multiple tapers in one competitive season.

The scenario reported by Hellard et al.[37] is analogous to the situation presented by McGregor et al. in data collected for an Olympic 1,500-meter finalist over the course of 7 years.[39] Using a simplified modeling approach, originally proposed by Coggan[36, 41] in cycling, McGregor et al. calculated daily training load measures termed *training stress score* (TSS) and generated estimates of fitness and fatigue termed *chronic training load* (CTL) and *acute training load* (ATL), respectively. Because conceptually, the physiological side of performance rests on the interaction of fitness and fatigue, and the balance of these two parameters dictates performance, the training stress balance (TSB) was developed to represent the simple relationship.

$$TSB = CTL - ATL$$

This modeling approach made conceptualization of the fitness and fatigue components of performance, which are typically manifested on different timescales, more readily attainable by coaches and athletes without a scientific background. Further background regarding the development of this approach is presented in chapter 22 of this text and outside references.[39, 41]

From this analysis, a similar scenario to that of the Olympic swimmer from the Hellard et al. study was observed. As can be seen in figure 23.3a, training load in TSS is highest at the beginning of the calendar year and then declines over the course of the year even though the primary objective of the season, the Olympics, occurred at the end of the season (arrow).[39]

Because of the relatively longer time constant of fitness (about 42 days), the CTL component remains elevated until approximately midseason, despite the persistent reductions in training load. As the CTL declines into the shaded region, performances are best (figure 23.3b; box). As training load is reduced further, CTL continues to drop out of the shaded region and performances decline. This pattern of tapering resulted in the best performances occurring at the period of the season that preceded the primary objective, the Olympics. The authors argued that after fitness declined below an acceptable level, performances declined as a result.

These results provide evidence for the arguments that

- reductions in training load for the taper should be relatively short in duration, on the order of 2 to 4 weeks, and
- multiple optimal peaks of performance are difficult to achieve during one season.

This contention is further supported by the modeling work of Fitz-Clarke et al.,[42] who used influence curves to model optimal training design and tapers that would lead to best performances in a single year. Their modeling again showed that optimal performances would result from the total cessation of

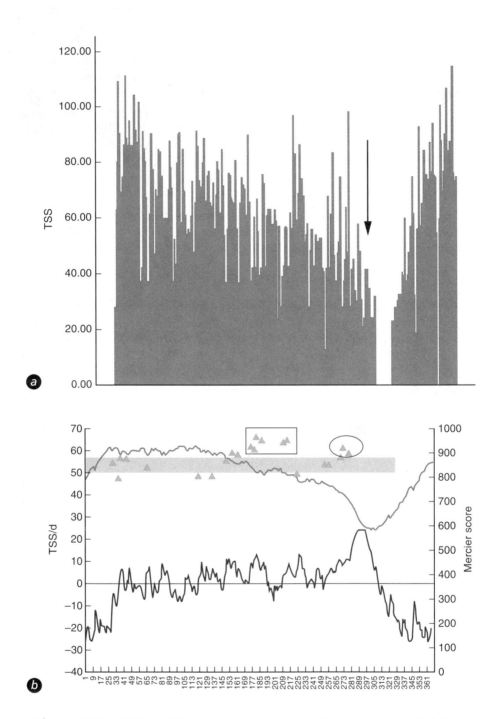

▶ **Figure 23.3** (*a*) Daily TSS training load during an Olympic year in which the runner made the 1,500-meter Olympic finals (arrow). (*b*) Performance modeling of the athlete presented in (*a*). The top line represents long-term fitness (CTL), and the bottom line represents predicted performance trends (TSB). Season-best performances occurred in the area surrounded by the box. Olympic performances occurred within the circle.

training for 16 days before the competition of interest. They also determined that optimal performance can be achieved for only one competition in a year because such a performance requires a reduced period of training that adversely affects subsequent performances.

Therefore, when planning the season, the ideal approach is to plan only one taper. Performance at all other competitions is somewhat compromised because training must be maintained at a higher level than what would produce optimized performance. In practical terms, however, as mentioned in chapter 22, modern competition schedules may not permit the luxury of planning for optimal performance in only one event at the end of a competitive season. Therefore, practical circumstances typically require a compromise when planning overall season periodization and tapering strategies.

Conclusion

From the available evidence presented in this chapter, several broadly applicable recommendations can be made with regard to taper optimization.

- In general, the taper should be composed of an approximate 40 to 60 percent reduction in training volume that comes with a minimal reduction in training frequency and intensity.
- Differences in optimal volume reduction may exist between triathlon disciplines, and smaller reductions in running volume (approximately 20 to 40 percent) may be warranted.
- Training intensities should be maintained during the taper, and frequency should be reduced no more than 20 percent.
- The duration of the taper should minimally be 2 weeks and preferably not more than 3, and the training load should be reduced in a progressive, exponential fashion.
- Further, the exponential reduction in training load should follow a fast-decay as opposed to a slow-decay pattern.

Although the area of tapering for performance in endurance sports has drawn substantial interest, much remains to be learned. In particular, for events lasting several hours, the optimized taper described in this chapter may require modification. Specifically with regard to triathlon, the aforementioned recommendations would certainly hold for sprint- and Olympic-distance events, but for long-course events (e.g. half-Ironman and Ironman), further investigation is warranted. Several studies[1,3,5,7] have argued that event duration does not seem to be a factor in taper optimization, but concrete evidence in this regard for events such as the Ironman distance is still lacking.

Therefore, these recommendations should be used only as guidelines. Coach and athlete discretion are an important consideration, particularly with increasing caliber of the triathlete. Nevertheless, in general, if these guidelines are followed, a triathlete and coach should feel confident that a performance improvement of 2 to 3 percent relative to pretaper levels can be expected with proper execution of the taper in triathlons from sprint- to Olympic-distance events and possibly for longer events as well.

CHAPTER 24

Physiology of Overtraining

—Matt Fitzgerald

Exercise imposes stress on the body. Elevated heart rate, increased blood flow to the extremities, heightened release of hormones including epinephrine and cortisol, even conscious perception of effort—all these acute responses to exercise combine with many others to create an overall stress state that enables the body to meet the demands of sustained exertion.

The physiological effects of such exertion do not cease when the workout ends but continue for some time afterward. The stress of exercise triggers processes of recovery, such as muscle tissue repair, which restore full function to the systems affected by the stress of exertion, and processes of adaptation, such as mitochondrial biogenesis, which enhance the body's ability to tolerate the stress of the next workout.

The most readily observed sign of the body's successful adaptation to repeated exercise stress is improved performance. The normal pattern in a systematic program of conditioning such as triathlon training is one of gradually increasing ability to sustain speed over distance. But exceptions occur. Triathletes at times experience an unexpected decline in performance despite executing the sort of incrementally increasing training workload that normally improves performance.

Several factors can cause this sort of unexpected decline in performance. Most are organic factors, such as an iron-deficiency anemia. Sometimes, however, performance declines expectedly in the absence of any clear organic cause.

Overtraining, or overtraining syndrome, is generally characterized as an unexpected decline in performance that is not caused by an organic factor such as anemia.[1] The name derives from the idea that, in such cases, excessive training itself is the primary cause of the performance decline. Like other stressors, exercise in excessive amounts can overwhelm the capacity of the body to adapt to it functionally. When this happens, the very workouts that once enhanced performance begin to worsen it.

Overtraining Versus Overreaching

All unexplained declines in performance are not automatically classified as overtraining syndrome. Only severe and prolonged cases earn this designation. Experts distinguish three levels of severity: functional overreaching, nonfunctional overreaching, and overtraining.

Functional Overreaching

Functional overreaching is a brief period of performance decline, lasting no longer than a few days, that is a normal intermediate outcome of intensive training. In colloquial terms, it is the 1 or 2 flat days that predictably follow an especially challenging individual workout or short block of training.

In a well-designed training program, the predictable onset of functional overreaching is quickly followed by a planned period of reduced training, typically lasting 1 to 7 days. In most instances such relative rest not only restores performance to preoverreaching levels but also yields a higher level of performance. The term *functional overreaching* is suggestive of the idea that this type of performance decline is, when properly managed, ultimately beneficial to the triathlete.

Scientists have developed a variety of popular software tools that triathletes can use to quantify their fatigue level and recovery needs so that flat days can be anticipated and functional overreaching can be easily managed. No algorithm, however, can make the body's response to training entirely predictable. Nearly all triathletes share the experience of sometimes feeling unexpectedly flat after a day or two of easy training and, conversely, feeling unexpectedly sharp despite fatigue from recent hard workouts.

In yet unpublished research, exercise physiologists Fabio Nakamura of the State University of Londrina, Brazil, and Samuele Marcora of the University of Kent, England, have documented large degrees of day-to-day variation in individual performance in standard endurance tests despite unchanging levels of fitness and preexisting fatigue. They speculate that daily variations in mood and motivation may partly account for the "good day–bad day" phenomenon, as they call it. Whatever the explanation, the important thing for triathletes to understand is that the occasional inexplicable bad day cannot be avoided in training and is in itself nothing to worry about.

Nonfunctional Overreaching

Nonfunctional overreaching is a state of performance decline that lasts longer than a few days but less than 2 weeks if responded to quickly with relative rest. It is qualitatively the same as functional overreaching in the sense that it is defined by an unexpected loss of performance. The difference is a matter of degree in two dimensions; the loss of performance is both more severe and longer lasting.

Nonfunctional overreaching is often colloquially referred to by triathletes as a stale patch in training. The condition typically occurs when two key errors occur in succession. First, a triathlete or her coach creates an overambitious training schedule that places the triathlete in a state of functional overreaching more quickly than anticipated and many days before the next period of scheduled recovery. The triathlete or coach then compounds this error by failing to respond to the situation with unscheduled relative rest, instead sticking to the plan. Consequently, the fatigue deficit increases and functional overreaching becomes nonfunctional overreaching.

Overtraining Syndrome

Overtraining syndrome (OTS) is defined as a state of severe performance decline that persists longer than 2 weeks even despite relative or total rest.[1] If nonfunctional overreaching results when a triathlete in a state of functional overreaching fails to respond quickly with rest, overtraining syndrome occurs when an triathlete in a state of nonfunctional overreaching continues to ignore his severe performance decline and persists in heavy training. The onset of overtraining syndrome is never sudden or unforeseeable, in other words.

The threshold of 2 weeks is somewhat arbitrary, having originated as a general observation agreed upon by a panel of experts that convened at Oxford University to "clarify the diagnostic criteria" of overtraining.[2] But it is useful nevertheless. Within the first 2 weeks of onset, nonfunctional overreaching and overtraining syndrome look much the same. Only time can distinguish them.

Differences Between Overreaching and Overtraining

Nonfunctional overreaching is resolved within 2 weeks if the triathlete rests. Most cases of overtraining syndrome last for many months, and some cases continue for years, despite rest. When a triathlete experiencing a loss of performance is unable to bounce back after 2 weeks of rest, it is usually possible to predict that she is unlikely to recover even with continued rest for many more weeks.

Although the signs and symptoms of functional overreaching are limited for the most part to performance decline and the accompanying fatigue, overtraining syndrome is more than merely a severe and prolonged state of performance decline; it is also characterized by a host of other symptoms, most of them psychological in nature. These will be discussed in more detail in the next section.

Another key difference between functional and nonfunctional overreaching, on the one hand, and overtraining syndrome, on the other, is that OTS occurs only in elite-level triathletes. Brazilian researchers recently found no symptoms or predisposing factors of OTS in a large sample of recreational triathletes training at fitness centers.[3]

The reason that full-blown overtraining syndrome is confined to the elite population of triathletes appears to be that an extremely high level of fitness and physical resilience is required to train through a period of declining performance and fatigue long enough for the syndrome to manifest fully. Subelite triathletes are likely to be forced to rest by injury or illness before reaching the level of maladaptation to exercise that defines OTS.

Motivation may be a factor as well. Subelite triathletes who have less at stake in their sport than elite triathletes are generally less willing to continue training intensively despite mounting fatigue and worsening performance decline.

Signs of Overtraining

Overtraining can be recognized by four major signs: decline in performance, fatigue, mood disturbances, and certain physiological changes. None of these signs alone indicates a problem, but when all of them appear together a state of overtraining is likely to be diagnosed.

Decline in Performance

The defining characteristic of overtraining syndrome is, again, a significant decline in performance that cannot be corrected with less than 2 weeks of relative rest.

As mentioned previously, in most cases of overtraining syndrome many months of relative rest are needed to restore performance fully. Significant rest is required because the decline in performance that is associated with overreaching is caused by normal physiological fatigue, whereas the decline in performance that is associated with overtraining syndrome is linked to a malfunctioning of the neuroendocrine system caused by excessive exposure to physiological fatigue. Recovering from overtraining syndrome is not simply a matter of removing the stressor of intensive training but of healing a systemic injury brought on by that stressor.

Fatigue

A second universal symptom of overtraining syndrome is fatigue. OTS sufferers feel both chronically fatigued in everyday life and abnormally fatigued during exercise. The relationship between exercise intensity and perceived exertion changes, so that any given intensity of exercise feels more challenging to the triathlete than normal. The underperformance and the fatigue that are always observed in overtrained triathletes are obviously linked. That is, the fatigued state of the triathlete has a causal relationship to compromised performance. What is less clear is the source of the fatigue.

Fatigue in triathletes may be either central or peripheral in nature. Central fatigue is an inability of the brain to drive muscle contractions at normal levels. Peripheral fatigue is an inability of the muscles to respond normally to simulation from the motor centers of the brain. Some evidence indicates that fatigue in overtraining is at least partly central in nature. For example, studies have demonstrated differences in patterns of central drive to the muscles between healthy and overtrained Olympic weightlifters.[4]

To the degree that overtraining is caused by fatigue centered in the brain, another unanswered question is whether that fatigue is wholly or partly psychological. Plenty of research demonstrates that endurance performance is compromised in situations in which perceived exertion is elevated. Therefore, the reduced performance in $\dot{V}O_2$max tests that is exhibited by overtrained triathletes is probably to some extent voluntary. In other words, triathletes quit such tests at lower levels of performance than normal because they have reached a maximum tolerable level of perceived exertion more quickly than normal.

Researchers have been unable to identify an underlying mechanism of overtraining syndrome to explain the fatigue and performance decline of OTS. A number of candidates have been considered. An increased blood level of creatine kinase, a biomarker of muscle damage, has been observed in many overtraining sufferers, but it is not seen in all cases; furthermore, creatine kinase levels cannot be used to distinguish overtraining from garden-variety acute postworkout muscle damage.

Low levels of glutamine, an important marker of immune function, are also often seen in the overtrained, but a recent scientific review declared the findings in this area inconclusive.[5] Researchers have also looked at the ratio of cortisol and testosterone, which yields a window into nervous system function, but the results of these investigations have been contradictory; some studies find a depressed ratio in subjects with unexplained performance decline, and others find no abnormalities in the cortisol–testosterone ratio.

Mood and Physiological Symptoms

Although the defining characteristics of prolonged performance decline and persistent fatigue are universal in overtraining syndrome cases, the condition is also associated with a long list of other symptoms that are present in many but not all cases. These indicators include mood symptoms such as depression, irritability, loss of motivation, and insomnia, and physiological symptoms such as changes in resting heart rate and decreased lactate production during exercise. Overtraining has also been shown to reduce performance in submaximal exercise tests including lactate threshold and $\dot{V}O_2$max. Either central or peripheral fatigue could cause these declines.

In 2003, Paula Robson of the University of Cape Town, South Africa, argued for what she called the interleukin-6 hypothesis of overtraining.[6] Interleukin-6 is a critical regulatory protein that is released in large amounts from damaged and glycogen-depleted muscle cells during exercise. Elevated interleukin-6 levels in the brain are also known to cause fatigue in exercise and contribute to postexercise tissue inflammation.

Robson suggested that repeated release of high levels of IL-6 in triathletes during and after exercise may precipitate a state of chronic, systemic inflammation that could explain all the signs and symptoms of overtraining syndrome. But in the several years since this hypothesis was put forward, it has received little confirmation.

Numerous other potential markers of overtraining have also been studied, including oxidative stress responses to exercise, blood viscosity, and salivary IgA levels. Although overtraining involves disturbances to the neural, immune, endocrine, and metabolic systems, scientists have been unable to find a single definitive physiological symptom of overtraining. Although there are seemingly obvious cases of overtraining in which triathletes experience major performance declines that persist despite prolonged rest, by and large these individuals are difficult to distinguish physiologically from triathletes who are not overtrained.

Diagnosing Overtraining

The lack of a definitive physiological marker of overtraining syndrome also means that no definitive diagnostic test exists for the condition. But tests can be performed to rule out other possible causes (such as iron-deficiency anemia) of the symptoms that a triathlete presents.

Because overtraining syndrome is defined by a performance decline, performance testing would be the ideal method of diagnosing OTS if it were practicable, but in most cases it is not. Performance testing would only work to identify a performance decrement characteristic of OTS if a baseline test result were available to compare with the result of a postonset test. Furthermore, as the authors of a 1995 scientific paper observed, "Using performance testing to diagnose overtraining is difficult because of the problem with standardizing procedures, the rarity of valid sport-specific tests, and the lack of generalization between laboratory test and field test performances."[7]

In addition to backing into a diagnosis of overtraining through a process of elimination of organic causes of performance loss, clinicians rely on standardized interviews and questionnaires to diagnose overtraining syndrome. The diagnosis is generally made when the triathlete reports most of the following signs and symptoms:

- Loss of performance
- Lack of energy and vigor
- Unusual fatigue and lethargy during training
- "Heavy" legs
- Muscle soreness
- Depression
- Moodiness and irritability
- Loss of motivation

- Compulsive need to exercise (possibly despite low motivation)
- Loss of enjoyment for sport
- Insomnia
- Lack of appetite
- Increased resting heart rate
- Increased number of upper respiratory tract infections

In a 1998 review, Canadian exercise physiologist Roy Shepherd wrote, "Overtraining remains more easily detected by decreases in physical performance and alterations in mood state than by changes in immune or physiological functions."[8] Nearly 20 years later the situation is largely unchanged.

Causes of Overtraining

We might assume, based on its name, that overtraining is caused simply by overtraining, or excessive training over a long period combined with inadequate rest. But science has not pinpointed the mechanisms by which training overload precipitates the signs and symptoms of overtraining with sufficient clarity to conclude that overtraining is in fact caused solely by too much exercise and not enough rest.

If overtraining were the sole cause of overtraining syndrome, then a certain training load would always cause overtraining syndrome in a particular triathlete. But the individual triathlete's maximum training tolerance clearly varies by circumstance. All sources of stress, whether physiologic or psychological, are processed by the body in similar ways, so that sources of stress outside of training (e.g., job stress, relationship stress, even psychological stress within the realm of sport) can combine with training to create a total allostatic load that results in overtraining signs and symptoms.

Overtraining syndrome is mainly a maladaptation to the stress of heavy training loads. For that reason, overtraining syndrome is never seen in triathletes shouldering light and moderate training loads. But other stressors in the life of the triathlete contribute. This fact suggests that reducing other stressors and improving the ability to manage stressors beyond training may constitute effective ways to reduce the risk of overtraining syndrome.

In 2000, scientists associated with the British Olympic Association put forth the idea of renaming overtraining syndrome "unexplained underperformance syndrome."[9] These researchers objected to the prevailing term because it implied a single known causation.

Although the British team made a good point, the new name failed to catch on, perhaps because the word *unexplained* almost seemed to suggest *unexplainable*. Overtraining may not be the sole cause of what most experts persist in calling overtraining syndrome, but it's close enough to qualify the popular name as a perfectly legitimate shorthand descriptor.

Overtraining as a Psychological Disorder

By definition, overtrained triathletes are unable to perform at normal levels. As we've seen, however, no clear physiological explanation for underperformance can be found in most cases. Although overtrained triathletes typically exhibit certain physiological abnormalities such as high levels of creatine kinase and low levels of glutamine, such markers are inconsistent, often indistinguishable from the same markers in triathletes who are merely in a state of normal fatigue, and thus insufficient to explain a the severe decline in performance capacity that characterizes OTS. For that reason, and because changes in mood and other psychological variables are the most pronounced symptoms of overtraining, some researchers characterize OTS as primarily a psychological disorder.

In 2002 Lawrence Armstrong and Jaci VanHeest at the University of Connecticut published a paper that explored the similarities between overtraining syndrome and clinical depression.[10] They noted that the two conditions share many symptoms, including loss of motivation, lethargy, and fatigue, and affect the same brain structures, neurotransmitters, endocrine pathways, and immune responses. Armstrong and VanHeest proposed that these similarities were not coincidental, but that the two conditions shared an etiology.

Specifically, these researchers hypothesized that overtraining syndrome begins when a highly motivated triathlete suffers a disappointing performance, as every triathlete does from time to time. Assuming that the disappointing performance was caused by inadequate training, the triathlete responds to this disappointment by increasing his training workload.

If this assumption is incorrect, the triathlete's response will lead to further performance decrements and possibly to further counterproductive increases in training. Over time a vicious cycle emerges, in which both the performance declines and the physical stress resulting from excessive training contribute to the development of the specific alterations in brain chemistry that are (or were) believed to underlie clinical depression.

The specific alteration in brain chemistry that has received the most notice in research on depression and overtraining syndrome is reduced transmission of the neurotransmitter serotonin. A 2006 study compared serotonin levels in overtrained and healthy triathletes and found no difference in serotonin levels between the two groups.[11]

By contrast, a 2010 study found that elite triathletes with overtraining syndrome (or unexplained underperformance syndrome, as these researchers called it) had higher levels of sensitivity in the serotonin receptors of the brain (which would reduce brain serotonin levels) than did healthy elite triathletes.[12]

Clearly, more research is needed to clarify whether alterations in serotonin activity are consistently associated with the overtrained state and whether patterns of serotonin activity in overtrained triathletes and depressed individuals are similar. In the meantime, the so-called serotonin hypothesis of depression has been seriously challenged by recent neuropsychology research. Experts in that field increasingly believe that the true nature and etiology of depression may be far more complex than a single neurochemical imbalance. In this regard, ironically, depression has a clear parallel with overtraining syndrome, which has defied every effort at reduction to a tidy explanation.

Regardless of what is happening in the physiology of the brains of overtrained triathletes, the syndrome has an obvious psychological component. Although the idea that OTS is fundamentally a type of depression has not acquired many adherents in the scientific community, the consensus within that community is that psychological factors—especially the motivation to persist in hard training despite declining performance—are evident at the origin of the condition and that its most salient symptoms are also psychological in nature.

Prevention and Treatment of Overtraining

Overtraining is easy to prevent in theory, because its onset is always gradual without being subtle. Every triathlete is sensitive to the telltale signs of fatigue and declining performance, which are always mild at first and then slowly become more severe, allowing the triathlete to address the developing condition long before a point of no return is passed. Triathletes in heavy training need only monitor their performance, fatigue level, and mood consistently and take measures that include but are not necessarily limited to relative rest when warning signs appear.

Performance monitoring should be as systematic as possible. Triathletes should keep a detailed training log that includes split times for swim workouts, ideally wattage data from cycling sessions, and pace data from runs. Scheduling standardized test workouts once every few weeks in each discipline will aid in systematizing this performance-monitoring process.

As mentioned previously, a moderate, short-term decline in performance over the course of training for an event is not necessarily a negative phenomenon and can even be beneficial in the case of functional overreaching. Triathletes, therefore, should not automatically panic every time they take a step backward in their training. As long as any performance decline, including an expected decline following a block of intensified training, is followed quickly with either planned relative rest or unscheduled rest to promote regeneration, nonfunctional overreaching and overtraining can be avoided.

Energy Levels and Mood State Monitoring

Monitoring subjective variables including energy levels and mood state may also help triathletes interpret any performance declines that occur or even anticipate performance declines and avoid them with unscheduled relative rest. In 2002 Owen Anderson developed a simple questionnaire for such self-monitoring that triathletes are encouraged to use daily throughout training.[13] The questionnaire consists of the following six statements:

- I slept well last night.
- I am looking forward to today's workout.
- I am optimistic about my future performance.
- I feel vigorous and energetic.
- My appetite is great.
- I have little muscle soreness.

Triathletes are asked to rate each statement on the following scale:

1: strongly disagree

2: disagree

3: neutral

4: agree

5: strongly agree

According to Anderson, a total score of 20 or more indicates that the triathlete is well recovered and ready to continue with planned training. A score below 20 indicates that the triathlete needs to train lightly to regenerate further.

Difficulty of Prevention

Because competitive triathletes are often resistant to making unplanned reductions to their training workload, preventing overtraining syndrome can be more difficult in practice than it is in theory. When full-blown overtraining syndrome has developed, prolonged rest is the only option.

In a 2006 paper published online, performance enhancement specialist François Gazzano recommended a treatment protocol of 1 week of complete rest followed by 6 to 12 weeks of a very gradual increase in training. Most clinicians agree, however, that each OTS case is highly individual. Although some overtrained triathletes can recover within 12 weeks on a planned schedule, others need much more time, and all overtrained triathletes must be willing to step back from their planned schedules of gradual return to full training in response to their symptoms. The recovering overtrained triathlete must always remember that not listening to her body got her into this mess and only listening to her body will get her out of it.

Conclusion

Effective triathlon training depends on balancing work and rest. Triathletes often work too much and rest too little. The consequences of such an imbalance include fatigue and stagnating or declining performance. Although the severe downward spiral of overtraining is relatively uncommon among age-group athletes, the less severe state of nonfunctional overreaching thwarts thousands of triathletes' race ambitions each year.

Use the information in this chapter to avoid nonfunctional overreaching and overtraining. Be aware of the early signs of a work–rest imbalance to spot incipient problems early, address them appropriately, and stay on track toward race goals.

PART

VII

Training Base Building for Triathlon

CHAPTER 25

Swim Base Building

—Jim Vance

Joe Friel once said, "As much as 80 percent of race-day fitness comes from the base period."[1] Considering the approach that a training year or season should be periodized from general preparation training to specific preparation, it makes sense that general skills and abilities would be the base or foundation from which most of performance for the season would derive. General preparation phase and base period being synonymous, the skills and energy systems that best generally prepare the triathletes for the season define this phase.

Swimming performance is highly skill dependent. This attribute makes it unique in the world of endurance sport. To improve performance in this discipline, coaches and triathletes primarily need to develop skills rather than endurance.

How long this phase should last varies from triathlete to triathlete based on goals, stage of skill development, initial fitness level, race schedule, injury history, and even training climate. Just as coaches and triathletes set goals for a season, setting training objectives or goals for the base period will help define the general preparation approach to all training sessions in this period.

The time of the season devoted to base training usually follows a period of rest and regeneration from a long prior season. Base training may also occur at a midpoint of the year during a multiple-peak season or when the coach or triathlete recognizes the need to reestablish basic physical attributes that have significantly eroded.

Swimming Fitness Goals During Base Period

Before beginning any training program, coaches and triathletes must have clear goals in place, both for performances for the season and for training, which will help in making all training decisions for the base period.

The first and most important step after setting goals for the base period is to assess what the limiting factors are for the triathlete. These limitations are any attributes that would prevent the triathlete from reaching those performance goals, either basic aerobic fitness, anaerobic fitness, muscular endurance, or specific skills and abilities. When these attributes are known, a coach can more easily determine how much time is needed in the base period. Triathletes new to the sport may spend an entire season training only basic skills and fitness. Because these triathletes may be lacking in physical attributes, simply training consistently with basic sessions can bring about steady improvement for many months, possibly the entire season.

Note that many studies have shown that body type plays a significant role in swim performance. Some aspects of body type may be beyond the control of the triathlete. Those that are manageable, such as body mass, could well be a swimming performance limiter to address away from the pool.[2, 3, 4, 5]

For an elite or advanced age-group triathlete coming into the base period with an ambitious race schedule, this phase may last only a few weeks, perhaps to be repeated later in the season. It could also be extended if the coach or triathlete believes that addressing aerobic fitness for a longer period is needed to prepare better for a long season.

Focusing on Technique and Skills

Swim technique is an important aspect of swim performance that must always be considered when making training decisions. If the triathlete lacks the technical abilities to perform at a high level in a triathlon swim, fitness-focused swim training as the central basis of performance training will likely be a waste of time that yields little improvement and only reinforces poor technique. A review of chapter 4 can clarify proper technique.

The skills that a coach or triathlete might focus on include lowering stroke counts, increasing stroke rate, mastering bilateral breathing ability, increasing distance per stroke, or some other individual marker or movement that needs attention. This point is discussed later in the chapter.

If the triathlete is highly skilled, endurance fitness becomes the likely limiting factor in performance. The limitation, identified by an assessment of past performances, could be aerobic, muscular, or anaerobic endurance fitness. For the latter, the focus could simply be to improve the triathlete's ability to stay with the lead pack at the start of a race. The goal could also be to prepare to race a 3,800-meter Ironman swim by developing better aerobic or muscular endurance. Generally, as the level of competition increases, the role of swimming endurance fitness becomes more important. But, as mentioned earlier, skill must never be compromised in an attempt to enhance fitness.

Determining the Balance of Training

The following are questions for a coach to ask about the triathlete to determine the balance needed in the base period for training focused on skill development versus training focused on endurance fitness:

- What are the triathlete's seasonal performance goals?
- How important is the swim leg for this triathlete as compared with bike and run abilities and relative to the performance goals?
- Where does the triathlete typically rank overall in the swim results of a triathlon? Could this be improved easily?
- How many years of experience does this triathlete have in the sport of triathlon?
- How many years of experience does this triathlete have in the sport of swimming?
- How much swim training has this triathlete done in past seasons?
- What have the base periods of previous years looked like from a swimming perspective?
- What is the range of motion in the key joints, especially the shoulder and ankle, which are important for swim technique?
- What injury history does this triathlete have?

After the coach or self-coached triathlete has determined whether the triathlete's base period should have a skill development focus, an endurance fitness focus, or a balanced approach, the structuring of the mesocycle can begin.

Base Period Mesocycle

The next consideration for a coach or triathlete is determining how much time is available to prepare for the major competitions of the season. Generally, the more time that is available for general preparation, the less risk a coach takes in training decisions and the more potential the triathlete has for improvement. Some experts suggest 8 to 12 weeks for triathletes who have not been training seriously for a period of several weeks, or a somewhat shorter time if the triathlete is starting at a high fitness level.[6, 7] Mesocycles are discussed in more detail in chapter 22.

For the triathlete who primarily needs skill development, frequency of swimming becomes arguably the most important aspect of training. Frequency is entirely an individual matter based on the triathlete's prior skill development. A minimum of three 60-minute sessions per week is recommended for skilled swimmers. Sessions should be more frequent and shorter in duration for the novice.[8]

Skill development sessions do not have to be complex. Studies show that simple efficiency improvements, such as better glide and reduced passive drag or even better pacing, can significantly improve a triathlete's performance.[9, 10, 11] As stated previously, however, these sessions do need to be consistent and frequent.

For the triathlete who needs greater endurance fitness, addressing the clear fitness weaknesses while maintaining or continuing to develop general fitness are the key considerations. The way in which coaches and triathletes choose to structure this period can be as varied as the triathletes themselves.

What does an endurance fitness approach to the base period look like? The energy systems that coaches or triathletes choose to focus on at this time are unique to the individual and are based on experience. Common goals and procedures of general preparation include improving aerobic capacity, developing anaerobic power, maintaining aerobic and anaerobic endurance, increasing specific joint flexibility, and even improving some stroke mechanics.[6]

Strength training, or dry-land resistance training, is a common aspect of training for many triathletes. Although evidence of improvement may be found in running and cycling, ample evidence indicates that the benefits of strength training do not transfer well to swim performance.[12, 13, 14] Therefore, improvements in performance from strength training may translate well to cycling or running but should not necessarily be expected in a skill-dependent sport like swimming.

Again, considering the individual triathlete's goals and background will help determine the optimum frequency, training intensity, and distances when planning the base mesocycle.

Base Period Microcycle

In a microcycle intended for a skill-focused triathlete, some key considerations should determine days in the water devoted to skill development. Microcycles are discussed in more detail in chapter 22.

The first consideration is whether group training with a coach on deck will be part of the program. These sessions are commonly called masters groups or swim clubs. Although some triathletes may resist or be afraid of these types of training groups, studies have shown that an effective coach on deck can greatly reduce swim errors and help triathletes better maintain the trained improvements.[15, 16]

Another major consideration is the structure of other training sessions, such as bike, run, and strength training in relationship to swim skill development sessions. Excessive pool time may well fatigue the triathlete and reduce the effectiveness of the skill development session. The central nervous system (CNS) needs to be in an optimal state for triathletes who are seeking skill development.[17] If the triathlete is doing more than one swim session per day, swimming after a long day of work, or swimming after other training sessions, the time of day and timing between these sessions must be considered if the optimal CNS state is desired.[18]

When focusing on endurance fitness development, the microcycle considerations are mostly limited to the highest intensity sessions as the basis for scheduling other training sessions. Just as with skill development, the CNS has many demands placed on it in maximal speed work, explosive strength work, and other high-intensity exercises, so triathletes need to come into these sessions with as little fatigue as possible to maximize their gains.[17] The more intense the sessions are, the more critical weekly planning becomes because 24 to 48 hours are needed to recover effectively from overload endurance sessions.[7]

Given the technical and high-intensity training demands on the CNS, the structuring of a microcycle should start with the key workouts for accomplishing the goals of the period. The restorative sessions are then interspersed between them to allow adequate recovery. The coach or self-coached triathlete must continually monitor the response to the mix of training dose to ensure positive adaptation.

Base Period Individual Sessions

When constructing an individual training session, whether for technical skill development or endurance fitness development, the most neurologically demanding aspects of the session should come early in the session, after an adequate warm-up but before the triathlete reaches a state of significant fatigue. In practical terms, the most technically demanding and physically intense efforts must occur early in the session and the longer, less intense or aerobic efforts can occur later.

Some of the most overlooked aspects of swim skill are those specific to open-water swimming. Open-water skills sessions throughout the base period can often produce the critical performance jumps necessary to achieve goals. This point is especially true for drafting skills that can conserve energy throughout the race.[4, 19, 20, 21, 22]

Simply developing the ability to swim straight in open water has produced marginal performance improvements.[23] A program, whether for beginner or advanced triathletes, that considers open-water skills is likely to yield positive performance results. Workouts and drills for simulating and improving open-water skills are listed later in this chapter.

Swimming skill development is key for many, if not all, swimmers and is typically found to be the biggest challenge facing novice triathletes. At least one study, however, showed that all triathletes who engaged in an aerobic swim training program saw fitness performance improvements, so training focused on skill development should not come solely at the expense of swimming endurance fitness training.[24] Conversely, focusing solely on endurance fitness and not attempting to fine-tune technical skill risks a reduction in race-day performance for even the best of swimmers in triathlon.

The goals of the individual session should consider the state of the triathlete's CNS; the time of day; and the needs, goals, and background of the individual triathlete.

Workout Creation and Monitoring for Adaptation

Workouts for skill development and endurance fitness enhancement can vary greatly but are often mutually beneficial. For example, an ability to apply a greater force and a longer distance per stroke has both skill and endurance fitness components. Focusing the purposes of the workouts and designing them to meet the goals of the triathlete, both for skill and endurance fitness, is one of the biggest challenges in triathlon.

After goals and objectives have been established for the season and the base phase, coaches and triathletes need to monitor progress toward those goals. This approach can help produce positive adaptation and prevent performance plateaus. Coaches and triathletes should determine a test set that represents the demands of the goal races and goal performances. Begin the base phase with this test and revisit it often throughout the period.

Monitoring Progress

If as much as 80 percent of race-day readiness is established in the base phase, then monitoring progress early in the phase to gauge progress toward race-day performance will provide feedback about the effectiveness of the program. If general preparation can yield significant improvement toward a specific goal, then confidence and motivation can be enhanced. After the general preparation is complete, continued monitoring with the same testing protocol during the ensuing mesocycles will continue to provide feedback about the effectiveness of the specific preparation.

After small changes in technique are observed or after consistent technique training has been performed, testing the triathlete and tracking the test results can help quantify skill improvement and training session effectiveness.

Perhaps the greatest argument for consistent monitoring and testing of triathletes is the prevention of performance plateaus. If a coach sees a plateau in performance before the triathlete is aware of it, consistent improvement is more likely to occur. A self-coached triathlete can use the test to aid in making training decisions. This process will keep the triathlete mentally fresh and motivated because he will note continued success.

Because of testing, when a coach or triathlete sees that training is no longer yielding the desired results, a change can be made quickly. Given the limited training time available, the more skilled that the triathlete is at making this determination, the more likely she is to experience positive performance gains.

Drills for Skill Improvement

Because fitness goals vary widely from triathlete to triathlete, the discussion of workouts here is limited to tools and drills for skill improvement.

The most effective technical skill development sessions require mental engagement. The more mentally engaged the triathlete is, the greater the opportunity is for positive training adaptations.[25] To be effective, the drills and workouts described require all the mental engagement that the coach or triathlete can summon. The following are intended to help the coach and triathlete recognize skill deficiencies while promoting improvement.

Swim Golf This drill provides objective feedback regarding technique changes. The triathlete swims a 50 (meters or yards) counting strokes (both hands). At the end of the 50, the stroke total is added to the time in seconds. The result is the score for that 50. Fatigue needs to be minimized because it affects results, so long recoveries should be used between the 50s and a consistent, moderate effort needs to be employed.

The ideal scenario is to lower the score by both time and stroke count over the course of a few such 50s. This drill provides the opportunity for triathletes to experiment with stroke counts or with other variables such as bilateral or single-side breathing to discover the effect on time. The drill helps the triathlete understand individual tendencies while experimenting with technique.

Tennis Balls In this drill triathletes simply swim with a tennis ball in each hand while focusing especially on the catch phase of the stroke. The tennis ball swim is somewhat better than closed-fist swim drills, which are rather common. With a tennis ball in the hand the triathlete is unable to cheat by slightly exposing more palm.

Bilateral Breathing Triathletes of all abilities tend to have a dominant breathing side. This predisposition ultimately means an imbalance of stroke mechanics and force application between the left and right sides throughout the stroke. Swimming easily and aerobically with bilateral breathing is an effective way to develop a balanced stroke, improve coordination, and reinforce technical changes. Bilateral breathing is a great workout tool for triathletes to build both technical skill and fitness.

Paddles Paddles have been discussed in chapters 7 and 18. The main purpose for using paddles is the development of force in the pull. Paddles may also correct technique both at the entry point of the hand into the water and in maintaining a high elbow for better leverage of the arm (see figure 25.1). Paddles are one of the best tools for advanced triathletes looking to improve endurance fitness and for triathletes at all levels needing technical improvements.

Snorkel A snorkel allows a triathlete to focus on technical aspects that she is attempting to improve without the distraction of turning the head to breathe. A snorkel gives the triathlete more time to view her own stroke underwater (see figure 25.2). As with bilateral breathing, using a snorkel helps to balance out both sides so that breathing does not occur continuously to one side.

▶ **Figure 25.1** Swimmer using paddles.

▶ **Figure 25.2** Swimmer using a snorkel.

Alternative Strokes By training with strokes other than freestyle, such as the butterfly and backstroke, triathletes can gain better body awareness, develop a feel for the water, and improve concentration and mental engagement in training sessions. In the case of butterfly, considerable endurance fitness improvements may occur because of the physical demands of the stroke.

Open-Water Pack Swimming Coaches and triathletes with access to a 50-meter pool can remove lane lines and place buoys near the corners of the pool. A small pack of triathletes then swims circuits around the buoys to simulate the conditions common to triathlon such as drafting, positioning, turns, and contact.

Drafting If a large pool with removed lane lines isn't available, triathletes can swim tightly in a line, switching leaders every lap or 100, thus encouraging them to stay on the feet of those in front of them. This drill allows them to deal with kicking feet while maintaining a close position for drafting.

Pontoon Starts Although pontoon starts are not common among age-group triathletes, they are common among the youth elite, junior elite, and elite racing in the United States and across the ITU circuit. Using the pool deck ledge as a simulated pontoon, triathletes dive start into an interval. By being closely bunched together, they develop their dive skill while becoming more confident on the starting pontoon. Safe pool depth must be considered before employing this drill.

Swimming Blind Having triathletes push off the wall with their eyes closed and swim until they touch a lane rope helps identify a tendency to drift either left or right in open water.

Conclusion

After determining goals and limiters, coaches and triathletes can begin to assess how to plan the general preparation or base phase of training to emphasize technical skill, endurance fitness, or both. While stressing mental engagement, a coach can monitor the triathlete for adaptation and change the program as needed to meet individual needs.

CHAPTER 26

Bike Base Building

—Neal Henderson, MSc

The base training phase is the single most important training period for endurance athletes preparing for competition or for those simply looking to improve their level. The majority of physiological improvements and endurance development occurs during this phase of training. Developing cycling-specific fitness during the base period for triathlon requires neuromuscular development, appropriate progression of endurance building, race-specific demands training, and work on the triathlete's weaker areas in cycling.

Intensity and Duration During Base Building

The intensity and duration for the majority of training that occurs while building endurance during the base period is best described as relatively low intensity with increasing duration. The greatest percentage of training performed by elite-level endurance athletes consists of low intensity base-building workouts.[1] Attempts to shortcut the base-building phase of training by increasing the intensity or decreasing the length of the base phase are counterproductive in the long run. At least one study showed that the intensification of endurance training, even for amateur endurance athletes training less than 10 hours per week, resulted in decreased performance compared with endurance training that was predominantly aerobic.[1]

These terms do have a relative basis in that a low-intensity base-level ride for a top male professional triathlete might be performed at 250 to 300 watts and a long ride for an athlete training for an Ironman distance race could be upward of 120 miles (190 km). For a novice triathlete, a similarly stressful ride might be performed at 60 to 80 watts for 20 miles (32 km). In both cases, the stress of the training session on the respective athlete might be similar.

Identifying Appropriate Training Intensity

With respect to intensity, it is a good idea to perform some sort of field or laboratory-based testing to identify appropriate training intensity for aerobic endurance base building. Laboratory testing can be performed to identify the upper limit of effort than can be sustained for about 1 hour in trained athletes. This test is typically referred to as a lactate profile test, and the point identified is called the lactate threshold. A lactate profile test typically consists of 6 to 10 stages of progressively harder exercise. Measurements of heart rate, perceived effort (or rating of perceived exertion, or RPE), and blood lactate concentration are taken at the end of each 3- to 5-minute-long stage.

A similar test can be performed using shorter stages and expired gas measurements (metabolic analysis, measuring oxygen and carbon dioxide fractions of expired air) to estimate the threshold. The laboratory-identified lactate threshold point is strongly correlated with the amount of power that can be generated for 1 hour by trained cyclists.[2]

Field tests are typically performed as maximum effort sustained for 20 to 60 minutes. Triathletes are encouraged to perform both laboratory and field testing several times throughout the season. The most important times to test would be at the beginning of the base phase to ensure that training is performed at the appropriate intensity and after the base phase as the triathlete is ready to begin the build for a more intense phase of training. Performing objective testing like this allows the tracking of improvements in fitness and performance.

Periodic field testing also gives critical information that can be used to help identify proper pacing, nutrition, and hydration strategies. These field tests can be performed either as all-out maximum performance tests for a specific duration or for a defined distance or course. Triathletes should perform their field tests on courses and in conditions that they are likely to encounter during their major competitions.[3]

Although the maximum power that can be generated during 1 hour of cycling is the gold standard and definition of threshold power, the task is difficult to complete effectively in training. Fortunately, because the relationship between power and duration for aerobic efforts shows that for each doubling of time the drop-off in power is approximately 8 percent, shorter field tests can yield good estimates of threshold power.

Most triathletes are capable of putting out a maximum effort for durations shorter than 1 hour in training. Therefore, a better test to estimate threshold power in a field test is to warm up appropriately and then perform a 5-minute effort at maximum power. The power achieved in a 5-minute maximum test is typically a good indication of the power at the triathlete's aerobic maximum, or power at $\dot{V}O_2$max. In a laboratory test, $\dot{V}O_2$max is typically measured with 1-minute-long stages with increasing power output at each stage until failure while measuring oxygen and carbon dioxide as well as the total volume of air expired to measure the absolute amount of oxygen that the triathlete consumes during maximal exercise.

The final stage of power achieved during the lab test is strongly correlated with the amount of power that can be sustained for 3 to 8 minutes of all-out exercise, which is why the 5-minute field test is a good analog to $\dot{V}O_2$max power. After a brief 5-minute active recovery, the triathlete then performs a maximum 20-minute effort to evaluate maximum sustainable power, or simply threshold power. This method of testing has been popularized by Dr. Andrew Coggan and his partner Hunter Allen.[4] The 5-minute maximum effort must precede the 20-minute effort, and the athlete must perform absolute maximum efforts for both tests to obtain reliable data.

Most triathletes who perform the testing correctly will see that the 5-minute power value is 125 to 135 percent of the 20-minute power value. A triathlete who achieves less than a 20 percent difference between 5-minute and 20-minute power likely held back during the 5-minute test to achieve a higher 20-minute value. In those instances, decrease the 20-minute power value by 5 to 10 percent to reflect threshold power accurately. A single 20-minute effort without any prior maximal effort will typically yield a power output that is 15 to 20 percent above the athlete's actual threshold power. Always look at the actual pacing used by the triathlete to achieve the result. This area can often provide critical feedback toward pacing for future tests and competition.

Another way to perform field testing is to constrain effort to a given variable such as heart rate. Knowing the heart rate associated with the triathlete's threshold from laboratory testing can give an excellent upper ceiling for both purely aerobic levels of effort and efforts that would be associated with threshold power or pace. Long-distance triathletes would gain more useful information on progression in race-specific power and pace by constraining the heart rate during a longer field test of 20 to 40 miles (32 to 64 km) at 15 beats below the threshold heart rate.

A short-course triathlete, on the other hand, would gain more relevant field-testing information from performing a 10- to 15-mile (16 to 24 km) test effort while holding the heart rate constant at his threshold heart rate value. In either case, the environmental conditions should be constant from one test to another, especially air temperature and wind speed. Also, the components, wheels, helmet, and clothing are variables that should be constant from one field test to the next to ensure comparable data and information.

In many cases, endurance athletes consider the appropriate training intensity for building their endurance foundation too easy. In fact, the correct intensity is simply appropriately easy. One of the adaptations that occur with low-intensity aerobic training is improving the body's ability to use fat as a fuel source during exercise, which allows carbohydrate stores to be maintained.

Other adaptations that occur are an increase in blood delivery to the active muscle through increased capillary density and improved cardiac output, which is increased by improvements in the stroke volume of the heart, or the amount of blood that is pumped with each beat.[5] Another benefit of slowly building endurance training volume with lower intensity is that it is a safe and healthy way to increase endurance while avoiding overuse injury and burnout.

Besides the specific methods of identifying training intensity such as heart rate, RPE, and power output, a simple method is effective—the talk test. When performing training at an aerobic base-building intensity, triathletes should be able to talk relatively comfortably, to string together nearly a complete sentence before needing to take a break for a breath.

For most people, the heart rate associated with this level of effort is 20 to 40 beats per minute lower than their threshold heart rate, which is typically between 85 and 90 percent of their sport-specific maximum heart rate and approximately 55 to 75 percent of their threshold power, the amount of power that they can sustain for 1 hour of all-out cycling. In terms of perceived effort, this effort will typically be between 2 and 4 on a 0 to 10 scale or between 11 and 15 on Borg's original 6 to 20 scale.

Rationale Behind Low Intensity and Long Duration

The aerobic endurance adaptations that result from low-intensity training take weeks, months, and years to develop to their maximum. For that reason, those who train for endurance sports performance need many years to reach their potential. Triathletes who try to shortchange the low-intensity aerobic training phase often end up sustaining overuse injuries and prematurely burning out. Keep in mind that not all training during the base phase has to be low intensity, but most of it should be. Adaptations to higher intensity training such as threshold, $\dot{V}O_2$max, and neuromuscular power occur much quicker, so those forms of training can be placed later in the training plan, often only weeks before competition.

Workout Volume and Structure

Triathletes should spend 50 percent of their total weekly training volume (hours) on the bike during the base phase. Typically, this volume of training is achieved with three to five cycling workouts per week. One to two workouts will be steady-state base endurance training, one workout will address peak neuromuscular development, and then one or two rides will address race-specific demands or personal weaknesses in cycling.

Steady-State Training

Steady-state training sessions predominantly consist of longer rides performed nearly exclusively at the aerobic base intensity (55 to 75 percent of lactate threshold power, or 60 to 70 percent of maximum heart rate). The goal of one workout each week would be to ride progressively longer, increasing by 10 to 20 percent each week. Every third or fourth week typically would be a recovery week that is significantly reduced in duration, normally a 30 to 60 percent reduction from peak volume. Triathletes should select appropriate training routes that are not too hilly and do not require a lot of starts and stops so that they can spend as much time as possible at the proper intensity. Indoor stationary bike trainer workouts can also be effective for building up aerobic base training ride volume.

Neuromuscular Development

Neuromuscular development is primarily developed through either sprinting or big-gear work. Also, the combination of these two can be effective. Neuromuscular training in cycling is all about recruiting the maximum amount of muscle fibers to produce peak torque and power. Peak power development in cycling typically occurs between 110 and 130 rpm and can be sustained for only 3 to 5 seconds. In trying to develop peak power the triathlete should select an appropriate starting gear at which the cadence is near 90 to 100 rpm to begin. Efforts can be performed both seated in the saddle as well as standing out of the saddle. Starting each sprint at a variety of cadences from low cadence in a big gear to high cadence in an easy gear helps develop the ability to produce high power output across a range of torque levels. This kind of effort is extremely important for off-road and draft-legal triathletes to perform. Triathletes who focus on long-distance nondrafting events have less need to incorporate neuromuscular workouts into their training, but such workouts can serve as a form of strength or resistance training for those with limitations to conventional strength training.

Triathletes should have complete rest after each sprint effort, typically at least 5 minutes. Between sprints, they should continue to pedal at an aerobic base training intensity. Triathletes can also perform neuromuscular development training by pushing a big gear at a slower cadence. One way to do this is to do a standing start, what track riders do at the start of their events. Using a gear such as a 53 × 15 or 53 × 16, they begin with 10 to 15 seconds of effort out of the saddle, trying to get up to the fastest speed possible. As with the high-speed sprint efforts, full recovery between efforts is critical. Most neuromuscular development workouts consist of only 6 to 12 total efforts during a 1-hour training session. This is the kind of workout in which quality trumps quantity.

Race-Specific Demands

Each race that a triathlete competes in might have certain features that make it unique, such as a steep or long uphill. A hallmark workout for triathletes preparing for these types of races might include two to four repeats of a similar climb in progressively harder gears and with variations in standing and seated climbing during the repeats. For those preparing for an off-road triathlon, performing mountain bike rides on terrain similar to the upcoming event at least once a week is important. In other races, a perfectly flat course that is subject to significant wind might be a special challenge. Even in the base phase of training triathletes should be including a workout each week or every other week that will address race-specific demands for the season's highest priority events. Being prepared both physically and mentally for the challenges of race day will give the triathlete confidence and proper preparation heading into a big race. Overdoing it is possible, however, so race-specific preparation workouts during the base phase of training should be performed only once each week or even just every other week. A progression of the training sessions focused on race-specific demands should occur throughout the base phase. Typically, these workouts should initially contain only 20 to 30 percent of full race-specific demands in a session. The amount of race-specific intensity will increase throughout the base phase, and for long-course triathletes a goal of achieving 75 to 100 percent of the race-specific demands in training is appropriate. Short-course racers often perform even more than 100 percent of race-specific demands in a single session to ensure appropriate capacity to perform the task in the race and still be able to run well afterward. Decreasing the rest between race-specific efforts and increasing the actual intensity are also effective means of increasing training stress without adding volume to any given race-specific workout.

Inherent Weaknesses

As much as we enjoy and are proficient at certain kinds of efforts and training sessions, we need to address areas in which we may be weak or not well prepared. A long-course triathlete who enjoys steady-state training needs to add some variable paced efforts to training. Training sessions that address weaknesses can be incorporated in many ways, but keeping these sessions specific and to the point is important. The goal of these kinds of sessions is not necessarily to turn a weakness into a true strength, but to decrease any possible deficit that the weakness may be causing. An honest evaluation of past training and racing results relative to the triathlete's peers will typically highlight the areas in which he is weak. Neuromuscular and race-specific training may possibly overlap with race-weakness training sessions. In these cases, the triathlete must be cautious to avoid performing more than one neuromuscular or race-specific intensity workout each week.

Workout Guidelines

Most riders are better off riding alone during their aerobic steady-state base building rides, because group riding almost always ends up incorporating more intense training. Performing the base building endurance training sessions at excessive intensity is counterproductive. Doing so will increase fatigue over time and not allow the body to achieve general aerobic fitness adaptations such as improved capacity to use fat as fuel.

The goal of aerobic endurance rides in training is to build the volume and duration of these rides gradually to exceed the longest goal race distance that a triathlete may be competing in during the season. Another goal of long endurance training rides is simply to increase confidence in being able to maintain a consistent strong effort for several hours. The long endurance rides are also an excellent time to practice hydration and fueling strategies that will be used during races.

Long Rides

Triathletes focused on Olympic-distance events should build up to at least a 40-mile (64 km) ride and even up to 50 miles (80 km) to build bike-specific endurance that will allow them not only to cycle at good intensity, speed, and power but also to be able to have the best possible run off the bike. For Half-Ironman (90 km cycle leg) races, triathletes should build up to 80- to 100-mile (130 to 160 km) rides at least two or three times before the race. Ironman-distance competitors should perform at least one epic ride of 130 to 160 miles (210 to 260 km) before the race and have several other rides of 100 to 120 miles (160 to 190 km) under their belts during the base phase.

These milestone long rides build not only endurance but also the psychological confidence that comes from being able to complete much more than the body will have to do on race day. These rides are also important in evaluating whether a given bike position can be maintained for the duration of the event, and they provide a good testing ground for on-bike nutrition and hydration experimentation.

Triathletes who live in climates that are not conducive to performing long rides outdoors during the winter can use stationary trainers and cross-training as a means of building up steady-state endurance volume. Athletes who live in cold and snowy areas can mix stationary bike training and cross-training with activities such as cross-country skiing and snowshoe hiking to put in long hours of steady-state endurance training without being exclusively on the bike. Even triathletes, the ultimate cross-trainers, can benefit from additional cross-training, especially during the base phase.

Weekly Progression

The weekly progression of training volume on the bike usually can be tolerated at greater levels with less risk of injury than can be done with swimming and especially running volume. In most cycling workouts, triathletes can increase the volume at least 15 to 25 percent per week on a weekly long ride. (In swimming or running, the recommended increase in the volume of sustained long sessions is only 5 to 10 percent.)

Because cycling doesn't involve the impact and eccentric muscle contractions of running and because the bigger muscles of the legs are less likely to suffer the overuse injuries that can affect the smaller muscles and mobile joints of the shoulders, which are stressed with swimming, triathletes can be more aggressive in increasing cycling volume compared with the two other disciplines.

Sample Weekly Schedule

The following is a typical weekly workout schedule to build endurance for a triathlete preparing for a hilly Half-Ironman (90 km cycle leg) race who is a good uphill rider but not as strong on the flats or downhills, especially tight turns on downhills.

1. **Long-distance ride:** Ride 80 miles (130 km) on rolling terrain primarily at base intensity. Include six 10-second seated sprint efforts in the time-trial position on flat sections of the course to work on recruiting aero position strength and power.

2. **Threshold interval ride:** Ride 35 to 40 miles (55 to 65 km) on a course that includes at least one hill that is .5 mile (.8 km) long. After an appropriate warm-up, perform six efforts at 90 percent of threshold power on the flat for .5 mile before the hill and then perform at 100 to 110 percent of threshold up the .5-mile hill. Rest with easy active recovery spinning for 5 to 10 minutes between intervals.

3. **Descending and cornering practice:** Warm up well and then practice four to six progressively faster 90-degree turns to both the right and the left. Focus on looking ahead, picking the fastest line through the turn, and steering the bike primarily by shifting body weight. The total ride might be only 10 to 15 miles (16 to 24 km) for this type of workout.

Conclusion

Building an effective cycling base is critical for success in triathlon. Spending significant portions of time developing a cycling base is the only way to build the endurance necessary to be a competitive triathlete. The foundation of fitness that all other phases of training will be built on depends on the cycling base. Being able to ride beyond the race distance of the goal event is important both physiologically and psychologically. Increasing neuromuscular power on the bike and building confidence with race-specific workouts will set up triathletes for later success. Reducing any weaknesses during the base phase is also smart, because triathletes will then be able to focus on improving the most important aspects of their fitness and performance for their competitive events.

CHAPTER 27

Run Base Building

—George M. Dallam, PhD

The classic concept of building a base in running refers to the idea of developing running performance by running increasingly larger volumes at a largely aerobic effort level or pace. It is widely, although not uniformly, believed that developing the ability to run very long distances at slow pace regularly is an important initial component of being able to run moderately long race distances at a faster pace later.

This concept is often referred to as laying the foundation on which higher intensity training will be built. This idea of base training fits into the use of a periodization training approach most commonly referred to as the general preparation phase of each macrocycle. Later periodization phases typically consist of a more diversified training program that includes a range of training intensities designed to be more specific to the stresses of triathlon or running racing. Such an approach is now broadly advocated in preparation for successful performance in endurance events.

Conflicting Evidence Regarding Base Building

But the utility of the base training or general preparation phase of periodization, and even periodization itself, has not been widely examined in carefully controlled scientific studies in running or triathlon.[1] In addition, the few studies that examine the concept indirectly in other sports are not supportive.[2] Research in running and other endurance sports that examine the current practices of elite athletes suggests that a mix of running intensities (about 20 percent of work at higher intensity and about 80 percent of work at aerobic threshold and below) is a far more common training model throughout most of the competitive year.[3, 4, 5, 6]

In addition, spending more relative training time at and below the aerobic threshold intensity in training also appears to be related to greater competitive success in running, assuming that a minimum amount of time is spent training in the higher intensity zones.[3] This minimum might be thought of as one or two sessions per microcycle that focus on both basic speed and speed endurance. A shift in this direction has also been documented in rowers who improved to an internationally competitive status over an extended period.[7] Of course, these observations may be explained by the greater capacity for total training volume likely to occur in higher ability endurance athletes who have a greater concentration of slow-twitch muscle fibers and the time necessary for recovery to respond favorably.

Although not directly studied, beginning triathletes may be well served by using a base training approach initially to build training tolerance gradually before entertaining a full range of training intensities. The most commonly cited reasons for doing so are preventing injury and preparing the body and mind for the rigors of greater intensity training as described previously. This approach also may be useful in the initial build-up for recreational triathletes who take considerable time off from training during the winter.

Elite and high-performing age-group triathletes, however, generally train nearly year round. The question of greatest importance for them is whether it is productive to cycle through periods of classical base training, systematically or not.

Base Training Versus Higher-Intensity Training

In a study examining this concept in highly competitive cross-country skiers, athletes who had not made significant progression following the use of a classic periodization approach, including a base training general preparation phase, over 1 year, were placed in a group that reduced the volume of low-intensity training and increased the volume of higher intensity training throughout the next training year. They essentially replaced base training with a more race-specific form of race preparation.[2]

The addition of an increased volume of higher intensity training and a reduction in overall training volume resulted in substantially larger improvements in the treatment group, both in comparison with themselves the previous year and in comparison with the initially higher performing control group who continued to follow a classical periodization approach through the second year.[2]

Further, a study has demonstrated in running that a training program using a variety of intensities evokes a greater response than one using higher volumes of primarily aerobic intensity training.[8] Although these findings do not definitively negate the value of using base training in the classical sense, they do bring into question the choice of method of periodization.

Tenets of Periodization

The basic tenets of periodization include the use of a systematic variation of volume and intensity of training in cyclical phases. In so doing, a variety of training intensities are combined to create a synergistic effect on performance capability at the target race distance. Typical elements of an endurance training periodization plan might include speed work, race-pace work, and endurance work, and, with the recent acknowledgement of the value of strength and peak power,[9] resistance training and plyometrics.

The cyclical phases, referred to as mesocycles, follow each other, and each has a specific focus. These most typically include a general preparation of high-volume aerobic running followed by increasingly more race-specific phases including the faster paced forms of training.

Arthur Lydiard's approach, which has been the basis for many current run training programs, follows a high volume of base training with successive mesocycles of strength focus using hill work and fartleks and then speed emphasis using flatter, faster running and interval training, specific preparation cycles before racing. But even in Lydiard's day, some athletes varied between different forms of training stress (long runs, hill runs, and speed runs, for instance) on a regular basis over a relatively short cycle of training throughout the training year. This approach has been referred to as mixed training.

Modern periodization approaches have evolved in at least two common forms that reflect these earlier ideas. These forms are referred to as linear periodization, which is similar to the Lydiard approach in having a different training emphasis in each phase, and undulating periodization, which is similar to the mixed training approach by regularly including all emphasis areas. Unfortunately, the relative effectiveness of each type of periodization has not been well studied in endurance sports, so any attempt to make inferences must come from another area, that being resistance training.

Comparing Linear to Undulating Periodization

The two common forms of periodization, linear and undulating, have been fairly broadly studied recently in resistance training.[10, 11, 12, 13, 14, 15, 16] Linear periodization, the classic approach, proceeds as follows. Each successive training mesocycle focuses on a single level of training intensity over multiple days of a microcycle, proceeding from relatively low intensity to relatively high intensity over successive mesocycles.

By contrast, undulating periodization proceeds without mesocycles, including only microcycles (typically 7 to 10 days) that incorporate a cyclical variation of differing intensity levels on differing training days within the microcycle. Examining the differences in these approaches helps address the underlying question of whether the systematic and sequential use of limited-focus training cycles is an effective approach.

The scientific literature on linear versus undulating periodization in resistance training, when equated for total training stimulus and addressed as whole, produces the following observations:

- both forms of periodization result in significant improvements among athletes in varying states of training;[10, 11, 12, 13, 14, 15, 16]
- no differences in strength are found after shorter periods (9 weeks) in untrained males[11] and untrained females;[12]
- linear periodization has been shown to produce greater increases in strength over longer periods (12 weeks) in recreationally trained males[10] as well as no difference in premenopausal women;[17]
- undulating periodization has been shown to produce statistically greater increases in strength among trained males over longer time frames (12 weeks)[15] and the inference of greater strength increases in trained males,[13,14] although neither of the last two results was statistically significant; and
- reverse linear periodization (working from high intensity to low intensity) has been shown to produce greater increases in muscular endurance than either linear periodization or undulating periodization.[15]

The first inference that we might draw from these data is that a complex training approach using multiple intensities is uniformly successful in creating improvement. Second, however, neither periodization organizational scheme is clearly more effective in the early phases of training, although an undulating approach may hold more promise for those who are already well trained. One theory concerning the reduced efficacy of a linear approach to periodization in comparison to an undulating one among well-trained athletes is that successive training cycles do not maintain previously acquired physiological abilities adequately, ultimately limiting performance improvement if the quantities under consideration are symbiotic in nature. An example would be the interaction of strength and endurance capacity.[9]

Last, when the target performance is more endurance focused than is possible in daily training efforts, it may be more effective to work from higher intensity training cycles toward lower intensity training cycles versus the opposite, which is more traditional.

Anecdotally, we know that many Ironman triathletes have used this approach, training with more emphasis on a variety of intensities at shorter distances and racing early in the year and then performing a block of training that is primarily endurance focused as the build-up to a specific Ironman event.

Consequently, the use of base training periods or mesocycles with a more single-minded focus on the development of increased endurance and movement strength capabilities seems to have the following applications in a periodization approach to training:

1. The early season development of both beginning triathletes and those who have taken a significant break from the training process

2. As a method of specific race preparation when the triathlete is attempting to race at distances significantly longer than typical daily training volumes

3. In triathletes who have become psychologically and physically fatigued following extended periods using an undulating periodization approach with a focus on multiple intensities of training

Building a Base Through a Periodized Run Training Program

Several widely accepted, although not scientifically validated, concepts surround the design of base training mesocycles. Following is a brief rundown on each of them.

Focusing on Aerobic Training Intensities

The first is that focusing primarily on aerobic training intensities offers the greatest potential to adapting successfully to progressively increasing training stress later. This is thought to be a function of the relatively lower level of autonomic nervous system fatigue[5, 6] and lower glycogen usage[18] associated with such training. Controlling training intensity so that it remains at an aerobic level can be accomplished by identifying the pace at which the aerobic threshold is reached and then progressively increasing the intensity of work.

The aerobic or first lactate threshold is identified by the first significant increase in blood lactate above the baseline (typically 1 or 2 millimoles) with each progressive increase in running speed during a progressive running test. This velocity, or the heart rate associated with it, can be identified using any of the following methods of determining the aerobic threshold:

1. Use heart rate monitoring to determine when 80 percent of the heart rate maximum has been reached. Determining relative training intensity reliably by heart rate requires that the maximum heart rate be measured, not estimated.

2. Use the predicted pace for the marathon distance and beyond. Predicted pace for various distances can be estimated using a variety of mathematical models.

3. Use ratings of perceived exertion (RPE of 12 to 14 on the Borg scale of 6 to 20) generated from a graded exercise test.

4. Identify the velocity at the aerobic or first lactate threshold by measuring lactate values during a graded exercise test or by using the simple talk test whereby the triathlete runs at the fastest speed at which he can still talk normally.

Gradually Increasing the Training Load

The second premise is that training load should be increased by no more than 10 percent in any given microcycle to reduce the potential for injury. This concept has been contradicted, however, by a recent study illustrating no reduction in injury among novice runners following a longer progression based on the 10 percent rule in comparison with a control group that progressed faster.[19]

One interpretation of this data is that the act of progressing training without a periodic break is the real culprit in creating injuries because of accumulated fatigue, not the rate of progression, because neither group appeared to do so.

Of course, if this interpretation is true, the faster progressing group should have produced more injuries sooner. This was the case in the previously mentioned study. Injury rates were compared at the end of the training period (8 weeks versus 13 weeks) and were nearly identical at 20 percent of those participating in each group, implying that the faster-progressing group reached that proportion of injuries sooner.[19]

Adding a Restoration Cycle

This idea leads to a third training concept—that several progressive training cycles during which training load has been increased should be followed by a reduced training load cycle, sometimes called a restoration cycle, to disburse the accumulated fatigue of the prior progressions and allow more successful adaptation.

The recently developed technological capacity to measure work output directly in cycling[20] has permitted the observation of this phenomenon in real-world training scenarios. Further, the concept has been modeled successfully in endurance training.[21] Consequently, when athletes increase their current training load over their recent historical average training load, which represents their adaptive status or fitness, they induce calculable fatigue (current load minus historical load) and a reduction in performance capacity. With successive increases in the training load beyond current capacity, fatigue increases further. Eventually this increasing or accumulated fatigue will result in injury or overtraining.

This understanding leads to the 3-to-1 rule: After several increases in training load over progressive microcycles of training, triathletes should proactively reduce training load to reduce accumulated fatigue and allow further progression before they incur an injury or become overtrained. In other words, after 3 weeks of increases in training load, the load should be reduced for 1 week. In theory, such an approach is likely to reduce both injury probability and the potential for overtraining. In application, training loads are reduced substantially (up to 50 percent) over a period of days to a full microcycle.

Incorporating Some Intensity

The last widely accepted belief regarding base training in running is that some elements of the broad spectrum of training intensity should be used for the purpose of maintaining the specific adaptations associated with them. Commonly, this is accomplished using alactates, or strides, as they are referred to in running. Strides are short, 15- to 20-second fast running efforts designed both to maintain running speed and to develop running technique at higher speeds. In addition, it has been observed that it is useful to maintain the steady-state speed associated with racing by periodically using a relatively shorter tempo or race-pace effort.

Sample Four-Week Mesocycle

Table 27.1 shows an example of a 4-week mesocycle in a base training plan for a typical competitive age-group triathlete, currently adapted to 18 miles (30 km) per week of running and focused on sprint- and international-distance competitions. The cycle is designed to increase endurance using the principles described previously while maintaining high-end speed, race speed endurance, and hill-running strength.

Table 27.1 Four-Week Base Training Mesocycle

Week	Day	Training
1	1	5 miles (8 km) aerobic running on a hilly course, 8 × 100-meter strides
	2	5 miles (8 km) aerobic running with 4 × 100-meter strides followed by 20-minute tempo effort
	3	8 miles (13 km) aerobic running
		Total distance: 18 miles (29 km)
2	1	5.5 miles (9 km) aerobic running on a hilly course, 8 × 100-meter strides
	2	5.5 miles (9 km) aerobic running with 4 × 100-meter strides followed by 20-minute tempo effort
	3	9 miles (14.5 km) aerobic running
		Total distance: 20 miles (32.5 km)
3	1	6 miles (9.5 km) aerobic running on a hilly course, 8 × 100-meter strides
	2	6 miles (9.5 km) aerobic running with 4 × 100-meter strides followed by 20-minute tempo effort
	3	10 miles (16 km) aerobic running
		Total distance: 22 miles (35 km)
4	1	3 miles (5 km) aerobic running on a hilly course, 4 × 100-meter strides
	2	3 miles (5 km) aerobic running with 4 × 100-meter strides followed by 10-minute tempo effort
	3	5 miles (8 km) aerobic running
		Total distance: 11 miles (18 km) (restoration)

Base Training Considerations

Several concepts are significant to maximizing the effectiveness of a base training period. These include evaluating the adaptive process in some way, quantifying training load in a manner that allows intelligent load progression and successful adaptation to occur, and incorporating additional elements of a complex training approach such as strength, strength endurance, and skill training.

Evaluating Adaptation

When training is aimed at increasing endurance first and foremost, this quality should be measured systematically to see whether the program is successful. Of course, the best measurements are part of the training process itself. An easy way to evaluate improving endurance without the need for time trials or racing is to measure the association between heart rate and pace in some commonly repeated element of the training process.

For instance, in the previous example, if the triathlete measures the heart rate and average pace of the tempo run and conducts it during each microcycle in the same conditions and location, evaluating the success of the adaptive process of the overall cycle will be relatively easy. When heart rate is reduced at a given pace or the pace is faster without a concomitant and proportionate increase in heart rate, then successful adaptation is taking place. When this is not the case, a reevaluation of the process should occur.

Of course, this evaluation helps in answering another fundamental question about base training: How long should this be carried out? An easy answer is that base training and progressive increases in training load should be carried out until successful adaption is no longer possible. Typically, this occurs over periods from about 4 weeks to as much as 24 weeks, depending on training background. At that point training tolerance has been reached, so moving to a more complex undulating approach or the next successive phase in a linear periodization approach is appropriate.

Further, a triathlete who has a method for quantifying total training load now has the most valid means possible of establishing an optimal training load, which is something just below that at which successful adaptation stopped occurring. This optimal load should be taken into consideration when designing successive training cycles that will contain a greater volume of higher intensity training. Typically, the total volume of training should be reduced to maintain a training load within the triathlete's current optimum range.

Measuring the Training Load

Quantifying loads in cycling is possible using power-measuring devices, but such devices are not yet available for running, for reasons discussed in chapter 7. But triathletes can create a rudimentary system for measuring running load if both pace and distance can be measured or calculated. Load is definable as the total work accomplished. The work rate of running is indirectly represented by time of running multiplied by the average pace of running. With most current GPS systems, the time and average pace in miles per hour of a run can be easily determined and used in a simple spreadsheet-based calculation. An example follows:

$$58 \text{ minutes total run time} \times 6.5 \text{ miles per hour average pace}$$
$$= 377 \text{ stress units}$$

Such a simple system for quantifying the outcome of work performed does not account for the change in work rate needed to facilitate running up or down hills. Consequently, an assumption is that training will be carried out on similar courses to produce reasonably meaningful microcycle-to-microcycle comparisons of training load.

After training load can be measured accurately and reliably, the basic principles of progression can be applied. The most fundamental progression principles are as follows.

Training load should increase gradually until successful adaptation is no longer occurring. This point represents a ceiling for any given person beyond which further training is counterproductive. This point has been reached when a reduction in work capacity occurs rather than an improvement.

Training load progression should be attempted using small adjustments, ideally of about 5 to 10 percent of the total load. Small relative increases in load reduce the likelihood of injury and increase the probability of successful adaptation.

Progressions in training load should occur only when successful adaptation to the previous load has occurred. For instance, following an increase in total microcycle running load, successful adaptation has occurred when average running velocity has become faster at any given heart rate or level of effort. When this is evident, training load can be further increased.

Temporary reductions in training load over several days, on the order of 30 to 50 percent of the present load, should occur systematically following successive increases in load. This plan permits the shedding of accumulated fatigue and increases the possibility that further progressions will be successful in creating adaptation.

Strength Training

For those who engage in the practice of strength training for triathlon, base or general training periods are probably the most useful time to make progressive increases in the resistance training load as well, following the principles already described. This approach has been demonstrated to minimize the loss in stride length acutely during intensive running training[22] and may help to offset losses in speed and range of motion occurring chronically from running large volumes at slower speeds. As with the endurance training process, the efficacy of the approach should be regularly assessed by evaluating effort and force levels across key resistance training sets.

Strength Endurance Training

Strength endurance training refers to the idea of increasing the resistance to forward motion to a small degree in swimming, cycling, or running by use of means that will minimally alter movement mechanics yet still allow sustained aerobic efforts. In running, both inclines[23] and weighted vests can be used for this purpose. The process creates increased muscle activations at the hip with each step[23] while reducing step rate slightly. Using inclines or weighted vests is analogous to using paddles in swimming or using a larger gear in cycling.

Such training has been hypothesized to recruit muscle fibers normally active only during higher intensity training, allowing a successful conversion of such fibers to a more oxidative or endurance-oriented profile that is more resistant to fatigue. Base training periods offer an opportune time to include and progress strength endurance running training in the overall training plan. The goal is to prepare the body for the rigors of both specific hill-focused training as well as higher speed training later.

Skill Development

Base training periods also offer an opportune time to focus on furthering skill development in running. This is often accomplished by including drill sets following training session warm-up periods and preceding the bulk of the aerobic running. Such a practice will ideally improve the runner's awareness and the use of intended mechanics throughout the remainder of the training session. High volumes of relatively slower running allow this process to occur with minimum distraction.

Running skill development methods likely to be successful include the use of limited barefoot running, the implementation of a learning method such as the pose method, or the use of functional training designed to improve total-body mobility.

Conclusion

The effectiveness of using traditional, narrowly focused base training periods in running is not clearly established in the published sport science research. Considering this finding, the decision to use a base training approach should be based on individual training considerations. Base training is likely to offer the greatest benefits to triathletes who are initiating a run training process for the first time or are returning to run training following extended periods of nonrunning.

For triathletes who train and race year round, periodic base training periods can be used to decompress from the physical and psychological stress created by more intensive complex training approaches. But during the bulk of the training year, a complex approach to training emphasizing a variety of speeds and distances is more likely to stimulate improvement over time.

To minimize any potentially deleterious effects of base training periods on the broader spectrum of running abilities, triathletes should incorporate maintenance-level work for basic running speed using strides and maintain steady-state speed endurance using tempo runs.

Further, strength training should be included in base training periods with a focus on progressive strength development. Adherence to basic progression principles including the use of aerobic intensities for most training (about 80 percent or more), slow progressions in total load using the 10 percent rule, and systematic periods of restoration training using the three-to-one rule may reduce the likelihood of overuse injury or overtraining. Finally, quantification of training load offers a useful method to guide the progression as well as to identify the optimal training load for successive training cycles.

PART

VIII

Multisport
Event-Specific Training
and Racing Tactics

CHAPTER 28

Sprint

—Gale Bernhardt

When triathletes enter a triathlon, both they and their coaches should have strategy and tactics in mind before race day. Strategy is the big-picture look at the event. If a triathlete is entering the Local Excellent Olympic-Distance Triathlon as her first triathlon, her strategy for training and race day will be different from that used by a seasoned triathlete looking to score a spot on the podium. Strategy is a long-term view of triathlon, how the sport fits into lifestyle, and the overall means for achieving goals.

Training and racing tactics are more fluid and change with current circumstances such as weather, opponents, level of fitness, and performance strengths, to name a few. Tactics are a blend of art, science, and individual triathlete capability.

Exertion Levels for Training and Racing

Before discussing how fast triathletes should be training and suggesting durations of each session, the best approach is to define exertion levels or training and racing zones. Unfortunately, not all exercise experts use the same system to define exercise intensity. To further the confusion, swim coaches use a different language to define exercise intensity than triathlon, bike, and run coaches do.

Endurance sport, triathlon, and exercise experts define specific exercise zones by drawing lines along the physiological function continuum discussed in part IV. The layperson might expect that these lines would be clearly defined. They are not.

When reading more information on triathlon, swim, bike, and run training, triathletes will find that the systems contain similarities. For the purposes of this part of the book, we will define seven training and racing zones, as seen in table 28.1.

Table 28.1 Reference Scale for Perceived Exertion and Training Zones

	Zone 1	Zone 2	Zone 3	Zone 4	Zone 5a	Zone 5b	Zone 5c
Rating of perceived exertion (RPE; original Borg scale)	6 to 9	10 to 12	13 or 14	15 or 16	17	18 or 19	20
Rating of perceived exertion (RPE; new Borg scale)	1 or 2	3 or 4	4 or 5	6	7	8 or 9	10
Swim pace	Work on form, no clock watching	T-pace + 10 s per 100	T-pace + 5 s per 100	T-pace	T-pace	T-pace – 5 s per 100	As fast as possible
Percentage of lactate threshold power	55 or less	56 to 75	76 to 90	91 to 99	100 to 105	106 to 120	121 or more
Percentage of lactate threshold heart rate (bike)	80 or less	81 to 88	89 to 93	94 to 99	100 to 102	103 to 105	106 or more
Percentage of lactate threshold heart rate (run)	84 or less	85 to 91	92 to 95	96 to 99	100 to 102	103 to 106	107 or more
Breathing and perceived exertion using runners as the example	Gentle rhythmic breathing. Pace is easy and relaxed. Intensity is a jog or trot.	Breathing rate and pace increase slightly. Many notice a change with slightly deeper breathing, although still comfortable. Running pace remains comfortable and conversation possible.	Aware of breathing a little harder. Pace is moderate. Holding a conversation is more difficult.	Starting to breathe hard. Pace is fast and beginning to become uncomfortable, approaching race pace for all-out 1- to 1.5-hour run.	Breathing is deep and forceful. Many notice a second significant change in breathing pattern. Pace is all-out sustainable for 1 to 1.5 hours. Mental focus is required, pace is moderately uncomfortable, and conversation is undesirable.	Heavy, labored breathing. Pace is noticeably challenging but sustainable for 15 to 30 minutes at race effort. Discomfort is high but manageable.	Maximal exertion in breathing. Pace is sprinting effort, causing high discomfort that is unsustainable for more than 1 minute.
Purpose and cross-reference of terms commonly used to describe each zone	Easy, aerobic, recovery.	Aerobic, extensive endurance, aerobic threshold endurance (Note: Some coaches call this region lactate threshold.)	Tempo, intensive endurance. *Ironman-distance race pace for intermediate and advanced athletes is typically within zones 1 to 3.*	Subthreshold, muscular endurance, threshold endurance, anaerobic threshold endurance.	Lactate threshold endurance, anaerobic threshold endurance, superthreshold, muscular endurance. *International-distance race pace is typically in zone 4 or 5a for advanced athletes.*	Aerobic capacity, speed endurance, anaerobic endurance. *Sprint-distance race pace is typically in zones 4 to 5b. Experienced athletes may be in zone 5c for limited time.*	Anaerobic capacity, power.

Adapted, with permission, from G. Bernhardt, 2007, *Training plans for multisport athletes* (Boulder, CO: VeloPress), 22-23, and G. Bernhardt, 2009, *Training plans for cyclists* (Boulder, CO: VeloPress), 28-29.

As triathletes investigate further, they will find that the various systems used by fitness experts are quite similar. Some of the training zone terminology is cross-referenced in table 28.1. The table can serve as a starting point to examine various training intensity charts used for heart rate, power, pace, and rating of perceived exertion (RPE) training.

Notice that a running pace column is not included. Multiple online calculators are available to estimate running pace based on a number of run tests, including races. As with the training zones, all run calculators are slightly different. Triathletes can use the running perceived exertion column to cross-reference pace charts.

Using Technology to Determine Pace

The world is filled with technological devices that can give triathletes instantaneous numbers for pace, power, and heart rate. Although many people value the usefulness of these devices, triathletes should never lose the ability to be in tune with their bodies and use perceived exertion for training and racing. Many successful high-level triathletes are so in tune with their bodies that they use perceived exertion alone to determine race pace.

Although perceived exertion works well for many triathletes, some, including those racing long distances, can often benefit from using heart rate, power, pace, or some combination of those tools. Using those tools prevents triathletes from beginning a race too fast and fading, making the end of the race a survival march rather than a run.

Sprint Training

Sprint races are typically 400 to 750 meters (450 to 800 yards) of swimming, 20 to 25 kilometers (12 to 15 miles) of cycling, and 4 to 5 kilometers (2.5 to 3.1 miles) of running. Slightly shorter or longer races can be found, but this range gives an idea of typical race distances. Sprint races are the perfect distance for people to begin to develop passion for triathlon. This distance is also ideal for triathletes who have a need for speed. Racing all out as fast as they can go is exhilarating for many people.

Depending on the specific race distance and the triathlete's athletic ability, sprint-distance races typically take 1 to 1 1/2 hours to complete. Triathletes with poor fitness can begin training and be ready to race in about 12 weeks. Triathletes who have fitness from a single sport, such as running, can be ready to race in about 6 to 8 weeks.[1]

Training Strategies

The number one strategy is to optimize the triathlete's fitness given current fitness level, daily time available to train, and the number of weeks available before race day.

Triathletes at a Lower Level of Fitness

When triathletes have a low level of fitness, training needs to emphasize building endurance, improving the aerobic system, strengthening tendons and ligaments, and minimizing the risk of injury. This phase of training is often referred to as general preparation by coaches and physiologists around the world and in various sports. Triathletes do this training at intensity zone 1 or 2.

If the triathlete has a low level of fitness and less than 12 weeks until race day, most of the training should be kept at zone 1 or zone 2 intensity. For triathletes who have low fitness but many weeks before race day, training can move from zone 1 to zone 2 intensity up to zone 5c. The progression of the training load will depend on the triathlete's profile, including single-sport history, triathlon history, training time available, the person's response to a given training load, and his race goals.

Slightly Experienced Triathletes

Triathletes who have completed at least one sprint race in the previous season and are looking to improve race performance can include more volume and intensity, or speed work, in training. The weekly training times in table 28.2 can be increased to accommodate the triathlete with more fitness. With a good base of zone 1 to zone 3 endurance in the 12 to 16 weeks before race day, these triathletes can add workouts at threshold pace or zone 4 or 5a intensity.

In the 8 to 12 weeks before the race, the triathlete can begin adding threshold intensity work in one workout in each discipline. The intensity can be structured intervals, or it can be accumulated time, driven by terrain. In either case, the triathlete begins with around 15 minutes of accumulated intensity in a single workout. For example, if the triathlete's long run for the week will be 45 to 60 minutes and that workout will include threshold-paced running, she should accumulate about 15 minutes at threshold pace. A convenient way to increase intensity and work on sport-specific strength is to run the uphill portions of a hilly course at threshold intensity.

Obviously, because threshold pace on hills is not equivalent to pace on a flat course or a track, triathletes will need to use perceived exertion, heart rate, or a combination of both. If the racecourse is hilly or on trails, the triathlete should use similar terrain in workouts to be prepared physically and mentally for race-day demands.

If triathletes are estimating time accumulated at threshold, downloading device data after the run can establish whether the time accumulated was high, low, or spot-on. The data can be used to help hone pacing skills.

If the triathlete decides to keep the long run aerobic and do threshold interval work in one of the shorter runs, a 3-to-1 or 4-to-1 ratio for work to rest is appropriate.[2] For example, if the workout is 45 minutes long, the triathlete should warm up for 15 to 20 minutes. After the warm-up, he does five 3-minute efforts at threshold pace, recovering for only 1 minute at zone 1 intensity between efforts. The work-to-rest ratio doesn't have to be exactly 3-to-1 or 4-to-1. Sufficient time should remain at the end of the workout for cool-down running at zone 1.

Sample Four-Week Progression for Running and Cycling   Depending on how much time remains between the beginning of threshold training and race day, the triathlete should build accumulated time at threshold up to 20 to 30 minutes. The intervals can be manipulated to build endurance at threshold pace. For example, a 4-week progression might look like the following:

   5×3 minutes at zone 4 or 5a (1-minute recovery interval at zone 1)

   5×4 minutes at zone 4 or 5a (1-minute recovery interval at zone 1)

   4×5 minutes at zone 4 or 5a (1.5-minute recovery interval at zone 1)

   3×6 minutes at zone 4 or 5a (2-minute recovery interval at zone 1)

   3×8 minutes at zone 4 or 5a (2-minute recovery interval at zone 1)

Of course, the triathlete can include a steady 15 or 20 minutes at threshold pace. To break the work into smaller segments, triathletes can include some recovery, though incomplete, to maintain a higher average pace for the speed portion of the workout.

   For cycling, a similar strategy and structure can be used for the intervals. The triathlete begins with around 15 to 20 minutes of time accumulated at zone 4 or 5a intensity and builds accumulated time at threshold to 30 to 40 minutes.

Sample Four-Week Progression for Swimming   In the pool, the triathlete can use intensity, pace, or a combination of both. Because intermediate triathletes have endurance, it is easy to conduct a 500-meter time trial to benchmark current fitness. From the time trial, an average pace per 100 meters can be determined. For example, if the 500- meter time-trial result is 8:50, the average 100-meter pace is 1:46. The triathlete should aim to improve that pace by swimming repeats slightly faster than time-trial pace.

   A 4-week progression is shown. The triathlete must be sure to do a 10- to 15-minute warm-up set before swimming fast. In the set, "send-off" means that the triathlete pushes off the wall each time the pace clock reads that time. Recovery time is the time between the end of the swim and the next send-off. Recovery in this case will be variable.

   5×100 on a 2:15 send-off, aiming to swim all 100s faster than 1:46

   5×100 on a 2:10 send-off, aiming to swim all 100s faster than 1:46

   5×100 on a 2:05 send-off, aiming to swim all 100s faster than 1:46

   5×100 on a 2:00 send-off, aiming to swim all 100s faster than 1:46

Triathletes With Higher Levels of Fitness

For racers with higher levels of fitness, a reasonable question is whether the triathlete is already a strong runner. Should one fast workout be dedicated to running, or would it be better to maintain running speed and dedicate a second workout to improving one of the other disciplines?

Doing more than one fast workout per discipline each week is a matter of personal preference and race strategy. Triathletes looking to improve overall race performance may be better off maintaining the strong discipline and emphasizing the other two disciplines, although this strategy may not be reasonable if the triathlete is prone to injury in one of the disciplines. For example, if the triathlete is a weak runner but has a chronic injury area, such as a knee, then adding another day of speed work in running may not be a good choice.

Another pertinent question is whether intermediate triathletes can do more than three fast workouts each week. A rule of thumb is that two to four fast, or otherwise stressful, workouts per week is enough. Most intermediate sprint-distance triathletes who train 4 to 6 hours per week find that four fast sessions are enough to bring about improvement.

Quality days should be fast and recovery days easy. The body makes performance gains after stress *and* recovery.

Advanced Triathletes

The advanced sprint triathlete is looking for performance improvements. These highly fit and experienced triathletes have race data. They know personal open times (discipline done alone, not part of a triathlon) for a 500-meter swim, 12- to 15-mile bike time trial, and a 3.1-mile run. They also have triathlon race data for various sprint-distance triathlons.

Advanced triathletes keep fit year-round, doing some type of endurance sport 5 or 6 days per week. These triathletes have completed a progression of training before race day that permits training at zone 5b paces in the 4 to 6 weeks before race day. Their training progression may resemble the following:

10 to 20 weeks before race day: zone 1 to 3 intensities.

6 to 13 weeks before race day: zone 4 or 5a. Using pace or power numbers to set interval speeds is preferable.

2 to 7 weeks before race day: zone 5b intensity. Specific race-pace data should be used to determine interval speeds in training sessions.

A wide variety of workouts can be used to improve speed. Work-to-rest ratios for intervals are 1-to-1 or greater. To allow more rest, a ratio such as 1-to-2 or 1-to-3 can be used. For single-discipline workouts, paces can begin at 6 to 10 percent faster than open race paces. For brick workouts, paces can begin at 6 to 10 percent faster than triathlon paces.

Training becomes more intentional and specific. If goal races are on hilly terrain, training is conducted on hills. If race-specific hills are not available on natural terrain, hills can be done on a treadmill for running or simulated on an indoor bike trainer.

A 30- to 60-minute swim session, a 2-hour bike ride, and a 1-hour run at an aerobic pace are all considered easy and normal for the advanced triathlete.

In some cases, advanced triathletes participate in multiple races in a 6- to 8-week period. Depending on the volume of training completed, some sprint triathletes reduce training volume and keep some intensity in the plan between races. Typically, triathletes use the 2 to 3 days after a race to go easy in zones 1 and 2. If the triathlete will race the next weekend, the few workouts before race day should be used for sharpening by keeping some race-pace efforts in training. If there are 2 weeks between races, more intensity will usually be included immediately after the recovery days and on the weekend between races.

Discipline workouts are only part of the advanced triathlete's training. Training to do well at racing includes attention to diet, mental skills training, and possibly strength training.

Sample 15-Week Plan

The sample 15-week plan (table 28.2) gives a snapshot of training progression for sprint race training. Approximate training hours are given so that triathletes can see a model of varying weekly work volume and volume reductions to allow recovery. Workout types, based on intensity descriptions given in table 28.1, can help guide the workouts that triathletes decide to put into a given training week. The primary focus for the week is a reminder that training is a progression and that triathletes cannot work on every item of fitness in every workout or even within every week. Finally, other comments are given to suggest plan modifications based on fitness levels.

Table 28.2 Sample 15-Week Training Plan For Sprint Triathlon

Week	Approximate training hours	Types of workouts	Primary focus for week	Other
1	3	Aerobic, technique, neuromuscular speed.	Work on proper technique and aerobic endurance; begin to introduce short segments (30 seconds or less) of accelerating speed.	Those with low fitness remain in zones 1 and 2. Those with higher levels of fitness can include work in zone 3.
2	3.5	Aerobic, technique, neuromuscular speed.	Work on proper technique and aerobic endurance; begin to introduce short segments (30 seconds or less) of accelerating speed.	Those with low fitness remain in zones 1 and 2. Those with higher levels of fitness can include work in zone 3.
3	2	Keep workouts similar to the previous 2 weeks but reduce training volume.	Recovery.	Aerobic time trials (TT) can be included at the end of the week. Duration of each TT depends on the triathlete's current fitness. Restrict intensity to around the top of zone 2 or low zone 3 within a narrow heart rate range of roughly three to five beats for cycling and running. For swimming, use the average pace achieved for 3×100 meters with 20 seconds of recovery. Highly experienced triathletes can make the TTs all-out efforts.
4	4	Aerobic, intensive endurance, technique, neuromuscular speed.	Continue focus from the last block and build long workout endurance.	Include zone 3 in some workouts in an unstructured manner, restricting total time in zone 3 by ability. Experienced and highly fit triathletes can begin adding lactate threshold work this week.
5	4.5	Aerobic, intensive endurance, technique, neuromuscular speed.	Continue focus from the last block and build long workout endurance.	Include zone 3 in some workouts in an unstructured manner, restricting total time in zone 3 by ability. Experienced and highly fit triathletes can include threshold work this week.
6	2.5	Keep workouts similar to the previous 2 weeks but reduce training volume.	Recovery.	Consider introducing a brick (bike-to-run) workout and practicing transitions.
7	4.5	Aerobic, intensive endurance intervals, technique, neuromuscular speed.	Build longest workouts to the limit of this training block.	Long swim workout roughly twice that of race distance. Long run builds to between 45 and 60 minutes. Long ride builds to 90 minutes.

Week	Approximate training hours	Types of workouts	Primary focus for week	Other
8	5	Aerobic, intensive endurance intervals, technique, neuromuscular speed.	Build longest workouts to the limit of this training block.	Long swim workout roughly twice that of race distance. Long run builds to between 45 and 60 minutes. Long ride builds to 90 minutes.
9	3	Keep workouts similar to the previous 2 weeks but reduce training volume.	Recovery.	Repeat the aerobic TT to measure progress.
10	5	Aerobic, threshold endurance intervals, technique, neuromuscular speed, unstructured and limited speed endurance.	Work on lactate threshold speed with the interval work. Include some limited time above threshold (zones 5b and 5c) within select workouts.	At this point in the training, it is tempting to make every workout fast, pushing the limits. Refrain from doing this. Most triathletes respond well to two to four challenging or key workouts per week. The remaining workouts should be aerobic, recovery, or technique focused.
11	5	Aerobic, threshold endurance intervals, technique, neuromuscular speed, unstructured and limited speed endurance.	Work on lactate threshold speed with the interval work. Include some time above threshold (zones 5b and 5c) within select workouts, limiting this time.	
12	3	Keep workouts similar to the previous 2 weeks but reduce training volume.	Recovery.	Consider doing a shortened distance race rehearsal workout this week.
13	4.5	Aerobic, race pace, technique, neuromuscular speed.	Intervals or long workouts should include race-pace work.	If brick workouts have not be done yet, include at least one this week.
14	4	Aerobic, race pace, technique, neuromuscular speed.	Intervals or long workouts should include race-pace work.	Final race rehearsal this week.
15	1.5 + race	Keep workouts similar to the previous 2 weeks but reduce training volume.	Include intensity segments at race pace or slightly faster.	An expected range of race paces can be plotted based on previous workout paces.

Racing Tactics

The tactics a triathlete should use for race day are directly related to that triathlete's fitness level and experience in the sport of triathlon. Triathletes doing their first race who have low levels of fitness should focus on comfortable completion of the event. Triathletes with high levels of fitness who are gunning for a personal best performance, and perhaps a podium spot, will use different tactics than the new racer.

Warm-Up

Beginner triathletes who have built just enough fitness to complete the event do not need to do an extensive warm-up. Most of the time, these triathletes will not warm up before the race. They will warm up during the swim, moving from relaxed zone 1 intensity to the highest swimming intensity they used during training. Most of the time this means beginning the swim in zone 1 and finishing it at zone 2 or zone 3 speed. The bike and run portions of the race will likely begin at zone 2 intensity and move to the highest intensity used during training.

Triathletes with some fitness and race experience may decide against a warm-up. The main difference between these triathletes and the beginners is that the race intensity tends to be higher during the last half of each event and for the overall race. Some of these experienced triathletes will prefer a very short warm-up of 5 to 10 minutes of easy bike spinning to check the gears, followed by a run of 2 to 5 minutes. These athletes may or may not include a short 100-meter warm-up swim.

Because the advanced triathlete's race is fast from the start, a prerace warm-up routine is necessary. These athletes may ride the bike for 20 to 30 minutes before the start on race day. They will likely also do a run of 10 to 15 minutes. In both the bike and run warm-ups, a few race-pace efforts should be included. These efforts are typically 60 seconds or less in length and include generous recovery times of at least 2 to 3 minutes.

A swim warm-up is also part of the race-day routine. Swimming 300 to 500 meters is not uncommon. A few 25-meter segments at race pace should be included in the warm-up. If swimming is not an option for warm-up, swim cords can be used.

Pacing

A negative-split tactic is the best way to enjoy a successful sprint event for newer triathletes. Plan to begin the race at a pace that seems too easy. Triathletes should plan to finish the race at the fastest pace practiced in training or slightly faster.

Experienced triathletes' race-day speeds should be similar to the speeds used in training. Because the experienced triathlete had some 4 to 8 weeks that included threshold work, a good portion of the race can be done at threshold intensity. Triathletes still green at racing should aim for a negative-split pace in each discipline. They should begin each discipline in zone 1 or 2 and push to zones 3 to 5a at the halfway point.

As soon as the gun goes off, faster triathletes are hitting zone 4 to 5a pace. Advanced triathletes use discretionary zone 5b and perhaps zone 5c. These anaerobic efforts are used tactically to advance overall race placement. In the swim these efforts are used to drop drafting competitors or bridge a gap to the feet of a competitor for purposes of drafting.

A negative-split strategy may be used by beginning the first half of each discipline at zone 4 and performing the second half of each discipline at zone 5b pace as much as possible. Although the triathlete may have a prerace strategy to perform a negative-split race, the competition may demand the use of higher race paces at times not favored by the triathlete. The best triathletes will be ready and willing to wield fitness at any time, regardless of time or location within the event.

In the most hotly contested races, triathletes must be ready for a final kick sprint to the finish line. The most competitive athletes, with the best competition, will need to train for this final kick.

Transitions

In sprint-distance racing, fast transitions are more important than they are at longer distances. Races can be easily won or lost in the transitions. When exiting the swim, running to the first transition (T1) is necessary. If the run to T1 is long or hilly, this element needs to be included in training.

Transition setup before the race has cycling shoes attached to the pedals. The shoes and pedals are held parallel to the ground by attaching lightweight rubber bands to the shoes and securing the shoes to the frame. This setup keeps shoes from wildly rotating while athletes run out of transition. Rotating shoes can catch on the ground, jamming and causing the shoe to release from the pedal. Obviously, stopping to retrieve a lost shoe is a time waster.

The fastest triathletes use a flying mount, similar to those used in cyclocross, to jump onto the bike and begin pedaling with their feet on top of the shoes. The light rubber bands break away. The feet can then be slipped into the shoes when the triathlete has settled into a comfortable pace.

Notice that socks are not mentioned. Fast transitions for short races do not allow the use of socks. This topic will be further discussed in chapter 33.

As in T1, the fastest triathletes perform a flying dismount before reaching the dismount line for the second transition (T2). To be ready to dismount, triathletes remove their feet from the cycling shoes and pedal with their feet on top of the shoes for the last 100 to 200 meters.

At the dismount line, these triathletes hit the pavement running. Slipping into running shoes sans socks, they head out on the run course. The fastest and most fit triathletes are capable of running the entire 5K in zones 5a and

5b. Those with less fitness are better off beginning the run in zone 3 or 4 and doing a negative-split effort by doing the last half of the run in zone 5b.

Weather and Altitude

In a perfect world, the weather on race day would be not too hot, not too cold, but just right. But because our world isn't perfect, triathletes need to be prepared for weather extremes. Although race directors often cancel or modify a race if weather is extreme, the decision of whether or not to race remains with the individual triathlete.

If a triathlete expects to race in hot and humid conditions on race day, doing some acclimatization is wise. A rule of thumb is that 10 to 14 days are needed to acclimatize to hot conditions. If triathletes can conduct training in a hot environment, doing an aerobic workout in the heat is wiser than doing a track workout. In all cases, triathletes should expect pace to decrease in any hot conditions, even after acclimatization.

If a triathlete lives in a cool location but is preparing for a hot race, wearing extra clothing for workouts to stimulate sweating is a proven tactic. But triathletes should not wear rubber sweat suits or other clothing that is not breathable.

Early spring and late fall races may be downright cold. Sipping on a hot beverage from a thermos before the swim can help triathletes keep warm at the start line and through a sprint race. If a triathlete gets cold easily, slipping on a jacket for the bike ride is worth the extra time.

If the triathlete is racing at altitude but lives at sea level, arriving at altitude 45 hours or more before the race will help performance in endurance events, according to at least one researcher.[3]

Conclusion

Although a relatively new triathlete and a highly experienced triathlete differ in many ways, the primary differences are whether the focus is on improving technique or speed, how much overall training volume is done, and how much of the volume is performed at higher intensities.

The best triathletes customize their training plans to fit their particular needs. New triathletes are at risk of injury or illness if they use a training plan built for highly experienced triathletes. Highly experienced triathletes who use a training plan that does not challenge them physically or mentally will not improve. The recommended approach is to determine individual needs and then plan accordingly.

CHAPTER 29

Olympic

—Gale Bernhardt

The Olympic- or international-distance triathlon standard is a 1.5-kilometer swim, a 40-kilometer bike ride, and a 10-kilometer run. The distances might be familiar to some single-sport triathletes. The 1,500-meter swim is a classic long-distance swim event. In cycling, performance in a 40K time trial is measured and compared by triathletes around the world. Of course, 10K events on and off the track are popular for runners. All three events are individual sports in the Olympics, so the name "Olympic" came to be used for this distance.

The sport of triathlon made its debut as an Olympic sport at the 2000 Games in Sydney, Australia. Professional triathletes representing their countries' colors race at venues around the globe, competing for valuable ranking points. Those points make them eligible for a spot on the starting line of the Olympic Games. Currently, the number of competitors is limited to 55 males and 55 females, and no country may have more than 3 triathletes on the starting line.

Although most age-group or nonprofessional triathletes race in a non-drafting format, the pros race in a draft-legal format, meaning that they can ride close to other riders on the bicycle leg, using the aerodynamic benefit of the group to their advantage. Race venues tend to be spectator-friendly multilap courses. Triathletes must be strong swimmers to make it into the early or bigger cycling packs. Triathletes in the first pack usually attempt to stay away from the main pack during the race, while those in chase packs aim to catch up. Whether triathletes are in the lead pack or the chase pack, they need to meter their work efforts so that they can perform a strong run after the bike ride.

Obviously, the training and racing tactics for a draft-legal format are different from those for a nondrafting event. This chapter focuses on training and race tactics for nondrafting events.

Race results of Olympic-distance events show that faster racers on flat courses turn in total finish times near the 2-hour mark. Other racers on the same course may be turning in finish times near the 5-hour mark. Because of the longer course, the spread in finish times is greater than it is in sprint-distance races.

Exertion Levels for Training and Racing

As the race distance increases, relative individual race speed decreases. The fastest average pace that any individual triathlete can sustain for an Olympic-distance event will be faster than the pace that he can achieve for a half-Ironman race yet slower than the pace that he will perform for a sprint-distance race.

Triathletes unfamiliar with training and racing intensities can review the information in table 29.1.

Olympic Training

The primary concern of most triathletes is comfortable completion of the event. They want to build enough endurance so that they can keep moving for 3 1/2 to 4 1/2 hours. For example, if the triathlete can swim at a pace of 2 minutes and 45 seconds per 100 meters, swim time will be 41 minutes. If she can ride 24.8 miles (39.9 km) at 15 miles per hour (24.1 km/h), her bike time will be about 1:40. By finishing the event at a 12-minute-per-mile (7:27/km) pace in the run, she will have a run split time of 1:15. Adding the individual sport times and including some transition time, her total race time will be 3:45 to 4:00.[1]

Enhancing Training

Serious Olympic-distance racers should have a base level of zone 1 to 3 (see table 29.1) fitness in swimming, cycling, and running 12 to 20 weeks before race day. The main difference between the sprint and the Olympic triathlete is volume of training time. The Olympic triathlete has more time available to train and recover from training than the sprint triathlete does.

Notice the point about recovery. To get faster, triathletes need to include more intensity in training and stay healthy. To do this, they need adequate recovery time. Some triathletes do well by increasing training time, intensity, or both for 3 or 4 weeks in a row before they take a recovery week. Recovery weeks typically include a 20 to 50 percent reduction in training volume but maintain some intensity in several workouts.[2]

Other triathletes see better progress when they build volume, intensity, or some combination of both over 2 weeks and then take a recovery week. The person who does the most training or the most intensity isn't the winner.

For swimming, the Olympic-distance triathlete aims to improve 1,500-meter pace or reduce the energy required to swim 1,500 meters. If he doesn't already know his pace for a 1,500-meter swim, a broken 900 meters is a good

Table 29.1 Reference Scale for Rating of Perceived Exertion and Training Zones

	Zone 1	Zone 2	Zone 3	Zone 4	Zone 5a	Zone 5b	Zone 5c
Rating of perceived exertion (RPE; original Borg scale)	6 to 9	10 to 12	13 or 14	15 or 16	17	18 or 19	20
Rating of perceived exertion (RPE; new Borg scale)	1 or 2	3 or 4	4 or 5	6	7	8 or 9	10
Swim pace	Work on form, no clock watching	T-pace + 10 s per 100	T-pace + 5 s per 100	T-pace	T-pace	T-pace − 5 s per 100	As fast as possible
Percentage of lactate threshold power	55 or less	56 to 75	76 to 90	91 to 99	100 to 105	106 to 120	121 or more
Percentage of lactate threshold heart rate (bike)	80 or less	81 to 88	89 to 93	94 to 99	100 to 102	103 to 105	106 or more
Percentage of lactate threshold heart rate (run)	84 or less	85 to 91	92 to 95	96 to 99	100 to 102	103 to 106	107 or more
Breathing and perceived exertion using runners as the example	Gentle rhythmic breathing. Pace is easy and relaxed. Intensity is a jog or trot.	Breathing rate and pace increase slightly. Many notice a change with slightly deeper breathing, although still comfortable. Running pace remains comfortable and conversation possible.	Aware of breathing a little harder. Pace is moderate. Holding a conversation is more difficult.	Starting to breathe hard. Pace is fast and beginning to become uncomfortable, approaching race pace for all-out 1- to 1.5-hour run.	Breathing is deep and forceful. Many notice a second significant change in breathing pattern. Pace is all-out sustainable for 1 to 1.5 hours. Mental focus is required, pace is moderately uncomfortable, and conversation is undesirable.	Heavy, labored breathing. Pace is noticeably challenging but sustainable for 15 to 30 minutes at race effort. Discomfort is high but manageable.	Maximal exertion in breathing. Pace is sprinting effort, causing high discomfort that is unsustainable for more than 1 minute.
Purpose and cross-reference of terms commonly used to describe each zone	Easy, aerobic, recovery.	Aerobic, extensive endurance, aerobic threshold endurance (Note: Some coaches call this region lactate threshold.)	Tempo, intensive endurance. *Ironman-distance race pace for intermediate and advanced athletes is typically within zones 1 to 3.*	Subthreshold, muscular endurance, threshold endurance, anaerobic threshold endurance.	Lactate threshold endurance, anaerobic threshold endurance, superthreshold, muscular endurance. *International-distance race pace is typically in zone 4 or 5a for advanced athletes.*	Aerobic capacity, speed endurance, anaerobic endurance. *Sprint-distance race pace is typically in zones 4 to 5b. Experienced athletes may be in zone 5c for limited time.*	Anaerobic capacity, power.

Adapted, with permission, from G. Bernhardt, 2007, *Training plans for multisport athletes* (Boulder, CO: VeloPress), 22-23, and G. Bernhardt, 2009, *Training plans for cyclists* (Boulder, CO: VeloPress), 28-29.

place to start. To do this, the triathlete swims 3 × 300 meters fast, recovering for 30 seconds after each swim. He watches the clock and gets a time for each 300 meters, aiming to have a difference of less than 15 seconds among the efforts. The average time for the three swims is the average 300-meter pace. That number divided by three determines the threshold pace (T-pace) per 100 meters.[3]

To work on endurance for the 1,500 meters, the triathlete should swim broken sets of 1,000 to 1,500 meters using T-pace and keeping recovery between swims at a minimum. For example, he can swim 10 to 12 × 100 meters on a send-off of T-pace plus 10 seconds. He should aim to swim the first half of the set at T-pace and the last half of the set at T-pace minus about 2 seconds.

For cycling and running, the sprint triathlete can include zone 4 to zone 5a intervals in training that total 20 to 30 minutes (table 29.1). Olympic triathletes can build this threshold training intensity to total 40 to 60 minutes in both cycling and running. The amount of time accumulated depends on the individual triathlete, recovery, and time limitations.

Most Olympic-distance triathletes do not have access to power meters. Bike training will have to be done using heart rate and perceived exertion. Running, however, is a different story. Nearly everyone has access to a track. Triathletes can use running pace from a recent 10K event to design intervals based on pace and distance, rather than heart rate and interval duration.

Unless doing a bike-to-run workout, a brick, the triathlete should use an open 10K running pace for run workouts. For a brick workout, the pace should be based on running performance in a race. Triathlon 10K paces are often 10 to 20 seconds per mile (6 to 12 seconds per kilometer) slower than open or standalone 10K runs.

If the goal race or races include hills, the triathlete should complete some of the threshold training with hill repeats or by riding a hilly course. The triathlete who lives in a flat area can simulate hills by riding into a stiff headwind, using a tougher gear than normal, or doing some combination of both.

Triathletes can consider doing some training on the racecourse if access is available.

Approach of Advanced Triathletes

The advanced triathlete is experienced and looking to maximize performance. In most cases, she is aiming for a podium spot or, at minimum, improving her placement in the overall field of racers. Competing at races that include a high-quality field is desirable.

Advanced racers may be looking for a position on their country's team to travel to the International Triathlon Union (ITU) World Championships. Each country has a slightly different qualification process. To find the process for their country, triathletes can visit the website of their national federation. A list of the world federations can be found on the ITU website.[4]

Whether they are looking to compete on the world stage or not, advanced triathletes are interested in performance, specifically, triathlon performance. They are competing 24 weeks a year or more. They may participate in other sports such as cyclo-cross or Nordic skiing or compete in swimming, cycling, or running single-sport events, but these activities are intended only to complement the triathlon season. These triathletes are serious about the sport of triathlon.

Racing at top age-group levels outside of local, small-town events requires three to four workout sessions per discipline per week. On some days, therefore, triathletes will do two workout sessions per day.

Optimizing personal performance in the sport requires analyzing triathlon performance in comparison with the competition. Triathletes should look at results and note where they fall in relation to others:

- **Where does swim time rank**? Is the triathlete the slowest or the fastest swimmer in the group? By how much time? Seconds or several minutes? Does rank change depending on the course (pool, lake, or ocean swim)?

- **Where does bike time rank**? Do the same evaluation for cycling. Is the triathlete at the top of the category or at the bottom? Does rank change if the course is flat, hilly, hot, cold, or windy?

- **Where does run time rank**? Evaluate the run rank in the same way.

- **Does the triathlete's head get in the way**? Does the triathlete become excessively nervous at races? Do negative thoughts creep into his mind? Can he visualize great performances?

- **Does the triathlete have nutrition problems on race day**? Does he run low on energy? Does he sweat excessively? Does his gastrointestinal tract cause problems?

The receding list, although not comprehensive, covers the major categories. When coaches and triathletes are looking to optimize performance, they need to look at all the variables that influence race-day outcomes. Identifying opportunities for improvement allows the coach and triathlete to prioritize training strategy.

A triathlete who is equal to the competition in cycling and running but loses time in swimming obviously needs to improve the swim. If the swim and run are in the top 10 percent of the category but bike time is in the lower 50 percent, cycling performance needs to be improved.

Depending on the individual needs for the triathlete's performance improvement, a variety of strategies can be used:

- **Single-sport focus**. The triathlete might consider spending the 4 to 6 months before the triathlon season training primarily on the discipline that is holding her back. If that is the swim, she could consider swimming 5 days per week, adding a stroke coach, swimming with a masters group, doing some swim competitions, or doing some combination of those options. If cycling is holding the triathlete back, she could consider riding with a fast group, doing some bike racing or mountain biking, or using a power meter to train. Or, if her running performance is inadequate, she could train for several 5K and 10K events. In all cases, the other two disciplines take a back seat to the developing discipline workouts.

• **Conduct select workouts at much higher intensities than race effort**. Although most of the race is spent at lactate threshold effort, the triathlete can do some training at intensities well above threshold and for extended periods. This goal can be accomplished with structured intervals or by including single-sport races in training. Certainly, well-placed group workouts can be advantageous, if used wisely.

• **Optimize recovery**. A triathlete who is running ragged because of life commitments may need more recovery than usual. For some triathletes, a 7-day reduced-volume recovery cycle is perfect. Other triathletes do well with only 5 days. Still others need 10 days. Optimizing individual performance means optimizing everything, including recovery.

• **Track and analyze training data**. Is the current training program producing the desired results? How can a coach or triathlete know? What mix of volume and intensity improves performance? What mix drives the triathlete to illness or injury? How long after a specific workout block should a triathlete evaluate training success? Today's workout does not mean instant performance improvement tomorrow or the next day.

Success takes time and seldom occurs by accident.

Sample 12-Week Plan

The 12-week plan shown in table 29.2 gives triathletes an idea of the overall progression of training. New triathletes can be ready to race within 12 weeks, but they will not be capable of racing at their personal potential. More than 12 weeks are needed to build the depth of fitness necessary to race at an advanced level.

Advanced triathletes who have years of endurance fitness built and multiple Olympic races on their race resumes will use the final 12 weeks before the race to push the envelope of threshold speed, looking for small improvements.

Racing Tactics

Race-day tactics will vary depending on the individual triathlete's fitness and previous race experience. New triathletes with limited fitness should aim to remain aerobic during most of the race. Advanced triathletes will push lactate threshold pace and sometimes exceed lactate threshold intensity during the event.

Table 29.2 Sample 12-Week Training Plan for Olympic Triathlon

Week	Approximate training hours	Types of workouts	Primary focus for week	Other
1	3 to 7	Aerobic, technique, neuromuscular speed.	Work on proper technique. Those with limited endurance should build aerobic endurance. Advanced triathletes should build zone 3 endurance. Introduce short segments (30 seconds or less) of accelerating speed.	Those with low fitness should remain in zones 1 and 2. Those with higher levels of fitness can include zone 3 in long workouts and perhaps some zone 3 intervals. Strength training once or twice per week is optional.
2	4 to 7	Same as week 1.	Same as week 1.	Those with low fitness should aim for a long ride (about 1 hour) and a long run (30 to 45 minutes). Those with higher fitness can aim for long rides (2 to 3 hours) and long runs (45 to 60 minutes).
3	4 to 8	Same as week 1.	Same as week 1.	Same as week 2.
4	2 to 5	Keep workouts similar to the previous 2 weeks but reduce training volume.	Recovery.	Bricks or time trials (TT) can be included at the end of the week. Duration of each TT depends on the triathlete's current fitness.
5 to 7	4 to 10	Aerobic, intensive endurance (for less fit triathletes), threshold endurance (for advanced triathletes), technique, neuromuscular speed.	Those with low fitness should continue to build long workouts, aiming for long rides to about 2 hours and long runs to about 60 minutes. For advanced triathletes, long rides are 3 hours and long runs are 60 to 75 minutes.	Triathletes with limited fitness should build endurance and intensive endurance. Advanced triathletes are at or near peak endurance and can focus on building speed and endurance at threshold.
8	2 to 5	Keep workouts similar to the previous 2 weeks but reduce training volume.	Recovery.	Bricks or TTs can be included at the end of the week. Duration of each TT depends on the triathlete's current fitness.
9 and 10	4 to 8	Aerobic maintenance, intensive endurance (for less fit triathletes), threshold endurance (for advanced triathletes), technique, neuromuscular speed.	Triathletes with low fitness should continue to build long rides to approximately 3 hours and long runs to 60 to 75 minutes. Advanced triathletes should focus on workouts that challenge threshold speed, and some may include limited aerobic capacity intervals.	The last high-volume training week is week 10.
11	4 to 6	Aerobic maintenance, intensive endurance (for less fit triathletes), threshold endurance (for advanced triathletes), technique, neuromuscular speed.	All triathletes should reduce training volume while keeping relative intensity in some workouts.	Training volume this week is less than week 10 to allow recovery heading into race day.
12	2 or 3 plus race	Recovery, threshold endurance intervals, technique, neuromuscular speed endurance.	Training volume decreases to create a rested state on race day. Limited intensity remains in the plan.	Triathletes should aim to race at intensities that they have practiced in training.

Pacing

Pacing strategy begins with the starting line of the swim. If the race is in open water and the start is a mass start (not organized in starting waves based on seed times), triathletes need to line up in a location that suits their swimming ability. Strong swimmers are in the front and closest to the buoy line. Slower swimmers who are more timid in open water should be at the back of the group and on the outside, away from the buoy line. Strong open-water swimmers will swim fast and aggressively along the shortest line. Although body contact is usually not intentional, those at the front should expect to have body contact from other swimmers. All competitors need to recognize that appropriate self-seeding makes the event more enjoyable for everyone.

For each discipline, triathletes should race at efforts similar to the paces held in training.

After completing the swim, intermediate-level triathletes should run at a mostly aerobic pace to their bikes. Depending on their depth of fitness and race experience, these triathletes should ride the first half of the bike course at mostly zone 1 to 2 or zone 2 to 3 intensity. At the halfway point, they can increase speed to include zone 3 to 5a, holding the higher intensity until a mile or so before transition. Heading into transition, they should decrease the force on the pedals and keep cadence high.

After a fast transition, intermediate triathletes should run the 10K at efforts similar to those used in the bike ride and similar to paces used in training.

Serious triathletes' race effort quickly goes to zone 3 or higher and is seldom below zone 3 for the entire event. Much of the time in each discipline is spent at lactate threshold; triathletes call this redlining the entire race. They will perform at anaerobic intensity at times to crest a hill, shake a competitor, or keep a competitor in sight.

All triathletes should begin the run at a slower pace and plan to finish at a faster pace. They need to avoid getting caught up in the frenzy of the transition area and starting the run at an unreasonably fast pace. The tactic of starting out slower often leads to a negative split, meaning that the second half of the run is faster than the first. Negative splits have proved to produce faster run performances in both elite[5] and highly trained triathletes.[6] A good place to start is to run the first kilometer at a pace roughly 5 percent slower than open 10K pace.

Triathletes who are aiming to be on the podium or finally slip past the rival who has gone faster in previous races must be willing to pay the uncomfortable price of high speed. Mental toughness and the ability to tolerate the discomfort of high paces are essential to success at high levels in sport, including this one.

Weather

As race distances get longer, weather plays a more prominent role in performance. When preparing for the event, triathletes should research weather patterns for the time of the year of the race. Early spring and late fall races can be cold. Sipping on a hot beverage from a carafe before the swim can help triathletes keep warm at the starting line. If a triathlete gets cold easily, slipping on a jacket for the bike ride is worth the extra time.

Midsummer events may include heat and humidity that can slow race pace significantly. The body uses a great deal of energy to cool down, particularly when triathletes attempt to produce high paces in hot, humid conditions. The thermal stress takes a toll, and triathletes are forced to slow down.

If a triathlete expects to compete in hot and humid conditions on race day, doing some acclimatization is wise. A rule of thumb is that 10 to 14 days are needed to acclimatize to hot conditions. If triathletes can conduct training in a hot environment, doing aerobic workouts is wiser than doing track workouts. In all cases, they should expect pace to decrease in any hot conditions, even after acclimatization.

If a triathlete lives in a cool location but is preparing for a hot race, wearing extra clothing for workouts to stimulate sweating is a proven tactic. But wearing rubber sweat suits or other clothing that is not breathable is not advised.

Altitude

If the triathlete is racing at altitude but lives at sea level, arriving at altitude 45 hours or more before the race will help performance in endurance events, according to at least one researcher.[7]

Conclusion

As race distance increases, the need for endurance conditioning increases. The first step is to perform long workouts and train consistently. As triathletes gain fitness and race experience, training volume can be held relatively constant. More advanced racers can emphasize muscular endurance, lactate threshold endurance, and even aerobic capacity.

As triathletes move to faster racing, the commitment to the sport of triathlon increases and so does the level of tactical training. Successful racing at the top levels is a direct result of carefully planned training.

CHAPTER 30

Half-Ironman

—Gale Bernhardt

Half-Ironman-distance events are typically composed of a 1.2-mile (1.9 km) swim, a 56-mile (90.1 km) bike ride, and a 13.1-mile (21.1 km) run. Added together, the distances of the individual disciplines come to 70.3 miles (113.1 km).

Covered more in depth in chapter 31, the World Triathlon Corporation (WTC) owns the Ironman brand and trademark. Any race director may host a half-Ironman-distance event. The races that carry the "Ironman 70.3" title are WTC-owned and branded half-Ironman-distance events.

Depending on the racecourse and race-day conditions, professional men may race a half-Ironman event in less than 4 hours and professional women may finish in less than 4 1/2 hours. Top age-group triathletes often come in under the 5-hour mark.

If courses become more difficult because of terrain or weather, race times become slower. A sampling of average race times for 35 races around the world yields a range from 5:09 to 6:33.[1]

A difference of 1 1/2 hours in average finish time is a big spread. When estimating race-day finish times in each discipline, the estimate should be based on current, proven athletic ability, not wished-for athletic ability.

Exertion Levels for Training and Racing

Experienced racers know that as the race distance increases, the pace in each discipline decreases. Triathletes unfamiliar with training and racing intensities can review table 30.1.

Half-Ironman Training

Having successfully raced one or two half-Ironman events, the intermediate triathlete is looking to improve time or placement in the field. If the triathlete races the same event from one year to the next, determining whether training has indeed had a positive effect on race results is easy. If the triathlete decides

Table 30.1 Reference Scale for Rating of Perceived Exertion and Training Zones

	Zone 1	Zone 2	Zone 3	Zone 4	Zone 5a	Zone 5b	Zone 5c
Rating of perceived exertion (RPE; original Borg scale)	6 to 9	10 to 12	13 or 14	15 or 16	17	18 or 19	20
Rating of perceived exertion (RPE; new Borg scale)	1 or 2	3 or 4	4 or 5	6	7	8 or 9	10
Swim pace	Work on form, no clock watching	T-pace + 10 s per 100	T-pace + 5 s per 100	T-pace	T-pace	T-pace – 5 s per 100	As fast as possible
Percentage of lactate threshold power	55 or less	56 to 75	76 to 90	91 to 99	100 to 105	106 to 120	121 or more
Percentage of lactate threshold heart rate (bike)	80 or less	81 to 88	89 to 93	94 to 99	100 to 102	103 to 105	106 or more
Percentage of lactate threshold heart rate (run)	84 or less	85 to 91	92 to 95	96 to 99	100 to 102	103 to 106	107 or more
Breathing and perceived exertion using runners as the example	Gentle rhythmic breathing. Pace is easy and relaxed. Intensity is a jog or trot.	Breathing rate and pace increase slightly. Many notice a change with slightly deeper breathing, although still comfortable. Running pace remains comfortable and conversation possible.	Aware of breathing a little harder. Pace is moderate. Holding a conversation is more difficult.	Starting to breathe hard. Pace is fast and beginning to become uncomfortable, approaching race pace for all-out 1- to 1.5-hour run.	Breathing is deep and forceful. Many notice a second significant change in breathing pattern. Pace is all-out sustainable for 1 to 1.5 hours. Mental focus is required, pace is moderately uncomfortable, and conversation is undesirable.	Heavy, labored breathing. Pace is noticeably challenging but sustainable for 15 to 30 minutes at race effort. Discomfort is high but manageable.	Maximal exertion in breathing. Pace is sprinting effort, causing high discomfort that is unsustainable for more than 1 minute.
Purpose and cross-reference of terms commonly used to describe each zone	Easy, aerobic, recovery.	Aerobic, extensive endurance, aerobic threshold endurance (Note: Some coaches call this region lactate threshold.)	Tempo, intensive endurance. *Ironman-distance race pace for intermediate and advanced athletes is typically within zones 1 to 3.*	Subthreshold, muscular endurance, threshold endurance, anaerobic threshold endurance.	Lactate threshold endurance, anaerobic threshold endurance, superthreshold, muscular endurance. *International-distance race pace is typically in zone 4 or 5a for advanced athletes.*	Aerobic capacity, speed endurance, anaerobic endurance. *Sprint-distance race pace is typically in zones 4 to 5b. Experienced athletes may be in zone 5c for limited time.*	Anaerobic capacity, power.

Adapted, with permission, from G. Bernhardt, 2007, *Training plans for multisport athletes* (Boulder, CO: VeloPress), 22-23, and G. Bernhardt, 2009, *Training plans for cyclists* (Boulder, CO: VeloPress), 28-29.

to race a different event, a measure of success is improved placement within category or percentage of field.

For example, if the triathlete placed in the bottom third of his category in his first half-Ironman race and later placed at the 50 percent mark or higher, his performance improved. Because of course difficulty, as mentioned previously, time at the second event might be slower than time at the first event.

Although new half-Ironman triathletes are completing some 50 to 100 percent of predicted race time within a 2-day training block, the intermediate triathlete is completing 90 to 110 percent of predicted race time in a 2-day block.

Training Plan for Intermediate Triathletes

The intermediate triathlete's biggest training week might look something like this:

Monday: Strength training or swim or bike for 60 minutes

Tuesday: Swim 60 minutes, run 45 minutes

Wednesday: Bike 60 to 90 minutes

Thursday: Swim 45 to 60 minutes, run 45 minutes

Friday: Day off or run 30 minutes

Saturday: Swim 45 to 60 minutes, bike 4 hours

Sunday: Run 90 to 120 minutes

Total training time: 11 1/2 to 13 1/2 hours

For the intermediate triathlete, both weekly volume and weekly intensity increase. Depending on individual ability and race limiters, the intermediate triathlete should begin by scheduling around 20 percent of the weekly training volume at zone 3 intensity (see table 30.1). For example, if the beginner triathlete trained 10 hours, 2 hours of that training time would be at zone 3 intensity. The 13 hours of intermediate triathlete training would have around 2 hours and 40 minutes of zone 3 intensity at the 20 percent load.

A second strategy for the intermediate triathlete is to keep weekly training hours lower but include more intensity. Although some triathletes might be able to handle 30 percent of weekly training volume at zone 3, others risk illness or injury. Constantly monitoring training load and triathlete response is critical to success. The aim should not be to include the most intensity; rather, the goal should be to include the least amount of volume and intensity possible to bring about continuous improvement.

Approach of Advanced Triathletes

Advanced triathletes have successfully completed a minimum of two half-Ironman races, and their preparation for a key race consumes a minimum of 6 months. These triathletes may complete multiple half-Ironman events in a single season of racing.

Goals for advanced triathletes vary. Some may be seeking to stand on the podium or qualify for a championship race. Others are looking to optimize personal performance, not necessarily to win any awards. Whatever their specific goals, most advanced triathletes are data driven.

These triathletes review personal race performances from past triathlons. Swim, bike, and run paces are collected for baseline performances. Transition times are reviewed from each event and compared with the best performances in the race. The goal of training is to improve race performance from baseline numbers.

The triathlete who is looking for a podium performance or championship qualification is more likely to select specific race venues and travel to events. For example, ocean swims or non-wetsuit swims favor strong swimmers. Hilly bike courses favor strong cyclists and discourage drafting. Some triathletes may prefer a hilly ride followed by a flat run, whereas others excel if both the bike and run courses are hilly.

Advanced triathletes use course selection in training. They review course profiles and replicate sections of the course in training.

Lactate Threshold Training

One training strategy is to do a lactate threshold training block, keeping training volume relatively low, before beginning to build event-specific endurance. If event-specific endurance begins building 12 to 15 weeks before race day, the lactate threshold training block is implemented 18 to 23 weeks before race day. The goal is to raise lactate threshold pace and power to give the triathlete a bigger aerobic engine.

The lactate threshold training block may include Olympic-distance races. When the triathlete is within the 12 to 15 weeks of race day, she may include Olympic-distance races at the end of a reduced-volume training week. These relatively shorter races help maintain speed.

Compared with the intermediate racer, the advanced racer devotes more time to triathlon training. These triathletes also have the capability to include more intensity in training. More intensity comes in the form of doing both a higher percentage of training load at higher intensities and more training at intensities above zone 3.

Training Plan for Advanced Triathletes

The golden question is, "What is the optimal percentage of intensity?" To date, no research has quantified the optimal load for triathletes. A study by Seiler and Espen examined the training load of elite cyclists and runners and concluded that roughly an 80:20 ratio of low- to high-intensity training yielded excellent long-term results in triathletes who train daily.[2]

Analysis becomes more difficult when a triathlete is training in three disciplines. A reasonable approach is to begin with an intensity load near the 20 percent mark and make adjustments from there.

If an intermediate triathlete's biggest training week is 11 to 13 hours, the advanced triathlete's load will be slightly more. An advanced triathlete's training week might be the following:[3]

Monday: Strength training or swim or bike for 60 minutes

Tuesday: Swim 60 minutes, run 60 minutes

Wednesday: Bike 75 to 90 minutes

Thursday: Swim 60 minutes, run 30 to 45 minutes

Friday: Bike 75 minutes

Saturday: Swim 60 to 90 minutes, run 2 hours

Sunday: Bike 5 hours

Total training time: 15 to 16 hours

If both intermediate and advanced triathletes are doing an intensity load of 20 percent of training volume, the advanced triathlete is doing more training hours at higher intensity simply because the overall load is larger.

The process is not quite as simple as assigning a 20 percent intensity load to each discipline. The triathlete must analyze strengths and performance limiters to decide how best to apply an intensity load.

Among elite swimmers, cyclists, and runners, cyclists and swimmers accumulate more weekly training volume than runners do. Although swimmers commonly perform two 2-hour sessions per day and cyclists regularly complete 5-hour training rides, neither of these training loads (hours of training sessions) typically happens in running. Running poses more injury risk from loads of high volume and high intensity.

The challenge is to find the appropriate blend of volume, frequency, intensity, and the other training parameters. Only after considering the triathlete's discipline history, injury history, and race goals can the optimal volume and intensity load, per discipline, be planned.

Sample 12-Week plan

The 12-week training plan (table 30.2) displays an overall roadmap for training progression for intermediate to advanced half-Ironman racers. These triathletes have a deep base of fitness when they reach the final few weeks before race day. Before the final 12 weeks preceding race day, these triathletes are already swimming at least 1.2 miles (1.9 km) once or twice per week. They are riding 3 or 4 days per week and doing a long ride of about 2 hours. They are running 3 or 4 days per week, including a long run of 60 to 90 minutes.

This base of fitness allows intermediate and advanced triathletes to push the intensity of workouts in the final 3 to 4 months before the race. Pushing intensive and lactate threshold endurance intensities before a solid aerobic base has been built risks illness and injury.

Table 30.2 Sample 12-Week Training Plan for Half-Ironman Triathlon

Week	Approximate training hours	Types of workouts	Primary focus for week	Other
1	7 to 10	Aerobic, technique, intensive endurance.	The primary focus is building endurance for event completion. The secondary focus is adding workouts with zone 3 intensity.	The most important aspect of half-Ironman racing is building event and discipline endurance. Advanced triathletes should include some threshold endurance in workouts.
2	7 to 10	Same as week 1.	Same as week 1.	Most triathletes adapt well with two to four key workouts (breakthrough, or hard, workouts) each week. Depending on individual race limiters, key workouts may be in only one discipline or spread among all disciplines.
3	7 to 10	Same as week 1.	Same as week 1.	Although the first 4 weeks of this plan show 2 weeks of high volume followed by 1 week of recovery (3:1), some athletes do better on a format of 2:1 or even 1:1.
4	6 to 8	Keep workouts similar to the previous 2 weeks but reduce training volume.	Recovery.	Bricks or time trials (TT) can be included at the end of the week. Although important, lightning-fast transitions are not as important for half-Ironman racing as for sprint- and Olympic-distance racing.
5	8 to 12	Aerobic, technique, intensive endurance.	The primary focus remains building long workout endurance. By the end of next week, the long swim should be a minimum of 1.2 miles (1.9 km). The long ride should be 3 to 4 hours. The long run is 1 1/2 to 2 hours.	Strong swimmers can often swim 2 days per week and have a successful race. Advanced racers may swim 4 or 5 days per week. Intermediate cyclists should be increasing the distance and volume of zone 3 intensity in long rides. Advanced athletes should be including some zone 4 to 5a work in a short interval ride or perhaps within the long ride.
6	8 to 12	Same as week 5.	Same as week 5.	Although some fatigue is expected during big training blocks, exhaustion must be avoided. Nonessential workouts should be eliminated if fatigue becomes excessive.
7	8 to 12	Same as week 5.	Same as week 5.	Individual discipline training distances are near race-day distances for advanced triathletes.
8	6 to 8	Keep workouts similar to the previous 2 weeks but reduce training volume.	Recovery.	Some triathletes make great gains by reducing training volume for 5 days, but others need 10. Adequate time must be allowed for recovery while training time and intensity are optimized.

Week	Approximate training hours	Types of workouts	Primary focus for week	Other
9	8 to 11	Aerobic, technique, intensive endurance.	Build final race endurance. If endurance has been built in previous weeks, the final volume of intensity peaks this week.	Advanced triathletes who respond well to high volume should continue to build long ride time this week and next. Run time may remain constant.
10	8 to 11	Aerobic, technique, intensive endurance.	Depending on individual triathlete needs, training volume may begin decreasing this week.	If week 9 was not the peak in training volume, the peak should occur no later than week 10.
11	6 to 10	Aerobic, technique, intensive endurance.	Decrease training volume but maintain some intensity.	Dress rehearsal for race day should be completed no later than this week.
12	2 to 3 plus race	Recovery, sharpening.	Training volume decreases to allow a rested state on race day. Limited intensity remains in the plan.	For intermediate and advanced triathletes, a good amount of zone 3 can be included on race day. Advanced triathletes will include zones 4 and 5a, depending on the individual. Certainly, the entire race cannot be executed above zone 3.

Notice that the types of workouts remain constant throughout the plan. Intermediate and advanced triathletes are aiming for three things: to build race endurance, to increase aerobic speed in all disciplines, and to increase lactate threshold heart rate so that the aerobic engine is larger.

Racing Tactics

When possible, intermediate and advanced triathletes should train on portions of the course for key races. When training on the course is not possible, these triathletes should try to see part or all of the course by driving it. After seeing the course, the triathlete can more easily develop a mental image of success specific to that course.

Pacing

Many top racers do not use technology when racing—no heart rate monitor, no power meter, often not even a watch. The pace that they need to travel during a race is so automatic that no technology is needed. Other racers are most successful if they have technology to help them during the race. Some racers use technology to limit pace early in the event. Others use technology to aim for specific power or heart rate outputs on the bike and specific pace and heart rate on the run.

Triathletes can decide for themselves whether to use technology to optimize race performance. Triathletes who do not want to monitor themselves with devices during races yet need the data can wear the devices but tape over the display. Data can be downloaded after the event for analysis.

Triathletes who do take advantage of technology on race day should set race-day goals based on training benchmark data. They can set a range of times from "best race possible in perfect conditions" to "wind and bad weather." Setting a race-day time range rather than a specific time for each discipline makes race times more realistic. This strategy also prevents taking on an all-or-nothing mind-set.

Advanced racers may need a short warm-up before the event. These triathletes will do little of the race at zone 1 intensity and most of it in zones 2 to 4. Although time in zone 4 does not make up most of the event, the advanced triathlete can push some zone 4 intensity. Obviously, racing an entire 6-hour event at lactate threshold is not possible, so using some discretion is important.

Weather

Average half-Ironman triathletes will be racing for 5 to 6 1/2 hours. Over this length of time, changing weather can play a significant role in race time. Triathletes need to be mentally prepared to adjust race-time goals if conditions become hot or windy. They must be willing to slow their pace to optimize race-day performance.

If a triathlete expects to race in hot and humid conditions on race day, doing some acclimatization is wise. A rule of thumb is that 10 to 14 days are needed to acclimatize to hot weather. If triathletes can conduct training in a hot environment, doing aerobic workouts in the heat is wiser than doing track workouts. In all cases, triathletes should expect pace to decrease in hot conditions, even after acclimatization.

If a triathlete lives in a cool location but is preparing for a hot race, wearing extra clothing for workouts to stimulate sweating is a proven tactic. Wearing rubber sweat suits or other clothing that is not breathable is not advised.

On the other end of the weather spectrum, early spring and late fall races can be cold. Sipping on a hot beverage from a carafe before the swim can help triathletes keep warm at the starting line. If a triathlete gets cold easily, slipping on arm warmers and a vest or a jacket for the bike ride may be worth the extra time.

Altitude

If the triathlete lives at sea level but is looking to race at altitude, arriving at altitude 45 hours or more before the race will help performance in endurance events, according at least one researcher.[4]

Conclusion

Racing the half-Ironman distance requires more training volume than racing the Olympic-distance event. Controlling pace early in the race is critical for success. Monitoring nutrition and hydration during this long event is also more important than it is for shorter races.

Practicing pacing, nutrition, and hydration plans during long training events creates a greater likelihood of success and reduces stress on race day.

CHAPTER 31

Ironman

—Gale Bernhardt

For some triathletes, Ironman-distance events are the pinnacle of the sport. Certainly, television coverage has helped make these events extremely popular. The human-interest stories featured throughout the program give many a reason to be inspired.

An Ironman event is composed of a 2.4-mile (3.9 km) swim, a 112-mile (180.2 km) bike ride, and a 26.2-mile (42.2 km) run. The name "Ironman" often refers to the championship race held in Hawaii each year, but it may refer to Ironman-branded races. The word "Ironman" and the famous M-dot logo are trademarks owned by the World Triathlon Corporation (WTC), a privately owned company. Races that are Ironman-distance events may not carry the word "Ironman" in the title or any advertising that might give triathletes the impression that these events are associated with WTC.

Ironman-branded events are the only events that are qualifying races for the world championship event in Hawaii. Triathletes may also gain entry into the world championship event through a lottery selection process.

The event distance of 140.6 miles (226.3 km) yields average finish times of 12 1/2 to 13 hours.[1] Racers must complete the event in less than 17 hours to be considered official finishers.

Because of the event distances and logistics, most Ironman-distance events have cutoff times for each segment of the race. In nearly all events, racers must complete the swim in less than 2 hours and 20 minutes. For events beginning at 7:00 a.m., the bike ride must be finished by 5:30 p.m. The marathon must be completed by midnight.

If triathletes are unable to meet the cutoff times, their race will end before they complete the full distance.

Exertion Levels for Training and Racing

For any individual triathlete, Ironman-distance race pace is slower than the pace used for the shorter race distances covered in chapters 28 through 30. To hone in on the right intensity to optimize training, triathletes can use table 31.1.

Table 31.1 Reference Scale for Rating of Perceived Exertion and Training Zones

	Zone 1	Zone 2	Zone 3	Zone 4	Zone 5a	Zone 5b	Zone 5c
Rating of perceived exertion (RPE; original Borg scale)	6 to 9	10 to 12	13 or 14	15 or 16	17	18 or 19	20
Rating of perceived exertion (RPE; new Borg scale)	1 or 2	3 or 4	4 or 5	6	7	8 or 9	10
Swim pace	Work on form, no clock watching	T-pace + 10 s per 100	T-pace + 5 s per 100	T-pace	T-pace	T-pace – 5 s per 100	As fast as possible
Percentage of lactate threshold power	55 or less	56 to 75	76 to 90	91 to 99	100 to 105	106 to 120	121 or more
Percentage of lactate threshold heart rate (bike)	80 or less	81 to 88	89 to 93	94 to 99	100 to 102	103 to 105	106 or more
Percentage of lactate threshold heart rate (run)	84 or less	85 to 91	92 to 95	96 to 99	100 to 102	103 to 106	107 or more
Breathing and perceived exertion using runners as the example	Gentle rhythmic breathing. Pace is easy and relaxed. Intensity is a jog or trot.	Breathing rate and pace increase slightly. Many notice a change with slightly deeper breathing, although still comfortable. Running pace remains comfortable and conversation possible.	Aware of breathing a little harder. Pace is moderate. Holding a conversation is more difficult.	Starting to breathe hard. Pace is fast and beginning to become uncomfortable, approaching race pace for all-out 1- to 1.5-hour run.	Breathing is deep and forceful. Many notice a second significant change in breathing pattern. Pace is all-out sustainable for 1 to 1.5 hours. Mental focus is required, pace is moderately uncomfortable, and conversation is undesirable.	Heavy, labored breathing. Pace is noticeably challenging but sustainable for 15 to 30 minutes at race effort. Discomfort is high but manageable.	Maximal exertion in breathing. Pace is sprinting effort, causing high discomfort that is unsustainable for more than 1 minute.
Purpose and cross-reference of terms commonly used to describe each zone	Easy, aerobic, recovery.	Aerobic, extensive endurance, aerobic threshold endurance (Note: Some coaches call this region lactate threshold.)	Tempo, intensive endurance. *Ironman-distance race pace for intermediate and advanced athletes is typically within zones 1 to 3.*	Subthreshold, muscular endurance, threshold endurance, anaerobic threshold endurance.	Lactate threshold endurance, anaerobic threshold endurance, superthreshold, muscular endurance. *International-distance race pace is typically in zone 4 or 5a for advanced athletes.*	Aerobic capacity, speed endurance, anaerobic endurance. *Sprint-distance race pace is typically in zones 4 to 5b. Experienced athletes may be in zone 5c for limited time.*	Anaerobic capacity, power.

Adapted, with permission, from G. Bernhardt, 2007, *Training plans for multisport athletes* (Boulder, CO: VeloPress), 22-23, and G. Bernhardt, 2009, *Training plans for cyclists*

Cross-Training Approach for Intermediate Triathletes

The intermediate Ironman triathlete has successfully completed at least one Ironman-distance race. The goal for the next event is to improve average pace or placement within the field. These triathletes have been training for years and are training specifically for long-distance racing 6 to 10 months before an Ironman-distance event. These triathletes may or may not be building weekly volume throughout that period, depending on their level of fitness and performance limiters.

Six months before the race, this triathlete has begun a specific preparation phase. Within this phase, the triathlete is doing workouts intended to improve performance on race day.

The first approach for an intermediate triathlete is to perform weight training, long rides of 2 to 3 hours, and 60- to 90-minute runs. Intensity is in the form of zone 3 interval work in the specific preparation phase. Those intervals are typically placed in shorter workouts midweek but can be placed in a long workout on a weekend.

This triathlete should be working in the weight room to build strength and muscular balance, eventually translating that work to power in swimming, cycling, and running. In one or two phases of strength training the gym work makes up two of the triathlete's key sessions for the week. Because of this focus, swim, bike, and run training stays mostly aerobic.

As the triathlete moves closer to race day, strength training is reduced to one session of maintenance work per week or every other week. The other strength days are replaced by running or cycling workouts. As the strength training load decreases, intensity in swimming, cycling, and running increases.

This format is suitable for triathletes who live in northern latitudes and compete in early summer races. Quality riding outdoors may be limited because of snow and cold temperatures. Doing three or four sessions per week on an indoor bike trainer becomes excessively boring. Replacing one or two bike workouts with a strength training workout helps prevent boredom and in most cases helps build strength for cycling.

For this triathlete outdoor runs may be easier, but because of slick conditions, workouts with intensity above zone 3 may be a problem. In this case, zone 3 training should be moved indoors to a treadmill.

This triathlete may replace long rides or runs with activities such as snowshoeing or cross-country skiing in the early phases of training. This type of aerobic cross-training allows the triathlete to maintain aerobic base fitness and enjoy the outdoors.

Lactate Threshold Approach for Intermediate Triathletes

A second approach for intermediate triathletes is to do a block of lactate threshold training (zone 4 to 5a) during the specific preparation phase. This work begins 6 to 12 months before the race and lasts 3 to 6 months, allowing enough time for a 1- to 2-week recovery period before beginning the final 12 to 14 weeks of precompetitive preparation leading to the Ironman race.

For this intermediate triathlete, the threshold training block includes threshold intervals similar to those used by triathletes training for sprint- and Olympic-distance races. This training block may include sprint- and Olympic-distance races as well.

For both intermediate and advanced triathletes, the specific preparation phase looks the same. Training volume is increasing, as is the distance or duration of long runs and rides. Using a 4:1, 3:1, or 2:1 ratio of higher volume weeks followed by a rest week helps keeps the triathlete healthy and promotes adaptation from the previous training load. The best ratio is the one that allows the triathlete to progress quickly while minimizing injury and illness.

Biggest Training Week for the Intermediate Triathlete

Approximately 3 or 4 weeks before race day, the intermediate triathlete has his biggest training week. Triathletes handling a bigger load and more training volume may want to taper volume for a longer period than a triathlete with less fitness. This triathlete's biggest week may look something like the following:[2]

Monday: Strength training maintenance for 60 minutes or off day

Tuesday: Swim 90 minutes, run 60 to 75 minutes

Wednesday: Bike 60 minutes

Thursday: Swim 60 minutes, run 30 minutes

Friday: Bike 60 minutes

Saturday: Swim 1 hour (can switch Tuesday and Saturday), run 3 to 3 1/4 hours

Sunday: Bike 6 hours

Total training time: 16 to 17 1/2 hours

Notice that the long swim is placed on Tuesday. Some triathletes may need to split long workouts to maintain quality or to meet personal schedule requirements. Also, notice that the long run is on Saturday and the long ride is on Sunday. Depending on the triathlete's personal schedule and performance limiters, these long workouts can be reversed or may be scheduled more than 24 hours apart.

For example, triathletes may prefer to do a group ride on Saturday if they are motivated by the group and enjoy the companionship. Another consideration for workout placement is triathlete durability and injury history. Triathletes who have had running injuries may be best served by doing the long run on Saturday, Friday, or Thursday on relatively fresh legs and completing the long ride on Sunday.

Training Strategies

Triathletes looking to place workouts more specific to the swim, bike, and run order will want to place the long swim on Saturday morning, in open water if possible, and ride immediately after the swim. The long run will then come on Sunday.

As for intensity, the intermediate triathlete will spend a lot of time in zone 3. Some consider zone 3 the beginning of lactate threshold training, but others believe that lactate threshold begins at low zone 4. Researchers found that elite athletes spend 80 percent or more of their training time below lactate threshold.[3] Intermediate and advanced triathletes can use this 20 percent guideline to improve performance. Because zone 3 isn't as taxing as zone 4 to 5a, intermediate triathletes may find that they can spend more than 20 percent of their training volume at zone 3 intensity. Accurate journaling and record keeping is needed to monitor the training load. The more comprehensive the data collection is, the easier it is for the triathlete to design an appropriate load. The goal is to improve continuously and not lose training time to having to recover from illness or injury.

Training for the Advanced Triathlete

The advanced triathlete has raced several Ironman events. More than likely, this triathlete is aiming to qualify for Kona, the Ironman World Championship event. At a minimum, this triathlete is looking to optimize training to obtain a personal best performance.

This triathlete has data collected on race pace and may have power data as well. Although a power meter is not required, it does help make training more accurate.

If the triathlete is looking to qualify for Kona, data analysis needs to be done to determine what is holding the triathlete back from placing higher in her category. Several questions need to be asked relative to others in her category.

Is the triathlete a weak swimmer?

Is the triathlete a weak cyclist?

Is the triathlete a weak runner?

Does the triathlete place better in her category on a hilly course?

Does the triathlete place better in her category in hot weather?

After the triathlete has identified where performance needs improvement relative to others in the category, training to improve performance in the weak or limiting discipline begins 6 to 10 months before the Ironman event. Additionally, a triathlete who is attempting to qualify for Kona should select a race based on the estimated ability to do well at on that course at that time of year.

Advanced triathletes typically train 12 to 15 hours on a normal basis and perform a recovery week of 9 to 10 hours during the specific preparation phase. During this time, these triathletes may be doing workouts in zone 4 to 5a as well as a limited amount of time above 5a.

Although the rule of thumb to perform 20 percent of volume at intensity is a place to begin, most triathletes will agree that 1 hour of zone 3 intensity is easier on the body than 1 hour of zone 4 intensity. To date, no comprehensive studies have examined training loads of advanced age-group triathletes. Advanced triathletes may be capable of handling 30 to 40 percent of the training load at intensities above zone 2. Generally, less than 10 percent of the advanced triathlete's volume is zone 4 and above.

Because advanced triathletes are training 12 to 15 hours per week in the specific preparation phase, they may be training 15 to 20 hours per week during the final 12 to 14 weeks before the Ironman. They will likely ride more than one century (160 km) ride during this time, whereas intermediate triathletes may have ridden only a single century ride in the same period.

Sample Big Training Week for an Advanced Triathlete

The following is an example of an advanced triathlete's big training week:[2]

Monday: Strength training maintenance or yoga or an easy spin on the bike for 60 minutes

Tuesday: Swim 75 minutes, run 30 to 60 minutes

Wednesday: Bike 60 minutes, run 30 to 45 minutes

Thursday: Swim 60 minutes, run 30 minutes

Friday: Bike 1 to 2 hours

Saturday: Swim 1 1/4 to 1 1/2 hours, run 2 to 3 hours

Sunday: Bike 5 to 7 hours (some triathletes may add an additional swim session on Friday or Sunday)

Total training time: 15 to 18 3/4 hours

It is fair to say that not all triathletes respond positively to intensity above zone 3, but others are bike racing in addition to preparing for an Ironman event. Some advanced triathletes have a lifestyle that allows them to train multiple times per day—training 18 to 20 hours per week, enjoying naps, and having recovery massages. Others do not have a lifestyle that can support this level of training volume, or their bodies do not respond well to high volume.

In any case, the training strategy should consider the individual triathlete's goals, performance limiters, lifestyle, and response to volume of training load and volume of intensity. The art of self-coaching requires constant fine-tuning to the training plan to make adjustments for how the triathlete is responding to the load.

Sample 13-Week Plan

The 13-week training plan (table 31.2) reveals a suggested progression for training for intermediate to advanced Ironman racers. These triathletes have a solid base of fitness before these final weeks. Before the final 13 weeks before race day, these triathletes are already swimming at least 1.75 to 2.4 miles (2.8 to 4.0 km) once or twice per week. They are riding 3 or 4 days per week, including a long ride of at least 3 hours. They are running 3 or 4 days per week, including a long run of 1 1/4 to 1 3/4 hours.

This base of fitness allows intermediate and advanced triathletes to push the intensity, or the volume of intensity, of workouts in the final 3 months before the race. Some triathletes work on increasing the pace at zone 3 intensity, whereas others work on increasing the volume of time tolerable at zone 3. Finally, some will attempt to work on both.

There is no single approach to improving race-day pace. Some strategies, such as increasing discipline volume, volume of zone 3 intensity, and volume of work done above zone 3, carry more risk for injury and illness. Optimizing pace, given individual responses to training loads, is part of the art of assembling a training plan.

Racing Tactics

A good training plan has triathletes well prepared and rested before race day. Often they get to the starting line with more eagerness and enthusiasm than patience. Ironman must be raced with the self-control to meter pace throughout the event. Holding back early in the race helps triathletes finish strong.

One way for intermediate Ironman racers to control pace is to limit effort to zone 1 and 2 intensity for the first half of the distance in each discipline—swim, bike, and run. Intensity can be increased to allow some zone 3 in the second half of the distance in each discipline. The goal is not to maximize zone 3 but to aim for a negative-split race in which the second half of the distance traveled in each discipline is done faster than the first half.

Table 31.2 Sample 13-Week Training Plan for Ironman Triathlon

Week	Approximate training hours	Types of workouts	Primary focus for week	Other
1	12 to 15	Aerobic, technique, intensive endurance.	The primary focus is building endurance for event completion. The secondary focus is adding workouts with zone 3 intensity.	The most important aspect of Ironman-distance racing is building event and discipline endurance. Advanced triathletes should include threshold endurance in some workouts.
2	12 to 15	Same as week 1.	Same as week 1.	Most triathletes adapt well with two to four key workouts each week (breakthrough, or hard, workouts). Intermediate racers with a strong swimming history can swim 2 days per week and have a successful race. Advanced racers may swim 4 or 5 days per week. Intermediate cyclists should increase the distance and volume of zone 3 intensity in long rides. Advanced triathletes may include some zone 4 to 5a work in a short interval ride or perhaps within the long ride.
3	12 to 15	Same as week 1.	Same as week 1.	Although the first 4 weeks of this plan show 2 weeks of high volume followed by 1 week of recovery (3:1), some triathletes do better on a format of 2:1 or even 1:1.
4	6 to 10	Keep workouts similar to the previous 2 weeks but reduce training volume.	Recovery.	Bricks, time trials (TT), or Olympic-distance races can be included at the end of the week. If racing is included, recovery from the race must be planned in the week following the race.
5	14 to 17	Aerobic, technique, intensive endurance.	The primary focus remains building long workout endurance. By the end of next week, long swim workouts should be around 2.4 miles (3.9 km). The long ride should be 5 hours. The long run should be 2 to 2 3/4 hours.	If advanced triathletes include half-Ironman racing in the final weeks heading into the Ironman event, these races are often placed in weeks 5 through 7.
6	14 to 17	Same as week 5.	Same as week 5.	Although some fatigue is expected during big training blocks, exhaustion must be avoided. Nonessential workouts should be eliminated if fatigue becomes excessive.

Week	Approximate training hours	Types of workouts	Primary focus for week	Other
7	6 to 10	Keep workouts similar to the previous 2 weeks but reduce training volume.	Recovery.	Some triathletes make great gains by reducing training volume for 5 days, but others need 10. Adequate time must be allowed for recovery while training time and intensity are optimized.
8	16 to 20	Aerobic, technique, intensive endurance.	Build final race endurance. If endurance has been built in previous weeks, the final volume of intensity peaks this week or next.	Advanced triathletes who respond well to high volume should continue to build long ride time this week and next. Run time may remain constant.
9	16 to 20	Aerobic, technique, intensive endurance.	Build final race endurance. If endurance has been built in previous weeks, the final volume of intensity peaks this week.	Advanced triathletes who respond well to high volume should continue to build long ride time this week and next. Run time may remain constant.
10	6 to 10	Keep workouts similar to the previous 2 weeks but reduce training volume.	Recovery.	Some triathletes make great gains by reducing training volume for 5 days, but others need 10. Adequate time must be allowed for recovery while training time and intensity are optimized.
11	14 to 16	Aerobic, technique, intensive endurance.	Training volume begins decreasing from maximum loads no later than this week.	Advanced triathletes may decrease the training volume in each discipline during different weeks before race day.
12	9 to 12	Aerobic, technique, intensive endurance.	Decrease training volume but maintain some intensity.	Dress rehearsal for race day (clothing, nutrition, hydration, race pace) is completed no later than this week.
13	3 to 5 plus race	Recovery, sharpening.	Training volume decreases to allow a rested state on race day. Limited intensity remains in the plan.	For intermediate and advanced triathletes, a good amount of zone 3 can be included on race day. Advanced triathletes will include zone 4, depending on the individual. Certainly, the entire race cannot be executed above zone 3.

Although a negative-split pace is desirable, achieving it is not always possible on some courses. If hills come early in the ride or the run, a negative-split effort needs to be employed. Data from long workouts will provide race-day guidelines for heart rate, power, and pace. Triathletes know from data collected what to expect on race day. Although selecting all the best long workouts and making those paces the race-day goals is tempting, smart triathletes make a range of race goals based on an optimal race and a suboptimal race depending on weather.

As discussed in the nutrition chapters, drinking too much or too little water during an Ironman event is a problem. Some triathletes do well allowing thirst and hunger to dictate hydration and fueling. For others, a guideline for fluid and fuel consumption rates per hour of racing works better. In either case, triathletes need to have a plan for race day and practice it in training.

A well-prepared triathlete with a race-day pacing plan has a better chance of successfully finishing the race than a well-prepared triathlete without one.

The advanced triathlete is keenly aware of pace and is aiming for a negative-split exertion on race day, although exertion levels are slightly higher than they are for the intermediate triathlete. Advanced racers are aiming to do most of the race at zone 2 to 3 intensity, and they may briefly go into zone 4. These periods may be related to catching a competitor or surging to drop one.

If possible, advanced triathletes aiming for a Kona slot should have spotters on course to let them know where they are relative to the competition. Triathletes can become remarkably inspired to push the pace if they know that they are in contention for a Kona slot.

For the advanced triathlete aiming for a personal best performance, the entire race is aimed at producing power and pace numbers achieved in training.

Weather

The average Ironman triathlete will race for 12 1/2 to 13 hours. In this time, weather can change and play a significant role in race time. Triathletes need to be mentally prepared to adjust race time goals if conditions are hot or windy. Triathletes must be willing to slow the pace to optimize race-day performance.

A triathlete who expects to race in hot and humid conditions on race day should do some acclimatization. A rule of thumb is that 10 to 14 days are needed to acclimatize to hot weather. If the triathlete can conduct training in a hot environment, doing aerobic workouts in the heat is wiser than doing track workouts. In all cases, triathletes should expect pace to decrease in any hot conditions, even after acclimatization.

If a triathlete lives in a cool location but is preparing for a hot race, wearing extra clothing for workouts to stimulate sweating is a proven tactic. Wearing rubber sweat suits or other clothing that is not breathable is not advised.

On the other end of the weather spectrum, early spring and late fall races can be cold. Sipping on a hot beverage from a carafe before the swim can help the triathlete keep warm at the starting line. If a triathlete gets cold easily, slipping on arm warmers and a vest or a jacket for the bike ride may be worth the extra time.

Conclusion

Ironman training and racing become more complicated as the triathlete's goals become higher. Because of the volume of training required to complete or compete in an Ironman event, close attention must always be given to the triathlete's response to the training load. Healthy and happy triathletes always race better than those who are injured, ill, or burned out.

CHAPTER 32

Duathlon

—Gale Bernhardt

The sport of duathlon is a great way for run–bike specialists to shine. Rather than beginning with a swim, duathlon begins with a run. A bike ride comes next, and a second run completes the event. The sport of duathlon carries some distance variability. The International Triathlon Union World Championship event distance standards are the following:[1]

Sprint: 5K run, 20K bike, 2.5K run

Standard: 10K run, 40K bike, 5K run

Long distance: 10K run, 150K bike, 30K run

Some nations have national championship events that are different distances than those contested at world championships. For example, the USA Triathlon National championship distance is often a 5K run, a 30K to 40K bike, and a 5K run.[2]

For this chapter, the 10K run, 40K bike, and 5K run distance will be used for training and racing discussion.

Table 32.1 gives some sample times from the finishers of a recent U.S. national championship.[3]

Because the data come from a national championship event, the finish times represent a faster overall average than most local events. Note some key items in the data:

- Duathletes over the age of 70 are competing at national championships for a slot on a world championship team.

- For top finishers, the difference between the first 5K time and the second 5K time is around 1 minute (roughly 20 seconds per mile [12 seconds per kilometer]). The midpack to final finishers had about a 2-minute difference (close to 40 seconds per mile [25 seconds per kilometer]) between the two run times.

- The difference in finish times between elites and top age-group athletes is 3 to 4 minutes. The elites travel 3 to 4.7 percent faster than age-group athletes do.

- Top age-group athletes are about 10 to 12 years older than elite athletes. Speed loss per year is in the range of 0.3 to 0.4 percent for the top performers in this data set.

For all duathletes, one training goal is to minimize the degradation of pace between the first run and the second run.

Table 32.1   Split Times for Competitors at a 5K–35K–5K Triathlon

	5K run	Pace in minutes per mile (min/km)	T1	35K bike	Pace in miles per hour (km/h)	T2	5K run	Pace in minutes per mile (min/km)	Overall time
First place elite male (age 28)	16:15	5:15 (3:15)	0:30	48:20	26.9 (43.3)	0:33	17:03	5:30 (3:25)	1:22:38
First place elite female (age 27)	18:38	6:01 (3:44)	0:42	54:33	23.9 (38.5)	0:34	19:44	6:22 (3:57)	1:34:10
First place age-group male (age 40)	16:21	5:17 (3:16)	0:32	51:59	25.4 (40.9)	0:41	17:24	5:37 (3:29)	1:26:14
First place age-group female (age 38)	19:15	6:13 (3:51)	0:54	55:34	23.4 (37.7)	0:43	20:38	6:40 (4:08)	1:37:00
Midpack age-group finisher (age 40)	20:21	6:34 (4:04)	0:45	1:06:00	19.2 (30.9)	1:10	22:48	7:21 (4:34)	1:50:56
Official final finisher (age 74)	50:07	16:10 (10:02)	2:37	2:00:32	10.8 (17.4)	2:12	52:08	16:49 (10:26)	3:47:34

Exertion Levels for Training and Racing

Individual duathletes can benefit by personalizing their training at the correct intensity. To assist in optimizing training, duathletes can reference table 32.2.

Enhancing Training

Intermediate racers have completed at least one duathlon and are looking to get faster. Although these duathletes are interested in more structured training and speed, typically they are not interested in increasing training hours. Improved performance beyond the entry level can be accomplished in about 3 months, even when keeping training time less than 6 1/2 hours per week.[4]

One strategy for training is to do at least one combo (run-to-bike) or brick (bike-to-run) workout per week. The structure of the workout can have both disciplines performed at an aerobic pace. Aerobic workouts, those in zone 1 to 2, help duathletes relax, let them settle in to a steady pace, and allow them to practice T1 or T2 (see table 32.2).

Table 32.2 Reference Scale for Rating of Perceived Exertion and Training Zones

	Zone 1	Zone 2	Zone 3	Zone 4	Zone 5a	Zone 5b	Zone 5c
Rating of perceived exertion (RPE; original Borg scale)	6 to 9	10 to 12	13 or 14	15 or 16	17	18 or 19	20
Rating of perceived exertion (RPE; new Borg scale)	1 or 2	3 or 4	4 or 5	6	7	8 or 9	10
Swim pace	Work on form, no clock watching	T-pace + 10 s per 100	T-pace + 5 s per 100	T-pace	T-pace	T-pace – 5 s per 100	As fast as possible
Percentage of lactate threshold power	55 or less	56 to 75	76 to 90	91 to 99	100 to 105	106 to 120	121 or more
Percentage of lactate threshold heart rate (bike)	80 or less	81 to 88	89 to 93	94 to 99	100 to 102	103 to 105	106 or more
Percentage of lactate threshold heart rate (run)	84 or less	85 to 91	92 to 95	96 to 99	100 to 102	103 to 106	107 or more
Breathing and perceived exertion using runners as the example	Gentle rhythmic breathing. Pace is easy and relaxed. Intensity is a jog or trot.	Breathing rate and pace increase slightly. Many notice a change with slightly deeper breathing, although still comfortable. Running pace remains comfortable and conversation possible.	Aware of breathing a little harder. Pace is moderate. Holding a conversation is more difficult.	Starting to breathe hard. Pace is fast and beginning to become uncomfortable, approaching race pace for all-out 1- to 1.5-hour run.	Breathing is deep and forceful. Many notice a second significant change in breathing pattern. Pace is all-out sustainable for 1 to 1.5 hours. Mental focus is required, pace is moderately uncomfortable, and conversation is undesirable.	Heavy, labored breathing. Pace is noticeably challenging but sustainable for 15 to 30 minutes at race effort. Discomfort is high but manageable.	Maximal exertion in breathing. Pace is sprinting effort, causing high discomfort that is unsustainable for more than 1 minute.
Purpose and cross-reference of terms commonly used to describe each zone	Easy, aerobic, recovery.	Aerobic, extensive endurance, aerobic threshold endurance (Note: Some coaches call this region lactate threshold.)	Tempo, intensive endurance. *Ironman-distance race pace for intermediate and advanced athletes is typically within zones 1 to 3.*	Subthreshold, muscular endurance, threshold endurance, anaerobic threshold endurance.	Lactate threshold endurance, anaerobic threshold endurance, superthreshold, muscular endurance. *International-distance race pace is typically in zone 4 or 5a for advanced athletes.*	Aerobic capacity, speed endurance, anaerobic endurance. *Sprint-distance race pace is typically in zones 4 to 5b. Experienced athletes may be in zone 5c for limited time.*	Anaerobic capacity, power.

Adapted, with permission, from G. Bernhardt, 2007, *Training plans for multisport athletes* (Boulder, CO: VeloPress), 22-23, and G. Bernhardt, 2009, *Training plans for cyclists* (Boulder, CO: VeloPress), 28-29.

For the combo workouts, two more strategies include a run at threshold pace followed by an easy ride or an easy run followed by a ride that includes threshold work. In both cases the threshold work can be broken into intervals or done for a steady time or distance.

When doing combo or brick workouts, intermediate duathletes should also be working on fast transitions during some of the workouts. For workouts that include fast transitions, duathletes may want to consider investing in special platform pedals, described in chapter 33.

A second strategy for intermediate duathletes is to keep most of the run and bike workouts separate, doing a brick or combo workout every 2 to 3 weeks. For some duathletes, keeping the focus on single-discipline workouts may yield better improvements. Duathletes may need to experiment to determine which strategy is best.

Biggest Training Week

For the duathlete looking to minimize training and maximize results, training around 6 hours per week will work. The biggest training week for this duathlete 8 weeks before race day might look something like the following:[4]

Monday: Off day

Tuesday: Run 30 minutes, mostly zone 1 or 2, and include pick-ups

Wednesday: Ride 45 minutes, mostly zone 1 or 2, and include skill drills

Thursday: Run 45 minutes and include threshold time totaling 15 to 20 minutes

Friday: Ride 45 minutes, mostly zone 1 or 2

Saturday: Long run for 90 minutes, mostly zone 1 or 2

Sunday: Long ride for 2 hours on a hilly course, zones 1 to 5a

Total training time: 6 1/4 hours

Additional Training Strategies

Many duathletes are familiar with doing intervals or steady efforts at lactate threshold. Duathletes can also build threshold fitness by accumulating time in zones 4 to 5a during an endurance ride and using the hills to drive intensity. Riding hills not only improves lactate threshold but also provides a discipline-specific strength workout. Obviously, the sample week does not include a combo or brick workout.

With the remaining weeks approaching race day, volume can be held constant during the week and the long weekend run can be reduced to 60 minutes. With volume held constant during nonrecovery weeks, threshold intervals can be done in cycling and running to improve race pace.

As a starting point for planning, the duathlete should observe the rule of doing two to four key workouts per week to provide both physical and mental stress. Second, the total volume of zone 4 to 5a work should be no more than 20 percent of total training volume.[5] The plan should be conservative at first until it is known what kind of load the duathlete can handle. When individual training response is documented, the training load can be adjusted up or down to achieve the best results.

Advanced Training

The advanced duathlete is experienced and is aiming for a personal best performance, a place on the podium, or perhaps a spot on a world championship team. Depending on predicted race finish time, most top age-group athletes will be racing at all intensities.

Advanced racers have a strong base of fitness and have performed 8 to 9 weeks of lactate threshold training, including unstructured threshold training followed by specific intervals.

Threshold training is followed by 6 to 10 weeks of training that includes anaerobic endurance and anaerobic capacity sessions. The blend of threshold training and anaerobic endurance training is not an exact science and is driven by the ability of the duathlete to respond to the training stimulus.

Like the intermediate duathlete, the advanced duathlete can approach training in single-discipline sessions, combo workouts, or brick workouts. The rules of thumb about doing two to four key workouts per week and limiting intensity to 20 percent of volume still apply for the advanced duathlete. Intensity for the advanced duathlete is defined as zone 4 and above.

Although the duathlete is running a 10K, doing a bike ride, and running a 5K, the duathlete should be training to develop the overall endurance to run a 15K. Any formulas used to calculate running paces for track workouts can be aimed at improving both 10K and 5K running speeds.

If duathletes examine the results from past world championship events on the International Triathlon Union website, they will find that running speed fades only about 10 to 20 seconds per mile (6 to 12 seconds per kilometer) from the pace of the first 10K to the pace for the final 5K of the race. Young adult age-group athletes are fast, running paces between 5:00 and 7:00 per mile (between 3:06 and 4:20 per kilometer).

For the lactate threshold bike training, intervals should be aimed at lactate threshold heart rate (zone 4 to 5a) or power improvement using a 3:1 or 4:1 work-to-rest ratio along with steady efforts at threshold. Steady efforts can be solo or repeats that are 10, 15, or 20 minutes long.

Advanced duathletes can also benefit from 3- to 5-minute intervals on the bike in zone 5b, followed by rest intervals equal to or double the work time.

In the final 4 to 6 weeks before race day, the advanced duathlete should include several combos, bricks, or shortened race simulation days at the track or use a device that yields pace running. The advanced duathlete must have the capability to minimize the difference between pace on the first and second runs.

Sample 12-Week Plan

The sample 12-week plan (table 32.3) gives general suggestions for the 12 weeks of training leading into race day. The plan assumes that duathletes have accomplished the preparatory training leading into this training block for 6 months.

Table 32.3 Sample 12-Week Training Plan for Duathlon

Week	Approximate training hours	Types of workouts	Primary focus for week	Other
1	3 to 7	Aerobic, technique, neuromuscular speed, lactate threshold.	Intermediate duathletes should focus on improving speed at lactate threshold. Advanced athletes may work on aerobic capacity in running or cycling.	Focus key workouts on success limiters until the final 6 weeks. Strength training once or twice per week is optional. Core strength training a minimum of once a week is recommended.
2	4 to 8	Same as week 1.	Same as week 1.	Duathletes often run 4 to 6 days per week.
3	4 to 10	Same as week 1.	Same as week 1.	The number of weeks to build intensity or training volume before inserting a recovery week depends on the individual duathlete. Some duathletes need only 4 or 5 days of reduced training volume, but others need 7 to 10 days.
4	4 to 6	Keep workouts similar to the previous 2 weeks but reduce training volume.	Recovery.	Combos, bricks, or time trials (TT) can be included at the end of the week. Duration of each TT depends on the duathlete's current fitness.

Week	Approximate training hours	Types of workouts	Primary focus for week	Other
5 to 7	6 to 12	Aerobic, technique, neuromuscular speed, lactate threshold.	Intermediate duathletes should keep the focus on improving speed at lactate threshold. If speed has peaked, they can increase duration at threshold speed appropriate for the race distances. Advanced duathletes should continue to work on aerobic capacity.	Both intermediate and advanced duathletes need the ability to run a fast 5K after a 10K run and a 40K ride. At minimum, duathletes want to minimize pace degradation between the first and second runs.
8	4 to 6	Keep workouts similar to the previous 2 weeks but reduce training volume.	Recovery.	Executing workouts on courses similar to the key race is important.
9 to 10	6 to 12	Same as weeks 5 to 7.	Same as weeks 5 to 7.	The last high-volume training week is week 10. Some duathletes need more taper before race day than others. For these duathletes, the last high-volume week may be week 9.
11	4 to 6	Same as previous weeks.	All duathletes reduce training volume compared with the previous week while keeping relative intensity included in some workouts.	Race-day gear should be chosen no later than this week, including clothing and gear selection on the bike.
12	2 to 3 plus race	Recovery, short segments of intervals done at race pace or slightly faster.	Training volume decreases significantly to allow a rested state on race day.	Duathletes should aim to race at intensities that have been practiced in training.

Racing Tactics

Duathletes should temper pace on the 10K, aiming for lactate threshold pace. Aiming to ride the 40K bike leg at mostly zone 3 to 5a intensity is possible for well-trained duathletes. They should finish strong on the final run, aiming for the final 5K to be no more than 10 to 20 seconds slower per mile (6 to 12 seconds per kilometer) than the 10K.

Because of the combo, brick, and race simulation training sessions, duathletes should be well aware of race pace and rate of perceived exertion. The first 10K should be run at the duathlete's self-selected race pace. Intermediate duathletes should aim for a bike ride that is a negative-split effort by riding the first half at zone 3 to 4 and the last half at zone 3 to 5a, spending more time at zone 4 to 5a. Advanced duathletes will ride a good portion of the first half of the bike at zone 4 intensity and the last half at zone 4 to 5b, keeping in mind that the 5K must be within 10 to 20 seconds per mile (6 to 12 seconds per kilometer) of the 10K.

In some cases, the course will determine where intensity is placed within the ride. If the course has most of the hills in the first half, a solid amount of intensity will be placed earlier in the ride. If course is rolling, intensity may be placed on the uphill portions and partial recovery can occur in the downhill sections.

In most races, the result is determined in the last half of the bike ride and the second 5K. Advanced duathletes can target other racers, whether in the same category or not. These targets can be used as an incentive to pass the next racer and keep pace high.

Weather

At race distances as long as a 10K run, a 40K ride, and a 5K run, weather can play a role in performance. When preparing for the event, duathletes should research weather patterns for the same time of the year as the race. Early spring and late fall races can be cold. Sipping on a hot beverage from a carafe before the 10K can help duathletes keep warm before the race begins. Keeping a warm-up suit on until the last moment also helps. If the race is on a chilly day the duathlete may choose to wear tights and arm warmers or a long-sleeved top.

If the race begins in cool conditions but temperatures are expected to increase, some duathletes don't mind starting the race a bit underdressed knowing that they will warm up during the race.

Midsummer events can be contested in heat and humidity that can slow race pace significantly. The body uses a great deal of energy to cool down, particularly if duathletes attempt to produce high paces in hot, humid conditions. Thermal stress takes a toll, so duathletes are forced to slow the pace.

If a duathlete expects to race in hot and humid conditions on race day, doing some acclimatization is wise. A rule of thumb is that 10 to 14 days are needed to acclimatize to hot weather. If the duathlete can conduct training in a hot environment, doing aerobic workouts in the heat is wiser than doing track workouts. In all cases, duathletes should expect pace to decrease in hot conditions, even after acclimatization.

If a duathlete lives in a cool location but is preparing for a hot race, wearing extra clothing for workouts to stimulate sweating is a proven tactic. Wearing rubber sweat suits or other clothing that is not breathable is not advised.

Altitude

If a duathlete is racing at altitude but living at sea level, arriving at altitude 45 hours or more before the race will help performance in endurance events, according to at least one researcher.[6]

Conclusion

Duathlon is a fantastic sport for many athletes. Because the swim is not part of the event, duathletes typically devote less time to training than triathletes do. A good portion of the time savings comes from eliminating the commute to the pool. Extremely efficient running and cycling can be done from the duathlete's own doorstep. Convenience can be a big attraction.

Duathletes who take a structured approach to training can make the most of limited training time. They need to begin with the appropriate foundation training to prepare muscles, tendons, and ligaments for the fast training to be done in the final weeks before the race.

Underprepared duathletes risk injury if they decide to train at fast paces every day of the week. This approach does not allow the body time to recover and advance to a new level of fitness.

For athletes of any level, fast performances relative to competitors in the same category can be achieved with strategic training and tactical racing.

CHAPTER 33

Combination Workout Training

—Gale Bernhardt

Although most triathlon training focus goes toward the primary disciplines of swimming, cycling, and running, the transitions that occur between disciplines are also important. Two main aspects of transition need to be considered. First is the body's ability to change from discipline to discipline, to change from swimming to cycling and from cycling to running. Each discipline puts different demands on the body.

The second consideration is the logistics of each transition, which includes equipment organization, sequence of movement, and speed of transition. For advanced triathletes racing short-course events, optimizing transition time may mean the difference between a podium position and no podium position. The speed of transitions is less critical in long-distance Ironman racing, but triathletes have no reason to be sloppy.

Practicing transitions is important for triathletes who are looking to improve performance. The workout most commonly used for this purpose is the bike-to-run workout to practice the second triathlon transition (T2), commonly called a brick. Triathletes can also practice the swim-to-bike transition (T1) in workouts. This workout, along with a run-to-bike workout for duathletes, is often called a combo.

Transition Considerations

Elite World Cup racers are the fastest at transitions because their racing success depends on it. Although this book does not cover International Triathlon Union (ITU)–style draft-legal racing, video clips of these racers give coaches and triathletes an idea of what the world's fastest transitions look like. One can find videos on the ITU website at www.triathlon.org and by searching the Internet.

Why are these racers so fast at T1? A fast T1 can mean the difference between making the first bike pack, making the chase pack, or being out alone. Chasing alone while everyone else is working within a peloton is a significant disadvantage on the bike. Peloton riders can usually take a break during a race, drafting while others are working. Chasing alone is a solo time trial effort that allows no rest.

Mastering T1 Challenges

Several issues during T1 encourage triathletes to be smart. Those who are the fittest and smartest are the fastest. The challenges begin immediately after exiting the swim. Triathletes run to their personal T1 spot, wanting to minimize the time spent standing in one location. They must do two things: minimize transition time with equipment choices and organize the sequence of activities so that any time *not* spent swimming, running to transition, or riding the bike is near zero.

More tips for T1:

• **Choosing a triathlon suit or swimsuit**. Some triathletes complete the entire race in a swimsuit, but most prefer a triathlon suit for speed and comfort. A tri suit has long legs like bike shorts, but the chamois pad is very light, providing some comfort on the bike but soaking up negligible water during the swim leg. Not changing from a swimsuit to cycling clothes in T1 makes the transition faster. Long-distance racers, however, may prefer a change of clothes because they want more comfort than a light chamois can provide during the long period on the bike.

• **Wearing a wetsuit**. If the swim temperatures require a wetsuit, preparing for T1 begins the moment when triathletes exit the water. While running to the T1 area, they remove cap and goggles. They unzip the wetsuit and peel it down to the waist to allow a fast stripping of the wetsuit at the individual T1 spot. Fit and leg length of the wetsuit likely will determine the speed at which the triathlete can remove it. To improve speed, the leg length can be cut to be shorter, allowing larger holes for ankle and foot removal at faster speed. Triathletes should also consider whether the length of the swim and water temperature provide a significant advantage to wearing a wetsuit given the possible increased T1 time.

• **Wearing socks**. Some short-course racers and long-distance triathletes may want to put on socks to reduce the possibility of blisters. Faster Olympic-distance racers nearly always ride without putting on socks because of the time savings. Some sport-lubrication or powder products can help improve transition times and prevent blisters if they are placed in the shoes or on the feet before the race start.

• **Clipping cycling shoes into the pedals**. Running in cycling shoes in a transition area for T1 or T2 can be awkward. Some cleats are slippery on an asphalt transition surface. Barefoot is much safer and faster, provided the ground is free of hazards.

• **Fastening shoes to the bike frame to keep them parallel to the ground while running to the mount or dismount line**. Triathletes can use thin rubber bands to attach the heel of the cycling shoes to the frame (see figure 33.1). This technique keeps the cranks from turning as the triathlete runs with the bike. The risk of turning cranks is that shoes can become hooked on the ground and be forced out of the pedals.

• **Mount the bicycle**. The fastest triathletes typically use a flying mount. They run with the bicycle and jump onto the seat while the bike is in motion. Cyclo-cross racers also use this technique. The benefit is a fast mount and quick acceleration to race speed. Triathletes should practice this technique regularly to make the mount fast but smooth, without hard landings or loss of bike control.

• **Pedal with feet on top of shoes**. After a fast transition, triathletes want to get the bike moving and up to race speed as quickly as possible. To accomplish this, racers pedal with their feet on top of the cycling shoes until it is convenient to slip their feet into the shoes with minimal coasting. Of course, triathlon-specific cycling shoes with one Velcro strap are easier to fasten than shoes with multiple straps.

▶ **Figure 33.1** Shoes fastened to the bike frame with rubber bands.

• **Wear sunglasses under helmet straps**. Sunglasses can be put on in transition or attached to the bike frame with light tape to be put on after the bike is rolling at race pace. If put on in transition, sunglasses usually are stored in the cycling helmet to keep them from being lost or knocked into traffic. No matter when sunglasses are finally put over the eyes, placing the frame under the helmet straps so that the helmet can be removed in T2 without removing the sunglasses is the fastest and best process for T2.

Mastering T2 Challenges

As in T1, triathletes want to minimize any time spent in transition during T2. By this time in the race, fatigue is beginning to accumulate. Most of the time, the race time is over the halfway mark. Tired legs are now asked to change from a circular pedaling motion to a stepping, running motion. This awkward change in activity can be made more comfortable with practice.

The best time to practice T2 is during brick workouts. Several tips can help triathletes practice T2 during brick workouts and on race day:

• **Drawing near T2**. As triathletes get within a quarter mile (.4 km) or so of the transition, they pull their feet out of their cycling shoes and pedal with their feet on top of the shoes, as they do when exiting T1. Triathletes looking for a fast dismount can do a flying dismount like that used by cyclo-cross racers, as opposed to a slower dismount that requires coming to a full stop and straddling the bike frame at the dismount line. For the flying dismount, one foot stands on the pedal as the other leg swings over the bike frame to the same side of the bike as the support leg. The free leg leads out front for a forward first step off the bike. The triathlete dismounts the bike at a full run from a moving bicycle.

• **Wearing socks**. Running without socks should be practiced in training before doing it in a race. Hot spots often develop into blisters when running sans socks. If the triathlete knows where the hot spots are, sport-lubrication or powder products can be put in the foot bed of the shoe to prevent or minimize blistering. Lubrication works for some triathletes, and powder products prevent blisters for others. Triathletes should practice to see what works.

• **Wearing shoes and a race belt**. With running shoes stacked on top of a hat and a race number belt, triathletes can quickly slip their feet into running shoes if the shoes have elastic laces. Triathletes grab the race number belt and a hat, and then begin running. Both items can be put on while running.

Making a Smooth Duathlon Transition

Many duathletes prefer to use a platform pedal attachment (see figure 33.2). The attachment runs the entire length of a running shoe so that more of the pedaling force can be used to propel the bicycle. A toe clip secures the shoe to the platform. The bottom of the platform has holes drilled for cleat attachment, similar to a cycling shoe. This device allows duathletes to transition from run to bike and back to run without a shoe change.

▶ **Figure 33.2** Platform pedal attachment.

Combination Workouts

Combination workouts bring two or more disciplines into a single workout, either for convenience or for specific race preparation. The most common combination workouts are swim to bike, bike to run (usually called a brick), and run to bike, depending on the goals of the triathlete and time of year.

Swim-to-Bike Workouts

A small segment of the triathlon population experiences some lightheadedness when transitioning from the prone position of swimming to the standing position of running, as triathletes do when moving from the swim to the first transition. Another small segment of the triathlon population experiences unusual leg fatigue going from swimming to running and then cycling. For these triathletes, one strategy is to set up a bike on a trainer on the pool deck.

Triathletes can begin with an easy swim of 500 meters or so and then transition to the trainer for an easy spin of around 10 minutes. They repeat this sequence two to four times in a single workout.

If the triathlete is not adapting or feels so lightheaded that passing out is a possibility, a doctor should be consulted to be certain that no medical issues are present. Depending on the severity of the problem, triathletes may want to be checked out before doing any swim-to-bike workouts.

As triathletes adapt to the easy swim-to-bike workouts on the pool deck, they should increase intensity by following a fast swim segment with an easy ride. The second round should be an easy swim followed by a faster ride. As adaptation to the transition between swimming and cycling continues, the triathlete can increase the intensity of both the swim and the ride.

Many triathletes do swim-to-bike workouts as a matter of convenience, particularly on weekends. Many do a pool workout and then head straight to a bike workout. With workouts sequenced in this manner, they can decide which workout or workouts should include intensity. As triathletes approach race day, they may want a swim-to-bike workout as a dress rehearsal for race day.

Bike-to-Run Workouts

Swim-to-bike and run-to-bike workouts are often called combination, or combo, workouts. The bike-to-run workout is often called a brick. Although the history of the word is not clear, one theory is that the name was given to the workout because when triathletes go from fast cycling to running, their legs feel like bricks.

To help triathletes adapt to the change of body movement and muscle recruitment from cycling to running, and the feeling that this change produces, aerobic brick workouts are a good place to start. Some prefer to do brick workouts every week throughout the training plan, but others limit brick workouts to once per month, perhaps as a workout during a recovery week. Others limit brick workouts to certain macrocycles. No standard has been set about how often to perform brick workouts, and some triathletes appear to make this adaptation better than others do.

In one study on elite international Olympic-distance racers, the intensity of cycling did not have an adverse effect on neuromuscular control and running economy.[1] Even moderately trained triathletes experienced little influence on running muscle recruitment after cycling.[2] These studies may lead the reader to believe that experience in the sport of triathlon eliminates any effect of cycling on running economy and muscle recruitment, but that is not true. A third study found that despite years of training, some elite triathletes do experience changes in leg movement and muscle recruitment in running after cycling.[3] The effects of cycling on neuromuscular control and running economy appear to vary among people.

When deciding how many bricks to include in a program, triathletes should consider their experience level, goal race distance, and race results. Slower sprint- and Olympic-distance racers are more likely to do short brick workouts. For faster sprint- and Olympic-distance racers, brick workouts are often in the range of 50 to 100 percent of race distance. For half-Ironman racers, bricks are often 25 to 50 percent of race distance. For Ironman racers, bricks become less important because the need for blazing fast transitions is not an issue except for the top triathletes.

For Ironman racers, the benefit-to-risk considerations of long brick workouts need to be evaluated. For example, how much value is gained from doing a 60-mile (100 km) bike ride followed by a 10- to 13-mile (16 to 20 km) run? Would this triathlete be better served by entering a half-Ironman race and using that race as part of the training strategy? Is the triathlete prone to running injuries? What is expected to be gained from the brick workout? Individual athlete strengths and weaknesses need to be considered when making training decisions. The bias should be toward conservative undertraining so that the triathlete remains injury free and mentally sharp.

Intermediate and advanced sprint- and Olympic-distance racers often complete brick workouts every 3 to 4 weeks. These workouts are done at the same intensity as other workouts in the macrocycle. The intensity portion of the brick can be structured in multiple ways:

- Aerobic ride followed by an aerobic run.
- Aerobic ride followed by a run that includes some portion at current training-cycle intensity. This run can be a steady effort or broken into intervals.
- Ride that includes some portion at current training-cycle intensity. This ride can be a steady effort or broken into intervals and is followed by an aerobic run.
- Ride followed by a run in which both disciplines include some portion at intensity.

Run-to-Bike Workouts

Duathlon T1 is easier to practice than triathlon T1 for most triathletes. Any yard or garage can be turned into a mock T1 area. The duathlete can go for the assigned run, return home, complete the transition, and head out on a bike ride.

The intensity for any run-to-bike workout should match the intensity of the rest of the workouts in that macrocycle. As workout intensity increases with an approaching race day, race-pace run-to-bike workouts can be included in the mix. Examples include the following:

- Run 5 kilometers, doing the last 1.5 kilometers at race pace. Immediately transition to an easy ride of 10 kilometers.
- Run 2.5 kilometers at aerobic intensity. Transition to a 15-kilometer negative-split ride. Begin at aerobic intensity for 7.5 kilometers and then ride the last 7.5 kilometers at close to race intensity. Faster duathletes can finish at zone 3 to 5a intensity and build from zone 3 to 5b in the second half of the ride.

- Run 5 kilometers, doing the last 1.5 kilometers at race intensity. Immediately transition to a ride of 15 kilometers. Make the first 7.5 kilometers at race intensity and finish at aerobic intensity.

The design of the workout should have intent for the duathlete. That intent may be transition practice, muscle recruitment when changing disciplines at an easy pace, or race-pace rehearsal. New and intermediate duathletes may consider making the workout distances less than race distances. Top duathletes may want the distances to be the same as race distances. They may perform only a portion of the workout at race pace so that they save the best performance for race day.

Conclusion

Whatever the level of the duathlete or the triathlete or the distance of goal races, an organized process for transition is helpful. The multisport athletes needs to be organized, smooth, and fast on race day. Rehearsing transitions at race intensity before race day helps eliminate errors and increases confidence when race day arrives.

Triathletes and duathletes may use only a few of the fast transition tips in this chapter to optimize T1 and T2 speeds. The more competitive the racer is, the more focus the racer will put on fast transitions.

The savvy racer will include combo and brick workouts to improve race time, not just to do a fun workout. When including these workouts in a program, the triathlete should be sure to have a specific purpose and goal for the workout.

Sports Medicine
for Triathletes

CHAPTER 34

Triathlete Body Maintenance and Medical Care

—John Post, MD

Picture a triathlete who has an injury or a nagging pain that's been slowing her down but who has an important race in the near future. How might she continue to train so that she doesn't worsen the pain but at the same time can prepare properly to arrive on race day at her peak of fitness? Many triathletes have done this balancing act at some point. This chapter focuses on preventing injuries and, if injury occurs, on knowing when to pull the trigger and involve the medical system. A triathlete who has a medical resource team in place before an injury can often get an accurate assessment of the problem and be back in training in a timely fashion.

Off-Season Recovery and Planning

Many annual training plans (ATPs) commence at the conclusion of the previous season with a rest period away from swim, bike, and run. This period is essential to cleanse the palate, so to speak. Psychologically, it ends one season and prepares the triathlete for the next, rekindling the fires of desire for what will likely be a long haul in the near future.

This period is definitely not one of inactivity. The triathlete is encouraged to engage in other activities and sports that he enjoys such as yoga, racquetball, basketball, and so on. Such activities veer away from the drudgery of a long swim or bike ride, thus helping to rejuvenate passion for the sport. Many people believe that 2 to 4 weeks is adequate to refresh and recharge.

During this time the foundation for the upcoming training year can be laid out in a structured fashion that first asks, Where am I physically? Triathletes can use this time to assess their health and fitness (see figure 34.1). In fact, such an assessment could possibly be one of the most important tasks of the off-season. Like the information exchanged in the doctor's office, the information that the triathlete produces here is important, because many coaching decisions and plans are based on it. Completeness is rewarded. Data should include any previous musculoskeletal surgery; triathlon-induced injuries, both recent and past, including cause if determined and remedy; accidents; and other areas of possible concern.

Armed with this information, the triathlete and coach can create the skeleton of a training plan for the upcoming year to decrease the potential for injury.

Review of previous triathlon-related injuries
- Injuries related to a previous season or sport
- Cause of each injury if known
- Remedy for each injury
- Plan to avoid these injuries in the future

Personal habits
- Adequate sleep
- Appropriate diet
- Weight concerns
- Spousal support

Health maintenance
- Tetanus up to date
- Colonoscopy
- Flu shot
- Skin review
- Other issues

Equipment and training site safety review
- Bike fit
- New batteries in lights
- Reflective clothing
- Day and night training location and surface evaluation

Injury resource team members identified
- Personal physician
- Bike injury expert
- Running injury expert

▶ **Figure 34.1** Personal health and fitness assessment.

If the triathlete understands from day 1 that reduction in the chance of injury is among the highest priorities, then deviation from the training plan will be minimized. In triathlon, the high volume of repetitive training makes it critical to use health assessments to lay a solid foundation for the season.

The serious triathlete keeps a detailed daily logbook, particularly when it comes to aches and pains, and most particularly when it comes to change. Often the solution to a physical problem can be found in those pages. The problem could involve a change in running shoes, the addition of hill work, pushing too hard on successive days, training hard when ill, altering cleat position, or other seemingly minor changes that are the keys to unlocking the causative factors of an injury. Coaches and others often incorrectly assume that a triathlete possesses a basic level of understanding about injuries, a misconception that can hinder diagnosis and recovery from an injury.

The whole point of training is the management of load, of the progressive increase of stress in a manner that does not produce unmanageable overload. The pages of the logbook contain clues about stress imbalance that might lead to injury. In some settings, complaining of pain or problems is seen as a sign of weakness. That circumstance is definitely not the case in triathlon, in which good information leads to good decisions.

Well before this stage the triathlete has defined a series of goals for the season, be they a physical challenge, weight loss or maintenance, fighting the effects of aging, or any number of other objectives. And now, like an athletic cartographer, the triathlete and coach can construct a map to triathlon success, giving the competitor the highest probability of toeing the start line in the first race of the season prepared for success with the lowest risk for injury. Decisions are made carefully by keeping previous injury patterns as part of the equation.

Triathlon can be risky business. As with any endurance sport, the triathlete's level of dedication (or perhaps level of addiction, because that term may be more accurate) may progress from fitness to overtraining to injury. Many bypass overtraining, instead proceeding straight to injury. If the risk is at one level for the single-sport competitor, we should consider the greater risk that applies to the multisport athlete. Triathlon participation is not a solo endeavor, so the triathlete's support system, including family and workmates, needs to be part of the analysis.

This personal health and fitness assessment can be done by triathletes of all levels at any time during the year. They should envision it as an ongoing process. A person who is taking a car on a long journey would perform just such an evaluation of the tire pressure, oil status, any recent nagging noises, and any changes in performance.

A similar review is done by the triathlete, perhaps if only on a subconscious level. This assessment is particularly important if there has been an annoying ache in the Achilles area, neck pain at the end of a swim workout, or worse. Part of the triathlete's query would include organ systems that had been a source of difficulty in the past. What am I likely to stress now? How is my training, focused on my race limiters, likely to exacerbate prior difficulties or injuries? In short, triathletes need to make honest, unbiased decisions about their abilities.

Being honest with oneself is hard. Minimizing or ignoring facts in this setting is incredibly easy. What active role are triathletes and coaches taking to correct the identified issues in the personal health and fitness assessment?

Note that many of those in coaching or teaching have never learned how to put an injury management plan in place, making it difficult for them to pass this skill on to the triathlete. Specific guidance is required for the triathlete to

- identify limiters early in the personal health and fitness assessment,
- become educated about the symptoms and causes of the current issue,
- seek clinical care to obtain an accurate diagnosis,
- follow some type of plan to remedy the condition just as she would follow a training plan, and
- understand that the plan comes not from the coach but from the clinical entity.

Injury Resource Team

In Joe Friel's *The Triathlete's Training Bible*[1] a good bit of time is spent defining and setting reasonable goals. We can't all win Hawaii. The thinking triathlete has created a seasonal road map that will allow him to meet certain racing performance criteria, ideally without incurring a short- or long-term injury. Part of this plan includes triathlete conduct (and a little bit of luck) in which measures are taken to avoid injury.

This process is continuous. The triathlete might strive to be the most careful bike rider in the group, the one least likely to crash or be struck by traffic. She is the one who pays attention to interval changes in footwear, watches the ever-changing weather, observes a schedule of bike maintenance and repair, and makes careful choices of when and where to ride.

But accidents and injuries happen even to the careful, prepared triathlete. Ankles get twisted on long runs, or shoulders may ache after a tough session in the pool. When the pain is not enough to consider altering the workout, medical intervention is likely not warranted.

Currently, medical professionals use the visual analog pain scale, or VAS, to quantify pain. It's a 0 to 10 scale, in which 0 is no pain, 1 or 2 is annoying pain, and 10 is the worst pain imaginable. If pain is a 3 or less, triathletes would probably benefit from an alteration or reduction in training without a visit to the medical team. But when the acuity of pain is higher and doesn't resolve with rest, seeking medical attention promptly is probably wise.

But if a person is in pain, where does he turn? A seasoned triathlete has a stable of resources, much like a golf bag full of clubs. The appropriate resource is chosen for the appropriate shot. Many consider it wise to have the following people as a part of an inner circle.

• **Local running shoe shop pro**. He has seen more running-related complaints—and come up with reasonable solutions—than any physician, and he has a stake in the triathlete's frequent return for more shoes and running-related products. If the search for a solution begins here, the triathlete may not need to seek medical attention at all. And besides, this consultation is probably free.

• **Local bike shop**. This is the place where triathletes may have purchased their bikes and other cycling gear. Many of the employees here have exceptional knowledge based on experience. For example, a nagging or chronic injury is often related to a poorly fitted bike. Many shops have professional bike fitters who can make adjustments and easily resolve such issues. The mechanics have not only turned wrenches on bikes for years but also race on the weekends. They will patiently answer the simplest of the triathlete's equipment and bike-fit questions.

• **Family physician**. Even triathletes get the flu and have hypertension, diabetes, asthma, and the like. The primary care physician's office is a great place to keep the engine tuned up, be reminded that a tetanus booster is needed, and much more.

• **Sports physician**. Many doctors include sports medicine as a small part of their practice. You might reflexively think of an orthopedic surgeon for those needs, and frequently, but not always, you'd be correct. But the trend in 21st century medicine is toward specialization, and a different choice would often be better. Increasingly, primary care doctors, physiatrists, and others emphasize the sports side. For example, Andy Pruitt, the director of the Boulder Center for Sports Medicine and world-renowned source for solving bike-related issues at the highest level (Lance Armstrong, Floyd Landis, Chris Carmichael, and Bobby Julich), is a doctor of education.[2] Such professionals have designed their practices with the athlete in mind.

• **Physical therapist, athletic trainer, or massage therapist**. States have various licensing requirements for these specialists. They also have a host of access variations. In some states, for example, a physical therapist can see patients only on physician referral. That said, after a condition has been diagnosed, these hands-on professionals may be an effective resource for a triathlete's return to normal activity levels. They may also play a role in triathlete recovery.

Triathletes normally experience some degree of pain while exercising and in the early recovery period. Usually the pain is just muscle soreness from a difficult workout effort. But if they begin to have specific pain in a joint or a muscle group, backing off a bit and reducing the load for a few days may be the appropriate action. Better to forego a full workout or two than risk potential peril.

If resolution of the pain does not occur, it may be time to see one of the members of the injury resource team. If these resource people have been identified before they are needed, activation at this juncture is a simple matter. One of the critical aspects of a smart training plan is the ability to get in specific volumes of intense quality training. If triathletes have underlying problems that keep them going easy day after day, they are not able to train optimally. Such training limiters need to be addressed.

Strength Training for Injury Prevention

Although chapter 18 covers strength and power training and chapter 36 deals with injury recovery, here we look at both from the point of view of the physician seeing the triathlete as a patient. In other words, what, if anything, can triathletes do (or not do) in their training to reduce or eliminate the potential for injury? We know that this process will never be foolproof. Even with the best planning and experience, unexpected outcomes occur.

Does strength training have a role in diminishing injuries in modern triathlon? Besides enhancing performance, increasing strength does play a role for many triathletes in decreasing their potential for becoming an injury statistic. The intelligent triathlete makes time in the training week to round out, or balance, the musculoskeletal system because doing so not only improves the probability of success on the racecourse but also diminishes the potential for injury.

Not all that long ago people thought that doing anything with weights was both foolish and arguably detrimental to the endurance athlete. The common misunderstanding in the past was that strength-related efforts would lead to bulking up—the Schwarzenegger look—and that although it might produce a striking appearance at the beach, it ultimately meant a slower, heavier, muscle-bound racer.

Six-time Hawaii Ironman champion Dave "The Man" Scott was among the first to understand the relationships among strength, performance, and injury. He did so quietly, amassing his first five wins before publishing *Dave Scott's Triathlon Training* in 1986.[3] He noted, "Most of the top athletes are faster runners than I am, yet I have been able to pass them at the end of triathlons, much to the surprise of many spectators" (p. 137). He goes on to point out, "Strength training . . . strengthens ligaments and tendons and joints and reduces injury potential" (p. 139). Tim Noakes, MD, in *Lore of Running*[4] states, "There is clear evidence to suggest that acute muscle injuries can be prevented by strengthening muscles and eliminating muscle imbalances between opposing muscles" (p. 783).

The National Strength and Conditioning Association (NSCA) defines strength as the ability of a muscle or muscle group to exert maximum force.[5] It is expressed as a one-repetition maximum, or 1RM. Similarly, muscle strength is the maximum amount of force that a muscle can exert against some form of resistance in a single effort.

Triathlon: A High-Risk Sport

Generally, although there are some notable exceptions, much of the current literature supports strength training for triathletes not only for performance gain but also for the purpose of its contribution to a lower injury rate. This point is of greater importance than many realize. Burns reported a 50 percent injury rate in 131 triathletes and noted that overuse accounted for 68 percent of preseason and 78 percent of in-season injuries reported.[6]

Unexpectedly, increasing years of triathlon experience was the most significant predictor of preseason injury risk. High preseason mileage increased the risk of injury during the season. In theory, shouldn't the overall triathlete population have a lower injury rate than a comparison group of single-sport endurance racers? If a triathlete comes from a cycling background, aren't the running and swimming workouts just cross-training? Well, maybe not. Some information does indeed point to a lower rate of overuse problems,[7] but many other studies show that the injury rate is much higher. Some report injury rates as high as 90 percent over a 5-year period.[8]

Some suggest that triathletes set themselves up for injury by participating in three endurance sports to excess. Thus, triathletes may tip the scale toward injury in all three areas instead of just one. In other words, if a running population sees metatarsal stress fractures, Achilles tendon strains, and IT band friction syndrome problems, and the folks at the swim club experience acromioclavicular and shoulder joint issues, they usually don't overlap. Not so in triathlon, which includes three endurance sports that usually require the athlete to perform longer and more frequent workouts compared with the single-sport participant. Using this logic, people suggest that triathlon is a high-risk sport.

Risk Factors

Risk factors for injury in triathlon have been identified as

- total weekly training distance,
- weekly cycling distance,
- cycling training pace,
- weekly swimming distance,
- number of weekly running workouts (not distance), and
- total number of workouts per week.

If the reader predicted that of all triathlon injuries, the rate of running injuries would be highest, that guess would be correct. Most, 58 to 64 percent, of these issues were running related, 16 to 34 percent were of cycling origin, and the remaining small percentage was related to swimming. The predominant areas of injury were the low back, knee, and Achilles. The final recommendation was this: "Triathletes should spend extra time strengthening those parts of their bodies in functional ways, i.e., during movement patterns which mimic those occurring naturally in their sports."[9]

Flexibility for Injury Prevention

When warming up before exercise, is being able to do a split that demonstrates a high degree of flexibility a desirable quality in all triathletes? Probably not. Flexibility has been defined as "the total achievable excursion (within the limits of pain) of a body joint through its range of motion."[10] The athlete today should know that flexibility is "an individual variable, joint specific, inherited characteristic that decreases with age, varies by gender and ethnic group, and bears little relation to body proportion or limb length."[10] To the benefit of the triathlon community, flexibility can be altered with appropriate exercise.

So why would a triathlete want to be more flexible, within certain boundaries? Many positives are associated with this practice, usually completed postworkout (infrequently before) or during a strength session. Some incorporate stretching into their workday routine by finding time intermittently throughout their day to practice. Flexibility can be too much of a good thing because the excessively flexible triathlete is at risk for joint dysfunction.[11]

The triathlete who has always been called double-jointed or was born with loose ligaments can be at risk. Joint dislocations to the shoulder, kneecap, and fingers are more common among such people, and although they make up only a small fraction of those who participate in triathlon, they account for a large proportion of those who have joint stability issues.

Various types of stretching have been proposed including ballistic, static, proprioceptive neuromuscular facilitation (PNF), and others. No single winner has emerged. Many good flexibility programs have been proposed, including an inventive regimen by Matt Fitzgerald in *The Complete Triathlon Book*.[12]

In short, although we have considered stretching and flexibility a required part of exercise, recent studies have shown that "increasing range of motion beyond function through stretching is not beneficial and can cause injury and decrease performance."[13]

Massage

The role of massage in triathlon is unclear. Athletes are told that massage speeds recovery, but no reliable scientific data supports this claim. But many say that it does feel good. They are told that massage increases or maintains soft-tissue mobility.

Reportedly, therapeutic massage functions as a collection of movements of both the deep and superficial layers of tissue to lengthen muscle units that have become contracted from lack of use, overuse, injury, or illness. Possibly by increasing blood and lymph circulation, massage can reduce anxiety and produce a sense of overall relaxation.

For the purposes of this text the word *massage* incorporates the classic understanding of the term, or the manipulation of superficial and deeper layers of muscle and connective tissue, as well as the Graston technique (inducing microtrauma with instruments)[14] and active release technique (ART), the soft-tissue, movement-based massage technique,[15, 16] and others.

Massage has been around for over a thousand years. More than 80 varieties of massage are recognized. A quick census today would show that the most commonly practiced specific technique is the well-known Swedish massage, which has been around for almost 200 years. It is classified as a relaxation sort of massage, and many types are known to Western practitioners.

The hands, feet, forearms, fingers, and other body parts can be used to perform it. Although some recommend massage preexercise, most use it for postexercise recovery and treatment of painful conditions. In a recovery situation, racers set their own schedules (often dependent on cost), be it weekly on an off-training day, biweekly, or even monthly. Many athletes perform self-massage. Injuries to the iliotibial band and quadriceps soreness respond well to treatment with foam rollers or other such devices.

Some believe that among the benefits are muscular relaxation and elimination of areas of spasm or trigger points, which they think reduces the potential for future injury. Others report that massage makes it possible for them to train harder because they believe it removes waste products from their muscles that would ordinarily persist.

In the athletic realm, the term *sports massage* is understood by many to incorporate a rehabilitative posture as might be found with strain and counterstrain, myofacial release, trigger point release, active release, and Graston. Supporters claim that techniques like ART can cure them of tendinitis, back pain, headaches, shoulder pain, carpal tunnel syndrome, and the like. These claims are difficult to validate. The ART website (www.activerelease.com) contains a plethora of ways to receive the treatment and courses to take, but it offers no research, no medical studies, and no peer-reviewed literature demonstrating that the technique is both safe and effective, achieves long-term success, and is based in science.

That said, the technique suggested is remarkably similar to the time-honored anchor and stretch or pin and stretch that massage and physical therapists and others use for deep soft-tissue work. Pin and stretch has been shown to be effective in scar tissue mobilization.

A similar finding persists at the Graston website, which describes the technique, supplies a possible explanation of its mechanism, and includes a list of providers.[14] But no scientific basis for the treatment is presented. Numerous athletes provide testimonials and stories of successes. So who are we to believe? When describing the Graston technique in *Science Based*

Medicine, Harriet Hall, MD, states, "The fact that lots of people use it and think it works does not constitute evidence that it actually works. Lots of people used bloodletting and thought it worked. Lots of people believe in astrology."[17]

Or, does the triathlete follow the teaching of Tom Holland, author of *The 12-Week Triathlete*,[18] who writes "While there are many claims about the supposed benefits of massage that I may question, I do believe that massage is extremely beneficial to athletes in general and triathletes in particular" (p. 128)? All those who have had a massage but have no knowledge of the specifics of the musculoskeletal system know that they felt better afterward. If they had sore legs from that interval workout or low-back pain from a long, hard bike ride, the massage made them feel better whether we (they) understand how it works on a cellular level or not.

But to the contrary, if a triathlete is in a situation in which a surgical procedure is recommended for some problem, what steps would he take to ensure that the procedure and the surgeon are safe and effective? Should we not expect the same from ART, Graston, and other practices? In short, massage is just one tool available to the triathlete. When used appropriately, it may play a role in both injury prevention and treatment. Further research may give us the tools needed to continue this discussion.

Conclusion

Health may be defined as the functional level or metabolic efficiency of a person. Health means being free from injury, pain, or illness. This definition relates well to this chapter because the more important aspects of triathlon health maintenance have been reviewed with a particular focus on information that is of practical value to the triathlete. Possibly the most important lesson is that triathletes themselves play a key role in the preemptive maintenance of their health, both body and spirit. Planning training with this in mind and having a medical resource team in place when things don't go according to plan contribute to the ultimate success of the season.

CHAPTER 35

Triathlon Injuries and Preventive Measures

—Nathan Koch, PT, ATC

The incidence of overuse injury is clearly prevalent in the sport of triathlon. To identify and treat overuse injury in a particular sport, it is critical to understand injury rates and causation. A study in the *Journal of Orthopedic Sports Physical Therapy* surveyed the training and injury patterns of 131 triathletes over a 10-week prospective period during the triathlon competition season and included a retrospective 6-month analysis of training history and prior overuse injuries. The study revealed that 50 percent of triathletes sustained an injury in the 6-month preseason at an injury exposure rate of 2.5 per 1,000 training hours. Thirty-seven percent were injured during the 10-week competition season at an injury exposure rate of 4.6 per 1,000 training hours. Overuse accounted for 68 percent of preseason injuries reported and 78 percent of competition season injuries reported. Increasing years of triathlon experience was the most significant predictor of preseason injury risk. A previous history of injury and high preseason running mileage increased the risk of injury during the competition season.[1]

In January 2010 the *Journal of Strength and Conditioning* published a study comparing the incidence of overuse injury between Ironman- (IM) and Olympic-distance (OD) triathletes (see table 35.1). The number of overuse injuries sustained over a 5-year period did not differ between OD and IM triathletes. Fewer OD triathletes (16.7 versus 36.8 percent) reported that their injury recurred. Although OD triathletes sustained fewer running injuries than IM triathletes did (1.6 ± 0.5 versus 1.9 ± 0.3), more athletes subsequently stopped running because of pain (41.7 versus 15.8 percent) and for longer periods (33.5 ± 43.0 versus 16.7 ± 16.6 days). In OD, the number of overuse injuries sustained inversely correlated with percentage of training time, number of intense run sessions, and bike hill repetitions. The IM overuse injury number correlated with the number of intensive sessions done (speed run and speed bike sessions).[2] In other words, higher intensity training reveals itself as a high-risk and high-reward activity.

Table 35.1 Comparing Overuse Injuries Between Ironman-Distance and Olympic-Distance Triathletes

	OD athletes	IM athletes
Injury recurrence	16.7%	36.8%
Running injuries sustained	1.6 ± 0.5	1.9 ± 0.3
Stopped because of pain	41.7%	15.8%
Number of days stopped because of pain	33.5 ± 43.0	16.7 ± 16.6

The entire musculoskeletal system plays a role in the optimal performance of the triathlete. If a link in the chain of movement is broken, the injury does not necessarily manifest itself immediately or even in the general vicinity of the breakdown. When attempting to diagnosis overuse injury in triathlon and create prevention programs, the entire chain of movement of the body must be addressed. Although each individual triathlete may have specific musculoskeletal and biomechanical concerns, some issues are unique to each discipline as well.

Swimming-Specific Injuries and Prevention

The most common swimming-specific injuries involve the shoulders, but injuries to the spine and neck are not uncommon.

Shoulder Injuries

Shoulder injuries are the most common injury among swimmers, typically resulting from increases in training intensity, volume, and distance. Because the shoulder is a ball-and-socket (glenohumeral) joint with a shallow socket and relatively large ball, it allows tremendous range of motion. This degree of mobility permits the shoulder to perform more movement than virtually any other joint, but it also makes the shoulder prone to breakdown under repeated stress. The average competitive swimmer swims approximately 60,000 to 80,000 meters per week. With a typical count of 8 to 10 strokes per 25-meter lap, each shoulder performs 30,000 rotations each week.[3] Although this training volume may be more than the typical triathlete performs, an understanding of how much movement is occurring in the shoulder is helpful in creating a picture of why it is so susceptible to overuse injury.

The most common swimming-related injury is described as *impingement syndrome* (generalized diagnosis that may include rotator cuff tendinitis or tendinosis, bursitis, long head of the biceps tendinitis or tendinosis, and so on) and presents as pain with overhead activity, pain at water entry or catch phase, and inability to sleep on the affected side.

Typically, these injuries are biomechanical in nature and can be addressed by modifying stroke pattern or in some cases by correcting the athlete's biomechanical restrictions. When dealing with an injured shoulder the triathlete should avoid the use of paddles and kickboards. Contributors to shoulder injury in the swim stroke are hand entry crossing midline, thumb down entry, asymmetric body roll, and unilateral breathing. Besides obtaining proper swim stroke instruction, the triathlete needs to increase spinal mobility and maintain good rotator cuff and scapular stabilizer strength. The following three exercises before or after each swim session can be helpful.

Thoracic Extension Over Half Foam Place the foam roll perpendicular to your midback. Extend your spine over the foam roll and lift both arms above your head (figure 35.1). Hold for 1 minute and repeat three to five times, moving the foam roller to higher segments of your thoracic spine.

▶ **Figure 35.1** Thoracic extension over half foam.

Rotator Cuff Strengthening Position 1 (figure 35.2a): Squeeze the towel roll down with the elbow and keep the elbow at 90 degrees at all times. Position 2 (figure 35.2b): Lift your hand while squeezing the towel roll and not moving the shoulder back. Slowly lower back to the starting position.

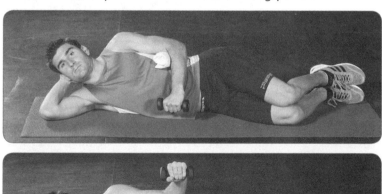

▶ **Figure 35.2** Rotator cuff strengthening: (a) position 1; (b) position 2.

Ts on a Physioball   Place your hips and core onto a physioball and place your feet on the ground for balance. Look at the ground to protect your neck. Keep your shoulders from rising up toward your ears. Concentrate on squeezing your shoulder blades together (figure 35.3). Keep your thumbs facing the ceiling.

▶ **Figure 35.3**   Ts on a physioball.

Spine and Neck Injuries

Although less common in swimming, a spinal injury may be more debilitating than an injury to the shoulder. Typically, spinal injuries become chronic in nature because they are adjusted or compensated for by the athlete's unknowingly changing the stroke pattern (i.e., turning out of one side only or rotating the trunk instead of the neck). Posture and positioning of the neck and shoulders during swimming, much like in sitting, plays a significant role in the amount of stress placed on the spine. In most cases, spinal injuries resulting from swimming are related to the aggravation of an already pathological spine by prolonged spinal positioning, meaning that the athlete has had a known or unknown spinal injury in the past.

Neck or cervical injuries can be described as radiculopathy, radiculitis, herniated or bulging disc, or degenerative disc disease with symptoms that may include radiating pain, numbness or tingling into the arm, scapular (shoulder blade) pain with turning or extending the head, a noticeable loss of head-turning ability, or sudden arm weakness or muscle atrophy. Low-back or lumbar injuries such as radiculopathy, radiculitis, spinal stenosis, herniated or bulging disc, degenerative disc disease, and sciatica may also include radiating pain, numbness or tingling in the lower extremity during or after swim, pain in the buttocks while sitting after a swim workout, or sudden leg or ankle weakness.

Preventing spinal injury in swimmers requires particular attention to the triathlete's symmetry of spinal rotation, mobility into extension, and overall posture. Exercises should focus on moving the spine with full range of motion. Exercises are particularly important for triathletes who have day jobs that require prolonged sitting or standing in one place. The following recommendations and exercises will help keep the spine mobile and its movement symmetrical.

Neck Rotation Stretch   Grab the right side of your head with your left hand and gently pull your head toward your left shoulder (figure 35.4a). Keep both shoulders down and relaxed. You should feel a stretch on the right side of the neck. You should never feel pain, numbness, or tingling. For a static stretch, hold the stretch for 1 minute and switch sides (figure 35.4b). Perform three stretches on each side.

If you perform stretches prior to swimming, perform dynamic stretches. Repeat the stretch multiple times without holding the stretch at the end range.

▶ **Figure 35.4**   Neck rotation stretch: (a) stretch the right side of the neck; (b) stretch the left side of the neck.

Seated Trunk Rotation on a Chair or Physioball Sit on a physioball with the hips, knees, and feet in line and the back straight. Lift your arms so that your hands are behind or to the sides of your head. Engage your abdominal muscles and core as you rotate your trunk as far as possible (figure 35.5). Do not allow the hips, knees, or feet to move. Feel the stretch around your midback and shoulders. Hold the stretch for 1 minute then stretch to the other side. Perform three stretches on each side.

▶ **Figure 35.5** Seated trunk rotation on a chair or physioball.

Standing Back Extension With Arms Overhead   Stand and lift your arms overhead, keeping the elbows straight and arms in. Gently extend your spine back, extending the neck and head last (figure 35.6). Think about moving each vertebrae individually from the bottom to the top. Feel the stretch in the spine, abdominal muscles, and shoulder blades. You should never feel pain, numbness, tingling, or dizziness. Hold the stretch for 1 minute then release. Stretch three times.

▶ **Figure 35.6**   Standing back extension with arms overhead.

Cycling-Specific Injuries and Prevention

Cycling is probably the most scientific of the three disciplines. A symbiotic relationship requires a perfect match of an athlete's unique biomechanical characteristics with a specific geometry to reach optimal performance. In other words, the bike must allow the body to function without excessive musculoskeletal resistance or wasted energy. When the body is pushed beyond its biomechanical limit, breakdown may occur and result in injury.

In December 2010 the *American Journal of Sports Medicine* published research on the incidence of cycling-related injury in professional cyclists. The researchers from Norway interviewed 109 professional cyclists about overuse injuries that they had sustained in the previous 12 months. Results of the study revealed that 45 percent of overuse injuries were located in the lower back and 23 percent in the knee. Twenty-three time-loss injuries were registered—57 percent in the knee, 22 percent in the lower back, and 13 percent in the lower leg. Few cyclists had missed competitions because of pain in the lower back (6 percent) or anterior knee (9 percent).[4] Note that lower-back injuries were the most common, although knee injuries resulted in the largest amount of training and racing time lost.

Although less common than low-back pain in cycling, cervical (neck) and thoracic (midback) injuries in cycling are frequent and typically related to the position of the head and neck over long periods. With the cervical spine maximally extended and the thoracic spine maximally flexed, tremendous stress is created at the transition, or breaking, point between the two. If the athlete has abnormal mobility or has sustained an injury in the past, this position can cause pain or create an overuse injury.

Neck and Midback Pain

In a 2007 study on the incidence of neck pain in multisport athletes published in the *Journal of Neurosurgery: Spine*, 164 athletes responded to a medical questionnaire. Approximately 64 percent of responding athletes reported that their neck pain was sports related. Total years in the sport and number of previous sports-related injuries were predictive.[5]

The most critical preventative measure that a triathlete can take with regard to neck and midback pain in cycling is proper positioning with a bike fit done by an experienced professional. Much like sitting at the computer all day, sitting on the bike causes postural stiffness and tension in the spine, creating potential for overuse injury. Prevention exercises for the neck and midback should focus on moving the spine in the direction opposite that which it remains in for long periods on the bike. Wall angels are good preventative exercises for the neck and midback. Thoracic extension over half foam (figure 35.1) and Ts on a physioball (figure 35.3) from the section on swimming injury prevention are also effective exercises.

Wall Angels Position 1 (figure 35.7a): Start with the back, hips, head, and arms against a wall. Position 2 (figure 35.7b): Raise the arms above the head. Slowly lower the arms down the wall, emphasizing squeezing the shoulder blades back and together. Complete two or three sets of 10 to 15 repetitions.

▶ **Figure 35.7** Wall angels: (a) position 1; (b) position 2.

Low-Back Pain

Low-back (lumbar) pain is an extremely frequent complaint in cycling, yet it is easily preventable. During cycling the lumbar spine is in a flexed or forward bend position, and the cyclist must be able to tolerate this position over long periods. To function optimally on the bike, the spinal, gluteal, and hamstring muscles and spinal and hip joints must be flexible enough to maintain this position with ease. In addition, muscles must be able to contract sufficiently to stabilize the pelvis and spine. Good strength and flexibility prevent excessive rotation and rocking on the saddle that can lead to overuse injury. The ability to stabilize becomes more important when positioning is aggressive or when power is increased.

Much like the cervical spine position on the bike, the lumbar spine position also mimics the sitting posture at a desk or in front of a computer. These prolonged postures create significant imbalances in muscle activation and restricted joint and soft-tissue mobility. The most critical preventative measure that a triathlete can take with regard to low-back injury is proper positioning on the bike facilitated by an experienced professional. Low-back exercises should focus on increasing spinal extension mobility and strengthening the back extensors and gluteal muscles. The following are preventative exercises for the lumbar spine.

Press-Ups   Lie face down. Push onto your elbows while keeping your hips against the floor or table (figure 35.8). Hold this position for 30 to 60 seconds or do 15 to 20 repetitions.

▶ **Figure 35.8**   Press-ups.

Back Extension Over Physioball   Lie over a physioball with your hips centered on the ball and your feet on the ground or supported against a wall. With your arms across your chest or your fingertips behind your ears, extend your torso up until your body forms a straight line with your legs (figure 35.9). Return to the starting position and repeat 30 times.

▶ **Figure 35.9**   Back extension over physioball.

Bridge With Long Arc Quad   Position 1 (figure 35.10a): Lie on your back with your knees bent and your feet flat on the ground. Tighten your abdominal muscles and squeeze your buttocks. Push your hips up so that they are level with your torso. Position 2 (figure 35.10b): While keeping your hips level and your thighs even with each other, gradually extend one leg so that the leg is straight. Do not allow the hips to drop. Alternate legs and repeat 10 to 15 times on each leg. Complete two or three sets. Use your arms to help you balance but not to lift you up. To increase the difficulty, cross your arms over your chest.

▶ **Figure 35.10**   Bridge with long arc quad: (a) position 1; (b) position 2.

Single-Leg Bridge Position 1 (figure 35.11a): Lie on your back with your knees bent and your feet flat on the ground. Bring one knee toward your chest. Position 2 (figure 35.11b): Lift your hips off the ground until your torso forms a straight line with your leg. Keep your knee bent. Slowly lower your hips to the ground, keeping your hips level. Alternate legs. Repeat 15 to 20 times on each leg. To increase the difficulty, straighten your lifted leg.

▶ **Figure 35.11** Single-leg bridge: (*a*) position 1; (*b*) position 2.

Pelvis and Hip Injuries

Pelvis and hip injuries in cycling, as in all sports, are becoming more common because medical professionals are gaining more knowledge and diagnosis is becoming faster and easier. On the bike, the skeletal and soft-tissue portion of the pelvis has four key contact points on the saddle that provide a stable platform from which the lower extremities can push and create momentum. The muscles surrounding the pelvis must be strong enough to act as stabilizers as momentum and forces increase. As the thigh gets closer to the chest at the top of the pedal stroke (extreme hip flexion), the lack of hip resistance becomes crucial to a stable pelvis, optimal power transfer, and avoidance of overuse injury.

Overuse hip injuries in cycling are preventable and are typically related to the millions of revolutions performed in this extreme hip-flexed position. Some cycling-related injuries to the pelvis and hip are discussed in the following paragraphs.

Femoral acetabular impingement (FAI) is a bony impingement of the femur on the acetabulum (hip socket located on the pelvis). The two basic types of bony impingement are CAM and pincer. CAM refers to a deformity of the femur at the head and neck junction. Pincer refers to an overgrowth of the acetabulum (socket). CAM and pincer deformity can occur independently or in combination. Pain is typically located in the groin or in front of the hip and is aggravated by a hyperflexed hip position (knee closer to the chest).

Athletica pubalgia (i.e., sports hernia) encompasses a variety of pelvic injuries involving the abdominal and pelvic musculature outside the ball-and-socket hip joint and on both sides of the pubic symphysis. Pain is typically located in the lower abdominal area and increases with hip extension or under abdominal strain.

Other injuries commonly seen in the hip are tendinitis and tendinosis of the hip flexor or hamstring tendons, bursitis, and proximal iliotibial band friction syndrome (ITBFS). These soft-tissue injuries typically resolve quickly, within 1 to 3 weeks, if properly cared for. Pain is usually localized to the tendon, is not deep, and increases with increased activity. These injuries may be irritated by sitting after workouts.

Preventing hip injury in a triathlete requires close attention to bike positioning as well as a specific exercise prescription. On the bike, the triathlete should consider reducing crank arm length, using an oblong or oval ring, emphasizing a flat ankle position at the top of the pedal stroke, and possibly raising the front end of the bike. Investigating saddle geometry that can best support the pelvis may be necessary. Proper positioning of the pelvis on the saddle, the amount of weight through the pelvis, and hip position during the pedal stroke will directly affect stability and subsequently the incidence of overuse injury.

Hip injury prevention exercises should focus on increasing hip mobility and increasing lateral and rotational hip strength.

Monster Walk   Place an exercise band around both ankles. Bend the knees and sit back while keeping body weight balanced on both feet. The shoulders stay directly over the knees and ankles throughout the exercise. Step to the side, reaching with the midfoot, and create resistance with the band (figure 35.12). Slowly follow the lead leg with the trail leg, working to control the resistance of the band. Do not allow the feet to touch. Keep the toes pointing straight ahead. Continue taking controlled steps with the abdominals and legs engaged while maintaining proper alignment and tension.

▶ **Figure 35.12**   Monster walk.

Sidesteps   Place an exercise band around both ankles. Stand tall with the abdominals engaged and knees extended. Maintaining this upright posture, step to the side, working to control the resistance of the band and reaching with the midfoot (figure 35.13). Keep the toes pointing straight ahead, abdominals engaged, hips level, and knees extended.

▶ **Figure 35.13**   Sidesteps.

Hip Flexor Stretch   Kneel with your trunk in a door frame, corner of a wall, or other sturdy frame. Keep your head, upper back, and gluteal muscles tight to the frame. Reaching your arms overhead, posteriorly tilt your pelvis to bring your lower back toward the frame (figure 35.14). For a greater stretch, reach your knee farther back.

▶ **Figure 35.14**   Hip flexor stretch.

Scorpions   Lie face down on the ground. Lift one leg toward the ceiling, keeping the knee bent. Next, keeping your chest close to the ground, rotate your hips so that your lifted leg crosses over your body (figure 35.15). Return to the starting position and repeat on the other leg. Complete 10 to 15 repetitions on each side.

▶ **Figure 35.15**   Scorpions.

Knee Injuries

The knee could be viewed as the center of activity for the lower body in cycling. In other words, the knee will go where the hip, foot, and ankle tell it to go. The knee functions primarily as a hinge joint and is powered by the prime movers in cycling, the quadriceps and the hamstrings. The kneecap and the femur create the patellofemoral joint. The patella, or kneecap, is a shallow saucerlike bone that floats when the knee is fully extended and gradually presses harder into a groove in the femur as the knee bends.

Hence, if conditions are present during the cycling motion that offset the tracking of the patella in the femoral groove, an overuse injury is likely to occur. Musculoskeletal conditions affecting biomechanics such as genu varus (bow legged), genu valgus (knock kneed), coxa varus (hip bowing), coxa valgus (hip angled inward), excessive or lack of femoral or tibial rotation, iliotibial band (ITB) tightness, leg-length discrepancy, and pelvic obliquity can create abnormal patellofemoral tracking and result in injury.

Anterior knee pain is pain in the front of the knee that is typically aggravated by actively extending the knee under load in an open (foot off the ground as a kicking motion) or closed (foot on the ground as in a squat) position. On the bike, pain typically occurs during the power phase of the pedal stroke (at approximately the 3 o'clock position) that increases under greater loads (seated climbing).

Lateral knee pain or iliotibial band friction syndrome (ITBFS) causes pain at the outside aspect of the knee. This pain is most common at the bottom of the pedal stroke as the knee extends. Therefore, it can be exacerbated by a saddle that is positioned too high.

Medial knee pain can occur as pes anserine tendinitis or tendinosis or bursitis. Pain is located at the medial or inside aspect of the knee below the kneecap. Swelling and tenderness are common at the location of the pes anserine. The pes anserine is an anatomical term used to describe the position of attachment for three tendons: sartorius, gracilis, and semitendinous. These tendons help control rotation between the upper leg and lower leg. During cycling, if rotation of the lower leg is excessive in relation to the upper leg, this condition may occur. This problem is sometimes related to type of pedal and cleat position.

Because the knee is so heavily influenced by hip and ankle mechanics during the pedal stroke, assessing the entire chain of movement is necessary to prevent injury. First, make sure that both knees are functioning symmetrically in the fore–aft pedal axle position and the knee flexion position at dead bottom center.

A comprehensive review study in *Sports Medicine* examined the effects of bicycle saddle height on knee injury risk and cycling performance. Most evidence suggests that a relatively small adjustment in saddle height (5 percent) affects knee joint motion by 35 percent.[6] Cleat alignment also heavily influences the position of the knee, and the alignment can be adjusted to reduce pressure or strain. A common recommendation is that pedals with float may assist in this reduction.

A research study in the *Journal of Biomechanical Engineering* concluded that everting the foot (turning it out) may be beneficial in either preventing or alleviating patellofemoral pain syndrome in cycling.[7] In some cases, such as a leg-length discrepancy, the knee may function differently on the left compared with the right. In this instance bike positioning becomes more complicated and requires a skilled medical bike fit to determine the cause and the amount of discrepancy. Assuming that a shim or lift between the shoe and cleat will solve all leg-length or asymmetrical issues is not safe. Although bike fit is critical to preventing knee injury, the triathlete can accomplish a lot by focusing on her own body through increasing the mobility of the hip and ITB and strengthening the hamstrings and gluteal muscles.

Foam Rolling for the ITB   Lie with the side of your thigh on a foam roller (figure 35.16). Roll up and down the iliotibial band in a slow, controlled fashion. The motion should stay above the knee and below the greater trochanter (hip bone). Repeat 10 to 15 times on each side and do two sets on each leg.

▶ **Figure 35.16**   Foam rolling for the ITB.

Hamstring Curls With Physioball   Lie flat on the ground with your heels centered on a physioball and your toes pointed at the ceiling. Dig your heels into the physioball, tighten the abdominals, and lift the hips (figure 35.17). Keeping the hips off the ground and pressure on the heels, pull the physioball toward your hips and then push it back out.

▶ **Figure 35.17**   Hamstring curls with physioball.

Dynamic Gluteal Muscles   Stand on one leg. Squat down and extend the opposite leg back, crossing it behind the squatting leg. (Think of the finish position in bowling.) Return to the starting position and alternate legs. Complete 30 to 40 repetitions on each leg.

▶ **Figure 35.18**   Dynamic gluteal muscles.

Foot and Ankle Injuries

Foot and ankle injuries in cycling are relatively uncommon, but they can be difficult to overcome. The foot and ankle create a small lever arm that should remain stable throughout the pedal stroke. Motion at the ankle should be minimal to provide a stable platform that allows the powerful quadriceps and gluteal muscles to transfer force to the pedals. The more the ankle moves, the more susceptible to injury it is.

Achilles tendinitis and tendinosis cause pain in the Achilles tendon that increases with increased intensity and is typically tender to the touch. Tendinosis refers to a chronic or degenerative condition of the tendon. This typically occurs in the cyclist because of a leg-length discrepancy, a shoe with a heel counter that is too high, or cleats that are too far forward.

Morton's neuroma, or in the early stages, hot spots, occurs in the forefoot (between the second and third toes or between the third and fourth toes). This inflammation of the nerve or nerve sheath is located between the bones of the foot, and it is typically very tender to the touch. Pain, numbness, and tingling get worse with increased cycling volume and training, with prolonged seated climbing, and when walking barefoot.

Metatarsalgia describes pain located at the forefoot that commonly is directly under the first or second metatarsal heads (ball of the foot). Callous formation will typically be found at the location of pain, and the athlete will overpronate and have increased pain with weight-bearing activity. Metatarsalgia usually occurs with increases in training intensity or volume, or with changes in footwear.

Prevention of foot and ankle injuries requires attention to pedal selection, cleat placement, and shoe preference. Although little research has been done on the optimal length, width, and shape of the actual pedal, the surface area of the pedal and cleat may influence foot pressures and subsequently result in overuse injury. Simply put, triathletes with bigger and wider feet may require a larger platform to reduce foot pain.

Cleat placement has recently been debated in the cycling world. Current efforts are to push the cleat position back from the metatarsalphalengeal location (forefoot) to the tarsometatarsal location (midfoot). This more rearward position of the cleat on the shoe can affect the foot and ankle positively by reducing pressure on the forefoot and by reducing the lever arm at the ankle. This positioning may result in less gastrocsoleus (calf) muscle activity and thus may reduce or eliminate forefoot numbing, reduce stress on the Achilles, and conserve the triathlete's calf muscles for running. At the same time, this more rearward position may negatively affect climbing performance.

Besides cleat position, actual shoe construction may contribute to injury. Proper width, length, height of heel counter, strap location, and material of the shoe insert are important considerations in selection of the proper cycling shoe. A research study done in *Foot and Ankle International* found that cycling shoes made with carbon fiber produced peak plantar pressures 18 percent higher than those of plastic design (121 kPa versus 103 kPa). Because most competitive shoes are made of carbon fiber, the addition of an insole, arch support, or metatarsal pad that will conform to the contours of the foot may be necessary.[8]

Foot and ankle injury prevention exercises during cycling should focus on maintaining gastrocsoleus muscle length, addressing tightness or restrictions in the soft tissue, and strengthening the small muscles in the foot that help stabilize the foot.

Gastrocsoleus Stretch With Midfoot Support   Stand with your hands on a wall and assume a lunge position. Align the outside of your back foot straight forward. Place a folded towel under the arch of your back foot and push your heel to the ground (figure 35.19). Hold the stretch for 30 to 60 seconds. Next, bend the knee of your stretching leg and repeat the stretch. This positioning will place more stretch on the soleus muscle.

▶ **Figure 35.19**   Gastrocsoleus stretch with midfoot support.

Foam Rolling the Gastrocsoleus   Sit on the ground with your legs straight and ankles crossed. Place the foam roller under your lower leg. Slowly roll up and down the length of the calf muscle (figure 35.20). Stay above the Achilles tendon and roll up underneath the knee. Roll 10 to 15 times on each leg and do two sets for each leg.

▶ **Figure 35.20**   Foam rolling the gastrocsoleus.

Arch Crunches   Place your foot on a towel and crunch your toes (figure 35.21), pulling the towel toward you. Continue this motion for 2 to 3 minutes and switch feet.

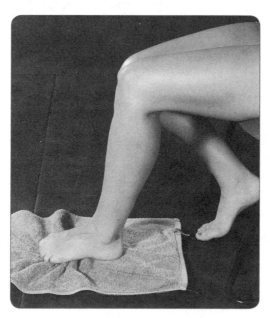

▶ **Figure 35.21**   Arch crunches.

Running-Specific Injuries and Prevention

Running injuries account for the most frequent and most debilitating injuries sustained by triathletes. Runners in general exhibit a higher incidence of overuse injury than cyclists or swimmers do. This discrepancy is typically attributed to the fact that running is a weight-bearing activity that results in forces acting on the body up to three times the athlete's body weight. This axial force coupled with the tremendous amount of eccentric (muscle working as it lengthens) muscle activity creates a stressful environment for the body and is the epitome of high risk–high reward training.

How likely is a runner to become injured during training? Where on the body do most injuries occur, and what are the significant factors? In a comprehensive review of 17 research studies on running injuries published in the *British Journal of Sports Medicine* in 2007, the incidence of lower-extremity running injuries in long-distance runners ranged from 19.4 percent to 79.3 percent. The predominant site of injury was around the knee (7.2 to 50 percent). The most significant results were that a long training distance per week in male runners and a history of previous injuries in males and females were significant risk factors for injuries.[9] Because of the wide range in running injury incidence reported, a specific study about the incidence of running injuries in triathletes would be a likely next step in the research.

For now, keeping a training log, having a coach, and listening to the body's response to training are the first steps to successful injury prevention. Additionally, assessing running technique and footwear under the expertise of an experienced coach or physical therapist is important. Much like the golf swing, run technique can be successful in many variations as long as the basic principles are observed. Additionally, exercise training in the form of resistance and plyometric training has resulted in enhanced running economy, possibly leading to decreased injury incidence.[10]

Lumbar Spine Injuries

Preventing lumbar spine injuries in the runner requires a review of the training program to assess body readiness for intense workouts, assessment of running gait and foot strike, and exercises that focus on spinal and hip mobility and core stability strengthening. Recent research suggests that by increasing hip extension mobility, the athlete can reduce anterior pelvic tilt and subsequently reduce compression and stress on the lumbar spine.[11]

Inchworm   Position 1 (figure 35.22*a*): Start in push-up position with the hands under the shoulders and the toes on the ground. Position 2 (figure 35.22*b*): Keeping the hands stationary, walk the feet toward the hands, lifting the hips in the air. Do not allow the knees to bend. Once in the uppermost position, keep the feet stationary and walk the hands forward to return to the starting position. For added stretch, drop the heels to the ground while lifting the hips in the air. Repeat 15 to 20 times while moving across the room.

▶ **Figure 35.22**   Inchworm: (*a*) position 1; (*b*) position 2.

Superman on BOSU   Lie on a BOSU ball, rounded side up, and have the hips centered on top. Keeping the arms forward and knees locked, lift both arms and both legs at the same time to Superman position (figure 35.23). Focus on squeezing the shoulder blades and the gluteal muscles. Hold for 30 to 60 seconds and complete two or three sets of 10 to 15 repetitions.

▶ **Figure 35.23**   Superman on BOSU.

Pike With Physioball   Begin in a push-up position with your feet on a physioball. Keeping the arms stationary and the legs straight, lift your hips and roll the physioball toward you until your body is in an inverted pike position (figure 35.24). Return to the starting position and repeat 30 to 40 times.

▶ **Figure 35.24**   Pike with physioball.

Pelvis and Hip Injuries

Pelvis and hip injuries in running differ from those that occur during cycling. The pelvis is more posteriorly rotated with the hip joint in extreme flexion on the bike, whereas in running the pelvis is typically tilted anteriorly and the hip joint must be able to flex and extend through the running gait cycle. As alluded to earlier, the ability of the hip joint to achieve hip extension during the swing phase of running is critical to efficiency, performance, and injury prevention.

Most pelvic and hip injuries occur because of poor running technique (lack of hip extension, excessive rotational or side-to-side movement, overstriding, heel striking), decreased muscle length (hip flexor or hamstrings), gluteal or adductor weakness, postural deficits (scoliosis, LLD), abnormal foot and ankle mechanics, training errors, or nutritional deficits. The number of female athletes with pelvic and hip pain has increased from less than 1 percent to 15.1 percent in the last two decades, and the most common activity is running.[12] These pelvic and hip injuries are discussed in the following paragraphs.

Femoral acetabular impingement (FAI), as in cycling, has bony impingements, CAM, or pincer, which commonly has symptoms of pinching sensation in the front of the hip or groin, groin pain, and deep ache in the hip with sitting or stretching. Pain is typically worse at the beginning of a run and may improve during the run, unlike the pain associated with a stress fracture.

Athletica pubalgia (i.e., sports hernia) encompasses a variety of pelvic injuries involving the abdominal and pelvic musculature outside the ball-and-socket hip joint and on both sides of the pubic symphysis. Athletes present with inguinal (groin) or lower abdominal pain that increases with running or physical activity. This condition can be challenging to diagnosis and is often misdiagnosed as a tendinitis or muscle strain.

Sacral, pelvic, or femoral stress fractures occur with significant increases in running volume or intensity. In addition to training errors, nutritional concerns and changes in footwear or orthotics may be related to stress fractures. More commonly affecting females, stress fractures present with generalized pain around the location of the fracture, and pain may increase during weight-bearing activity. Athletes cannot typically run through this injury.

Trochanteric bursitis is inflammation of the bursa sac, a sac of fluid that provides lubrication between a bone and a tendon. Pain is typically on the outside of the hip. The hip is tender to the touch and may be swollen.

Hamstring tendinitis or tendinosis in the posterior hip or buttocks region is inflammation or degeneration of the hamstring tendon where it attaches to the ischial tuberosity (sit bone). This injury occurs with increases in training intensity and is the result of increased strain on the tendon as stride length increases.

Piriformis syndrome refers to a painful condition located in the buttocks where the piriformis muscle is in spasm, injured, or irritated. Compression of the sciatic nerve may occur. Pain typically is located in the buttocks, although it may be referred into the back of the thigh (hamstring), and it increases with sitting, squatting, and athletic activity.

As with the lumbar spine, preventing pelvic and hip injuries in the runner requires a review of the training program to assess body readiness for intense workouts, assessment of running gait and foot strike, and exercises that focus on hip mobility and core stability strengthening. Changes to running gait posture and technique may also help. Recent research suggests that subtle increases in step rate can substantially reduce the loading to the hip and knee joints during running and may prove beneficial in the prevention and treatment of common running-related injuries.[13]

Hip injury prevention exercises should focus on increasing hip extension mobility and hip lateral and rotational strength. Along with the exercise presented here, sidesteps (see figure 35.13) and scorpions (see figure 35.15) are good for preventing hip injuries.

Clams With an Exercise Band Position 1 (figure 35.25a): Lie on your side and place an exercise band above both knees. Bend your legs so that your heels, buttocks, and shoulders align. Position 2 (figure 35.25b): Engage your abdominal muscles to maintain proper alignment. Keeping your feet together, slowly lift the upper leg from the lower leg.

▶ **Figure 35.25** Clams with an exercise band: (a) position 1; (b) position 2.

Knee Injuries

Knee injuries are the most common injury sustained during running. The most common knee injury occurring in runners is patellofemoral syndrome, which appears to be related to excessive coronal (side-to-side) and transverse (rotational) plane motion during the running gait cycle.

Excessive movement or lack of movement at the joints above and below the knee can negatively affect the function of the knee or patellofemoral joint and create increased stress. The knee must be allowed to function primarily in the sagittal (straightforward) plane with the least amount of load and time on the ground as possible. The knee joint undergoes a five-fold increase in quadriceps activity to support body weight on the ground. This increase is associated with a five-fold increase in the ground reaction force moment about the knee.[14] The muscles surrounding the knee joint must be strong enough to assist with absorption of this force.

The entire chain of movement above and below the knee joint must be examined to determine the cause of increased stress and injury. Additional research suggests that knee pain can be affected by alignment of the lower extremity (the amount of ankle motion, the presence of knee varus, or bowing, and the functional position of the forefoot).[15] Specific knee injuries that can occur in running are discussed in the following paragraphs.

Anterior knee pain (patellofemoral syndrome, fat pad impingement, patellar tendinitis or tendinosis, patellar bursitis, and chondromalcia patella) is pain in the front of the knee that is aggravated by actively extending the knee under load in an open (foot off the ground as in a kicking motion) or closed (foot on the ground as in a squat) position. During running, pain typically occurs at the impact and loading phases of the gait cycle.

Lateral knee pain or iliotibial band friction syndrome (ITBFS), as in cycling, is pain located at the outside aspect of the knee. During running, pain typically occurs at the end of the swing phase or at impact.

Medial knee pain or pes anserine tendinitis or tendinosis or bursitis, as mentioned earlier, is pain located at the medial or inside aspect of the knee below the kneecap. During running, if lower leg rotation is excessive in relation to the upper leg, this condition may occur.

Meniscus (cartilage) tear or injury can be located on the medial or lateral aspect of the knee and is typically along the joint line. Acute tearing occurs from a traumatic twisting or hyperextension event and is usually accompanied by swelling, tenderness, and locking or catching in the joint. A degenerative meniscal tear is a wear-and-tear condition that occurs over time and is typically related to either an old injury or abnormal running mechanics over many years.

Hamstring strain (tear in the belly of the hamstring muscles) exhibits pain in the back of the thigh. The athlete usually recalls the exact moment when the injury occurred. Typically, it is accompanied by swelling, bruising, pain, and difficulty walking. Evidence suggests that during the terminal swing of the running gait, the hamstrings demonstrate the most dramatic increase in biomechanical load when speed is progressed toward maximal sprinting.[16] Therefore, this injury typically occurs during sprint or interval workouts.

Prevention of knee injuries in the runner requires a review of the training program to assess body readiness for intense workouts. A recent research study concluded that an 8-week rehabilitation program focusing on strengthening and improving neuromuscular control of the hip and core musculature produces positive patient outcomes, improves hip and core muscle strength, and reduces excessive movement at the knee, which is associated with developing patellofemoral syndrome.[17]

Knee injury prevention exercises include the monster walk (see figure 35.12), sidesteps (see figure 35.13), and foam rolling for the ITB (see figure 35.16), as well as the exercise presented here.

Windmill Deadlift   Position 1 (figure 35.26a): Stand straight and balance on one leg. Hold a dumbbell in the hand on the side of the lifted foot. Position 2 (figure 35.26b): Slowly lean forward while maintaining a straight line from the foot through the hip and shoulder. Reach to the outside of the opposite foot. Keep leaning until hamstring flexibility limits the movement and slowly return to position 1. Position 3 (figure 35.26c): Hold the dumbbell in the hand on the side of the grounded foot. Slowly lean forward while your swinging leg turns away from your body.

▶ **Figure 35.26**   Windmill deadlift: (a) position 1; (b) position 2; (c) position 3.

Foot and Ankle Injuries

Foot and ankle injuries in running are common, and potential causes and prevention techniques are heavily debated. The barefoot running craze has had more effect on injuries to the foot and ankle than to any other joint. Although some studies found that running barefoot with a forefoot gait results in less axial forces, they did not examine the impact and strain on surrounding muscle and tendon.[18]

Experts generally accept that running with a forefoot gait technique is more efficient and creates less impact, although running barefoot has its own issues of safety and practicality. No research studies are currently available on barefoot running injuries. A study in *Medicine and Science in Sports and Exercise* demonstrated that using a more forefoot style of running results in a 33 percent decrease in stride length, a 45 percent decrease in vertical displacement of center of mass, and a 35 percent decrease in vertical impacts compared with rear-foot strike patterns.[19] The difference between a trained (forefoot running) shoe runner and a barefoot runner on incidence of injury requires more research. Proper footwear selection and running technique instruction may be the best option for prevention of injury.

Results from a study in *Clinical Biomechanics* revealed that high-arched runners reported a greater incidence of ankle injuries, bony injuries, and lateral lower-leg injuries. Low-arched or flatfooted runners exhibited more knee injuries, soft-tissue injuries, and medial lower-leg injuries.[20] Common injuries of the foot and ankle during running are discussed in the following paragraphs.

Achilles tendinitis, tendinosis, tenosynovitis, and bursitis all describe pain located at the Achilles tendon that increases with increased intensity. The tendon is typically tender to the touch, swollen, or thickened. This condition may occur because of increases in training intensity or volume or changes in footwear.

Posterior tibialis tendinosis, tendinitis, or medial tibial stress syndrome (shin splints) describes pain located on the inside of the shin. The posterior tibialis muscle and tendon, located on the inside portion of the tibia (lower leg), are under tremendous load as they work eccentrically to control the foot and ankle during pronation in the loading phase. Typically caused by repetitive overload, overpronation during the load phase, and muscle imbalances, this condition may also be initiated by changes in footwear or training.

Peroneal tendinosis or tendinitis describes pain located on the outside of the shin. The peroneal muscles and tendons are primary stabilizers of the foot and ankle during the loading phase. When injured, they are tender to the touch. This condition occurs more frequently in a cavus or supinated foot.

Plantar fasciitis or fasciosis is an extremely common inflammatory or degenerative condition that occurs because of repeated microtrauma to the plantar fascia as it inserts into the calcaneus (heel). When injured, significant heel pain occurs. The pain is worse with the first few steps in the morning, but the tissue typically warms up and feels a bit better throughout the day. During running, pain usually occurs in the first few minutes but improves as the plantar fascia warms up. A tear or stress fracture will cause pain that does not improve with activity and may exhibit localized swelling or bruising.

Morton's neuroma, or hot spots, occurs in the forefoot (between the second and third toes or the third and fourth toes) and is characterized by inflammation of the nerve or nerve sheath located between the bones of the foot. Typically, the area is tender to the touch and may feel like a marble is in the shoe. Pain, numbness, and tingling will increase as running volume and training increase. Walking barefoot is usually avoided.

Metatarsalgia describes pain located at the forefoot that commonly is directly under the first or second metatarsal heads (ball of the foot). Callous formation typically occurs at the location of pain, and the athlete overpronates and has increased pain with weight-bearing activity. Metatarsalgia usually occurs with increases in training intensity or volume or with changes in footwear.

Calcaneal cuboid syndrome is a condition that presents as pain on the outside or outside bottom of the foot, and it typically occurs in runners with a history of ankle sprain. This condition refers to a subluxation or abnormal movement of the cuboid bone toward the sole of the foot. It typically presents as localized tenderness, a slight indentation, and pain on the outside of the foot with walking, and it seems to occur more frequently in the overpronated foot.

Stress fracture of a metatarsal bone in the foot is the most common fracture that occurs in runners. Usually presenting as localized tenderness and pain with weight-bearing activity, a stress fracture often occurs following a sudden increase in training or a change in footwear. Runners with a supinated or rigid foot are most at risk for this injury. Caution should be used when using orthotics made of hard materials (plastic, carbon fiber) for this population. Additional attention should be paid to the fifth metatarsal because pain there should be differentiated from an acute fracture versus a stress fracture. Tibial (lower-leg) stress fractures may also occur in runners, especially those who have poor lower-extremity mechanics during the stance phase of running.[21]

Compartment syndrome or chronic exertional compartment syndrome is not fully understood, although it is theorized that increases in intramuscular pressure during exercise impair blood flow and subsequently cause pain. This condition typically occurs in the front, or anterior, portion of the lower leg and is more common in runners as a chronic syndrome. It is thought to be caused by lower-extremity malalignment, muscle imbalances, training errors, improper footwear, or poor running gait technique.

Evaluating shoe selection while actually running is critical to prevention of injury. Research has shown that motion control shoes caused the greatest percentage of runners to be injured regardless of foot type.[22] Furthermore, running shoes with more wear resulted in less trunk lean and longer stance time during running, emphasizing the need to replace running shoes frequently.[23]

Running technique training, footwear selection assistance by a knowledgeable professional, and possible integration of custom orthotics can provide significant injury prevention. In addition, strengthening the foot and ankle will provide stability when the foot hits the ground under the tremendous load of the runner's body.

Arch crunches (see figure 35.21) should be used in conjunction with the exercise presented here to prevent ankle and foot injuries.

Eccentric Ankle Inversion With Exercise Band   Begin with the foot relaxed and the band placing tension to the inside of the foot (figure 35.27). Scoop the bottom of the foot as far to the inside as possible, moving only your ankle. Do not let your knee move with your foot. Slowly return to the starting position and repeat Perform the action 30 to 40 times on each foot.

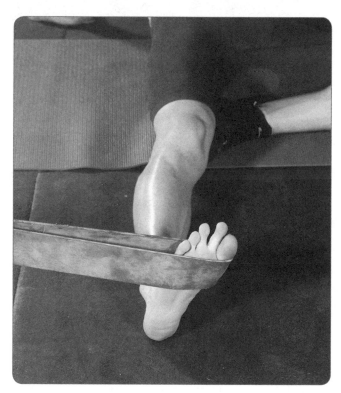

▶ **Figure 35.27**   Eccentric ankle inversion with exercise band.

Heel Raise   Stand on the balls of your feet on the edge of a box or step. Lift your heels up while keeping the knees straight (figure 35.28). Maintain pressure on the big toes. Do not allow the heels to move outward. After the heels are in the uppermost position, slowly lower the heels to the starting position. Repeat 30 to 40 times. To progress, try doing heel raises one leg at a time.

▶ **Figure 35.28**   Heel raise.

Training Through Injury

Although training through injuries is normally unwise, in some circumstances training can proceed under the guidance of a sports medicine physician or physical therapist. Table 35.2 provides general guidelines, although their applicability will vary with the severity and location of the injury. The various tissues in the body undergo different physiological methods of healing; some may require full rest, whereas others may even require exercise to stimulate the body's natural healing process.

Table 35.2 Training Through Injury

Type of injury	Yes	No	What can I do? (may depend on location of injury)
Bone		X	Swim and bike
Muscle	X		Swim, bike, and possibly run
Tendon	X		Swim and bike
Ligament		X	Bike
Cartilage		X	Swim and bike
Nerve		X	See physician
Fascia	X		Swim, bike, and run
Swelling		X	Swim and possibly bike
Redness or fever		X	See physician

Conclusion

Being successful in an endurance sport such as triathlon, in which triathletes can compete at any age, requires persistence and knowledge of injury prevention. Understanding how each triathlete's unique body responds to training, what signs warn of potential injury, and what preventative measures can be taken can mean the difference between ringing the cowbell on the side of the road and qualifying for world championships. The information provided in this chapter is not intended to diagnosis a current injury but to provide a resource to healthy triathletes so that they can sustain a lifelong passion for competition and health.

CHAPTER 36

Triathlon Injury Recovery Techniques

—Nathan Koch, PT, ATC

Full recovery from injury is critical to a executing a successful training program and ultimately achieving the triathlete's goals. Recovery from injury is typically multifactorial and may require a team of experts to determine the path to full recovery. Finding a sports medicine clinician with experience in helping triathletes recover from injury is the first and most critical step in resolving injury. Determining the cause of the injury, and not just treating symptoms, may take more commitment from the athlete and the treating clinician, but doing so will set the course of treatment in the right direction.

The following are some, but not all, injury recovery techniques used by sports medicine clinicians. In the sports medicine world and the medical world in general, the phrase *practicing medicine* is used for a reason. A technique or treatment that works well for one triathlete may not work for the next with the same condition. "More research is needed" is a common statement in the medical literature; hence, the athlete's treatment is based on the current research available, the clinician's experience, and trial and error.

Therefore, these techniques or procedures are provided as potential solutions to overcoming injury for the triathlete. The following are grouped into three categories: DIY with a bit of guidance, conservative clinician-assisted treatments, and invasive clinician-assisted treatments. They may be used in combination or individually, depending on the clinician's preference, the specific injury and, most important, the triathlete's preference.

DIY (Do It Yourself) With a Bit of Guidance

Several injury recovery methods can be initiated by the triathlete with a little instruction. Although an appointment with a sports medicine professional is not necessary to begin these treatments, occasionally a consultation is helpful to address technique or form.

Core Strengthening

Core strengthening can be described as control of the trunk during complicated movements such as swimming, cycling, and running involving a complex interaction between the nervous, muscular, and skeletal systems. Although many exercises are available to athletes, establishing a core strengthening program that focuses on the triathlete's specific weak muscles and movements is critical to injury recovery and injury prevention.

In other words, programs designed to increase core strength in the triathlete should have specific goals. The scapular, back, abdominal, and hip muscles should all be considered when implementing a core training program.

Although researching every available core exercise to determine which one best activates the intended muscle is virtually impossible, one study at least got the ball rolling. A study in the *Journal of Orthopedic and Sports Physical Therapy* tested the ability of eight Swiss ball exercises (roll-out, pike, knee-up, skier, hip extension right, hip extension left, decline push-up, and sitting march right) and two traditional abdominal exercises (crunch and bent-knee sit-up) on activating core (lumbopelvic hip complex) musculature.[1]

Results revealed that the roll-out and pike (figure 36.1) were the most effective exercises in activating upper and lower rectus abdominis, external and internal obliques, and latissimus dorsi muscles, while minimizing lumbar paraspinals (back extensors) and rectus femoris (quadriceps) activity. The pike with physioball exercise in chapter 35 is a good example of the pike exercise that activates these muscles.

▶ **Figure 36.1** Pike with physioball. See chapter 35.

Eccentric Strengthening

Eccentric strengthening is the gold standard in the research literature for treating overuse tendon injuries (tendinosis or tendinopathy). For instance, eccentric exercises have the most evidence of effectiveness in treatment of Achilles tendinopathy compared with extracorporeal shockwave therapy, local corticosteroid treatments, prolotherapy (an injection of an irritant solution such as dextrose or sugar water that is thought to increase blood supply and repair damaged connective tissue), and topical nitroglycerine application.[2]

Eccentric contractions occur when the muscle is contracting as it is lengthening. These contractions are commonly described as negatives. They are more forceful contractions than concentric (muscle shortening) contractions, and they strengthen the connective tissue to a greater degree. This type of strengthening is critical to fixing a tendon injury long term and preventing future injury. Achilles tendinosis, patellar tendinosis, and hamstring tears are three common overuse injuries that are frequently cited in the literature as responding favorably to eccentric strengthening.

Ice

Ice or cold plunge has been used for decades to control swelling and inflammation from acute injuries. It may not be as beneficial for chronic injuries except for temporary pain relief. Ice is the simplest form of injury recovery, and it should be used early and often in an acute injury such as ligament sprain, muscle sprain, or joint irritation. Temperature should be between 33 and 59 degrees Fahrenheit (between 0.5 and 15 degrees Celsius) for 10 to 20 minutes.

Although ice should be applied immediately in the case of acute injury, ice baths used as a preventative measure may make sense to avoid aches immediately after hard efforts. Because ice constricts the blood vessels that involve normal protein synthesis in the muscle, recovery could possibly be slowed by using ice sooner than 2 or 3 hours after hard efforts. To address this theory, more research is needed on how ice or vasoconstriction of blood vessels affects muscle recovery and how soon after activity to apply ice.

Spinal Stabilization

Spinal stabilization refers to a group of exercises focusing on segmental spinal stabilization. Exercises focused on deep abdominal and spinal muscles (transversus abdominis and the multifidus) have been shown to be superior to exercises focused on superficial muscles (rectus abdominis, obliques, and erector spinae) in reducing pain and decreasing disability in people with low-back pain.[3]

People with chronic low-back pain typically exhibit atrophy or weakening of spinal and hip flexors muscles. This weakness typically correlates with the painful or injured side and would indicate a strong necessity for exercises that isolate this musculature. Typically, these exercises are prescribed by physical therapists and may include exercises such as back or hip extension or supine bridging exercises such as the bridge with long arc quad and single-leg bridge exercises discussed in chapter 35 (figures 36.2 and 36.3).

▶ **Figure 36.2** Bridge with long arc quad. See chapter 35.

▶ **Figure 36.3** Single-leg bridge. See chapter 35.

Stretching

Stretching is a heavily debated topic that requires continued research and, more important, good clinical judgment. Research and opinions vary dramatically on what stretches to do, how long to hold them, when to perform them, and whether stretching can be detrimental to athletic performance.

When used for specific injuries, stretching or range of motion exercises that are prescribed specifically to target damaged or restricted tissue are crucial to recovery. Current thinking in the sports medicine world suggests the use of dynamic or movement stretching that mimics the athlete's movement in sport before activity and static or sustained position hold stretching after training.

Evidence for stretching hamstring and hip flexors (specifically the rectus femoris) in runners was presented in a study in *Gait and Posture* in February 2010.[4] The peak length of the right (trailing limb) hip flexor was nearly identical between walking and running, whereas the maximum length of the rectus femoris, a hip flexor and knee extensor, increased during running. The maximum length of the left (leading limb) biceps femoris (hamstring) was also unchanged between walking and running. Further, the timing of peak hip flexor length and peak opposite-leg hamstring length occurred essentially simultaneously during running, at a time during gait when the hamstrings are most vulnerable to stretch injury.

Therefore, hip flexor stretching in combination with hamstring stretching may be beneficial in the treatment and prevention of running-related hamstring injury. Although an entire book could be written on the topic of stretching, an excellent clinical research review titled "To Stretch or Not to Stretch: The Role of Stretching in Injury Prevention and Performance" in the *Scandinavian Journal of Medicine and Science in Sports* by M.P. McHugh and C.H. Cosgrave provides a fantastic summary of the available research.[5]

Water Running

Water running, or reduced-body-weight running, is a common prescription for runners who sustain a stress fracture or for athletes as they recover from surgery. Water running is used to reduce vertical forces through the bone and soft tissue. A recent study comparing running in water at chest level versus hip level revealed vertical forces corresponding to 0.80 and 0.98 times the subject's body weight at the chest and hip level, respectively. Anteroposterior (forward to backward) forces corresponded to 0.26 and 0.31 times the subject's body weight at the chest and hip level, respectively. As the water level decreased, the subjects ran faster.

Therefore, the immersion level and speed must be considered because they can affect the force components, mainly in the anteroposterior direction.[6] The advent of antigravity treadmills has allowed greater control of these conditions, although they are expensive to use and not widely available.

Conservative Clinician-Assisted Treatments

Some injury recovery methods require the assistance of a licensed sports medicine clinician. In most cases, an appointment for an evaluation is necessary before initiating treatment.

Compression Machines

Compression machines have been used for years in the medical profession. Significant research has shown that these machines are effective in treating wound healing, venous insufficiency, and lymphedema. More recently, compression machines have entered the sports medicine world in the treatment of postoperative and postfracture swelling in addition to muscle recovery.

Although results are quantifiable in the treatment of joint or limb swelling after an acute injury or postsurgery, more research is needed to determine the effectiveness of their use for muscle recovery and injury prevention. The most effective devices appear to be those that mimic normal human physiology and provide segmented and milking compression.

Dry Needling

Dry needling is a medical treatment modality to produce inoculations in the injured tissue leading to increased blood and nutrient delivery. Besides causing localized response in the affected tissue, dry needling is also believed to create nervous system stimulation leading to endorphin release and reduced transmission of pain signals.

Dry needling requires specialized training and is performed by physicians, physical therapists, and chiropractors. It is typically performed every 48 to 72 hours to allow continuation of the process.

Minimal research is available about using dry needling for treatment in overuse injuries, although it appears promising for overuse tendon and muscle injuries. Little to no pain is involved with this technique, but some injuries or conditions such as injuries to the chest or abdomen may be contraindicated secondary to use of needles.

Electrotherapy

Electrotherapy agents and electrical stimulation are used in a variety of forms (high-volt galvanic, Russian, TENS, microcurrent, ultrasound, laser therapy, and others). Electrotherapy is typically used in physical therapy clinics, athletic training rooms, and chiropractic offices to help alleviate pain by blocking pain signals, reduce swelling, or activate an atrophied or weak muscle. These modalities are typically used within the first 1 to 2 weeks after an acute injury such as an ankle sprain or postsurgery to reduce pain and swelling.

High-voltage galvanic electrical stimulation has been shown to heal wounds and reduce swelling. Russian electrical stimulation is useful in the rehabilitation of an atrophied muscle such as the quadriceps after knee surgery. Electrical stimulation in any form does not fix or cure injury and is only an adjunct to other treatments. Low-level laser therapy is the application of light by a low-powered laser to an injury. Its clinical effectiveness is debated, and agreement is limited about the appropriate settings or parameters of the machines.

Instrument-Assisted Tissue Mobilization

Instrument-assisted tissue mobilization, such as augmented soft-tissue mobilization (ASTYM) and Graston, is used by certified clinicians to address fibrotic adhesions that develop in a tendon because of prolonged stress and trauma over time.

Basic medical science describes an injured tendon (tendinopathy) as a chronic or degenerative condition rather than inflammation. This degenerative condition creates abnormal orientation of tendon fibers and scar-tissue-like properties. An analogy used to describe what is occurring during this type of treatment is that the injured tissue is like spaghetti in a bowl, whereas normal tissue should look like spaghetti in a box.

ASTYM may be used only by physical therapists, whereas Graston may be used by chiropractors or physical therapists. ASTYM uses plastic tools, graded pressure, and a treatment philosophy that focuses on stimulating the body's natural healing process and includes specifically prescribed exercises. Graston uses metal tools and graded pressure with or without exercises.

These instrument-assisted techniques are most beneficial for tendinosis, tendinitis, tenosynovitis, muscle strains, carpal tunnel, and postop scarring. They require as little as 1 treatment to 12 treatments to resolve the issue.[7] They may also accelerate early healing following an acute ligament injury.[8] An added bonus of these two treatments is that the athlete is instructed to continue with training and exercise, albeit with possible limitations depending on severity of injury.

Spinal Manipulations and Mobilizations

Spinal mobilizations and manipulations are performed by physical therapists, chiropractors, and osteopathic physicians. These manual techniques (clinicians using their hands to treat) are used to increase joint mobility and motion. Typically, they are used to treat spinal injuries and pain, although they may be used effectively in other joints.

Thoracic (midback) thrust manipulations have been shown to provide greater improvements in pain, cervical (neck) range of motion, and disability in the short and long term when compared with passive treatment involving electrical stimulation (TENS) and deep heat (infrared).[9]

With a lesser degree of effectiveness, the athlete can perform self-mobilization of a joint to increase joint mobility and range of motion. Examples would include thoracic spine (midback) stretches over a half foam roller for shoulder and neck injuries or prone press-ups for low-back and disc injuries. Thoracic extension over half foam (figure 36.4) and press-ups (figure 36.5) are described in chapter 35.

▶ **Figure 36.4**   Thoracic extension over half foam. See chapter 35.

▶ **Figure 36.5**   Press-ups. See chapter 35.

Massage

Massage is extremely variable in technique and form throughout the world of massage therapy. Although little research supports the use of massage as a long-term recovery technique, it may serve as a good adjunct to other treatment techniques because it can improve range of motion in the limbs and spine.

Anecdotal improvements are frequently reported by athletes who use massage as a body maintenance or prevention technique, whether using device-assisted (i.e., foam roller) techniques or when provided by a skilled therapist. Massage appears most helpful in the recovery of muscle strains and fascia injuries such as ITB syndrome.

Current research evidence has not affirmed the use of massage to reduce pain associated with delayed onset muscle soreness (DOMS), to enhance sports performance or recovery significantly, or to play a significant role in the rehab of sports injuries.[10] Further, using massage immediately after a hard effort or race may have detrimental effects on removal of lactate from the muscle and hence muscle recovery.[11]

Nerve-Gliding Techniques

Nerve-gliding techniques are used by physical therapists to floss the sheath that surrounds an injured peripheral nerve, such as the median nerve in carpal tunnel syndrome or the ulnar nerve in handlebar or cyclist palsy. In other words, these stretching techniques are prescribed by physical therapists to assist in recovery of nerve injuries that occur away from and are unrelated to the spine and are typically the result of excessive compression forces.

NSAIDS

Non-steroidal anti-inflammatory drugs (NSAIDS), such as Ibuprofen and Aleve, are effective at controlling injury pain and inflammation. NSAIDS appear to provide pain relief in the short term, but their effectiveness in the long term has not been demonstrated. For most triathletes, a bottle of NSAIDS is as important as swim goggles in the gear bag.

A recent study in the *British Journal of Sports Medicine* involving triathletes competing in the 2008 Brazil Ironman found a high prevalence of NSAID consumption, limited awareness of their effects and side effects, and a high rate of nonprescribed use.[12] Because these drugs are available over the counter, have a long history, and provide the ultimate ease of use (pill), they are extremely common and often abused. Although effective for tendon, muscle, and joint injuries, they should be used with caution. Long-term use of NSAIDS for pain management can negatively affect the cardiovascular system, gastrointestinal tract, liver, and kidneys.

Orthotics

Significant debate continues regarding the effectiveness of custom and over-the-counter orthotics in reducing and correcting overuse injury. Because of the extreme variability of opinion among medical practitioners about process, materials, and examination, it is not hard to understand the persistence of this debate.

Orthotics are commonly prescribed by sports medicine clinicians such as physical therapists, chiropractors, and podiatrists. Certainly, a degree of science and art is involved when designing custom orthotics. Significant evidence is available proving the effectiveness of orthotics in pain reduction and reduction of functional impairment in runners.

A recent study in *Medicine and Science in Sports and Exercise* found that custom foot orthotics used in running shoes alter the muscle activation of the peroneal muscles (higher preactivation before foot strike) in runners with overuse injuries.[13] Although this study has some limitations, it suggests that orthotics provide enhanced dynamic control of ankle stability.

A review of the available research reveals many positive and unremarkable or negative findings with regard to over-the-counter or prefabricated and custom-made foot orthotics. Thus, the individualistic nature of each athlete must be recognized, and the need should be assessed based on a dynamic running or cycling examination.

Orthotics should be considered when dealing with patellofemoral injuries and foot and ankle conditions. Note that orthotics for cycling and running should be examined individually because the mechanics of how the foot and ankle load are dramatically different in these two sports.

Tape

Clinicians and athletes use various types of tape to reduce pain and improve performance. There is no evidence to prove that tape application has a direct effect on athletic performance. There is likely no increase in power, muscle firing, or proprioception (limb awareness in space) when tape is applied to healthy subjects. Tape has some capability to increase muscle firing patterns and decrease load on an injured knee or shoulder joint.

Note that the tape should be applied by a licensed sports medicine clinician, not by the triathlete himself. Taping alone does not address the underlying culprit of the injury, although it may help speed the healing process. Taping techniques can be beneficial for the following conditions: calcaneal cuboid syndrome, patellofemoral syndrome, plantar fasciitis, shoulder impingement, and elbow tendinitis or tendinosis.

Topical Pharmaceuticals

Topical pharmaceuticals such as nitroglycerine, ketoprofen, and dexamethasone can be delivered in an absorbable patch, in a cream, or in a physical therapy clinic through an electrotherapy method such as ultrasound or iontophoresis. Nitroglycerine (NTG) is a vasodilator commonly used in heart conditions that has been used in the form of a nitrous oxide patch, controversially, in chronic tendon injuries that require increased blood flow to heal. This treatment is most commonly used in the Achilles tendon because its blood supply is poor.

One meta-analysis review article concluded that in chronic tendinopathy, strong evidence supported the use of NTG for relieving pain during activities of daily living and increasing tendon strength.[14] Ketoprofen and dexamethasone are anti-inflammatory medications that can be delivered directly to the injured tendon, ligament, or joint by a form of electrical stimulation (iontophoresis) or ultrasound (phonophoresis) without some of the side effects of ingesting medication. But the evidence is questionable regarding its effectiveness, and theoretical concerns remain about its repeated use and long-term effects on soft tissue.

Traction

Traction or decompression is used to create disc decompression in conditions such as herniated disc, degenerative disc, and sciatica. It can be used in the treatment of cervical (neck) or lumbar (low-back) injuries. Typically prescribed and performed by physical therapists or chiropractors, spinal decompression is achieved by a traction or decompression machine.

Traction is a conservative treatment that should be attempted before considering spinal injections or surgery. Traction appears most effective for spinal conditions that refer pain into the extremities and have signs of nerve root compression such as numbness and tingling.

Invasive Clinician-Assisted Treatments

The following injury recovery methods are more aggressive in nature or invasive. These treatments may be more controversial in the medical literature, have more significant side effects, and should typically be considered after conservative care has failed.

Corticosteroid Injections

Corticosteroid injections (sometimes referred to as cortisone or steroid injections) are the most commonly used injections in the treatment of sports injury and arthritis. Despite the effectiveness of corticosteroid injections in the short term, noncorticosteroid injections offer fewer immediate and long-term side effects.

A review of the medical literature involving complications associated with the use of corticosteroids in the *Clinical Journal of Sports Medicine* revealed that the existing medical literature does not provide precise estimates for complication rates following the therapeutic use of injected or systemic corticosteroids in the treatment of athletic injuries. Tendon and fascial ruptures are often reported complications of injected corticosteroids, whereas tibial stress fractures and multifocal osteonecrosis (bone death) were described with systemic corticosteroids (i.e., drugs taken by mouth).[15]

Hyaluronic Acid Injections

Hyaluronic acid (HA) injections, commonly referred to as viscosupplementation, are injections indicated for the treatment of pain in osteoarthritis of the knee in patients who have failed to respond adequately to conservative care. These joint-lubricating injections must be prescribed and performed by a trained physician. Although significant improvement appears to occur in the treatment of joint arthritis, more research is needed to determine effectiveness in other joints and injuries.

Platelet-Rich Plasma Therapy

Platelet-rich plasma therapy, or PRP therapy, is a relatively new and controversial injection therapy that uses the athlete's own blood to assist with tissue healing. The first available study about using PRP therapy for Achilles tendonitis did not exhibit favorable results.[16] More research is needed on how effective it is, what conditions are appropriate, what specific quantity of cells should be used, and how many and over what timeframe injections should be given.

PRP therapy can be prescribed and performed by sports medicine physicians. The high cost of treatment and the amount of time off from training (ranges from 1 week to months depending on physician protocol) are typically the primary concerns from athletes. Platelet-rich plasma has also been used for chronic conditions such as plantar fasciitis, ankle sprains, lateral epicondylitis, and hamstring insertion strains.

Prolotherapy

Prolotherapy is an injection therapy that typically uses a sugar-based compound that is intended to irritate the region and promote tissue healing. It is not effective for complete tendon tears and is minimally effective for degenerative joint disease. More research is needed to identify the conditions that respond best to these injections. They are used primarily by naturopathic physicians, who have reported success for tendon and ligament injuries. Eccentric loading exercises combined with prolotherapy may provide more rapid improvements in symptoms than eccentrics alone.[17]

Stem Cell Therapy

Stem cell therapy (autologous bone-marrow-derived mesenchymal stem cells) is a controversial topic that may have potential either to fade away or to become the latest and greatest in sports injury recovery. It is currently being used experimentally for injuries to cartilage, disc, bone, tendon, and ligament.

Little research is currently available about the effectiveness in the short and long term. Much like PRP therapy, this treatment is cost prohibitive and requires athletes to refrain from training for a significant time. A recent study reported that reinjury rates in horses following tendon injury are high with conventional treatment but that the use of stem cells has resulted in a significant reduction in tendon reinjury in National Hunt racehorses.[18]

Surgery

In most cases, surgery is a last resort, because it never restores the injured area to normal. An athlete dedicated to training will need equal dedication to conservative treatment measures before resorting to surgery. Unfortunately, some injuries will probably fail to respond to conservative measures.

For instance, surgery is indicated if a tendon is completely torn. Most partial tears can be rehabbed and must be given 3 months of rehab at the very least before surgery is considered. If a tendon is completely torn, surgery is the only available option to restore function to the tendon and its muscle. Common examples would be rotator cuff tear, patellar tendon tear, and Achilles tendon tear.

Additional injuries that should have surgery as a viable option would be disc herniation that causes muscle weakness, cartilage (articular or hyaline) damage in a joint, some grade 3 ligament tears, displaced or unstable fractures, acute compartment syndrome, and athletic pubalgia, or sports hernia.

In any of the aforementioned cases the triathlete needs to seek the consult of an experienced orthopedic surgeon who has done a significant number of the indicated surgery and understands the triathlete's goals. Setting realistic goals for return to sport with the surgeon is critical to a satisfactory outcome following surgery.

Physical Exam

The final and most critical piece of the injury recovery process is what should happen before using a treatment method with a triathlete: the physical exam.

A physical examination to determine cause is the most critical injury recovery technique. The exam should include a thorough musculoskeletal and biomechanical assessment to look for muscular imbalances, asymmetric motion or strength, abnormal postural conditions such as a leg-length discrepancy or scoliosis, and a review of injury and training history.

Evaluating and treating the entire chain of movement is usually necessary. The assessment would ideally include video analysis of movement to understand how the triathlete's individual body functions during a specific activity. The sports medicine professional treating the injured triathlete must understand the biomechanics of swimming, cycling, and running to fix the injury effectively and prevent reoccurrence.

For example, in the case of a recent study on patellofemoral pain syndrome in runners, gait retraining using real-time feedback to improve hip mechanics was used as an evaluation tool and treatment.[19] Results revealed a significant decrease in knee pain and improved function. The results suggest that treatment strategies for patellofemoral pain syndrome should focus on addressing the underlying mechanics associated with this injury.

This example of assessing movement to address the underlying cause or dysfunction related to an injury should be equally applied to swimming, cycling, and running. Complicated movement analysis of a specific sport requires a highly trained professional with years of experience.

Treatment Suggestions

After a biomechanical assessment, a combination of injury recovery strategies works most effectively and gets the athlete back to training faster. The following treatment suggestions can provide some guidance when addressing an injury specific to the type of tissue injured. These suggestions are common treatment approaches by sports medicine clinicians who assist triathletes. They are not intended to supersede the diagnosis and treatment plan of a health care professional.

Tendon injuries (Achilles tendinosis)

1. Augmented soft-tissue mobilization—tool assisted (ASTYM)
2. Dry needling
3. Eccentric strengthening

If no improvement occurs over the course of a couple of months with conservative measures, rule out a tear in the tendon and consider prolotherapy, nitric oxide patches, or PRP therapy.

Muscle injuries (hamstring strain or tear)

1. Augmented soft-tissue mobilization—tool assisted (ASTYM) or massage
2. Isolated strengthening (injured muscle) and core strengthening
3. Modalities (electrotherapy, infrared, and cold laser technology)

Ligament injuries (ankle sprain)

1. Augmented soft-tissue mobilization—tool assisted (ASTYM)
2. Compression machine because this type of injury typically results in swelling
3. Taping techniques

If no improvement occurs after a couple of months with conservative measures, rule out a complete tear and consider prolotherapy or PRP therapy.

Fascial injuries (plantar fasciitis or fasciosis)

1. Augmented soft-tissue mobilization—tool assisted (ASTYM) or massage
2. Isolated and core strengthening
3. Static and dynamic stretching

Bone injuries (stress fracture)*

1. Water running or antigravity treadmill running
2. Core strengthening exercises to address muscle imbalances
3. Assessment of nutrition, running gait, and footwear

Cartilage injuries (meniscus tear in the knee)

1. Core and specific joint-isolated strengthening exercises
2. Injection therapies (prolotherapy, PRP, cortisone, stem cell), mostly experimental
3. Surgery

Dysfunctional joint movement (patellofemoral syndrome)

1. Core strengthening with particular attention to stabilizing the musculature that controls the injured joint
2. Taping techniques
3. Massage and stretching to address soft-tissue restrictions (i.e., ITB)

Spinal disc injuries (herniated disc in the lumbar spine or sciatica)

1. Spinal mobilization techniques
2. Spinal stabilization and core strengthening exercises
3. Spinal decompression or traction

If no improvement occurs after a couple of months with conservative measures, further assessment may be required to determine the benefit of injections (prolotherapy, PRP, or cortisone).

Conclusion

When injury strikes a triathlete, she typically hits the panic button faster than the speed of light. But the triathlete must take a deep breath, step back and review the options, search for the cause, and seek the counsel of experienced sports medicine professionals. This chapter provides the injured triathlete with greater knowledge of the treatment tools available. Ultimately,

---

*Requires diagnostic imaging

overcoming injury requires a specific plan, much like a race plan, that must be adhered to if the outcome is to be successful. This process becomes extremely difficult when the defined recovery plan takes longer than initially expected or interferes with race goals. But triathletes are known for their persistence, and never is this trait more important than when they face injury.

Nutrition for Triathletes

CHAPTER 37

Energy Needs, Sources, and Utilization

—Bob Seebohar, MSc, RD

Efficiency is a commonly used term in the sport of triathlon. From a physical standpoint, triathletes seek to improve their efficiency in moving their bodies in an effort to use less oxygen. Participating in triathlon training leads to a high degree of energy expenditure, so triathletes must replenish their energy needs efficiently to fuel their bodies properly.

From a nutrition perspective, being efficient means being able to use the proper nutrients stored in the body at the right times throughout training based on the duration and intensity. Efficiency is about maximizing the use of some nutrients while preserving others to provide sustained energy levels to support performance.

Metabolic Efficiency

The oxidation of fat by the mitochondria is the main source of energy when the intensity of exercise is low, typically defined in scientific research as ranging from 35 to 65 percent of maximum intensity.[1, 2, 3] Depending on gender and size, a triathlete has about 1,300 to 2,000 calories stored as carbohydrate, which is distributed in the liver, muscles, and blood.

Under normal conditions, the body has enough glycogen stores to fuel 2 to 3 hours of continuous training at moderate intensity.[4] But for durations longer than this or for higher intensity training sessions, the body must either receive energy from supplemental sources or be efficient at using its internal stores. Note that as the intensity of exercise increases, the working muscles require more blood flow, thus diverting blood flow from the digestive tract. This effect is often referred to as the blood shunting response.

When a triathlete consumes a large amount of calories under these conditions, the body must decide whether to redistribute blood back to the digestive tract and take away some of the oxygen-rich blood from the muscles used to exercise or to keep the blood in the muscles and risk not being able to digest the calories consumed. By improving the body's efficiency at using its internal stores of fat and preserving its limited stores of carbohydrate, triathletes can reduce the amount of calories ingested per hour, supply enough energy to the body for locomotion, and decrease the risk of gastrointestinal (GI) distress. The term used to describe this ability is metabolic efficiency.[5]

To improve the body's efficiency in using its stored nutrients, a mixture of macronutrients is required at each meal or snack to provide proper blood sugar control. Lean protein and fiber, found in carbohydrate-rich foods such as fruits, vegetables, and whole grains, are the two main components in providing blood sugar stabilization. Stable blood sugar will lead to enhanced fat oxidation throughout the day, which will reduce the amount of calories that need to be consumed during exercise after the body adapts to a higher fat oxidation rate.

Macronutrients

An understanding of macronutrients is needed to have proper foundational knowledge before implementing a nutrition periodization or weight management plan. Macronutrients consist of carbohydrate, protein, fat, water, vitamins, and minerals. Although they all have different functions in the body, they interact with one another to support the triathlete's training program.

Carbohydrate

Carbohydrate is the ultimate source of energy for the body and brain. Carbohydrate is vital to triathletes because of its ability to maintain energy levels and high cognitive functioning. Besides providing energy, carbohydrate plays a protein-sparing role. When glycogen (stored carbohydrate) levels become low, the body begins to make glucose from protein and fat, but that process is inefficient and uses energy to make only a small amount of additional energy.

Simple and Complex Carbohydrates

The two main classifications of carbohydrates, simple and complex, have different chemical structures. Simple carbohydrates, often referred to as simple sugars, are made up of short chains of sugars and are classified as mono-, di-, and oligosaccharides. Complex carbohydrates are made up of longer chains, also called polysaccharides, and include starch and fiber.

Monosaccharides include glucose, fructose, and galactose. These are the simplest form of carbohydrate. They are made up of one simple sugar molecule and are the easiest to digest.

Disaccharides include sucrose (glucose, fructose), lactose (glucose, galactose), and maltose (glucose, glucose). These are made up of two monosaccharides and are not as easy to digest.

Oligosaccharides contain three to nine monosaccharides and include malto-dextrins, corn syrup, and high-fructose corn syrup. Artificially sweetened foods often contain oligosaccharides. The digestion rate of oligosaccharides is longer than that of the two previously mentioned.

Polysaccharides are often referred to as complex carbohydrates. They include starch and fiber. They are made up of long, complex chains of sugars and require more complex mechanisms for digestion than simple carbohydrates do, which extends their digestion time.

Molecular Weight Carbohydrates

Another fairly new topic in the performance arena pertaining to carbohydrate is high molecular weight carbohydrates. The reason that this type of carbohydrate is important is related to blood sugar regulation and movement. Blood glucose concentrations are influenced by the movement of glucose from the stomach to the intestine and into the blood.

This process is important because the osmolality of a solution has been shown to influence the gastric emptying rate from the stomach. Gastric emptying times can be of extreme importance to triathletes during training and competition. Carbohydrate sources with high osmolality may delay glucose transportation by slowing gastric emptying. A steady supply of glucose without much delay of delivery to the blood and the working muscles and brain is ideal to maintain physical and cognitive functioning.

High molecular weight (HMW) carbohydrates, polyglucosides or glucose polymers, have low osmolality, which make their entry and exit time out of the stomach quick and efficient.

Glycemic Index

Another important, and somewhat controversial, area in carbohydrate knowledge is glycemic index. Each sugar has a different glycemic index value, which means that it will be digested faster or slower. The glycemic index (GI) of foods can be affected by many variables, such as preparation method, presence of protein and fat, and fiber content. It is rare to find a food that has only one sugar in it that will not be affected by other factors that alter its glycemic index value.

Even more important is understanding the various parts that make up the GI. The glycemic response (GR) of a food is a measure of the ability of that food to raise blood sugar. The two main components in determining GR are GI and glycemic load (GL). Many triathletes have used GI at some point in their training to maintain steady energy levels throughout the day or to increase glycogen storage after a quality workout, but unfortunately they do not often use the GL in conjunction with it; therefore, they are plagued with misinformation and are using only half of the equation.

GI is a standard measure of how quickly 50 grams of carbohydrate of a particular food are converted to sugar and thus affect blood sugar over a 2-hour period. In the past, simple carbohydrates were classified as having a high GI, whereas complex carbohydrates were classified as providing sustained energy with a gentler rise in blood sugar. Nonrefined, or wholesome, carbohydrates are typically preferred because they provide important nutrients whereas refined carbohydrates do not. But many triathletes correlate wholesome with complex and simple with refined, which is sometimes not accurate.

For example, fruit is considered a simple carbohydrate, but the carbohydrate in fruit is unrefined and fruit is dense in nutrients and full of vitamins, minerals, and fiber. Each food produces its own blood sugar profile, and the correlation is not strong with whether it contains simple or complex carbohydrates. Some complex carbohydrates can be digested, absorbed, and used as quickly as simple sugars can, meaning that they have similar glycemic responses.

Many factors aside from being classified as a simple or complex sugar can affect the GI of foods. Some of these are the following:

- Biochemical structure of the carbohydrate
- Absorption process
- Size of meal
- Degree of processing
- Contents and timing of previous meal
- Fat, fiber, and protein content
- Ripeness

Glycemic Response

The GI of a food reveals how fast a carbohydrate will increase blood sugar levels, but it does not provide the information regarding how much of that carbohydrate is in a serving of that food. Hence, the importance of GL enters the equation. Both the GI and GL are needed to determine the glycemic response of a food.

Glycemic load is the numerical value of the GI divided by 100 and multiplied by the available carbohydrate content of the food in grams. GL takes the GI into account, but it is based on how much carbohydrate is in the food or drink. The GL is numerically lower than the glycemic index.

Here is an example. Watermelon has a GI of 72. A recommended serving of half a cup is 4 ounces, or 120 grams, of watermelon. This serving has 6 grams of carbohydrate. To calculate the GL, divide the GI by 100 and multiply by the carbohydrate content in grams:

$$(72/100) \times 6 = 4.32, \text{ or 4 when rounded}$$

In this example, a high-GI food becomes a low-GL food. Thus, based on the serving size and quantity eaten, watermelon will have a better GR and therefore result in a lower rise in blood sugar than its GI indicates. Keep in mind that as the serving size of a food increases, the amount of carbohydrate also increases, which will increase the GR of the food.

In many cases, GL is not based on a typical amount of food eaten, so GL does not provide realistic information unless the food is weighed before consumption. The important take-home lesson about GL is that it provides an understanding of the relationship between a specific amount of food and its biochemical response.

Protein

Protein provides the muscles with the amino acids needed to resynthesize and rebuild new muscle cells. In the body, protein plays key roles in chemical reactions, hormone structure, antibodies, fluid and electrolyte balance, and structural components of the body such as muscles, tendons, and ligaments.

A protein is composed of amino acids. Each amino acid consists of an amine group (the nitrogen-containing part), a carbon atom with a side chain, and an acid. Each amino acid has a specific side chain that gives it its identity and chemical nature. Amino acids can also be used to build new proteins.

If the body has a surplus of amino acids and energy, the carbon backbone of the amino acid is converted to fat and the nitrogen is excreted in the urine. The protein from food travels to the stomach where stomach acid separates the protein strands into shorter strands and amino acids. These then travel to the small intestine where they are broken down further and absorbed into the blood for delivery to the cells in need of amino acids.

The two types of proteins are classified as essential and nonessential. By definition, essential proteins provide all the amino acids that the body cannot make and thus must be obtained through food. These proteins are found in abundance in any animal product such as meat, fish, and dairy products; soy products; and some grains such as quinoa. The essential amino acids are histidine, isoleucine (branched chain amino acid), leucine (branched chain amino acid), valine (branched chain amino acid), lysine, methionine, phenylalanine, threonine, and tryptophan.

Nonessential proteins provide the amino acids that the body can make. These proteins are found in foods such as legumes, seeds and nuts, grains, and vegetables. The nonessential amino acids are alanine, arginine, asparagine, aspartic acid, cysteine, glutamic acid, glutamine, glycine, proline, serine, and tyrosine.

Fat

The body has abundant stores of fat, in excess of 80,000 calories for some triathletes.[6] These almost unlimited stores can be used as energy. Fat is essential for body processes such as body insulation, internal organ protection, nerve transmission, and metabolizing fat-soluble vitamins.

The two classifications of fats are unsaturated and saturated. Unsaturated fats have three additional subcategories: monounsaturated, polyunsaturated, and trans fats. Chemically, saturated fats have most of their fatty acids saturated with hydrogen. Unsaturated fats have one or more fatty acids that are unsaturated.

The unsaturated fats, specifically the polyunsaturates omega-6s and omega-3s, have gained much popularity among triathletes. These unsaturated fats cannot be made by the body because the cells cannot convert one fat to another. Thus, triathletes must receive these fats through food or by supplementation. Omega-6 fats do not normally need to be supplemented in the diet because triathletes receive so many through processed and packaged foods. Omega-3 fats should be increased in the diet. Good food examples include walnuts, salmon, flax, and chia seeds, to name a few. Because food sources are limited, especially for omega-3 fats, taking supplements is usually the first choice for triathletes who want to increase dietary intake of these beneficial fats.

Essential fatty acids (EFA) have many important functions in the body, including the following:

- Regulation of blood pressure and blood lipids
- Formation of blood clots
- Assistance in the immune response
- Improvement of the inflammation profile

A common misconception among triathletes is that polyunsaturated fats are created equal. In fact, the opposite is true, and understanding the biochemical differences is important. The most significant difference is in the metabolic process of these two fats. In the biochemical metabolic pathway of the omega-3 and omega-6 fats, there is one step in which both compete for one shared enzyme. This process can be problematic because omega-6 fats predominate in the eating program of most triathletes. These fats are preferentially metabolized instead of omega-3 fats.

The result is a metabolic dominance of omega-6 fats, which can have a negative effect on health and performance, specifically the inflammatory response. To alter this situation in a favorable way, triathletes should reduce their omega-6 fat intake and increase the amount of omega-3 fat that they receive through food and supplementation. This change will lead to a better metabolic conversion that favors improved health by providing more of the beneficial compounds EPA and DHA (eicosapentaenoic and docosahexaenoic acids) to the body.

Water

Of the essential nutrients required for life, water is by far the most important. Water makes up 60 to 75 percent of total body weight.[7] Water improves fluid balance, acts in the blood as a transport mechanism, eliminates metabolic waste products, dissipates heat, helps to digest food, and lubricates joints. Water is an essential nutrient that is crucial to survival as well as athletic performance.

An interesting side note on the topic of water is thirst. Thirst is defined as a conscious awareness of the desire for water and other fluids, and it usually controls water intake. The physiological drive to drink is controlled by a decrease in blood volume, an increase in blood osmolarity (the total concentration of particles in solute), and a decrease in the flow of saliva.[8] These markers ultimately lead to sending a signal to the brain, which will increase thirst.

Vitamins and Minerals

Vitamins are metabolic catalysts that regulate biochemical reactions within the body. They are catalysts needed for metabolic processes to occur, but they do not provide energy directly. Vitamins are extremely important for sustaining optimal health and can play a significant role in athletic performance.

Minerals are elements that combine to form structures of the body and regulate body processes. Minerals are found in abundance in most foods, but they do not serve as a source of energy. The minerals magnesium, sodium, calcium, potassium, zinc, and iron are the most popular among triathletes because of their effects on hydration and cramping, oxygen delivery, and immune system health. Minerals are discussed in chapter 40.

Weight Management and Body Composition

Many triathletes want to manipulate their body weight or body composition at some point in their sport participation for a variety of reasons including aesthetic, performance, or health. The strategies used are of key importance, and although these plans must be individualized for each triathlete, some general recommendations are useful.

Although the energy balance equation (calories in versus calories out) can be a valuable education tool, many triathletes fail to realize that manipulating body weight is never as easy as counting calories because macronutrients have different metabolic fates in the body. Rather than counting calories and attempting to configure daily deficits and surpluses of calories, an easier approach is to learn about the mind and body connection associated with food. The quantity of macronutrients that triathletes should eat is discussed in chapter 38, and the strategy is applicable to quantifying the volume of food to eat on a daily basis for specific training cycles.

The most important step when it comes to controlling and manipulating body weight is to relearn the body's cues for hunger and satiety. Letting hunger and satiety guide feeding patterns is difficult at first, because of the psychological and emotional connection to food and the disconnect with cognitive decision making about food choices that triathletes lose with age. This change will lead to long-term success because it allows the body's physiological systems to align with its psychological systems. The point is that people need to let hunger and satiety be their primary guides to developing a healthy relationship with food.

Instinctual eating is a concept that describes feeding the body when it is biologically hungry. Biological hunger can be identified when physical hunger pangs exist in the stomach or when cognitive functioning and the ability to concentrate and focus decrease. Letting hunger and satiety be the primary guides to feeding will allow a healthy relationship with food to develop. The cornerstone of using this concept and changing body weight or body composition is controlling blood sugar. When blood sugar is high, the hormone insulin is released. When that happens, the body's ability to use fat as fuel is significantly diminished.[9] Preventing high ebbs and flows of blood sugar will help control insulin release, which will in turn help regulate body weight and body composition.

Controlling Blood Sugar

Controlling blood sugar through the manipulation of diet is much simpler than triathletes expect. As stated previously, eating sources of lean protein and fiber together will produce a blood sugar stabilization effect and improve satiety while improving the body's ability to use fat and preserve carbohydrate. Eating a diet high in carbohydrate or not including good sources of protein with carbohydrate will promote the oxidation of carbohydrate and thus cause consistent ebbs and flows of blood sugar. This fluctuation will not contribute to satiety or optimal fat oxidation opportunities.

Additionally, focusing on a metabolically efficient eating plan will improve the body's thermogenic response. This concept describes the metabolic heat loss associated with food intake. Protein has the highest heat loss, approximately 20 to 30 percent, followed by carbohydrate at approximately 5 to 10 percent and fat at approximately 3 to 5 percent.[10] Many triathletes shy away from eating lean protein because they are consuming a high-carbohydrate diet, but eating a bit more lean protein will lead to higher metabolic heat loss, which will aid in achieving goals pertaining to weight loss or body fat loss.

In normal nondisease states, the body's blood sugar ebbs and flows about every 3 to 4 hours. Thus, by following the eating plan described earlier, triathletes should be feeding their bodies along these intervals throughout the day, depending on the timing of training sessions. Triathletes who tend to eat every 1 to 2 hours usually do so because blood sugar is not stable. Eating a higher carbohydrate load will lead to a higher degree of carbohydrate oxidation, which means that the body requires more supplemental carbohydrate consumed through food at more frequent intervals.

Weight Loss Strategies

To complement the hunger and satiety cues and responses offered here, the following chapter provides quantitative implementation strategies associated with weight loss in the discussion of the concept of nutrition periodization. These weight loss strategies usually include using the energy balance equation to track calories in versus calories out. Many triathletes do this with online calculators or software programs. Although keeping a food and training log for energy consumption and expenditure reasons is educational and may assist the triathlete in making a behavior change, long-term success is usually not achievable.

Understanding nutrition facts labels, ingredients, and serving sizes of food is valuable, but when triathletes use numbers without first understanding their physiological hunger response, they tend to yo-yo with weight and body composition because of lack of connection between the body and mind. The nutrition periodization quantitative prescription for weight loss is an important piece of weight management, but it should not be used before a clear association is understood with hunger and satiety.

Conclusion

Having a good understanding of the various macronutrients and their importance in the triathlete's body is paramount to sustaining optimal performance. The information in this chapter can help develop the ability to use nutrients in a methodical manner to fuel and recover from training sessions and improve health.

CHAPTER 38

Nutrition Periodization

—Bob Seebohar, MSc, RD

The future of sports nutrition embraces the relationship of aligning a triathlete's daily nutrition plan with her physical training plan, a concept termed *nutrition periodization*.[1] This process will promote the physiological adaptations with the training response as volume and intensity change from day to day, week to week, and month to month.

Instead of focusing on proper nutrition in the days leading up to a competition, nutrition periodization should be used to support the training load shifts that occur throughout the year. Each time the physical training program cycle changes, the nutrition program should change to support the changing energy needs. The goal of nutrition periodization is to provide the body the nutrients needed to improve health, strength, speed, power, and endurance while helping to maintain a healthy immune system, body weight, and body composition.

The easier a nutrition plan that a triathlete can have, the more successful he will be at implementing it on a year-round basis. Further, he will not be subject to the negative effects of dietary fads. The goals of nutrition periodization are simple and straightforward:

- To enhance health
- To improve performance
- To manipulate body weight and composition

Triathletes who are not nutritionally prepared before training sessions will likely not receive the same positive physiological training adaptations as triathletes who are prepared and place nutrition on the top of their priority list. Adequately fueling the body before, during, and after training sessions allows the body to accomplish the physiological objectives of the workout in addition to promoting a faster recovery.

Daily macronutrient ranges have been published in scientific research pertaining to endurance athletes. These numbers provide triathletes, coaches, and health professionals a starting place for how to build a triathlete's daily nutrition plan. The ranges are large but will be properly separated into more manageable ranges based on training cycles.

The ranges seen in research, from 3 to 19 grams of carbohydrate per kilogram of body weight, from 1.2 to 2.5 grams of protein per kilogram of body weight, and from 0.8 to 3.0 grams of fat per kilogram of body weight,[2, 3, 4, 5, 6] are large because of the many differences among triathletes, body weight and body composition changes, and competition cycles. Because of these differences, it cannot be stated which macronutrient range a triathlete should follow based purely on gender or even the race distance for which the triathlete trains.

The training cycle and the physical demands along with body weight and body composition goals should be considered when devising a nutrition plan. What follows is a description of how to use the general concept of nutrition periodization and the numbers within each of the training cycles that triathletes will follow throughout the year, from the overall macrocycle down to the daily microcycle.

Macrocycle Nutrition Guidelines

A handful of nutrition guidelines apply year round on the macrocycle level of planning. Specifically, managing oxidative stress, inflammation, and iron deficiency should be main focal points throughout a triathlete's annual training plan.

Oxidative Stress

Oxidative stress, sometimes referred to by researchers as reactive oxygen species, is more commonly known to triathletes as free radicals. Free radicals are atoms with unpaired electrons that can be formed when oxygen interacts with certain molecules. These highly reactive free radicals can impart damage to the cell membrane and DNA.

When this happens, cellular functioning can decrease, which can affect many body processes. The body has internal enzyme systems that help to scavenge these free radicals, but the body can be overloaded at certain times, such as when performing strenuous exercise, being at altitude, being in a polluted environment, or when experiencing stress.

Antioxidants act as scavengers and interact with free radicals to stop the destructive chain reaction of cellular damage. Triathletes should choose foods year round that are rich in beta-carotene, vitamin E, vitamin C, selenium, and zinc because they can help support immune function and quench free radical production. Acquiring these antioxidants through food is the preferred method rather than relying solely on supplements.

Inflammation

Aerobic capacity declines when the body is in an inflammatory state. This condition can be detrimental to athletic performance because systemic inflammation can have a negative effect on both health and performance.

Inflammation includes many aspects, but in terms of athletics, the main detriment to performance is linked to the endothelial lining of the artery and the inflammation that incurs there. When this lining becomes inflamed, vasoconstriction is greater and less blood is delivered to working muscles. Less blood flow equates to less oxygen and nutrient delivery and less waste removal from the muscles.

Triathletes encounter bacteria and viruses on a regular basis, but the body is typically well equipped to attack and destroy these invaders through the inflammation response. A certain amount of inflammation in the body is beneficial, but excess inflammation begins to cause problems.

The two main types of inflammation are classic and silent. Classic inflammation is the most common because it is the type that is indicated by a bruise. Triathletes have undoubtedly experienced this type of inflammation because of falls, scrapes, and muscle contusions. In situations like this, the body is typically prepared to handle the recovery process. Additionally, triathletes have used the concept of rest, ice, compression, and elevation to promote faster recovery.

Silent inflammation, which has no visual symptoms such as those found in classic inflammation, can have significant negative health and performance effects. This type of inflammation is often involved in disease states such as heart disease, Alzheimer's, rheumatoid arthritis, and cancer.

One of the methods of determining the amount of silent inflammation in the body is through blood testing that looks at the level of C-reactive protein (CRP) in the body. CRP is a marker of total-body inflammation. This type of inflammation is more difficult to manage, which is why improving the overall daily nutrition plan to include more anti-inflammatory omega-3 fats is highly beneficial.

The differences between the omega-6 and omega-3 fats were explained in chapter 37, but to appreciate the importance of these fats and their role in inflammation, more of the science should be understood. The metabolism and effects of fatty acids are complex, and understanding what happens when certain types of fats become more or less initiated in their biochemical pathways is important.

Omega-6 fats, found in corn, safflower, sunflower, and soybean oils, are separated into two main constituents through their metabolic process: arachidonic acid (AA) and gamma-linolenic acid (GLA). Having an overabundance of AA leads to a higher degree of inflammation. AA is usually high because triathletes typically consume many of the oils listed.

GLA is an omega-6 fat, but it has anti-inflammatory properties because it is not converted to the proinflammatory AA compound. Instead, GLA is converted to dihomogamma-linolenic acid (DGLA), which competes with AA in the metabolic pathway. If DGLA is present more than AA, DGLA will negate the proinflammatory effects of AA.

The underlying message is that triathletes should reduce their consumption of oils and foods rich in omega-6 and increase their intake of omega-3 food sources, such as salmon, walnuts, flax, and chia seeds. The metabolic fate of omega-3 fats concludes with the compounds EPA and DHA but only if omega-6 fats are reduced so that the shared enzyme can allow omega-3 to convert to EPA and DHA rather than allow omega-6 fats to convert to AA.

Iron

The last macrocycle nutrition component is iron. Iron stores and training load are inversely related, so as the volume and intensity increase in a triathlete's training program, body iron stores may decrease. Menstruating females are more susceptible to low iron stores, but males can also be vulnerable.

About two-thirds of the iron found in the body is contained in hemoglobin, and the rest is distributed in the liver, spleen, and bone marrow, with small amounts in myoglobin. Some triathletes are susceptible to high iron losses, and some are not. Several signs and symptoms may classify a triathlete as at risk for iron deficiency or anemia:

- Unrecognized bleeding from the intestinal tract
- Hematuria (presence of blood in the urine)
- Heavy sweating (iron is found in small amounts in sweat)
- Foot strike hemolysis (destruction of red blood cells because of the impact of the foot strike on the ground)
- Females who regularly menstruate
- Inflammation (which can lead to an increase in hepcidin, a protein that reduces gastrointestinal iron absorption)
- Restriction of calories

Role of Iron

Iron has many roles in the body, such as being part of neural and immune function, thyroid hormone metabolism, and mitochondrial oxidative enzymes and being involved in the formation of new red blood cells. One of the most important roles that iron plays is as a component of the protein hemoglobin, which carries oxygen from the lungs to the body's cells.

Iron stores can be hard for triathletes to maintain because the typical iron absorption from food is rather low. Some foods may be high in iron, but their absorption rates are low. In addition, iron inhibitors found in the diet can decrease iron absorption even more. These inhibitors include calcium, zinc, phytates, and fiber found in whole grains and nuts; tannins found in coffee and tea; bran; and soy products.

Additionally, triathletes with Celiac disease or Crohn's disease may have lower rates of iron absorption because of the effects on the gastrointestinal system. But on a positive note, iron promoters found in the diet promote a higher rate of absorption. These foods include meat, fish, poultry, broccoli, Brussels sprouts, tomatoes, potatoes, green and red peppers, and other foods rich in vitamin C.

The two types of iron in foods are heme and nonheme. Heme iron comes from animal sources such as beef, chicken, shrimp, oysters, sardines, and fish and has a high absorption rate. Nonheme iron comes from vegetable sources such as enriched cereals, blackstrap molasses, pumpkin seeds, beans, lentils, and tofu and has a much lower absorption rate compared with heme iron sources.

Consequences of Low Iron Stores

Triathletes often wonder what it feels like to have low iron stores. Without a laboratory blood work analysis, the easiest way to know whether iron deficiency is present is fatigue that worsens with exertion during exercise. Fatigue is common in sport, of course, and it can result from many causes such as other nutritional imbalances, illness, or stress. If a triathlete experiences normal fatigue throughout the day that does not worsen with exercise, the cause is likely not iron deficiency by itself, although a blood test should be done to rule out this possibility.

Other signs and symptoms are associated with iron deficiency, but note that an iron stores blood work test is needed make an accurate diagnosis of iron deficiency or anemia. The other signs and symptoms are the following:

- Decreased performance
- Sleepiness and fatigue (outside of normal)
- Poor concentration
- Moodiness or irritability
- Always feeling cold
- Decreased immune function
- Eating nonnutritive substances such as dirt, clay, and ice (often referred to as pica)

Three Stages of Iron Deficiency

Three stages are associated with iron deficiency, which can be determined through laboratory blood work analysis and proper interpretation by a sports physician or sports dietitian:

1. Stage 1, iron depletion, is the mildest form of iron deficiency. Normally, serum ferritin levels will be decreased. If the condition is detected early enough, this stage can be easily managed through food and does not normally require supplementation.
2. Stage 2, iron deficiency without anemia, is characterized by a low serum ferritin, a decrease in percent transferrin saturation, and an increase in total iron binding capacity. This stage can also be treated with food if caught early enough, although supplementation may be needed.
3. Stage 3, anemia, is the most serious stage. It includes all the previously mentioned blood clinical markers in addition to a decrease in hemoglobin.

Triathletes should be aware of the four types of anemia can be diagnosed with laboratory blood work analysis:

1. **Macrocytic:** Red blood cells are larger than normal. The most common type is called megaloblastic, or pernicious, anemia. It is caused by a deficiency of vitamin B_{12} or folic acid.

2. **Microcytic:** Red blood cells are smaller than normal. The main cause is iron deficiency anemia.

3. **Normocytic:** Red blood cells are normal in size but low in quantity and have a low hemoglobin level. Typical causes are chronic illness, medications, pregnancy, and hemolysis.

4. **Sports:** This is not a clinically recognized type but is common among triathletes in the initial phases of training. Because of higher plasma volume (training response), iron in the body appears to be diluted and hemoglobin levels are lower. A triathlete should not worry or supplement with iron if this occurs because the body will adapt. Performance has not been shown to be compromised.

High training loads may cause a decrease in iron stores; therefore, a triathlete's nutrition should be periodized to include more iron-rich foods at certain times of the annual training year. In a perfect world, supplementation would not be necessary, but some triathletes may need supplementation in addition to a sound, iron-rich nutrition program. Those with clinically diagnosed iron deficiency anemia must consume foods high in iron as well as take an iron supplement. If iron stores are too low, increasing those stores through food alone is extremely difficult, especially if a triathlete is in a high training load period or in race season.

Iron Supplements

A triathlete who is clinically diagnosed with iron deficiency or anemia may be asked to take an iron supplement. Supplemental iron may cause gastrointestinal (GI) distress such as constipation, which can negatively affect training sessions. Luckily, the replenishment of iron stores typically takes about 6 to 8 weeks depending on the stage, and in cases of the first stage of iron deficiency, supplementation may not be necessary.

Triathletes should emphasize eating iron-rich foods, pay special attention to scheduled changes in training load, and be sure to have frequent blood tests to monitor the status of iron stores throughout the year in relation to training, competitions, and possible supplementation. Iron supplements should be used wisely and only after iron stores blood testing has been completed and evaluated by a qualified sports physician or sports dietitian.

After the aforementioned macrocycle nutrition guidelines are understood, mesocycle and microcycle nutrition plans and goals can be introduced.

Base Period Nutrition Plan

As stated previously, nutrition should be aligned with the physiological goals and objectives for each training cycle. The common foundational goals among triathletes during the base season are improving endurance, strength, and flexibility. Additional ancillary goals may be included, such as improving technique and economy, but in general training intensity is low and volume is low to moderate.

During this cycle, changing body weight or composition may be the primary goal. Triathletes who want to pursue that goal should do so only during the first three-quarters of the cycle so that energy demands do not exceed energy consumption as training load increases. Refer to the section about weight management in table 38.1 for more information.

Table 38.1 provides ranges of the macronutrients that can be used to help build a triathlete's eating plan.

Carbohydrate intake should range from 3 to 7 grams per kilogram of body weight during base training depending on body weight or composition goals. On the average, 3 or 4 grams per kilogram can be used for weight loss, and 5 to 7 grams per kilogram can be used for triathletes who do not have a weight loss goal.[1]

Protein intake should range from 1.2 to 2.0 grams per kilogram.[1] The higher end of the protein range may be needed for triathletes engaging in a heavier strength training program or for those seeking weight loss because it will have a more positive effect on satiety.

Fat intake should range from 0.8 to 1.2 grams per kilogram. For triathletes who have weight or body composition goals, daily fat intake can range from 0.8 to 1.0 grams per kilogram, and those in a weight maintenance phase can consume 0.9 to 1.2 grams per kilogram.[1]

Research does not support a definitive daily hydration recommendation, but triathletes can use a few simple assessment tools to monitor daily hydration status. The first is urine color. The normal color of urine throughout the day should ideally be pale yellow. Many factors can alter this color, such as the first void of the morning and certain dietary supplements, so triathletes should assess urine after the first void in the morning.

The second tool is frequency. Urinating every 2 to 3 hours throughout the day will provide a rough indication of hydration status for triathletes in non-disease states. Urinating too often or not often enough can indicate improper hydration.

Table 38.1 Nutrition Consumption for Body Weight Goals

Body weight goal	Carbohydrate	Protein	Fat
Weight loss	3 to 4 g/kg (1.4 to 1.8 g/lb)	1.6 to 2.0 g/kg (0.7 to 0.9 g/lb)	0.8 to 1.0 g/kg (0.4 to 0.5 g/lb)
Weight management	5 to 7 g/kg (2.3 to 3.2 g/lb)	1.2 to 1.6 g/kg (0.5 to 0.7 g/lb)	0.9 to 1.2 g/kg (0.4 to 0.5 g/lb)

Specific Preparation Period Nutrition Plan

This training cycle progresses from mostly aerobic training to triathlon-specific training goals such as improving strength, speed, power, force, and economy. Training sessions will likely be focused on specificity and the intensity is higher, so energy expenditure is greater. Therefore, nutrient needs will be different. Triathletes need to enter training sessions well fueled and hydrated. Table 38.2 lists nutrition consumption for various training loads.

Daily carbohydrate intake will likely need to be increased during this cycle, and it should range from 5 to 12 grams per kilogram per day.[1] The range is large to account for the volume of training. Less carbohydrate may be needed on days that have a lower training load, and the opposite also holds true.

Protein intake should range from 1.4 to 2.0 grams per kilogram.[1] Normally, triathletes tend to follow a lower range for protein during a competition build or race cycle because carbohydrate consumption is higher.

Fat intake should range from 1.0 to 1.5 grams per kilogram.[1] Most triathletes will find themselves needing only the lower end of this range, but endurance and ultraendurance triathletes may need a larger amount of daily fat to maintain energy stores.

A triathlete may be going through multiple competitions during this training cycle, and that schedule offers multiple tapering opportunities. Although the distance of the upcoming race and tapering schedule are factors, training volume is generally reduced and intensity is usually maintained or lessened during a taper. Therefore, carbohydrate intake can be decreased to 5 to 7 grams per kilogram, protein can be maintained at 1.4 to 1.6 grams per kilogram, and fat can be held at around 1.0 grams per kilogram.[1]

As with the base training cycle, triathletes should monitor their daily hydration by the color and frequency of urination. Because of the higher intensity and duration of training sessions, however, triathletes may have a higher degree of fluid loss, so they should monitor their daily hydration status closely.

Table 38.2 Nutrition Consumption for Training Loads

Training load	Carbohydrate	Protein	Fat
Low	5 to 8 g/kg (2.3 to 3.6 g/lb)	1.6 to 2.0 g/kg (0.7 to 0.9 g/lb)	1.0 to 1.2 g/kg (0.45 to 0.5 g/lb)
High	7 to 12 g/kg (3.2 to 5.5 g/lb)	1.4 to 1.6 g/kg (0.6 to 0.7 g/lb)	1.2 to 1.5 g/kg (0.5 to 0.7 g/lb)

Off-Season Cycle Nutrition Plan

With less structured training or complete rest comes significant changes in energy expenditure. The off-season typically includes a reduction in volume, intensity, and frequency of training for triathletes. Because of the quick transition from competition season to the off-season, triathletes often have difficulty making the necessary nutrition changes that are needed to coincide with reduced energy expenditure. With that challenge comes potential gains in weight and body fat.

But by following macronutrient ranges that support lower energy expenditure, triathletes can successfully manage the transition from competition season to off-season without unnecessary weight gain.

During the off-season (table 38.3), daily carbohydrate intake should range from 3 to 4 grams per kilogram if the triathlete is exercising without specific objectives and training less than 2 hours per day.[1]

Protein intake should range from 1.5 to 2.0 grams per kilogram.[1] The higher range can be used by triathletes to improve satiety, stabilize hunger response throughout the day, and contribute to positive net protein synthesis if strength training will be part of the program.

Fat intake should range from 1.0 to 1.2 grams per kilogram.[1] Fat is still important to include in the daily nutrition program, and healthier sources should be the focal points.

During this time of the year, triathletes should attempt to establish their fluid balance instinct again without adhering to specific hydration guidelines. Water alone does not have to be the focus because some portion of fluid requirements can be achieved by eating foods such as fruits and vegetables that contain a lot of water.

Table 38.3 Nutrition Consumption for Training Cycles

BASE TRAINING CYCLE			
Training cycle	Carbohydrate	Protein	Fat
Weight loss	3 to 4 g/kg (1.4 to 1.8 g/lb)	1.6 to 2.0 g/kg (0.7 to 0.9 g/lb)	0.8 to 1.0 g/kg (0.36 to 0.45 g/lb)
Weight management	5 to 7 g/kg (2.3 to 3.2 g/lb)	1.2 to 1.6 g/kg (0.5 to 0.7 g/lb)	0.9 to 1.2 g/kg (0.4 to 0.5 g/lb)
SPECIFIC PREPARATION			
Training cycle	Carbohydrate	Protein	Fat
Low training load	5 to 8 g/kg (2.3 to 3.6 g/lb)	1.6 to 2.0 g/kg (0.7 to 0.9 g/lb)	1.0 to 1.2 g/kg (0.45 to 0.5 g/lb)
High training load	7 to 12 g/kg (2.3 to 5.5 g/lb)	1.4 to 1.6 g/kg (0.2 to 0.7 g/lb)	1.2 to 1.5 g/kg (0.5 to 0.7 g/lb)
Off-season	3 to 4 g/kg (1.4 to 1.8 g/lb)	1.5 to 2.0 g/kg (0.7 to 0.9 g/lb)	1.0 to 1.2 g/kg (0.45 to 0.5 g/lb)

Conclusion

Using the quantitative ranges associated with nutrition periodization will help triathletes better manage their caloric intake relative to the ever-changing energy expenditure that results from the cycle shifts in the training program that happen throughout the year. Energy needs must be reassessed when the training cycle changes to keep triathletes properly fueled without under- or overeating.

Guiding a nutrition program and associating energy needs with fluctuating energy expenditures based on training load changes throughout the year is the primary goal of nutrition periodization. This approach will lead to better management of weight, body composition, and energy needs associated with training.

CHAPTER 39

Nutrient Timing for Triathlon Training and Racing

—Bob Seebohar, MS, RD

Specific nutrient timing protocols are of great benefit when used before, during, and after certain training sessions. A specific nutrient timing schedule for a triathlete must consider that a triathlete's energy needs may be higher or lower depending on the type, duration, and intensity of workouts and the overall physical goals for the specific training cycle. The following guidelines will be separated based on the nutrient to allow a customized approach to training for triathlons of different distances.

Before Training

Nutrition needs before training depend largely on whether the upcoming training session will be short or long.

Shorter Sessions

Carbohydrate is necessary before most training sessions, but if the training cycle does not have high energy demands as defined by long duration (greater than 2 to 3 hours) or high intensity, then a carbohydrate feeding may not be necessary until after the workout. This circumstance is typical during the off-season and early preparatory (base) training cycles and for athletes using the metabolic efficiency concept described in chapter 37.

Teaching the body to use more of its internal fat stores as energy and thus preserving the limited carbohydrate stores means that fewer calories are needed for any training session. For sessions that are less than 2 hours in duration and are of low to moderate intensity, focusing on hydration may be the only nutrient timing recommendation needed.

The form of carbohydrate that an athlete chooses depends largely on the mode (swim, bike, or run) of the training session and the athlete's individual digestive system response. Liquid sources of carbohydrate are much easier and quicker to digest compared with semisolid sources and, especially, solid sources.

For example, Kevin Collington, elite short-course triathlete, chooses high-carbohydrate foods such as oatmeal with honey to eat before training sessions. He states that these foods provide him the quick energy that he needs before training and do not weigh him down. They also help him prepare for his next workout, often 1 to 2 hours later.

In contrast, Matt Chrabot, elite short-course triathlete, typically eats white toast and eggs before some training sessions and races. (Kevin and Matt are two of several triathletes whom I have interviewed about nutritional aspects of training and competing. All quotes and information from triathletes in this chapter came from my personal interviews with them.)

Longer Sessions

For longer training sessions (more than 3 hours), the normal pretraining carbohydrate recommendation is to consume 200 to 300 grams, 1 to 4 hours beforehand.[1] As the start of the workout approaches, less carbohydrate should be consumed to allow adequate digestion. For sessions lasting 2 to 3 hours, triathletes need to assess their hunger cues and energy needs. Often, no calories are needed during a 2- to 3-hour moderate-intensity aerobic training session, but if any higher intensity will occur within the session, energy expenditure and thus energy needs will increase.

Protein needs depend on many factors, including the triathlete's training session goal, mode of training, intensity, and digestive challenges, but the normal recommendation is to consume 5 to 20 grams of protein before training.[2] This nutrient can be taken in the form of a liquid such as a smoothie with milk or protein powder or a semisolid such as yogurt or cottage cheese. Alternatively, protein-enhanced sports drinks can be used.

The guidelines for consuming fat before a workout are not concrete, and many triathletes try to minimize their intake of fat before training because it has a slower rate of digestion. If it is consumed, fat should be kept to a minimum so that it does not significantly disrupt the digestive response.

Surprisingly, the nutrient often forgotten in a triathlete's pretraining nutrition plan is fluid. Triathletes typically wake up dehydrated, and this condition can impair their performance. Thus, triathletes need to begin the day with an adequate hydration plan.

At least 4 hours before exercise, triathletes should consume approximately 5 to 7 milliliters of fluid per kilogram of body weight. For example, a 160-pound (73 kg) triathlete would consume 364 to 509 milliliters of fluid. Additional fluid should be consumed slowly, approximately 3 to 5 milliliters per kilogram of body weight, 2 hours before exercise if the triathlete is not urinating or if the urine is dark in color.[3] For the sample triathlete described here, this quantity would be 218 to 364 milliliters of fluid.

Consuming sodium-rich foods during this time can help stimulate thirst and retain fluids. If sodium is consumed in a beverage, the recommended amount is 460 to 1,150 milligrams per liter.[3] But triathletes can obtain sodium from food sources and add additional sodium to foods or beverages if needed.

Sarah Haskins, 2008 Olympian, structures what she eats before training based on the mode and the intensity of the session. For a lower intensity workout, she chooses a meal with more protein (like eggs) before the workout. For a longer or higher intensity workout, she chooses something that is easier to digest. As she explains,

> Before a longer brick session (3-hour bike and 45-minute run), I will have 8 ounces of Greek yogurt, strawberries, and two slices of toast with natural peanut butter. During the workout, I will have an entire First Endurance Liquid Shot Gel Flask, two bottles of First Endurance EFS sport drink, and one bottle of water. After the workout I will have one bottle of water and one bottle of First Endurance Ultragen recovery drink.

During Training

As stated previously, nutrition must be periodized based on the triathlete's current training cycle. Nutrition recommendations during training sessions will differ based on fluctuating energy expenditures and needs throughout the year. During most off-season training, nutritional needs during exercise will be low to nonexistent. Even during the early phases of the preparatory (base) training cycle, nutritional needs during training will be low. Not until the duration of training sessions exceeds 2 to 3 hours will triathletes need to consume calories during training.

A classic example of this concept is Kevin Collington. He consumes nothing for workouts that are 90 minutes or shorter. For workouts longer than 90 minutes he consumes 200 to 300 calories per hour from sports drinks, energy gels, and energy bars.

The following information can be used to assist a triathlete in building a nutrient timing protocol for training sessions or races, but it should be customized to the time of year and the triathlete's individual goals, as discussed in chapter 38.

Carbohydrate Consumption

Scientific research has long supported the hourly consumption of 30 to 60 grams of carbohydrate. Recent research, however, has supported increasing the maximum grams of carbohydrate if multiple sources of carbohydrate are consumed[4] because of multiple transport mechanisms of carbohydrate across the small intestine. These guidelines suggest the consumption of up to 90 to 105 grams of carbohydrate per hour of exercise.[4]

Note that the body has enough stored carbohydrate to fuel about 2 to 3 hours of moderately intense exercise; thus, as discussed previously, some training sessions may either not need supplemental carbohydrate or need only a small amount. Additionally, if a triathlete has developed metabolic efficiency and is better at using fat as an energy source during training, less carbohydrate may be needed during certain workouts.[5] Matt Chrabot consumes only an energy gel during competitions because they last less than 2 hours.

Note that many triathletes who consume too much carbohydrate during training experience GI distress. Thus, triathletes should seek to develop metabolic efficiency during the off-season or early preparatory training cycle to reduce their hourly calorie needs from carbohydrate. This, in turn, will decrease the risk of GI distress in triathletes who have experienced it in the past or have sensitive stomachs. Matt Chrabot explains his individual concerns:

> *I experience GI distress during run workouts; thus, the amount of fiber I eat throughout the day if I'm running in the afternoon plays an important role. What's considered healthy by most people's standards isn't in a runner's best interest. Healthy in many cases translates to high in fiber.*

Protein Consumption

The research in support of consuming protein during training is inconclusive, but it does suggest that consuming protein during training may decrease posttraining muscle soreness and damage.[6] For the sport of triathlon, however, offering protein as an energy source during training is generally not necessary. If protein is to be used during training, the mainstream consensus is to use branched chain amino acids rather than whole protein sources. Many branched chain amino acids can be found in popular sports drinks and sports nutrition products.

Fat Consumption

Similarly, triathletes are not likely to need to consume any fat during most workouts or competitions. One exception is with ultraendurance triathletes who may have competitions spanning multiple days and may require more calories overall. In general, most triathletes do not need to include fat in their during-training or competition nutrition plan. They should focus on carbohydrate and possibly protein.

Sodium Consumption

The quantity of sodium consumed during training is one of the most controversial topics among researchers, athletes, and coaches. Because of the positive role that sodium plays in helping maintain fluid balance, triathletes need to consume sodium, but the quantities and the timing are debated in the scientific community. Some research supports the consumption of 460 to 1,150 milligrams per liter[3] of fluid consumed, whereas the American College of Sports Medicine recommends consuming 0.5 to 0.7 grams of sodium per liter of fluid per hour. Other researchers recommend a higher range of 1.7 to 2.9 grams of sodium per liter of fluid per hour.[7]

For triathletes who have high sweat rates or have difficulty staying hydrated, more sodium per hour may be required. Experimentation is encouraged to identify their sodium needs. Many sport drinks cannot provide the amount of sodium that most triathletes need, so sodium supplementation is an option.

Sodium supplements can be found in many forms including capsules, tablets, powders, liquids, and strips. The triathlete should choose a product that provides the amount of sodium required by his body and find a delivery system that is simple to implement and easy on his digestive system.

Fluid Consumption

Dehydration is a key concern for triathletes. The most serious consequence of exercise-induced dehydration is hyperthermia, which places added stress on the cardiovascular system. The increase in the body's core temperature through exercise combined with warm environmental conditions can quickly predispose a triathlete to becoming dehydrated.

As fluids are lost from the body, an increase occurs in the concentration and osmolality of dissolved substances and particles in the body's fluids, including sodium. These increases in osmolality and sodium concentration reduce blood flow to the skin and thus decrease the rate of sweating. The cooling mechanism for the body becomes less efficient, which can accelerate the process of contracting a heat illness.

Another negative consequence of dehydration-induced hyperthermia is a large decline in cardiac output. Less blood is delivered to the muscles and the extremities, so less oxygen is delivered to the working muscles, both of which will negatively affect training.

The primary benefit of sufficient fluid replacement during training is maintaining cardiac output and allowing blood flow to the skin to increase to high levels, which will promote heat dissipation from the skin, thereby preventing excessive storage of body heat.

Dehydration of as little as 1 percent loss of body weight through sweat can have a negative effect on training and racing. For a 160-pound (73 kg) triathlete, this loss equates to only 1.6 pounds (.7 kg). Most triathletes can lose this amount of fluid in a short time, especially if training in a warm and humid environment. Some research supports the recommendation of drinking 3 to 8 ounces (90 to 240 ml) of fluid every 15 to 20 minutes during training.[3, 8]

This approach, known as drinking ahead of thirst, is being challenged in the scientific community. Some suggest that drinking according to thirst instead of ahead of thirst may be more beneficial. Although no scientific studies to date have determined which approach is best, triathletes need to adapt their fluid replacement strategies to their training and environment and experiment with their approach throughout the year.

After Training

Triathletes need to consume nutrients within 30 to 60 minutes following quality training because during this period insulin sensitivity is at its highest and muscles are more apt to accept nutrients. Refueling and rehydrating in the first 30 to 60 minutes following a training session or competition is particularly important for glycogen-depleting workouts, typically those longer than 2 or 3 hours or shorter (about 90 minutes) with higher intensity intervals. Both scenarios produce stress to the internal glycogen stores and can contribute to dehydration at a faster rate, particularly in warmer environments.

Recommended carbohydrate intake posttraining is based on body weight. The current guidelines for replenishing carbohydrate are to consume 1.0 to 1.2 grams of carbohydrate per kilogram of body weight.[9] Protein intake is based on the absolute quantity consumed, 10 to 25 grams,[10] and the triathlete's body weight is not a factor.

Most research agrees that higher glycemic index sugars and essential amino acids are preferred sources of carbohydrate and protein, respectively. After challenging training sessions or races, triathletes often do not feel hungry, but they still need to provide their bodies with nourishment. Thus, a good strategy is to consume a liquid source of calories that includes both carbohydrate and protein.

Fat is typically not included in the first feeding following training because it can impede carbohydrate absorption. But it can certainly be included in the second feeding, usually about 2 hours after the initial feeding. When fat is consumed, healthy sources, including mono- and polyunsaturated fats, are recommended. Sodium is also a necessary component of the postworkout or race nutrition plan. Current guidelines suggest consuming 2 to 5 grams of sodium per liter of fluid when triathletes have lost a significant amount of fluid (more than 2 liters) during the workout.[10]

Triathletes often do not consume enough fluids after training or competition to replenish what they lost during their efforts. Research suggests that for proper rehydration, 150 percent of fluid losses should be consumed following training sessions.[11] The recommendation of drinking 24 ounces of fluid for every pound (1.5 liters for every kilogram) of body weight lost during training will accomplish this goal.[11]

For example, if a triathlete loses 4 pounds (1.8 kg) in a training session or competition, she should consume 96 ounces (2.7 L) of fluid for optimal rehydration. Of course, this is quite a bit of fluid, so instead of having to make up for a significant amount of dehydration after training or competition, the triathlete can hydrate before and during the effort to prevent a large fluid loss that may be unrealistic to handle afterward.

After the last workout of the day, Kevin Collington likes to have something like a salad with vegetables and a good protein source.

Conclusion

Implementing a nutrient timing system to use before, during, and after training sessions is an evolving task that will change as energy needs, training cycles, and environmental factors change. But as triathletes progress closer to their competition days, they should have a well-formed race-week and race-day nutrition plan already developed from their experimentation with nutrient timing strategies during each of their training cycles.

Race-week nutrition should be implemented by simply following what has worked during higher training loads but accounting for reduced energy expenditure within the taper. Race-day nutrition will no longer be a mystery because the athlete has been developing nutrient timing strategies for higher intensity and longer training sessions during the specific preparation training cycle. Using the knowledge presented in this chapter along with individual experimentation, the triathlete will already have developed a race-day nutrition plan during training and will have tested it many times before the competition.

CHAPTER 40

Supplements for Triathletes

—Bob Seebohar, MSc, RD

It is no surprise that triathletes use nutrition supplements throughout the year. Some do so with good reason, but others have with no reason at all besides having viewed them in a magazine or having heard testimonials from professional triathletes. Supplements encompass a wide range of nutrition products and extend beyond the popular vitamins and minerals. Supplement categories are discussed after a brief description of the supplement industry is given.

Supplement Regulation

The Dietary Supplements Health and Education Act (DSHEA) of 1994 states that nutritional supplements that do not claim to diagnose, prevent, or cure disease are not subject to regulation by the Food and Drug Administration (FDA). Unfortunately, many supplement manufacturers have concluded that DSHEA guidelines mean that they have no need to prove claimed benefits, to show safety with acute or chronic administration, to commit to accepted quality assurance practices, or to follow the stringent labeling regulations required for food products.

As a result, dietary ingredients used in dietary supplements are no longer subject to the premarket safety evaluations required of other new food ingredients or for new uses of old food ingredients.

The intent of DSHEA was to meet the concerns of manufacturers and consumers that safe and well-labeled products would be available to people who wanted to use them.

The purposes of DSHEA included the following:

- Define dietary supplements and dietary ingredients
- Establish a new framework for assuring safety
- Outline guidelines for literature displayed where supplements are sold

- Provide for use of claims and nutritional support statements
- Require ingredient and nutrition labeling
- Grant the FDA the authority to establish good manufacturing practice (GMP) regulations

The nutritional supplement industry is a multibillion-dollar-a-year growth industry. The industry is moving toward compiling more scientific data and validating products and claims for formulation and marketing purposes. For that reason, companies will continue to outsource their production to contract manufacturers who already have good quality control procedures and laboratories in place.

Oversight of Supplement Manufacturing

Some supplements do not contain the stated amounts of ingredients or, even worse, have additional substances that are not listed on the label. These inaccuracies can be of concern to triathletes who have health issues because a certain herbal product or manufactured supplement could interfere with medications. Likewise, elite athletes who undergo regular drug testing could face sanctions if they unknowingly consume a prohibited substance.

Contamination of a supplement can occur at many levels in the supply and manufacturing process. Luckily, several industry-driven good manufacturing practices (GMP) programs are in place to assist athletes and coaches. One industry program is overseen by the National Nutritional Foods Association (NNFA), which has certified dozens of companies and has a strategic alliance with NSF International, a third-party institution that provides supplement contamination testing.

Membership in NNFA requires compliance with its GMPs, and its website lists companies that are members. NSF International has an athlete-certification program and can test specific products for interested athletes. Other resources include consumerlab.com, which has independently tested dietary supplements and has an Athletic Banned Substances Screened Products Program; the FDA, which has also presented an outline of a GMP program on its website at www.cfsan.fda.com; and Informed Choice (www.informed-choice.org), another third-party institution that provides supplement contamination testing.

Evaluating the Efficacy of a Supplement

The following criteria can be used to help evaluate the efficacy of using a supplement:

- The label carries the USP (United States Pharmacopoeia) mark. The USP mark means that the supplement passes tests for dissolution (how well it dissolves), disintegration, potency, and purity. The manufacturer should also be able to demonstrate that the product passes tests for content potency, purity, and uniformity.

- A nationally known food and drug manufacturer made the supplement. Reputable manufacturers follow strict quality control procedures.
- Research supports product claims. Reputable companies should provide research from peer-reviewed scientific journals to support claims.
- Claims are accurate and appropriate. If statements are unclear or the label makes preposterous claims, the company probably did not follow good quality control procedures.

Additionally, a few simple criteria can be employed when advising triathletes about supplements. Figure 40.1 is a simple, 12-step checklist that can be used to educate triathletes. When a supplement is being considered, a triathlete should progress through this checklist before purchase. If any of the statements on the checklist is true, there is good reason to be skeptical of taking the supplement. The triathlete should investigate the supplement in question in greater depth.

- The product promises quick improvement in health or physical performance.
- The product contains some secret ingredient or formula.
- The product is advertised mainly with anecdotes, case histories, or testimonials.
- The product features popular personalities or star athletes in its advertisements.
- The product takes a simple truth about a nutrient and exaggerates that truth in terms of health or physical performance.
- The product questions the integrity of the scientific or medical establishment.
- The product is advertised in a health or sports magazine whose publishers also sell nutritional aids.
- The product is sold by the person who recommends it.
- The product uses the results of a single study or outdated and poorly controlled research to support its claims.
- The product is expensive, especially when compared with the cost of obtaining the equivalent nutrients from ordinary foods.
- The product is a recent discovery not available from any other source.
- The product makes claims that are too good to be true and promises the impossible.

▶ **Figure 40.1** Checklist for evaluating a supplement.

Primary Types of Supplements for Triathletes

Many nutrition supplements on the market claim to improve performance in some way, shape, or form. To make it easier to navigate the supplement world, supplements can be classified into three categories:

1. **Dietary:** micronutrients such as calcium, iron, zinc, and multivitamins. These supplements are used to counter certain vitamin and mineral deficiencies. Triathletes typically use these supplements because laboratory testing has identified vitamin and mineral deficiencies or because they want to have an insurance policy in place to mask inadequate food choices.

2. **Sports:** energy bars, gels, sports drinks, and electrolyte supplements. Their primary use is before, during, and after training.

3. **Ergogenic:** performance-enhancing substances such as amino acids, creatine, caffeine, sodium bicarbonate, energy drinks with extra ingredients added for mental focus or energy production, adaptogens, androstendione, beta-hydroxy-beta-methylbutyrate (HMB), carnitine, conjugated linoleic acid (CLA), glucosamine, chondroitin, and others. Triathletes typically do not take these substances in great amounts, but they may take them throughout the day and possibly before exercise, depending on the ergogenic aid.

Popular Supplements Used by Triathletes

Discussing all supplements used by triathletes is not feasible, but the following are among the more popular in terms of efficacy and use in endurance sport. Table 40.1 shows some of the common benefits and drawbacks of supplements.

Iron

Iron is a supplement that should be taken only under the supervision of a medical or nutrition professional in response to a laboratory-tested proven deficiency. Iron is a component of hemoglobin, the protein found in red blood cells that carries oxygen to cells, and myoglobin, the protein found in heart and skeletal muscle that carries oxygen to those muscles. The daily recommended intake of iron does not account for what is lost because of a high training load; iron stores and training load are inversely related. Although iron stores may be compromised in the body when training load is high, taking any supplement is not recommended until a sports physician or sports dietitian conducts an evaluation.

Some athletes, particularly menstruating females, vegetarians, and those following calorie-restricted diets, are more prone to iron deficiency anemia, but any athlete can be prone to iron deficiency. Maintaining iron balance and getting enough iron in the body can be difficult because iron is lost through sweat, urine, the GI tract, and foot-strike hemolysis. If an athlete has low

Table 40.1 Benefits and Drawbacks of Supplements

Supplement	Benefits	Drawbacks
Iron	Improves oxygen-carrying capacity	Iron overload; supplementing iron possibly fatal for athletes who have the disease hemochromatosis
Calcium	Maintains bone health, muscle function	None
Multivitamins	Correct deficiencies	Possible overload of fat-soluble vitamins (A, D, E, K)
Energy gels	Provide immediate energy	Possible GI distress because of high carbohydrate concentration
Electrolytes	Improve fluid balance	Increases thirst in some athletes
Adaptogens	Increase resistance to stress	Inconclusive but strengthening evidence to validate its use
Beta-alanine	Serves as buffering tool in delaying fatigue	No scientific validation yet of its worth in endurance sport
Caffeine	Stimulates central nervous system, which can improve mental alertness, increase usage of fat as fuel, and spare glycogen	Anxiety, irritability, possible GI distress at excessive doses
MCTs	Converts to energy faster; spares glycogen	Anecdotal reports of GI distress
Creatine	Improves anaerobic energy system training	No data regarding its safety for use in young athletes

iron stores, the body's ability to make red blood cells is limited, which leads to a decrease in the oxygen-carrying capacity of the blood. Because athletes depend on oxygen delivery to working muscles, even a slight imbalance of iron stores can have significant effects on performance. All triathletes should have a full blood draw, including iron stores, taken once per year, preferably in the base training cycle. This information will provide a baseline regarding iron stores and will indicate whether a supplement should be taken.

Calcium

Calcium is the most abundant mineral in the body. The majority of calcium is present in the bones and teeth. The remaining stores are used for muscular contractions and metabolic functions such as activating enzymes that break down muscle glycogen for energy production.

The regulation of calcium in the body requires two hormones, parathyroid and calcitonin, and vitamin D. When blood calcium levels decrease, parathyroid hormone is released and increases the activation of vitamin D in the kidneys, which act to decrease the amount of calcium lost in the urine. In addition, vitamin D increases the absorption of calcium from the small intestine and resorption from the bones.

The body is efficient in regulating calcium. Thus, excessive or poor dietary intake of calcium rarely results in acute changes in calcium levels in the body. A dietary imbalance coupled with an athlete's demanding training schedule can result in calcium alterations over time that can create a chronic deficiency state over years. There is really no deficiency test for calcium, nor do symptoms become evident. But triathletes can have their bone mineral density measured, which can show whether adequate dietary calcium is being consumed.

But some athletes may not be meeting their bodies' calcium needs. Specifically, athletes who restrict their daily caloric intake for the purpose of aesthetics, health, or performance or those who did not consume adequate amounts of calcium during childhood could be susceptible to poor calcium deposition. This situation could lead to bone deformities and the possibility of having a lower peak bone mass at an early age, thus increasing the risk of osteoporosis. Eating lower amounts of calcium as an adult athlete can lead to excessive calcium resorption from the bone, which increases the risk of osteomalacia, a softening of the bones.

Intakes of calcium may be higher for athletes than for nonathletes because calcium is lost in sweat. Current daily recommendations for calcium intake are to consume between 1,300 to 1,500 milligrams of calcium per day. The tolerable upper intake level (UL) per day is 2,500 milligrams. Toxicity symptoms over the UL include constipation, kidney stones, cardiac arrhythmia, and malabsorption of iron, magnesium, and zinc.

Multivitamins

The use of a daily multivitamin has always been controversial. Whether to take one is not an easy question to answer. Experts generally believe that athletes who engage in strenuous or long-duration training may have increased needs for some vitamins and minerals. What is not known exactly is which vitamins and minerals are specifically needed in excess by some athletes, so no specific recommendations can be made. Generally, a good practice for some athletes may be to take a multivitamin that meets their expenditure needs and is associated with their gender and possible micronutrient deficiencies as long as its use is aligned with the athlete's physical periodization cycles.

Energy Gels

Energy gels are a mix between a sports drink and an energy bar in a semisolid structure. These products are extremely popular among triathletes because they are a source of concentrated calories that is easy to carry and consume. The primary purpose of energy gels is to provide carbohydrate that can be used immediately during training or competition to fuel working muscles. The type and quantity of carbohydrate contained in the energy gel should be evaluated to determine whether it will meet the athlete's energy needs.

Additionally, energy gels have roughly a 55 to 65 percent carbohydrate concentration (compared with 4 to 8 percent in most sports drinks), which makes gels more challenging for an athlete to digest during training and competition. Athletes with sensitive stomachs may have difficulty absorbing these high-concentration gels, and higher intensity training will sometimes lead to a reduction in digestion of calories. Adequate water must be consumed with an energy gel, and consuming a gel simultaneously with a sports drink is not recommended.

Electrolyte Supplements

Electrolyte supplements are typically seen as tablets, capsules, powders, fluids, and strips. Also available are full-spectrum electrolyte supplements that offer additional minerals such as calcium, magnesium, and potassium. The basis for including more minerals in electrolyte supplements is to make up for what is lost in sweat. Many compounds are found in sweat including ammonia, copper, creatinine, iodine, iron, lactic acid, manganese, phosphorus, urea, uric acid, sodium, chloride, calcium, potassium, and magnesium. The last five are the micronutrients found in higher quantity in sweat.

For athletes who have a high sweat rate and sodium concentration and train in a hot and humid environment, additional electrolyte supplements may be needed. No sports drink on the market can supply the necessary quantities of electrolytes for these athletes. A typical sodium loss per hour for athletes is 1 gram,[1] but anecdotal information from coaches and athletes is that sodium losses can be as high as 5 grams per hour.

Adaptogens

Adaptogens, consisting mostly of herbal compounds, are a fairly new inclusion to the supplement market even though they have existed for thousands of years. An adaptogen is a substance that increases resistance to physical and emotional stress, stress-related imbalances, and environmental pollution.[2] Some also contain polysaccharides. These have been reported to stimulate the immune system, which works in a synergistic way to increase the body's ability to prevent illness. Some common examples of adaptogens include ginseng, ashwagandha, schisandra, rhodiola, cordyceps, reishi, and maitake.

One of the major actions of adaptogens relative to athletes is their ability to increase resistance to the catabolic effects of high-intensity training and stress. As the intensity of training increases, the body has to use its natural defense mechanisms to help repair and replace the damage that occurs. Using adaptogens could allow this defense mechanism to work more efficiently.

The benefits of taking adaptogens are more likely to occur in the more intense training cycles. Most of the current research has targeted physiological markers important to athletes such as $\dot{V}O_2$peak, pulmonary ventilation, time to exhaustion, and others, such as creatine kinase and C-reactive protein activity. Some recent research has shown a link to prevention of overtraining syndrome, providing protective effects from inflammation and infection, increasing fat utilization, and slowing glycogen utilization.

Beta-Alanine

Beta-alanine, a nonessential amino acid, is part of the amino acid carnosine and is needed to replenish the body's stores of carnosine to fuel high-intensity exercise. Carnosine is a potent buffer of hydrogen ions, and increased amounts of this amino acid have direct correlation with improved anaerobic and aerobic performance. Muscle carnosine synthesis is limited by the availability of beta-alanine. Thus, supplementing with beta-alanine would cause an increase in carnosine stores, which could then provide a buffering mechanism during training.

Consistent, high-intensity exercise increases the amount of muscle carnosine, but research has shown that taking a daily beta-alanine supplement increases it more than training and eating carnosine-rich foods[3] such as beef, pork, poultry, and fish does. Beta-alanine, through its effect on carnosine, can also synthesize lactic acid to be reused as fuel and can generate nitric oxide synthase, which makes the vasodilator nitric oxide.[3]

Although no definitive agreement has been reached among researchers who have studied endurance athletes, it is generally accepted that supplemental beta-alanine can increase carnosine levels, which can have a positive effect in delaying neuromuscular fatigue, using lactic acid as fuel, improving intra- and extracellular buffering capabilities, augmenting total work completed, and increasing time to exhaustion.[3]

Caffeine

Caffeine is one of the most well-researched ergogenic aids. Caffeine acts on the central nervous system as a stimulant by increasing the release of adrenaline, which can improve mental alertness, using body fat as fuel, and sparing glycogen at low- to moderate-intensity exercise.[4] In higher intensity exercise, caffeine has been shown to decrease the rating of perceived exertion, increase carbohydrate oxidation when consumed with a carbohydrate source, and allow athletes to reach a higher levels of lactate.

Caffeine is often mistakenly classified as a diuretic. Recent research, however, suggests that over a 24-hour period, caffeine does not exhibit a dehydrating effect on the body.[5] Moderate amounts of caffeine can be consumed throughout the day as long as other beverages are consumed to aid in positive net fluid balance.

The protocol that can be used to seek improvement in performance with caffeine includes the following:

- Consume 3 to 9 milligrams of caffeine per kilogram of body weight 60 to 75 minutes before competition.[6]

- If the competition is prolonged, consuming 1 to 3 milligrams of caffeine every 90 to 120 minutes may be justified.[7] More is not better in this scenario because an excessive dose taken too frequently can cause GI distress.

Caffeine has been proved to improve performance when used correctly. But using caffeine as an ergogenic aid should be done with caution because of the higher levels needed to stimulate the central nervous system. Too much caffeine can cause athletes to become anxious, delirious, and irritable. Athletes must not abuse it in sport.

Medium Chain Triglycerides (MCTs)

Most athletes do not view fat as a supplement or even as an ergogenic aid. But MCTs are different. Some athletes have used these fats to enhance performance during longer duration training and competition.

MCTs are a type of saturated fat with shorter lengths of carbon molecules that allow them to have characteristics different from other fats. MCTs are digested and metabolized more quickly by the liver and can be converted to energy faster. MCTs act similarly to carbohydrate, which has led to the belief that they could be used as a glycogen-sparing fuel source.

Unfortunately, research has shown mixed results. Evidence that supports the use of MCTs as an ergogenic aid to improve performance is not convincing, although anecdotal reports continue to come from athletes who have had great success using it.

Creatine

Creatine, a nitrogenous organic compound, is made from the amino acids arginine, glycine, and methionine. Most creatine in the body is found in the skeletal muscle, although a small amount is synthesized in the liver, kidneys, and pancreas. The theory behind the use of creatine among athletes is that supplementing with it can improve athletic performance in events that last between 90 seconds and 4 minutes. The proposed mechanism underlying the benefit of creatine is that it decreases the stress on anaerobic glycolysis and reduces lactate levels. This, in turn, would delay fatigue. Although the benefits for anaerobic athletes are obvious, creatine could benefit endurance athletes for specific training sessions that are targeted at improving anaerobic endurance or for heavier strength training cycles.

As mentioned previously, creatine exhibits its positive effect on the anaerobic energy pathway, specifically the phosphocreatine system (sometimes referred to as the creatine phosphate system). This energy system is the first to be initiated in any training session, and it can become depleted quickly, usually in less than 15 seconds. The benefit of supplementing with creatine is that it can improve the ability to generate more ATP (adenosine triphosphate), which can improve energy supply during shorter, more intense interval training sessions. The result could be more forceful muscle contractions and possibly higher velocities of movement.

Many methods of supplementing with creatine are used. The traditional method has been to use loading phase consisting of consuming 20 grams of creatine per day for 5 to 7 days and then to implement a maintenance dose of 3 to 5 grams per day. Another method is to consume 3 to 5 grams per day on a consistent basis without a loading phase. Additionally, research has provided shorter protocol testing, consisting of up to only 5 days of creatine loading, and has discovered improvements in anaerobic markers of performance.[9]

Regardless of the method chosen, creatine supplementation should be customized based on each triathlete's needs. Cycling the use of creatine is important because some evidence suggests that using creatine for an extended period may reduce its positive effects. Normal cycling patterns include using creatine for 3 to 8 weeks and then discontinuing its use for 3 to 4 weeks.

Supplementing with creatine has not come without controversy. In the past, concerns have surfaced about using creatine in warmer climates and its possible effects on decreasing performance in warmer environments, usually because of dehydration concerns. But research has concluded that using creatine does not decrease an athlete's ability to dissipate heat, nor does it negatively affect the fluid balance state as long as recommended doses are taken.[8]

Creatine supplementation has been studied in normal, healthy adults but not in youth under 18 years of age. No conclusive data suggests that using creatine is unsafe for adults, but no information is available regarding the use of creatine in young athletes or over extended periods with this age group. Additionally, because the physiological benefit of creatine lies in regenerating ATP to improve energy, athletes should not use creatine without making sure that they are consuming adequate calories on a daily basis. The use of creatine should be justified and used carefully by each triathlete.

Conclusion

Because many triathletes use supplements in their training and competition, it is important to know about the three categories of supplements and to understand why triathletes use them. Often times, supplements are not necessary if nutrition periodization and nutrient timing protocols are used consistently. In some cases, a triathlete may reach for a supplement depending on its specific category, the way in which it may improve health or performance, and the specific deficiency that needs to be addressed. In most cases, triathletes can obtain a large portion of their vitamin and mineral needs through whole foods, but the use of sport supplements and ergogenic aids, such as energy bars, energy gels, sports drinks, and caffeine, will be efficacious before, during, and after some training sessions and competitions.

PART
XI

Psychology
of Multisport

CHAPTER 41

Mental Toughness for Triathlon

—JoAnn Dahlkoetter, PhD

Triathletes face significant psychological barriers in their training and competitions as they push themselves to their physical limits. Whether it's the fear of a recurring injury, going out too fast in the swim, losing focus during the last section of the bike leg, or hitting the wall at mile 20 of the marathon, athletes all have mental or physical obstacles to overcome. With proper mental training, triathletes can learn to work through these blocks and enhance their motivation and self-confidence. Triathletes can find that as beliefs about their limits change, the limits themselves begin to shift. Beliefs give rise to goal realization.

In some cases, research has revealed that mental practices are almost as effective as true physical practice, and that doing both is more effective than either alone.[1] Thus, more triathletes are seeking out mental training tools and sport psychology experts to assist them with the mental side of their performance. Both males and females are seeking this help, but some interesting gender differences are appearing when examining who is searching for help in the mental training area. One study by Dolan, Houston, and Martin found that female triathletes were more likely than male triathletes to train with others, use mental preparation strategies, and report feeling anxious before competitions.[2]

In triathlon training and racing, the mind and body are so well connected that achieving good consistent race outcomes is difficult when the proper mind-set is not present. The right internal state must be created first. After a triathlete feels right inside, a quality triathlon performance can occur more naturally and with less effort. The appropriate internal state can bridge the gap between what the triathlete thinks she can accomplish and what she actually achieves. The right mind-set can make the difference between just having the capacity and realizing true potential.

One top triathlete recently noted that during his best event,

It was like I was in an invisible envelope where the only thing that existed was this race. I was essentially unaware of myself . . . like my body was being directed from an unconscious part of myself, rather than by my thoughts. I did not have to think about each move . . . I was on automatic pilot.

This is exactly the mind-set that will help triathletes achieve their best, but that mind-set can be elusive to achieve. This chapter explores the keys to achieving that mind-set, beginning with performance motivation.

Achieving Peak Performance

Triathletes should ask themselves a few questions. Have they ever had both their mind and body totally in sync with their triathlon training or racing. Have they ever had the sense that, for a single moment, they were in complete control of what they were doing? Have they ever felt such an intense pleasure and motivation in an action that they could continue doing it all day just for the experience, regardless of the outcome?

Research, interviews, and mental performance coaching with a wide variety of athletes over 30 years have established the foundation for a better understanding of the peak motivation state. Through this experience, it's been discovered that several emotional and behavioral patterns and mind-sets are clearly linked to achieving this state. This chapter describes how triathletes can achieve this ideal state of high-level motivation more often, and it identifies the circumstances that allow it to occur.

What do triathletes report about their motivation and peak performance or zone experience? This is a state of mind at which a person becomes completely immersed in the task at hand, to the exclusion of most other outside influences. Triathletes are completely focused on the present moment; the rest of the world seems to fade into the background. During the peak performance they feel more self-confident and more fully integrated. Their mind, body, and spirit are tuned in to the moment. These are the times when they feel most energetic and alive.

Psychologist Abraham Maslow first studied people with peak experiences, called *self-actualizations*, in the early 1940s. He researched human behavior at its most personally fulfilling levels. He found that during peak experience, "The human powers come together in a particularly efficient and intensely enjoyable way . . . in which the person is more open to experience, more expressive or spontaneous, fully functioning, more truly oneself, more fully human."[3]

Motivated triathletes also report a feeling of power during optimal performance that transcends their usual level of strength and energy. This outpouring of power is often apparent to other triathletes or spectators. In personal interviews, spectators reported watching the eyes of Mark Allen in the marathon section of the Hawaii Ironman Triathlon, stating, "He looks so driven, so consumed by the momentum of the race itself, that nothing can stop him." The act of swim, bike, and run itself takes over and the person feels completely synchronized within it.

Maintaining this type of internal balance is key for staying motivated, for performing well, and for producing an enjoyable experience. Performing well is a natural outcome of having the right kind of internal thoughts and feelings. When an athlete feels good, training improves. Level of performance is a direct reflection of motivation, mind-set, and the way that the triathlete thinks and feels. Thus, to deliver an optimal performance, triathletes need to build and sustain the right type of internal environment regardless of what is going on around them.

Key characteristics of motivation and peak performance include having a feeling of being totally immersed in an activity, of being completely in tune with the task at hand. Triathletes have an expectation that they have the ability to meet the challenge ahead. They are focused on the present moment so intensely that they can often foresee actions before they occur. This focus gives triathletes a sense of unusual power that appears to come from a new source within themselves. From this, they have a sense of total joy and elation, a harmonious experience of mind, body, and spirit. They have a perception that the past and future are fading away and the present action is the only thing that matters.

Anyone can experience high levels of motivation and peak performance in a wide range of triathlon settings. We discuss specific techniques for developing motivation through goal setting in the next section.

Goal Setting and Commitment

Goal setting is essential for making steady progress in any triathlon training program. Without goals we tend to flounder, like a ship without a rudder. We may go a long way, but we might well end up running in circles without a sense of direction to our training.

The question of how goal setting and perfectionism affects performance is highly debated. One research study investigated how perfectionism affected race performance and what role competitive triathletes' goals played in this relationship (study 1: N = 112; study 2: N = 321).[4]

The research analysis indicated that perfectionistic personal standards, high performance-approach goals, low performance-avoidance goals, and high personal goals predicted race performance beyond the triathletes' normal performance level.

The implications from this study are that triathletes need to set high personal goals that are specific but attainable based on their training records (e.g., run at a 6:30 per mile [4:00 per km] pace for the next half-Ironman). The more specific the goals are and the more that the triathlete can incorporate mental rehearsal and visualization into the goals, the more likely he is to achieve them.

The way that triathletes approach goals can have a powerful effect on the results. How can triathletes make goal setting more effective? Several factors can improve success and results, including the types of goals set and the way that they are measured and evaluated. Here are some principles to keep in mind when establishing a program.

- **Focus on aspects within the triathlete's control**: Triathletes should direct energy toward aspects of training and competition that are potentially within their control, such as triathlon training schedule, plan, diet, warm-up, form, mental focus, and effort level. They should avoid focusing on elements that are beyond their control such as placing, winning, the weather, and their competitors.

- **Create measurable goals**: Triathletes should write goals in a logbook so that they see them every day. Goals should be specific rather than general, and they should provide a framework for evaluating progress, such as a time. If necessary, goals can be adjusted. Triathletes can give themselves a reward for progress made or readjust the goal if it is unrealistic.

- **Set both long-term and short-term goals**: Successful triathletes devise short-term goals that bring them closer to their final goals. Many make the mistake of skipping short-term goals.

- **Make the goal public**: Research has shown that those who make their goals public in some way perform significantly better than those who keep their goals to themselves.

Mental Discipline: The Champion's Mind-Set

How do triathletes develop the mental discipline to keep the training schedule on course with all of life's setbacks and distractions? To excel as triathletes, they need to be eager for success and results, and they must focus on becoming the best triathlete they can be. It should begin with a vision, but then the triathlete must be disciplined to reach the goal.

We often read about triathletes who overcome physical barriers. Out of these challenges triathletes develop an intense, burning desire to succeed. They need to demonstrate to themselves that they can complete their goals even with their physical limits. Through these kinds of examples triathletes and coaches can begin to understand that mental discipline and desire are sometimes more important than genetic capacity or a healthy body.

To be a disciplined triathlete, the drive must come from within, whether a novice, a serious triathlete, or an elite competitor. Few people realize that building and maintaining a high level of self-motivation is a learned skill that anyone can acquire. Discipline and motivation is energy, and that sense of self-directedness is one of the most powerful sources of energy available to an athlete. From internal discipline triathletes gain the willingness to persevere with training, to endure discomfort and stress, and to make priorities with time and energy as they move closer to fulfilling their goal.

In a 2004 study Grand'Maison reported that although two-thirds of the Ironman respondents stated that their knowledge of sport psychology was limited or inexistent, 97 percent said that they believed strongly or very strongly that discipline and mental skills were key to success.[5] In addition, the survey revealed two deep-rooted misconceptions about the use of sport psychology: that sports psychology is mainly for those with deep emotional issues and that it's only for top-level elite triathletes. Ironman triathletes' issues clearly reflect what many performers want and what sport psychology consultants should be providing—practical and effective guidelines that work in the real world of performance.

Key Traits of the Highly Disciplined Triathlete

What are the key characteristics of well-disciplined triathletes? Through extensive work with numerous triathletes over several years, a constellation of traits that defines the champion's mentality has developed. High-level triathletes do not possess superhuman powers or extraordinary traits limited to a select few. Anyone who wants to excel in triathlon can develop the characteristics that make a champion.

• **Internal discipline and self-direction**: Champion triathletes decide from the outset that they are training and competing for themselves, not for the awards, not for the prize money, not for their coaches. Direction and drive need to come from within. The objectives must be chosen because that's precisely what they want to be doing. Triathletes should ask themselves, "What keeps me swimming, biking, and running? Who am I doing it for?"

• **Commitment to excellence**: Does the triathlete set a high standard for herself? Elite triathletes know that to excel at their sport, they must decide to make it a priority in their life, to be the best at what they do. They set challenging yet realistic standards that are specific, and they are honest in evaluating their abilities and the amount of time and energy that they can put into their program.

• **Determination, consistency, organization**: Winning triathletes know how to self-energize and work hard on a daily basis. Because they are passionate about what they do, they find it easier to maintain consistency in training and competition. Regardless of personal problems, fatigue, or difficult circumstances, they can generate the excitement and energy needed to do their best.

• **Concentration and focus**: Disciplined triathletes have the ability to maintain focus for long periods. They can tune in what's critical to their performance and tune out what's not. They can easily let go of distractions and take control of their attention, even under pressure. They put their attention on the aspects of the competition that are within their control and recognize that they can make that choice.

• **Capacity to deal with obstacles**: Top triathletes know how to deal with difficult situations. Adversity builds character and becomes an opportunity for learning, opening the way for personal growth and renewal. When elite triathletes know that the odds are against them, they embrace the opportunity to explore the outer limits of their potential. Rather than avoiding pressure they feel challenged by it. They are calm and relaxed under fire, realizing that nervousness is normal and that some nervousness can contribute to performance. Breathing deeply and doing a mental rehearsal of exactly how the race should go can also help triathletes remain calm and relaxed.

• **Enthusiasm and desire, love for the sport**: Triathletes who win have a drive, a fire inside that fuels their passion to achieve a key goal, regardless of their level of talent or ability. They begin with a vision, and as they see that vision with more clarity, it becomes more likely to turn into reality. Wherever attention goes, energy flows.

Mental Imagery

Images are the mental representations of experience. Although verbal language is the most common means for communicating with the external world, imagery is a powerful means for internal communication. The visualization process can be defined as the conscious creation of mental or sensory images for the purpose of enhancing training and life. It is the deliberate attempt to select positive mental images to affect how the body responds to a given situation.

By using imagery or visualization, athletes can create, in vivid detail, a replay of a best performance in the past. Alternatively, they can mentally rehearse an upcoming event and see themselves doing it right. Imagery guides much of an athlete's experience because it is a more efficient, complete language than self-talk. For example, trying to describe to someone how to execute the perfect freestyle swim stroke, in detail, using words is difficult. A person could write an entire book. The same stroke shown through a video replay of a top triathlete conveys the same message in a few seconds.

Most athletes daydream and reexperience situations in their minds in a haphazard way. The fact that people can remember previous experiences in detailed fashion is why visualization works so well for athletes. Most good triathletes have discovered this technique on their own and may use it occasionally to improve learning and performance. For maximum results, however, they need to control their imagery and practice it on a regular basis rather than just let thoughts pass in and out. Through imagery, triathletes can re-create their best performances in detail and then use that energy to help them through any situation that they may encounter.

Principles for Building Discipline and Maximizing Performance

With the constellation of traits that disciplined triathletes possess, how do triathletes begin to build them into their lives? How do they turn these qualities into useful behaviors that will make a difference in the way that they train and race?

The following suggestions have helped many athletes excel in their sport.

• **Create a disciplined mind-set**: Direct focus to what is possible, to what can happen, on the path toward success. Rather than complaining about the weather or criticizing the competition, mentally trained triathletes attend to only those things that they can control. They have control over thoughts, emotions, training form, and perception of each situation. Triathletes have a choice in what they believe about themselves. Positive energy makes peak performances possible.

• **Practice being focused yet relaxed**: Develop the ability to maintain concentration for longer periods. Tune in to what's critical to performance and tune out what's not. Triathletes can easily let go of distractions and take control of their attention. As they focus more on the task at hand (e.g., training form, how they're feeling), negative thoughts will have fewer ways to enter the mind. Athletes at any level can experience the same single-minded focus and drive seen in elite athletes. Concentration is a learned skill that can improve with practice. The key is to recognize that good concentration is a constant vigil. The mind is like a gypsy; a certain amount of mind drifting will always occur. But if triathletes regularly work on their attention span, they can begin to take control of the most distracting situations. When athletes want to concentrate on something, they must find a way to become more attracted to it, such as thinking of a song that has an upbeat cadence and synchronizing their movements to that rhythm.

• **Picture goals every day**: Enter a relaxed state through deep abdominal breathing. Then, as vividly as possible, create an image in the mind of what you want to achieve in the sport. Triathletes can produce a replay of one of their best performances in the past and then use all those positive feelings of self-confidence, energy, and strength in the mental rehearsal of an upcoming event. See yourself doing it right and then use the imagery during the event itself.

• **Build a balanced lifestyle**: Create a broad-based lifestyle with a variety of interests. Strive for a balance among work and fun, social time, personal quiet time, and time to be creative. Develop patterns of healthy behavior.

Eat regularly, get a consistent amount of sleep each night, reduce workload at times if possible, and allow time to relax and reflect between activities. Develop a social support network of close friends and family, some who are sports oriented and some who have other interests. Learn to communicate openly. Resolve personal conflicts as they occur, so that they don't build to a crisis on the night before an important race.

• **Enjoy the process and take the pressure off**: Triathletes should make a deliberate effort each day to create enjoyment in triathlons, to renew their enthusiasm and excitement for training, and to avoid trying to force physical improvement. Especially when in the recovery phase after a race or when healing from an injury, lighten up on the rigid training schedule and exercise according to feelings each day. Remove the strict deadlines and race dates that have been cast in stone. Let the next breakthrough occur naturally, at its own pace, when the internal conditions are right. Trust that there's a time to push hard in races and a time to hold back during recovery.

• **Use setbacks as learning opportunities**: Draw out the constructive lessons from every workout and race and then move on. Look for advantages in every situation, even if conditions are less than ideal.

Conclusion

Mental toughness is the key to performing well on a consistent basis for triathletes at all levels. The mind and body are so well connected that achieving a good outcome becomes difficult when mental toughness is not present. The right internal state must be created first. When a triathlete feels right inside, a quality performance can occur naturally. The appropriate internal state can bridge the gap between what a triathlete thinks he can accomplish and what he actually achieves. The right mind-set can make the difference between just having the ability and realizing true potential. Triathletes should incorporate the mental toughness profile into mental preparation to train more healthfully and perform at their best.

CHAPTER 42

Psychology of Triathlon Training

—JoAnn Dahlkoetter, PhD

For most people who are passionate about their sport, triathlon training provides a sense of self-assurance, a feeling of control over life, and the chance to test personal limits and reach for new challenges. Yet when goals become unrealistically high, internal pressure builds, making workouts more like an obligation than a pleasure. When this happens, triathletes may cross the line into obsession. They may become desensitized to their body's feedback and unknowingly overtrain, creating serious risk for injury, stress, or burnout.

A study by Main et al. reported that exposure to stressors (either training or psychological) had significant effects on several negative health factors including mood disturbance and burnout.[1]

The disciplines of swimming, biking, and running are effective ways of handling so many needs that for some triathletes, training becomes an all-consuming obsession that preempts all other interests in life. Having a focused commitment to physical improvement is not in itself harmful, but when triathletes become so attached to their training that it becomes the sole means for coping with life, its positive effects can quickly fade away.

Obsession and Staleness

Triathletes frequently make comments such as, "I'm working harder than ever, putting in more time training, and there's absolutely no progress. Is it something in my head?" Or they say, "I'm recovered from my injury, but I can't seem to get my form back." Others might offer, "I'm at 100 percent physically, but the motivation just isn't there."

These statements may sound familiar. Plateaus and staleness are universal experiences that all triathletes and performers have gone through, regardless of ability level or type of sport. Experiencing peaks and valleys is normal, but there are ways to regain passion and ensure that high points are experienced more often than low ones.

Research examining obsession and the overtraining syndrome in elite athletes indicates an incidence rate of about 20 to 30 percent. A relatively higher occurrence is seen in individual-sport athletes, females, and those competing at the highest representative levels.[2]

Symptoms of Obsession

Any triathlete who has challenged himself for a long time has probably experienced a period of frustration. How long this period lasts depends largely on his ability to recognize the symptoms and seek help early.

The most commonly reported symptoms are similar to those observed in overtrained athletes: increased perception of effort during exercise, frequent upper respiratory tract infections, muscle soreness, sleep disturbances, loss of appetite, mood disturbances, shortness of temper, decreased interest in training and competition, decreased self-confidence, and inability to concentrate. The appearance of these many symptoms underlines the importance of taking a holistic approach when trying to treat or prevent overtraining in the triathlete; both training and nontraining stressors must be considered.

Obsession Profile

The obsessed triathlete who displays a high risk for injuries, staleness, or burnout often shows classic type A personality characteristics: a high-achieving perfectionist who is independent, has a strong need to be in control, finds it difficult to relax, and is unexpressive emotionally. If the triathlete's training pattern fits the following description, she may have moved from passion to obsession and be unknowingly setting herself up for disappointment.

• **Obsession and obligation**: Triathletes believe that they must complete the daily distance in their program regardless of weather, personal state of health, or enjoyment level. Training becomes a duty.

• **Lack of balance**: They tend to avoid developing a broad-based lifestyle that includes social support, a variety of interests, and a firm sense of self. They cling to training as their primary coping mechanism and use exercise to deal with most of life's stresses.

• **Never-ending goals**: Triathletes may use their athletic goals as a way to prove themselves, but they are rarely satisfied even when they reach their goals. They are constantly looking toward the next target, but they can't relax and enjoy the journey.

• **No pain, no gain**: Triathletes continue to train through pain that worsens during a workout, a sure road to injury or loss of motivation. Triathletes often get into trouble by testing pain thresholds on a daily basis. Many triathletes are afraid to rest because they have trouble changing gears. They can't relax and trust that their bodies will remember what to do.

• **Lack of variety**: Doing the same repetitive activity week after week with little or no variation can bring about a sense of boredom or declining interest. Even if physical injury doesn't affect enthusiasm, mental strain can eventually take its toll.

• **Continual pressure and seriousness**: With the demands of a rigid training schedule and the pressures of competition, triathletes can lose the element of fun in workouts. Building more enjoyable periods into a training routine is critical for preventing burnout.

• **Negative thinking**: Triathletes may frequently condemn themselves for failures, setbacks, and mistakes rather than realizing that these things are inevitable and may offer good opportunities for learning.

• **Avoidance**: They can become overanxious about meeting a goal, which may lead to their subconsciously seeking a way out. A sick or injured triathlete doesn't have to face the pressures of the real competition.

Obsession and burnout are barriers that prevent triathletes from fully enjoying their training and reaching their best performances. Overtraining without having regular breaks can often lead to injury and suboptimal performances.

Tips for Preventing Staleness

The following strategies may help build variety into a triathlete's life and create renewed interest and passion in training. A triathlete who notices any of the symptoms of staleness should address them immediately, because they will not go away on their own.

• **Change the routine by cross-training**: Modify the normal training schedule, even if only for a few days. Try active rest by doing a different sport such as hiking, in-line skating, or cross-country skiing for a few days. Breaks and variation in routine can give triathletes the emotional energy that they need to make them hungry again for training and racing.

• **Build in more diversity**: Go to a new, scenic place to train at least once a week. Take a running or biking vacation to explore new trails in national parks, tropical beaches, or high mountain peaks.

• **Listen to the body**: Coaches and triathletes should become partners with the triathlete's body, giving it regular attention and dialoguing with it. Triathletes need to become acutely aware of what the body and mind need each day for proper recovery. Both body and mine need to know when it's time to push hard and when there is a need to back off.

The tips offered in chapter 41 on mental toughness apply here as well: Create a disciplined mind-set, practice being focused and relaxed, picture goals every day, build a balanced lifestyle, reduce pressure, and use setbacks as learning opportunities.

For triathletes, the overall goal is to stay passionate but not become obsessed. Coaches and triathletes should create a healthy, sustainable training program and lifestyle to prevent slumps, injuries, and burnout. Triathletes need to discover the point of pushing just hard enough without going over the edge in training. In each area of life they need to know how much is enough. They should try to put these mental training techniques to work and learn to live more fully, train more healthfully, and perform best when it counts the most.

Mind–Body Awareness

Sport psychologists working with triathletes at every level often hear their patients say, "Whenever an important race comes up something goes wrong, either mentally or physically. I can't seem to pull my mind and body together when it really counts. I seem to be continually sabotaging myself."

For example, running requires so many bones, muscles, and connective tissue to work well together that the triathlete can easily misjudge the body's limits and incur an injury.

Coaches often teach triathletes not to pay too much attention to the body's subtle messages of aches and pains. Coaches might say, "Don't be a wimp. Just get through the workout. We have a race this Sunday." So triathletes often ignore the subtle symptoms and plod on, making sure to complete the designated weekly distance, doing a small amount of tissue damage each day, until the body screams for attention. After an injury sets in, the healing and recovery process then takes much longer because they did not have the mind–body awareness skills to pay attention each day.

Tuning in Early to the Body's Messages

In fact, the body has critical information for triathletes and coaches. They need only to listen carefully, sense its subtle messages, and follow its direction regularly. Triathletes first need to check in with their bodies before they blindly move ahead with a training plan. To train consistently and stay healthy, triathletes need to treat and care for their bodies as they would a finely tuned machine.

When working to improve mind–body awareness, a technique involving listening and dialoguing allows triathletes to tune in to the body and mind with a sense of compassion and curiosity. Many athletes have successfully used this dialoguing technique. The process does not take extra time, only greater awareness during the time when athletes are training. Triathletes can learn a method of sensing how they feel, physically and mentally. They can then have a dialogue with their feelings and sensations, and do most of the listening. Triathletes tend to be action oriented, driven, and goal directed. They are accustomed to telling their bodies what to do, most of the time not so tactfully.

A triathlete may say to himself, "Pick up the pace, you slug. Your shoulders are too stiff. Why aren't you catching that guy in front of you?" What do triathletes do when an uncomfortable feeling develops in the body (e.g., calf cramping or knee aching)? The typical reaction is to try to override it. Perhaps yell at it a bit. "Why does this stupid pain have to come on right now, when I've got 13 miles to go in the run?" Or they might beat themselves up mentally, "If only I had trained harder, my knee wouldn't freeze up like this."

Mind–Body Awareness Strategies

The key to doing well in triathlon and preventing injuries is to become quiet and listen to the body's sensations on a daily basis. The key to mind–body awareness for preventing injury is for triathletes to let the body give this crucial feedback, especially while warming up for regular workouts. Then they can take in and respect its wisdom before deciding on a course of action.

When triathletes let the body speak, they are allowing themselves to be open to the depth and richness of their whole self—body, mind, and spirit. When they pay attention to a sensation such as tension or pain, it is more likely to be resolved so that they can go on with their training in a clear, focused way. Coaches and triathletes may also gain a better sense of what they need to do, if anything, to help the body function more efficiently (e.g., alter posture, training form, breathing, and so on). Often they don't need to change anything at all. The body can heal and correct itself. For instance, if a minor calf strain occurs, awareness and backing off on the training plan can often take care of the problem.

During a workout, triathletes may wonder about many issues: "Am I doing the right thing for my body today? Should I be going this far or this fast when I'm just returning from an injury? Is this workout helping to strengthen that area, or is it further aggravating the tendons that are still weak and vulnerable? Am I ready to take my training to the next level, or should I be conservative and stay with the same workouts for another week?" Regular listening and dialoguing with the body, as described in the following section, can fully answer all these questions and give triathletes a strong sense that they are doing the right thing.

Checking in With the Mind and Body

The body is wise in many ways beyond what the average person acknowledges. If it is allowed to do so, the body can show the path to optimal health and fitness. The body carries knowledge not only about how the triathlete is training but also about how she is treating herself, what she values and believes, how she has been hurt emotionally, and how she is living her life. Triathletes' physical selves know the best path to follow to move up to the next level in performance.

Many triathletes recognize that they can confer with their bodies to assess whether they are eating the proper food and getting enough sleep. They understand that their bodies know what it feels like to be in good health and what it feels like when they are on the edge of a cold or flu or injury. They know the positive sensations of having energy to spare and being focused, and when they've become too tired or let their bodies get torn down.

Indeed, coaches and triathletes understand how to identify the extreme states, but do they recognize the subtle stages in between? By training arduously and regularly challenging the muscles and tissues to work harder, triathletes are continually tearing down the body. And they need to remember that they are also challenging the mind. It, too, needs recovery. This repair and healing process is going on constantly, for both the body and mind. The question is, What can triathletes do to be more aware and to facilitate the healing process? With some practice and exercises, triathletes can improve their mind–body awareness.

Mind–Body Awareness Exercise

Triathletes should think about an area of the body that they would like to work on and begin a dialogue with. They should ask themselves, "What bodily sensation am I most aware of? What part needs my attention?" After they identify a certain area, they should ask, "What exactly does it feel like?" Triathletes should find the right words to describe it, making sure that they have the best words to articulate how it feels (e.g., tight shoulders, heavy feet, mind racing, and so on). They can write down these thoughts in a journal later.

Now they can begin asking that part of the body what it needs: "What needs to happen next for it to get better?" They can learn, for instance, whether it needs more rehab care or more rest. Does it need some special treatment?

Next, they could ask the body to show how it would feel to be completely healed. How would it feel to have the problem cleared up, resolved satisfactorily? The body knows how it would feel to have the situation resolved, even though a triathlete's analytical mind may have no idea how that could happen. That kind of suggestion helps create an opening for new ways of being and perhaps healthier ways of treating the body.

The body's solutions are infinitely better, more creative, and healthier than anything the logical mind can dream up. Triathletes may feel stuck, but the body isn't. After they begin to listen, understand, and dialogue with their bodies, their bodies will show their wisdom. The body will show better ways for staying healthy and moving forward with training. Triathletes can then train more consistently and remain healthy throughout the year, gaining a new level of sensitivity to the body that can take them to new performance highs.

Relaxation

One of the most overlooked elements in triathlon training programs also happens to be the one most crucial for good performance—the ability to relax the mind and body. Championship performances look smooth and effortless because the top athletes know how to relax. Elite triathletes consistently report that the key to smoother, faster training is to focus on being relaxed rather than trying to create more power.

Triathletes who try to muscle through a workout can create a lack of synchronicity in the muscle groups. For instance, for an athlete to run efficiently, the hamstrings must be relaxed as the quads are contracting. This aspect can be critical in the final stages of a race when fatigue sets in and the pressure mounts. Remaining loose and calm can make all the difference, enhancing the ability to perform when it really counts.

One study examined the relationship between basic psychological skills usage (i.e., goal setting, imagery, self-talk, and relaxation) and the intensity and dimensions of competitive anxiety.[3] Interviews were conducted on a sample of elite athletes from a variety of team and individual sports. Findings revealed that the participants maintained the intensity of their anxiety response before competition but could then use goal setting, imagery, or self-talk to reinterpret their anxiety-related symptoms and enhance performance. Higher levels of self-confidence and an optimistic outlook toward forthcoming competitions were also expressed. The athletes reported that they perceived control over their anxiety responses when they used relaxation techniques.

Triathletes are continually moving between tension and relaxation, both mentally and physically. They need a certain amount of tension to perform well, but if their muscles become too tight, they lose fluidity and sense of control. Each triathlete needs to find that right balance to move and stay within the comfort zone.

What Happens When Triathletes Relax

Relaxation can be done both while being active and while being still. Relaxation does for the mind what stretching does for the body. It is both a mental and physical experience. Relaxation is state of physical and mental stillness characterized by the absence of tension and anxiety. It means letting go and sometimes doing absolutely nothing with the mind and muscles. Although relaxation is one of the more natural and satisfying states that human beings can attain, the feeling of calmness must be experienced to be fully understood.

Two positive effects occur when people discover how to relax. First, a physiological response occurs. Those who are most relaxed go into a slow, deep abdominal breathing pattern and experience a decrease in heart rate. The electromyograph (EMG) shows diminished muscle tension, and the hand thermometer shows warmth, indicating more blood flow to the hands and feet.

Second, a psychological response ensues. The electroencephalograph (EEG) indicates that relaxed triathletes who are still while visualizing go into an alpha state, creating more brain waves in this creative and healthful state of consciousness. This state enhances their ability to concentrate and move away from anxiety and negative thoughts, a state of mind more conducive to performing well. Relaxation is also an enabling condition. Those who are physically and mentally relaxed are empowered to accomplish feats not possible at other levels of consciousness.

Benefits of Relaxation

Learning relaxation has many positive rewards that extend far beyond the arena of sport. People can begin to see gains in every part of life. Triathletes need to clear their minds and calm themselves more completely for a number of reasons.

• **Prepare for a triathlon:** Calm the mind and conserve energy in the body to perform well in an important event. Triathletes need to be fully rested for maximal exertion.

• **Decrease tension levels:** Find the optimal stress level and reduce unnecessary tension and anxiety.

• **Create fluidity of muscles:** Triathletes can train more efficiently because their antagonistic (nonworking) muscles are loose. Their coordination and strength are greatly enhanced because they are using only the muscles necessary to perform the task at hand.

• **Lower the risk of injury:** Injury is often a result of muscle tightness. The healthiest muscles are those that are loose and relaxed.

• **Decrease fatigue:** Triathletes often exhaust themselves with the day's activities. Those who are overanxious are unconsciously contracting their muscles throughout the day, which slows the blood flow process needed for rapid recovery. Periodic relaxation exercises can help triathletes feel recharged and energetic.

• **Enhance quality of sleep:** Triathletes need to be able to reduce their internalized pressure and fall into a deep and restful sleep on the night before a competition or after traveling to a new environment.

• **Accelerate the natural healing process:** During any given winter, chances are high that triathletes will have a flu virus. Yet their own healing system (immune system) will deal with it effectively without their awareness, as long as they are allowing enough relaxation and recovery time.

• **Repair of bone and soft tissue:** Running and other weight-bearing activities are high-maintenance activities. The body is constantly repairing itself. Some have found that broken bones and connective tissue strains can be healed in a shorter time when they use mental relaxation and imagery techniques.

• **Recharge the mind:** Triathletes who learn the art of relaxation can quickly discharge any pressure and restore the feelings of excitement and joy about training.

• **Open and expand consciousness:** When the mind is fully relaxed, negative thinking and self-criticism are greatly reduced. The right brain becomes more open to new ideas, and triathletes can begin to work with visualization techniques in a powerful way. They can create vivid mental images of exactly what they want to happen and increase the chances of turning those images into reality.

Self-Assessment for Tension and Stress

The key to successful performance in any sport is to recognize the early warning signs of rising stress levels. Triathletes then need to take immediate action to bring stress levels down before the body screams at them for attention. Each person typically has a characteristic pattern in the response to stress. What system in the body overacts to pressure? Do triathletes notice any of the following reactions? Triathletes should rate themselves on each of the reactions listed on a scale of 1 to 10 (10 being the highest or worst) by putting a number next to each symptom:

- Racing heart
- Muscle tension in jaw, neck, shoulders
- Rapid, shallow breathing
- Stomach upset or vomiting
- Desire to urinate
- Irritability
- Forgetting details
- Inability to focus or make decisions
- Resorting to old habits
- Feeling fatigued
- Catching colds frequently

Triathletes should know their individual responses to stressful situations such as a competition and begin doing relaxation exercises before the symptoms get out of hand.

Muscle Relaxation Exercise

When Usain Bolt broke the world record in the relay in the 100 meters at the world championships, his face looked peaceful and serene as he was coming in to the finish line. Triathletes often report, "Relaxed running seems so easy that it feels as if you're hardly working at all."

With regular practice of relaxation techniques, triathletes can begin to look and feel like world-class competitors. Here is a useful exercise to reach deeper levels of relaxation and higher levels of performance.

When doing various tasks, triathletes should try monitoring the muscle tension levels that accompany common activities throughout the day. They should notice how they hold their wrists and shoulders while typing at the computer, how tightly they are gripping the steering wheel while driving, what muscles they are using to hold the phone (is their neck crimped?), how tight their neck and shoulders are while they are doing the last interval in a workout. Triathletes frequently use far more muscle power than needed to accomplish a task effectively. When they muscle through a workout, they block the body's natural timing, flow, and rhythm. The movement becomes jerky and uncoordinated, causing fatigue to develop more quickly.

The goal in this exercise is to match the effort with the task. Top triathletes are skilled in detecting subtle differences in tension levels and fine-tuning their responses, adjusting muscle tension to whatever job they are doing. They should relax the muscles not needed for the task.

Conclusion

The long-range challenge for triathletes in using the psychology of training is to create a healthy, balanced lifestyle and prevent staleness, injuries, and burnout. Triathletes need to find that point where they are pushing just hard enough without going over the edge in each part of their training. After practicing these techniques both at home and during training, triathletes will find that triathlons begin to feel easier. They can take their minds off the feeling of tension and fatigue and move straight into focusing on the task at hand. They'll look forward to pressure situations as an opportunity to fine-tune relaxation and have their bodies and minds perform well when it really counts.

CHAPTER 43

Mental Skills for Peak Triathlon Performance

—JoAnn Dahlkoetter, PhD

Confidence, self-worth, and optimism are all key elements in determining how triathletes view a triathlon challenge and transform it into a powerful performance. Developing a realistic, healthy self-image is the foundation for success in sport and in life. When triathletes know themselves well and are confident in their abilities, they're well on their way to realizing their goals. Self-confidence gives them the ability to create and sustain an optimal performance state regardless of the external conditions.

For example, many triathletes gain a confidence boost when their fast training times indicate that they can do well in an upcoming race. A study by Knechtle, Wirth, and Rosemann showed that faster training runs and setting a fast personal best time in a marathon and in an Olympic-distance triathlon were associated with a subsequent fast Ironman race time.[1]

Top triathletes have a strong, solid belief in themselves and their ability to perform well. Their confidence is so deep that it is almost indestructible, unaffected by outside influences. Extremely self-confident triathletes are resilient to setbacks, can deal with pressure, and are not easily intimidated. For example, six-time Hawaii Ironman Champion Mark Allen had a presence about him, an extraordinary self-assurance that at times could appear intimidating to others. His belief in himself was reflected in his performances.

Confidence, like determination, discipline, and strength, are fortunately all part of a constellation of mental skills that are learned and not inherited. Therefore, with regular practice they can become part of a triathlete's skill set.

Self-Confidence

Self-esteem and positive self-image are essential for performing well in any sport. One of the main factors differentiating humans from other animals is the awareness of self. Humans have the ability to form an identity and then attach a value to it. They define themselves by certain standards and then decide whether they like themselves.

The struggle that often occurs comes from the human capacity for self-judgment. If a triathlete rejects or criticizes himself for doing poorly in a race, he'll find himself avoiding anything that might bring on the pain of further self-rejection. He may then take fewer risks in training and racing, as well as in social and professional situations. In short, people may limit their ability to realize their full potential.

The good news is that people can learn to stop making these judgments and direct their energies toward building a more constructive self-image. Triathletes can change how they feel about themselves. They can learn to recognize their positive qualities and acquire an attitude of acceptance toward themselves and others. After those perceptions change, they will see improvements in training and in every part of their life with a gradually expanding sense of inner freedom.

Transforming Weaknesses Into Strengths

If triathletes are content with a mediocre performance, they will never challenge themselves to reach their full potential in a competition. If they really want to improve their training and build confidence, they need to go out of their way to address and correct their weaknesses.

Many triathletes fail in their workouts because they are unable to overcome a singular personal deficiency. They adopt a negative attitude toward weaknesses. They justify a shortcoming by saying that they were born with this particular problem or have since acquired it and that they can do nothing about it. Alternatively, they defend a weakness, such as their swimming ability, and in the process start to structure their lives around it, saying, "I'm not a good swimmer, I'll never get faster." They make the weakness the center of their thinking instead of facing the issue head on and conquering it by joining a masters swim program or taking a swim class or lessons.

So to build confidence, triathletes must first understand their specific problem areas and then go to work. By making the weakest link in their chain strong, they can't help but improve. The best triathletes in the world are those who actively work to overcome their weaknesses. Practicing strengths is fun because we excel in those areas and can easily get positive feedback. But the way for triathletes to improve is to test themselves, to learn where they are making mistakes, to face them, and to turn them around.

For instance, in a race in which a competitor surges ahead of them, dedicated triathletes try to stay with the competitor and use that triathlete's energy to pull them along to a personal best. If they cannot meet the challenge, they'll know that it's time to go back to the pool or the track and work on their ability to increase the pace and recover quickly within the workout.

When a race is on the line, there is no substitute for both physical and mental skill. If triathletes have addressed their weaknesses, they won't be vulnerable.

They'll be fully prepared, confident, and ready to encounter anything that the competition might give them.

Building Confidence

Triathletes should try using some of the following techniques and choose the strategies that seem to fit them best, including modeling positive qualities, engaging in healthy self-talk, building self-acceptance, and making positive self-statements.

Modeling Positive Qualities

Let's say that a triathlete wants to train more efficiently, with a sense of confidence, lightness, and power. She should select another triathlete who possesses those qualities and visualize that person's style during her workout. She imagines being that triathlete, floating effortlessly with endless amounts of energy and self-assuredness. For example, a triathlete who runs with tight shoulders or a posture either too far forward or too straight up and down can model a training partner who has a better form. A triathlete who slows down at the end of races can mimic her partner, who always finishes strong, in both practices and events.

Engaging in Healthy Self-Talk

Triathletes can work to diminish the intensity of negative self-attacks while nourishing more healthy self-talk. They may never entirely turn off the inner voice that says, "You really screwed up that workout; you're stupid," but they can tone down its volume and significance. An effective way to go about quieting this negative voice is to imagine turning down the volume on a radio or portable media player. Triathletes can do the same thing. With each breath out, they can turn down the volume on the negative voice. And when someone gives them a compliment, rather than dismissing it they should take it in and let it enhance their self-esteem.

Building Self-Acceptance

Triathletes frequently use their watches, their scores, or their performances to define their self-worth. They may say, "I need to run a sub-40 minute 10K to feel OK about myself." A disappointing race performance does not indicate that they are poor triathletes, nor is it a commentary on their real potential. Triathletes need to begin with a firm foundation, a secure sense of self. They must consciously lighten up on harsh self-judgments and come to accept themselves as valuable people regardless of the outcome.

Boosting confidence is critical to good performance, and many other attributes follow in its wake. Self-confident triathletes are also optimistic, motivated, focused, and unafraid to take risks. They move toward challenges with inner strength and courage and find personal rewards in each endeavor regardless of the outcome. As their self-image becomes more positive, the degree of excellence will correspondingly rise in all areas of their lives.

Making Positive Self-Statements

Triathletes should write out their list of personal strengths and build positive affirmations around each one. They should create simple positive phrases to say to themselves silently or aloud to reinforce their positive qualities. Here are some examples:

- I am a strong, efficient triathlete; I am improving rapidly.
- I believe in myself; I radiate confidence.
- I strive to be positive and enthusiastic, no matter what happens.
- I feel a sense of power, confidence, and inner strength when I compete.
- I thoroughly enjoy myself as I train and compete.
- I am consistently working to address my weaknesses.
- The results will take care of themselves; I simply perform.
- My body and mind are growing stronger and healthier every day.
- Mistakes are simply feedback; I am open to learning.
- I focus on doing the very best that I can at every moment.
- I am willing to do whatever it takes to meet my goal.

Focus and Determination

Success in triathlon training requires total concentration and determination, for both novices and those at the highest levels of performance. If the mind begins to wander, a triathlete can easily become distracted and lose the edge. The decline affects not only performance but also the quality of the experience. The person cannot take pleasure in an activity when not fully present.

For instance, a 2011 study by Memmert indicated that skilled athletes who had high attention scores performed better than skilled players who had low attention scores, in accordance with specific creative-thinking abilities.[2]

Complete and undivided attention is difficult to come by. Triathletes can easily become sidetracked by myriad external factors or the mind's thought processes. Focusing is a challenge when numerous tasks compete for attention (e.g., preparation for their event, work responsibilities, family demands, children's needs, and so forth).

Triathletes may have input from several sources at once—a coach, a training group, or a sports medicine doctor. The challenge is to integrate all this information, separate the important issues from the nonessential ones, and make important decisions about training. Knowing how to focus and being able to maintain concentration throughout the day is critical for triathletes at any level.

Present-Centered Focus

Successful concentration depends on a present-centered focus in which triathletes are totally connected to the current task. A present-centered focus is one in which all attention is directed to what is occurring now. So, for instance, in a race, a triathlete may be focusing on what the competitor in front of him is doing, or on how his body is feeling, or what decision he is going to make by having that information.

Concentration is the learned skill of fully attending to the task at hand and excluding irrelevant external cues and internal distractions. Internal factors for triathletes might include self-doubt, fears, expectations, or fatigue. External distractions may involve heavy traffic on the travel route to a competition, a rival competitor showing up unexpectedly, or equipment problems. Triathletes need to be able to concentrate in spite of those disruptions. The true test comes when the requirements of a particular situation to stay focused extend beyond their current abilities.

Unfortunately, deep concentration is not as simple as it appears on the surface. The brain is not programmed to stay in the present moment. The capability to assimilate large quantities of information can make it difficult to sustain attention on any one subject for a long period. Thoughts about the past or future can cry out for attention whenever people try to focus on one subject.

The critical mind often focuses on the mistakes and the what-ifs—what might have occurred and what should have occurred. Triathletes think about the training that they should have done, or the critical move that was made late in the competition, or the great shape that they were in last year. Focusing on what could have happened will not change the past, but the present can suffer because of trying to change it.

Now look at how top triathletes tune in to the current moment during a peak performance. Throughout these periods, triathletes focus on the precise details of the event that allow them to respond optimally. They often report intense focus on one activity—cycling up a hill and choosing the right gears or finishing the race at a certain pace. Top triathletes are flexible enough to assess and make changes in their mental focus easily.

Triathletes need to focus on the present to be successful. Key aspects and tools needed to do so include process goals, refocusing, and changing focus.

Process Goals

Besides tuning into the present moment, a triathlete needs to focus on the right objective to do well in training and competition. What are they focusing on? Attending to process goals is far more effective than thinking about the outcome. A process focus involves concentration on the specific task being done rather than the result. So, for instance, a triathlete may focus on technique, breathing, pace, or mental attitude. A process goal keeps attention directed toward what needs to be done right now.

Refocusing

If triathletes lose their focus, their aim should be to regain it as quickly as possible. When distracting thoughts interrupt their flow, they want to retune the brain into the correct psychological channel. Awareness of inattention is the first step. The sooner that triathletes notice the lapse in attention, the quicker they can turn it around. The second step is selecting another point at which to direct the mind. They can return their attention to the same focus that they had before they were interrupted, or they can go to something else of importance at that moment.

When doing a triathlon, for example, the right focus depends on what is happening at that moment (e.g., finishing the swim or making a quick transition to the bike). So concentration becomes dynamic and changes according to particular challenges of the event. Knowing what to focus on is a skill that can be developed with time and experience. As triathletes encounter a variety of scenarios, they can store their responses in memory, improve their ability to take action, and learn to return their focus to a relevant object more quickly.

Changing Focus

Triathletes also need to be flexible in their range of focus, able to switch gears whenever necessary. For instance, during the start of a triathlon they need to have a wide focus and attend to what is happening all around. They want to be aware of others so that they don't get run over by the people behind them. By the middle of the race, they are more attuned to proper pacing, their breathing, and their form. In the final stages of the race, they switch to a narrower focus, pouring all their energies into putting one foot in front of the other and getting themselves to the finish line. In other words, they are focusing on the present, what is in front of them at that moment.

Three Focusing Exercises

The following exercises will help triathletes hone their ability to maintain focus and determination.

Breathing Exercise #1

Practice this exercise before beginning training each day. Find a comfortable, quiet place where you will not be interrupted and note the time on a watch. Close your eyes and narrow your focus to one point—breathing. Notice the inhale and exhale. Continue this exercise for as long as you can sustain your focus. When your mind begins to wander, open your eyes and note the time on the watch. How much time passed since you started the task? Ten seconds? One minute?

Breathing Exercise #2

Begin by doing deep abdominal breathing. Feel your belly rise and fall with each breath. Upon the inhale, imagine that your breath is carrying particles of concentration and determination into your body. With the exhale, notice that all the distractions and stress are drifting away. The incoming breath is like a sedative that supplies the peace needed to focus on the present.

Mental Rehearsal Exercise

Successful triathletes prepare for their events in advance. They have practiced every scenario in their minds a hundred times before it occurs. The more they rehearse their plan ahead of time in training, the more automatic it will become and the less thought will be required during the actual performance. They will be able to react appropriately to what is happening each moment. After they have a game plan in place, they can keep their mind on what is relevant and follow the plan when it really counts.

Triathletes at any level can experience the same single-minded focus and drive that elite athletes use. Concentration is a learned skill that can improve with practice. The key is to recognize that good concentration is a constant vigil.

But if triathletes regularly work on their attention span, they can begin to take control of the most distracting situations. As they sharpen their focus, they can experience the effortless stretching of the mind and body because they are totally immersed in the present. They will gain a keen sense of the big picture and be able to anticipate the correct moves to handle any training or racing situation that comes their way.

Visualization

A powerful resource for channeling performance energies more efficiently is visualization, also known as mental imagery. In the Olympics a wide range of elite triathletes have reported using visualization in their training to improve performance. Practicing visualization can make all the difference in how triathletes of any ability level experience their workouts and races.

For example, in a 2004 study by Ranganathan et al., exercise psychologists compared "people who went to the gym with people who carried out virtual workouts in their heads." They found a 30 percent muscle increase in the group who went to the gym. But the group of participants who conducted mental exercises of the weight training increased muscle strength as well, achieving nearly half as much gain (13.5 percent) as those who really worked out. Those in the virtual workout group maintained their average for 3 months following the mental training.[3]

The use of mental imagery for enhanced performance is not new. The practice of martial arts in Asia, meditation and yoga in ancient India, and hypnotherapy are other illustrations of how the mind's capacity to picture situations can be a critical part of athletic performance. Whereas mental training may have been viewed skeptically in the past, imagery and other similar techniques have now become an integral part of most sport competitions. Serious triathletes who want to engage in complete preparation train both the body and mind for top-level performance.

To test the effect of imagery in the training of skilled movements, in 2007 Fontani et al. designed an experiment in which athletes learned a new motor action and trained themselves for a month either by overt action or by mental imagery of the action. The results show that mental imagery can influence muscular abilities such as strength and power.[4]

Just as athletes work out their bodies, they also need to exercise their brains. Visualization and mental training is like taking the brain to the gym. Coaches and triathletes want their bodies to have many different gears and speeds. They also need the mind to be flexible, to be able to shift into different gears depending on the task. Mental imagery is a powerful tool for achieving this purpose.

Images are the mental representations of our experience. Although verbal language is the most common means for communicating with the external world, images are a powerful means for internal communication. By using imagery or visualization, triathletes can create, in vivid detail, a replay of one of their best past performances or mentally rehearse an upcoming event and learn to see themselves doing it right.

Imagery guides much of a triathlete's experience because it is a more efficient, complete language than self-talk. Using words to describe to someone how to execute the perfect running style in detail could fill an entire book. Showing the same running form through a video replay of a top triathlete doing hill training can convey the same message in a few seconds.

Incorporating Visualization Into Training

Most people daydream and reexperience situations in their minds in a haphazard way. The fact that they can remember previous experiences in detailed fashion is why visualization works so well for triathletes. Most good triathletes have discovered this technique on their own and may use it occasionally to improve learning and performance. For maximum results, they need to control their imagery and practice it regularly rather than just let thoughts pass in and out. Through their visualization they can re-create the past in detail and transform it to fit any situation that they encounter.

Types of Imagery

There are three primary types of imagery:

1. Internal visual imagery: With this type of imagery, triathletes mentally rehearse what they see with their own eyes as they execute an event. It's as if they have a video camera on their head that records what they are seeing as they are moving.

2. External visual imagery: Triathletes become outside observers, as though they are watching a movie of themselves performing. This method is useful for analyzing form or distancing themselves from pain during a race.

3. Kinesthetic imagery: Triathletes don't see anything but experience the event through their sense of touch. For instance, they feel the wind on their face or notice their arms propelling themselves forward as they run.

Visualization is not wishful thinking or daydreaming about being a great triathlete. It is a learned skill that requires effort, concentration, discipline, and regular practice to gain the maximum benefits. Following are the key principles for triathletes to use in creating effective mental imagery.

Guidelines for Effective Visualization

Use visualization almost any time—at home or before, during, or after training and racing. In the learning phases imagery is easier to do in a quiet, nondistracting environment. Visualization is most effective when the mind is calm and the body is relaxed.

Begin the session with a few minutes of deep abdominal breathing. Put one hand on your belly about 2 inches (5 cm) below the belly button and feel your hand rise and fall with each breath. With each inhale, imagine filling up a balloon inside your abdomen; during the exhale, the balloon collapses back down.

Create in your mind an image as vivid as possible of what you want to achieve in the sport. Just let distracting thoughts and feelings float away and refocus on the image.

Bring in the senses to see, hear, and feel what it's like to have a great training run or race. Sight, hearing, and touch are the most powerful senses for incorporating day-to-day visualization into training. Bring the scene into the present tense to be focused totally on the task at hand.

Don't replay the mistakes. You should see what you want to see, not what you don't want to see. Strive to remove the memory of errors. If you see yourself doing something incorrectly, edit the film in your mind and replay it exactly as you wish it to happen, imagining that your performance is equal to or better than your previous best.

Mentally rehearse training at the same rhythm and pace that you want to achieve in actual execution to establish the appropriate neurological pattern within your brain.

Use visual models. Before going to sleep at night, try watching a video of a superior performance (go to YouTube or find recordings from the last Olympics). Then visualize yourself moving just as fluidly and powerfully as your favorite triathlete does.

To train the body properly, you must first train the mind. Inspiring images can create powerful emotions and produce superior performances. So the best approach is to focus on positive images and memories.

At first, triathletes may not fully believe that they can perform up to the level of their visualizations. Acting as if it is already happening is OK. With practice the body will come into line with mental images. If a negative image comes into the mind, triathletes just need to breathe deeply, let it go with the exhale, and then bring in a positive image with the next breath. As they practice and refine their mental training, their images will become clearer and more convincing.

Remember that visualization can be effective at any level of triathlon training or competition. Mental and physical training can complement one another. The more familiar that triathletes become with the intricacies of triathlon, the more effective their mental practice will be.

Of course, visualization is not a substitute for physical training; triathletes still have to put in the distances. But visualization can make all the difference in the quality and enjoyment of training and racing. It will move triathletes much closer to realizing their true potential.

Conclusion

Gaining mental skills can give triathletes an edge in training and racing. Triathletes are indeed multidimensional, a synthesis of body and mind, capable of accomplishing extraordinary things. This chapter has explained the many elements of the successful triathlete, both psychological and physical.

The purpose of mental skills training is to nurture and develop all these attributes so that each part supports every other part. Triathletes should seek to experience the broader, deeper elements of the sport. By doing so, they can begin to comprehend the profound connection between mental training and the subsequent changes in performance.

After they understand these concepts, triathletes can take the lessons from triathlon and enhance the way that they think, feel, and behave in everyday life. They can enjoy and appreciate the value of the triathlete lifestyle and realize their true potential.

Epilogue

The Application of Science in Triathlon

—Joe Friel, MSc

Is training to perform at a high level in triathlon only about training longer, harder, and more often? Having read this book and now perhaps having a deeper understanding of the science of training for triathlon, you know the answer: A lot more goes into triathlon performance than just lots of swimming, biking, and running.

In the early days of triathlon, training was simple—work out long, hard, and often. Science has taken us well beyond this oversimplified approach to performance. The requirements for success in triathlon are many and varied, from physiology and genetics to equipment and psychology—and much more. Therein lies the challenge for you.

The sport of triathlon is complex. Many variables are involved, not the least of which is the unique characteristics of the athlete. As a coach, athlete, sport scientist, or student of sport, you must give a great deal of thought to what is deemed necessary for boosting performance given these individual considerations. Where should the triathlete invest time, energy, and money? What approach is best to meet the triathlete's particular needs? There are no easy or one-size-fits-all answers; there are only options. And that is what makes sport, especially one as complex as triathlon, so intriguing.

Science has not come up with any guaranteed training methods that fit all athletes all the time. If we have learned one thing from research, it is that what works on average for a group of subjects doesn't affect all the same way. In the final analysis, it boils down to the individual. And an effective, well-planned approach isn't even a fixed position for any given athlete. Changes are always taking place in the triathlete's physiological and psychological makeup, lifestyle, goals, and more. What works—and what doesn't—depends not only on what is known from science but also on what the triathlete has experienced and how he currently responds to a training dose.

So now the fun begins. Application. I hope that *Triathlon Science* has given you a platform on which to begin applying what you have learned from the best that sport science has to offer.

References

Chapter 1 Physiology and the Multisport Athlete

1. Tannerstedt, J., Apro, W., and Blomstrand, E. 2009. Maximal lengthening contractions induce different signaling responses in the type I and type II fibers of human skeletal muscle. *Journal of Applied Physiology, 106,* 1412–1418.

2. Wernbom, M., Augustsson, J., and Thomee, R. 2007. The influence of frequency, intensity, volume and mode of strength training on whole muscle cross-sectional area in humans. *Sports Medicine, 37,* 225–264.

3. Yan, Z., Okutsu, M., Akhtar, Y.N., and Lira, V.A. 2011. Regulation of exercise-induced fiber type transformation, mitochondrial biogenesis, and angiogenesis in skeletal muscle. *Journal of Applied Physiology, 110,* 264–274.

4. Bentley, D.J., Millet, G.P., Vleck, V.E., and McNaughton, L.R. 2002. Specific aspects of contemporary triathlon: Implications for physiological analysis and performance. *Sports Medicine, 32,* 345–359.

5. Laursen, P.B. 2011. Long distance triathlon: Demands, preparation and performance. *Journal of Human Sport and Exercise, 6,* 247–263.

6. Laursen, P.B., and Rhodes, E.C. 2001. Factors affecting performance in an ultraendurance triathlon. *Sports Medicine, 31,* 195–209.

Chapter 2 Genetics and Inheritance in Triathlon Performance

1. Lettre, G. 2009. Genetic regulation of adult stature. *Current Opinion in Pediatrics, 21,* 515–522.

2. Yang, J., Benyamin, B., McEvoy, B.P., Gordon, S., Henders, A.K., Nyholt, D.R., Madden, P.A., et al. 2010. Common SNPs explain a large proportion of the heritability for human height. *Nature Genetics, 42,* 565–569.

3. Knechtle, B., Wirth, A., Baumann, B., Knechtle, P., Rosemann, T., and Oliver, S. 2010. Differential correlations between anthropometry, training volume, and performance in male and female Ironman triathletes. *Journal of Strength & Conditioning Research, 24*(10), 2785–2793.

4. Peterson, R.E., Maes, H.H., Holmans, P., Sanders, A.R., Levinson, D.F., Shi, J., Kendler, K.S., Gejman, P.V., and Webb, B.T. 2011. Genetic risk sum score comprised of common polygenic variation is associated with body mass index. *Human Genetics, 129,* 221–230.

5. Bray, M.S., Hagberg, J.M., Pérusse, L., Rankinen, T., Roth, S.M., Wolfarth, B., and Bouchard, C. 2009. The human gene map for performance and health-related fitness phenotypes: The 2006–2007 update. *Medicine and Science in Sports and Exercise, 41,* 35–73.

6. Flynn, M.G., Costill, D.L., Kirwan, J.P., Fink, W.J., and Dengel, D.R. 1987. Muscle fiber composition and respiratory capacity in triathletes. *International Journal of Sports Medicine, 8*(6), 383–386.

7. Simoneau, J.A., and Bouchard, C. 1995. Genetic determinism of fiber type proportion in human skeletal muscle. *FASEB Journal, 9,* 1091–1095.

8. Ahmetov, I.I., and Rogozkin, V.A. 2009. Genes, athlete status and training—an overview. *Medicine and Sport Science, 54,* 43–71.

9. Ahmetov, I.I., Druzhevskaya, A.M., Lyubaeva, E.V., Popov, D.V., Vinogradova, O.L., and Williams, A.G. 2011. The dependence of preferred competitive racing distance on muscle fibre type composition and *ACTN3* genotype in speed skaters. *Experimental Physiology, 96,* 1302–1310.

10. Bouchard, C., An, P., Rice, T., Skinner, J.S., Wilmore, J.H., Gagnon, J., Pérusse, L., Leon, A.S., and Rao, D.C. 1999. Familial aggregation of $\dot{V}O_2$max response to exercise training: Results from the HERITAGE Family Study. *Journal of Applied Physiology, 87,* 1003–1008.

11. Timmons, J.A., Knudsen, S., Rankinen, T., Koch, L.G., Sarzynski, M., Jensen, T., Keller, P., Scheele, C., Vollaard, N.B., Nielsen, S., Akerström, T., et al. 2010. Using molecular classification to predict gains in maximal aerobic capacity following endurance exercise training in humans. *Journal of Applied Physiology, 108,* 1487–96.

12. Bouchard, C., Sarzynski, M.A., Rice, T.K., Kraus, W.E., Church, T.S., Sung, Y.J., Rao, D.C., and Rankinen, T. 2011. Genomic predictors of the maximal O_2 uptake response to standardized exercise training programs. *Journal of Applied Physiology, 110,* 1160–1170.

13. Collins, M., Xenophontos, S.L., Cariolou, M.A., Mokone, G.G., Hudson, D.E., Anastassiades, L.C., and Noakes, T.D. 2004. The *ACE* gene and endurance performance during the South African Ironman triathlons. *Medicine and Science in Sports and Exercise, 36,* 1314–1320.

14. Saunders, C.J., Xenophontos, S.L., Cariolou, M.A., Anastassiades, L.C., Noakes, T.D., and Collins, M. 2006a. The bradykinin beta 2 receptor (*BDKRB2*) and endothelial nitric oxide synthase 3 (*NOS3*) genes and endurance performance during Ironman triathlons. *Human Molecular Genetics*, 15, 979–987.

15. Posthumus, M., Schwellnus, M.P., and Collins, M. 2011. The *COL5A1* gene: A novel marker of endurance running performance. *Medicine and Science in Sports and Exercise*, 43, 584–589.

16. O'Connell, K., Posthumus, M., and Collins, M. 2011. *COL6A1* Gene and Ironman triathlon performance. *International Journal of Sports Medicine*, 32(11), 896–910.

17. Woods, D. 2009. Angiotensin-converting enzyme, renin-angiotensin system and human performance. *Medicine and Sport Science*, 54, 72–87.

18. Yang, N., Garton, F., and North, K. 2009. Alpha-actinin-3 and performance. *Medicine and Sport Science*, 54, 88–101.

19. Saunders, C.J., September, A.V., Xenophontos, S.L., Cariolou, M.A., Anastassiades, L.C., Noakes, T.D., and Collins, M. 2007. No association of the *ACTN3* gene R577X polymorphism with endurance performance in Ironman triathlons. *Annals of Human Genetics*, 71, 777–781.

20. Ahmetov, I.I., Druzhevskaya, A.M., Astratenkova I.V., Popov, D.V., Vinogradova, O.L., and Rogozkin, V.A. 2010. The *ACTN3* R577X polymorphism in Russian endurance athletes. *British Journal of Sports Medicine*, 44, 649–652.

21. Ahmetov, I.I., Williams, A.G., Popov, D.V., Lyubaeva, E.V., Hakimullina, A.M., Fedotovskaya, O.N., Mozhayskaya, I.A., Vinogradova, O.L., Astratenkova, I.V., Montgomery, H.E., and Rogozkin, V.A. 2009. The combined impact of metabolic gene polymorphisms on elite endurance athlete status and related phenotypes. *Human Genetics*, 126(6), 751–761.

22. Maciejewska, A., Sawczuk, M., Cieszczyk, P., Mozhayskaya, I.A., and Ahmetov, I.I. 2012. The *PPARGC1A* gene Gly482Ser polymorphism in Polish and Russian athletes. *Journal of Sports Sciences*, 30, 101–113.

23. Tucker, R., and Collins, M. 2012. Athletic performance and risk of injury: Can gene explain all? *Dialogues in Cardiovascular Medicine*, 17(1), 31–39.

24. Dallam, G.M., Jonas, S., and Miller, T.K. 2005. Medical conditions in triathlon competition: Recommendations for the triathlon organisers, competitors and coaches. *Sports Medicine*, 35, 143–161.

25. Collins, M., and Raleigh, S.M. 2009. Genetic risk factors for musculoskeletal soft tissue injuries. *Medicine and Sport Science*, 54, 136–149.

26. September, A.V., Mokone, G.G., Schwellnus, M.P., and Collins, M. 2006. Genetic risk factors for Achilles tendon injuries. *International Sport Medicine Journal*, 7, 201–215.

27. Collins, M., and Posthumus, M. 2011. Type V collagen genotype and exercise-related phenotype relationships: A novel hypothesis. *Exercise and Sport Sciences Reviews*, 39, 191–198.

28. Noakes, T.D., Sharwood, K., Speedy, D., Hew, T., Reid, S., Dugas, J., Almond, C., Wharam, P., and Weschler, L. 2005. Three independent biological mechanisms cause exercise-associated hyponatremia: Evidence from 2,135 weighed competitive athletic performances *Proceedings of the National Academy of Sciences of the United States of America*, 102, 18550–18555.

29. Saunders, C.J., de Milander, L., Hew-Butler, T., Xenophontos, S.L., Cariolou, M.A., Anastassiades, L.C., Noakes, T.D., and Collins, M. 2006b. Dipsogenic genes associated with weight changes during Ironman triathlons. *Human Molecular Genetics*, 15, 2980–2987.

30. de Milander, L., Kun, M.A., September, A.V., Schwellnus, M.P., Noakes, T.D., and Collins, M. 2012. *AVPR2* gene and weight changes during triathlons. *International Journal of Sports Medicine*, 33(1), 67–75.

Chapter 3   Gender and Age Considerations in Triathlon

1. Lepers, R., and Cattagni, T. 2012. Do older athletes reach limits in their performance during marathon running? *Age (Dordr)*, 34(3), 773–781.

2. Whipp, B.J., and Ward S.A. 1992. Will women soon outrun men? *Nature*, 335(6355), 25.

3. Sparling, P.B., O'Donnell E.M., and Snow T.K. 1998. The gender difference in distance running performance has plateaued: An analysis of world rankings from 1980 to 1996. *Medicine and Science in Sports and Exercise*, 30, 1725–1729.

4. Knechtle, B., Knechtle, P., and Rosemann, T. 2011. Upper body skinfold thickness is related to race performance in male Ironman triathletes. *International Journal of Sports Medicine*, 32(1), 20–27.

5. Lepers, R. 2008. An analysis of Hawaii Ironman performances in elite triathletes from 1981 to 2007. *Medicine and Science in Sports and Exercise*, 40, 1828–1834.

6. Tanaka, H., and Seals, D.R. 1997. Age and gender interactions in physiological functional capacity: Insight from swimming per-

formance. *Journal of Applied Physiology*, 82(3), 846–851.

7. Schumacher, Y.O., Mueller, P., and Keul, J. 2001. Development of peak performance in track cycling. *Journal of Sports Medicine and Physical Fitness*, 41, 139–146.

8. Swain, D.P. 1994. The influence of body mass in endurance bicycling. *Medicine and Science in Sports and Exercise*, 26, 58–63.

9. Knechtle, B., Knechtle, P., and Lepers, R. 2010. Participation and performance trends in ultra-triathlons from 1985 to 2009. *Scandinavian Journal of Medicine & Science in Sports*, doi:10.1111/j.1600-0838.2010.01160.x

10. Lepers, R., Knechtle, B., Knechtle, P., and Rosemann, T. 2011. Analysis of ultra-triathlon performances. *Open Access Journal of Sports Medicine*, 2, 131–136.

11. Ransdell, L.B., Vener, J., and Huberty, J. 2009. Master athletes: An analysis of running, swimming and cycling performance by age and gender. *Journal of Exercise Science & Fitness*, 7, S61–S73.

12. Lepers, R., and Maffiuletti, N. 2011. Age and gender interactions in ultra-endurance performance: Insight from triathlon. *Medicine and Science in Sports and Exercise*, 43(1), 134–139.

13. Reaburn, P., and Dascombe, B. 2008. Endurance performance in masters athletes. *European Review of Aging and Physical Activity*, 5, 31–42.

14. Bernard, T., Sultana, F., Lepers, R., Hausswirth, C., and Brisswalter, J. 2010. Age related decline in Olympic triathlon performance: Effect of locomotion mode. *Experimental Aging Research*, 36(1), 64–78.

15. Lepers R., Sultana F., Bernard T., Hausswirth C., and Brisswalter, J. 2010. Age-related changes in triathlon performances. *International Journal of Sports Medicine*, 31(4), 251–256.

16. Lepers, R., and Stapley, P.J. 2011. Age-related changes in conventional road versus off-road triathlon performance. *European Journal of Applied Physiology*, 111(8), 1687–1694.

17. Balmer, J., Bird, S., and Davison, R. 2008a. Indoor 16.1-km time-trial performance in cyclists aged 25–63 years. *Journal of Sports Sciences*, 26, 57–62.

18. Mittendorfer, B., and Klein, S. 2001. Effect of aging on glucose and lipid metabolism during endurance exercise. *International Journal of Sport Nutrition and Exercise Metabolism*, 11, S86–91.

19. Sial, S., Coggan, A.R., Hickner, R.C., and Klein, S. 1998. Training-induced alterations in fat and carbohydrate metabolism during exercise in elderly subjects. *American Journal of Physiology*, 74, E785–790.

20. Lepers, R., Rüst, C.A., Stapley, P., and Knechtle, B. 2012 Relative improvements in endurance performance with age: Evidence from 25 years of Hawaii Ironman racing. *Age (Dordr)*, doi: 10.1007/s11357-012-9392-z

Chapter 4 Swimming Biomechanics for Triathlon

1. Toussaint, H.M. 1990. Differences in propelling efficiency between competitive and triathlon swimmers. *Medicine and Science in Sports and Exercise*, 22(3), 409–415.

2. Toussaint, H.M., Beelen, A., Rodenburg, A., Sargeant, A.J., deGroot, G., Hollander, A.P., et al. 1988. Propelling efficiency of front-crawl swimming. *Journal of Applied Physiology*, 65(6), 2506–2512.

3. Zamparo, P. 2006. Effects of age and gender on the propelling efficiency of the arm stroke. *European Journal of Applied Physiology*, May 97(1), 52–58.

4. Bixler, B. 2005. Resistance and propulsion. In J.M. Stager and D.A. Tanner (Eds.), *Handbook of sports medicine and science: Swimming* (2nd ed., pp. 59–101). Malden, MA: Blackwell Science.

5. Counsilman, J.E. 1969. The role of sculling movements in the arm pull. *Swimming World*, December, 6, 7, 43.

6. Counsilman, J.E. 1971. The application of Bernoulli's principle to human propulsion in water. In *Biomechanics in swimming, waterpolo, and diving* (pp. 59–72). Brussels, Belgium: Universite Libre de Bruxelles.

7. Miller, D.I. 1975. Biomechanics of swimming. *Exercise and Sport Sciences Reviews*, 3, 219–48.

8. Rushall, B.S., Sprigings, E.J., Holt, L.E., and Cappaert, J.M. 1994. A re-evaluation of forces in swimming. *Journal of Swimming Research*, Fall 10, 6–30.

9. Schleihauf, R.E. 1979. A hydrodynamic analysis of swimming propulsion. *International symposium on biomechanics in swimming* (pp. 70–109). Baltimore: University Press.

10. Schleihauf, R.E., Higgins, J., Hinricks, R., Luedtke, D., Maglischo, C., Maglischo, E., et al. 1984. Biomechanics of swimming propulsion. *American Swimming Coaches Association world clinic yearbook*, 19–24.

11. Toussaint, H.M., and Truijens, M. 2005. Biomechanical aspects of peak performance in human swimming. *Animal Biology*, March 55(1), 17–40.

12. Toussaint, H.M., Van den Berg, C., and Beek, W.J. 2002. "Pumped-up propulsion" during front crawl swimming. *Medicine and Science in Sports and Exercise*, February 34(2), 314–319.

13. Maglischo, E.W. 2003. *Swimming fastest*. Champaign, IL: Human Kinetics.

14. Costill, D.L., Kovaliski, J., Porter, D., Fielding, R., and King, D. 1985. Energy expenditure during front crawl swimming: Predicting success in middle distance events. *International Journal of Sports Medicine*, 6, 266–270.

15. Craig, A.B.J., Skehan, P.L., Pawelczyk, J.A., and Boomer, W.L. 1985. Velocity, stroke rate, and distance per stroke during elite swimming competition. *Medicine and Science in Sports and Exercise*, 17(6), 625–634.

16. Toussaint, H.M., Bruinink, L., Coster, R., De Looze, M., Van Rossem, B., Van Veenen, R., et al. 1989. Effect of a triathlon wet suit on drag during swimming. *Medicine and Science in Sports and Exercise*, 21(3), 325–328.

Chapter 5 Cycling Biomechanics for Triathlon

1. Sharp, A. 1896. *Bicycles and tricycles*. Longmans Green (reprinted MIT Press, Cambridge, 1977).

2. Broker J. 2003. Cycling biomechanics: Road and mountain. In E. Burke (Ed.), *High tech cycling II* (pp. 119–146). Champaign, IL: Human Kinetics.

3. Cavanaugh, P., and Sanderson, D. 1986. The biomechanics of cycling: Studies of the pedaling mechanics of elite pursuit riders. In E. Burke (Ed.), *Science of cycling* (pp. 91–122). Champaign, IL: Human Kinetics.

4. LaFortune, M., and Cavanaugh, P. 1983. Effectiveness and efficiency during bicycle riding. In Matsui and Kobayashi (Ed.), *Biomechanics VIIB; International Series on Sport Science 4B*. Champaign, IL: Human Kinetics

5. Kautz, S., and Hull, M. 1993. A theoretical basis for interpreting the force applied to the pedal in cycling. *Journal of Biomechanics* 14, 843–855

6. Broker J. 2003. Cycling power: Road and mountain. In E. Burke (Ed.), *High tech cycling II* (pp. 147–174). Champaign, IL: Human Kinetics.

7. Chapman, A., Vicenzino, B., Blanch, P., and Hodges, P. 2007. Leg muscle recruitment during cycling is less developed in triathletes than cyclists despite matched cycling training loads. *Experimental Brain Research*, 181 (3), 503–518.

8. Munro, C., and Miller, D. 1987. Ground reaction forces in running: A re-examination. *Journal of Biomechanics*, 20 (2), 147–155.

9. Ryan, M., and Gregor, R. 1992. EMG profiles of lower extremity muscles during cycling at constant workload and cadence. *Journal of Electromyography and Kinesiology*, 2(2), 69–80.

10. Chapman, A., Vincenzino, B., Blanch, P., Dowlan, S., and Hodges, P. 2008. Does cycling effect motor coordination of the leg during running in elite triathletes? *Journal of Science and Medicine in Sport*, 11, 371–380.

11. Chapman, A., Vincenzino, B., Hodges, S., Dowlan, A., Alexander, M., and Milner, T. 2009. Cycling impairs neuromuscular control during running in triathletes: Implications for performance, injury and intervention. *Journal of Science and Medicine in Sport*, 12S, S1–S83, 142.

12. Bonacci, J., Green, D., Saunders, P., Blanch, P., Franettovich, M., Chapman, A., and Vicenzino, B. 2010. Changes in running kinematics after cycling are related to alterations in running economy in triathletes. *Journal of Science in Medicine in Sport*, 13, 460–464.

13. Sutter, K., Sayers, M., and Askew, C. 2009. The effects of cycling intensity on running economy in triathletes. *Journal of Science in Medicine in Sport*, 12S, S1–S83, 143.

14. Bonacci, J., Green, D., Saunders, P., Franettovich, M., Blanch, P., and Vicenzino, B. 2011. Plyometric training as an intervention to correct altered neuromuscular control during running alter cycling in triathletes: A preliminary randomized controlled trial. *Physical Therapy in Sport*, 12, 15–21.

Chapter 6 Running Biomechanics for Triathlon

1. Anderson, T. 1996. Biomechanics and running economy. *Sports Medicine*, 22(2), 76–89.

2. Fletcher, G., Bartlett, R., Romanov, N., and Fotouhi, A. 2009. Pose Method technique improves running performance without economy changes. *International Journal of Sports Science and Coaching*, 3(3), 365–380. doi: 10.1260/174795408786238506

3. Hausswirth, C., and Brisswalter, J. 2008. Strategies for improving performance in long duration events: Olympic distance triathlon. *Sports Medicine*, 38(11), 881–891. doi: 1 [pii]

4. Kyröläinen, H., Belli, A., and Komi, P.V. 2001. Biomechanical factors affecting running economy. *Medicine and Science in Sports and Exercise*, 33(8), 1330–1337.

5. Saunders, P.U., Pyne, D.B., Telford, R.D., and Hawley, J.A. 2004. Factors affecting running

economy in trained distance runners. *Sports Medicine*, 34(7), 465–485. doi: 3475 [pii]

6. Williams, K.R. 2007. Biomechanical factors contributing to marathon race success. *Sports Medicine*, 37(4–5), 420–423. doi: 37NaN38 [pii]

7. Lake, M.J., and Cavanagh, P.R. 1996. Six weeks of training does not change running mechanics or improve running economy. *Medicine and Science in Sports and Exercise*, 28(7), 860–869.

8. Hausswirth, C., and Lehénaff, D. 2001. Physiological demands of running during long distance runs and triathlons. *Sports Medicine*, 31(9), 679–689.

9. Arendse, R.E., Noakes, T.D., Azevedo, L.B., Romanov, N., Schwellnus, M.P., and Fletcher, G. 2004. Reduced eccentric loading of the knee with the pose running method. *Medicine and Science in Sports and Exercise*, 36(2), 272–277. doi:10.1249/01.MSS.0000113684.61351.B0

10. Dallam, G.M., Wilber, R.L., Jadelis, K., Fletcher, G., and Romanov, N. 2005. Effect of a global alteration of running technique on kinematics and economy. *Journal of Sports Science*, 23(7), 757–764. doi: W6T5U3W0436V0U52 [pii]10.1080/02640410400022003

11. Romanov, N., and Fletcher, G. 2007. Runners do not push off the ground but fall forwards via a gravitational torque. *Sports Biomechanics*, 6(3), 434–452. doi:10.1080/14763140701491625

12. Divert, C., Mornieux, G., Baur, H., Mayer, F., and Belli, A. 2005. Mechanical comparison of barefoot and shod running. *International Journal of Sports Medicine*, 26(7), 593–598. doi: 10.1055/s-2004-821327

13. Lieberman, D.E., Venkadesan, M., Werbel, W.A., Daoud, A.I., D'Andrea, S., Davis, I.S., Pitsiladis, Y. 2010. Foot strike patterns and collision forces in habitually barefoot versus shod runners. *Nature*, 463(7280), 531–535. doi: nature08723 [pii]10.1038/nature08723

14. Williams, K.R. 1985. The relationship between mechanical and physiological energy estimates. *Medicine and Science in Sports and Exercise*, 17(3), 317–325.

15. Arampatzis, A., Knicker, A., Metzler, V., and Bruggemann, G. 2000. Mechanical power in running: A comparison of different approaches. *Journal of Biomechanics*, 33(4), 457–463. doi: 10.1016/S0021-9290(99)00187

16. Unnithan, V.B., Dowling, J.J., Frost, G., and Bar-Or, O. 1996. Role of cocontraction in the O2 cost of walking in children with cerebral palsy. *Medicine and Science in Sports and Exercise*, 28(12), 1498–1504.

17. Støren, Ø., Helgerud, J., and Hoff, J. 2011. Running stride peak forces inversely determine running economy in elite runners. *Journal of Strength and Conditioning Research*, 25(1), 117–123. doi: 10.1519/JSC.0b013e3181b62c8a

18. Bentley, D.J., Cox, G.R., Green, D., and Laursen, P.B. 2008. Maximising performance in triathlon: Applied physiological and nutritional aspects of elite and non-elite competitions. *Journal of Science and Medicine in Sport*, 11(4), 407–416. doi: S1440-2440(07)00155-7 [pii] 10.1016/j.jsams.2007.07.010

19. Squadrone, R., and Gallozzi, C. 2009. Biomechanical and physiological comparison of barefoot and two shod conditions in experienced barefoot runners. *Journal of Sports Medicine and Physical Fitness*, 49(1), 6–13.

20. Hanson, N.J., Berg, K., Deka, P., Meendering, J.R., and Ryan, C. 2011. Oxygen cost of running barefoot vs. running Shod. *International Journal of Sports Medicine*, 32(6), 401–406. doi: 10.1055/s-0030-1265203

21. Robbins, S.E., and Hanna, A.M. 1987. Running-related injury prevention through barefoot adaptations. *Medicine and Science in Sports and Exercise*, 19(2), 148–156.

22. Giuliani, J., Masini, B., Alitz, C., and Owens, B.D. 2011. Barefoot-simulating footwear associated with metatarsal stress injury in 2 runners. *Orthopedics*, 34(7), e320–323. doi: 10.3928/01477447-20110526-25

23. Jenkins, D.W., and Cauthon, D.J. 2011. Barefoot running claims and controversies: A review of the literature. *Journal of the American Podiatry Medical Association*, 101(3), 231–246. doi: 101/3/231 [pii]

24. Egermann, M., Brocai, D., Lill, C.A., and Schmitt, H. 2003. Analysis of injuries in long-distance triathletes. *International Journal of Sports Medicine*, 24(4), 271–276. doi: 10.1055/s-2003-39498

25. Neely, F.G. 1998. Biomechanical risk factors for exercise-related lower limb injuries. *Sports Medicine*, 26(6), 395–413.

26. Siegele, J., Horstmann, T., Bunc, V., Shifta, P., Verle, S., and Niess, A. 2010. [Relation between pelvis malposition and functional knee pain by long distance running]. *Sportverletz Sportschaden*, 24(3), 144–149. doi: 10.1055/s-0029-1245638

27. Wen, D.Y. 2007. Risk factors for overuse injuries in runners. *Current Sports Medicine Reports*, 6(5), 307–313.

28. Hreljac, A. 2004. Impact and overuse injuries in runners. *Medicine and Science in Sports*

and Exercise, 36(5), 845–849. doi: 00005768-200405000-00017 [pii]

29. Kerrigan, D.C., Franz, J.R., Keenan, G.S., Dicharry, J., Della Croce, U., and Wilder, R.P. 2009. The effect of running shoes on lower extremity joint torques. *PM & R*, 1(12), 1058–1063. doi: S1934-1482(09)01367-7 [pii]10.1016/j.pmrj.2009.09.011

30. Bentley, D.J., Millet, G.P., Vleck, V.E., and McNaughton, L.R. 2002. Specific aspects of contemporary triathlon: Implications for physiological analysis and performance. *Sports Medicine*, 32(6), 345–359. doi: 320601 [pii]

31. Millet, G.P., and Vleck, V.E. 2000. Physiological and biomechanical adaptations to the cycle to run transition in Olympic triathlon: Review and practical recommendations for training. *British Journal of Sports Medicine*, 34(5), 384–390.

32. Bernard, T., Vercruyssen, F., Grego, F., Hausswirth, C., Lepers, R., Vallier, J.M., and Brisswalter, J. 2003. Effect of cycling cadence on subsequent 3 km running performance in well trained triathletes. *British Journal of Sports Medicine*, 37(2), 154–158; discussion 159.

33. Guezennec, C.Y., Vallier, J.M., Bigard, A.X., and Durey, A. 1996. Increase in energy cost of running at the end of a triathlon. *European Journal of Applied Physiology and Occupational Physiology*, 73(5), 440–445.

34. Hausswirth, C., Bigard, A.X., and Guezennec, C.Y. 1997. Relationships between running mechanics and energy cost of running at the end of a triathlon and a marathon. *International Journal of Sports Medicine*, 18(5), 330–339. doi: 10.1055/s-2007-972642

35. Cala, A., Veiga, S., García, A., and Navarro, E. 2009. Previous cycling does not affect running efficiency during a triathlon world cup competition. *Journal of Sports Medicine and Physical Fitness*, 49(2), 152–158.

36. Hue, O., Valluet, A., Blonc, S., and Hertogh, C. 2002. Effects of multicycle-run training on triathlete performance. *Research Quarterly for Exercise and Sport*, 73(3), 289–295.

37. Lucía, A., Hoyos, J., and Chicharro, J.L. 2001. Preferred pedalling cadence in professional cycling. *Medicine and Science in Sports and Exercise*, 33(8), 1361–1366.

38. Gottschall, J.S., and Palmer, B.M. 2002. The acute effects of prior cycling cadence on running performance and kinematics. *Medicine and Science in Sports and Exercise*, 34(9), 1518–1522. doi: 10.1249/01.MSS.0000027712.03976.B6

39. Garside, I., and Doran, D.A. 2000. Effects of bicycle frame ergonomics on triathlon 10-km running performance. *Journal of Sports Science*, 18(10), 825–833. doi: 10.1080/026404100419883

40. Chapman, A.R., Vicenzino, B., Blanch, P., and Hodges, P.W. 2007. Leg muscle recruitment during cycling is less developed in triathletes than cyclists despite matched cycling training loads. *Experimental Brain Research*, 181(3), 503–518. doi: 10.1007/s00221-007-0949-5

41. Toussaint, H.M. 1990. Differences in propelling efficiency between competitive and triathlon swimmers. *Medicine and Science in Sports and Exercise*, 22(3), 409–415.

42. Chapman, A.R., Vicenzino, B., Blanch, P., and Hodges, P.W. 2008. Is running less skilled in triathletes than runners matched for running training history? *Medicine and Science in Sports and Exercise*, 40(3), 557–565. doi: 10.1249/MSS.0b013e31815e727a

Chapter 7   In the Water

1. Dallam, G.M., Jonas, S., and Miller, T.K. 2005. Medical considerations in triathlon competition: Recommendations for triathlon organisers, competitors and coaches. *Sports Medicine*, 35(2), 143–161.

2. Foster, S. 2007. *Open water swimming: Some basic principles*. Retrieved from www.fluidmovements.com/ss/documents/30.pdf

3. Glover, D. 2009. When "stuff" happens during the swim. *Triathlon Life*, 12(3), 42–43.

4. *International Triathlon Union—competition rules*. 2011 Retrieved from www.triathlon.org/images/uploads/itusport_competition-rules_20110222.pdf

5. *British Triathlon Federation*. 2011. Retrieved from www.britishtriathlon.org/events/page.php?article=383&category=/events/&folder=rules/

6. Clarys, J.P. 1979. Human morphology and hydrodynamics. In *Third International Symposium of Biomechanics in Swimming* (pp. 3–41). Edmonton, Canada: University of Alberta, and Baltimore: University Park Press.

7. *USA Triathlon*. 2011. Retrieved from www.usatriathlon.org/resources/for-race-directors/sanctioning/getting-started

8. *Triathlon Canada—Triathlon medical manual*. 2000. Retrieved from www.triathlon.mb.ca/admin/images/Seasons/sanction_triathlon-canada_medicalmanual.pdf

9. *International Triathlon Union—uniform rules—age group*. 2011. Retrieved from www.triathlon.org/images/uploads/itusport_uniform-rules-age-group_2010-11-29_1.pdf

10. *International Triathlon Union—uniform rules— juniors/U23/elite athletes.* 2011. Retrieved from www.triathlon.org/images/uploads/ itusport_uniform-rules-elite-junior-u23_09-11-2010-clean-vf.pdf

11. *Triathlon Australia policy documents.* 2011. Retrieved from www.triathlon.org.au/ Assets/Triathlon+Australia+Digital+Assets/ Resources/Technical/TA+Policy+Document_ June+2011.pdf

12. *International Triathlon Union—approved national federation AG uniforms 2011.* 2011 Retrieved from www.triathlon.org/images/uploads/ approved_catalogue_ag_2011.pdf

13. *International Triathlon Union—approved national federation uniforms 2011.* 2011. Retrieved from www.triathlon.org/images/uploads/ approved_catalogue_ag_2011.pdf

14. *Triathlon Australia—approved unifrom design.* 2011. Retrieved from www.triathlon.org.au/ Assets/Triathlon+Australia+Digital+Assets/ Resources/High+Performance/Australian +Elite+Tri-Suit+-+revision+18+November +2010.pdf

15. FINA. 2011. *List of FINA approved swim suits.* Retrieved from www.fina.org/H2O/index. php?option=com_content&view=article&id= 917&Itemid=461

16. *Triathlon Australia competition rules.* 2011. Retrieved from www.triathlon.org.au/ Assets/Triathlon+Australia+Digital+Assets/ Resources/Technical/TA+Race+Competition+ Rules.pdf

17. *USA Triathlon list of approved swimsuits.* 2011. Retrieved from www.usatriathlon.org/ resources/about-events/rules/approved-skinsuits-speedsuits

18. Parsons, L., and Day, S. 1986. Do wet suits affect swimming speed? *British Journal of Sports Medicine,* 20(3), 129.

19. Toussaint, H.M., DeLooze, M., Van Rossem, B., Leijdekkers, M., and Dignum, H. 1990. Differences in propelling efficiency between competitive and triathlon swimmers. *Medicine and Science in Sports and Exercise,* 22(3), 409–415.

20. Chatard, J., and Millet, G. 1996. Effects of wetsuit use in swimming events. Practical recommendations. *Sports Medicine* (Auckland, NZ), 22(2), 70.

21. Chatard, J.C., Senegas, X., Selles, M., Dreanot, P., and Geyssant, A. 1995. Wet suit effect: A comparison between comeptitive swimmers and triathletes. *Medicine and Science in Sports and Exercise,* 27(4), 580–586.

22. Tomikawa, M., Shimoyama, Y., and Nomura, T. 2008. Factors related to the advantageous effects of wearing a wetsuit during swimming at different submaximal velocity in triathletes. *Journal of Science and Medicine in Sport,* 11(4), 417–423.

Chapter 8 On the Bike

1. Ricard, D., Hills-Meyer, P., Miller, M., and Michael, T. 2006. The effects of bicycle frame geometry on muscle activation and power during a Wingate anaerobic test. *Journal of Sports Science and Medicine,* 5, 25–32.

2. Browning, R. 1991. *Lower extremity kinetics during cycling in elite triathletes in aerodynamic cycling.* Unpublished master's thesis, University of California at Los Angeles.

3. Garside, I., and Doran, D. 2000. Effects of bicycle frame ergonomics on triathlon10-km running performance. *Journal of Sport Sciences,* 18(10), 825–833.

4. International Triathlon Union. 2011. *ITU competition rules.* Author: North Vancouver, British Columbia, Canada.

5. Kyle, C. 2003. Selecting cycling equipment. In E. Burke (Ed.), *High tech cycling II* (pp. 1–48). Champaign, IL: Human Kinetics.

6. *USA Triathlon competitive rules, article V—cycling conduct.* 2011. Retrieved from www.usatriathlon.org/about-multisport/rulebook.aspx

7. Hamley, E., and Thomas, V. 1967. Physiological and postural factors in the calibration of a bicycle ergometer. *Journal of Physiology,* 191, 55–57.

8. LeMond, G., and Gordis, K. 1987. *Greg LeMond's complete book of bicycling* (pp. 118–145). New York: Perigree Books.

9. Pruitt, A., and Matheny, F. 2001. *Andy Pruitt's medical guide for cyclists.* Chapel Hill, NC: RBR.

10. Norgren, K. 2011. *Validation of an on-road motion capture system for cycling research and bicycle fitting.* Unpublished master's thesis, University of Colorado at Colorado Springs.

11. Hagberg, J., and McCole, S. 1996. Energy expenditure in cycling. In E. Burke (Ed.), *High tech cycling* (pp. 167–184). Champaign, IL: Human Kinetics.

12. Broker, J. 2003. Cycling power: Road and mountain. In E. Burke (Ed.), *High tech cycling II* (pp. 147–174). Champaign, IL: Human Kinetics.

Chapter 9 For the Run

1. Boyer, K.A., and Nigg, B.M. 2004. Muscle activity in the leg is tuned in response to impact force characteristics. *Journal of Biomechanics,*

37(10), 1583–1588. doi: S0021929004000314 [pii] 10.1016/j.jbiomech.2004.01.002

2. Nigg, B.M., and Wakeling, J.M. 2001. Impact forces and muscle tuning: A new paradigm. *Exercise and Sport Sciences Reviews*, 29(1), 37–41.

3. Dixon, S.J., Collop, A.C., and Batt, M.E. 2000. Surface effects on ground reaction forces and lower extremity kinematics in running. *Medicine and Science in Sports and Exercise*, 32(11), 1919–1926.

4. Kerdok, A.E., Biewener, A.A., McMahon, T.A., Weyand, P.G., and Herr, H.M. 2002. Energetics and mechanics of human running on surfaces of different stiffnesses. *Journal of Applied Physiology*, 92(2), 469–478. doi: 10.1152/japplphysiol.01164.2000

5. Brughelli, M., and Cronin, J. 2008. Influence of running velocity on vertical, leg and joint stiffness: Modelling and recommendations for future research. *Sports Medicine*, 38(8), 647–657. doi: 3883 [pii]

6. Bosco, C., Saggini, R., and Viru, A. 1997. The influence of different floor stiffness on mechanical efficiency of leg extensor muscle. *Ergonomics*, 40(6), 670–679. doi: 10.1080/001401397187964

7. McMahon, T.A., and Greene, P.R. 1979. The influence of track compliance on running. *Journal of Biomechanics*, 12(12), 893–904. doi: 0021-9290(79)90057-5 [pii]

8. Zamparo, P., Perini, R., Orizio, C., Sacher, M., and Ferretti, G. 1992. The energy cost of walking or running on sand. *European Journal of Applied Physiology and Occupational Physiology*, 65(2), 183–187.

9. Janakiraman, K., Shenoy, S., and Sandhu, J.S. 2011. Intravascular haemolysis during prolonged running on asphalt and natural grass in long and middle distance runners. *Journal of Sports Sciences*, 29(12), 1287–1292. doi: 10.1080/02640414.2011.591416

10. Miller, B.J., Pate, R.R., and Burgess, W. 1988. Foot impact force and intravascular hemolysis during distance running. *International Journal of Sports Medicine*, 9(1), 56–60. doi: 10.1055/s-2007-1024979

11. Paradisis, G.P., Bissas, A., and Cooke, C.B. 2009. Combined uphill and downhill sprint running training is more efficacious than horizontal. *International Journal of Sports Physiology and Performance*, 4(2), 229–243.

12. Peeling, P., Dawson, B., Goodman, C., Landers, G., Wiegerinck, E.T., Swinkels, D.W., and Trinder, D. 2009. Training surface and intensity: Inflammation, hemolysis, and hepcidin expres-

sion. *Medicine and Science in Sports and Exercise*, 41(5), 1138–1145. doi: 00005768-200905000-00021 [pii]10.1249/MSS.0b013e318192ce58

13. Damavandi, M., Dixon, P.C., and Pearsall, D.J. 2011. Ground reaction force adaptations during cross-slope walking and running. *Human Movement Science*. doi: S0167-9457(11)00098-4 [pii]10.1016/j.humov.2011.06.004

14. Fields, K.B., Sykes, J.C., Walker, K.M., and Jackson, J.C. 2010. Prevention of running injuries. *Current Sports Medicine Reports*, 9(3), 176–182. doi: 00149619-201005000-00014 [pii] 10.1249/JSR.0b013e3181de7ec5

15. Richards, C.E., Magin, P.J., and Callister, R. 2009. Is your prescription of distance running shoes evidence-based? *British Journal of Sports Medicine*, 43(3), 159–162. doi: bjsm.2008.046680 [pii] 10.1136/bjsm.2008.046680

16. Robbins, S.E., and Hanna, A.M. 1987. Running-related injury prevention through barefoot adaptations. *Medicine and Science in Sports and Exercise*, 19(2), 148–156.

17. Warburton, M. 2001. Barefoot Running. *Sportscience*, 5(3), online.

18. Divert, C., Mornieux, G., Freychat, P., Baly, L., Mayer, F., and Belli, A. 2008. Barefoot-shod running differences: Shoe or mass effect? *International Journal of Sports Medicine*, 29(6), 512–518. doi: 10.1055/s-2007-989233

19. Stefanyshyn, D.J., and Nigg, B.M. 2000. Energy aspects associated with sport shoes. *Sportverletz Sportschaden*, 14(3), 82–89. doi: 10.1055/s-2000-7867

20. Roy, J.P., and Stefanyshyn, D.J. 2006. Shoe midsole longitudinal bending stiffness and running economy, joint energy, and EMG. *Medicine and Science in Sports and Exercise*, 38(3), 562–569. doi: 00005768-200603000-00023 [pii] 10.1249/01.mss.0000193562.22001.e8

21. Nigg, B.M., Bahlsen, H.A., Luethi, S.M., and Stokes, S. 1987. The influence of running velocity and midsole hardness on external impact forces in heel-toe running. *Journal of Biomechanics*, 20(10), 951–959.

22. Wakeling, J.M., Von Tscharner, V., Nigg, B.M., and Stergiou, P. 2001. Muscle activity in the leg is tuned in response to ground reaction forces. *Journal of Applied Physiology*, 91(3), 1307–1317.

23. McKenzie, D.C., Clement, D.B., and Taunton, J.E. 1985. Running shoes, orthotics, and injuries. *Sports Medicine*, 2(5), 334–347.

24. Nigg, B.M. 2001. The role of impact forces and foot pronation: A new paradigm. *Clinical Journal of Sports Medicine*, 11(1), 2–9.

25. Van Meerhaeghe, T. 2006. [When and why functional orthotics?]. *Revue médicale de Bruxelles*, 27(4), S327–329.

26. Landorf, K.B., and Keenan, A.M. 2000. Efficacy of foot orthoses. What does the literature tell us? *Journal of the American Podiatric Medical Association*, 90(3), 149–158.

27. Landorf, K.B. 2011. Foot orthoses can reduce lower limb overuse injury rate. *Journal of Physiotherapy*, 57(3), 193. doi: S1836-9553(11)70041-8 [pii] 10.1016/S1836-9553(11)70041-8

28. Nigg, B.M., Nurse, M.A., and Stefanyshyn, D.J. 1999. Shoe inserts and orthotics for sport and physical activities. *Medicine and Science in Sports and Exercise*, 31(7 Suppl.), S421–428.

29. Burkett, L.N., Kohrt, W.M., and Buchbinder, R. 1985. Effects of shoes and foot orthotics on $\dot{V}O_2$max and selected frontal plane knee kinematics. *Medicine and Science in Sports and Exercise*, 17(1), 158–163.

30. Ely, M.R., Cheuvront, S.N., Roberts, W.O., and Montain, S.J. 2007. Impact of weather on marathon-running performance. *Medicine and Science in Sports and Exercise*, 39(3), 487–493. doi: 00005768-200703000-00012 [pii] 10.1249/mss.0b013e31802d3aba

31. Montain, S.J., Ely, M.R., and Cheuvront, S.N. 2007. Marathon performance in thermally stressing conditions. *Sports Medicine*, 37(4–5), 320–323. doi: 37NaN12 [pii]

32. Gosling, C.M., Gabbe, B.J., McGivern, J., and Forbes, A.B. 2008. The incidence of heat casualties in sprint triathlon: The tale of two Melbourne race events. *Journal of Science and Medicine in Sport*, 11(1), 52–57. doi: S1440-2440(07)00196-X [pii] 10.1016/j.jsams.2007.08.010

33. Dallam, G.M., Jonas, S., and Miller, T.K. 2005. Medical considerations in triathlon competition: Recommendations for triathlon organisers, competitors and coaches. *Sports Medicine*, 35(2), 143–161. doi: 3524 [pii]

34. Buskirk, E.R., Iampietro, P.F., and Bass, D.E. 2000. Work performance after dehydration: Effects of physical conditioning and heat acclimatization. 1958. *Wilderness and Environmental Medicine*, 11(3), 204–208.

35. Garrett, A.T., Rehrer, N.J., and Patterson, M.J. 2011. Induction and decay of short-term heat acclimation in moderately and highly trained athletes. *Sports Medicine*, 41(9), 757–771. doi: 5 [pii] 10.2165/11587320-000000000-00000

36. Wehrlin, J.P., and Hallén, J. 2006. Linear decrease in $\dot{V}O_2$max and performance with increasing altitude in endurance athletes. *European Journal of Applied Physiology*, 96(4), 404–412. doi: 10.1007/s00421-005-0081-9

37. Rusko, H.K., Tikkanen, H.O., and Peltonen, J.E. 2004. Altitude and endurance training. *Journal of Sports Sciences*, 22(10), 928–944; discussion 945. doi: 10.1080/02640410400005933

38. Beidleman, B.A., Muza, S.R., Fulco, C.S., Cymerman, A., Sawka, M.N., Lewis, S.F., and Skrinar, G.S. 2008. Seven intermittent exposures to altitude improves exercise performance at 4300 m. *Medicine and Science in Sports and Exercise*, 40(1), 141–148. doi: 10.1249/mss.0b013e31815a519b

39. Saunders, P.U., Pyne, D.B., and Gore, C.J. 2009. Endurance training at altitude. *High Altitude Medicine and Biology*, 10(2), 135–148. doi: 10.1089/ham.2008.1092

40. Stray-Gundersen, J., and Levine, B.D. 2008. Live high, train low at natural altitude. *Scandinavian Journal of Medicine and Science in Sports*, 18(Suppl. 1), 21–28. doi: SMS829 [pii] 10.1111/j.1600-0838.2008.00829.x

41. Chapman, R., and Levine, B.D. 2007. Altitude training for the marathon. *Sports Medicine*, 37(4–5), 392–395. doi: 37NaN31 [pii]

42. Wilber, R.L. 2007. Application of altitude/hypoxic training by elite athletes. *Medicine and Science in Sports and Exercise*, 39(9), 1610–1624. doi: 00005768-200709000-00024 [pii] 10.1249/mss.0b013e3180de49e6

43. Millet, G.P., Roels, B., Schmitt, L., Woorons, X., and Richalet, J.P. 2010. Combining hypoxic methods for peak performance. *Sports Medicine*, 40(1), 1–25. doi: 1 [pii] 10.2165/11317920-000000000-00000

44. Kargarfard, M., Poursafa, P., Rezanejad, S., and Mousavinasab, F. 2011. Effects of exercise in polluted air on the aerobic power, serum lactate level and cell blood count of active individuals. *International Journal of Preventive Medicine*, 2(3), 145–150.

45. Pierson, W.E., Covert, D.S., Koenig, J.Q., Namekata, T., and Kim, Y.S. 1986. Implications of air pollution effects on athletic performance. *Medicine and Science in Sports and Exercise*, 18(3), 322–327.

46. Sacha, J.J., and Quinn, J.M. 2011. The environment, the airway, and the athlete. *Annals of Allergy, Asthma, and Immunology*, 106(2), 81–87; quiz 88. doi: S1081-1206(10)00601-0 [pii] 10.1016/j.anai.2010.06.004

47. Poussel, M., and Chenuel, B. 2010. [Exercise-induced bronchoconstriction in non-asthmatic athletes]. *Revue des maladies respiratoires*,

27(8), 898–906. doi: S0761-8425(10)00370-0 [pii]10.1016/j.rmr.2010.08.004

48. Campbell, M.E., Li, Q., Gingrich, S.E., Macfarlane, R.G., and Cheng, S. 2005. Should people be physically active outdoors on smog alert days? *Canadian Journal of Public Health*, 96(1), 24–28.

49. Daigle, C.C., Chalupa, D.C., Gibb, F.R., Morrow, P.E., Oberdörster, G., Utell, M.J., and Frampton, M.W. 2003. Ultrafine particle deposition in humans during rest and exercise. *Inhalation Toxicology*, 15(6), 539–552. doi: 00F0G36CKYU-W1B7B [pii] 10.1080/08958370304468

Chapter 10 Triathlon Training Technologies

1. Friel, J. 2009. *The triathlete's training bible* (3rd ed., pp. 54–55). Boulder, CO: VeloPress.

2. Friel, J. 2009. *The triathlete's training bible* (3rd ed., p. 49). Boulder, CO: VeloPress.

3. Coggan, A., and Allen, H. 2009. *Training and racing with a power meter* (2nd ed., p. 48). Boulder, CO: VeloPress.

4. McGregor, S., and Fitzgerald, M. 2010. *The runner's edge*. Champaign, IL: Human Kinetics.

Chapter 11 Aerobic Capacity

1. Hill, A.V. 1925. *Muscular activity* (pp. 1–115). London: Bailliere Tindall and Cox.

2. Taylor, H.L., Buskirk, E., and Henschel, A. 1955. Maximal oxygen uptake as an objective measure of cardio-respiratory performance. *Journal of Applied Physiology*, 8, 73–80.

3. Day, J.R., Rossiter, H.B., Coats, E.M., et al. 2003. The maximally attainable $\dot{V}O_2$ during exercise in humans: The peak vs. maximum issue. *Journal of Applied Physiology*, 95, 1901–1907.

4. Lucia, A., Rabadan, M., Hoyos, J., et al. 2006. Frequency of the $\dot{V}O_2$max plateau phenomenon in world-class cyclists. *International Journal of Sports Medicine*, 27, 984–992.

5. Doherty, M., Nobbs, L., and Noakes, T.D. 2003. Low frequency of the "plateau phenomenon" during maximal exercise in elite British athletes. *European Journal of Applied Physiology*, 89, 619–623.

6. Noakes, T.D., St. Clair Gibson, A., and Lambert, E.V. 2005. From catastrophe to complexity: A novel model of integrative central neural regulation of effort and fatigue during exercise in humans: Summary and conclusions. *British Journal of Sports Medicine*, Feb. 39(2), 120–124.

7. Hawley, J.A., and Noakes, T.D. 1992. Peak power output predicts maximal oxygen uptake and performance time in trained cyclists. *European Journal of Applied Physiology and Occupational Physiology*, 65(1), 79–83.

8. Padilla, S., Mujika, I., Angulo, F., and Goiriena, J.J. 2000. Scientific approach to the 1-h cycling world record: A case study. *Journal of Applied Physiology*, Oct. 89(4), 1522–1527. Erratum in *Journal of Applied Physiology*, Dec. 89(6).

9. Van Schuylenbergh, R., Eynde, B.V., and Hespel, P. 2004. Prediction of sprint triathlon performance from laboratory tests. *European Journal of Applied Physiology*, Jan. 91(1), 94–99.

10. Laursen, P.B., and Rhodes, E.C. 2001. Factors affecting performance in an ultraendurance triathlon. *Sports Medicine*, 31(3), 195–209.

11. Laursen, P.B., Knez, W.L., Shing, C.M., Langill, R.H., Rhodes, E.C., and Jenkins, D.G. 2005. Relationship between laboratory-measured variables and heart rate during an ultra-endurance triathlon. *Journal of Sports Sciences*, Oct 23(10), 1111–1120.

12. Hue, O., Le Gallais, D., Chollet, D., and Préfaut, C. 2000. Ventilatory threshold and maximal oxygen uptake in present triathletes. *Canadian Journal of Applied Physiology*, Apr. 25(2), 102–113.

13. Bunc, V., Heller, J., Horcic, J., and Novotny, J. 1996. Physiological profile of best Czech male and female young triathletes. *Journal of Sports Medicine and Physical Fitness*, Dec. 36(4), 265–270.

14. Galy, O., Manetta, J., Coste, O., Maimoun, L., Chamari, K., and Hue, O. 2003. Maximal oxygen uptake and power of lower limbs during a competitive season in triathletes. *Scandinavian Journal of Medicine and Science in Sports*, June 13(3), 185–193.

15. Lucía, A., Hoyos, J., Pérez, M., Santalla, A., and Chicharro, J.L. 2002. Inverse relationship between VO₂max and economy/efficiency in world-class cyclists. *Medicine and Science in Sports and Exercise*, Dec. 34(12), 2079–2084.

16. Coyle, E.F. 2005. Improved muscular efficiency displayed as Tour de France champion matures. *Journal of Applied Physiology*, June 98(6), 2191–2196. Epub 2005 Mar 17.

17. Bouchard, C., Sarzynski, M.A., Rice, T.K., et al. 2011. Genomic predictors of the maximal O_2 uptake response to standardized exercise training programs. *Journal of Applied Physiology*, 110, 1160–1170.

18. Bouchard, C., Leon, A.S., Rao, D.C., et al. 1995. The HERITAGE Family Study. Aims, design, and measurement protocol. *Medicine and Science in Sports and Exercise*, 27, 721–729.

19. Morss, G.M., Jordan, A.N., Skinner, J.S., et al. 2004. Dose Response to Exercise in Women aged 45–75 yr (DREW): Design and rationale. *Medicine and Science in Sports and Exercise*, 36, 336–344.

20. Kraus, W.E., Torgan, C.E., Duscha, B.D., et al. 2001. Studies of a targeted risk reduction intervention through defined exercise (STRRIDE). *Medicine and Science in Sports and Exercise*, 33, 1774–1784.

21. Helgerud, J., Høydal, K., Wang, E., Karlsen, T., Berg, P., Bjerkaas, M., Simonsen, T., Helgesen, C., Hjorth, N., Bach, R., and Hoff, J. 2007. Aerobic high-intensity intervals improve $\dot{V}O_2$max more than moderate training. *Medicine and Science in Sports and Exercise*, Apr. 39(4), 665–671.

22. Gibala, M.J., Little, J.P., van Essen, M., Wilkin, G.P., Burgomaster, K.A., Safdar, A., Raha, S., and Tarnopolsky, M.A. 2006. Short-term sprint interval versus traditional endurance training: Similar initial adaptations in human skeletal muscle and exercise performance. *Journal of Physiology*, Sep. 15, 575(Pt. 3), 901–911.

Chapter 12 Economy

1. Foster, C., and Lucia, A. 2007. Running economy: The forgotten factor in elite performance. *Sports Medicine*, 37(4–5), 316–319.

2. Capelli, C., Pendergast, D.R., and Termin, B. 1998. Energetics of swimming at maximal speeds in humans. *European Journal of Applied Physiology and Occupational Physiology*, Oct., 78(5), 385–393.

3. Lucía, A., Hoyos, J., Pérez, M., Santalla, A., and Chicharro, J.L. 2002. Inverse relationship between $\dot{V}O_2$max and economy/efficiency in world-class cyclists. *Medicine and Science in Sports and Exercise*, Dec., 34(12), 2079–2084.

4. Noakes, T.D., and Tucker, R. 2004. Inverse relationship between $\dot{V}O_2$max and economy in world-class cyclists. *Medicine and Science in Sports and Exercise*, June, 36(6), 1083–1084; author reply 1085–1086.

5. Hausswirth, C., Bigard, A.X., and Guezennec, C.Y. 1997. Relationships between running mechanics and energy cost of running at the end of a triathlon and a marathon. *International Journal of Sports Medicine*, 18, 330–339.

6. Hue, O., Gallais, D.L., Chollet, D., Boussana, A., and Prefaut, C. 1997. The influence of prior cycling on biomechanical and cardiorespiratory response profiles during running in triathletes. *European Journal of Applied Physiology and Occupational Physiology*, 77, 98–105.

7. Millet, G.P., Millet, G.Y., Hofmann, M.D., and Candau, R.B. 2000. Alterations in running economy and mechanics after maximal cycling in triathletes: Influence of performance level. *International Journal of Sports Medicine*, 21, 127–132.

8. Kjendlie, P.L., Ingjer, F., Stallman, R.K., and Stray-Gundersen, J. 2004. Factors affecting swimming economy in children and adults. *European Journal of Applied Physiology*, Oct., 93(1–2), 65–74. Epub 2004 Jul 8.

9. Hopker, J., Passfield, L., Coleman, D., Jobson, S., Edwards, L., and Carter, H. 2009. The effects of training on gross efficiency in cycling: A review. *International Journal of Sports Medicine*, Dec., 30(12), 845–850.

10. Sacchetti, M., Lenti, M., Di Palumbo, A.S., and De Vito, G. 2010 Different effect of cadence on cycling efficiency between young and older cyclists. *Medicine and Science in Sports and Exercise*, 42, 2128–2133.

11. Louis, J., Hausswirth, C., Easthope, C., Brisswalter, J. 2011. Strength training improves cycling efficiency in master endurance athletes. *European Journal of Applied Physiology*, June 3. [Epub ahead of print]

12. Hopker, J.G., Coleman, D.A., and Wiles, J.D. 2007. Differences in efficiency between trained and recreational cyclists. *Applied Physiology, Nutrition and Metabolism*, 32(6), 1036–1042.

13. Hopker, J.G., Coleman, D.C., and Passfield, L. 2009. Changes in cycling efficiency during a competitive season. *Medicine and Science in Sports and Exercise*, 41(4), 912–919.

14. Hopker, J., Coleman, D., Passfield, L., and Wiles J. 2010. The effect of training volume and intensity on competitive cyclists' efficiency. *Applied Physiology, Nutrition and Metabolism*, Feb., 35(1), 17–22.

15. Lucía, A., Pardo, J., Durantez, A., Hoyos, J., and Chicharro, J.L. 1998. Physiological differences between professional and elite road cyclists. *International Journal of Sports Medicine*, 19(5), 342–348.

16. Jeukendrup, A.E., Craig, N.P., and Hawley, J.A. 2000. The bioenergetics of World Class Cycling. *Journal of Science and Medicine in Sport*, Dec., 3(4), 414–433.

17. Bonacci, J., Chapman, A., Blanch, P., and Vicenzino, B. 2009. Neuromuscular adaptations to training, injury and passive interventions: Implications for running economy. *Sports Medicine*, 39(11), 903–921.

18. Paavolainen, L., Häkkinen, K., Hämäläinen, I., Nummela, A., Rusko, H. 1999. Explosive-strength training improves 5-km running time

by improving running economy and muscle power. *Journal of Applied Physiology*, May, 86(5), 1527–1533.

19. Nummela, A.T., Paavolainen, L.M., Sharwood, K.A., Lambert, M.I., Noakes, T.D., and Rusko, H.K. 2006. Neuromuscular factors determining 5 km running performance and running economy in well-trained athletes. *European Journal of Applied Physiology*, May, 97(1), 1–8.

20. Gleim, G.W., Stachenfeld, N.S., and Nicholas, J.A. 1990. The influence of flexibility on the economy of walking and jogging. *Journal of Orthopaedic Research*, Nov., 8(6), 814–823.

21. Craib, M.W., Mitchell, V.A., Fields, K.B., Cooper, T.R., Hopewell, R., and Morgan, D.W. 1996. The association between flexibility and running economy in sub-elite male distance runners. *Medicine and Science in Sports and Exercise*, June, 28(6), 737–743.

22. Godges, J.J., MacRae, P.G., and Engelke, K.A. 1993. Effects of exercise on hip range of motion, trunk muscle performance, and gait economy. *Physical Therapy*, 73, 468–477.

23. Nelson, A.G., Kokkonen, J., Eldredge, C. et al. 2001. Chronic stretching and running economy. *Scandinavian Journal of Medicine and Science in Sports*, 11, 260–265.

24. Godges, J.J., MacRae, H., Longdon, C. et al. 1989. The effects of two stretching procedures on hip range of motion and gait economy. *Journal of Orthopaedic and Sports Physical Therapy*, 10, 350–357.

25. Chapman, A., Vicenzino, B., Blanch, P. et al. 2007. Leg muscle recruitment during cycling is less developed in triathletes than cyclists despite matched cycling training loads. *Experimental Brain Research*, 181, 503–518.

26. Bonacci, J., Green, D., Saunders, P.U., Blanch, P., Franettovich, M., Chapman, A.R., et al. 2010. Change in running kinematics after cycling are related to alterations in running economy in triathletes. *Journal of Science and Medicine in Sport*, 13, 460–464.

27. Millet, G.P., and Vleck, V.E. 2000. Physiological and biomechanical adaptations to the cycle to run transition in Olympic triathlon: Review and practical recommendations for training. *British Journal of Sports Medicine*, 34, 384–390.

Chapter 13 Anaerobic Threshold

1. Wasserman, K., and McIlroy, M.B. 1964. Detecting the threshold of anaerobic metabolism in cardiac patients during exercise. *American Journal of Physiology*, 14, 844–852.

2. Solberg, G., Robstad, B., Skjønsberg, O.H., and Borchsenius, F. 2005. Respiratory gas exchange indices for estimating the anaerobic threshold. *Journal of Sports Science and Medicine*, 4, 29–36.

3. Anderson, G.S., and Rhodes, E.C. 1989. A review of blood lactate and ventilatory methods of detecting transition thresholds. *Sports Medicine*, 8, 3–55

4. Quinn, T.J., and Coons, B.A. 2011. The Talk Test and its relationship with the ventilatory and lactate thresholds. *Journal of Sports Science*, Aug., 29(11), 1175–1182.

5. Gaskill, S.E., Ruby, B.C., Walker, A.J., Sanchez, O.A., Serfass, R.C., and Leon, A.S. 2001. Validity and reliability of combining three methods to determine ventilatory threshold. *Medicine and Science in Sports and Exercise*, Nov., 33(11), 1841–1848.

6. Brooks, G.A. 2007. Lactate: Link between glycolytic and oxidative metabolism. *Sports Medicine*, 37(4–5), 341–343.

7. Brooks, G.A. 2009. Cell-cell and intracellular lactate shuttles. *Journal of Physiology*, Dec. 1, 587(Pt. 23), 5591–5600.

8. Bernard, T., Hausswirth, C., Le Meur, Y., Bignet, F., Dorel, S., and Brisswalter, J. 2009. Distribution of power output during the cycling stage of a Triathlon World Cup. *Medicine and Science in Sports and Exercise*, June, 41(6), 1296–1302.

9. Laursen, P.B., Rhodes, E.C., Langill, R.H., McKenzie, D.C., and Taunton, J.E. 2002. Relationship of exercise test variables to cycling performance in an Ironman triathlon. *European Journal of Applied Physiology*, Aug., 87(4–5), 433–440.

10. Hopker, J., Coleman, D., Passfield, L., and Wiles, J. 2010. The effect of training volume and intensity on competitive cyclists' efficiency. *Applied Physiology, Nutrition and Metabolism*, Feb., 35(1), 17–22.

11. Gibala, M.J., Little, J.P., van Essen, M., Wilkin, G.P., Burgomaster, K.A., Safdar, A., Raha, S., and Tarnopolsky, M.A. 2006. Short-term sprint interval versus traditional endurance training: Similar initial adaptations in human skeletal muscle and exercise performance. *Journal of Physiology*, Sep. 15, 575(Pt. 3), 901–911.

12. Van Schuylenbergh, R., Eynde, B.V., and Hespel, P. 2004. Prediction of sprint triathlon performance from laboratory tests. *European Journal of Applied Physiology*, Jan., 91(1), 94–99. Epub 2003 Sep 4.

13. Schabort, E.J., Killian, S.C., St. Clair Gibson, A., Hawley, J.A., and Noakes, T.D. 2000. Prediction

of triathlon race time from laboratory testing in national triathletes. *Medicine and Science in Sports and Exercise*, Apr., 32(4), 844–849.

14. Hue, O. 2003. Prediction of drafted-triathlon race time from submaximal laboratory testing in elite triathletes. *Canadian Journal of Applied Physiology*, Aug., 28(4), 547–560.

15. Swart, J., and Jennings, C.L. 2004. Use of blood lactate concentration as a marker of training status: Review article. *South African Journal of Sports Medicine*, 16, 1–5.

16. Pyne, D.B., Lee, H., and Swanwick, K.M. 2001. Monitoring the lactate threshold in world-ranked swimmers. *Medicine and Science in Sports and Exercise*, Feb., 33(2), 291–297.

Chapter 14   Muscle Types and Triathlon Performance

1. Andersen, J.L., Schjerling, P., and Saltin, B. 2000. Muscle, genes and athletic performance. *Scientific American*, 283, 48–55.

2. Andersen, J.L., and Aagard, P. 2010. Effects of strength training on muscle fiber types and size; consequences for athletes training for high-intensity sport. *Scandinavian Journal of Medicine and Science in Sports*, 20(Suppl. 2), 32–38.

3. Zierath, J.R., and Hawley, J.A. 2004. Skeletal muscle fiber type: Influence on contractile and metabolic properties. *PLoS Biology*, Oct. 2(10), e348.

4. Harridge, S.D. 1996. The muscle contractile system and its adaptation to training. In P. Marconnet, B. Saltin, P.V. Komi, and J. Poortmans (Eds.), *Human muscular function during dynamic exercise* (pp. 82–94). Basel, Switzerland: Karger.

5. Bottinelli, R. 2001. Functional heterogeneity of mammalian single muscle fibres: Do myosin isoforms tell the whole story? *Pflugers Archiv*, 443, 6–17.

6. Lionikas, A., Li, M., and Larsson, L. 2006. Human skeletal muscle myosin function at physiological and non-physiological temperatures. *Acta Physiologica*, 186, 151–158.

7. Simoneau, J.A., and Bouchard, C. 1989. Human variation in skeletal muscle fiber-type proportion and enzyme activities. *American Journal of Physiology*, Oct. 257(4 Pt. 1), E567–572.

8. Tesch, P.A., and Karlsson, J. 1985. Muscle fiber types and size in trained and untrained muscles of elite athletes. *Journal of Applied Physiology*, Dec., 59(6), 1716–1720.

9. Fink, W.J., Costill, D.L., and Pollock, M.L. 1977. Submaximal and maximal working capacity of elite distance runners. Part II: Muscle fiber composition and enzyme activities. *Annals of the New York Academy of Sciences*, 301, 323–327.

10. Costill, D.L., Daniels, J., Evans, W., Fink, W.J., Krahenbuhl, G., and Saltin, B. 1976. Skeletal muscle enzymes and fiber composition in male and female track athletes. *Journal of Applied Physiology*, 40, 149–154.

11. Parcell, A.C., Sawyer, R.D., and Craig Poole, R. 2003. Single muscle fiber myosin heavy chain distribution in elite female track athletes. *Medicine and Science in Sports and Exercise*, Mar., 35(3), 434–438.

12. Saltin, B., Henriksson, J., Nygaard, E., and Andersen, P. 1977. Fiber types and metabolic potentials of skeletal muscles in sedentary man and endurance runners. *Annals of the New York Academy of Sciences*, 301, 3–44.

13. Gollnick, P.D., and Matoba, H. 1984. The muscle fiber composition of skeletal muscle as a predictor of athletic success. An overview. *American Journal of Sports Medicine*, May–June, 12(3), 212–217.

14. Holloszy, J.O., and Coyle, E.F. 1984. Adaptations of skeletal muscle to endurance exercise and their metabolic consequences. *Journal of Applied Physiology*, Apr., 56(4), 831–838.

15. Luden, N., Hayes, E., Minchev, K., Louis, E., Raue, U., Conley, T., and Trappe, S. 2011. Skeletal muscle plasticity with marathon training in novice runners. *Scandinavian Journal of Medicine and Science in Sports*, Apr 8, 662–670.

16. Aagaard, P., Andersen, J.L., Bennekou, M., Larsson, B., Olesen, J.L., Crameri, R., Magnusson, S.P., and Kjaer, M. 2011. Effects of resistance training on endurance capacity and muscle fiber composition in young top-level cyclists. *Scandinavian Journal of Medicine and Science in Sports*, Mar. 1. e298–307.

17. Wang, Y.X., Zhang, C.L., Yu, R.T., Cho, H.K., and Nelson, M.C., et al. 2004. Regulation of muscle fiber type and running endurance by PPAR\gd\. *PLoS Biology*, 2, e294.

18. Gollnick, P.D., Armstrong, R.B., Saltin, B., Saubert, C.W. 4th, Sembrowich, W.L., and Shepherd, R.E. 1973. Effect of training on enzyme activity and fiber composition of human skeletal muscle. *Journal of Applied Physiology*, Jan., 34(1), 107–111.

19. Simoneau, J.A., Lortie, G., Boulay, M.R., Marcotte, M., Thibault, M.C., and Bouchard, C. 1985. Human skeletal muscle fiber type alteration with high-intensity intermittent training. *European Journal of Applied Physiology and Occupational Physiology*, 54(3), 250–253.

20. Helgerud, J., Høydal, K., Wang, E., Karlsen, T., Berg, P., Bjerkaas, M., Simonsen, T., Helgesen, C., Hjorth, N., Bach, R., and Hoff, J. 2007. Aerobic high-intensity intervals improve V̇O₂max more than moderate training. *Medicine and Science in Sports and Exercise*, Apr., 39(4), 665–671.

21. Burgomaster, K.A., Howarth, K.R., Phillips, S.M., Rakobowchuk, M., Macdonald, M.J., McGee, S.L., and Gibala, M.J. 2008. Similar metabolic adaptations during exercise after low volume sprint interval and traditional endurance training in humans. *Journal of Physiology*, Jan., 1;586(1), 151–60. Epub 2007 Nov 8.

22. Gibala, M.J., Little, J.P., van Essen, M., Wilkin, G.P., Burgomaster, K.A., Safdar, A., Raha, S., and Tarnopolsky, M.A. 2006. Short-term sprint interval versus traditional endurance training: Similar initial adaptations in human skeletal muscle and exercise performance. *Journal of Physiology*, Sep. 15, 575(Pt. 3), 901–911.

Chapter 15 Fatigue Resistance and Recovery

1. Nybo, L., and Nielsen, B. 2001. Hyperthermia and central fatigue during prolonged exercise in humans. *Journal of Applied Physiology*, Sep., 91(3), 1055–1060.

2. Nybo, L., and Nielsen, B. 2001. Perceived exertion is associated with an altered brain activity during exercise with progressive hyperthermia. *Journal of Applied Physiology*, Nov., 91(5), 2017–2023.

3. Drust, B., Rasmussen, P., Mohr, M., Nielsen, B., and Nybo, L. 2005. Elevations in core and muscle temperature impairs repeated sprint performance. *Acta Physiologica Scandinavica*, Feb., 183(2), 181–190.

4. Tucker, R., and Noakes, T.D. 2009. The physiological regulation of pacing strategy during exercise: A critical review. *British Journal of Sports Medicine*, June, 43(6), e1. Epub 2009 Feb 17.

5. Lambert, E.V., St. Clair Gibson, A., and Noakes, T.D. 2005. Complex systems model of fatigue: Integrative homoeostatic control of peripheral physiological systems during exercise in humans. *British Journal of Sports Medicine*, Jan., 39(1), 52–62.

6. Noakes, T.D., St. Clair Gibson, A., and Lambert, E.V. 2005. From catastrophe to complexity: A novel model of integrative central neural regulation of effort and fatigue during exercise in humans: Summary and conclusions. *British Journal of Sports Medicine*, Feb., 39(2), 120–124.

7. Tucker, R. 2009. The anticipatory regulation of performance: The physiological basis for pacing strategies and the development of a perception-based model for exercise performance. *British Journal of Sports Medicine*, June, 43(6), 392–400. Epub 2009 Feb 17.

8. Rowell, L.B., Marx, H.J., Bruce, R.A., et al. 1966. Reductions in cardiac output, central blood volume, and stroke volume with thermal stress in normal men during exercise. *Journal of Clinical Investigation*, 45, 1801–1816.

9. Nadel, E.R., Cafarelli, E., Roberts, M.F., and Wenger, C.B. 1979. Circulatory regulation during exercise in different ambient temperatures. *Journal of Applied Physiology*, Mar., 46(3), 430–437.

10. Savard, G.K., Nielsen, B., Laszczynska, J., Larsen, B.E., and Saltin, B. 1988. Muscle blood flow is not reduced in humans during moderate exercise and heat stress. *Journal of Applied Physiology*, Feb., 64(2), 649–657.

11. Cheung, S.S., and Sleivert, G.G. 2004. Multiple triggers for hyperthermic fatigue and exhaustion. *Exercise and Sport Sciences Review*, 32, 100–106.

12. Tatterson, A.J., Hahn, A.G., Martin, D.T., and Febbraio, M.A. 2000. Effects of heat stress on physiological responses and exercise performance in elite cyclists. *Journal of Science and Medicine in Sport*, June, 3(2), 186–193.

13. Kay, D., Marino, F.E., Cannon, J., et al. 2001. Evidence for neuromuscular fatigue during high-intensity cycling in warm, humid conditions. *European Journal of Applied Physiology*, 84, 115–121.

14. Marino, F.E., Lambert, M.I., and Noakes, T.D. 2004. Superior performance of African runners in warm humid but not in cool environmental conditions. *Journal of Applied Physiology*, 96, 124–130.

15. Tucker, R., Rauch, L., Harley, Y.X., and Noakes, T.D. 2004. Impaired exercise performance in the heat is associated with an anticipatory reduction in skeletal muscle recruitment. *Pflugers Archiv*, July, 448(4), 422–430.

16. Rauch, H.G., St. Clair Gibson, A., Lambert, E.V., and Noakes, T.D. 2005. A signalling role for muscle glycogen in the regulation of pace during prolonged exercise. *British Journal of Sports Medicine*, Jan., 39(1), 34–38.

17. Noakes, T.D. 2000. Physiological models to understand exercise fatigue and the adaptations that predict or enhance athletic performance. *Scandinavian Journal of Medicine and Science in Sports*, June, 10(3), 123–145.

18. Noakes, T.D. 2004. Linear relationship between the perception of effort and the duration of constant load exercise that remains. *Journal of Applied Physiology*, Apr., 96(4), 1571–1572; author reply 1572–1573.

19. Amann, M., Eldridge, M.W., Lovering, A.T., Stickland, M.K., Pegelow, D.F., and Dempsey, J.A. 2006. Arterial oxygenation influences central motor output and exercise performance via effects on peripheral locomotor muscle fatigue in humans. *Journal of Physiology*, Sep. 15, 575(Pt. 3), 937–952. Epub 2006 Jun 22.

20. Amann, M., Proctor, L.T., Sebranek, J.J., Pegelow, D.F., and Dempsey, J.A. 2009. Opioid-mediated muscle afferents inhibit central motor drive and limit peripheral muscle fatigue development in humans. *Journal of Physiology*, Jan. 15, 587(Pt. 1), 271–283. Epub 2008 Nov 17.

21. Amann, M., and Dempsey, J.A. 2008. The concept of peripheral locomotor muscle fatigue as a regulated variable. *Journal of Physiology*, Feb. 14. [Epub ahead of print]

22. Nielsen, B., and Davies, C.T. 1976. Temperature regulation during exercise in water and air. *Acta Physiologica Scandinavica*, Dec., 98(4), 500–508.

23. St. Clair Gibson, A., Baden, D.A., Lambert, M.I., Lambert, E.V., Harley, Y.X., Hampson, D., Russell, V.A., and Noakes, T.D. 2003. The conscious perception of the sensation of fatigue. *Sports Medicine*, 33(3), 167–176.

Chapter 16 Warm-Up and Cool-Down

1. Wright, V., and Johns, R.J. 1961. Quantitative and qualitative analysis of joint stiffness in normal subjects and in patients with connective tissue diseases. *Annals of the Rheumatic Diseases*, 20, 36–46.

2. Buchthal, F., Kaiser, E., and Knappeis, G.G. 1944. Elasticity, viscosity and plasticity in the cross striated muscle fibre. *Acta Physiologica Scandinavica*, 8(1), 16–37.

3. Brechue, W.F., Ameredes, B.T., Barclay, J.K., and Stainsby, W.N. 1995. Blood flow and pressure relationships which determine $\dot{V}O_2$max. *Medicine and Science in Sports and Exercise*, 27(1), 37–42

4. Barcroft, J., and King, W.O. 1909. The effect of temperature on the dissociation curve of blood. *Journal of Physiology*, 39(5), 374–384.

5. Andzel, W.D. 1982. One mile run performance as a function of prior exercise. *Journal of Sports Medicine and Physical Fitness*, 22(1), 80–84.

6. Bruyn-Prevost, P. 1980. The effects of various warming up intensities and durations upon some physiological variables during an exercise corresponding to the WC170. *European Journal of Applied Physiology and Occupational Physiology*, 43(2), 93–100.

7. Proske, U., Morgan, D., and Gregory, J. 1993. Thixotropy in skeletal muscle and in muscle spindles: A review. *Progress in Neurobiology*, 41(6), 705–721.

8. Orlick, T., and Partington, J. 1987. The sport psychology consultant: Analysis of critical components as viewed by Canadian Olympic athletes. *Sport Psychologist*, 2, 105–130.

9. Law, R.Y., and Herbert, R.D. 2007. Warm-up reduces delayed-onset muscle soreness but cool-down does not: A randomised controlled trial. *Australian Journal of Physiotherapy*, 53, 91–95.

10. Murphy, J.R., Di Santo, M.C., Alkanani, T., and Behm, D.G. 2010. Aerobic activity before and following short-duration static stretching improves range of motion and performance vs. a traditional warm-up. *Applied Physiology, Nutrition, and Metabolism*, 35(5), 679–690.

11. Stewart, I.B., and Sleivert, G.G. 1998. The effect of warm-up intensity on range of motion and anaerobic performance. *Journal of Orthopaedic and Sports Physical Therapy*, 27(2), 154–161.

12. Gregson, W.A., Drust, B., Batterham, A., and Cable, N.T. 2002. The effects of pre-warming on the metabolic and thermoregulatory responses to prolonged submaximal exercise in moderate ambient temperatures. *European Journal of Applied Physiology*, 86(6), 526–533.

13. Gonzalez-Alonso, J., Teller, C., Andersen, S.L., Jensen, F.B., Hyldig, T., and Nielsesn, B. 1999. Influence of body temperature on the development of fatigue during prolonged exercise in the heat. *Journal of Applied Physiology*, 85(3), 1032–1039.

14. Bishop, D., Bonetti, D., and Dawson, B. 2001. The effect of three different warm-up intensities on kayak ergometer performance. *Medicine and Science in Sports and Exercise*, 33(6), 1026–1032.

15. Saltin, B., Gagge, A.P., and Stolwijk, J.A. 1968. Muscle temperature during submaximal exercise in man. *Journal of Applied Physiology*, 25(6), 679–688.

16. Ozyener, F., Rossiter, H.R., Ward, S.A., and Whipp, B.J. 2001. Influence of exercise intensity on the on- and off-transient kinetics of pulmonary oxygen uptake in humans. *Journal of Physiology*, 533, 891–902.

17. Tomaras, E.K., and MacIntosh, B.R. 2011. Less is more: Standard warm-up causes fatigue and less warm-up permits greater cycling power output. *Journal of Applied Physiology,* 111(1), 228–235.

18. Burnley, M., Doust, J.H., and Jones, A.M. 2006. Time required for the restoration of normal heavy exercise VO$_2$ kinetics following prior heavy exercise. *Journal of Applied Physiology,* 101(5), 1320–1327.

19. Kenny, G.P., Reardon, F.D., Zaleski, W., Reardon, M.L., Haman, F., and Ducharme, M.B. 2003. Muscle temperature transients before, during, and after exercise measured using an intramuscular multisensor probe. *Journal of Applied Physiology,* 94, 2350–2357.

20. Ahmaidi, S., Granier, P., Taoutaou, Z., Mercier, J., Dubouchaud, H., and Prefaut, C. 1996. Effects of active recovery on plasma lactate and anaerobic power following repeated intensive exercise. *Medicine and Science in Sports and Exercise,* 28(4), 450–456.

21. Wilmore, J.H., and Costill, D.L. 2008. *Physiology of sport and exercise* (4th ed., pp. 116–117). Champaign, IL: Human Kinetics.

22. Wilmore, J.H., and Costill, D.L. 2004. *Physiology of sport and exercise* (3rd ed.). Champaign, IL: Human Kinetics, p. 100.

23. De Pauw, K., De Geus, B., Roelands, B., Lauwens, F., Verschueren, J., Heyman, E., and Meeusen, R.R. 2011. Effect of five different recovery methods on repeated cycle performance. *Medicine and Science in Sports and Exercise,* 43(5), 890–897.

24. Foss, M.L., Ketevian, S.J., and Fox, E.L. 1998. *Fox's Physiological Basis for Exercise and Sport.* New York: WCB/McGraw-Hill.

25. Vaile, J., Halson, S., Gill, N., and Dawson, B. 2008. Effect of hydrotherapy on recovery from fatigue. *International Journal of Sports Medicine,* 29(7), 539–544.

26. Ingram, J., Dawson, B., Goodman, C., Wallman, K., and Beilby, J. 2009. Effect of water immersion methods on post-exercise recovery from simulated team sport exercise. *Journal of Science and Medicine in Sport,* 12(3), 417–421.

Chapter 17 Flexibility and Core Strength

1. Araujo, C.G. 1999. Body flexibility profile and clustering among male and female elite athletes. *Medicine and Science in Sports and Exercise,* 31(5), S115.

2. McCullough, A., Kraemer, W., Volek, J., Solomon-Hill, G.F., Hatfield, D., Vingren, J.,

and Maresh, C. 2009. Factors affecting flutter kicking speed in women who are competitive and recreational swimmers. *Journal of Strength and Conditioning Research,* 23(7), 2130–2136.

3. Hahn, T., Foldspang, A., Vestergaard, E., and Ingemann-Hansen, T. 1999. Active knee joint flexibility and sports activity. *Scandinavian Journal of Medicine and Science in Sports,* 9(2), 74–80.

4. Jones, A.M. 2002. Running economy is negatively related to sit-and-reach test performance in international-standard distance runners. *International Journal of Sports Medicine,* 23(1), 40–43.

5. Ibid., 40.

6. Treheam, T.L., and Buresh, R.J. 2009. Sit-and-reach flexibility and running economy of men and women collegiate distance runners. *Journal of Strength and Conditioning Research,* 23(1), 158–62.

7. Craib, M.W., Mitchell, V.A., Fields, K.B., Cooper, T.R., Hopewell, R., and Morgan, D.W. 1996. The association between flexibility and running economy in sub-elite male distance runners. *Medicine and Science in Sports and Exercise,* 28(6), 737–743.

8. Ibid., 737.

9. Nelson, A.G., Kokkonen, J., Eldredge, C., Cornwell, A., and Glickman-Weiss, E. 2001. Chronic stretching and running economy. *Scandinavian Journal of Medicine and Science in Sports,* 11(5), 260–265.

10. Mojock, C.D., Kim, J.S., Eccles, D.W., and Panton, L.B. 2011. The effects of static stretching on running economy and endurance performance in female distance runners during treadmill running. *Journal of Strength and Conditioning Research,* 25(8), 2170–2176.

11. Allison, S., Bailey, D., and Folland, J. 2008. Prolonged static stretching does not influence running economy despite changes in neuromuscular function. *Journal of Sports Sciences,* 26(14), 1489–1495.

12. Hayes, P.R., and Walker, A. 2007. Pre-exercise stretching does not impact upon running economy. *Journal of Strength and Conditioning Research,* 21(4), 1227–1232.

13. Prichard, B. 1984. *Lower extremity injuries in runners induced by upper body torque (UBT).* Lecture presented at Biomechanics and Kinesiology in Sports U.S. Olympic Sports Medicine Conference, Colorado Springs, CO.

14. Egermann, M., Brocai, D., Lill, C.A., and Schmitt, H. 2003. Analysis of injuries in long-

distance triathletes. *International Journal of Sports Medicine*, 24(4), 271–276.

15. Byrnes, W.C., McCullagh, P., Dickinson, A., and Noble, J. 1992. Incidence and severity of injury following aerobic training programs emphasising running, racewalking, or step aerobics. *Medicine and Science in Sports and Exercise*, 25(5), S81.

16. Korkia, P.K., Tunstall-Pedoe, D.S., and Maffulli, N. 1994. An epidemiological investigation of training and injury patterns in British triathletes. *British Journal of Sports Medicine*, 28(3), 191–196.

17. Krivickas, L., and Feinberg, J.H. 1996. Lower extremity injuries in college athletes: Relation between ligamentous laxity and lower extremity muscle tightness. *Archives of Physical Medicine and Rehabilitation*, 77(11), 1139–1143.

18. Wilber, C.A., Holland, G.J., Madison, R.E., and Loy, S.F. 1995. An epidemiological analysis of overuse injuries among recreational cyclists. *International Journal of Sports Medicine*, 16(3), 201–206.

19. American College of Sports Medicine position stand. The recommended quantity and quality of exercise for developing and maintaining cardiorespiratory and muscular fitness, and flexibility in healthy adults. 1998. *Medicine and Science in Sports and Exercise*, 30(6), 975.

20. Pereles, D., Roth, A., and Thompson, D. 2011, February. *The impact of a pre-run stretch on the risk of injury in runners*. American Academy of Orthopaedic Surgeons 2011 Annual Meeting Paper Presentations, San Diego, California.

21. Thacker, S.B., Gilchrist, J., Stroup, D.F., and Kimsey, C.D. 2004. The impact of stretching on sports injury risk: A systematic review of the literature. *Medicine and Science in Sports and Exercise*, 36(3), 371–378.

22. Alter, M.J. 2004. *Science of flexibility*. Champaign, IL: Human Kinetics.

23. Khaund, R., and Flynn, S.H. 2005. Iliotibial band syndrome: A common source of knee pain. *American Family Physician*, 71(8), 1545–1550.

24. Maffulli, N., Pankaj, S., and Luscombe, K.L. 2004. Achilles tendinopathy: Aetiology and management. *Journal of the Royal Society of Medicine*, 97(10), 472–476.

25. Hodges, P.W., and Richardson, C.A. 1997. Contraction of the abdominal muscles associated with movement of the lower limb. *Physical Therapy*, 77(2), 132–142.

26. Ireland, M.L., Wilson, J.D., Ballantyne, B.T., and Davis, I.M. 2003. Hip strength in females with and without patellofemoral pain. *Journal of Orthopaedic and Sports Physical Therapy*, 33(11), 671–676.

27. Leetun, D.T., Ireland, M.L., Willson, J.D., Ballantyne, B.T., and Davis, I.M. 2004. Core stability measures as risk factors for lower extremity injury in athletes. *Medicine and Science in Sports and Exercise*, 36(6), 926–934.

28. Fredericson, M., Cookingham, C., Chaudhari, A.M., Brian, C., Oestreicher, N., and Sahrmann, S.A. 2000. Hip abductor weakness in distance runners with iliotibial band syndrome. *Clinical Journal of Sport Medicine*, 10(3), 169–175.

29. Sherry, M.A., and Best, T.M. 2004. A comparison of 2 rehabilitation programs in the treatment of acute hamstring strains. *Journal of Orthopaedic and Sports Physical Therapy*, 34(3), 116–125.

30. Morton, D.P., and Callister, R. 2010. Influence of posture and body type on the experience of exercise-related transient abdominal pain. *Journal of Science and Medicine in Sport*, 13(5), 483–488.

31. Sato, K., and Mokha, M. 2009. Does core strength training influence running kinetics, lower-extremity stability, and 5000-M performance in runners? *Journal of Strength and Conditioning Research*, 23(1), 133–140.

32. Schibek, J.S., Guskiewicz, K.M., Prentice, W.E., Mays, S., and Davis, J.M. 2001. *The effect of core stabilization training on functional performance in swimming*. Master's thesis, University of North Carolina, Chapel Hill.

33. Stanton, R., Rearburn, P.R., and Humphries, B. 2004. The effect of short-term Swiss ball training on core stability and running economy. *Journal of Strength and Conditioning Research*, 18, 522–528.

34. Okada, T., Huxel, K.C., and Nesser, T.W. 2011. Relationship between core stability, functional movement, and performance. *Journal of Strength and Conditioning Research*, 25(1), 252–261.

Chapter 18 Strength Training

1. Telephone interview with Tudor O. Bompa, PhD [Interview by D.W. Warden]. (2007, November 28). Retrieved from www.tri-talk.com

2. Bompa, T.O. 1999. *Periodization: Theory and methodology of training* (4th ed., p. 316). Champaign, IL: Human Kinetics.

3. Ibid., p. 318.

4. Weyland, P.G., Sternlight, D.B., Bellizzi, M.J., and Wright, S. 2000. Faster top running speeds are achieved with greater ground forces not more rapid leg movements. *Journal of Applied Physiology*, 89(5), 1991–1999.

5. Hickson, R.C., Dvorak, B.A., Gorostiaga, E.M., Kurowski, T.T., and Foster, C. 1988. Potential for strength and endurance training to amplify endurance performance. *Journal of Applied Physiology*, 65(5), 2285–2290.

6. Marcinik, E.J., Potts, J., Schlabach, G., Will, S., Dawson, P., and Hurley, B.F. 1991. Effects of strength training on lactate threshold and endurance performance. *Medicine and Science in Sports and Exercise*, 23(6), 739–743.

7. Paavolainen, L., Hakkinen, K., Hamalainen, I., Nummela, A., and Rusko, H. 1999. Explosive-strength training improves 5-km running time by improving running economy and muscle power. *Journal of Applied Physiology*, 89(5), 1527–1533.

8. Mikkola, J., Vesterinen, V., Taipale, R., Capostagno, B., Hakkinen, K., and Nummela, A. 2011. Effect of resistance training regimens on treadmill running and neuromuscular performance in recreational endurance runners. *Journal of Sports Science*, 29(13), 1359–1371.

9. Storen, O., Helgerud, J., Stoa, E.M., and Hoff, J. 2008. Maximal strength training improves running economy in distance runners. *Medicine and Science in Sports and Exercise*, 40(6), 1087–1092.

10. Millet, G.P., Jaquen, B., Borrant, F., and Candau, R. 2002. Effects of concurrent endurance and strength training on running economy and VO_2 kinetics. *Medicine and Science in Sports and Exercise*, 34(8), 1351–1359.

11. Yamamoto, L.M., Lopez, R.M., Klau, J.F., Casa, D.J., Kraemer, W.J., and Maresh, C.M. 2008. The effects of resistance training on endurance distance running performance among highly trained runners: A systematic review. *Journal of Strength and Conditioning Research*, 22(6), 2036.

12. Yamamoto, L.M., Klau, J.F., Casa, D.J., Armstrong, L.E., and Maresh, C.M. 2010. The effects of resistance training of road cycling performance among highly trained cyclists: A systematic review. *Journal of Strength and Conditioning Resistance*, 24(2), 560.

13. Esteve-Lanao, J., Rhea, M.R., Fleck, S.J., and Lucia, A. 2008. Running-specific, periodized strength training attenuates loss of stride length during intense endurance running. *Journal of Strength and Conditioning Research*, 22(4), 1176–1163.

14. Ploutz, L.L., Tesch, P.A., Biro, R.L., and Dudley, G.A. 1994. Effect of resistance training on muscle use during exercise. *Journal of Applied Physiology*, 76(4), 1675–1681.

15. Goreham, C., Green, H.J., Ball-Burnett, M., and Ranney, D. 1999. High-resistance training and muscle metabolism during prolonged exercise. *American Journal of Physiology, Endocrinology and Metabolism*, 276(3), E489–E496.

16. Johnston, R.E., Quinn, T.J., Kertzer, R., and Vroman, N.B. 1997. Strength training in female distance runners: Impact on running economy. *Journal of Strength and Conditioning Research*, 11(4), 224–229.

17. Aagaard, P., Andersen, J.L., Bennekou, M., Larsson, B., Olesen, J.L., Crameri, R., Kjaer, M. 2011. Effects of resistance training on endurance capacity and muscle fiber composition in young top-level cyclists. *Scandinavian Journal of Medicine and Science in Sports*. doi: 10.1111/j.1600-0838.2010.01283.x

18. Louis, J., Hausswirth, C., Easthope, C., and Brisswalter, J. 2012. Strength training improves cycling efficiency in master endurance athletes. *European Journal of Applied Physiology*, 112(2), 631–640.

19. Bishop, D., Jenkins, D., Mackinnon, L.T., McEniery, M., and Carey, M.F. 1999. The effects of strength training on endurance performance and muscle characteristics. *Medicine and Science in Sports and Exercise*, 31(6), 886–891.

20. Ferrauti, A., Bergermann, M., and Fernandez-Fernandez, J. 2010. Effects of a concurrent strength and endurance training on running performance and running economy in recreational marathon runners. *Journal of Strength and Conditioning Research*, 24(10), 2770–2778.

21. Aagaard, P., and Andersen, J.L. 2010. Effects of strength training on endurance capacity in top-level endurance athletes. *Scandinavian Journal of Medicine and Science in Sports*. doi: 10.1111/j.1600-0838.2010.01197.x

22. Tanaka, H., Costill, D.L., Thomas, R., Fink, W.J., and Widrick, J.J. 1993. Dry-land resistance training for competitive swimming. *Medicine and Science in Sports and Exercise*, 25(8), 952–959.

23. Trappe, S.W., and Pearson, D.R. 1994. Effects of weight assisted dry-land strength training on swimming performance. *Journal of Strength and Conditioning Research*, 8(4), 209–275.

24. Swimming, Athens and Aquaman: Michael Phelps interview [Interview by P. Mauro]. (2008, August 13). *IGN Sportsw.*

25. Michaelis, V. 2008, August 3. Built to swim, Phelps found a focus and refuge in water. *USA Today*.

26. Tanaka, H., and Swensen, T. 1998. Impact of resistance training on endurance performance. A new form of cross-training. *Sports Medicine*, 25(3), 191.

27. Ibid, 191.

28. Friel, J. 2009. *The triathlete's training bible* (3rd ed., pp. 242–247). Boulder, CO: VeloPress.

29. Chtara, M., Chamari, K., Chaouachi, M., Chaouachi, A., Koubaa, D., Feki, Y., and Amri, M. 2005. Effects of intra-session concurrent endurance and strength training sequence on aerobic performance and capacity. *British Journal of Sports Medicine*, 39(8), 555–560.

30. Ronnestad, B.R., Hansen, E.A., and Raastad, T. 2010. In-season strength maintenance training increases well-trained cyclists' performance. *European Journal of Applied Physiology*, 110(6), 1269–1282.

31. Kraemer, W.J., and Fry, A.C. 1991. Strength testing: Development and evaluation of methodology. In P.J. Maud and C. Foster (Eds.), *Physiological assessment of human fitness* (2nd ed., pp. 129–130). Champaign IL: Human Kinetics.

32. Brzycki, M. 1993. Strength testing: Predicting a one-rep max from reps-to-fatigue. *JOPERD*, 64, 88–90.

33. Gourgoulis, V., Aggeloussis, N., Vezos, N., Kasimatis, P., Antoniou, P., and Mavromatis, G. 2007. Estimation of hand forces and propelling efficiency during front crawl swimming with hand paddles. *Journal of Biomechanics*, 41(1), 208–215.

34. Toussaint, H.M., and Vervoom, K. 1990. Effects of specific high resistance training in the water on competitive swimmers. *International Journal of Sports Medicine*, 11(3), 228–233.

35. Girold, S., Calmels, P., Maurin, D., Milhau, N., and Chatard, J.C. 2006. Assisted and resisted spring training in swimming. *Journal of Strength and Conditioning Research*, 20(3), 547–554.

36. Turner, A.M., Owings, M., and Schwane, J.A. 2003. Improvement in running economy after 6 weeks of plyometric training. *Journal of Strength and Conditioning Research*, 17(1), 60–67.

37. Saunders, P.U., Telford, R.D., Pyne, D.B., Peltola, E.M., Cunningham, R.B., Gore, C.J., and Hawley, J.A. 2006. Short-term plyometric training improves running economy in highly trained middle and long distance runners.

Journal of Strength and Conditioning Research, 20(4), 947–954.

Chapter 19 General and Specific Training

1. Duffield, R., Dawson, B., and Goodman, C. 2005. Energy system contribution to 400-metre and 800-metre track running. *Journal of Sports Sciences*, 23(3), 299–307.

2. Wilmore, J.H., Costill, D.L., and Kenney, W.L. 2008. *Physiology of sport and exercise* (p. 241). Champaign, IL: Human Kinetics.

3. Seiler, K.S., and Kjerland, G.O. 2006. Quantifying training intensity distribution in elite endurance athletes: Is there evidence for an "optimal" distribution? *Scandinavian Journal of Medicine and Science in Sports*, 16(1), 49–56.

4. Esteve-Lanao, J., Juan, A.S., Earnest, C.P., Foster, C., and Lucia, A. 2005. How do endurance runners actually train? Relationship with competition performance. *Medicine and Science in Sports and Exercise*, 37(3), 496–504.

5. Esteve-Lanao, J., Foster, C., Seiler, S., and Lucia, A. 2007. Impact of training intensity distribution on performance in endurance athletes. *Journal of Strength and Conditioning Research*, 21(3), 943.

6. Coggan, A., Raguso, C., Gastaldelli, A., Sidossis, L., and Yeckel, C. 2000. Fat metabolism during high-intensity exercise in endurance-trained and untrained men. *Metabolism*, 49(1), 122–128.

7. Toussaint, H.M., and Beek, P.J. 1992. Biomechanics of competitive front crawl swimming. *Sports Medicine*, 13(1), 8–24.

8. Lucia, A., Hoyos, J., and Chicharro, J.L. 2001. Preferred pedalling cadence in professional cycling. *Medicine and Science in Sports and Exercise*, 33(8), 1361–1366.

9. Leirdal, S., and Ettema, G. 2011. The relationship between cadence, pedalling technique and gross efficiency in cycling. *European Journal of Applied Physiology*, 111(12), 2885–2893.

10. Chavarren, J., and Calbet, J.L. 1999. Cycling efficiency and pedalling frequency in road cyclists. *European Journal of Applied Physiology*, 80(6), 555–563.

11. Gottschall, J.S., and Palmer, B.M. 2002. The acute effects of prior cycling cadence on running performance and kinematics. *Medicine and Science in Sports and Exercise*, 34(9), 1518–1522.

12. Dantas, J.L., Smirmaul, B.P., Altimari, L.R., Okano, A.H., Fontes, E.B., Camata, T.V., and Moraes, A.C. 2009. The efficiency of pedaling

and the muscular recruitment are improved with increase of the cadence in cyclists and non-cyclists. *Electromyography and Clinical Neurophysiology*, 49(6–7), 311–319.

13. Nimmerichter, A., Eston, R., and Williams, C. 2012. Effects of low and high cadence interval training on power output in flat and uphill cycling time-trials. *European Journal of Applied Physiology*, 112(1), 69–78.

14. Paton, C.D., Hopkins, W.G., and Cook, C. 2009. Effects of low- vs. high-cadence interval training on cycling performance. *Journal of Strength and Conditioning Research*, 23(6), 1758–1763.

Chapter 20 Interval Training

1. Margaria, R., Oliva, R.D., Di Prampero, P.E., and Cerretelli, P. 1969. Energy utilization in intermittent exercise of supramaximal intensity. *European Journal of Applied Physiology*, 26(6), 752–756.

2. Billat, V., Pinoteau, J., and Petit, B. 1996. Calibration de la duree des repetitions d'une seance d'interval training a la vitesse associee a VO_2max en reference au temps limite continu. *Science and Motricite*, 28, 13–20.

3. Billat, V.L., Slawinski, J., Bocquet, V., Demarle, A., Lafitte, L., Chassaing, P., and Koralsztein, J. 2000. Intermittent runs at the velocity associated with maximal oxygen uptake enables subjects to remain at maximal oxygen uptake for a longer time than intense but submaximal runs. *European Journal of Applied Physiology*, 81(3), 188–196.

4. Esfarjani, F., and Laursen, P.B. 2007. Manipulating high-intensity interval training: Effects on VO_2max, the lactate threshold and 3000 m running performance in moderately trained males. *Journal of Science and Medicine in Sport*, 10(1), 27–35.

5. Laursen, P.B., Shing, C.M., Peake, J.M., Coombes, J.S., and Jenkins, D.G. 2002. Interval training program optimization in highly trained endurance cyclists. *Medicine and Science in Sports and Exercise*, 34(11), 1801–1807.

6. Sperlich, B., Zinner, C., Heilemann, I., Kjendlie, P., Holmberg, H., and Mester, J. 2010. High-intensity interval training improves VO_2peak, maximal lactate accumulation, time trial and competition performance in 9-11-year-old swimmers. *European Journal of Applied Physiology*, 110(5), 1029–1036.

7. Ziemann, E., Grzywacz, T., Luszczyk, M., Laskowski, R., Olek, R.A., and Gibson, A.L. 2011. Aerobic and anaerobic changes with high-intensity interval training in active college-aged men. *Journal of Strength and Conditioning Research*, 25(4), 1104–1112.

8. Bartlett, J.D., Close, G.L., MacLaren, D.P., Gregson, W., Drust, B., and Morton, J.P. 2011. High-intensity interval running is perceived to be more enjoyable than moderate-intensity continuous exercise: Implications for exercise adherence. *Journal of Sports Science*, 29(6), 547–553.

9. Ekkekakis, P., Hall, E.E., and Petruzzello, S.J. 2008. The relationship between exercise intensity and affective responses demystified: To crack the 40-year-old nut, replace the 40-year-old nutcracker! *Annals of Behavioral Medicine*, 35(2), 136–149.

10. Nekoliczak, A., and Petruzzello, S. 2011. *Effect of differing intensities of exercise on affect and enjoyment.* Unpublished master's thesis. IDEALS College of Applied Health Sciences.

11. Williams, D., Dunsiger, S., Ciccolo, J., Lewis, B., Albrecht, A., and Marcus, B. 2008. Acute affective response to a moderate-intensity exercise stimulus predicts physical activity participation 6 and 12 months later. *Psychology of Sport and Exercise*, 9(3), 231–245.

12. Tomlin, D.L., and Wenger, H.A. 2001. The relationship between aerobic fitness and recovery from high intensity intermittent exercise. *Sports Medicine*, 31(1), 1–11.

13. Wilkinson, J.G., Martin, D.T., Adams, A.A., and Liebman, M. 2002. Iron status in cyclists during high-intensity interval training and recovery. *International Journal of Sports Medicine*, 23(8), 544–548.

14. Seller, S. 2010. What is best practice for training intensity and duration distribution in endurance athletes? *International Journal of Sports Physiology and Performance*, 5(3), 276–291.

15. Laursen, P.B. 2010. Training for intense exercise performance: High-intensity or high-volume training? *Scandinavian Journal of Medicine and Science in Sports*, 20, 1–10.

16. Lindsay, F.H., Hawley, J.A., Myburgh, K.H., Schomer, H.H., Noakes, T.D., and Dennis, S.C. 1996. Improved athletic performance in highly trained cyclists after interval training. *Medicine and Science in Sports and Exercise*, 28(11), 1427–1434.

17. Westgarth-Taylor, C., Hawley, J.A., Rickard, S., Myburgh, K.H., Noakes, T.D., and Dennis, S.C. 1997. Metabolic and performance adaptations to interval training in endurance-trained cyclists. *European Journal of Applied Physiology and Occupational Physiology*, 75(4), 298–304.

18. Stepto, N.K., Hawley, J.A., Dennis, S.C., and Hopkins, W.G. 1999. Effects of different interval-training programs on cycling time-trial performance. *Medicine and Science in Sports and Exercise*, 31(5), 736–741.

19. Helgerud, J., Hoydal, K., Wang, E., Karlsen, T., Berg, P., Bjerkaas, M., and Hoff, J. 2007. Aerobic high-intensity intervals improve VO₂max more than moderate training. *Medicine and Science in Sports and Exercise*, 39(4), 665–671.

20. Smith, T.P., Coombes, J.S., and Geraghty, D.P. 2003. Optimising high-intensity treadmill training using the running speed at maximal O₂ uptake and the time for which this can be maintained. *European Journal of Applied Physiology*, 89(3), 337–343.

21. Weston, A.R., Myburgh, K.H., Lindsay, F.H., Dennis, S.C., Noakes, T.D., and Hawley, J.A. 1996. Skeletal muscle buffering capacity and endurance performance after high-intensity interval training by well-trained cyclists. *European Journal of Applied Physiology*, 75(1), 7–13.

22. Franch, J., Madsen, K., Djurhuus, M., Mogens, S., and Pedersen, P.K. 1998. Improved running economy following intensified training correlates with reduced ventilatory demands. *Medicine and Science in Sports and Exercise*, 30(8), 1250–1256.

23. Paton, C.C., and Hopkins, W.G. 2004. Effects of high-intensity training on performance and physiology of endurance athletes. *Sportscience*, 8, 25–40.

24. Laursen, P.B., Blanchard, M.A., and Jenkins, D.G. 2002. Acute high-intensity interval training improves Tvent and peak power output in highly trained males. *Canadian Journal of Applied Physiology*, 27(4), 336–348.

25. Belcastro, A.N., and Bonen, A. 1975. Lactic acid removal rates during controlled and uncontrolled recovery exercise. *Journal of Applied Physiology*, 39(6), 932–936.

26. Declan, A.J., Brennan, K.M., and Lauzon, C.D. 2003. Effects of active versus passive recovery on power output during repeated bouts of short term, high intensity exercise. *Journal of Sports Science and Medicine*, 2, 47–51.

27. Felix, S.D., Manos, T.M., Jarvis, A.T., Jensen, B.E., and Headley, S.A. 1997. Swimming performance following different recovery protocols in female collegiate swimmers. *Journal of Swimming Research*, 12, 1–6.

28. Dalleck, L., Bushman, T.T., Crain, R.D., Gajda, M.M., Koger, E.M., and Derksen, L.A. 2010. Dose-response relationship between interval training frequency and magnitude of improvement in lactate threshold. *International Journal of Sports Medicine*, 31(08), 567–571.

29. Fox, E.L., Bartels, R.L., Billings, C.E., O'Brien, R., Bason, R., and Mathews, D.K. 1975. Frequency and duration of interval training programs and changes in aerobic power. *Journal of Applied Physiology*, 38(3), 481–484.

30. Paton, C.D., and Hopkins, W.G. 2005. Combining explosive and high-resistance training improves performance in competitive cyclists. *Journal of Strength and Conditioning Research*, 19(4), 826–830.

Chapter 21   Duration, Frequency, and Intensity

1. Powers, S., and Howley, E.T. 2008. *Exercise physiology: Theory and application to fitness and performance level.* New York: McGraw-Hill.

2. Zaryski, C., and Smith, D.J. 2005. Training principles and issues for ultra-endurance athletes. *Current Sports Medicine Reports*, 4(3), 165–170.

3. Main, L.C., Landers, G.J., Grove, J.R., Dawson, B., and Goodman, C. 2010. Training patterns and negative health outcomes in triathlon: Longitudinal observations across a full competitive season. *Journal of Sports Medicine and Physical Fitness*, 50(4), 475–485.

4. Gosling, C.M., Forbes, A.B., McGivern, J., and Gabbe, B.J. 2010. A profile of injuries in athletes seeking treatment during a triathlon race series. *American Journal of Sports Medicine*, 38(5), 1007–1014.

5. Vleck, V.E., Bentley, D.J., Millet, G.P., and Cochrane, T. 2010. Triathlon event distance specialization: Training and injury effects. *Journal of Strength and Conditioning Research*, 24(1), 30–36.

6. Gosling, C.M., Gabbe, B.J., and Forbes, A.B. 2008. Triathlon related musculoskeletal injuries: The status of injury prevention knowledge. *Journal of Science and Medicine in Sport*, 11(4), 396–406.

7. Hickson, R.C., Hagberg, J.M., Ehsani, A.A., and Holloszy, J.O. 1981. Time course of the adaptive responses of aerobic power and heart rate to training. *Medicine and Science in Sports and Exercise*, 13(1), 17–20.

8. Hickson, R.C., Overland, S.M., and Dougherty, K.A. 1984. Reduced training frequency effects on aerobic power and muscle adaptations in rats. *Journal of Applied Physiology*, 57(6), 1834–1841.

9. Knechtle, B., Knechtle, P., Rust, C.A., and Rosemann, T. 2011. A comparison of anthropometric

and training characteristics of Ironman triathletes and Triple Iron ultra-triathletes. *Journal of Sports Sciences*, 29(13), 1373–1380.

10. Neal, C.M., Hunter, A.M., and Galloway, S.D. 2011. A 6-month analysis of training-intensity distribution and physiological adaptation in Ironman triathletes. *Journal of Sports Sciences*, 29(14), 1515–1523.

11. Iaia, F.M., and Bangsbo, J. 2010. Speed endurance training is a powerful stimulus for physiological adaptations and performance improvements of athletes. *Scandinavian Journal of Medicine and Science in Sports*, 20(suppl. 2), 11–23.

12. Iaia, F.M., Hellsten, Y., Nielsen, J.J., Fernstrom, M., Sahlin, K., and Bangsbo, J. 2009. Four weeks of speed endurance training reduces energy expenditure during exercise and maintains muscle oxidative capacity despite a reduction in training volume. *Journal of Applied Physiology*, 106(1), 73–80.

13. Laursen, P.B., and Jenkins, D.G. 2002. The scientific basis for high-intensity interval training: Optimising training programmes and maximising performance in highly trained endurance athletes. *Sports Medicine*, 32(1), 53–73.

14. Laursen, P.B., Shing, C.M., Peake, J.M., Coombes, J.S., and Jenkins, D.G. 2002. Interval training program optimization in highly trained endurance cyclists. *Medicine and Science in Sports and Exercise*, 34(11), 1801–1807.

15. Esteve-Lanao, J., Foster, C., Seiler, S., and Lucia, A. 2007. Impact of training intensity distribution on performance in endurance athletes. *Journal of Strength and Conditioning Research*, 21(3), 943–949.

16. Seiler, S. 2010. What is best practice for training intensity and duration distribution in endurance athletes? *International Journal of Sports Physiology and Performance*, 5(3), 276–291.

17. Laursen, P.B., Shing, C.M., Peake, J.M., Coombes, J.S., and Jenkins, D.G. 2005. Influence of high-intensity interval training on adaptations in well-trained cyclists. *Journal of Strength and Conditioning Research*, 19(3), 527–533.

18. Londeree, B.R. 1997. Effect of training on lactate/ventilatory thresholds: A meta-analysis. *Medicine and Science in Sports and Exercise*, 29(6), 837–843.

19. Tabata, I., Irisawa, K., Kouzaki, M., Nishimura, K., Ogita, F., and Miyachi, M. 1997. Metabolic profile of high intensity intermittent exercises. *Medicine and Science in Sports and Exercise*, 29(3), 390–395.

20. Tabata, I., Nishimura, K., Kouzaki, M., Hirai, Y., Ogita, F., Miyachi, M., et al. 1996. Effects of moderate-intensity endurance and high-intensity intermittent training on anaerobic capacity and $\dot{V}O_2$max. *Medicine and Science in Sports and Exercise*, 28(10), 1327–1330.

21. Green, H., Tupling, R., Roy, B., O'Toole, D., Burnett, M., and Grant, S. 2000. Adaptations in skeletal muscle exercise metabolism to a sustained session of heavy intermittent exercise. *American Journal of Physiology, Endocrinology, and Metabolism*, 278(1), E118–E126.

22. Green, H.J., and Fraser, I.G. 1988. Differential effects of exercise intensity on serum uric acid concentration. *Medicine and Science in Sports and Exercise*, 20(1), 55–59.

23. Laursen, P.B., Blanchard, M.A., and Jenkins, D.G. 2002. Acute high-intensity interval training improves Tvent and peak power output in highly trained males. *Canadian Journal of Applied Physiology*, 27(4), 336–348.

24. Lindsay, F.H., Hawley, J.A., Myburgh, K.H., Schomer, H.H., Noakes, T.D., and Dennis, S.C. 1996. Improved athletic performance in highly trained cyclists after interval training. *Medicine and Science in Sports and Exercise*, 28(11), 1427–1434.

25. Stepto, N.K., Hawley, J.A., Dennis, S.C., and Hopkins, W.G. 1999. Effects of different interval-training programs on cycling time-trial performance. *Medicine and Science in Sports and Exercise*, 31(5), 736–741.

26. Weston, A.R., Myburgh, K.H., Lindsay, F.H., Dennis, S.C., Noakes, T.D., and Hawley, J.A. 1997. Skeletal muscle buffering capacity and endurance performance after high-intensity interval training by well-trained cyclists. *European Journal of Applied Physiology and Occupational Physiology*, 75(1), 7–13.

27. Westgarth-Taylor, C., Hawley, J.A., Rickard, S., Myburgh, K.H., Noakes, T.D., and Dennis, S.C. 1997. Metabolic and performance adaptations to interval training in endurance-trained cyclists. *European Journal of Applied Physiology and Occupational Physiology*, 75(4), 298–304.

28. Iaia, F.M., Perez-Gomez, J., Thomassen, M., Nordsborg, N.B., Hellsten, Y., and Bangsbo, J. 2011. Relationship between performance at different exercise intensities and skeletal muscle characteristics. *Journal of Applied Physiology*, 110(6), 1555–1563.

29. Iaia, F.M., Thomassen, M., Kolding, H., Gunnarsson, T., Wendell, J., Rostgaard, T., et al. 2008. Reduced volume but increased training intensity elevates muscle Na+-K+ pump

alpha1-subunit and NHE1 expression as well as short-term work capacity in humans. *American Journal of Physiology, Regulatory, Integrative, and Comparative Physiology*, 294(3), R966–974.

30. Balsom, P.D., Gaitanos, G.C., Ekblom, B., and Sjodin, B. 1994. Reduced oxygen availability during high intensity intermittent exercise impairs performance. *Acta Physiologica Scandinavica*, 152(3), 279–285.

31. Gaitanos, G.C., Williams, C., Boobis, L.H., and Brooks, S. 1993. Human muscle metabolism during intermittent maximal exercise. *Journal of Applied Physiology*, 75(2), 712–719.

32. Parolin, M.L., Spriet, L.L., Hultman, E., Hollidge-Horvat, M.G., Jones, N.L., and Heigenhauser, G.J. 2000. Regulation of glycogen phosphorylase and PDH during exercise in human skeletal muscle during hypoxia. *American Journal of Physiology, Endocrinology, and Metabolism*, 278(3), E522–E534.

33. Trump, M.E., Heigenhauser, G.J., Putman, C.T., and Spriet, L.L. 1996. Importance of muscle phosphocreatine during intermittent maximal cycling. *Journal of Applied Physiology*, 80(5), 1574–1580.

34. Parolin, M.L., Chesley, A., Matsos, M.P., Spriet, L.L., Jones, N.L., and Heigenhauser, G.J. 1999. Regulation of skeletal muscle glycogen phosphorylase and PDH during maximal intermittent exercise. *American Journal of Physiology*, 277(5 Pt. 1), E890–E900.

35. Harmer, A.R., McKenna, M.J., Sutton, J.R., Snow, R.J., Ruell, P.A., Booth, J., et al. 2000. Skeletal muscle metabolic and ionic adaptations during intense exercise following sprint training in humans. *Journal of Applied Physiology*, 89(5), 1793–1803.

36. McKenna, M.J., Heigenhauser, G.J., McKelvie, R.S., Obminski, G., MacDougall, J.D., and Jones, N.L. 1997. Enhanced pulmonary and active skeletal muscle gas exchange during intense exercise after sprint training in men. *Journal of Physiology*, 501(Pt. 3), 703–716.

37. Fiskerstrand, A., and Seiler, K.S. 2004. Training and performance characteristics among Norwegian international rowers 1970–2001. *Scandinavian Journal of Medicine and Science in Sports*, 14(5), 303–310.

38. Billat, V., Bernard, O., Pinoteau, J., Petit, B., and Koralsztein, J.P. 1994. Time to exhaustion at $\dot{V}O_2$max and lactate steady state velocity in sub elite long-distance runners. *Archives Internationales de Physiologie, de Biochimie et de Biophysique*, 102(3), 215–219.

39. Bosquet, L., Leger, L., and Legros, P. 2002. Methods to determine aerobic endurance. *Sports Medicine*, 32(11), 675–700.

40. Lydiard, A. 1990. *Osaka lecture*. Retrieved from www.lydiardfoundation.org/pdfs/al_lecture.pdf

41. McGregor, S.J., and Fitzgerald, M. 2010. *The runner's edge*. Champaign, IL: Human Kinetics.

42. Allen, H., and Coggan, A. 2010. *Training and racing with a power meter*. Boulder, CO: VeloPress.

Chapter 22 Periodization

1. Bompa, T.O. 2009. *Periodization: Theory and methodology of training* (5th ed.). Champaign, IL: Human Kinetics.

2. Selye, H. 1978. *The stress of life*. New York: McGraw-Hill.

3. Bompa, T.O. 2005. *Periodization training for sports* (2nd ed.). Champaign, IL: Human Kinetics.

4. Issurin, V.B. 2010. New horizons for the methodology and physiology of training periodization. *Sports Medicine*, 40(3), 189–206.

5. Rowbottom, D.G., Keast, D., Garcia-Webb, P., and Morton, A.R. 1997. Training adaptation and biological changes among well-trained male triathletes. *Medicine and Science in Sports and Exercise*, 29(9), 1233–1239.

6. Rowbottom, D.G., Keast, D., and Morton, A.R. 1998. Monitoring and preventing of overreaching and overtraining in endurance athletes. In R.B. Kreider (ed.) *Overtraining in sport* (pp. 47–66). Champaign, IL: Human Kinetics.

7. Friel, J. 2009. *The triathlete's training bible* (3rd ed.). Boulder, CO: VeloPress.

8. Matveyev, L.P. 1965. *Periodization of sports training*. Moscow: Fizkultura i Sport.

9. Smith, D.J. 2003. A framework for understanding the training process leading to elite performance. *Sports Medicine*, 33(15), 1103–1126.

10. Stone, M.H., O'Bryant, H., and Garhammer, J. 1981. A hypothetical model for strength training. *Journal of Sports Medicine and Physical Fitness*, 21(4), 342–351.

11. Turner, A. 2011. The science and practice of periodization: A brief review. *Strength and Conditioning Journal*, 33(1), 34–46.

12. Baechle, T.R., and Earle, R.W. (Eds.). 2008. *Essentials of strength training and conditioning*. Champaign, IL: Human Kinetics.

13. Zaryski, C., and Smith, D.J. 2005. Training principles and issues for ultra-endurance athletes. *Current Sports Medicine Reports*, 4(3), 165–170.

14. Mujika, I. 2009. *Tapering and peaking for optimal performance*. Champaign, IL: Human Kinetics.

15. Friel, J. 2009. *The cyclist's training bible*. Boulder, CO: VeloPress.

16. Fry, R.W., Morton, A.R., and Keast, D. 1991. Overtraining in athletes. An update. *Sports Medicine*, 12(1), 32–65.

17. Brown, L.E. 2001. Nonlinear versus linear periodization models. *Strength and conditioning journal*, 23(1), 42–44.

18. Issurin, V.B. 2008. Block periodization versus traditional training theory: A review. *Journal of Sports Medicine and Physical Fitness*, 48(1), 65–75.

19. Kiely, J. 2010. New horizons for the methodology and physiology of training periodization: Block periodization: New horizon or a false dawn? *Sports Medicine*, 40(9), 803–805 [author reply].

20. McGregor, S.J., Weese, R.K., and Ratz, I.K. 2009. Performance modeling in an Olympic 1500-m finalist: A practical approach. *Journal of Strength and Conditioning Research*, 23(9), 2515–2523.

21. Lydiard, A. 1990. *Osaka lecture*. Retrieved from www.lydiardfoundation.org/pdfs/al_lecture.pdf

22. Lydiard, A., and Gilmour, G. 2000. *Running with Lydiard* (2nd ed.). Oxford, UK: Meyer and Meyer Sport.

23. Stewart, A.M., and Hopkins, W.G. 2000. Seasonal training and performance of competitive swimmers. *Journal of Sports Sciences*, 18(11), 873–884.

24. Mujika, I., Chatard, J.C., Busso, T., Geyssant, A., Barale, F., and Lacoste, L. 1995. Effects of training on performance in competitive swimming. *Canadian Journal of Applied Physiology*, 20(4), 395–406.

25. Pyne, D.B., Lee, H., and Swanwick, K.M. 2001. Monitoring the lactate threshold in world-ranked swimmers. *Medicine and Science in Sports and Exercise*, 33(2), 291–297.

26. Issurin, V.B. 2009. Generalized training effects induced by athletic preparation. A review. *Journal of Sports Medicine and Physical Fitness*, 49(4), 333–345.

27. Bondarchuk, A.P. 1988. Constructing a training system. *Track Technique*, 102, 3254–3269.

28. Apel, J.M., Lacey, R.M., and Kell, R.T. 2010. A comparison of traditional and weekly undulating periodized strength training programs with total volume and intensity equated. *Journal of Strength and Conditioning Research*, 25(3), 694–703.

29. Buford, T.W., Rossi, S.J., Smith, D.B., and Warren, A.J. 2007. A comparison of periodization models during nine weeks with equated volume and intensity for strength. *Journal of Strength and Conditioning Research*, 21(4), 1245–1250.

30. Hartmann, H., Bob, A., Wirth, K., and Schmidtbleicher, D. 2009. Effects of different periodization models on rate of force development and power ability of the upper extremity. *Journal of Strength and Conditioning Research*, 23(7), 1921–1932.

31. Miranda, F., Simao, R., Rhea, M., Bunker, D., Prestes, J., Leite, R.D., et al. 2011. Effects of linear vs. daily undulatory periodized resistance training on maximal and submaximal strength gains. *Journal of Strength and Conditioning Research*, 25(7), 1824–1830.

32. Prestes, J., Frollini, A.B., de Lima, C., Donatto, F.F., Foschini, D., de Cassia Marqueti, R., et al. 2009. Comparison between linear and daily undulating periodized resistance training to increase strength. *Journal of Strength and Conditioning Research*, 23(9), 2437–2442.

33. Rhea, M.R., Ball, S.D., Phillips, W.T., and Burkett, L.N. 2002. A comparison of linear and daily undulating periodized programs with equated volume and intensity for strength. *Journal of Strength and Conditioning Research*, 16(2), 250–255.

34. Rhea, M.R., Phillips, W.T., Burkett, L.N., Stone, W.J., Ball, S.D., Alvar, B.A., et al. 2003. A comparison of linear and daily undulating periodized programs with equated volume and intensity for local muscular endurance. *Journal of Strength and Conditioning Research*, 17(1), 82–87.

35. Vanni, A.C., Meyer, F., da Veiga, A.D., and Zanardo, V.P. 2010. Comparison of the effects of two resistance training regimens on muscular and bone responses in premenopausal women. *Osteoporosis International*, 21(9), 1537–1544.

36. Banister, E.W., Carter, J.B., and Zarkadas, P.C. 1999. Training theory and taper: Validation in triathlon athletes. *European Journal of Applied Physiology and Occupational Physiology*, 79(2), 182–191.

37. Busso, T., Candau, R., and Lacour, J.R. 1994. Fatigue and fitness modelled from the effects of training on performance. *European Journal of Applied Physiology and Occupational Physiology*, 69(1), 50–54.

38. LeMond, G., and Gordis, K. 1987. *Greg LeMond's Complete Book of Bicycling*. New York: Perigree.

39. Calvert, T.W., Banister, E.W., Savage, M.V., and Bach, T. 1976. A systems model of the effects of training on physical performance. *IEEE Transactions on Systems, Man and Cybernetics*, 6, 94–102.

40. Allen, H., and Coggan, A. 2010. *Training and racing with a power meter*. Boulder, CO: VeloPress.

41. Coggan, A.R. 2006. *The Performance Manager*. Paper presented at the USA Cycling Coaching Summit. Retrieved from http://home.trainingpeaks.com/articles/cycling/the-science-of-the-performance-manager.aspx

42. McGregor, S.J., and Fitzgerald, M. 2010. *The runner's edge*. Champaign, IL: Human Kinetics.

43. Mureika, J.R., Covington, D., and Mercier, D. 2000. The 1999 Mercier scoring tables: A how-to guide. *Athletics: Canada's National Track and Field / Running Magazine* (April/May).

44. Fitz-Clarke, J.R., Morton, R.H., and Banister, E.W. 1991. Optimizing athletic performance by influence curves. *Journal of Applied Physiology*, 71(3), 1151–1158.

Chapter 23   Tapering and Peaking for Races

1. Bosquet, L., Montpetit, J., Arvisais, D., and Mujika, I. 2007. Effects of tapering on performance: A meta-analysis. *Medicine and Science in Sports and Exercise*, 39(8), 1358–1365.

2. Thomas, L., Mujika, I., and Busso, T. 2009. Computer simulations assessing the potential performance benefit of a final increase in training during pre-event taper. *Journal of Strength and Conditioning Research*, 23(6), 1729–1736.

3. Mujika, I. 2009. *Tapering and peaking for optimal performance*. Champaign, IL: Human Kinetics.

4. Houmard, J.A. 1991. Impact of reduced training on performance in endurance athletes. *Sports Medicine*, 12(6), 380–393.

5. Mujika, I., and Padilla, S. 2003. Scientific bases for precompetition tapering strategies. *Medicine and Science in Sports and Exercise*, 35(7), 1182–1187.

6. Mujika, I., Padilla, S., Pyne, D., and Busso, T. 2004. Physiological changes associated with the pre-event taper in athletes. *Sports Medicine*, 34(13), 891–927.

7. Pyne, D.B., Mujika, I., and Reilly, T. 2009. Peaking for optimal performance: Research limitations and future directions. *Journal of Sports Science*, 27(3), 195–202.

8. Mujika, I., Padilla, S., and Pyne, D. 2002. Swimming performance changes during the final 3 weeks of training leading to the Sydney 2000 Olympic Games. *International Journal of Sports Medicine*, 23(8), 582–587.

9. Jeukendrup, A.E., Hesselink, M.K., Snyder, A.C., Kuipers, H., and Keizer, H.A. 1992. Physiological changes in male competitive cyclists after two weeks of intensified training. *International Journal of Sports Medicine*, 13(7), 534–541.

10. Martin, D.T., Scifres, J.C., Zimmerman, S.D., and Wilkinson, J.G. 1994. Effects of interval training and a taper on cycling performance and isokinetic leg strength. *International Journal of Sports Medicine*, 15(8), 485–491.

11. Steinacker, J.M., Lormes, W., Kellmann, M., Liu, Y., Reissnecker, S., Opitz-Gress, A., et al. 2000. Training of junior rowers before world championships: Effects on performance, mood state and selected hormonal and metabolic responses. *Journal of Sports Medicine and Physical Fitness*, 40(4), 327–335.

12. Mujika, I., and Padilla, S. 2000. Detraining: Loss of training-induced physiological and performance adaptations. Part II: Long term insufficient training stimulus. *Sports Medicine*, 30(3), 145–154.

13. Mujika, I., and Padilla, S. 2000. Detraining: Loss of training-induced physiological and performance adaptations. Part I: Short term insufficient training stimulus. *Sports Medicine*, 30(2), 79–87.

14. Mujika, I., and Padilla, S. 2001. Muscular characteristics of detraining in humans. *Medicine and Science in Sports and Exercise*, 33(8), 1297–1303.

15. Hickson, R.C., Foster, C., Pollock, M.L., Galassi, T.M., and Rich, S. 1985. Reduced training intensities and loss of aerobic power, endurance, and cardiac growth. *Journal of Applied Physiology*, 58(2), 492–499.

16. Mujika, I. 2010. Intense training: The key to optimal performance before and during the taper. *Scandinavian Journal of Medicine and Science in Sports*, 20(suppl. 2), 24–31.

17. Costill, D.L., King, D.S., Thomas, R., and Hargreaves, M. 1985. Effects of reduced training on muscular power in swimmers. *Physician and Sportsmedicine*, 13, 94–101.

18. Shepley, B., MacDougall, J.D., Cipriano, N., Sutton, J.R., Tarnopolsky, M.A., and Coates, G. 1992. Physiological effects of tapering in highly trained athletes. *Journal of Applied Physiology*, 72(2), 706–711.

19. Houmard, J.A., Scott, B.K., Justice, C.L., and Chenier, T.C. 1994. The effects of taper on

performance in distance runners. *Medicine and Science in Sports and Exercise,* 26(5), 624–631.

20. Houmard, J.A., Costill, D.L., Mitchell, J.B., Park, S.H., Fink, W.J., and Burns, J.M. 1990. Testosterone, cortisol, and creatine kinase levels in male distance runners during reduced training. *International Journal of Sports Medicine,* 11(1), 41–45.

21. Houmard, J.A., Costill, D.L., Mitchell, J.B., Park, S.H., Hickner, R.C., and Roemmich, J.N. 1990. Reduced training maintains performance in distance runners. *International Journal of Sports Medicine,* 11(1), 46–52.

22. Houmard, J.A., Kirwan, J.P., Flynn, M.G., and Mitchell, J.B. 1989. Effects of reduced training on submaximal and maximal running responses. *International Journal of Sports Medicine,* 10(1), 30–33.

23. McConell, G.K., Costill, D.L., Widrick, J.J., Hickey, M.S., Tanaka, H., and Gastin, P.B. 1993. Reduced training volume and intensity maintain aerobic capacity but not performance in distance runners. *International Journal of Sports Medicine,* 14(1), 33–37.

24. Houmard, J.A., and Johns, R.A. 1994. Effects of taper on swim performance. Practical implications. *Sports Medicine,* 17(4), 224–232.

25. Neufer, P.D., Costill, D.L., Fielding, R.A., Flynn, M.G., and Kirwan, J.P. 1987. Effect of reduced training on muscular strength and endurance in competitive swimmers. *Medicine and Science in Sports and Exercise,* 19(5), 486–490.

26. Banister, E.W., Carter, J.B., and Zarkadas, P.C. 1999. Training theory and taper: Validation in triathlon athletes. *European Journal of Applied Physiology and Occupational Physiology,* 79(2), 182–191.

27. Zarkadas, P.C., Carter, J.B., and Banister, E.W. 1995. Modelling the effect of taper on performance, maximal oxygen uptake, and the anaerobic threshold in endurance triathletes. *Advances in Experimental Medicine and Biology,* 393, 179–186.

28. Margaritis, I., Palazzetti, S., Rousseau, A.S., Richard, M.J., and Favier, A. 2003. Antioxidant supplementation and tapering exercise improve exercise-induced antioxidant response. *Journal of the American College of Nutrition,* 22(2), 147–156.

29. Vollaard, N.B., Cooper, C.E., and Shearman, J.P. 2006. Exercise-induced oxidative stress in overload training and tapering. *Medicine and Science in Sports and Exercise,* 38(7), 1335–1341.

30. Coutts, A.J., Slattery, K.M., and Wallace, L.K. 2007. Practical tests for monitoring performance, fatigue and recovery in triathletes. *Journal of Science and Medicine in Sport,* 10(6), 372–381.

31. Coutts, A.J., Wallace, L.K., and Slattery, K.M. 2007. Monitoring changes in performance, physiology, biochemistry, and psychology during overreaching and recovery in triathletes. *International Journal of Sports Medicine,* 28(2), 125–134.

32. Banister, E.W., and Calvert, T.W. 1980. Planning for future performance: Implications for long term training. *Canadian Journal of Applied Sport Science,* 5(3), 170–176.

33. Busso, T. 2003. Variable dose-response relationship between exercise training and performance. *Medicine and Science in Sports and Exercise,* 35(7), 1188–1195.

34. Busso, T., Candau, R., and Lacour, J.R. 1994. Fatigue and fitness modelled from the effects of training on performance. *European Journal of Applied Physiology and Occupational Physiology,* 69(1), 50–54.

35. Busso, T., and Thomas, L. 2006. Using mathematical modeling in training planning. *International Journal of Sports Physiology and Performance,* 1(4), 400–405.

36. Coggan, A.R. 2006. *The Performance Manager.* Paper presented at the USA Cycling Coaching Summit. Retrieved from http://home.trainingpeaks.com/articles/cycling/the-science-of-the-performance-manager.aspx www.cyclingpeakssoftware.com/pmc_summit.pdf

37. Hellard, P., Avalos, M., Lacoste, L., Barale, F., Chatard, J.C., and Millet, G.P. 2006. Assessing the limitations of the Banister model in monitoring training. *Journal of Sports Science,* 24(5), 509–520.

38. Hellard, P., Avalos, M., Millet, G., Lacoste, L., Barale, F., and Chatard, J.C. 2005. Modeling the residual effects and threshold saturation of training: A case study of Olympic swimmers. *Journal of Strength and Conditioning Research,* 19(1), 67–75.

39. McGregor, S.J., Weese, R.K., and Ratz, I.K. 2009. Performance modeling in an Olympic 1500-m finalist: A practical approach. *Journal of Strength and Conditioning Research,* 23(9), 2515–2523.

40. Calvert, T.W., Banister, E.W., Savage, M.V., and Bach, T. 1976. A systems model of the effects of training on physical performance. *IEEE Transactions on Systems, Man and Cybernetics,* 6, 94–102.

41. Allen, H., and Coggan, A. 2010. *Training and racing with a power meter.* Boulder, CO: VeloPress.

42. Fitz-Clarke, J.R., Morton, R.H., and Banister, E.W. 1991. Optimizing athletic performance by influence curves. *Journal of Applied Physiology*, 71(3), 1151–1158.

Chapter 24 Physiology of Overtraining

1. Purvis, D., Gonsalves, S., and Deuster, P.A. 2010. Physiological and psychological fatigue in extreme conditions: Overtraining and elite athletes. *PM & R*, 2, 442–450.

2. Budgett, R., Newsholme, E., Lehmann, M., Sharp, C., Jones, D., Peto, T., Collins, C., Nerurkar, R., and White, P. 2000. Redefining the over training syndrome as the unexplained underperformance syndrome. *British Journal of Sports Medicine*, 34, 67–68.

3. Ackel-D'Elia, C., Vancini, R.L., Castelo, A., Nouailhetas, V.L., and Silva, A.C. 2010. Absence of the predisposing factors and signs and symptoms usually associated with overreaching and overtraining in physical fitness centers. *Clinics (Sao Paulo)*, 65(11), 1161–1166.

4. Koutedakis, Y., Frischknecht, R., Vrbová, G., Sharp, N.C., and Budgett, R. 1995. Maximal voluntary quadriceps strength patterns in Olympic overtrained athletes. *Medicine and Science in Sports and Exercise*, 27(4), 566–572.

5. Agostini, F., and Biolo, G. 2010. Effect of physical activity on glutamine metabolism. *Current Opinion in Clinical Nutrition and Metabolic Care*, 13(1), 58–64. Review.

6. Robson, P. 2003. Elucidating the unexplained underperformance syndrome in endurance athletes: The interleukin-6 hypothesis. *Sports Medicine*, 33(10), 771–781.

7. Urhausen, A., Gabriel, H., and Kindermann, W. 1995. Blood hormones as markers of training stress and overtraining. *Sports Medicine*, 20, 251–276.

8. Shephard, R.J., and Shek, P.N. 1998. Acute and chronic over-exertion: Do depressed immune responses provide useful markers? *International Journal of Sports Medicine*, 19(3), 159–171. Review.

9. Budgett, R., Newsholme, E., Lehmann, M., Sharp, C., Jones, D., Peto, T., Collins, D., Nerurkar, R., and White, P. 2000. Redefining the overtraining syndrome as the unexplained underperformance syndrome. *British Journal of Sports Medicine*, 34(1), 67–68.

10. Armstrong, L.E., and VanHeest, J.L. 2002. The unknown mechanism of the overtraining syndrome: Clues from depression and psychoneuroimmunology. *Sports Medicine*, 32(3), 185–209.

11. Uusitalo, A.L., Vanninen, E., Valkonen-Korhonen, M., and Kuikka, J.T. 2006. Brain serotonin reuptake did not change during one year in overtrained athletes. *International Journal of Sports Medicine*, 27(9), 702–708. Epub 2006 Feb 1.

12. Budgett, R., Hiscock, N., Arida, R.M., and Castell, L.M. 2010. The effects of the 5-HT2C agonist m-chlorophenylpiperazine on elite athletes with unexplained underperformance syndrome (overtraining). *British Journal of Sports Medicine*, 44(4), 280–283.

13. Anderson, O. 2002. How do you know when you are at risk of overtraining? It's a simple matter of well you feel, sleep and eat. *Peak Performance*, 163, 1–4.

Chapter 25 Swim Base Building

1. Friel, J. 2010. *Your best triathlon*. Boulder, CO: VeloPress.

2. Knechtle, B., Baumann B., Knechtle, P., and Rosemann, T. 2010. Speed during training and anthropometric measures in relation to race performance by male and female open-water ultra-endurance swimmers. *Perceptual and Motor Skills*, 111(2), 463–474.

3. Naemi, R., and Sanders, R.M. 2008. A "hydrokinematic" method of measuring the glide efficiency of a human swimmer. *Journal of Biomechanical Engineering*, 130(6), 061016.

4. Chatard, J.C., Chollet, D., and Millet, G. 1998. Performance and drag during drafting swimming in highly trained triathletes. *Medicine and Science in Sports and Exercise*, 30(8), 1276–1280.

5. Toussaint, H.M., and Beek, P.J. 1992. Biomechanics of competitive front crawl swimming. *Sports Medicine*, 13(1), 8–24.

6. Maglischo, E. 2003. *Swimming fastest*. Champaign, IL: Human Kinetics.

7. Sterkel, J. 2001. Long and short range planning. In D. Hannula and N. Thornton (Eds.), *The swim coaching bible* (pp. 107–108). Champaign, IL: Human Kinetics.

8. Byrn, G., and Friel, J. 2009. *Going long* (2nd ed.). Boulder, CO: VeloPress.

9. Naemi, R., Easson, W.J., and Sanders, R.H. 2010. Hydrodynamic glide efficiency in swimming. *Journal of Science and Medicine in Sport*, 13(4), 444–451. Epub 2009 Jun 18.

10. Robertson, E., Pyne, D., Hopkins, W., and Anson, J. 2009. Analysis of lap times in international swimming competitions. *Journal of Sports Science*, 27(4), 387–395.

11. Zaidi, H., Taiar, R., Fohanno, S., and Polidori, G. 2008. Analysis of the effect of swimmer's

head position on swimming performance using computational fluid dynamics. *Journal of Biomechanics*, 41(6), 1350–1358.

12. Tanaka, H., Costill, D.L., Thomas, R., Fink, W.J., and Widrick, J.J. 1993. Dry-land resistance training for competitive swimming. *Medicine and Science in Sports and Exercise*, 25(8), 952–959.

13. Trappe, S.W., and Pearson, D.R. 1994. Effects of weight assisted dry-land strength training on swimming performance. *Journal of Strength and Conditioning Research*, 8(4), 209–275.

14. Tanaka, H., and Swensen, T. 1998. Impact of resistance training on endurance performance. A new form of cross-training. *Sports Medicine*, 25(3), 191.

15. Koop, S., and Martin, G.L. 1983. Evaluation of a coaching strategy to reduce swimming stroke errors with beginning age-group swimmers. *Journal of Applied Behavior Analysis*, 16(4), 447–460.

16. Moreno, F.J., Saavedra, J.M., Sabido, R., Luis, V., and Reina, R. 2006. Visual search strategies of experienced and non-experienced swimming coaches. *Perceptual and Motor Skills*, 103(3), 861–872.

17. Issurin, V. 2008. The workout: General concepts and structure guidelines. In M. Yessis (Ed.), *Block periodization* (pp. 62–63). Michigan: Ultimate Athlete Concepts.

18. Arnett, M.G. 2001. The effect of a morning and afternoon practice schedule on morning and afternoon swim performance. *Journal of Strength and Conditioning Research*, 15(1), 127–131.

19. Peeling, P., and Landers, G. 2009. Swimming intensity during triathlon: A review of current research and strategies to enhance race performance. *Journal of Sports Sciences*, 27(10), 1079–1085.

20. Chatard, J.C., and Wilson, B. 2003. Drafting distance in swimming. *Medicine and Science in Sports and Exercise*, 35(7), 1176–1181.

21. Chollet, D., Hue, O., Auclair, F., Millet, G., and Chatard, J.C. 2000. The effects of drafting on stroking variations during swimming in elite male triathletes. *European Journal of Applied Physiology*, 82(5–6), 413–417.

22. Basset, D.R. Jr., Flohr, J., Duey, W.J., Howley, E.T., and Pein, R.L. 1991. Metabolic responses to drafting during front crawl swimming. *Medicine and Science in Sports and Exercise*, 23(6), 744–747.

23. Gatta, G., Ditroilo, M., Sisti, D., Cortesi, M., Benelli, P., and Bonifazi, M. 2008. The assess-

ment of path linearity in swimming: A pilot study. *International Journal of Sports Medicine*, 29(12), 959–964. Epub 2008 Jun 11.

24. Wakayoshi, K., Yoshida, T., Ikuta, Y., Mutoh, Y., and Miyashita, M. 1993. Adaptations to six months of aerobic swim training. Changes in velocity, stroke rate, stroke length and blood lactate. *International Journal of Sports Medicine*, 14(7), 368–372.

25. Goldsmith, W. 2011, August 1. Mental skills training in swimming: A new approach. Message posted to www.swimcoachingbrain.com

Chapter 26 Bike Base Building

1. Seiler, S., and Tonnessen, E. 2009. Intervals, threshold, and long slow distance: The role of intensity and duration in endurance training. *Sportscience*, 13, 32–53.

2. St. Pierre, A., and Henderson, N. 2009. Laboratory performance evaluations, time trial performance, and training intensity distribution in elite masters cyclists. *Medicine and Science in Sports and Exercise*, 41(6), 461–462.

3. National Strength and Conditioning Association. 2012. *Developing endurance*, edited by Reuter, B. Champaign, IL. Human Kinetics.

4. Allen, H., and Coggan, A. 2010. *Training and racing with a power meter* (2nd ed.). Boulder, CO: VeloPress.

5. Wilmore, J., Stanforth, P., Gagnon, J., Rice, T., Mandel, S., Leon, A., Rao, D.C., Skinner, J., and Bouchard, C. 2001. Cardiac output and stroke volume changes with endurance training: The HERITAGE Family Study. *Medicine and Science in Sports and Exercise*, 33(1), 99–106.

Chapter 27 Run Base Building

1. Midgley, A.W., McNaughton, L.R., and Jones, A.M. 2007. Training to enhance the physiological determinants of long-distance running performance: Can valid recommendations be given to runners and coaches based on current scientific knowledge? *Sports Medicine*, 37(10), 857–880. doi: 37103 [pii]

2. Gaskill, S.E., Serfass, R.C., Bacharach, D.W., and Kelly, J.M. 1999. Responses to training in cross-country skiers. *Medicine and Science in Sports and Exercise*, 31(8), 1211–1217.

3. Esteve-Lanao, J., Foster, C., Seiler, S., and Lucia, A. 2007. Impact of training intensity distribution on performance in endurance athletes. *Journal of Strength and Conditioning Research*, 21(3), 943–949. doi: R-19725 [pii]10.1519/R-19725.1

4. Esteve-Lanao, J., San Juan, A.F., Earnest, C.P., Foster, C., and Lucia, A. 2005. How do endurance runners actually train? Relationship with competition performance. *Medicine and Science in Sports and Exercise*, 37(3), 496–504. doi: 00005768-200503000-00022 [pii]

5. Seiler, K.S., and Kjerland, G. 2006. Quantifying training intensity distribution in elite endurance athletes: Is there evidence for an "optimal" distribution? *Scandinavian Journal of Medicine and Science in Sports*, 16(1), 49–56. doi: SMS418 [pii]10.1111/j.1600-0838.2004.00418.x

6. Seiler, S., Haugen, O., and Kuffel, E. 2007. Autonomic recovery after exercise in trained athletes: Intensity and duration effects. *Medicine and Science in Sports and Exercise*, 39(8), 1366–1373. doi: 00005768-200708000-00020 [pii]10.1249/mss.0b013e318060f17d

7. Fiskerstrand, A., and Seiler, K.S. 2004. Training and performance characteristics among Norwegian international rowers 1970–2001. *Scandinavian Journal of Medicine and Science in Sports*, 14(5), 303–310. doi: SMS370 [pii]10.1046/j.1600-0838.2003.370.x

8. Enoksen, E., Shalfawi, S.A., and Tønnessen, E. 2011. The effect of high- vs. low-intensity training on aerobic capacity in well-trained male middle-distance runners. *Journal of Strength and Conditioning Research*, 25(3), 812–818. doi: 10.1519/JSC.0b013e3181cc2291

9. Yamamoto, L.M., Lopez, R.M., Klau, J.F., Casa, D.J., Kraemer, W.J., and Maresh, C.M. 2008. The effects of resistance training on endurance distance running performance among highly trained runners: A systematic review. *Journal of Strength and Conditioning Research*, 22(6), 2036–2044. doi: 10.1519/JSC.0b013e318185f2f0

10. Apel, J.M., Lacey, R.M., and Kell, R.T. 2011. A comparison of traditional and weekly undulating periodized strength training programs with total volume and intensity equated. *Journal of Strength and Conditioning Research*, 25(3), 694–703. doi: 10.1519/JSC.0b013e3181c69ef6

11. Buford, T.W., Rossi, S.J., Smith, D.B., and Warren, A.J. 2007. A comparison of periodization models during nine weeks with equated volume and intensity for strength. *Journal of Strength and Conditioning Research*, 21(4), 1245–1250. doi: R-20446 [pii]10.1519/R-20446.1

12. Kok, L.Y., Hamer, P.W., and Bishop, D.J. 2009. Enhancing muscular qualities in untrained women: Linear versus undulating periodization. *Medicine and Science in Sports and Exercise*, 41(9), 1797–1807. doi: 10.1249/MSS.0b013e3181a154f3

13. Miranda, F., Simão, R., Rhea, M., Bunker, D., Prestes, J., Leite, R.D., and Novaes, J. 2011. Effects of linear vs. daily undulatory periodized resistance training on maximal and submaximal strength gains. *Journal of Strength and Conditioning Research*, 25(7), 1824–1830. doi: 10.1519/JSC.0b013e3181e7ff75

14. Prestes, J., Frollini, A.B., de Lima, C., Donatto, F.F., Foschini, D., de Cássia Marqueti, R., and Fleck, S.J. 2009. Comparison between linear and daily undulating periodized resistance training to increase strength. *Journal of Strength and Conditioning Research*, 23(9), 2437–2442. doi: 10.1519/JSC.0b013e3181c03548

15. Rhea, M.R., Ball, S.D., Phillips, W.T., and Burkett, L.N. 2002. A comparison of linear and daily undulating periodized programs with equated volume and intensity for strength. *Journal of Strength and Conditioning Research*, 16(2), 250–255.

16. Rhea, M.R., Phillips, W.T., Burkett, L.N., Stone, W.J., Ball, S.D., Alvar, B.A., and Thomas, A.B. 2003. A comparison of linear and daily undulating periodized programs with equated volume and intensity for local muscular endurance. *Journal of Strength and Conditioning Research*, 17(1), 82–87.

17. Vanni, A.C., Meyer, F., da Veiga, A.D., and Zanardo, V.P. 2010. Comparison of the effects of two resistance training regimens on muscular and bone responses in premenopausal women. *Osteoporosis International*, 21(9), 1537–1544. doi: 10.1007/s00198-009-1139-z

18. Vøllestad, N.K., and Blom, P.C. 1985. Effect of varying exercise intensity on glycogen depletion in human muscle fibres. *Acta Physiologica Scandinavica*, 125(3), 395–405.

19. Buist, I., Bredeweg, S.W., van Mechelen, W., Lemmink, K.A., Pepping, G.J., and Diercks, R.L. 2008. No effect of a graded training program on the number of running-related injuries in novice runners: A randomized controlled trial. *American Journal of Sports Medicine*, 36(1), 33–39. doi: 0363546507307505 [pii]10.1177/0363546507307505

20. Jobson, S.A., Passfield, L., Atkinson, G., Barton, G., and Scarf, P. 2009. The analysis and utilization of cycling training data. *Sports Medicine*, 39(10), 833–844. doi: 3 [pii] 10.2165/11317840-000000000-00000

21. Busso, T. 2003. Variable dose-response relationship between exercise training and performance. *Medicine and Science in Sports and Exercise*, 35(7), 1188–1195. doi: 10.1249/01.MSS.0000074465.13621.37

22. Esteve-Lanao, J., Rhea, M.R., Fleck, S.J., and Lucia, A. 2008. Running-specific, periodized strength training attenuates loss of stride length during intense endurance running. *Journal of Strength and Conditioning Research*, 22(4), 1176–1183. doi: 10.1519/JSC.0b013e31816a861f

23. Klein, R.M., Potteiger, J.A., and Zebas, C.J. 1997. Metabolic and biomechanical variables of two incline conditions during distance running. *Medicine and Science in Sports and Exercise*, 29(12), 1625–1630.

Chapter 28   Sprint

1. Bernhardt, G. 2004. Triathlon training basics. Boulder, CO: VeloPress.

2. Bernhardt, G. 2007. Training plans for multi-sport athletes (2nd ed.). Boulder, CO: VeloPress.

3. Burtscher, M., et al. 2006. Effects of short-term acclimatization to altitude (3200 m) on aerobic and anaerobic exercise performance. International Journal of Sports Medicine, 27, 629–635.

Chapter 29   Olympic

1. Bernhardt, G. 2007. Training plans for multi-sport triathletes (2nd ed). Boulder, CO: VeloPress.

2. Bernhardt, G. 2004. Triathlon training basics. Boulder, CO: VeloPress.

3. Bernhardt, G., and Hansen, N. 2011. Swim workouts for triathletes (2nd ed). Boulder, CO: VeloPress.

4. International Triathlon Union, listing of federations. Retrieved from www.triathlon.org/federations/

5. Le Meur, Y., et al. 2011. Relationships between triathlon performance and pacing strategy during the run in an international competition. International Journal of Sports and Physiology Performance, 6(2), 183–194. Retrieved from www.ncbi.nlm.nih.gov/pubmed/21725104

6. Hausswirth, C., et al. 2009. Pacing strategy during the initial phase of the run in triathlon: Influence on overall performance. European Journal of Applied Physiology, 108(6), 1115–1123. Retrieved from www.ncbi.nlm.nih.gov/pubmed/20024576

7. Burtscher, M., et al. 2006. Effects of short-term acclimatization to altitude (3200 m) on aerobic and anaerobic exercise performance. International Journal of Sports Medicine, 27, 629–635.

Chapter 30   Half-Ironman

1. Britt, R. 2010. Easiest half-Ironman 70.3? Hardest? RunTri's ranking of best half-Ironman races. Retrieved from www.runtri.com/2010/08/toughesthardest-vs-easiestfastest-half.html

2. Seiler, S., and Espen, T. 2009. Intervals, thresholds, and long slow distance: The role of intensity and duration in endurance training. Sportscience, 13, 32–53. Retrieved from www.sportsci.org/2009/ss.htm

3. Bernhardt, G. 2007. Training plans for multi-sport athletes (2nd ed.). Boulder, CO: VeloPress.

4. Burtscher, M., et al. 2006. Effects of short-term acclimatization to altitude (3200 m) on aerobic and anaerobic exercise performance. International Journal of Sports Medicine, 27, 629–635.

Chapter 31   Ironman

1. Britt, R. 2011. How much time does it take to finish an Ironman triathlon? Average Ironman finish times. Retrieved from www.runtri.com/2011/06/how-long-does-it-take-to-finish-ironman.html

2. Bernhardt, G. 2007. Training plans for multi-sport triathletes (2nd ed.). Boulder, CO: VeloPress.

3. Seiler, S., and Espen, T. 2009. Intervals, thresholds, and long slow distance: The role of intensity and duration in endurance training. Sportscience, 13, 32–53. Retrieved from www.sportsci.org/2009/ss.htm

Chapter 32   Duathlon

1. International Triathlon Union website, www.triathlon.org

2. USA Triathlon website, www.usatriathlon.org

3. USA Triathlon. 2011. National Championship Results. Retrieved from http://ultramaxtri.com/timing/2011/2011_USAT_Du_Nat/USATDuN_results.html

4. Bernhardt, G. 2007. Training plans for multi-sport athletes (2nd ed.). Boulder, CO: VeloPress.

5. Seiler, S., and Espen, T. 2009. Intervals, thresholds, and long slow distance: The role of intensity and duration in endurance training. Sportscience, 13, 32–53. Retrieved from www.sportsci.org/2009/ss.htm

6. Burtscher, M. et al. 2006. Effects of short-term acclimatization to altitude (3200 m) on aerobic and anaerobic exercise performance, International Journal of Sports Medicine, 27, 629–635.

Chapter 33   Combination Workout Training

1. Bonacci, J., et al. 2011. Neuromuscular control and running economy is preserved in elite

international triathletes after cycling. Sports Biomechanics, 10(1), 59–71. Retrieved from www.ncbi.nlm.nih.gov/pubmed/21560752

2. Bonacci, J., et al. 2010. Altered movement patterns but not muscle recruitment in moderately trained triathletes during running after cycling. Journal of Sports Science, 28(13), 1477–87. Retrieved from www.ncbi.nlm.nih.gov/pubmed/20945251

3. Chapman, A.R., et al. 2008. Does cycling effect motor coordination of the leg during running in elite triathletes? Journal of Science and Medicine in Sport, 11(4), 371–80. Epub 2007 Apr 26. Retrieved from www.ncbi.nlm.nih.gov/pubmed/17466592

Chapter 34   Triathlete Body Maintenance and Medical Care

1. Friel, J. 2009. The triathlete's training bible (3rd ed.). Boulder, CO: VeloPress.

2. Pruitt, A. 2006. Andy Pruitt's complete medical guide for cyclists. Boulder, CO: VeloPress.

3. Scott, D. 1986. Dave Scott's triathlon training. New York: Simon and Schuster.

4. Noakes, T. 2001. Lore of running (4th ed.). Champaign, IL: Human Kinetics.

5. Dale, P. 2011. Definition of muscular strength and endurance. www.livestrong.com/article/106346

6. Burns, J. 2003. Factors associated with triathlon-related overuse injuries. Journal of Orthopedic Sports Physical Therapy, 33(4), 177–184.

7. Korkia, P. 1994. An epidemiological investigation of training and injury patterns in British triathletes. British Journal of Sports Medicine, 28(3), 191–196.

8. O'Toole, M. 1989. Overuse injuries in ultra endurance athletes. American Journal of Sports Medicine, 17, 514–518.

9. Meehan, H. 2000. Do triathletes really have fewer injuries, and which ones get hurt? www.sportsinjurybulletin.com.

10. Jenkins, J. 2010. Flexibility for runners. Clinics of Sports Medicine, 29, 365–377.

11. McCann, P. 2010. Flexibility in the athlete. University of Virginia Foundation, University of Virginia. Personal communication.

12. Fitzgerald, M. 2003. Staying healthy. The complete triathlon book. New York: Grand Central.

13. Ingraham, S.J. 2003. The role of flexibility in injury prevention: Have we stretched the truth? MN Med, 86(5), 58–61.

14. www.grastontechnique.com

15. www.activerelease.com

16. Leahy, P., and Michael, D.C. 2011. Founder, active release technique. Personal communication.

17. Hall, H. 2009. The Graston technique: Inducing microtrauma with instruments. Science Based Medicine, Dec. 29, www.sciencebasedmedicine.org/index.php/the-graston-technique-inducing-microtrauma-with-instruments

18. Holland, T. 2011. The 12-week triathlete (2nd ed.). Beverly, MA: Fair Winds Press.

Chapter 35   Triathlon Injuries and Preventive Measures

1. Burns, J., Keenan, A.M., and Redmond, A.C. 2003. Factors associated with triathlon-related overuse injuries. Journal of Orthopaedic and Sports Physical Therapy, 33(4), 177–184.

2. Vleck, V.E., Bentley, D.J., Millet, G.P., and Cochrane, T. 2010. Triathlon event distance specialization: Training and injury effects. Journal of Strength and Conditioning Research, 24(1), 30–36.

3. Heinlein, S.A., and Cosgarea, A.J. 2010. Biomechanical considerations in the competitive swimmer's shoulder. Sports Health: A Multidisciplinary Approach, 2(6), 519–525.

4. Clarsen, B., Krosshaug, T., and Bahr, R. 2010. Overuse injuries in professional road cyclists. American Journal of Sports Medicine, 38(12), 2494–2501.

5. Villavicencio, A.T., Hernández, T.D., Burneikiene, S., and Thramann, J. 2007. Neck pain in multisport athletes. Journal of Neurosurgery: Spine 7(4), 408–413.

6. Bini, R., Hume, P.A., and Croft, J.L. 2011. Effects of bicycle saddle height on knee injury risk and cycling performance. Sports Medicine, 41(6), 463–476.

7. Gregersen, C.S., Hull, M.L., and Hakansson, N.A. 2006. How changing the inversion/eversion foot angle affects the nondriving intersegmental knee moments and the relative activation of the vastii muscles in cycling. Journal of Biomechanical Engineering, 128(3), 391–398.

8. Jarboe, N.E., and Quesada, P.M. 2003. The effects of cycling shoe stiffness on forefoot pressure. Foot and Ankle International, 24(10), 784–788.

9. Van Gent, R.N., Siem, D., Van Middelkoop, M., Van Os, A.G., Bierma-Zeinstra, S.M.A., and Koes, B.W. 2007. Incidence and determinants of lower extremity running injuries in long

distance runners: A systematic review. British Journal of Sports Medicine, 41(8), 469–480.

10. Bonacci, J., Chapman, A., Blanch, P., and Vicenzino, B. 2009. Neuromuscular adaptations to training, injury and passive interventions: Implications for running economy. Sports Medicine, 39(11), 903–921.

11. Franz, J.R., Paylo, K.W., Dicharry, J., Riley, P.O., and Kerrigan, D.C. 2009. Changes in the coordination of hip and pelvis kinematics with mode of locomotion. Gait and Posture, 29(3), 494–498.

12. Myers, W.C., Kahan, D.M., Joseph, T., Butrymowicz, A., Poor, A.E., and Zoga, A.C. 2011. Current analysis of women athletes with pelvic pain. Medicine and Science in Sports and Exercise, 43(8), 1387–1393.

13. Heiderscheit, B.C., Chumanov, E.S., Michalski, M.P., Wille, C.M., and Ryan, M.B. 2011. Effects of step rate manipulation on joint mechanics during running. Medicine and Science in Sports and Exercise, 43(2), 296–302.

14. Biewener, A.A., Farley, C.T., Roberts, T.J., and Temaner, M. 2004. Muscle mechanical advantage of human walking and running: Implications for energy cost. Journal of Applied Physiology, 97(6), 2266–2274.

15. Lun, V., Meeuwisse, W.H., Stergiou, P., and Stefanyshyn, D. 2004. Relation between running injury and static lower limb alignment in recreational runners. British Journal of Sports Medicine, 38(5), 576–580.

16. Chumanov, E.S., Schache, A.G., Heiderscheit, B.C., and Thelen, D.G. 2011. Hamstrings are most susceptible to injury during the late swing phase of sprinting. British Journal of Sports Medicine, 45(9), 684–685.

17. Earl, J.E., and Hoch, A.Z. 2011. A proximal strengthening program improves pain, function, and biomechanics in women with patellofemoral pain syndrome. American Journal of Sports Medicine, 29(1), 154–163.

18. Lieberman, D.E., Venkadesan, M., Werbel, W.A., Daoud, A.I., D'Andrea, S., Davis, I.S., Mang'Eni, R.O., and Pitsiladis, Y. 2010. Foot strike patterns and collision forces in habitually barefoot versus shod runners. Nature, 463(7280), 531–535.

19. Arendse, R.E., Noakes, T.D., Azevedo, L.B., Romanov, N., Schwellnus, M.P., and Fletcher, G. 2004. Reduced eccentric loading of the knee with the pose running method. Medicine and Science in Sports and Exercise, 36, 272–277.

20. Williams, D.S., McClay, I.S., and Hamill, J. 2001.

Arch structure and injury patterns in runners. Clinical Biomechanics, 16(4), 341–347.

21. Milner, C.E., Hamill, J.D., and Davis, I.S. 2010. Distinct hip and rearfoot kinematics in female runners with a history of tibial stress fracture. Journal of Orthopedic and Sports Physical Therapy, 40(2), 59–66.

22. Ryan, M.B., Valiant, G.A., McDonald, K., and Taunton, J.E. 2009. The effect of three different levels of footwear stability on pain outcomes in women runners: A randomized control trial. British Journal of Sports Medicine, 45, 715–721.

23. Kong, P.W., Candelaria, N.G., and Smith, D.R. 2009. Running in new and worn shoes: A comparison of three types of cushioning footwear. British Journal of Sports Medicine, 43, 745–749.

Chapter 36   Triathlon Injury Recovery Techniques

1. Escamilla, R.F., Lewis, C., Bell, D., Bramblet, G., Daffron, J., Lambert, S., Pecson, A., Imamura, R., Paulos, L., and Andrews, J.R. 2010. Core muscle activation during Swiss ball and traditional abdominal exercises. Journal of Orthopedic and Sports Physical Therapy, 40(5), 265–276.

2. Magnussen, R.A., Dunn, W.R., and Thomson, B.A. 2009. Nonoperative treatment of midportion Achilles tendinopathy: A systematic review. Clinical Journal of Sports Medicine, 19(1), 55–64.

3. Franca, F.R., Burke, T.N., Hanada, E.S., and Marques, A.P. 2010. Segmental stabilization and muscular strengthening in chronic low back pain: A comparative study. Clinics, 65(10), 1013–1017.

4. Riley, P.O., Franz, J., Dicharry, J., and Kerrigan, C.D. 2010. Changes in hip joint muscle tendon lengths with mode of locomotion. Gait and Posture, 31(2), 279–283.

5. McHugh, M.P., and Cosgrave, C.H. 2010. To stretch or not to stretch: The role of stretching in injury prevention and performance. Scandinavian Journal of Medicine and Science in Sports, 20, 169–181.

6. Haupenthal, A., Ruschel, C., Hubert, M., de Brito Fontana, H., and Roesler, H. 2010. Loading forces in shallow water running at two levels of immersion. Journal of Rehabilitation Medicine, 42(7), 664–669.

7. Wilson, J.K., Sevier, T.L., Helfst, R.H., Honing, E.W., and Thomann, A.L. 2000. Comparison of rehabilitation methods in the treatment of patellar tendinitis. Journal of Sports Rehabilitation, 9(4), 304–314.

8. Loghmani, M.T., and Warden, S.J. 2009. Instrument-assisted cross-fiber massage accelerates knee ligament healing. Journal of Orthopaedic and Sports Physical Therapy, 39(7), 506–514.

9. González-Iglesias, J., Fernández-De-Las-Peñas, C., Cleland, J.A., and Gutiérrez-Vega, M.D.R. 2009. Thoracic spine manipulation for the management of patients with neck pain: A randomized clinical trial. Journal of Orthopaedic and Sports Physical Therapy, 39(1), 20–27.

10. Brummitt, J. 2008. The role of massage in sports performance and rehabilitation: Current evidence and future direction. North American Journal of Sports Physical Therapy, 3(1), 7–21.

11. Wiltshire, E.V., Poitras, V., Pak, M., Hong, T., Rayner, J., and Tschakovsky, M.E. 2010. Massage impairs postexercise muscle blood flow and "lactic acid" removal. Medicine and Science in Sports and Exercise, 42(6), 1062–1071.

12. Gorski, T., Cadore, L.E., Pinto, S.S., Silva, E.M., Correa, S.C., Beltrami, G.F., and Kruel, M.L.F. 2011. The use of NSAIDs in triathletes: Prevalence, level of awareness and reasons for use. British Journal of Sports Medicine, 45, 85–90.

13. Baur, H., Hirschmuller, A., Muller, S., and Mayer, F. 2011. Neuromuscular activity of the peroneal muscle after foot orthoses therapy in runners. Medicine and Science in Sports and Exercise, 43(8), 1500–1505.

14. Gambito, E.D., Gonzales-Suarez, C.B., Oquiñena, T.I., and Agbayani, R.B. 2010. Evidence on the effectiveness of topical nitroglycerin in the treatment of tendinopathies: A systematic review and meta-analysis. Archives of Physical Medicine and Rehabilitation, 91(8), 1291–1305.

15. Nichols, A. 2005. Complications associated with the use of corticosteroids in the treatment of athletic injuries. Clinical Journal of Sports Medicine, 15(5), E370.

16. Weir, A., van Schie, H.T.M., Bierma-Zeinstra, S.M.A., Verhaar, J.A.N., Weinans, H., and Tol, J.L. 2010. Platelet-rich plasma injection for chronic Achilles tendinopathy. JAMA, 303(2), 144–149.

17. Yelland, M.J., Sweeting, K.R., Lyftogt, J.A., Ng, S.K., Scuffham, P.A., and Evans, K.A. 2011. Prolotherapy injections and eccentric loading exercises for painful Achilles tendinosis: A randomized trial. British Journal of Sports Medicine, 45, 421–428.18. Avella, C.S., and Smith, R.K. 2010. Ultrasound evaluation of stem cell treated tendon injuries in the horse: Repair or regeneration. Lancet, 376(9754), 1751–1767.

18. Avella, C.S., and Smith, R.K. 2010. Ultrasound evaluation of stem cell treated tendon injuries in the horse: Repair or regeneration. Lancet, 376(9754), 1751–1767.

19. Noehren, B., Scholz, J., and Davis, I. 2011. The effect of real-time gait retraining on hip kinematics, pain and function in subjects with patellofemoral pain syndrome. British Journal of Sports Medicine, 45, 691–696.

Chapter 37   Energy Needs, Sources, and Utilization

1. Arnos, P.M., Sowash, J., and Andres, F.F. 1997. Fat oxidation at varied work intensities using different exercise modes. Medicine and Science in Sports and Exercise, 29, S199.

2. Jeukendrup, A.E. 2004. Carbohydrate intake during exercise and performance. Nutrition, 20, 669–677.

3. Acheton, J., Gleeson, M., and Jeukendrup, A.E. 2002. Determination of the exercise intensity that elicits maximal fat oxidation. Medicine and Science in Sports and Exercise, 34, 92–97.

4. Coyle, E.F. 1995. Substrate utilization during exercise in active people. American Journal of Clinical Nutrition, 61, 968S–979S.

5. Seebohar, B. 2009. Metabolic efficiency training: Teaching the body to burn more fat. Fuel-4mance.

6. van Loon, L.J.C. 2004. Use of intramuscular triacylglycerol as a substrate source during exercise in humans. Journal of Applied Physiology, 97(4), 1170–1187.

7. Dunford, M., and Doyle, J.A. 2008. Nutrition for sport and exercise. Belmont, CA: Thompson Higher Education.

8. Kenney, W.L., and Chiu, P. 2001. Influence of age on thirst and fluid intake. Medicine and Science in Sports and Exercise, 33(9), 1524–1532.

9. Horowitz, J.F., Mora-Rodriguez, R., Byerley, L.O., and Coyle, E.F. 1997. Lipolytic suppression following carbohydrate ingestion limits fat oxidation during exercise. American Journal of Physiology, 273(4), E768–E775.

10. Halton, T.L., and Hu, F.B. 2004. The effects of high protein diets on thermogenesis, satiety and weight loss: A critical review. Journal of the American College of Nutrition, 23(5), 373–385.

Chapter 38   Nutrition Periodization

1. Seebohar, B. 2010. Nutrition periodization for athletes (2nd ed.). Boulder, CO: Bull.

2. Burke, L.M., Cox, G.R., Cummings, N.K., and Desbrow, B. 2001. Guidelines for daily carbohydrate intake: Do athletes achieve them? Sports Medicine, 31(4), 92–97.

3. Burke, L.M., Kiens, B., and Ivy, J.L. 2004. Carbohydrates and fat for training and recovery. Journal of Sports Sciences, 22, 15–30.

4. Tarnopolsky, M. 2004. Protein requirements for endurance athletes. Nutrition, 20, 662–668.

5. Rodriguez, N.R., DiMarco, N.M., and Langley, S. 2009. Nutrition and athletic performance. Journal of the American Dietetic Association, 109(3), 509–527.

6. Campbell, B., Kreider, R.B., Ziegenfuss, T., La Bounty, P., Roberts, M., Burke, D., Landis, J., Lopez, H., and Antonio, J. 2007. International society of sports nutrition position stand: Protein and exercise. Journal of the International Society of Sports Nutrition, 4, 8.

Chapter 39   Nutrient Timing for Triathlon Training and Racing

1. Hargreaves, M., Hawley, J.A., and Jeukendrup, A. 2004. Pre-exercise carbohydrate and fat ingestion: Effects on metabolism and performance. Journal of Sports Sciences, 22, 31–38.

2. Tipton, K.D., and Wolfe, R.R. 2004. Protein and amino acids for athletes. Journal of Sports Sciences, 22, 65–79.

3. Sawka, M.N., Burke, L.M., Eichner, E.R., Maughan, R.J., Montain, S.J., and Stachenfeld, N.S. 2007. Exercise and fluid replacement position stand. Medicine and Science in Sports and Exercise, 39(2), 377–389.

4. Jeukendrup, A.E. 2010. Carbohydrate and exercise performance: The role of multiple transportable carbohydrates. Current Opinion in Clinical Nutrition and Metabolic Care, 13(4), 452–457.

5. Seebohar, B. 2009. Metabolic efficiency training: Teaching the body to burn more fat. Fuel4mance.

6. Luden, N.D., Saunders, M.J., and Todd, M.K. 2007. Postexercise carbohydrate-protein-antioxidant ingestion decreases plasma creatine kinase and muscle soreness. International Journal of Sports Nutrition and Exercise Metabolism, 17(1), 109–123.

7. Maughan, R.J. 1991. Fluid and electrolyte loss and replacement in exercise. Journal of Sports Sciences, 9, 117–142.

8. Jeukendrup, A.E., Jentjens, R., and Moseley, L. 2005. Nutritional considerations in triathlon. Sports Medicine, 35, 163–181.

9. Burke, L.M., Kiens, B., and Ivy, J.L. 2004. Carbohydrates and fat for training and recovery. Journal of Sports Sciences, 22, 15–30.

10. Burke, L., and Deakin, V. 2006. Clinical sports nutrition (3rd ed.). McGraw-Hill.

11. Maughan, R., and Shirreffs, S.M. 2008. Development of individual hydration strategies for athletes. International Journal of Sports Nutrition and Exercise Metabolism, 18, 457–472.

Chapter 40   Supplements for Triathletes

1. Burke, L., and Deakin, V. 2006. Clinical sports nutrition (3rd ed.). McGraw-Hill.

2. Panossian, A., Wikman, G., and Wagner, H. 1999. Plant adaptogens III. Earlier and more recent aspects and concepts on their mode of action. Phytomedicine 6(4), 287–300.

3. Artioli, G.G., Gualano, B., Smith, A., Stout, J., and Lancha, A.H. 2010. Role of beta alanine supplementation on muscle carnosine and exercise performance. Medicine and Science in Sports and Exercise, 42(6), 1162–1173.

4. Graham, T.E. 2001. Caffeine and exercise: Metabolism, endurance and performance. Sports Medicine, 31, 785–807.

5. Armstrong, L.E., Pumerantz, A.C., Roti, M.W., Judelson, D.A., Watson, G., Dias, J.C., Sokmen, B., Casa, D.J., Maresh, C.M., Harris, L., and Kellogg, M. 2005. Fluid, electrolyte and renal indices of hydration during 11 days of controlled caffeine consumption. International Journal of Sport Nutrition and Exercise Metabolism, 15, 252–265.

6. Hoffman, J.R., Kang, J., Ratamess, N.A., Jennings, P.F., Mangine, G.T., and Faigenbaum, A.D. 2007. Effect of nutritionally enriched coffee consumption on aerobic and anaerobic exercise performance. Journal of Strength and Conditioning Research, 21(2), 456–459.

7. Yeo, S.E., Jentjens, R.L., Wallis, G.A., and Jeukendrup, A.E. 2005. Caffeine increases exogenous carbohydrate oxidation during exercise. Journal of Applied Physiology, 99, 844–850.

8. Lopez, R.M., Casa, D.J., McDermott, B.P., Ganio, M.S., Armstrong, L.E., and Maresh, C.M. 2009. Does creatine supplementation hinder exercise heat tolerance or hydration status? A systematic review with meta-analyses. Journal of Athletic Training, 44(2), 215–223.

9. Law, Y.L., Ong, W.S., GillianYap, T.L., Lim, S.C., and Von Chia, E. 2009. Effects of two and five days of creatine loading on muscular strength and anaerobic power in trained athletes. Journal of Strength and Conditioning Research, 23(3), 906–914.

Chapter 41   Mental Toughness for Triathlon

1. Ranganathan, V.K., Siemionow, V., Liu, J.Z., Sahgal, V., and Yue, G.H. 2004. From mental power to muscle power: Gaining strength by using the mind. Neuropsychologia, 42(7), 944–956.

2. Dolan, S.H., Houston, M., and Martin, S.B. 2011. Survey results of the training, nutrition, and mental preparation of triathletes: Practical implications of findings. Journal of Sports Science July 29(10), 1019–1028.

3. Maslow, A.H. 1943. A theory of human motivation. Psychological Review, 50(4), 370–396.

4. Stoeber, J., Uphill, M.A., and Hotham, S. 2009. Predicting race performance in triathlon: The role of perfectionism, achievement goals, and personal goal setting. Journal of Sport and Exercise Psychology, 31(2), 211–245.

5. Grand'Maison, K. 2004. What mental skills Ironman triathletes need and want. Journal of Excellence, 10, 86–87.

Chapter 42   Psychology of Triathlon Training

1. Main, L.C., Landers, G.J., Grove, J.R., Dawson, B., and Goodman, C. 2010. Training patterns and negative health outcomes in triathlon: Longitudinal observations across a full competitive season. Journal of Sports Medicine and Physical Fitness, 50(4), 475–485.

2. Winsley, R., and Matos, N. 2011. Overtraining and elite young athletes. Medicine and Sport Science, 56, 97–105.

3. Wadey, R., and Hanton, S. 2008. Basic psychological skills usage and competitive anxiety responses: Perceived underlying mechanisms. Research Quarterly for Exercise and Sport, 79(3), 363–373.

Chapter 43   Mental Skills for Peak Triathlon Performance

1. Knechtle, B., Wirth, A., and Rosemann, T. 2010. Predictors of race time in male ironman triathletes: Physical characteristics, training, or prerace experience? Perceptual and Motor Skills, 111(2), 437–446.

2. Memmert, D. 2011. Creativity, expertise, and attention: Exploring their development and their relationships. Journal of Sports Sciences, 29(1), 93–102.

3. Ranganathan, V.K., Siemionow, V., Liu, J.Z., Sahgal, V., and Yue, G.H. 2004. From mental power to muscle power: Gaining strength by using the mind. Neuropsychologia, 42(7), 944–956.

4. Fontani, G., Migliorini, S., Benocci, R., Facchini, A., Casini, M., and Corradeschi, F. 2007. Effect of mental imagery on the development of skilled motor actions. Perceptual and Motor Skills, 105(3 Pt. 1), 803–826.

Index

Note: The italicized *f* and *t* following page numbers refer to figures and tables, respectively.

About the Editors

Joe Friel, MSc, has trained endurance athletes since 1980. He served as head coach of the USA National Triathlon Team at the World Championships in 2000, and athletes he has worked with have appeared in the Olympic Games, world and national championships. He is co-founder of the USA Triathlon's National Coaching Association and served on the USA Triathlon Coaching Certification Committee. Friel is a Colorado State Masters Triathlon champion, a Rocky Mountain region and Southwest region duathlon age-group champion, and has been a perennial USA Triathlon All-American duathlete. As a member of several national duathlon teams, Friel was a top-five contender in world class events and competed in road running and United States Cycling Federation races. He is the author of *The Triathlete's Training Bible, Your First Triathlon, Your Best Triathlon, Total Heart Rate Training,* and *The Paleo Diet for Athletes,* and he is a contributor to *Precision Heart Rate Training* and USA Triathlon's *Complete Triathlon Guide.*

Jim Vance is a triathlon/duathlon, running, and cycling coach at TrainingBible Coaching and the founder and head coach of TriJuniors, a USAT High Performance Team in San Diego. For his coaching, he was awarded the 2009 Tri Club of San Diego Coach of the Year and was appointed US Elite National Team coach for the Duathlon World Championships in 2011 and 2012. He has coached athletes who have won or qualified for events including the US Elite National Championship, Elite ITU World Championship, Ironman World Championship, 70.3 World Championship, and XTERRA European Tour Elite. A former elite triathlete who spent  time at the US Olympic Training Center, Vance placed third in the Florida Ironman and was an International Triathlon Union Age Group World Champion, a XTERRA Amateur World Champion, and a Letter winner at the University of Nebraska in track and field and cross country.

About the Contributors

Ildus I. Ahmetov is the head of the Laboratory of Molecular Genetics at Kazan State Medical University. He also serves as a Senior Research Fellow of the Sports Genetics Laboratory at the St. Petersburg Research Institute of Physical Culture and as a Senior Research Fellow of the Laboratory of Exercise Physiology at the Institute for Biomedical Problems of the Russian Academy of Sciences. He won Young Investigators Awards in 2007 and 2010 for projects documenting genetic variants in athletes and is author of *Molecular Sports Genetics.*

Hunter Allen is a former professional cyclist, renowned coach, and expert in using power meters to train endurance athletes. As a professional racer for 17 years, he earned more than 40 career victories in competitions around the world. Upon retiring from racing, Allen became a USA Cycling elite-level cycling coach and certified nutrition consultant. He has coached more than 400 athletes, including the 2008 USA Cycling BMX Olympic team, champions of the European road racing circuit, and champion mountain bikers. He writes for *Road* magazine and *Cycling Weekly,* and he coauthored

Training and Racing with a Power Meter and *Cutting-Edge Cycling.* Allen is the founder of Peaks Coaching Group, and is a co-developer of TrainingPeaks WKO software, a leading program for analyzing data from power meters.

Gale Bernhardt is a triathlon, cycling, and endurance coach. She served as the 2004 USA Triathlon Olympic coach for both the men's and women's teams and was selected by USA Triathlon to serve as the 2003 Pan American Games men's and women's coach. She has served as a USA Triathlon World Cup coach for the International Triathlon Union (ITU) Sport Development squad, and has worked internationally for the ITU as an expert World Cup coach. She has worked with Olympic athletes and winners of the USA Cycling Pro National Championship race. Bernhardt is author of five books for triathletes: *Training Plans for Multisport Athletes; Triathlon Training Basics; Bicycling for Women; Training Plans for Cyclists;* and *Swim Workouts for Triathletes.* She is also a contributor to *The Woman Triathlete.*

Jeff Broker, PhD, has been involved in the study of pedaling mechanics and optimal integration of rider and bicycle since 1987. He worked at the United States Olympic Committee (USOC) as a Senior Sport Biomechanist for nearly 10 years, through which he worked with the USA Triathlon and US National Cycling team to optimize rider/bicycle integration. He has worked with nine United States sports federations including the US Cycling Federation, USA Triathlon, and USA Track & Field. Broker is author of *Bicycle Accidents: Biomechanics, Engineering, and Legal Aspects* and is a contributor to *High-Tech Cycling* and *International Olympic Committee's Olympic Handbook of Sports Medicine: Road Cycling.* He currently serves as an Associate Professor and Chair of the Biology department at the University of Colorado.

Professor **Malcolm Collins** leads a productive research group investigating the biological mechanisms of musculoskeletal soft tissue injuries and endurance performance. His research interests include genetic elements that determine the endurance phenotype and the inter-individual physiological responses during participation in endurance events. He has published more than 70 papers in scientific journals and book chapters, several focused on the Ironman triathlete. He serves as a professor in the Research Unit for Exercise Science and Sports Medicine (ESSM) at the University of Cape Town.

JoAnn Dahlkoetter, PhD, is founder of Performing Edge Coaching International, a global resource and certification training program for sports psychology coaches. She is an internationally recognized keynote speaker and world-class athlete. She is a past winner of the San Francisco Marathon (2:43:20), placed 2nd in the Hawaii Ironman Triathlon, and was rated the No. 1 triathlete in the U.S. by *Triathlete Magazine*. The author of the bestselling book *Your Performing Edge*, her work has been published in *Runners World*, *Fitness Magazine*, *Time*, and *Sports Illustrated*. She is currently a regular contributor

to the *Huffington Post* and *Triathlete Magazine*. Dr. Dahlkoetter has appeared as an expert guest on numerous shows including Oprah and Friends, ABC sports, and NBC Olympics. She is a licensed clinical psychologist and medical staff member at Stanford University Medical Center and currently maintains a fulltime private practice. In her 30 years of clinical practice Dr. Dahlkoetter has worked with five Olympic Gold Medalists and numerous Olympic and professional athletes. She continues to train and race in the San Francisco Bay Area.

George M. Dallam, PhD, a 30-year triathlete participant and coach, is the founding member of the National Coaching Commission of USA Triathlon and was USA Triathlon's first national team coach. Throughout his coaching career, Dallam has served as a personal coach to several elite triathletes including Hunter Kemper, Amanda Stevens, Marcel Vifian, Callahan Hatfield, Michael Smedley, Ryan Bickerstaff, Nick Radkewich, Susan Williams, Laura Reback, Becky Lavelle, and Doug Friman. Athletes under his direction have won seven National Elite Championships, Pan American Games gold and silver medals, World Cup medals, World and USA Age Group Championships, as well as qualifying for and being among the top American male finishers in three Olympic Games. In 2005, he was a finalist for the United States Olympic Committee's esteemed "Doc" Counsilman Award for Science in Coaching. He was named USA Triathlon's Elite Coach of the Year in 2006. Dallam has been a professor in Exercise Science and Health Promotion at Colorado State University at Pueblo for 15 years. As a sport scientist he has authored and coauthored numerous scientific papers and books relating to triathlon, including *Championship Triathlon Training*. He is a contributor to USA Triathlon's *Complete Triathlon Guide*.

Matt Fitzgerald is a running and triathlon coach, sports nutritionist, and USA Triathlon All-American. He placed second overall in the 2004 Long Beach Triathlon and was an Ironman finisher. He has contributed to many triathlon publications including *Triathlete Magazine* (for which he was the former senior editor), *Triathlete*, and *Inside Triathlon*. He has been featured on TrainingPeaks and Active.com. His many writing accomplishments include authoring *Triathlete Magazine's Complete Triathlon Book*, *Triathlete Magazine's Essential Week-by-Week Training Guide*, *Racing Weight*, *Iron War*, *RUN: The Mind-Body Method of Running by Feel*, and *Brain Training For Runners* and co-authoring *Run Faster from the 5K to the Marathon* and *The Runner's Edge*.

Neal Henderson is a triathlon coach, the sports science director at the Boulder Center for Sports Medicine, and a consultant to USA Cycling, USA Triathlon, and Specialized Bicycle Components. He has coached numerous elite triathletes including Cameron Dye, Flora Duffy, Seth Wealing, and Jamie Whitmore, and has worked with cyclists Taylor Phinney and Roman Kreuziger. He was named USA Cycling National Coach of the Year in 2009 and USA Cycling Developmental Coach of the Year in 2007. He is a USA Triathlon Level 3 Elite Coach and USA Cycling Level 1 Elite Coach. He was a member of the USA Triathlon National Coaches Commission from 2003 to 2008. As a triathlon participant, he was a Top American Finisher at the International Triathlon Union Winter Triathlon World Championships in 2002 and 2003 and was 1st Place Amateur Overall at XTERRA Keystone in 1999.

Nathan Koch is founder, director, and owner of Endurance Rehab LLC, the official training center for Joe Friel's Ultrafit. He is also an instructor of Advanced Bike Fit Classes at the Serotta International Cycling Institute. He writes regularly about sports injuries and recovery for *Triathlete Magazine* and *LAVA Magazine*. Koch has provided sports medicine to NCAA Division I men's and women's athletics at Saint Louis University and the University of Nebraska, and he spent three seasons working for the St. Louis Rams and a sports medicine clinic (ProRehab) in St. Louis, where he 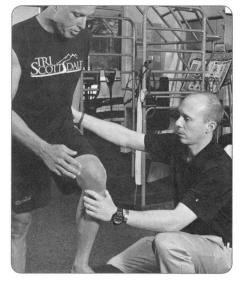 worked with professional athletes. He has presented "Core Strengthening for the Endurance Athlete" to teams of elite medical professionals and has worked closely with them to provide the most technologically-advanced sports medicine available.

Sean Langlais is a consultant for Biomechanics Engineering, where he examines the biomechanics of injuries, including those occurring due to cycling. He recently had his "Grip Pressure Distributions and Associated Variability in Golf: A Two-Club Comparison" published in the *Journal of Biomechanics*. After receiving his MSc in Exercise Science from the University of Colorado, Langlais worked with Carmichael Training Systems where he helped train cyclists and triathletes in endurance. At CTS, he also served as the in-house bicycle mechanic. He has also worked with USA cycling as the team mechanic for the Junior National Mountain Bike skills camp.

Romuald Lepers is an assistant professor at the Faculty of Sport Sciences in Dijon at Burgundy University in France where his research interests include exercise physiology, neuromuscular fatigue, and the effects of age and gender on endurance performances. He has published more than 70 articles, many on triathlon and endurance in publications including *Journal of Sports Sciences*, *European Journal of Applied Physiology*, and *Scandinavian Journal of Medicine & Science in Sports*. He is a frequent triathlon participant, having completed 21 Ironman races, four of which were the Hawaii Ironman.

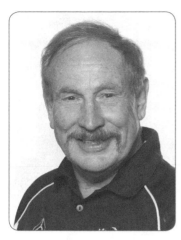

Bruce R. Mason is the head of the Aquatics Testing Training and Research Unit at the Australian Institute of Sport where he provides biomechanical servicing to the Australian Institute of Sport swim team and Australian swim team. He was the chief biomechanical advisor to the Australian swim team from 1994 to 2002, for which he received the Order of Australia Medal and Australian Sports Medal from the Australian government. He also twice received awards for Outstanding Contribution to Swimming in Australia from the Australia Swim Coaches & Teachers Association. His research in swimming biomechanics has led him to present at ISBS and BMS international conferences. Mason has contributed to three books on swimming: *The Swim Coaching Bible*, *World Book of Swimming*, and *Triathlon Into the Nineties*.

Stephen J. McGregor, PhD, a former triathlete and elite competitive cyclist, coached endurance athletes for more than 15 years, advising numerous cyclists, triathletes, and runners at the national and international level. He has been appointed as physiological advisor to both the 2008 U.S. Olympic BMX team and Eastern Michigan University men's cross country/distance track team and has presented at numerous conferences including USA Triathlon Art and Science of Coaching. He is a USA Cycling Level I coach and is an instructor for the USA Cycling Level II Coaching Certification Sports Sciences,

USA Cycling Power Training Certification Course, USA Cycling Level I (Elite) Coaching Certification Interval Training, and South African Coaching and Power Training Certification. He is currently the director of both the Applied Physiology Laboratory and the Human Factors-Dynamical Systems Laboratory at Eastern Michigan University. He is co–author of *The Runner's Edge*.

David Pease is a senior biomechanist and the deputy head of discipline in the Aquatic Testing, Training, and Research Unit at the Australian Institute of Sport where he conducts research into enhancing swimming performance and helps the swim program monitor athletes during training sessions. With more than 20 years' experience in swimming biomechanics, he has served as a biomechanist for USA Swimming and New Zealand Swimming. He has also worked with United States Swimming's International Center for Aquatic Research (ICAR) and the United States Olympic Committee's Sport Science division. He was a competitive swimmer from the age of 6 through university level, when he swam for the University of Southern California.

John Post, MD, is the medical director at TrainingBible Coaching and an orthopedic surgeon at Martha Jefferson Hospital in Charlottesville, Virginia. He is a widely-read medical and triathlon author and lecturer who presents nationally and runs his own endurance athlete blog. For more than 20 years, his focus has included surgical and nonsurgical knee and shoulder care in endurance athletes. A veteran triathlete, Post has finished the Hawaii Ironman six times, in addition to participating in the Manhattan Island Marathon Swim and the English Channel Relay Swim.

Gina Sacilotto is a research assistant in the Aquatics Testing Training and Research Unit at the Australian Institute of Sport Aquatics where she assists Bruce R. Mason in research for athletes and coaches to enhance performance. An open-water competitive swimmer herself, through her research she has explored topics including active drag in swimming, anthropometry in swimming, and the development of new aquatics biomechanical systems to enhance swimmer performance.

Bob Seebohar, MS, RD, CSSD, CSCS, is owner of Fuel4mance, a leading nutrition consulting firm serving amateur and elite athletes; Kids that TRI, 501c3 Youth Triathlon Team; Performance Webinars, an educational webinar company; and a co-owner of Elite Multisport coaching. In 2008, Seebohar traveled to the summer Olympic Games in Beijing as a sport dietitian for the U.S. Olympic team and as the personal sport dietitian and exercise physiologist for the Olympic triathlon team. He has worked closely with triathletes including Susan Williams (2004 Olympic Bronze medalist), Sarah Haskins, and Jasmine Oeinck (2009 National Elite Champion). He has also been appointed a sports nutrition consultant for the USA Triathlon Olympic and Developmental teams. Seebohar is a USA Triathlon Elite Level III coach and a frequent presenter for USA Triathlon coaching certification clinics. In 1996, he represented the United States as a member of the duathlon team at the World Championships. He has competed in numerous endurance events including the Boston Marathon and six Ironman races. He is author of eight books on endurance and nutrition including *Performance Nutrition: Applying the Science of Nutrient Timing* and *Nutrition Periodization for Athletes.* He is a contributor to USA Triathlon's *Complete Triathlon Guide.*

Dr. Ross Tucker is senior lecturer with the University of Cape Town's Exercise Science and Sports Medicine department where he has studied topics including fatigue and the role of the brain in determining pacing strategy and exercise performance. He serves as a sports scientist and strategist for the Springbok Sevens rugby team and has recently worked with Olympic kayakers Shaun Rubenstein and Mike Arthur in preparation for the 2012 London Olympics. He currently serves as the scientific editor of *Runner's World South Africa* and as a contributor and editor to Health24, South Africa's largest fitness- and health-related website. He is a consultant technical expert and physiologist with Adidas South Africa and consults Discovery Health, Powerade, and *Sports Illustrated*. He has co-authored *Runner's World Magazine's The Runner's Body* and participates regularly in 10k races and half-marathons.

David Warden is co-founder of PowerTri. com. He is the founder of David Warden Coaching where he coaches triathletes of all abilities. An internationally-recognized triathlon coach and overall winner of 19 triathlon events, he is former vice president of the USA Triathlon Rocky Mountain Regional Council. He has more than 15 years of experience in endurance sports, having been named 2011 USA Triathlon Rocky Mountain Region sprint-distance champion and a three-time USA Triathlon All-American. He also produces the Tri Talk Triathlon Podcast, the #1 multi-sport podcast on iTunes, and he has had articles published in *Triathlete* and *Inside Triathlon* magazines.

Randall L. Wilber is a senior sport physiologist at the U.S. Olympic Training Center in Colorado Springs. He has worked with the U.S. National Team in triathlon since 1993, has worked with every U.S. Olympic Team in triathlon since 2000, has been named a member of the official U.S. Olympic Team delegation in three summer Olympics and three winter Olympics, and has provided support for Team USA at two Pan American Games. He has worked with many famous triathletes including Hunter Kemper, Barbara Lindquist, Sheila Taormina, Nick Radkewich, Susan Williams, Laura Bennett, and Matt Charbot. A well-published author, his scientific papers have appeared in numerous journals. He is author of two books, *Altitude Training and Athletic Performance* and *Exercise-Induced Asthma: Pathophysiology and Treatment*. He has been an invited speaker at several USA Triathlon coaching clinics as well as International Triathlon Union sponsored conferences. Wilber has been recognized as a fellow of the American College of Sports Medicine (ACSM) and has served on the ACSM Olympic and Paralympic Sports Medicine Issues Committee since 2005. He was named chair of that committee in 2009.